PENGUIN BOOKS

The Fear and the Freedom

'An eloquent meditation o[n] ... psychological tentacles of th[e] ... written and profoundly percep[tive] ... Lowe as one of our fin[est] ...

'A deft blend of historical research, moving int[o] ... [c]hallenging psychological insights. Lowe writes with elegance and perception. A truly illuminating read' Jonathan Dimbleby

'Provocative, insightful and at times profoundly moving. I hope everyone – and our politicians especially – will read it and learn its vitally important lesson' James Holland

'Books about the causes and course of the Second World War continue to pour off the presses. Yet there are far fewer books about the worldwide geopolitical, economic and personal effects of the most catastrophic event of the twentieth century. So Keith Lowe's concise, lucid and highly readable book, which also includes the testimony of individual memories of the immediate years after the end of the war and their hopes of a cleansed new world of social justice and prosperity, is to be welcomed. In Lowe's opinion, the reconfiguration and realignment of nations that followed the war led ultimately to Brexit, with Europe once again divided in a potentially dangerous and certainly disruptive way' Juliet Gardiner

'This powerful book serves as a timely reminder of what our forefathers [f]orged out of the ashes of the Second World War – an international order [b]ased on cooperation and interdependence together with a bold, fearless domestic agenda that set about creating a new society' David Lammy

'An intelligent and far-reaching history of the post-war world . . . couldn't be more timely' Gavin Jacobson, *Financial Times*

'A compelling work of historical scholarship' John Gray, *New Statesman*

'Perceptive, compelling, a masterpiece: painstakingly researched, ... [T]elegraph

'Lowe has assembled a remarkable chorus of voices and asks the most probing of questions . . . a very readable and startling book' David Olusoga, *Guardian*

'A provocative book, a talented historian' Gerard DeGroot, *The Times*

'Well-written, well-researched and riveting. The echoes of most wars die away over time; this thought-provoking book shows how the Second World War's echoes seem to grow louder' Andrew Roberts, *Evening Standard*

'Extraordinary. An important book, profound in its humanity' Brian Morton, *Herald*

ABOUT THE AUTHOR

Keith Lowe is widely recognized as a leading authority on the Second World War. He is the author of *Inferno: The Devastation of Hamburg, 1943* and *Savage Continent*, which was a *Sunday Times* top ten bestseller and won the PEN Hessell-Tiltman Prize. He has spoken often on television and radio, both in Britain and in the United States, and his books have been translated into twenty languages. He lives in north London with his wife and two children.

The Fear and the Freedom

Why the Second World War Still Matters

KEITH LOWE

PENGUIN BOOKS

To Gabriel and Grace

PENGUIN BOOKS

UK | USA | Canada | Ireland | Australia
India | New Zealand | South Africa

Penguin Books is part of the Penguin Random House group of companies
whose addresses can be found at global.penguinrandomhouse.com.

First published by Viking 2017
Published in Penguin Books 2018
001

Copyright © Keith Lowe, 2017

The moral right of the author has been asserted

Typeset by Jouve (UK), Milton Keynes
Printed in Great Britain by Clays Ltd, St Ives plc

A CIP catalogue record for this book is available from the British Library

ISBN: 978-0-241-96648-8

www.greenpenguin.co.uk

MIX
Paper from
responsible sources
FSC® C018179

Penguin Random House is committed to a
sustainable future for our business, our readers
and our planet. This book is made from Forest
Stewardship Council® certified paper.

Contents

List of Illustrations

Inset section

Picture credits

Miura Kazuko, 1; Keith Lowe, 2, 6, 7, 14, 17, I-4, I-5, I-9, I-13, I-15; Atlas Van Stolk, Rotterdam, 3; Adam Nadel, 4; Atta Awisat, 5; Nagai Tokusaburou, 8; Getty Images, 9, 23, 28, I-1, I-2, I-16; US Library of Congress, 10, 16; *Ogonyok*/Kommersant, 11; Harry S. Truman Library, 18; © The Oxford Group, 19; Delhi Art Gallery Archives, 20, 21, 22, 34; UN Archives, 24; Benjamin Ferencz, 25, 27; David Low/Solo Syndication, 26; Herb Block Foundation, 29; Rex Features, 32, 37, I-8; George Rodgers/MG Camera Press, 35; Tim Gidal Collection, The Israel Museum, Jerusalem, 38; George C. Marshall Foundation, 40; House of Sharing/Museum of Sexual Slavery by the Japanese Military, 41, I-3; Dittmann Mendel, 42; Imperial War Museum, London, 45; *Wprost*, I-7; China Film Group Corporation, I-11; Columbia Pictures, I-12; Mike Peel (www.mikepeel.net), I-14; *Philadelphia Daily News*, I-17.

Author's Note on Asian Names

Throughout the text I have tried always to refer to people by the names that they themselves would use. Thus, Chinese, Japanese, Korean and Vietnamese names are written with family name first and given name last, as is the convention in those countries. I have necessarily made one or two exceptions where a person is already well known in the West according to the opposite, Western order. Thus the postwar South Korean leader is rendered Syngman Rhee, and the wartime prime minister of Japan is given as Hideki Tojo, when their family names are, respectively, Rhee and Tojo. Occasionally an author who has lived in the West for a long time will give his or her name in the Western order, and I have therefore followed suit in the endnotes. If in doubt, the reader can turn to the index and the bibliography, where individuals are listed alphabetically by their family names. In Indonesia it is common for people to have a single name. Thus, for example, readers should not be concerned about discovering President Sukarno's first name: Sukarno was his full name.

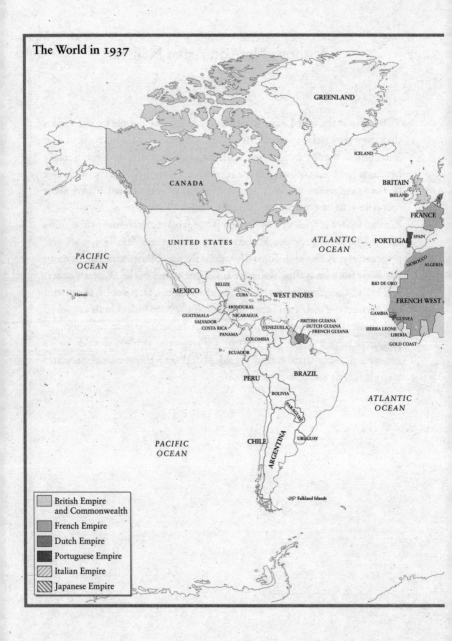

The World in 1937

GREENLAND

ICELAND

CANADA

BRITAIN

IRELAND

FRANCE

UNITED STATES

ATLANTIC OCEAN

PORTUGAL SPAIN

PACIFIC OCEAN

MOROCCO ALGERIA

RIO DE ORO

MEXICO BELIZE

CUBA WEST INDIES

FRENCH WEST

Hawaii

GUATEMALA HONDURAS
SALVADOR NICARAGUA
COSTA RICA
PANAMA

GAMBIA GUINEA

VENEZUELA BRITISH GUIANA
DUTCH GUIANA
FRENCH GUIANA

SIERRA LEONE LIBERIA

COLOMBIA

GOLD COAST

ECUADOR

PERU BRAZIL

BOLIVIA

ATLANTIC OCEAN

PARAGUAY

CHILE URUGUAY

PACIFIC OCEAN

ARGENTINA

Falkland Islands

British Empire
and Commonwealth

French Empire

Dutch Empire

Portuguese Empire

Italian Empire

Japanese Empire

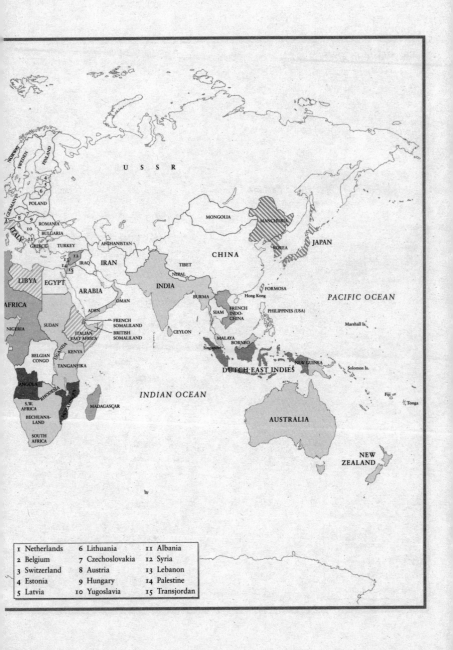

NORWAY
SWEDEN
FINLAND

U S S R

GERMANY
4
5
6
POLAND
8 9
10
ROMANIA
ITALY
11
BULGARIA
GREECE
TURKEY
AFGHANISTAN
12
13
14
15
IRAQ
IRAN

MONGOLIA

MANCHURIA

KOREA

JAPAN

CHINA

TIBET

LIBYA
EGYPT
ARABIA
NEPAL
INDIA
FORMOSA

AFRICA
OMAN
BURMA
Hong Kong
PACIFIC OCEAN

NIGERIA
SUDAN
ADEN
FRENCH
SOMALILAND
SIAM
FRENCH
INDO-
CHINA
PHILIPPINES (USA)

Marshall Is.

ITALIAN
EAST AFRICA
BRITISH
SOMALILAND
CEYLON
MALAYA
BORNEO

BELGIAN
CONGO
UGANDA
KENYA
Singapore

TANGANYIKA
DUTCH EAST INDIES
NEW GUINEA

Solomon Is.

ANGOLA
RHODESIA
INDIAN OCEAN
Fiji
Tonga

S.W.
AFRICA
MADAGASCAR

BECHUANA-
LAND
AUSTRALIA

SOUTH
AFRICA

NEW
ZEALAND

1 Netherlands	6 Lithuania	11 Albania
2 Belgium	7 Czechoslovakia	12 Syria
3 Switzerland	8 Austria	13 Lebanon
4 Estonia	9 Hungary	14 Palestine
5 Latvia	10 Yugoslavia	15 Transjordan

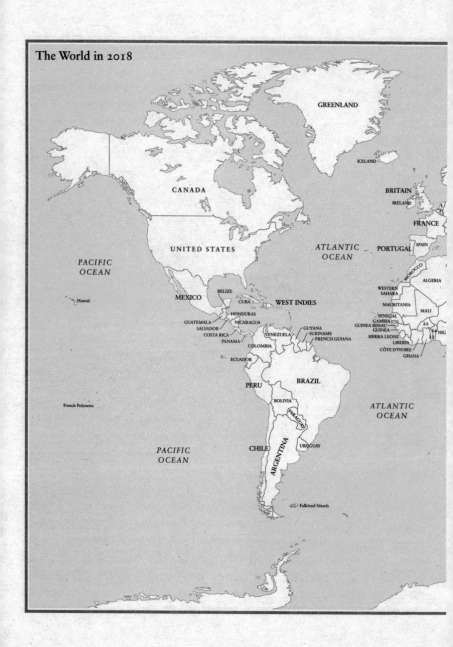

The World in 2018

GREENLAND

ICELAND

CANADA

BRITAIN

IRELAND

FRANCE

ATLANTIC OCEAN

PORTUGAL

SPAIN

PACIFIC OCEAN

Hawaii

MEXICO

BELIZE

CUBA

WEST INDIES

MOROCCO

ALGERIA

WESTERN SAHARA

MAURITANIA

MALI

HONDURAS

GUATEMALA

SALVADOR

NICARAGUA

COSTA RICA

PANAMA

VENEZUELA

GUYANA

SURINAME

FRENCH GUIANA

COLOMBIA

SENEGAL

GAMBIA

GUINEA BISSAU

GUINEA

SIERRA LEONE

LIBERIA

CÔTE D'IVOIRE

GHANA

22

NIG

ECUADOR

PERU

BRAZIL

BOLIVIA

French Polynesia

PACIFIC OCEAN

CHILE

ARGENTINA

PARAGUAY

URUGUAY

ATLANTIC OCEAN

Falkland Islands

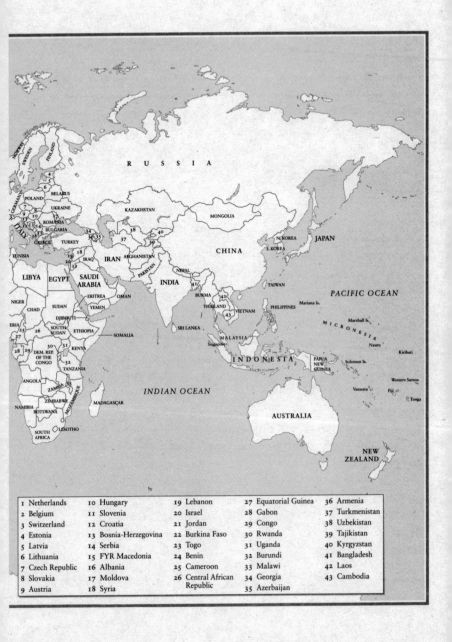

1 Netherlands	10 Hungary	19 Lebanon	27 Equatorial Guinea	36 Armenia
2 Belgium	11 Slovenia	20 Israel	28 Gabon	37 Turkmenistan
3 Switzerland	12 Croatia	21 Jordan	29 Congo	38 Uzbekistan
4 Estonia	13 Bosnia-Herzegovina	22 Burkina Faso	30 Rwanda	39 Tajikistan
5 Latvia	14 Serbia	23 Togo	31 Uganda	40 Kyrgyzstan
6 Lithuania	15 FYR Macedonia	24 Benin	32 Burundi	41 Bangladesh
7 Czech Republic	16 Albania	25 Cameroon	33 Malawi	42 Laos
8 Slovakia	17 Moldova	26 Central African	34 Georgia	43 Cambodia
9 Austria	18 Syria	Republic	35 Azerbaijan	

Introduction

'I was never happy in my life.' That is how Georgina Sand, well into her eighties at the time when I interviewed her, summed herself up. 'I never really belonged anywhere. If I'm in England I still consider myself a refugee. Even now I'm asked where I come from – I have to say to some of them that I've been here longer than they've been alive. But when I'm in Vienna I don't feel any more like an Austrian. I feel a stranger. A sense of belonging has gone.'[1]

From the outside, Georgina appears elegant and self-assured. Intelligent and erudite, she is never afraid to express an opinion. She is also quick to laugh, not only at the absurdities of the world, but also often at herself and at the quirks and eccentricities of her family, which she finds endlessly endearing.

She knows that she has a lot to feel thankful for. For more than fifty years she was married to her childhood sweetheart, Walter, with whom she had children and then a grandchild, of whom she is enormously proud. She is an accomplished artist, and since the death of her husband has had exhibitions both in Britain and in Austria. She lives a life that most people would consider comfortable, in a large and stylish apartment on London's South Bank, with a view over the River Thames towards St Paul's Cathedral.

But beneath her easy smile, beneath her accomplishments and her elegance and all the apparent comfort of her surroundings, lies a shaky foundation: 'I have a lot of insecurities. I always have had . . . My life was a constant worry . . . For example, I was always overanxious with my children. I was always worried that I was going to lose them or something. Even now I dream that I have lost them somewhere. The insecurity is always there . . . My son says there was always an undercurrent in our house – an undercurrent of unease.'

She is unequivocal about the source of this unease. It comes, she says, from the events that she and her husband experienced during the Second World War – events that she describes unashamedly as a 'trauma'. The war changed her life massively and irrevocably, and the memory of what it did to her still haunts her today. And yet she feels an obligation to tell her story because she knows that it has affected not only her own life, but also those of her family and her community. She senses too the echoes that her story has in the wider world. The events that she lived through changed the lives of millions of people just like her throughout Europe and beyond. In its own small way, her story is emblematic of our age.

Georgina was born in Vienna at the end of 1927, at a time when the city had lost its status as the centre of an empire and was struggling to find a new identity. When the Nazis marched into Vienna in 1938, the people cheered, imagining the return of a greatness they felt they deserved. But as a Jew, Georgina had no cause to celebrate. Within days she was told to sit at the back of her classroom at school, and several of her friends said that their parents had forbidden them to speak to her. She witnessed the painting of anti-Semitic slogans on the windows of Jewish shops, and the harassment of Orthodox Jews in the street. On one occasion she saw a crowd of people gathered around some Jewish men who were being forced to lick spittle from the pavement. 'And the people around were laughing and spurring them on. It was terrible.'

Georgina's family also had other reasons to feel anxious at the arrival of the Nazis: her father was a committed Communist, and was already under surveillance by the government. Deciding that the new environment was too dangerous, he silently disappeared – to Prague. A couple of months later Georgina and her mother followed him. Under the pretence that they were going on a picnic in the countryside they gathered a few belongings and took a train to the border, where a 'strange-looking man' smuggled them across to Czechoslovakia.

For the next year the family lived together in her grandfather's apartment in Prague, and Georgina was happy; then the Nazis arrived here as well, and the process began all over again. Her father once again went into hiding. To make her safe, Georgina's mother enrolled her on a new British initiative designed to save vulnerable children from Hitler's clutches – a programme known as the *Kindertransport*. Her grandfather, who had been to Britain several times, told her that she was going to live in a big house, in luxury, with a rich family. Her mother told her that she would be joining her very soon. And so eleven-year-old Georgina was put on a train and sent to Britain to live amongst strangers.

Though she did not know it at the time, she would never see her mother again.

Georgina arrived in London on a summer's day in 1939, full of excitement, as if she were starting a holiday rather than a new life. It did not take long for the excitement to wear off. The first guardians she was sent to were a military family in Sandhurst. They seemed cold and dour, especially the mother. 'I think she wanted a little cuddly girl, you know, because she had two sons. But I was always crying, because I missed my family.'

From there she was sent to live with a very old couple in a damp, dilapidated house – effectively a slum – in a poor district of Reading. 'That's where [the authorities] dumped me. Literally dumped me. I think they must have paid this couple a bit of maintenance, but they were incapable of looking after me. I was very, very unhappy. They had a grandson who was a bully – he was a grown-up man, and he was living in the house. He tried to do unpleasant things with me . . . I was so scared of him.'

Over the next six months she developed boils under her arms and grew increasingly fearful of the grandson's attentions. She was eventually rescued by her father, who had somehow managed to smuggle himself to Britain and who now came and collected her. But her father could not look after her for long either because the British authorities, suspicious of German-speaking men, wanted to intern him as a potential enemy alien. So once again she found herself amongst strangers, this time on the south coast of England.

So began the series of displacements that would characterize her teenage years. She was soon evacuated from the south coast because of the threat of invasion. She spent a while in the Lake District, and then at a boarding school in North Wales, before returning to London to live with her father in the autumn of 1943. She never stayed in one place for more than a year or two, and she developed a fear of English people, none of whom really seemed to understand or care about her.

When the war came to an end Georgina was seventeen years old. Her greatest wish was to be reunited with her mother. She returned to Prague, where she managed to find her aunt, but of her mother there was no trace. Her aunt told her how many of them had been rounded up and sent to Theresienstadt concentration camp. Georgina's mother had been put on a transport to Auschwitz, where she had almost certainly perished.

These events haunt Georgina to this day: the repeated displacements, the loss of her mother, the anxiety and uncertainty of the war and its aftermath, and all the time the background threat, never fully acknowledged, of violence. Though she has lived in London since 1948, she cannot forget the ten years of continual disruption that characterized her life between the ages of ten and twenty. That this was infinitely better than the alternative is undeniable, but the thought of what might have happened to her had she stayed in central Europe does not console her. She can't bear to think about what happened to her family and friends who died in the concentration camps, and yet she cannot escape from thinking about them either. Even today she cannot bring herself to watch films of Jews being deported during the war for fear of seeing her mother amongst the victims.

She is also haunted by what might have been: 'When I go to Vienna, and when I used to go to visit my aunt in Germany and so on, I saw families – healthy, beautiful families with young kids. I don't ski, but we sometimes went to the mountains and I watched, you know, and looked at children, all German speaking, and all hale and hearty. And I thought, I could have had a better life. I could have been with my family, growing up in a more secure environment. And certainly knowing where I belong. I never really belonged anywhere.'

My interest in Georgina's story is threefold. Firstly, as a historian of the Second World War and its aftermath I am an inveterate collector of stories. Georgina's is just one of twenty-five I collected for this book, one for each chapter. Some I gathered personally through interviews or by email correspondence, others were gleaned from archival documents or published memoirs; some are from famous people and others from people who are unknown to anyone but their family and friends. These stories are in turn just a tiny sample of the hundreds I have sifted through out of the thousands – millions – of individual stories that make up our communal history.

Secondly, and more importantly, Georgina is related to my wife, and hence part of my family. What she has to tell me makes sense of that branch of my family's tree – their fears and anxieties, their obsessions, their longings, some of which have been transmitted silently to my wife, to me, and to our children, almost as if by osmosis. No person's experience belongs exclusively to them – it is part of a web that families and communities build together, and Georgina's story is no different.

Lastly, and most importantly, at least in the context of this book, there is something emblematic about her tale. Like Georgina, hundreds of thousands of other European Jews – those who survived the war – were displaced from their homes and scattered across the globe. They and their offspring can be found today in every major city from Buenos Aires to Vladivostok. Like Georgina, millions of other German speakers, perhaps as many as 12 million in total, were also uprooted and exiled from their homes in the chaotic aftermath of the war. Her narrative has echoes throughout not only Europe, but also China, Korea and Southeast Asia, where tens of millions were likewise displaced; and in North Africa and the Middle East, where the to-ing and fro-ing of vast armies caused irreversible disruption throughout the war years. The echoes are fainter, but still recognizable, in the stories of refugees from later conflicts, such as Korea, Algeria, Vietnam, Bosnia – conflicts which also have roots in the Second World War. They have been passed on to the children of refugees, and to their communities – just as Georgina has shared her memories with her family and friends – and are now woven into the very fabric of nations and diasporas around the world.

The more one studies the events that Georgina and others like her lived through, the deeper and more widespread their consequences seem to be. The Second World War was not just another crisis – it directly affected more people than any other conflict in history. Over 100 million men and women were mobilized, a figure that easily dwarfs the number who fought in any previous war, including the Great War of 1914–18. Hundreds of millions of civilians around the world were also dragged into the conflict – not only as refugees like Georgina, but also as factory workers, as suppliers of food or fuel, as providers of comfort and entertainment, as prisoners, as slave labourers, and as targets. For the first time in modern history the number of civilians killed vastly outweighed the number of soldiers, not just by millions, but by tens of millions. Four times as many people were killed in the Second World War as in the First. For every one of those people there were dozens who were indirectly affected by the vast economic and psychological upheavals that accompanied the war.[2]

As the world struggled to recover in 1945 entire societies were transformed. The landscapes that rose from the rubble of the battlefield looked nothing like the landscapes that had existed before. Cities changed their names, economies changed their currencies, people changed their nationalities. Communities that had been homogeneous for centuries were suddenly inundated with strangers of all nationalities, all races, and all colours – people like Georgina, who didn't belong. Entire nations were set free, or newly enslaved. Empires fell and were replaced with new ones, equally glorious and equally cruel.

The universal desire to find an antidote to war spawned an unprecedented rush of new ideas and innovations. Scientists dreamed of using new technologies – many of them created during the war – to make the world a better, safer place. Architects dreamed of building new cities out of the rubble of the old, with better housing, brighter public spaces and more contented populations. Politicians, economists and philosophers fantasized about egalitarian societies, centrally planned and efficiently run for the happiness of all. New political parties, and new moral movements, sprang up everywhere. Some of these changes built on ideas that had come about as a result of earlier upheavals, such as the First World War or the Russian Revolution, and some of them were entirely new; but even the older ideas were adopted after 1945 with a speed and an urgency that would have been unthinkable at any other time. The overwhelming nature of the war, its uniquely horrific violence and its unparalleled geographical scope, had created a thirst for change that was more universal than at any other time in history.

The word that came to everyone's lips was 'freedom'. America's wartime leader, Franklin D. Roosevelt, had spoken of four freedoms – freedom of speech, freedom of worship, freedom from want and freedom from fear. The Atlantic Charter, drawn up in consultation with the British prime minister, Winston Churchill, had also spoken of the freedom of all peoples to choose their own form of government. Communists spoke of freedom from exploitation while economists spoke of free trade and free markets. And in the wake of the war, some of the world's most influential philosophers and psychologists wrote of even deeper freedoms, fundamental to the human condition.

The call was taken up all over the world, even in those countries far removed from the fighting. As early as 1942 the future Nigerian statesman Kingsley Ozumba Mbadiwe was demanding that liberty and justice be extended to the colonial world once the war was won. 'Africa,' he wrote, 'will accept no other prize than freedom.'[3] Some of the most enthusiastic founder members of the United Nations were the Central and South American countries, who envisaged an international system that would see 'injustice and poverty banished from the world', and a new era in which 'all nations, large and small', would 'cooperate as equals'.[4] The winds of change were blowing everywhere.

According to the American statesman Wendell Willkie, the atmosphere during the Second World War was far more revolutionary than it had been during the First. After touring the globe in 1942, he returned to Washington inspired by the way that men and women all over the world were struggling to throw off imperialism, reclaim their human and civil rights and build 'a new society . . . invigorated by independence and freedom'. It was, he said, enormously exciting, because people everywhere seemed to have a new-found confidence 'that with freedom they can achieve anything'. But he also confessed that he found this atmosphere more than a little frightening. No one seemed able to agree on a common goal. If they did not do so before the war was over, Willkie predicted a collapse of the spirit of cooperation that was holding the Allies together, and a return to the same discontents that had led to war in the first place.[5]

Thus the Second World War sowed the seeds not only of a new freedom, but also of a new fear. As soon as the war was over people began to eye their former allies with distrust once again. Tension returned between the European powers and their colonies, between right and left and, most importantly, between the USA and the Soviet Union. Having only recently witnessed an unprecedented global catastrophe, people everywhere began to worry that a new, even bigger war was coming. The 'undercurrent of unease' described by Georgina Sand was a universal phenomenon after 1945.

In this respect, Georgina's story in the immediate aftermath of the war is perhaps also emblematic. After peace was declared she returned to Prague in the hope of finding the sense of belonging she had lost as a child; but when she did not find it, she hoped instead that she could create it anew. She met Walter again, whom she had known as a girl, and fell in love. She got married, made friends, prepared to settle down. With all the optimism of youth, she imagined that her future could only be bright, despite the obstinate shadow that the war was still casting over her life. Even after discovering the death of her mother she truly believed that she would be able to put the misery of the war years behind her, because she wanted to move on, to reinvent herself. She wanted to be free.

Unfortunately the Czech authorities had different ideas. In 1948, when the Communists seized control, she and Walter were instructed to pledge their unquestioning loyalty to the new regime, and by extension to the Soviet superpower. Since they were not prepared to do so, they were forced to flee the country once again. Their flight was symbolic of yet another consequence of the Second World War – the new Cold War, which saw the whole world polarized between West and East and between right and left. To use Churchill's phrase, an iron curtain was drawn across the centre of Europe; revolutions, coups and civil wars broke out across the developing world. More refugees, more stories.

This book is an attempt to survey the major changes – both destructive and constructive – that took place in the world because of the Second World War. It necessarily covers the major geopolitical events: the emergence of the superpowers, the start of the Cold War, the long, slow collapse of European colonialism and so on. It also covers the great social and economic consequences of the war: the transformation of our physical environment; the massive changes in living standards, in world demographics, in world trade; the rise and fall of free-market controls; the birth of the nuclear age. But more importantly, it attempts to look beyond these events and trends to consider the mythological, philosophical and psychological effects of the war. How did the memory of bloodshed affect our relationships with one another and with the world? How did it change our view of what human beings were capable of? How did it influence our fears of violence and power, our craving for freedom and belonging, our dreams of equality and fairness and justice?

In order to dramatize these questions I have chosen to place at the heart of each chapter the story of a single man or woman who, like Georgina Sand, lived through the events of the war and its aftermath, and was profoundly affected by them. In each chapter, this individual story is used as a starting point to guide the reader towards glimpses of the wider picture that lies beyond – the story of that person's community, their nation, their region, the whole world. This is not just a stylistic device – it is absolutely fundamental to what I am trying to express. I do not pretend that one person's account can ever sum up the full range of experiences lived by the rest of the world; but there are elements of the universal in everything we do and everything we remember, particularly in what we tell each other about ourselves and about our past. History has always involved a negotiation between the personal and the universal, and nowhere is this relationship more relevant than in the history of the Second World War.

In 1945 there was a general understanding that the actions and beliefs of every individual, and by extension their memories and past experiences, concerned not only themselves but also mankind as a whole. This was an era when psychoanalysts like S. H. Foulkes and Erich Fromm were first beginning to investigate the relationship between the individual and the groups to which they belonged. 'The basic entity of the social process,' said Fromm in 1942, 'is the individual . . . Any group consists of individuals and nothing but individuals, and psychological mechanisms which we find operating in a group can therefore only be mechanisms that operate in individuals.'[6] Sociologists and philosophers of the time were also exploring the way that the individual is reflected in the whole, and vice versa: 'In fashioning myself, I fashion man,' said Jean-Paul Sartre at the end of 1945, and many of his fellow existentialists were keen to draw universal conclusions from the events that they had witnessed during the war. These are principles that are as applicable today as they were then: we have collectively adopted the stories of people like Georgina as if they were our own.[7]

Of course, I am aware that the stories people tell do not always reflect the absolute truth. Those told by survivors of war are notoriously unreliable. Facts get forgotten, or misremembered, or embellished. People's opinions of themselves or their deeds can change quite dramatically and, when they do, they can be backdated and inserted as original opinion. Nations and societies act similarly. The myths and downright lies we have told ourselves over the decades since the Second World War are just as important in forming our world as the truths ever were. It is the historian's responsibility to check these stories against the record of the time, and try to fashion something that is as close to the objective truth as possible. I have tried not to sit in judgement of the individuals whose accounts I pass on, even when I do not personally agree with them. Instead, since this is a global history, I have reserved my criticism for those instances where our *collective* emotions have got the better of us and embedded in us a collective memory that is entirely contradictory to the evidence. Thus the individual stories are exactly that – stories. It is in the way that they interact with the collective narrative that 'story' ends, and history begins.

I have tried to include case studies from all around the world, and from a variety of political perspectives, some of which are far from my own political and geographical point of view. There are stories here from Africa and Latin America, as well as from Europe, North America and Asia, because these regions were also deeply affected by the war. Nevertheless, there is a higher proportion of stories from the parts of the world that were directly involved in the fighting, because they undoubtedly experienced greater changes as a consequence of the war. There are more stories from the USA than anywhere else. This is not out of my own liberal Western bias – or, at least, not only because of that – but because it reflects the balance of power that emerged from the war: like it or not, the twentieth century was called the 'American century' for a reason. Japan also features heavily in the opening part of the book, because I feel that its symbolic importance is under-represented in Western narratives of the war.

The reader will also notice that there are more stories here from those who held leftist political views than from those on the right. Once more, this is deliberate. In global history, 1945 was probably the high-water mark for the left – those with socially progressive, even openly Communist ideas dominated the political agenda as they never have since. But I am a firm believer that nobody is entirely consistent in their political beliefs, and I have included stories of people who underwent dramatic changes in their beliefs as a result of their experiences, both from right to left and vice versa.

Finally, it is important to say that this book is supposed to be at least a little bit challenging. In the following pages the reader will find much that is familiar, but also, hopefully, many things that are less so, perhaps even alienating. In today's echo-chamber world, where more and more of us are exposed only to those points of view that chime closely with our own, it is more important than ever to have our views challenged occasionally, and to allow ourselves to be open to that challenge. The world looks very different when considered from the viewpoint of a soldier or a civilian, a man or a woman, a scientist or an artist, a businessman or a trade unionist, a hero, a victim or a criminal. All these points of view are represented in the following pages. But I would urge the reader to approach this book rather with the eyes of an outsider – a refugee – whose own preconceptions must be put temporarily to one side if the context of what follows is to be understood. I myself have struggled with this. Historians can be just as prejudiced as anyone else, and in the following pages I have tried to be honest about some of my own preconceived ideas and beliefs. Once or twice, as in the chapter on postwar European nationalism, I have taken the difficult decision to put my own fears and longings under the spotlight. I would urge the reader occasionally to do the same.

A historian is also a kind of refugee: if the past is another country, it is one to which he or she can never return, no matter how enthusiastic his or her efforts to recreate it. I embarked upon this book knowing that it could only ever be a blurred representation of the bright new world that emerged from the ashes of 1945, which in any case was always too vast to be contained comfortably between the covers of a single volume. I can only hope that the fragments I have found and glued together will inspire readers to explore further, and fill in some of the wider cracks and omissions for themselves.

But then, in many respects, this book is not really about the past at all. It is about why our cities look the way they do today, why our communities are becoming so diverse, and why our technologies have developed in the way that they have. It is about why nobody believes in Utopia any more, why we champion human rights even as we undermine them, and why there is such despair over the possibilities of ever reforming our economic system. It is about why our efforts at world peace are so punctuated by violence, and why our countless quarrels and civil conflicts still have not been resolved despite decades of politicking and diplomacy. All of these issues and more fill our newspapers on a daily basis, and have their roots in the Second World War.

Above all else, this book is about the eternal conflict between our desire on the one hand to unite with our neighbours and allies, and our desire on the other to keep ourselves separate – a conflict that was played out on a worldwide scale in the aftermath of the Second World War and which continues to inform our personal and communal relationships today. Our nature, but also our history, keeps us in an ambiguous space that is neither entirely inside nor entirely outside our communities. Like Georgina Sand, none of us can truly say that we belong.

PART I

Myths and Legends

1. The End of the World

On the morning of 6 August 1945, a Japanese lecturer named Ogura Toyofumi was making his way into the city of Hiroshima when he witnessed a sight that would change history. About four kilometres away, over the centre of town, he saw a blinding flash of light: it was bluish white, like the light from a photographer's magnesium flash, but on such a scale that it seemed to have split the sky open. In astonishment, he threw himself down on the ground and watched. The flash was followed by a huge column of red flame and smoke, 'like lava from a volcano that had erupted in midair', rising miles into the sky.

The sight was as beautiful as it was terrifying. 'I don't know how to describe it. A massive cloud column defying all description appeared, boiling violently and seething upward. It was so big it blotted out much of the blue sky. Then the top of it began to spill down, like the breakup of some vast thundercloud, and the whole thing started to seep out and spread to the sides . . . Its shape was constantly changing and its colours were kaleidoscopic. Here and there it glittered with some small explosions.'

Never having seen anything like this before, he imagined himself for a moment in the presence of some divine event: the pillar of fire seen by Moses in the Old Testament, perhaps, or a manifestation of the Buddhist *shumisen* cosmos. But as religious and mythical images passed rapidly through his mind, he realized that none of them came close to the awesome sight that was unfolding before him. 'The unsophisticated concepts and fantasies dreamed up by the ancients were useless to describe this horrible pageant of clouds and lights staged in the firmament.'[1]

Moments later Ogura was hit by the atomic blast, which he weathered by pressing himself flat to the ground. All around him he could hear 'tremendous ripping, slamming and crashing sounds as houses and buildings were torn apart'. He also thought he could hear screams, although afterwards he was never sure if these had been real or were just products of his imagination.

By the time Ogura was able to rise to his feet again, just a few moments later, his environment had been utterly transformed. Where once there had been a thriving city – the seventh largest in Japan – there was now suddenly nothing but rubble, skeletons of houses, blackened ruins. In a state of shock he climbed to the top of a nearby hill to survey the damage, before heading off into the city centre to get a closer look.

What he saw astonished him. 'Hiroshima had ceased to exist . . . I couldn't believe it. All around me was a vast sea of smoking rubble and debris, with a few concrete buildings rising here and there like pale tombstones, many of them shrouded in smoke. That's all there was, as far as the eye could see . . . There was no difference at all between the distant view and the scene close-up . . . No matter how far I walked, the sea of ruins stretching back on both sides of the road still burned and smoked . . . I had expected to see a great deal of devastation, but I was dumbfounded to see that the area had been completely obliterated.'[2]

Ogura's description of Hiroshima was one of the first to be published in Japan. Written in the form of a series of letters to his wife, who had been killed in the blast, it is an attempt to understand how the author's home town was transformed instantaneously from a world of the living into a world of the dead. It is filled with hellish scenes of grotesquely deformed corpses and survivors so horrifically injured that they are barely recognizable as human beings. There are regular references to the 'inferno', to the 'Buddhist versions of hell' and to the 'fiery end of Sodom and Gomorrah'. In the final pages there is even mention of a typhoon that hit Hiroshima a month after the war was over, which reminded the author of 'the Flood of Noah's time'. The implication is that what Ogura had experienced was not merely the destruction of a single city, but something akin to Armageddon itself, as the English title of his book, *Letters from the End of the World*, testifies.[3]

Such apocalyptic visions were common amongst Hiroshima survivors. The novelist Ota Yoko, who wrote another of the earliest accounts of the bombing, could find no other reasonable explanation for the speed with which everything had been vaporized: 'I just could not understand why our surroundings had changed so greatly in one instant . . . I thought it might have been something which had nothing to do with the war, the collapse of the earth which it was said would take place at the end of the world, and which I had read about as a child.'

Ogura Toyofumi and his family. This was the last photograph of the family all together: Ogura's wife would die of radiation sickness two weeks after the bomb destroyed Hiroshima.

Like Ogura, she groped for supernatural causes, wondering if the whole of the war were not a kind of 'cosmic phenomenon' brought about by some vast phantasm intent on destroying the world.[4]

Thousands of other survivors also believed, for a while at least, that what they were witnessing was the end of days. Any researcher making a detailed study of eyewitness accounts from Hiroshima will come across the same phrases again and again: 'scenes from hell', 'a living hell', 'hell on earth', 'the world of the dead', 'it felt like the sun had fallen out of the sky', 'I had a terrible lonely feeling that everybody else in the world was dead'. Some survivors are still unable to reconcile what they saw that day with the world as it had been before the bombing, or indeed with the world as it has since become: it is as if they had witnessed something in an alternative reality entirely unrelated to our own. 'Looking back to that day,' wrote one survivor forty years later, 'I feel that it was not a human world, and that what I saw was the hell of another world.'[5]

Such thoughts echo the experiences of countless other witnesses to countless other events during the Second World War across the globe. Horrific though the experience of Hiroshima was, it was still only a single event in a worldwide conflict that had already been taking place for many years. As the Vatican newspaper, *L'Osservatore Romano*, made clear on the day after Hiroshima, there was something terrifyingly familiar about the atomic bomb: it was just the final episode in a war that seemed to have no end to its 'apocalyptic surprises'.[6] Even some of those who experienced the atomic bomb were forced to admit that it was merely the 'ugly after-echo of a war that had already ended'. In her memoir, Ota Yoko conceded that what she had experienced was only the symptom of something much greater, and much more horrific: a single catastrophe in a never-ending chain of 'suffocating, apocalyptic horror'.[7]

The experiences of civilians in Germany were similar to those in Japan. Germany was never subjected to the atomic bomb, but its cities, even more than Japan's, suffered years of conventional bombing that was no less catastrophic. Hamburg, for example, was virtually wiped from the face of the map in 1943 when a combination of high explosives and incendiary bombs caused a firestorm to engulf the city. In the days after the bombing, the novelist Hans Erich Nossack described his return to Hamburg as a 'descent into the underworld'. His book about the experience was entitled, succinctly, *Der Untergang* ('The End').[8]

By the end of the war, apocalyptic imagery, particularly biblical imagery, was omnipresent: Dresden, like Hiroshima, was consumed by a 'biblical pillar of fire'; Munich looked like the scene of the 'Last Judgement'; Dusseldorf was 'not even a ghost'.[9] The authorities in Krefeld referred to their bomb shelters as 'Noah's Ark' – the implication being that the few who found refuge there would be saved from an apocalypse that would inexorably consume the rest of the world.[10] The same imagery appears with virtually every city destroyed during the war. Stalingrad was 'the city of the dead'.[11] Warsaw was a 'city of vampires', so badly destroyed that 'it seemed as if the world had fallen apart'.[12] The liberation of Manila in the Philippines was 'Just shells and bombs and shrapnels . . . we thought it was the end of the world!'[13]

People used such language because they could find no other way to express the magnitude of the trauma they had experienced. Many of those who wrote memoirs of the war, even professional writers, lament the inadequacy of ordinary language to describe the experience of such total loss. They know that the word 'hell' is a cliché, but can find no alternative.[14]

It was not only individuals who reacted to the war in this way: communal reactions were equally uncomprehending. The newspapers of 1944 and 1945 regularly portrayed the war as something so all-encompassing, and so unprecedented, that it seemed to have destroyed the prewar world entirely. A particularly good example appeared in *The New York Times Magazine* in March 1945. Their correspondent Cyrus Sulzberger declared Europe to be the new 'dark continent', before painting a picture of unprecedented destruction 'which no American can hope to comprehend'. The language used in his article was remarkably similar to that used by Ogura Toyofumi to describe Hiroshima after the atom bomb. In an astonishingly short time, according to Sulzberger, the civilized Europe that he had known before the war had simply ceased to exist. In its place was a new, alien landscape of moral and physical devastation, where the everyday experience of ordinary people was one of 'battle, civil war, imprisonment, famine or disease'. Markets did 'not exist in large areas'. The continent's youth had been indoctrinated with ideas 'which biblical philosophers would have associated with Antichrist'. After the wholesale genocide of the war years there was 'not yet any way of knowing just how many Europeans have slaughtered each other'. In short, Europe resembled 'a Luca Signorelli Day of Judgment fresco', and the entire continent, from its centre to its periphery, had been filled with 'all the horrors envisioned centuries before in the Book of Revelation'.[15]

As with Ogura Toyofumi's description of Hiroshima, Sulzberger's article was replete with biblical and apocalyptic imagery – indeed, it was illustrated with a half-page drawing of the Four Horsemen of the Apocalypse. Other newspapers around the world did likewise, as did institutions and governments. They reacted in this way because, much like the individuals who were caught up in the worst episodes of the war, they were incapable of expressing, or even understanding, events on this scale.

After 1945 a wide variety of national and international institutions compiled studies on the physical, economic and human damage caused by the war, but the statistics they produced made no sense on a human level. The devastation was presented as a series of snapshots: Berlin was 33 per cent destroyed, Tokyo was 65 per cent destroyed, Warsaw was 93 per cent destroyed; France lost more than three-quarters of its railway trains, Greece lost two-thirds of its shipping, the Philippines lost at least two-thirds of its schools and so on, city after city, country after country, like items on some baleful inventory.[16] In an attempt to engage our imagination, government statisticians tried to break the numbers down into manageable chunks: we were told that the bombing of Dresden produced 42.8 cubic metres of rubble for every surviving inhabitant, and that the $1.6 trillion spent on the war represented $640 for every man, woman and child on the planet. But what this meant in reality – what the totality of the physical and economic devastation was really like – was always beyond imagining.[17]

The same was true of the scale of the killing, which has never been properly quantified: some historians guess a figure of around 50 million while others suggest 60 or 70 million, but nobody pretends that they really know.[18] In a sense the absolute numbers do not really matter – 50 million or 70 million or 500 million, it all sounds like the end of the world. Human beings do not – cannot – understand such numbers objectively. Much like Ogura, or any of the other millions of people who experienced the trauma of the Second World War, we reach for absolutes in an attempt to express the inexpressible.

As a consequence, much of the terminology used to describe the war still has a portentous quality today. The word 'holocaust', for example, originally meant the burning of a sacrifice until it was entirely consumed by fire: to many people today the term is understood not as a metaphor but as a literal description of what happened to European Jewry during the Second World War (an impression that is only enhanced by references to Jews being sent 'to the ovens', 'to the crematoria', or being turned into 'ashes').[19] Likewise the term 'total war', famously coined by the German propaganda minister Joseph Goebbels, is pregnant with ominous promise: it implies an inexorable process towards 'total devastation' and 'total death'.[20] Historians today regularly write about the war in these terms: indeed, one internationally bestselling historian entitled his book about the final months of the war *Armageddon*.[21] Documentary film-makers do likewise: a ground-breaking French series on the Second World War, for example, which was aired around the world, bore the title *Apocalypse*.[22] The Second World War was 'the greatest catastrophe in human history', the 'world-historical global cataclysm', the 'greatest man-made disaster in history' – to quote three bestselling historians.[23] In the words of Russian President Vladimir Putin it was a 'burning storm' that 'ravaged not only through Europe, but also through Asian and African nations'.[24] According to China's President Hu Jintao, it brought 'an untold disaster to the world and an unparalleled catastrophe to human civilization'.[25] The impression conveyed by such statements is not the traditional message that 'the end of the world is nigh', but that, on the contrary, the end of the world has already happened.

Of course, objectively speaking, the world did not end. Large areas of the globe experienced no destruction at all, including the whole of mainland North America as well as Central and South America. The vast bulk of sub-Saharan Africa also remained physically untouched, and although Australians were shocked by the bombing of Darwin in 1942, the rest of their continent experienced almost nothing at all of the war's devastation. Large parts of Europe and east Asia, where the conflict was at its most intense, remained steadfastly undestroyed. A large proportion of Germany's small towns and villages remained havens of peace right up until the end of the war, despite the comprehensive desolation of its cities. Even the likes of Dresden, the ruins of which postwar planners believed would take 'at least seventy years' to rebuild, were patched up and functioning again within just a few years of the armistice.[26]

The loss of life, though horrific, did not constitute an end of the world either. Despite Nazi boasts of a 'final solution' to the Jewish question, even the most pessimistic estimates of Jewish mortality show that they failed: at least a third of Europe's Jews would live to remember the crimes that were committed against their families.[27] A cold look at the statistics shows that other races and nationalities fared proportionally better. About one in every eleven German people lost their lives during the war, one in twenty-five Japanese, one in thirty Chinese, one in eighty Frenchmen, around one in 160 British people and less than one in three hundred Americans. On a global scale, the Second World War certainly put a sizeable dent in the world's population, but it was still only a dent: 70 million deaths represents about 3 per cent of the world's prewar population – a sickening thought, certainly, but still not Armageddon.[28]

Why, then, do we persist in characterizing the war in this way? It is true that the idea of the end of the world has a symbolic and emotional resonance that no mere statistics can replicate. And it is also true that some parts of the world still, even now, have not come to terms with the trauma they experienced during those catastrophic years. But the fact that images of the apocalypse continue to be so popular, and so widespread, suggests that there is also something else going on, that there is in fact something *comforting* about the thought that in wartime life as it was known came to such a violent end.

There are two explanations for this. Firstly, as the coming chapters will show, the myth of apocalypse does not exist in isolation: it is merely one part of a network of mythology which also allows other, more hopeful myths to thrive. In particular, it allows us to believe that the old, rotten prewar system was entirely purged, leaving a blank slate for us to rebuild a new, purer, happier world. There is nothing more comforting than the belief that we have created our own universe, untainted by the failed ideas of our predecessors that led us to war in the first place. It allows us to believe that we, wiser than they, will not repeat their mistakes.

But there is also a darker explanation, less pleasant to contemplate. According to Freud, man's urges towards destruction and self-destruction are every bit as primal as his urges to live and to create.[29] The wartime delight in annihilation – the more total, the more satisfying – is well documented, especially with regards to the uncompromising directives given by some of the Nazi leaders.[30] But this delight was not something exclusive to those we have come to think of as monsters, it is something that was also felt by the war's heroes. When the head of the atom bomb project at Los Alamos, Robert Oppenheimer, witnessed the first A-bomb test, he was so impressed with the power he now held that he uttered the words of the Hindu god Vishnu in the *Bhagavad Gita*: 'I am become death, the destroyer of worlds.' Whenever he repeated these words in later years he always did so with great solemnity, but at the time of the explosion he is reputed to have accompanied them with a strut, like Gary Cooper in the Hollywood western *High Noon*.[31] There is such a delight in destruction, and the sense of raw power that it bestows, that sometimes even the victims of that destruction can be seduced by its intoxicating effects. In his description of the bombing of Hamburg, Hans Erich Nossack admitted to willing the bombers on, eager to see the total destruction of his city despite his simultaneous horror of it.[32] The exaggerations that came after the bombing, where survivors spread rumours of up to 300,000 deaths in the city (the actual figure was about 45,000), were not only an attempt to express the enormity of what the people of Hamburg had been through, but also an attempt to participate in its power.[33]

If we look again at Ogura Toyofumi's description of the devastation of Hiroshima we can see hints of similar emotions. Ogura not only documents his shock at witnessing the power of the atom bomb, but also his perverse fascination with its terrible beauty, its immensity and the 'kaleidoscopic colours' that 'glittered' in its mushroom cloud.[34] He describes it as a divine event, almost holy in its significance. After the initial experience of the atomic flash, and the ensuing blast, he felt compelled to walk into the centre of the city, to experience for himself the full extent of the power of what he had seen, almost as if he wanted to *take part* in it. There is a sense of reluctant satisfaction, almost of pride, in his announcement nine months later that the destruction he had witnessed was 'the greatest of its kind that man had ever experienced'.[35]

I sometimes wonder if our perpetual fascination with the destruction of the Second World War does not also stem, at least partly, from our own subconscious wish to take part in the end of the world. When we indulge in myths of Armageddon, do we not also have a taste of what it means to destroy? I suspect that, like Ogura, we are fascinated by this feeling, even while we are also repelled by it; but unlike Ogura, most of us in the twenty-first century are not constrained by immediate and personal loss. Perhaps this is why we want the destruction to be bigger, more beautiful, more total – not because it explains anything more clearly, but because it gives us a taste of the divine.

Our need to describe the war in divine terms remains almost as strong today as it was in the 1940s, but our reasons for doing so have changed. What was once an understandable reaction to vast and inhuman events has since become an unconscious method of satisfying other, more disturbing urges, some of which have little to do with the war at all.

As we shall see in the coming chapters, this urge to clutch at absolutes is a recurring theme in all our dominant myths of the Second World War. And its effects – on the way we see ourselves, as well as on our relationships with one another – have often been quite profound. The 'end of the world' was not only a self-contained 'event'. It was also an idea that provided the perfect context for a plethora of other myths to take root.

2. Heroes

The Second World War was an age not only of catastrophes but also of heroes. One man who knows what it is like to be celebrated as a war hero is a former infantryman with the US 232nd Regiment named Leonard Creo, and his story demonstrates just how powerful, and just how hollow, such celebrations can be.

For Creo, the Second World War had many beginnings.[1] As a teenager in New York he was aware of the turmoil that suddenly engulfed Europe in 1939 and 1940: he used to follow the news with great excitement, 'like it was a football game'. It became more personal at the end of 1941 when the Japanese bombed Pearl Harbor and the USA was dragged into the war. Three months later, at the age of nineteen, he volunteered for the army: he started out in the artillery, then retrained as a signaller before training once again as a rifleman in the 42nd Infantry Division. But it was not until 1944 that he finally found himself on a troop ship bound for Europe, and his war began for real.

Creo first set foot in France at the end of that year. His unit was sent ahead of the rest of the division to help guard the city of Strasbourg, on the front line between France and Germany. The city was not at all secure. So many American troops had been sucked into other battles further north that this part of the front was only thinly defended, and Creo often found himself patrolling the line or guarding short stretches of the River Rhine more or less alone.

One day in January 1945, the Germans mounted an attack across the river. What happened next is a blur in his mind. He ran from one position to another to avoid being killed. He fired his bazooka at the enemy troops. He doesn't remember getting scared, just excited – 'I was happy as hell!' But then he was hit by a bullet in the side, and caught in an explosion from a German shell which peppered his leg with shrapnel. 'And that was the end of my war.'

There followed a series of other endings. Creo was patched up and sent home to the USA to recover from his wounds. Despite being badly disabled, he was not released from the army but kept on in case he could be used in a back-up role following recuperation. He celebrated VE Day in Long Island, but not too enthusiastically because he knew that this too was not really the end: Japan still had to be defeated. He celebrated the dropping of the atom bomb with more enthusiasm, as well as VJ Day, because these were more emphatic endings. But he was not finally discharged until October 1945.

The atmosphere that surrounded these various endings to the war was utterly transformative. When the divisional commander heard about Creo's exploits in Strasbourg, he awarded him a bronze star. The citation spoke of Creo's 'indomitable courage', and how he had 'single-handedly' prevented enemy forces from crossing the river 'in the face of murderous machine-gun and artillery fire'. It was enough to make any man proud of himself.[2]

Meanwhile, almost *all* returning GIs were treated as heroes in America. Their efforts on behalf of their country were officially recognized in the G. I. Bill, which granted them a host of benefits, such as low-interest mortgages, free access to higher education and a guaranteed income of $20 a week for a year if they could not find a job. Creo eventually made use of these provisions by going to study art at university – something that would have been unthinkable before the war. After college he also used his generous disability payments to support himself while he established himself as an artist – a career that he would follow for the rest of his life. Things certainly looked good for men like Creo after the war.

This attitude of respect towards veterans, both formal and informal, has followed him throughout his life. Creo has often been called a hero – sometimes in generic terms, but sometimes with specific reference to his war record and his medal. It is a label he once found gratifying, but which gradually became an embarrassment. When he thinks back to that day in Strasbourg, he realizes that some of the specific details in his citation are not accurate, and that, in any case, there was probably nothing special about what he did. 'This is what any ordinary guy would do in the circumstances. If you didn't run away, you did *that*.' Furthermore, 'At the end of the war they decided that every infantryman who saw active combat deserved a bronze star, so I got an oak leaf cluster. So that means I got two [medals]. One of which is worthless, and the second doesn't mean anything.'

Today, he finds the automatic reverence that is given to Second

Leonard Creo in 2017, wearing his old US Army uniform.

World War veterans 'uncomfortable' and 'absurd'. He never attends commemorations of the war, because he can't bear the culture of turning every cook and clerk into a hero just by virtue of his age and his uniform. 'We're seeing more and more adulation every day that passes, because we're getting fewer and fewer. Pretty soon they'll see who's the last one, just as they did with World War One. And they'll put it all on one little guy, who could have been a clerk up in Company A or something.'

The Second World War changed Creo's life. It was his involvement in the war that allowed him to take advantage of the G.I. Bill, study, become an artist: he now has paintings in the permanent collections of museums and universities across America. The injuries he sustained during the war prompted him to take up walking – first for the purpose of rehabilitation, but later as a sport. He is today a champion race walker, and has set world records for his age group in veterans' races. It was the war that first took him abroad: he now speaks three languages, has travelled all over the world and has spent long periods living in Mexico, Italy, Spain, France and now Britain. None of these things would have happened without the Second World War. When I interviewed him he was quite emphatic on this point. 'It changed my life in just about every way possible,' he said. 'Everything that's ever happened to me is from the war.'

There is only one other point that he makes with quite as much emphasis. 'I am not a hero. And if *I* say that, you've got to believe me.'

Leonard Creo's story reflects a deep-rooted problem in the way that the world – and particularly the victorious nations – remembers the Second World War. Creo did not choose to become a hero, it was a label foisted upon him, one that seems to have grown and developed over the years quite independently of Creo himself. As he understands better than most, the actual events of the war and how we *remember* those events are two very different things, and the ever-widening discrepancy makes him very uncomfortable.

Most of our images of the Second World War's heroes date from 1944 and 1945 – the years when nation after nation was liberated, and when the Allies gradually emerged victorious. Probably the most famous image of the war – and indeed, one of the iconic images of the entire century – is Alfred Eisenstaedt's photograph of a sailor kissing a nurse in New York's Times Square on VJ Day. This single picture contains all the elements of the Allied myth of the end of the war. It is a moment of unbridled joy. It is a moment of unity in celebration. The focus of the picture is of two people in uniform – who are thus representative of the country they serve – and as neither of their faces is visible they are also everyman and everywoman. But most importantly they represent a fairy tale: the hero, who has vanquished a monster, returning home to get the girl. If the Second World War were a Hollywood movie, this is exactly how we would choose to end it.

The British and American press often featured similar stories of male heroes being kissed or otherwise worshipped by women during and after the war. The American army newspaper, *Stars and Stripes*, showed regular photographs of European women kissing their liberators, or dancing with them, or merely gazing at them ecstatically. *Life* magazine did likewise. Britain's *Daily Express* gladly portrayed France during the liberation as a nation filled with damsels in distress, 'springing at the soldiers to put their arms around them and say: "Oh, we have waited so long, so impatiently."'[3]

This was not mere propaganda: it reflected the experience of many ordinary British and American soldiers, who were often overwhelmed by the outpourings of gratitude they experienced. Local populations showered them with flowers, food and wine, and women of all ages turned out to bestow kisses. One British captain remembers being served a four-course meal on beautiful china plates, while sitting in his jeep, although 'unfortunately the column moved on just as I was getting to the liqueurs'.[4] Another remembers being lifted off his feet by a 'huge woman' who hugged him, kissed him, and finally danced with him in the middle of the road: 'My feet, I swear, never touched the ground.'[5]

Sometimes the passion of the crowd, and particularly of the women in the crowd, was like some kind of erotic frenzy: indeed, one historian has described it as a 1940s version of Beatlemania.[6] But for most people the liberation was predominantly a spiritual rather than an erotic event. The Australian war reporter Alan Moorehead described the 'hysteria' he witnessed during the liberation of Paris as a kind of patriotic fervour: 'Women were lifting their babies to be kissed. Old men were embracing. Others were sitting weeping in the gutters. Others again just standing and crying aloud with joy.'[7]

During the liberation of the Netherlands one young woman remembered her first sight of an Allied soldier almost as a religious experience. Maria Haayen was living in The Hague when the Canadians arrived in their tanks: 'All the blood drained from my body, and I thought: *there comes our liberation*. And as the tank came nearer, I lost my breath and the soldier stood up – he was like a saint.'[8] Similarly, a Dutch man recalled that it 'was a privilege even to touch the sleeve of a Canadian uniform. Each Canadian private was a Christ, a saviour'.[9] Even hardened prisoners of war could respond to their liberation with a kind of spiritual ecstasy. One former captive in the German prison at Colditz described the moment when an American soldier entered the courtyard and announced that the prisoners were free:

> Suddenly, a mob was rushing towards him, shouting and cheering and struggling madly to reach him, to make sure that he was alive, to touch him and from the touch to know again the miracle of living . . . They welled up like gushing springs, they overflowed, they burst their banks, they tumbled unhindered and uncontrolled. Frenchmen with tears streaming down their faces kissed each other on both cheeks – the salute

of brothers. They kissed the G.I., they kissed everyone within range . . .
Man was at his finest amidst the grandeur of this moment of liberation.
A noble symphony arranged by the Great Composer had reached its
thunderous finale and, as the last triumphal chord swelled into the
Hymn of Nations, man looked into the face of his Creator turned
towards him, a vision of tenderness, mirrored for an instant by the
purity of his own unrepressed torrent of joy and thankfulness. At such a
moment, mountains move at the behest of man, he has such power in the
sight of God.[10]

The focus of this mystical experience – the bringer of this divine
message of 'the miracle of living' – is the single American soldier who
entered the castle courtyard on that day. As a representative of the
victorious Allies he is a hero; more than that, he is a messiah.

In the years since 1945, Britain and America have often succumbed to
the temptation to take all of this at face value. One of the most potent
legacies of the Second World War is the way that the Allies have culti-
vated an idea of themselves as 'Freedom's warriors', the people who
fought 'the Good War' or even, most famously, 'the greatest generation
any society has ever produced'.[11]

Group analysts have long noted the tendency of national groups to
proclaim themselves the greatest, or the fairest, or the best, often to a
degree that would seem megalomaniacal in an individual.[12] Even so, the
Second World War has allowed the victorious nations to take this tendency to new heights. On the fiftieth anniversary of VE Day, America's
President Bill Clinton proclaimed that each and every American who
served in war deserved our undying adulation: 'no matter their rank,
every soldier, airman, marine, sailor, every merchant marine, every
nurse, every doctor was a hero'. Not only that, but also, 'Millions were
heroes here on the home front.' These millions upon millions of heroes
had not merely won a war, they had 'saved the world'; and later, through
their continued heroism, they 'brought half a century of security
and prosperity to the West', and even 'brought our former enemies back
to life'.[13]

It is easy to find instances of Americans – both Democrat and
Republican – aggrandizing themselves and their wartime generations.
What is perhaps more interesting is the fact that, when it comes to the

Second World War, so many other nationalities continue to feel honour-bound to agree with them. On the sixtieth anniversary of D-Day, France's President Jacques Chirac not only thanked the Americans for liberating his country in 1944 – as indeed was right and proper of him – but also went on to proclaim them 'legendary heroes' who had 'reshaped the course of history', 'conferred a new stature on mankind' and even 'raised the human conscience onto a higher plane'. Even after all these decades, the simple American GI was still being proclaimed a messiah.[14]

The problem with this heroic ideal, as veterans like Leonard Creo recognize, is that it is completely impossible to live up to. The Allies might have produced their fair share of stereotypically brave and selfless men, but millions also took part in the war without ever having their bravery seriously tested. Cooks and clerks deserve as much respect as the next man – but do they deserve the title 'hero'? And what about those men who *were* tested in battle, but who were pushed beyond their breaking point? In the European theatre alone around 150,000 British and American soldiers deserted their posts, and over 100,000 had to be treated for nervous disorders because they were unable to cope with the stress of combat.[15] These men were certainly not 'legendary heroes', but if they are to be excluded from that title, so liberally bestowed upon the other Allied soldiers, what does it make them? Surely those of us who have never faced the prospect of a violent death have no right to pass judgement.

If Allied soldiers were not uniformly brave, neither were they uniformly 'noble' or 'gallant'. In Normandy, Allied soldiers routinely broke into civilian houses, destroyed property in search of loot, intimidated the local population and stole valuables. One woman in Colombières claimed that the Canadian troops who liberated the village also subjected it to an 'onslaught' of looting and vandalism: 'the men stole, pillaged, sacked everything . . . They snatched clothing, boots, provisions, even money from our strong box. My father was unable to stop them. The furniture disappeared; they even stole my sewing machine.'[16] One British artillery officer was appalled after witnessing the wanton destruction of a Norman farmer's house by his fellow soldiers: 'Three hundred Germans, apparently, had lived hereabouts and respected the owner's property, livestock and goods. How would he on his return react to this outrage except to curse his liberators?'[17] By all accounts, American soldiers behaved just as badly, if not worse. According to

French and Belgian police files, in the wake of the liberation the overwhelming majority of Allied assaults, thefts and instances of public
drunkenness were committed by GIs.[18]

If the women of western Europe were expecting the Allies to be
chivalrous heroes, what they sometimes got was an army of battle-
hardened and sexually frustrated young men, most of them barely out
of their teens. The US Army alone stands accused of raping as many as
17,000 women in North Africa and Europe between 1942 and 1945.[19]
While this is a fraction of the hundreds of thousands of women raped by
Soviet soldiers in the eastern half of the continent, it is still a long way
from the popular legend of the Americans as 'knights in shining
armour'.[20] The British were not much better. According to Yvette Levy,
a French Jew who was liberated from a labour camp in Czechoslovakia,
'The Tommies behaved just as badly as the Russians. A man in uniform
loses all his dignity. The English soldiers said they would give us food
only if we slept with them. We all had dysentery, we were sick, dirty . . .
and here was the welcome we got! I don't know what these men thought
of us – they must have taken us for wild animals.'[21]

If the Allies were sometimes badly behaved in Europe, their behaviour in Asia and the Pacific was sometimes atrocious.[22] The Asian civilian
population were certainly not always glad to see them. For many people
in Burma, Malaya and Singapore, the return of the British was just as
unwelcome as the return of the Soviets had been in eastern Europe: some
regarded it as merely one colonial occupier replacing another. The price
of liberation was also sometimes considered far too high. The retaking of
Manila, for example, might have cost the lives of 1,000 US soldiers and
around 16,000 Japanese soldiers – but it also killed anything up to 100,000
Filipinos.[23] 'I spat on the very first American soldier I saw,' claimed one
Manila woman afterwards. 'Damn you, I thought. There's nobody here
but us Filipino civilians, and you did your best to kill us.'[24]

There are thousands upon thousands of similar stories of resentment
and anger towards the Allies – indeed, it would be quite a simple matter
to construct a history of the liberation in which the Allies appear not as
saints, but as monsters. The point here is not to belittle either the
achievements of the Allies or the fundamental goodness of their intentions, merely to puncture the myth that they were somehow perfect.
This might seem a rather obvious point; but the emotional framework
that surrounds our popular understanding of the war does not always

allow for such nuance. We *want to* believe that our heroes were flawless, even today. We all instinctively bristle against any suggestion that they might also have been selfish, bungling, ignorant, chauvinist, occasionally brutal – in short, human. In the final account, the Allied soldiers who fought and won the Second World War were neither heroes nor monsters, but ordinary men like Leonard Creo.

The illusion of Allied perfection during the Second World War has had profound effects on the postwar world. Having told themselves that they had been involved in a 'good war', the British and Americans have been searching for a new good war ever since. That is not to say that they have consciously gone out looking for trouble, but rather that when they have found themselves in trouble they have shamelessly exploited their position as the good guys of history to justify their cause.

Or perhaps that is too cynical: both countries have also often found themselves dragged into conflicts that they never wanted to be involved in, but which they have made their own out of a feeling of responsibility towards the world. America in particular has often been called on to act as the world's policeman. When they step forward to do their duty, Americans summon the courage to do so by reminding themselves that, since they are heroes, they are obliged to act as heroes.

Since 1945, virtually every war in which Britain and America have become embroiled has been accompanied by invocations of their Second World War heroism. After the Korean War broke out in June 1950, President Truman repeatedly appealed to the memory of 1945 in his television addresses and speeches to Congress.[25] Both President Kennedy and President Johnson compared the 'vigorous young Americans' who were fighting in Vietnam to the 'legion of American heroes' who fought in the Second World War.[26] And in 1982, during the Falklands War, British journalists joined Margaret Thatcher in comparing the heroism of the British task force to that of earlier heroes who had 'built the empire' and 'won the Second World War'.[27]

There is nothing unique about this. *Every* nation, almost without exception, exploits its past to justify its present. It is simply that Britain and America, who see themselves as the greatest heroes of the greatest war, have more to exploit than most.

A perfect example of how America in particular does this was given by President Ronald Reagan in June 1984. On the fortieth anniversary of D-Day, at a ceremony on the Normandy coast, Reagan made a speech that was as much about the Cold War as it was about the commemoration.

He began with a familiar, formulaic invocation of the myth of the Second World War as a titanic battle between the forces of good and the forces of evil:

> We're here to mark that day in history when the Allied armies joined in battle to reclaim this continent to liberty. For four long years, much of Europe had been under a terrible shadow. Free nations had fallen, Jews cried out in the camps, millions cried out for liberation. Europe was enslaved, and the world prayed for its rescue. Here in Normandy the rescue began. Here the Allies stood and fought against tyranny in a giant undertaking unparalleled in human history.[28]

From this moment on he repeatedly painted an idealized, mythical picture of the perfect Allied heroes: 'These are the champions who helped free a continent', 'These are the heroes who helped end a war', 'everyone was brave that day', 'The men of Normandy had faith that what they were doing was right, faith that they fought for all humanity, faith that a just God would grant them mercy on this beachhead or the next.' The Allies, he claimed, were motivated purely by 'faith and belief', by 'loyalty and love' and by the knowledge 'that God was an ally in this great cause'.

Midway through his speech, however, Reagan took a new direction, as he turned to events that occurred after the war was over. Unlike the Americans, 'Soviet troops that came to the center of this continent did not leave when peace came. They're still there, uninvited, unwanted, unyielding, almost forty years after the war.' Because of this, American heroism was obliged to continue. While the Soviets persisted in the ways of conquest, America would continue to protect the freedom of Europe's democracies: 'We are bound today by what bound us forty years ago, the same loyalties, traditions and beliefs . . . We were with you then; we are with you now.'

Listening to this speech, it would be easy to imagine that the Second World War had never finished. There is a direct and explicit link between 'then' and 'now': the same forces of good are fighting the same forces of evil. Importantly, the enemy is not the Germans or the Nazis, who are never once mentioned in the speech, but the much more abstract forces of 'tyranny' – a term that can be applied to both the Nazis and the Soviets. It is as if the mindset of June 1944 had somehow been frozen in time.

Fast forward another couple of decades and, despite some huge historical shifts in the world, the rhetoric does not seem to have changed. In 2001 America had a new enemy. After the 9/11 attacks it launched a 'war against terror', starting with a military strike against Afghanistan. In order to garner international support, when President George W. Bush addressed the United Nations that November he deliberately invoked parallels with wartime America:

> In [the] Second World War, we learned there is no isolation from evil. We affirmed that some crimes are so terrible, they offend humanity itself. And we resolved that the aggressions and ambitions of the wicked must be opposed early, decisively, and collectively, before they threaten us all. That evil has returned, and that cause is renewed.[29]

A few weeks later he declared that 'terrorists are the heirs to fascism' in a speech that directly compared 9/11 to the Japanese bombing of Pearl Harbor.[30]

In the coming months Bush repeatedly made parallels between the Second World War and the war against terror. He compared America's alliances to her Second World War alliances; he compared the fortitude of the American people to their fortitude in the 1940s; he even called his Secretary of State a modern-day version of the wartime general George Marshall (and implied that he himself was a modern-day Roosevelt).[31] But perhaps it was his speech on Memorial Day in 2002 that best demonstrated his attempts to portray his modern war as an echo of the 'good war' of 1945. Bush chose not to spend Memorial Day in the United States, as his predecessors always had, but at the American war memorial in Normandy. In a speech littered with religious stories and imagery, he reminded the world that American soldiers 'came to liberate, not to conquer', that they 'sacrificed' themselves 'for the future of humanity', and that they came bearing 'a light that scattered darkness' from the world. While this makes good rhetoric, it is unfair on American soldiers themselves. In 2002, just as in 1945, they were still being forced into an unrealistic role as messiahs in uniform.[32]

British and American politicians are by no means unique in their constant claims to heroism, nor their constant harping back to the Second

World War. The Russians are often as bad, and President Putin has been just as quick as President Bush to invoke the Russian people's wartime heroism (and indeed use it to justify his own war on terror).[33] Likewise, the Chinese proudly proclaim their own 'heroic deeds' in the 'people's war of resistance against Japanese aggression', but quietly draw a veil over the savagery of the civil war that was taking place at the same time.[34] Those European countries that had significant underground movements during the war, such as the French, the Italians, the Dutch, the Norwegians or the Poles, also exaggerate their heroism and play down the nature of their resistance activities, which often involved violence, crime and the use of targeted terror against their own people.[35] The only reason I have concentrated on the British and Americans in this chapter is that these are the two nationalities whose Second World War heroism remains largely untainted, even today. They are perhaps the most interesting examples, because they are the ones who have the most to lose. America is also the only 'hero' nation that continues to wield power on a truly global scale: the psychology of American heroism is therefore not an issue confined to Americans, but a problem that affects us all.

And it is a problem. Heroes, no matter their nationality, can get so caught up in their own idea of themselves that they become blind to their own faults. Moreover, they are often quick to see faults in others. The problem with heroes is that they will always need a monster to fight; and the more perfect the hero, the more correspondingly threatening the monster must be.

This leads us to another of the potent myths that has been bequeathed to us by the Second World War: 1945 not only gave us our dominant psychological template for heroism, but also provided us with a corresponding template for evil. These two archetypes are so intimately entwined that it is often impossible to refer to one without also referring to the other – but their effects on society are quite distinct. The myth of the hero can sometimes be hollow. But as I shall show next, the myth of the monster, and its impact on society, can be downright toxic.

3. Monsters

According to psychoanalysts there is an intimate relationship between heroes and demons. Nations rarely extol their own virtues without contrasting them against the evils of outsiders. This is a good way of projecting everything we do not like about ourselves onto others, and it is also an excellent way to distract ourselves from the difficulties and splits that exist amongst ourselves. We embrace our enemies – both real and imagined – because they allow us to focus all our negative feelings elsewhere. To paraphrase Freud, whole nations can pull together in brotherly love, as long as they have someone to hate.[1]

In wartime, the demonization of one's enemies becomes an even greater priority, because the need for social cohesion is greater. There is nothing like an external threat to create what the British still call the 'Blitz spirit'. In any case, a nation is obliged to portray its enemies as evil in order to justify going to war against them in the first place. In addition it will call them evil in order to inspire its people to do what they must: war is essentially the business of killing, and it is much easier to kill one's enemies when one believes them to be monsters.

During the Second World War all sides demonized their enemies. Studies of wartime propaganda show how strikingly similar this demonization was, almost regardless of which country it came from. At the very least, the 'enemy' – whomever that enemy might be – was depicted as somehow warped, depraved or racially 'inferior'. Thus German and Italian propaganda often portrayed the Americans as gangsters, negroes and Jews; the Japanese characterized the British as callous imperialists who had enslaved south Asia; while the Soviets were portrayed as a new incarnation of the Barbarian hordes.[2] Meanwhile, the Allies portrayed the Germans as godless, emotionless killers, and thieves in the night, and the Japanese as the 'yellow hordes of Asia'.[3] All sides depicted their enemies as power-hungry, duplicitous, exploitative, manipulative, violent, psychopathic and particularly fond of attacking women and children.[4]

More often the enemy was not given the courtesy of being human at all – or if he was, then he was at best deformed or somehow 'subhuman'.

The Japanese routinely characterized the Chinese as apes, rats or donkeys, and drew cartoons of them with claws, horns or short, stubby tails. In return, Chinese propaganda routinely characterized their Japanese invaders as 'dwarves' or devils.[5] The Nazis famously depicted Jews and Slavs as rats: in return they themselves were depicted as various beasts, ranging from pigs to rabid dogs, tigers, snakes, scorpions, cockroaches, mosquitoes and even bacteria.[6] Perhaps the most vicious anti-German propaganda came from Soviet newspapers, which urged their soldiers to exterminate Germans as if they were vermin. 'We cannot live as long as these grey-green slugs are alive,' proclaimed the Red Army newspaper in August 1942. 'Today there is only one thought: Kill the Germans. Kill them all and dig them into the earth. Then we can go to sleep.'[7]

All sides dehumanized their enemies for precisely this purpose: because it was easier to kill them if they were perceived as animals. Thus the Japanese were described in American propaganda as a 'plague' whose 'breeding grounds around the Tokyo area must be completely annihilated'; while the Japanese replied with exhortations to 'Beat the Americans to Death!'[8]

In the most extreme cases, however, the enemy was depicted as something altogether darker and more terrifying than mere subhumans. Mythical beasts were conjured up: hydras, winged demons, flying skeletons, soulless robots, the Grim Reaper, Frankenstein's monster, the Horsemen of the Apocalypse.[9] One of the most common images, which was used by every side, was that of the vampire. The cover of *Collier's* magazine in the USA depicted the Japanese air force as a vampire bat carrying bombs to Pearl Harbor, while the cover of *Manga* in Japan showed President Roosevelt as a green-faced, grasping monster with Dracula fangs.[10] These images were often not merely caricatures: they were meant to express a very real fear. During the German occupation of the Netherlands, for example, *De Groene Amsterdammer* printed a darkly disturbing cartoon of a vampire with a gas mask for a face, sucking the lifeblood out of the naked body of a Dutch patriot.

America produced similar images of the 'yellow peril': in one famous cartoon from 1942, the Japanese prime minister, Hideki Tojo, was depicted as an ape-like monster leaning over the body of an American airman with blood dripping from his mouth.[11]

Looking back from the twenty-first century, there is something truly frightening about such images. We now know all about the atrocities

L. J. Jordaan's haunting depiction of the Nazi invasion of the Netherlands in 1940, as printed in *De Groene Amsterdammer*.

that characterized the Second World War: the Holocaust, the vast Nazi networks of slave labour throughout Europe, the use of human beings for scientific experimentation or bayonet practice and, perhaps most disturbingly, the way that some Japanese soldiers in parts of Southeast Asia slaughtered prisoners of war in order to eat their flesh. Armed with such hindsight, it is tempting to imagine that much of the demonization, at least from the Allied side, was entirely justified. But we have to remember that the vast majority of the images and diatribes quoted above were created *before* the worst atrocities occurred, and certainly before they were widely known. Demonization of the enemy was therefore not a reaction to atrocity, but a precursor to it. Indeed, as countless sociological and psychological studies show, it was one of the factors that made such atrocities possible in the first place. We are rightly horrified when we see how Nazi film-makers portrayed Jews as rats; but knowing what we know now, we should be equally concerned at the way Allied propaganda portrayed the Japanese as lice, or the Germans as bacteria.[12]

★

Front-line soldiers frequently report a sense of reawakening to the humanity of their enemy after the battle is won. Robert Rasmus, a rifleman with the US 106th Division, tells how he and his fellow soldiers entered the Second World War with an absolute hatred of Germans, before finally coming face to face with some of their dead in the spring of 1945.

> It was sunshine and quiet. We were passing the Germans we killed. Looking at the individual German dead, each took on a personality. These were no longer an abstraction. These were no longer the Germans of the brutish faces and the helmets we saw in the newsreels. They were exactly our age. These were boys like us.[13]

During the normal course of events, one might imagine a similar process occurring on a societal level. Once Germany and Japan had been defeated they would no longer have appeared quite so threatening – the Allies might therefore have been able to acknowledge their humanity once again. According to traditional renderings of history this is exactly what happened: Germany and Japan were 'rehabilitated', helped back to their feet, allowed to become the 'good pupils' of the superpowers. In the words of US President Bill Clinton, 'we brought our former enemies back to life'.[14]

Unfortunately, one of the most potent legacies of the Second World War is the degree to which this rehumanization of the 'enemy' did *not* happen. If anything, in the immediate aftermath of the war, when the realities of German and Japanese wartime atrocities became widely known, attitudes towards the Allies' enemies hardened. Cartoons of walking skeletons and piles of corpses had been replaced with photographs and newsreels of the real thing. Rumours and stories of isolated atrocities had been replaced with hard evidence of the systematic abuse, torture and extermination of millions upon millions of civilians – and what is more, this was publicized across the globe by newspapers covering the various war-crimes trials. Until 1945, some of the more extreme cartoon images of the enemy might easily have been dismissed as metaphors: after the war-crimes trials they no longer seemed metaphorical at all.

The move to rehabilitate Germany and Japan therefore took place against a background of many competing voices that demonized the Allies' wartime enemies like never before. If today we more readily remember the calls for moderation it is only because it suits us to do so: in fact, wartime hatreds lingered at an official level for months after the war. The American GIs who occupied southern Germany were issued with pamphlets describing its civilians as 'trapped rats' who had 'shared in the profits of Germany's inhumanity'.[15] According to some Scandinavian historians, public hatred towards the Germans endured for some twenty years.[16] Many politicians of the day were quite forthright about their feelings. 'I do not want ever to see the re-establishment of a Reich again,' said President Charles de Gaulle at the end of 1945.[17] Prokop Drtina, the future justice minister of Czechoslovakia, was fond of saying, 'There are no good Germans, only bad and even worse ones.' Even clergymen were prepared to pronounce the German race so 'evil' that 'the commandment to love thy neighbour . . . does not apply'.[18]

Throughout the Pacific, attitudes towards the Japanese were somewhat similar. In popular Filipino literature after the war, the Japanese were almost always portrayed as 'savage', 'bow-legged', 'slant-eyed' rapists and conquerors, whose only role was that of the villain. Such characterizations predominated right up into the 1960s, and have remained common ever since.[19] Yukawa Morio, Japan's first postwar ambassador to the Philippines, recalls that when he first arrived there in 1957, 'although I had prepared, I was so surprised at the depth of the bad feeling toward Japan'.[20] In Malaysia and Singapore, according to some sources, demonization of the Japanese after the war was even stronger.[21] Meanwhile, in Korea, hatred of the Japanese was perhaps strongest of all: so toxic were Korean attitudes towards Japan that when the two nations finally signed a treaty to normalize their diplomatic relations in 1965, after nearly fourteen years of negotiations, it caused widespread rioting and members of the opposition party resigned from the National Assembly in protest.[22]

In the years since 1945, anti-Japanese feeling in America, directly inherited from the Second World War, has never been far from the surface. After the rapid rise of Japan's economic power in the 1960s and 70s, all levels of American society returned to denigrating the Japanese, or 'Jap bashing' as it became known. US senators in the mid-1980s began to refer to the importation of Japanese cars as 'an economic Pearl Harbor', while presidential hopefuls like Howard Baker used the fortieth anniversary of the end of the war to proclaim two 'facts': 'First, we're still at war with Japan. Second, we're losing.' In 1985, the Pulitzer

Prize-winning author Theodore H. White wrote an article in *The New York Times Magazine* entitled 'The Danger from Japan', in which he warned that the Japanese were using 'martial' trade practices to create a new version of their wartime East-Asia Co-Prosperity Sphere. Such sentiments were echoed across Asia and Australia in the 1980s.[23]

In China, an explosion of anti-Japanese sentiment is even more recent, provoked by a massive resurgence of public memory about the war. Tragic images of children brutalized during the Rape of Nanjing have become 'virtually ingrained on the Chinese collective unconscious' through their continual reuse in Chinese documentary films, and the story of the massacre is repeated every few years in ever more popular feature films.[24] By 2013, Chinese television companies were making over 200 programmes a year dramatizing the 1937–45 war. In February 2014 the Chinese government instituted two new national holidays: one to mark the anniversary of the Nanjing massacre and the second to mark the anniversary of Japan's final surrender.[25]

Anti-German sentiment linked to the Second World War is also still very much alive, particularly in Europe. In 2013 the presidential election in the Czech Republic descended into racial insults, with politicians and the press accusing one of the candidates, Karel Schwarzenberg, of being too 'German' to deserve election.[26] In Greece, those who opposed EU austerity measures in the wake of the 2008 financial crisis frequently burned swastikas at demonstrations. In February 2012 the right-wing Greek newspaper *Dimokratia* went so far as to print a front-page picture of the German Chancellor, Angela Merkel, wearing a Nazi uniform, above an astonishingly tasteless headline comparing Greece to Dachau concentration camp.[27] In August the same year, the Italian prime minister, Silvio Berlusconi, ran a political campaign based on anti-German sentiment, with frequent references to the Second World War. One of his newspapers, *Il Giornale*, printed a front-page photograph of Angela Merkel raising her hand in a gesture similar to the Nazi salute, beneath the headline 'Quarto Reich'.[28]

Many of these perceptions of Germans and Japanese have more to do with contemporary politics than with the Second World War – for example China's anti-Japanese rhetoric has grown during their territorial dispute over a group of islands in the East China Sea, and many European nations are angry at Germany's increasing political and economic dominance inside the European Union. Nevertheless, it is the

Second World War that every nation instinctively reaches for when looking for a template for modern demons.

In our collective imagination, the Nazis in particular have become our standard template for evil. A worldwide succession of postwar bogeymen have been compared to Hitler, including Egypt's President Nasser in the 1950s, Palestine's Yasser Arafat in the 1970s, Argentina's General Galtieri in the 1980s, and Iraq's Saddam Hussein and Serbia's Slobodan Milošević in the 1990s.[29] Political groups often characterize their rivals as fascist in ways that are historically meaningless: thus Indian Members of Parliament accuse one another of being 'like Hitler', and prominent Australians compare gay rights activists to the Gestapo.[30] In the run-up to the 2016 American presidential campaign the *Philadelphia Daily News* even published a front-page picture of Donald Trump with his arm raised as if in a Nazi salute, above the headline 'The New Furor' (a deliberate pun on 'Führer').[31]

Today, 'Nazi' is routinely employed as a conceptual shorthand for wickedness everywhere. The figure of Adolf Hitler in particular has become what one cultural critic has called 'the epitome of evil', employed by novelists, film-makers and politicians to highlight the people and ideas they most fear. Thus Richard Nixon and Osama bin Laden have both been portrayed as modern 'Hitler's.[32] Nazis pop up as villains in thousands of our best-known films, from *The Sound of Music* to the Indiana Jones movies. Even the 'storm troopers' in the Star Wars films are based on the German Wehrmacht – the shape of their helmets alone immediately identifies them as the 'enemy'. A comprehensive list of all the many and varied postwar cultural references to this 'epitome of evil' would be virtually endless. In the decades since the Second World War, the Nazi, ersatz or otherwise, has developed into a monster every bit as enduring as any of the mythological demons that were portrayed in wartime propaganda.

The Face of 'Evil'

Was Hitler really evil? Were the men who served in the SS or the Gestapo evil? And what about those who conducted medical or scientific experiments on human beings? So strong is the mythology around this subject that even to suggest that these people might not have been monsters but 'ordinary men' can seem sacrilegious.[33] Entire schools of history have been founded upon the notion that the Nazis were not only evil, but uniquely so: those who claim otherwise have provoked cries of outrage in academic circles, in parliaments and in the media throughout the world.[34]

While no reputable historian would deny that the actions of the Nazis or the Japanese Kempeitai (military secret police) were often evil, it is perhaps a mistake to characterize all the people who carried out these acts in the same way. From a psychological point of view there is no such thing as an evil person, only a sick person, or someone caught within a sick system. From a philosophical point of view, too, there is a difference between an evil person and a person who carries out evil acts. The great tragedy of the Second World War is the way that it not only propelled people with psychopathic tendencies into positions of great power, but also nurtured and magnified the sickness within social systems to such a degree that even ordinary men became both capable of committing evil acts and enthusiastic about doing so.

It is extremely rare that someone is willing to speak openly about the atrocities they committed during the Second World War, and even more unusual for a perpetrator to exhibit genuine interest in the human consequences of their actions. One such person was Yuasa Ken, a Japanese doctor who performed vivisections on several Chinese prisoners during the war. His story is a good indicator of exactly what has been missing in postwar Japan, and in the world in general.

Yuasa was born in 1916 in Tokyo, the son of a medical practitioner. By his own account, he was the perfect product of his upbringing: obedient, hard-working, keen to prove himself to his superiors. He was used to hearing about Japanese racial superiority, and never questioned his country's right to invade its neighbours: he had a strong memory of his teacher in elementary school saying, 'The Japanese people are a superior race. They must conquer China and become the masters of all Asia.' He never questioned this idea: indeed, the thought of questioning or criticizing his superiors in any respect never occurred to him.[35]

Following in his father's footsteps, Yuasa graduated from medical school in 1941 at the age of twenty-four. However, he was keen to contribute to Japan's war effort in China, so he immediately applied to become an army surgeon. He was trained for two months, commissioned as a first lieutenant army surgeon and finally sent to north-east China.

In March 1942, less than six weeks after his assignment to the Luan Army Hospital near the city of Taiyuan in China's Shanxi Province, Yuasa was summoned to attend a practice surgery session. He had already heard that army surgeons performed vivisections, and knew that all junior staff were expected to attend; so despite a nagging feeling of fear, coupled with a certain curiosity about what he was about to witness, he reluctantly made his way to the autopsy room.

When he arrived, he found it filled with hospital and divisional staff – not only junior doctors like him, but all of the senior ranks. In one corner were two Chinese farmers with their hands tied behind their backs. One of them stood in silence, apparently resigned to his fate; the other, however, was obviously terrified and kept crying out in fear. Yuasa watched them anxiously, but made sure to keep his composure in front of his superiors. He remembers asking if the two men had committed any crime that warranted the death penalty, but was fobbed off with the answer that it made no difference – the war would probably claim their lives anyway.

After everyone was assembled, the hospital director announced that they would get started. Some Japanese guards prodded the two farmers to step forward. The braver of the two walked calmly to the operating table and lay down on it but the other continued crying out, and started backing away. He backed right into Yuasa. Not wanting to appear weak before his superiors, Yuasa hesitated for a moment before giving the terrified man a shove and commanding him to 'Move forward!' By doing this he felt as though he had undergone some sort of test, or rite of passage.

Once the two Chinese men had been stripped and anaesthetized, the surgeons began their practice session. First they performed an appendectomy, followed by an amputation of one of the men's arms. Next they practised cutting out sections of the men's intestines and reattaching them; and finally they performed a tracheotomy. The purpose of all this was to familiarize the surgeons with the sort of surgery that would be common in the aftermath of battle. Thus Yuasa was able to justify the vivisection in his mind as preparation to save the lives of his countrymen. The lives of Japanese soldiers were, as he had been taught, of far greater worth than the lives of Chinese peasants.

After three hours of surgery, the two Chinese men were still breathing, but only weakly. Now that the practice session was over, all that was left to do was to finish the farmers off and dispose of their bodies.

The hospital director attempted to kill them by injecting air into their hearts, but it did not work. At this point Yuasa himself was called upon to help: 'I strangled one of them with my hands and applied pressure to the carotid artery, but I still could not get him to stop breathing . . . First Lieutenant O and I tied the man's belt around his neck and strangled him by pulling hard on both ends, but still his breathing did not stop.' In the end one of the doctors suggested injecting chloroethane directly into their veins, which Yuasa did, and the two men finally expired.[36] That night, after work, Yuasa went out with his colleagues. He was strangely restless, but after a few drinks he felt better, and did not give the day's events any more thought.

During the following three years Yuasa participated in six further vivisections on fourteen Chinese people. Some of the sessions were of little use in training army doctors: they included testicular extractions, a brain extraction and general anatomy lessons. On one occasion bullets were fired into the bodies of four men before army surgeons practised removing them, without anaesthesia. On another occasion, when the session was too sparsely attended to make practice worthwhile, the hospital director took the opportunity to try his hand at beheading one man with a sword. After April 1943 Yuasa himself took responsibility for arranging vivisections. He did this unquestioningly, despite knowing that the Kempeitai picked the victims more or less at random.

'It was never the case that we used prisoners for vivisections just because there were extra prisoners available. It was always, "We need them, so get them for us." They were necessary for surgery practice in order to save the lives of Japanese soldiers, you see. Chinese people were arrested for that purpose alone.'[37]

Yuasa freely admitted that, at the time, he felt no guilt for committing murder in this way. 'We felt they were like waste. Garbage.'[38]

When the war came to an end in August 1945, Yuasa had to decide whether to return home to Japan or to remain in China. Like thousands of other Japanese, he decided to stay on. It never occurred to him that the Chinese might want revenge for what Japanese doctors like him had done, because in his own mind he had done nothing wrong. So he remained in China, married, had children. For the next few years he continued to practise medicine, seeing both Chinese and Japanese patients and giving instruction to Chinese junior doctors.

He was not arrested until two years after the Communists had won control of the country. In January 1951 he was sent to a prison camp, but he was not unduly concerned, because he still did not think conducting surgery practice on living human beings was a serious offence, let alone in any way evil: 'Inside, I was making all sorts of rationalizations to justify what I had done. "I was just following orders. There was nothing I could do about it. There was a war going on. It was not the first time something like this had been done. Everybody was doing it." Things like that. Plus, the war was already over.'[39]

He did not begin to feel uneasy until the Communists instructed him to make a full and frank confession, but even then he was reassured by the promise that all prisoners who genuinely repented would be pardoned: all he had to do was to admit to his crimes and he would be repatriated to Japan. Accordingly, he made a half-hearted confession – he left out some of the more shameful details, such as the brain extraction he had performed, but he hoped it would be enough to satisfy the investigators. It wasn't. His confession was rejected as insincere and he remained in captivity.

At the end of 1952, after almost two years in jail and numerous attempts at confession, Yuasa was transferred back to Shanxi Province, where he was put into Taiyuan Prison. It was here that he received a letter from the mother of one of his victims – the man whose brain he had removed. The letter described the mother's anguish when her son was arrested by the Kempeitai. It described how she had tried to follow the police truck on her bicycle, but had been unable to keep up; how she had searched everywhere before being told that her son had been taken to the hospital to be dissected alive. 'I was so sad,' she wrote, 'so sad I thought my eyes would burst from weeping. I could not tend the rice paddies I had been cultivating. I could not eat. Yuasa, I hear that you are now under arrest. I asked the government to please punish you severely.'[40]

This letter, more than anything else, finally brought home to Yuasa the enormity of his wartime actions. Before, he had seen his victims as mere bodies, specimens for surgical instruction – indeed, he had found it difficult to picture what their faces looked like. Now he realized that these people had also been living human beings, with families and communities, and he was able for the first time to recall the look of helpless terror on their faces as he began to operate on them.

Yuasa spent a further three and a half years in his gloomy prison cell reflecting on these images, and trying to understand how on earth he had been capable of doing such terrible things. In the summer of 1956 he was finally released and sent back to Japan.

Denial runs through Yuasa's story almost from start to finish. In the beginning he denied to himself that what he was doing was wrong. He continued denying it throughout the war with an apparently clean conscience: by his own admission he had no sleepless nights, no nightmares and certainly no remorse. After the war he remained in denial, and saw no reason to be afraid of any Chinese retaliation. The only thing that brought Yuasa out of his obliviousness was a prolonged period of soul-searching – enforced at first, but more voluntary later on, after the letter from his victim's mother opened his eyes to the terrible acts he had committed. Had Yuasa returned home directly after the war, it is likely that he would never have begun the process of coming to terms with his, and Japan's, past.

This certainly seems to have been the case with Yuasa's old colleagues. When he came back to Japan in 1956 he was given a reception to welcome him home. Amongst the guests were some of the army surgeons and nurses with whom he had once worked. To Yuasa's complete surprise, he discovered that almost none of them seemed to have given their wartime actions a second thought. One even asked him why the Chinese had labelled Yuasa a war criminal when he, like all the other surgeons, had acted perfectly correctly during the war. Yuasa simply asked him, 'Do you remember what we did?' but his fellow doctor had no idea what he was referring to.

Over the following years Yuasa worked with hundreds of medical staff who had taken part in the occupation of China, but not one of them said a word about guilt. In the early 1960s he decided to write a book describing what he had seen and done in China. He thought it was important to speak out about his own guilt, and thereby shine a light on a part of Japanese history that had never been publicly acknowledged. But as soon as it was published he immediately started receiving hate mail calling him a 'disgrace', or 'the epitome of stupidity', for drawing attention to an aspect of the war that much of Japan thought better forgotten. Other letters came from fellow vivisectionists who felt 'threatened' by his book, because they did not want to face up to the past. Denial was everywhere.

Yuasa Ken shortly before his death in 2010.

According to psychiatrist Noda Masaaki, who interviewed Yuasa extensively, such attitudes are symptomatic of the entire medical establishment in Japan, and indeed Japanese society as a whole.

> What have we lost, I wonder, by denying the past in this way? When we deny our life experiences, we invite psychological self-destruction. When wounds to the spirit are repressed they eventually explode in the form of emotional dysfunction and mental illness. Are the Japanese living in a spiritual state any different than the one we lived in during the war of aggression? Through our denial of the past, what sort of future have we destined for ourselves?[41]

The painful process of facing up to his crimes that Yuasa underwent is one that very few people, let alone societies, are willing to engage in.

Germany has been much praised for the way it has come to terms with the past – especially by Japanese academics, who cannot conceive of any similar process taking place in their own country. And yet, like Yuasa, Germany took this path only because it was forced to do so: firstly by the Allies, who insisted on re-educating Germans about their nation's misdeeds with newsreels and enforced trips to concentration camps, and later by the generation born after the war, who reached maturity in the 1960s and demanded to know what their parents and grandparents had done during the Nazi times. Neither of these processes was duplicated in Japan on anything like the same scale.

And yet even in Germany it remains a struggle to remind people that it was not monsters but ordinary people who oversaw the Holocaust, who shot prisoners of war, who raped and murdered their way across eastern Europe. In recent years, the figure of Hitler as a demonic, Mephistophelean character has dominated Germany's collective memory of the war; and the war itself is increasingly viewed in the same way as in Britain or America, as a gigantic conflict between good and evil. This is a much easier narrative to embrace, since it seems to absolve 'ordinary' Germans from responsibility – if war crimes are committed only by 'monsters' then the rest of us can sleep easy.[42]

Stories like Yuasa's remind us that it is not only the victims of war that are human, but the perpetrators too. Acknowledging their humanity does not exonerate them, as some people claim – quite the opposite, in fact, since only our fellow humans can be condemned for not taking responsibility for their actions.[43] Labelling such men as 'monsters' has the opposite effect: it lets them off the hook. And yet we still feel compelled to do this, because it is a convenient way of keeping our distance from them. So we ignore the huge body of historical, sociological and psychological evidence which suggests that ordinary people – people not so different from ourselves – are eminently capable of committing truly atrocious crimes, given the right set of circumstances. Effectively, we too are in denial.[44]

The Second World War not only magnified existing prejudices between peoples and nations to a vast and unprecedented degree but also provided opportunities for those prejudices to become hatreds, and for those hatreds to become murderous. In some cases it created demons where before there had been none. Such events occurred on a vast scale, in places as far apart as Norway and New Guinea.

One of the aspects that distinguishes this conflict from others is the sheer extent of its cruelty. Atrocities occurred in every theatre, perpetrated by every side, and were often directly encouraged by states and their institutions to such a degree that it was sometimes difficult, even dangerous, to act towards one's enemies with any human decency at all. All sides invoked demons and, once invoked, these demons very quickly became real.

We still live with these demons today, both in their original form and in the form of new enemies, which – unsurprisingly – bear a remarkable resemblance to the old ones. Our mutual animosities will never be laid to rest while we continue to represent the war as a conflict between the forces of absolute good and absolute evil. Such concepts make it easy for the victors to deny their faults, and difficult for the vanquished to confront their sins: they remain the main stumbling block to our collective understanding of why human beings of all nationalities and classes acted the way they did.

There are very good reasons why these myths of good and evil will not go away – reasons that have little to do with either the victors or the vanquished. The vast majority of people who experienced the Second World War do not see themselves as heroes or monsters, but rather as victims. Indeed, in many ways our understanding of the war is defined by this overwhelming experience of victimhood. It is the plight of the victim that both damns the villain and gives the hero his moral authority; and it is our need to commemorate this sense of victimhood that forces us to return to the war again and again. Heroes and villains at least have the option to put the past aside and let bygones be bygones. Victims, as I shall show next, do not have that luxury.

4. Martyrs

In 2013 a university professor in Jerusalem published a memoir of his experiences during the Second World War, and how they had affected him in later life. Otto Dov Kulka's story serves as a good example of the kind of psychological issues that faced millions of people in the years after the war. It is at once entirely unique, and yet representative of something much greater; in its own way it provides a metaphor for the way that the world as a whole has experienced both the Holocaust in particular, and the Second World War in general.[1]

Kulka was just six years old when the Germans invaded his home country of Czechoslovakia in 1939. As Jews, he and his family were particularly at risk from German repression, but his father was arrested in any case for anti-Nazi activities. Kulka and his mother were also arrested and imprisoned, along with the rest of Czechoslovakia's Jewish population.

In the autumn of 1943 at the age of ten, Kulka was sent to Auschwitz-Birkenau concentration camp. He and his mother were housed in a specially designated 'Family Camp', which was to be kept as a show-piece for the international community in case the Red Cross should decide to inspect Auschwitz. As a consequence he was allowed 'privileges' that were not available to inmates of other parts of the complex. He did not have to undergo the infamous 'selection' at the station, which separated those who were fit for work from those who were destined immediately for the gas chambers. He did not have his head shaved, or his clothes and belongings confiscated. He and his mother were allowed to continue some semblance of normal life: he attended a makeshift school, where he and his friends put on plays and concerts, and he even joined a choir, in which, within sight of the crematoria, he learned to sing Beethoven's 'Ode to Joy'.

Everyone in the Family Camp was aware that this was highly unusual, and could not understand why they should have been singled out for such special treatment. But their good fortune did not last long. In March 1944, exactly six months after their arrival, the entire group was rounded up and taken to the gas chambers. There were no selections, and no possibility of escape – they were simply disposed of en masse. Their place was then taken by a new group, which was again to be granted the same privileges and the same freedoms – but only until their six months had, in turn, come to an end. Kulka and his mother survived the first culling by sheer luck: they both happened to be in the infirmary on the night of the liquidation. But they were under no illusion that this was anything but a temporary reprieve.

Despite many other brushes with death, Kulka eventually survived Auschwitz, but he spent the rest of his life trying to come to terms with the trauma he had experienced there. As an adult he became a historian specializing in the study of the Third Reich, including the creation of Auschwitz and similar extermination camps. In 1984 he wrote a meticulously documented history of the Family Camp where he had been imprisoned, in which he carefully unravelled the motivation behind the creation of the camp and its final liquidation.

At the same time he began to construct a deeply private metaphorical landscape, based around his childhood emotions and experience. In his mind he transformed Auschwitz into 'the Metropolis of Death', the centre of a vast empire of annihilation that spread across the entire world. The gas chambers and crematoria became eternal symbols, quite separate from their existence in reality; and the Vistula, into whose tributaries the ashes of the dead were emptied, became a mythological River Styx or the 'River of Truth'.

Kulka was aware that this internal world was incompatible with his academic work. At the university where he was a historian, he had become renowned for the dispassionate, scientific nature of his research – metaphors, symbols and personal mythology had no place here. He therefore kept his internal world and his academic world scrupulously separate; and yet he recognized that they mirrored one another – that one was not possible without the other.[2]

Despite his own survival, and despite the dismantling of the Nazi state and all its killing centres, Kulka was convinced that he would never escape the symbolic power of Auschwitz. He was haunted by recurring, circular nightmares in which he would repeatedly be saved from the gas chambers, only to find himself back where he started, facing the same ordeal over again. In an attempt to exorcize himself of these dreams, in the 1970s Kulka made a journey to the ruins of

Otto Dov Kulka, distinguished historian and former inmate of the 'Family Camp' at Auschwitz.

Auschwitz. He made a point of stepping into one of the former gas chambers as a symbolic completion of the death narrative that haunted him. It did not work. The dreams continued, and Kulka retained for the rest of his life the sense that death – not ordinary death, but the 'Great Death' that presided over Auschwitz – was the 'sole certain perspective ruling the world'.[3]

Kulka's memoir is a particularly eloquent description of a phenomenon that many survivors of the war experienced: not only those who lived through the Holocaust but also survivors of bombing campaigns, torture, displacement, ethnic cleansing or the many, many other wartime traumas that occurred across the globe. Those who had experienced such misfortunes were often compelled to recycle them endlessly in dreams, flashbacks, writings or conversations. Some, like Kulka, felt compelled to study the events they had experienced or witnessed, or even re-enact them in a fruitless attempt to master them. For these people there could be no wiping of the slate. The symbolic 'ending of the world' that they had experienced did not pave the way for any kind of personal resurrection: on the contrary, it trapped them in a state where an awareness of death and the possibility of apocalypse was ever present – a state that psychologist Robert Jay Lifton, writing about atomic bomb survivors, famously termed 'death in life'.[4]

For such people the war was both over and not over: they inhabited a sort of no-man's-land, severed from a past that had been destroyed and yet unable to immerse themselves fully in a future that promised rebirth. Otto Dov Kulka's experience of the 'Metropolis of Death' was therefore far from being a mere 'memory' as we would conventionally understand it. In his mind the end of the world was not something that was over, but something that was 'perpetually part of my present'.[5] Throughout his life he retained the conviction that Auschwitz, or what Auschwitz represented, would inevitably consume him, just as it had consumed everyone he had known in 1944.

Victim Communities

What is true of individuals is also true, to a certain degree, of communities. It was almost impossible to be Jewish after 1945 without also having an intense relationship with the Holocaust, and millions of Jews who had no direct experience of that terrible event nevertheless lived with an awareness of its shadow constantly hanging over them.[6] British journalist Anne Karpf has written eloquently about what it was like to grow up with parents who were Holocaust survivors. Despite an atmosphere of enforced optimism at home, Karpf quickly developed a variety of very strong anxieties, beneath which was an unhealthy obsession with death:

> Death was alive and present in our home. My parents had a few rescued pre-war photo albums containing group pictures of chillingly merry people. They would point out who was who and how they died. With so few living relatives dead ones had to suffice . . . It seemed as if from birth I was obsessed with death.[7]

The Holocaust has, for better or worse, become increasingly central to the Jewish identity. With the decline of both religious beliefs and the Zionist movement, Jews around the world have sometimes struggled to find any single big idea that unifies them: to a certain degree, the shadow of the Holocaust has filled that gap. This is not something that all Jews feel comfortable with. But just as individuals like Otto Dov Kulka have

A shrine to the victims of the Holocaust – the Hall of Names at Yad Vashem, Jerusalem.

been obliged to incorporate the memory of Auschwitz into their daily emotional lives, so too must the Jewish community as a whole live with the Holocaust as a constant, inescapable presence.[8]

Many events have reawakened intense anxieties amongst Jews: to name just a few, the show trials of Jewish political and intellectual figures in the USSR during the early 1950s, the capture and trial of Adolf Eichmann in the 1960s, the 1967 Arab–Israeli War, the 1973 Yom Kippur War, the Arab intifada, the post-9/11 rise in anti-Semitic attacks around the world, the growth of Iran's nuclear capability, the huge popularity of the anti-Semitic Jobbik political party in Hungary, and so on. In the light of what happened during the Second World War, the world's Jewish community does not – indeed, cannot – take such events lightly.

Jews are not alone in reacting this way. The war caused similarly large-scale trauma in many other communities: one needs only to look at the statistics associated with the war to get a feel for the staggering scale of their losses. Around one in six Poles was killed between 1939 and 1945 as well as up to one in five Ukrainians. At least 20 million Soviet citizens are thought to have died, probably more: the numbers are so huge, and the disruption to society so massive, that historians' margins of error are always in the millions.[9] The same is true in China, where even conservative estimates of the number of people killed during the war range from 15 to 20 million, and some Chinese historians put the number as high as 50 million.[10] The word 'holocaust' was frequently used in 1945 to describe not the genocide of European Jews, but the war as a whole.

Jews are therefore not the only community whose experience of the Second World War has left them with a morbid identification with the dead. One of the most important symbols of the war in France, for example, is the village of Oradour-sur-Glane, which was destroyed in 1944 as a reprisal for Resistance activity in the area. The original village has been preserved exactly as it was on the day when its population was massacred, a fossilized symbol of negation, and today this ghost town occupies a special place in French memory. There are similar martyred villages, towns and cities throughout Europe that are equally morbid, and equally important to the national consciousness. The Czechs have the village of Lidice, which was entirely razed as a reprisal for the assassination of the Nazi leader Reinhard Heydrich. The Greeks have the village of Distomo, the Italians have Marzabotto, the Belgians have Vinkt. The defining symbol of Polish martyrdom was the systematic

The nation as holy martyr – the memorial to the Dutch war dead in Amsterdam.

destruction of Warsaw, when the city was deliberately razed by the Nazis after a failed uprising in 1944. The Chinese feel similar emotions about Nanjing, which was destroyed in 1937 and its population systematically raped and massacred by the Japanese. Even the so-called perpetrator nations have their own symbols of martyrdom: the Germans remember the bombing of Dresden, and the Japanese have Hiroshima and Nagasaki.

In 1945 every participating nationality, to a greater or lesser degree, was considered a victim of the war; and their communal reactions to their various traumas mirrored those of individuals. Many nations have experienced flashbacks to the sense of powerlessness they felt during the war, especially in the 1960s, 70s and 80s, when there were widespread fears that a third world war might be about to break out. Some have experienced the compulsion to repeat the past, even to the point of re-enacting the aggression they felt in 1945 – the waves of anti-Japanese sentiment that have periodically rocked South Korea immediately spring to mind. Books have been written psychoanalysing the way that Israel appears to have taken on some of the characteristics of the very perpetrators who oppressed Jews during the 1930s and 40s (and, naturally, other books have been written refuting such claims). In the worst cases, nations have been unable to cope with the trauma of the war, and have subsequently suffered complete psychic breakdown. For example the violent disintegration of Yugoslavia in the 1990s took place in an atmosphere suffused with the rhetoric of the Second World War, and involved episodes of ethnic cleansing that were virtual re-enactments of events that took place fifty years previously. To this day there are communities across the region that continue to live in denial or fear, and who have little or no trust of their neighbours because of the continuing cycle of atrocity and counter-atrocity that began during the Second World War. The 2014 crisis in Ukraine bears many of the same hallmarks: a country torn apart by war and ethnic cleansing during the 1940s which has been unable to create a stable, single identity since.

Rise of the Martyr

Of all the different groups who were persecuted during the war, and who now bicker about who was responsible for their suffering, one has emerged as pre-eminent – the Second World War's quintessential victim. There are many reasons why the world has chosen Jews to fulfil this role. As the main focus of Nazi vitriol before and during the war, it seems appropriate that they should become the main focus of our sympathy afterwards. They were murdered more efficiently and in higher numbers than any other racial group. And the industrial methods that were employed to annihilate them seem to epitomize the inhumanity both of the Nazi system and of the war itself. In these ways, Jews are an ideal symbol of our collective victimhood.

Just as significant, however, are the sociological motives behind our choice. Since Jews had no nation, they effectively belonged to all nations. As a consequence, all of us can identify with their suffering without reawakening the dangerous national rivalries that might once again lead us into the abyss. In the same way, every nation in the West is able to acknowledge a degree of complicity in the Holocaust – whether as active participants or as passive bystanders – safe in the knowledge that they do not have to bear that guilt alone. The culpability of our fore-bears in standing by while Jews were murdered is one thing that we are all willing to admit. A universal victim can be just as useful as a univer-sal scapegoat in bringing nations and peoples together.

It is important to remember that this state of affairs did not come about overnight. People in the West are so used to expressing communal grief at the unique suffering of Jews that they assume every right-thinking person does so, and that they have always done so; but actually it took decades to develop. Contrary to what we think we remember, the Allied soldiers who rode into Auschwitz, Belsen and Dachau did not immediately gather up Jews into what Bill Clinton characterized as 'the warm embrace of freedom'.[11] In reality, most soldiers recoiled from the horror of these places, and often found their sympathy overwhelmed with disgust for the 'creatures' and 'ape-like living skeletons' they found there.[12] The humanitarian agencies that looked after displaced persons in the following months had a similarly complicated relationship with Jews. While trying to remain sympathetic to this particularly trauma-tized group, they became increasingly frustrated at their inability to behave 'normally', or indeed gratefully, and came to regard Jews as vengeful troublemakers and 'future criminals'. Even the director of the United Nations Relief and Rehabilitation Administration in West Ger-many characterized them as 'desperate men who will stick at nothing'.[13]

Later, when these Jews returned home, their communities made it painfully clear that they were not interested in listening to what they had been through – indeed, many communities were openly hostile to Jews returning at all. Everyone had suffered during the war. No one was interested in learning how someone else's suffering might have been greater than their own.[14]

Sympathy for Jews did not grow much in the years that followed. According to several recent historical studies, Europeans in the 1940s and 50s actively avoided hearing stories of the genocide, because it revealed the darkest consequences of their wartime collaboration with the Nazis – a collaboration that they were anxious to distance themselves from. It also contradicted the comforting myth that all Europeans had suffered equally together.[15] Americans were not much more sympathetic: in the 1950s Jewish suffering was old news, and people were more concerned about the new evil of communism than they were about the old spectre of Nazism.[16] Even in the new state of Israel, sympathy for Holocaust survivors was distinctly lacking. Israeli Jews wanted to think of themselves as fighters, heroes, strong enough to seize and hold their own country: they often despised the European Jews who had gone meekly to their deaths, 'like sheep to the slaughter'. The survivors were, in the words of Israeli poet Leah Goldberg, 'ugly, impoverished, morally unstable and hard to love'.[17] Even David Ben-Gurion, one of Israel's founding fathers, characterized some of the survivors as 'harsh, evil, and egotistical people' whose ordeal had taken away 'every good part of their souls'.[18]

Far from identifying with the victims, therefore, it seems that much of the world still felt quite hostile towards them. It was not until a new generation came of age in the 1960s that the world finally started to embrace the sufferers and actively engage with the full horror of the Holocaust. There are various reasons why this change took place, some of which are inextricably linked to historical events. The capture in Buenos Aires by Mossad agents of the Nazi war criminal Adolf Eichmann in 1960 was perhaps the most important of these: his trial the following year was deliberately constructed to provide the world with an education in what the Nazis had done to the Jewish people, and its reportage by luminaries such as Hannah Arendt was eagerly consumed throughout the West.[19] But societal changes also played their part. The 1960s generation was eager to reject authority, and to embrace the role of the outsider. The Jew, in the words of Jean-Paul Sartre, was not only 'the stranger, the intruder, the unassimilated at the very heart of our society', but also the 'quintessence of man'. The 1960s was the time when all kinds of groups began to identify themselves as persecuted minorities: it was the era of love and peace, feminism, civil rights for African-Americans, and so on. When students took to the streets of Paris in 1968 with the slogan 'Nous sommes tous des Juifs allemands' ('We are all German Jews'), they were expressing not only solidarity with the archetypal outsider but also a shared sense of victimhood.[20]

Alongside such shifting attitudes, the 1960s saw the beginning of an explosion of Holocaust histories, memoirs, novels, TV dramas, documentaries and Hollywood movies – a trend that only accelerated in the 1970s and 80s – making the 'Holocaust story' a genre in its own right. This was when memoirists like Primo Levi and Elie Wiesel first found a mass audience, and when Raul Hilberg's landmark book, *The Destruction of the European Jews*, opened the way for subsequent studies on Holocaust history. Perhaps the most important turning point in the portrayal of the genocide was the American TV drama miniseries *Holocaust* in 1978, which shocked and enthralled tens of millions of viewers both in America and in West Germany. Its reception in Germany was particularly influential: this was the first time that a mass audience had been presented with an unflinching portrayal of the Holocaust, and some historians credit the miniseries with kick-starting Germany's process of coming to terms with its Nazi past.[21] Other watershed moments include the epic 1985 documentary *Shoah*, made by French director Claude Lanzmann, and Steven Spielberg's hugely successful, multi-Oscar winning 1993 film *Schindler's List*.

What almost all depictions of the Holocaust have in common is the way that they enshrine the suffering of the victim as the central experience of the Second World War. Holocaust stories are entirely unconcerned with traditional versions of the war as a titanic fight between heroes and villains – instead, the dichotomy they explore is one between perpetrator and victim, the powerful and the powerless, the innocent and the guilty. The victims are almost always idealized in these stories: they are, in the words of one American critic, 'gentle, scholarly, middle-class, *civilized* people' – people 'like us'. Quarrelsome Jews, ignorant Jews – the bullies, liars and layabouts that are found in every community – are rarely, if ever, portrayed.[22] The perpetrators, by contrast, are almost always demonized. Concentration camp guards are uniformly sadistic and Nazi officials uniformly corrupt and treacherous. In many of the most important memoirs and dramas there is also a brooding sense of some vast and nameless evil lurking unseen in the background – what Holocaust survivor and Nobel Peace laureate Elie Wiesel has called 'a demonic convulsion' in the forces that form our world.[23]

This perception of the Holocaust as the struggle between good, blameless people and a vast, unstoppable evil has lodged itself firmly in our collective unconscious. Journalists and academics who try to question this dichotomy are often vilified as a result. For example Hannah Arendt's book about the Eichmann trial provoked fury amongst American Jews because of the way she questioned both of these moral absolutes. On the one hand she insisted that Eichmann was 'neither monstrous nor demonic', but merely bland and banal; on the other hand she brought attention to the way that some Jewish leaders had actively collaborated with the Nazi regime. She was consequently denounced as a 'self-hating Jewess' in one Jewish newspaper, while a prominent American Jewish institution mounted a campaign against what it called her 'evil book'.[24] Journalist John Sack received similar treatment when he tried to publish a book about the way some Jews committed acts of revenge after the war was over. A variety of publishers in America and Europe cancelled publication of the book for fear of bad publicity, and Sack himself was accused both on TV and in print of Holocaust denial.[25] When Professor Christopher Browning wrote a book suggesting that the perpetrators of the Holocaust were not monsters inspired by hatred or fanaticism, but merely 'ordinary men', fellow academic Daniel Goldhagen was so incensed that he wrote a 600-page rebuttal. His book, *Hitler's Willing Executioners*, demonized Germany as a nation inspired by murderous hatred of Jews. It is interesting that while Browning's book won more praise in academic circles, it was Goldhagen's comforting portrayal of the monster that became a runaway bestseller.[26]

Today, we idealize 'the Jews' of the Second World War and demonize 'the Nazis' almost without thinking. Jews who came through the Holocaust are treated with a public reverence that is usually reserved for war heroes – indeed, they are often called 'heroes' in memorial speeches and editorials.[27] We rarely emphasize how many Jews have been embittered by what they have suffered; instead, we describe their lives as 'the triumph of good over evil', 'a testament to courage', or 'a shining example of the survival of the human spirit'.[28] Memorial speeches by popes and presidents continually remind us that wartime Jews were 'innocent victims, innocent people', or 'six million innocent . . . men, women, children, babies'.[29] This mantra of innocence is not merely the righteous and long-overdue rejection of anti-Semitic stereotypes: it is an appeal to something greater – a spiritual purity that is directly related to their status as victims. They are routinely described as 'sacred', the 'Jewish equivalent of saints' and the holders of holy secrets that 'others will never know'. In 1974 the Bishop of New York described them as 'Holy Innocents', whose 'sacrifice' had the potential to redeem us all. 'The survivor has become a priest,' claimed the education director of the Israeli Holocaust memorial, Yad Vashem, in 1993; 'because of his story, he is holy.'[30]

Many historians, sociologists and psychologists have noted the way that the Holocaust has developed into something akin to a 'mystery religion', complete with sacred texts, holy relics and hallowed places.[31] On the surface this 'mystery religion' bears some resemblance to the personal mythology that Otto Dov Kulka revealed in his memoir, with its 'empire of death' and its immutable and unknowable laws. However, there are also many ways in which this communal mythology is nothing like Kulka's personal one at all. To begin with, Kulka was always scrupulous in keeping his personal mythology and his scientific understanding of the facts entirely separate: those outside the academic world are not always quite so conscientious.[32] Secondly, while Kulka's mythological world remained immutable, almost fossilized by the trauma he suffered, our own perceptions tend to change with the political and cultural weather. The mystical way we view the Jewish story today bears no resemblance to the stories of heroic resistance that formed the dominant Jewish narrative in the 1950s, nor to the heavy sense of depression that used to hang over the subject during the 1980s. In fact, in some respects our narrative no longer even appears particularly Jewish. In his scholarly dissection of the way that the Holocaust has been portrayed in American life, Peter Novick drew attention to this curious fact:

> One of the things I find most striking about much of recent Jewish Holocaust commemoration is how 'un-Jewish' – how *Christian* – it is. I am thinking of the ritual of reverently following the structured pathways of the Holocaust in the major museums, which resembles nothing so

much as the Stations of the Cross on the Via Dolorosa; the fetishized objects on display like so many fragments of the True Cross or shin bones of saints . . . Perhaps most significantly, there is the way that suffering is sacralized and portrayed as the path to wisdom – the cult of the survivor as secular saint. These are themes that have some minor and peripheral precedent in Jewish tradition, but they resonate more powerfully with major themes in Christianity.[33]

The more 'global' the mythology of the Holocaust has become, the more it has adopted the language and symbolism of the dominant culture, which in the West is predominantly a Christian one. In this context, Auschwitz has become the Jewish equivalent of Golgotha, and the huge memorials and museums in Jerusalem, Washington and Berlin have become national Jewish cathedrals. Thus, in our collective imagination, the victims have slowly been transformed from 'lambs for the slaughter' to the Lamb of God himself – a sort of collective Christian Messiah. In Christian thinking Europe's wartime Jews are often referred to as 'the martyrs of the Holocaust' whose 'sacrifice' finally brought the world to its senses; and crucifixion imagery has often been used to portray their 'passion'. Thus, in the eyes of the world, a specifically Jewish experience has been subtly converted into a Christian one.[34]

The logical end point of this narrative is one of redemption and resurrection. The Holocaust is slowly changing from a straightforward horror story, which demonstrates the depth of man's capacity for evil, to one of hope. We now congratulate ourselves for having learned the lessons of the war. We note with satisfaction the way that Europe has risen from the ashes to become a stable, tolerant, peaceful continent. As a global community we take pride in our international institutions and international system of laws, and declare that the terrors of the Holocaust will never be allowed to happen again. All of which is a much more hopeful form of mythology than the one of previous decades, but mythology nonetheless.[35]

Competitive Martyrdom

Where does this leave the actual victims – the real people who experienced the Holocaust for themselves? To be sure, the sacralization of the

Holocaust does suit many of the survivors. It makes them feel respected and listened to, even gives their lives meaning as they proselytize the message of 'never again'. However, it leaves others feeling profoundly uneasy, not only because of the way they are pressured to find something redemptive in their experiences, but also because they find the received view of the Holocaust unnecessarily stifling. In his memoir, Otto Dov Kulka confessed that he never watched films about Auschwitz or read the accounts of fellow inmates – not because they brought back painful memories, but because he never recognized the place they described. Auschwitz memoirs, he observed, had a 'uniform language' – one might even say a uniform mythology – which has come to be accepted throughout the world; but this did not chime with his own language, his own mythology, his own Auschwitz. To his great discomfort, listening to other survivors never aroused fellow feeling, only 'total alienation'.[36] Other survivors have said similar things. Their individual stories, while individually respected, have been sacrificed on the altar of a more general, and more convenient, mythology; in the eyes of the world, the Holocaust survivor has been reduced to little more than 'a museum piece, a fossil, a freak, a ghost'.[37]

It is not only individuals who find themselves alienated by the sanctification of Jewish suffering. Poland is one nation amongst many that suffers from what has been called, perhaps a little tastelessly, 'Holocaust envy'. For the past two centuries the Poles have defined themselves as a nation of martyrs, perpetually struggling for freedom but repeatedly victimized by their bigger, more powerful neighbours. What happened to Poland during the Second World War seemed like the ultimate confirmation of this belief: the country was repeatedly dismembered, and emerged from the war with a smashed economy, razed cities and entirely redrawn borders. Unlike western Europe, which regained its freedom in 1945, Poland found itself enslaved by a new totalitarian system that continued to crucify it until the fall of communism more than forty years later. In absolute terms, it suffered the same number of deaths as did Jews – indeed, half of the Jews who were murdered were in fact also Polish. But because of the way that many Poles collaborated in the Holocaust, the rest of the world often remembers them not as victims but as perpetrators. Poles today really struggle with this idea – not because they are any more anti-Semitic than other people, or any less capable of accepting responsibility for their misdeeds, but because they are so used to seeing themselves as the 'Christ among nations' that they cannot yet reconcile themselves to the fact that Jews have appropriated their title.[38]

There are many other groups that envy the status of Jews as the world's archetypal martyr. When the United Nations General Assembly held a day-long commemoration of the Holocaust in 2005, some of the delegates made a point of drawing attention to their own national tragedies during the Second World War. The South Korean spokesman wanted to point out that the war's atrocities had not been confined to Europe: other regions of the globe had 'also endured massive human rights violations and forced brutality'. He presumably had in mind the fate of the Korean 'comfort women' – those women who were coerced into a life of sexual slavery at Japanese military brothels and who have symbolized the Korean sense of victimhood ever since the 1990s. The Chinese representative highlighted the appalling slaughter in his country – 35 million deaths, according to him. Nazi Germany might have committed innumerable atrocities, he said, but the 'militaristic butchers' of Japan 'took no second seat' to them.

Other delegates at this commemoration wanted to widen the discourse about victimhood still further. The special envoy of Guinea, speaking on behalf of the African states, took the opportunity to bring up the horrors of slavery, colonialism and apartheid. The Rwandan delegate spoke at length about the genocide in his own country, as did the spokesman from neighbouring Tanzania. The Armenian delegate mentioned not only the Armenian genocide but also many others, and complained of the 'double standards' of the UN when comparing one genocide to another. The Venezuelan speaker even dared to condemn the 'conquests waged by America and its allies' during the second half of the twentieth century.

This may signal the beginning of a shift in our views on Second World War victimhood, but for the moment at least the Holocaust remains the central symbol around which all the other victims congregate. During this special session of the UN General Assembly, at least, the centrality of the Holocaust was never seriously under threat, and it remained the benchmark against which all other atrocities were measured. It was still 'the twentieth century's ultimate crime', 'the absolute moral abomination', 'the ultimate act of man's inhumanity to man'. Even those who pressed for a similar recognition of their own tragedies still acknowledged the value of a universal victim. As the Armenian delegate said, echoing the sentiments of many other 'victims' before him, 'We are all Jews.'[39]

In truth, the main reason we have communally adopted Second World War Jews as our archetypal victims is simply that it suits almost everyone. For Europe, the Holocaust provides a cautionary tale and allows for a form of collective guilt that binds the continent together – it is virtually the only thing that everyone in Europe agrees on.[40] For many nations in South America it has provided an indirect way of coming to terms with their own troubled pasts: the Holocaust memorial in Montevideo, for example, was used as a template for the later memorials to the victims of Uruguay's own fascist dictatorship.[41] In Africa and Asia the Holocaust is the final nail in the coffin of the myth of white superiority: it gives added vindication, if any were needed, to the decision to throw off colonial rule.[42] Americans, meanwhile, continue to use the Holocaust as a way not only to demonstrate their heroism in liberating the world from Nazism but also to show the difference between the rotten Old World and the superior New.[43] Lastly, for Jews themselves, their victimhood status has bestowed a sense of moral power that is in marked contrast to the powerlessness they felt during the war. In the world's imagination, the Holocaust has made them almost a holy race, blessed by a seemingly eternal innocence.[44]

With only a few exceptions, the whole world benefits from the myth of the universal victim, not because it has learned any lessons from the Holocaust, but because it believes it has. This is the final myth of the Holocaust, and one that I shall turn to next – the comforting belief that the horror of the Second World War led us to some kind of redemption and rebirth. Of all the myths that came out of the war, this is probably the most seductive.

5. The Beginning of the World

On 9 August 1945, just three days after Hiroshima was destroyed, a second atom bomb was dropped on Japan. Nagai Takashi was working in his office at Nagasaki's university hospital when the bomb went off. Unlike Ogura Toyofumi, he did not see the terrible beauty of the explosion: the first he knew of it was when a blinding flash came through the window, followed by a blast of wind which threw him into the air and then buried him beneath a heap of rubble and broken glass.

Like virtually all atom bomb survivors, Nagai's account of that day has an apocalyptic quality. He describes large objects hurtling through the sky in 'a macabre dance', and charred bodies lying everywhere in a 'world of the dead'. He even reports a group of his colleagues trying to make sense of what had just happened by speculating that the sun itself had just exploded. A few days later, Emperor Hirohito's announcement of Japan's capitulation only seemed to underline the sense of apocalypse, at least on a national level: 'Our Japan – the Japan symbolized by Mount Fuji piercing the clouds and enlightened by the sun that rose in the eastern sea – was dead. Our people, the people of Yamato, were cast to the very depths of an abyss. We who were alive lived only in shame. Happy indeed were our companions who had left this world in the holocaust of the atomic bomb.'[1]

Remarkably, Nagai seems to have been able to accept his, and Japan's, fate without much bitterness. As a devout Christian he certainly had a strong framework for coming to terms with loss, but even so the speed and depth of his psychological recovery seem extraordinary. When one of his former students came to him later that year talking of revenge, Nagai chided him gently: 'My wife is dead; my property is lost, my house is destroyed. I've lost everything. I have nothing. I gave everything I had but I was defeated. Why should I say that it's a tragedy or a pitiful situation? Why is it pitiful? Our situation now is like that of a man who looks at the moon after the rain. It was a war. We lost. I have no regrets.'[2]

What Nagai began to experience now was a period of spiritual rebirth. As a university radiologist, he was familiar with the science behind nuclear physics, and he quickly guessed that what he had experienced was one of the first atom bombs. The very idea fascinated him. Even as his own world was collapsing around him, he immediately recognized that 'the curtain was rising on a new age: the atomic age'. Despite his crushing grief, he and his colleagues 'nevertheless felt rising within us a new drive and a new motivation in our search for truth. In this devastated atomic desert, fresh and vigorous scientific life began to flourish.'[3] Over the next few months, he and his fellow scientists charted for the first time the effects of radiation sickness, both in the population at large and in themselves. Nagai, who already had leukaemia, was particularly badly affected. He would die from the after-effects of the bomb six years later.

This progression from despair to mourning, acceptance and spiritual rebirth is something that psychologists would recognize as a relatively healthy response to the extremely traumatic events Nagai had experienced. Through his Christianity and his passion for science, he had managed to transform his loss into something meaningful; though he

Nagai Takashi with his children, shortly before his death in 1951. His best-selling books gave hope to a despondent Japan in the aftermath of defeat.

would live with the consequences of that loss for the rest of his short life, he was at least able to start again.

Nagai's personal journey seemed to strike something of a chord in Japan. His memoir, *The Bells of Nagasaki*, became a bestseller and was also turned into a hugely successful movie, whose theme tune became something of an anthem for the times. The book was recommended by the Japanese Education Ministry as a set text for all Japanese schools. Over the following months, Nagai came to be seen as something of a saint: indeed, the Japanese newspapers often referred to him as 'the saint of Nagasaki', and comparisons with Gandhi were common. The city of Nagasaki awarded him honorary citizenship, and he was formally declared a national hero by the state. His books also brought him international renown: he was visited on his sick bed by Helen Keller, Emperor Hirohito and an emissary of the Pope. After his death in May 1951, he was regarded by some as a Christ-like figure whose suffering was emblematic of Japan's sacrifice during and after the war.[4]

Part of Nagai's appeal was the way he managed to transform catastrophe into triumph. The bomb had not destroyed him, it had transformed him: he had effectively been born again through martyrdom. This was certainly the message that he himself preached in his books and other writings. In November 1945 Nagai gave a speech at a Requiem Mass in the ruins of Nagasaki's Urakami Cathedral in which he described the atom bomb not as a bringer of destruction, but as a gift from God:

'It was not the American crew, I believe, who chose our suburb. God's providence chose Urakami and carried the bomb right above our homes. Is there not a profound relationship between the annihilation of Nagasaki and the end of the war? Was not Nagasaki the chosen victim, the lamb without blemish, slain as a whole-burnt offering on an altar of sacrifice, atoning for the sins of all the nations during World War II? . . . Let us be thankful that Nagasaki was chosen for the whole-burnt sacrifice. Let us be thankful that through this sacrifice peace was granted to the world . . .'[5]

This extraordinary speech reflected what many other cultural and political figures were also saying. In the same month, the president of Tokyo University told his returning students that they too should celebrate their defeat as the beginning of a new era of 'reason and truth'.[6] One of the country's most influential postwar philosophers, Tanabe

Hajime, also characterized Japan's despair as a natural step on the way to 'resurrection and regeneration': the nation, he claimed, would not only be reborn, but also would show the way to a safer, more peaceful planet.[7] Even before the American occupation began, at the end of August 1945, the head of the government's Information Bureau was touting the experience of the atom bomb as the key to turning Japan from the 'losers of the war' to the 'winners of the peace'.[8] Japan at last had a special place in the world – not through conquest, but through defeat: as the world's first and only atomic martyr it could serve as an example to all of mankind of the perils of war.

Partly as a consequence of such ideas, Japan underwent a transformation that was every bit as rapid as Nagai Takashi's. In the immediate postwar years it changed from one of the most militaristic societies in the world to one of the most pacific. Later it would undergo similar economic, political and cultural transformations, reinventing itself repeatedly. All this stemmed from Japan's experience of the Second World War, and particularly the atom bomb, which remains the single most iconic moment in the foundation of contemporary Japan.

Impressive though all this might be, there is still something slightly disturbing about it, on both a personal and a societal level. For all Nagai's supposed saintliness, he was not a figure without controversy. There were those who were appalled at his notion that the atom bomb was some sort of gift from God, and many who attended the Requiem Mass were reportedly angry at his characterization of their dead families as 'holy sacrifices' rather than victims of an atrocity. There was also something suspect about Nagai's portrayal of Nagasaki as a symbol of martyred innocence. Neither Nagasaki nor Japan was quite the 'lamb without blemish' they liked to believe they were: it was not 'the sins of all nations' that had started the war, but *Japan's* sins. Nagai never quite made the connection between his own unconditional support for the wartime government and the crimes that were committed in Japan's name. This is a problem that has plagued the nation ever since: alongside Japan's collective martyrdom was an element of collective guilt, but this is a notion that has never been embraced in the same way, and still is not today.

In the long run, the miraculous rebirth of the nation after the war was only ever a partial one. The Japanese might have reinvented their economy, but neither the Americans nor the postwar government ever managed to break up the cartels that had controlled Japan's wartime industrial system. None of the country's industrial leaders was ever brought to trial, despite the way they had both paved the road to war and enjoyed huge profits from it, particularly from the use of slave labour. Throughout the postwar period there has remained a strong sense that the Japanese economic miracle was partly built on rotten foundations. Even in the twenty-first century some of the most important Japanese corporations – such as Mitsubishi, Mitsui and Nippon Steel – still have to fight court cases because of their alleged behaviour during the Second World War.[9]

The Japanese also completely overhauled their political system after the war: under American tutelage they dissolved their empire, introduced a new constitution and granted women the vote for the first time. And yet their highest symbol of authority remained the emperor in whose name the war was fought. Some of the leading political figures who were responsible for the war either remained in their positions throughout the immediate postwar years or were returned to power soon after the Americans handed the reins back to the Japanese. Indeed, one politician was elected to parliament for the first time in 1952 on the back of his notoriety as a war criminal who had escaped justice.[10]

While Japanese culture has also undergone a massive transformation since 1945, in another sense the country has never really been able to move on. According to one Japanese psychiatrist, Japan's manic pursuit of material gain in the second half of the twentieth century was partly a way of hiding the scars of war. The whole nation, says Noda Masaaki, has become adept at making 'sophisticated-sounding excuses for ourselves' in order to avoid an honest confrontation with the issues of war and guilt. Even the peace movement, with its narrative of Japanese victimhood, is based on a form of denial. Japan today is 'a culture that still refuses to recognize its emotional wounds': no matter how often the nation has reinvented itself, it has never achieved a true spiritual rebirth because it has never fully managed to embrace its wartime responsibilities.[11]

The Rebirth of Nations

There is, of course, nothing unique in any of this. The myth of resurrection has been a constant theme throughout the world ever since the end of the war. If one takes a closer look at the metaphors that were used by witnesses of the devastation in 1945, many of them are far more hopeful than they immediately seem. The Last Judgement, Gomorrah, Noah's Flood, Vishnu's scorching of the universe – these are images not only of total destruction but also of rebirth. The war may have brought about the end of the old world, but it also promised the beginning of a new one, better and fairer than the last. Regardless of whether this rebirth ever actually took place, just the idea of it brought enormous hope and comfort to a world population thoroughly demoralized by years of hardship, violence and oppression.

Just about everyone had a vested interest in propagating this myth of a new world rising from the ashes of the old. It certainly chimed well with the victors. In his speeches to the nation, President Truman underlined again and again the fact that the American people were about to witness a 'new era', that they were standing 'on the threshold of a new world', and that with the death of the 'world at war' came the birth of a 'world of peace'. On 16 August 1945, the day after Japan's capitulation, he proclaimed, 'This is the end of the grandiose schemes of the dictators to enslave the peoples of the world, destroy their civilization, and institute a new era of darkness and degradation. This day is a new beginning in the history of freedom on this earth.'[12] There could be no better encapsulation of all the myths I have covered so far: the victory of good over evil, the martyrdom of the world and, finally, the resurrection brought about by Allied heroes.

The USSR, meanwhile, was slower to embrace 1945 as the start of something *completely* new. Soviet ideology had always emphasized 1917 as the USSR's foundation year, and while the Second World War remained a massive influence on all aspects of Soviet society, it took a few decades before it eclipsed the symbolism of the October Revolution. Nevertheless, by the late 1960s the Soviets had begun producing hundreds of films, books and artworks devoted to the war. Memorials and museums were opened all over the country and the celebration of Victory Day became a major national event. The principal narrative of the war was one of enormous loss leading to eventual triumph: the people of the Soviet Union had been slaughtered, but through their sacrifice the nation had been not only saved but also reborn to glorious victory.[13]

In the end, the Soviets adopted the same myths about the Second World War that the communist parties in eastern Europe had embraced all along. It was the war that had brought 'the birth of a new

Czechoslovakia', that had created 'a magnificent vision of a new life' in Yugoslavia and that had 'burst the chains of the [East] German people'.[14] In a VE Day speech in 1985, the Albanian defence minister, Prokop Murra, summed up the standard Communist view in eastern Europe: the Second World War was 'one of the greatest events in world history, which dealt the irreparable blow to the capitalist system, instigated the national liberation struggles, marked the decline of colonialism and created a new ratio of forces in favour of socialism and revolution'.[15] Despite its vast legacy of death and destruction, the war was never mourned by the Communists it brought to power; rather it was celebrated as the force that had ushered in a brave new world.[16]

The same was true in much of Africa and Asia, where nationalists saw the war as a crucible out of which their states might be re-forged, free from colonial rule. In a debate on independence at the end of 1946 the future Indian prime minister, Jawaharlal Nehru, invoked the Second World War and its tumultuous aftermath as one of the major factors in India's rebirth:

> We have just come out of the World War and people talk vaguely and rather wildly of new wars to come. At such a moment this New India is taking birth – renascent, vital, fearless. Perhaps it is a suitable moment for this new birth to take place out of this turmoil in the world.[17]

Indonesia's future president, Sukarno, was even clearer about the way that the Second World War was responsible for forging his nation. 'Do not forget that we live in a time of war,' he told a government committee preparing for independence in June 1945:

> It is during this time of war that we are going to establish the state of Indonesia – in the midst of war's thunder. I even utter thanks to God that we are going to establish an Indonesian state not under a clear sky, but with the sound of the drums of war and in the fire of warfare. Indonesia Merdeka ['free Indonesia'] shall emerge a tempered Indonesia, an Indonesia Merdeka tempered in the fire of war.[18]

There were similar sentiments in much of Southeast Asia, North Africa and the Middle East where the war unleashed an unstoppable wave of independence struggles. Because of the war, 'everything has changed and is changing'.[19] Because of the war the moral imperative for self-determination was growing across 'the whole surface of the earth'.[20]

Those with perhaps the greatest incentive to proclaim 1945 a rebirth were the victims and the perpetrators of the war. Both had good reason to want to put the past behind them and start anew. In the war's aftermath, nations like France, Belgium and the Netherlands expended a great deal of political energy proclaiming themselves not only reborn but also rendered stronger and more unified by their wartime experience. So compelling was this communal longing for a return to stability and potency that we now remember this time as a period of celebration, unity and rebuilding in these countries, when in fact there was also a great deal of unrest and violence for years after the war.[21]

In Germany, meanwhile, 1945 was proclaimed *Stunde Null*, a phrase which can loosely be translated as 'Year Zero'.[22] This concept expressed not only the fear that the country had been bombed back into a kind of pre-Christian Dark Age, but also the hope that it could make a new start: much like the Japanese, postwar Germans fervently hoped that their recent past had been buried for ever beneath the rubble. It is easy to criticize them for this, but in the context of a world where most nations were announcing a new beginning, it would have been highly unusual had Germany and Japan not done likewise. Although German and Japanese motives might have been very different from those of other nations, *Stunde Null* was a universal idea.

A Global Rebirth

While many countries adopted a myth of national rebirth after the war, what is perhaps more interesting is the way that the same myth was adopted internationally, even globally. It was not Japan or France or India alone that was reborn, but the whole world: 1945 was a communal Year Zero and has remained such in our collective imagination ever since. A world of violence, repression and evil had been destroyed. And a new world, inspired by the values of the Atlantic Charter and the United Nations, was created.

From the very beginning, however, this global vision came into conflict with the myths of individual nations. All of the national myths that came out of the war depended, to varying degrees, on a sense of victimization. France, Britain, America and all the other Allies had been attacked by a monster, but had triumphed; Communists were breaking

free of the bonds of capitalism; colonial countries were liberating themselves from the slave masters who had oppressed them for centuries; and
so on. But the *international* myth of rebirth was quite different. It imagined a future in which there was not even the potential for such quarrels
and conflicts: in the new world we would all be governed by a mutual
desire for peace. In such a world we would experience both fraternity
and prosperity, the rule of law and the careful regulation of extreme
political and market forces. Nationalism, and all the irrational passions
it fostered, would gradually become redundant.

Perhaps the strongest expression of this new Utopia can be seen in the
foundation myths of today's European Union, which has gone further
than any other international body to break down the barriers between
nations. EU leaders have always acclaimed the way in which 'the European Union was born from the ashes and rubble of the Second World
War'; indeed, it is difficult to find a major European document or statement by an EU leader that does *not* make reference to the foundation of
the new Europe as a reaction to the war.[23] From the very beginning, the
EU was conceived not only as a 'new Europe' but as a new *kind* of Europe, in which catastrophes like the Second World War would no longer
be possible.[24] In the words of Konrad Adenauer, Germany's first postwar Chancellor, and one of the founding fathers of the EU, the postwar
world was the 'beginning of a new historical epoch':

> The age of national states has come to an end. Everyone must feel that a
> change has taken place, that an era has vanished and that a new age is
> dawning in which men will look beyond the borders of their own coun-
> try and work in fraternal co-operation with other nations for the true
> aims of humanity.[25]

What began as an economic partnership between France and Germany quickly spread to include most of western Europe and, since 1989,
eastern Europe too. Many former Eastern Bloc countries consider their
Communist years as an effective continuation of the Second World
War: gaining membership of the European Union became one of the
main ways in which they could symbolically leave the repression of the
past behind, and join a new world of 'freedom' and 'democracy'. Even
today this founding myth remains the central justification for the expansion of the EU and ever closer union between Europe's member states.[26]

The very same ideas are expressed on a global level in the foundation myths of the United Nations. The opening words of the United Nations Charter state explicitly that the organization was set up in 1945 in order to prevent another world war from bringing 'untold sorrow to mankind'. As with the European Union, one is hard pressed to find any major speech or document coming from the UN that does not mention the fact that it was 'born out of the ashes of World War Two', and that its founding purpose was to create a new era of 'peace and respect for human rights' and to 'spare the world from another cataclysm'.[27] To this day, the United Nations Security Council chamber is dominated by a huge mural of a phoenix rising from the rubble of warfare.

The Cost of Myth

None of the myths and legends I have described so far came from nowhere. There was much truth in each of them: the vast destruction that overtook large parts of Europe and Asia did indeed resemble the end of the world; the war undeniably involved a great deal of heroism, monstrousness and martyrdom; and the rebirth of hope that occurred everywhere after 1945 was certainly miraculous. But these truths are not the whole truth. They hide many of the doubts and anxieties that the people of all nations suffered while the world was at war, and provide excuses for people today not to look too closely at their history. We can only indulge in these myths – which seem so absolute and clear-cut – by turning our eyes away from the messy and morally ambiguous reality of what actually took place during those terrible years.

Neither do any of these myths exist in isolation. One of the reasons they have persisted so long is that, no matter how shaky they are individually, as a group they support one another, *amplify* one another. Our images of total devastation provide the perfect backdrop for our folk memories of the Second World War as a titanic struggle for the very soul of mankind. Our heroes are made more heroic by the image of absolute evil against which they were fighting and our monsters are made more monstrous by our belief in the unqualified innocence of the martyrs they tortured. Tying all this together – the total destruction, the selfless heroism and the infinite suffering – is our myth of the new world risen from the ashes of the old. This is the final prize granted to our heroes and martyrs: it ennobles their sacrifice and makes all the suffering seem worthwhile. Taken all together, this network of myths represents a belief system that has been adopted all over the world – with many local variations, naturally, but nevertheless global.

It is important to acknowledge that a belief system like this takes hold for good reason. During the war the belief in moral absolutes was entirely necessary, because the crisis that confronted people all over the world required them to take decisive action. The mythology they adopted in the face of this crisis not only gave individuals the courage and fortitude to meet the demands that were being made of them, but also created the sense of unity that was necessary for them to band together and fight the war successfully. In the process, however, these moral absolutes also satisfied deep emotional needs. There is nothing more gratifying than knowing that you have right on your side, that you are fighting a good war against an evil that must be destroyed. While these myths made perfect sense in 1945, therefore, there was also a danger in them, because they allowed no room for subtlety, for nuance – for doubt.

Today there are no practical reasons why we should hold on to these myths. They are no longer necessary for our survival, as they once were. We no longer need them to explain the unexplainable. The world has moved on, but we have not: we have become stuck in the same mindset that we indulged in 1945. And yet we show no inclination to do anything about it. We simply accept our myths as they are, for no better reason than that they are familiar, and because they still fulfil the same emotional needs that we experienced all those years ago: we crave the old wartime certainties of good and evil, heroes and villains, monsters and martyrs, which contrast so strongly with the day-to-day uncertainties of our own contemporary lives. Thus, we nurture a shameless nostalgia for the war, regardless of whether it is appropriate or not, and we feel comforted by this nostalgia, even when it risks rekindling the very fires that we fought so hard to extinguish in 1945.

All of these myths contribute to the instabilities that continue to plague our international system, even those that at first appear relatively benign. It is easy to criticize our beliefs in heroes, monsters and martyrs for the way they divide us, but the idea of the world reborn like a phoenix in 1945 is also suspect. It is sometimes difficult to acknowledge this, because it frustrates some of our most cherished desires. We *want* to imagine the myth of rebirth as a positive force, full of healing and forgiveness. We *want* to believe that a line can be drawn under all the violence, and that we can rise above our past without resentment or regret. But when these values are imposed upon society without a proper examination of the events we are leaving behind, it is both dishonest and unhealthy. Noble as it is to let bygones be bygones, the insistence that we have moved on, that we have been cleansed by our rebirth after the war, denies us the opportunity to mourn what was lost, or acknowledge our culpability.

For the people who emerged from the shadow of war in 1945, none of this was yet an issue. Of all the myths that came out of this time, the one that was not yet fully formed was precisely this myth of rebirth. As the bombs stopped falling and people all over the world took to the streets to celebrate the end of the war, the image of the phoenix rising from the ashes was not yet a myth but a very real hope that lived in the hearts of millions. As people's thoughts turned to rebuilding, it was only natural that new luminaries would step forward, with visions of new ways of living, new relationships and new forms of expression. Much of the rest of this book will concern itself with the dreams of freedom that they had, and how they were both realized and frustrated amidst the other after-effects of the war.

But within these dreams there were also nightmares. From the very beginning, the new world always seemed painfully fragile, because what had been destroyed once could easily be destroyed again. The fear of repetition was one that haunted everyone the world over. Perhaps the most eloquent expression of that fear came from the new Indian prime minister, Jawaharlal Nehru, in 1949:

> If you look back during the last thirty years or more which have comprised two wars and the period between these wars, you will find the same cries, changing slightly with the changed situation of course, but nevertheless the same cries, the same approaches, the same fears and suspicions and the same arming on all sides and war coming. The same talk of this being the last war, the fight for democracy and all the rest of it is heard on every side. And then the war ends, but the same conflicts continue and again the same preparation for war. Then another war comes . . . Nobody and no country wants war. As war becomes more and more terrible they want it still less. Yet some past evil or karma or some destiny goes on pushing people in a particular direction, towards

the abyss, and they go through the same arguments and they perform
the same gestures like automatons.[28]

The true message of the end of the war was, therefore, not only one
of freedom but also one of fear. With the dawn of the atomic age, the
world could no longer afford to follow the endless cycle of destruction
and rebuilding that had characterized the worlds that had gone before.
After Hiroshima and Nagasaki everyone knew that the next global war
might result in an actual, rather than a symbolic, apocalypse.

PART II

Utopias

6. Science

If any one group felt themselves burdened in 1945 with both the world's dreams and its nightmares, it was the scientists who had spent the war years working on the atomic bomb.

One of these scientists was Eugene Rabinowitch, a Russian-born chemist. Rabinowitch had already experienced some of the most turbulent events of the twentieth century. As a young man he had been forced to flee St Petersburg in the wake of the Russian Revolution. Later he had also fled Germany to escape anti-Semitic persecution at the hands of the Nazis. In 1938, when Europe was on the brink of war, he joined the general exodus of European scientists for America. But it was his time as a senior chemist on the Manhattan Project in Chicago, at the height of the war, that would most change his life. Rabinowitch was only one of hundreds of scientists employed to research and build nuclear weapons – but the experience, and the consequences of the discoveries that he and his fellow scientists made, would haunt him for the rest of his days.[1]

Rabinowitch was first invited to join the atomic bomb project in 1943 by James Franck, a Nobel laureate he had worked with in Germany before the war. He first expressed his doubts about a nuclear future shortly afterwards. He would go for long walks with Franck or other senior scientists such as Leo Szilard, and discuss his worries in hushed tones. While he understood the urgent need to build the bomb, he strongly felt that the American establishment was failing to consider the long-term implications of what they were doing. The secrets of nuclear power could not remain an American monopoly for long. Once other nations also discovered these 'secrets' a new arms race was bound to ensue. The consequences of such an arms race, if it were ever allowed to get out of control, were unthinkable.

In the spring of 1945 Rabinowitch's concerns gained a new urgency: it was an open secret amongst the scientists that an atom bomb would soon be ready for testing. That June, a committee was hastily set up to consider the social and political implications of nuclear weaponry, particularly if it were used in the war against Japan. Rabinowitch would become one of the principal authors of its report.

'It was unbearably hot in Chicago at that time,' he remembered years later. 'As I walked through the streets of the city, I was overcome by the vision of crashing skyscrapers under a flaming sky. Something had to be done to warn humanity. Whether on account of the heat or my own inward excitement, I could not sleep that night. I began writing our report long before daybreak. James Franck had given me a draft of one and a half pages as his contribution. But my own treatment of the matter became very much more detailed.'[2]

The 'Franck Report', as it has come to be known, made two very carefully reasoned points.[3] Firstly, the advent of nuclear power represented to mankind not only an opportunity but also a greater threat than had ever before existed. If the nations of the world were to avoid a future arms race, it was essential that America give up its temporary monopoly on the atom bomb and help instead to set up an international body with the power to control atomic energy for the good of all mankind.

Secondly, it argued, the bomb should not be used in an 'unannounced attack' on Japan, since this would seriously undermine the possibility of any international agreement on atomic energy ever being reached. It would be far better if the bomb were demonstrated to the world openly – perhaps in an uninhabited desert or barren island. That way, Japan might be frightened into surrender without the need for a massive loss of life. If the Japanese military insisted upon continuing the war despite such a demonstration, the bomb could still be used against them.

The scientists' report was delivered to Washington with some urgency, but the US government simply ignored it. 'We waited for some reaction, and we waited and waited,' Rabinowitch later remembered. 'We had the feeling we could have dropped the report into Lake Michigan.'[4] Less than two months later, atomic bombs were dropped on Hiroshima and Nagasaki, bringing the war to its sudden, climactic close. While the rest of the world celebrated, many members of the scientific establishment were plunged immediately into a deep gloom.

In the following months Rabinowitch decided to dedicate himself to publicizing their fears. He and a fellow scientist, Hyman Goldsmith, set up a new journal called the *Bulletin of the Atomic Scientists*, whose purpose was 'to awaken the public to full understanding of the horrendous reality of nuclear weapons, and of their far-reaching implications for the

Eugene Rabinowitch, atomic scientist and long-time voice of conscience for the
nuclear age.

future of mankind'.[5] In the coming years, as the unofficial mouthpiece
of the 'scientists movement', Rabinowitch's journal would become a
voice of conscience for the atomic age. It would publish articles by the
world's leading physicists – such as Albert Einstein, J. Robert Oppenheimer, Niels Bohr and Edward Teller – but also included among its
contributors were several philosophers and sociologists (Bertrand Russell and Raymond Aron), politicians (Henry J. Morgenthau and Andrei
Gromyko), economists (Abba P. Lerner) and even theologians (Reinhold
Niebuhr). Every aspect of the atom bomb and its consequences was discussed and dissected in the hope of 'scaring men into rationality'.[6]

By Rabinowitch's own admission, the hopes embodied in his journal
were always likely to be dashed. Talks between the superpowers to inter-
nationalize atomic energy finally broke down in 1948. The following year,
the Soviet Union detonated its own nuclear bomb and, just as Rabinowitch had feared, an arms race quickly started, one that would eventually

include Britain, France, China, India, Pakistan, Israel and – well into the twenty-first century – North Korea. In the seventy years after the first atomic bomb test in 1945, some 125,000 warheads were built and deployed all over the world. Despite the best efforts of international bodies like the UN and the International Atomic Energy Agency, Eugene Rabinowitch's fears about nuclear proliferation were eventually confirmed.[7]

And yet he never abandoned his faith that science still represented the best hope for mankind – not only in unlocking the secrets of the universe, but also in the way that scientists everywhere insisted on ignoring the quarrels of politicians and collaborating with one another. 'The scope of the scientific revolution of our time is so immense, and so pregnant with still greater future potentialities, that it is transforming the very bases of human existence,' he wrote in later life. 'Our era may appear, to a myopic mind . . . as an era of alienation in which mankind has become separated as never before . . . but to future generations it will appear as an era of beginning world-wide co-operation of mankind.'[8]

The revelation of atomic power in 1945 produced a global sense of shock that is hard to appreciate today. When President Truman announced the dropping of the bomb on Hiroshima, the world's media was entirely unprepared for the story, and did not know how to respond. The power of the bomb, the sheer scale and expense of America's secret project to build it, the possibility of an end to the war – all of these subjects vied for headline space. But what garnered most attention was Truman's comment that scientists had succeeded in 'harnessing the basic power of the universe'. This one line, which was reproduced in newspapers all over the world, seemed to capture everyone's imagination.

One of the first people to describe the combined sense of shock and wonder produced by the events of that summer was the American novelist E. B. White. 'For the first time in our lives we can feel the disturbing vibrations of complete human readjustment,' he wrote in the *New Yorker* just two weeks after the bombing of Hiroshima. 'Usually the vibrations are so faint as to go unnoticed. This time they are so strong that even the ending of a war is overshadowed.' Other writers were quick to agree. 'In an instant, without warning,' claimed *Time* magazine two days later, 'the present had become the unthinkable future.' With the atom bomb's first explosion, claimed another journalist, 'your world and mine, the world we knew, came to an end. A new world was born in that mountain of fire.'[9]

Man harnesses the 'basic power of the universe': Bikini Atoll, 1946.

While everyone agreed that something fundamental had changed, there was no consensus over whether this was a good or a bad thing. In America, there very quickly arose a strong polarization between those who regarded atomic power as a new dawn for mankind and those who feared it would lead to Armageddon.

Prominent amongst the former group was William Laurence of *The New York Times*, the only journalist who had been given access to the Manhattan Project while it was still secret. In September 1945 he wrote a series of articles in which he likened the advent of the atomic age to a spiritual awakening. By harnessing this power, he claimed, mankind had found 'the veritable "Philosopher's Stone" . . . a key to the fountainhead of the very power that keeps the universe going'.[10] He also described the first atom bomb test in the New Mexico desert, which he himself had witnessed: 'One felt as though he had been privileged to witness the Birth of the World – to be present at the moment of Creation when the Lord said: Let There be Light!'[11]

A variety of other American journalists likewise proclaimed the birth of a new age. Atomic power, they suggested, brought the opportunity to 'abolish war', to usher in a future of 'inexhaustible' power and 'unlimited wealth', and even create 'an earthly paradise'.[12] In 1946 *Time* magazine's Gerald Wendt went so far as to suggest that atomic power would one day be available in 'capsule form', and man would no longer want for anything: 'Then at last science will have freed the human race not only from disease, famine, and early death, but also from poverty and work.'[13]

At the same time, however, other prominent thinkers could not help imagining an altogether darker future. Max Lerner, writing in *PM*, was one of many who saw in atomic power the threat of a 'world of which the fascists have been long dreaming, in which a small pitiless elite could hold the power of life and death over the large mass of mankind'.[14] Jean-Paul Sartre considered the atom bomb, 'the negation of man'; Einstein called the new situation 'the most terrible danger in which man has ever found himself'; while General Carl Spaatz, the US Air Force chief who had overseen the bombing of Japan, foresaw a future in which an atomic war 'may end in the most tragic of paradoxes: the good society, in attempting to destroy evil, may destroy itself'.[15]

Many other parts of the world expressed their hopes and fears about this new scientific wonder in similarly Manichean terms. Typical was the reporting of Britain's *Picture Post*, which brought out a special edition at the end of August 1945 focusing on the implications of the bomb. 'The harnessing of atomic energy is probably the greatest event of our lifetimes,' the opening article claimed, one that 'opens up wide new horizons of both hope and horror'. The cover showed a haunting photograph of a child on a beach in twilight, with the caption 'Dawn – Or Dusk?'[16] The *Illustrated Weekly of India* likewise ran stories on how mankind might 'destroy itself in the last and most frightful of wars; or it may live henceforth in a Utopia like the dreams of Edward Bellamy'. Within a few weeks of the bombs on Hiroshima and Nagasaki it was already imagining 'limitless quantities of power . . . at a cost so low that for all practical purposes it would be free' – but at the same time ran articles about how such power might endanger the whole 'economic and industrial future of the world'.[17]

In the following years this polarization of views manifested itself in almost every nation. In the Soviet Union there was a virtual news blackout about the bomb until the Soviets themselves had created one: at which point it was hailed as a triumph of socialism that heralded a new

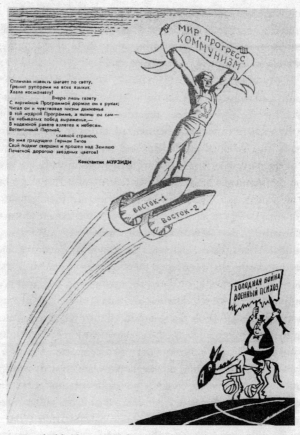

Soviet propaganda, like this cartoon from the early 1960s, pushed the dream of 'Peace, progress and communism' through nuclear power. America, meanwhile, is depicted as a frustrated warmonger, impotently clutching its Cold War weaponry.

era of unlimited power for all. In Germany the opposing views of the nuclear age depended on which half of the country one lived in: the destructive potential of atomic power was emphasized in the West while socialist ideals of a utopian atomic future were more often emphasized in the East. In Japan, which eventually embraced nuclear technology despite its awful wartime experience, the dichotomy was between 'evil' military uses of nuclear power and 'good' civilian ones. Smaller countries, meanwhile, often saw themselves as helpless bystanders in a world of atomic superpowers. In the Netherlands, for example, the atomic age was often portrayed as a force of nature which had driven mankind to a crossroads: whichever road they went down, whether the road to doom or the road to paradise, the people of the Netherlands would be swept along without much choice.[18]

This polarized picture of science and scientists was partly a result of the way that they have always been regarded in the popular imagination, which throughout history has demonized its Fausts and Frankensteins even as it has celebrated its Galileos and Newtons.[19] But it was also a result of the prevailing myths that were first taking shape at the end of the war – of Armageddon followed by rebirth, of heroes and monsters, of sin and redemption. The astonishing progress of nuclear physics in the space of just a few short years, and the dramatic and violent way in which it was revealed to the world, fitted in very neatly with all of these ideas.

But what about the other sciences? How were chemistry, biology, mathematics, technology and so on viewed in the aftermath of the war? The answer is that they also slotted themselves into the same myths as nuclear physics, but with a different and much more hopeful emphasis. To be sure, these sciences had also produced their fair share of monsters during the war – people like the Nazi eugenicist Josef Mengele and the many Japanese doctors and researchers who conducted human experiments in China. The engines of destruction they created, while not as dramatic as the atom bomb, could be no less devastating: it is estimated, for example, that the Japanese killed more than half a million people in China through their innovations in bacteriological warfare.[20] But on the whole, the stories about science that took hold after 1945 were not of monsters but of heroes, and not of destruction but of rebirth and redemption. The sheer volume of scientific discovery that had taken place during the war, and its seemingly miraculous uses in the years that followed, underlined the message that 1945 was the start of a brand-new world.

The Second World War had changed the face of science. The new sense of urgency it had engendered, the sudden government intervention and the injection of vast amounts of public money had transformed the pace at which all kinds of scientific discoveries were made. The progress in aeronautical engineering, for example, was almost as incredible as that of nuclear science. In 1939 pilots of all nations were still routinely flying biplanes; but by 1945 they were flying jets. Helicopters, which had been mere oddities before the war, were being mass produced by the end of it. Likewise, rocketry was still relatively unsophisticated at the start of the war, but by 1945 mankind was already capable of sending missiles to the edge of space. It was the war itself that created these wonders. Often the basic technology had already existed before the conflict – the first ever jet plane, for example, was flown in Germany on 27 August 1939, just a few days before the war in Europe began – but it was the war that provided the incentive to develop and refine such inventions to the point where they were capable of transforming our understanding of the world.[21]

In the fields of medicine and disease prevention, similar quantum leaps were also made. The treatment of burns and physical trauma was transformed – largely because army surgeons had so much practice dealing with them. But other advances came out of the pure determination inspired by the war effort. The wartime development of penicillin is a perfect example. Discovered by Alexander Fleming in 1929, and developed by Howard Florey and Ernst Chain in the late 1930s, penicillin was still little more than a medical curiosity at the beginning of the war. In 1941, the commercial production of penicillin in the USA was zero; by the end of the war, as a result of a massive effort to research, refine and develop the drug, American manufacturers were producing over 646 billion units of penicillin *per month*. This only came about because of an unprecedented collaboration between British and American scientists, between governments and commercial interests and even between rival companies. Just ten days after the bombing of Pearl Harbor, for example, a meeting of American drug companies agreed to share their research with the US government, to which the US government responded by heavily subsidizing that research, and even financing the construction of penicillin plants. The subsequent development of other breakthrough antibiotics, such as streptomycin, was a consequence of such work.[22]

The history of the insecticide DDT followed the same pattern. Like penicillin, it had been discovered before the war – but only when tens of thousands of Allied troops began contracting malaria in the Pacific theatre did the US government see the need to fund its use on a wide scale. By 1945 it was being sprayed from low-flying aeroplanes wherever Allied soldiers in that theatre were stationed. After the liberation of Manila and Singapore it was sprayed routinely over the entire cities in order to protect the civilian population from disease: appreciative newspaper journalists from the *Straits Times* hailed it as a 'boon to humanity'.

It was also used during the liberation of prisons and concentration camps to kill the lice that carried typhoid. Though its disastrous environmental effects would be revealed in the late 1960s and 1970s, it was largely due to DDT that the epidemics that everyone feared in the wake of the war never materialized.[23]

Computer technology also made several leaps as a result of the war. In 1941 Konrad Zuse built the world's first programmable digital computer, the Z3, which was used by the German Aircraft Research Institute to perform complex calculations related to aircraft design. In Britain, meanwhile, even more powerful computers were being created to decipher encrypted German messages. The most important of these was Thomas Flowers's Colossus – a huge machine, funded by the British Post Office Research Station, which was capable of processing thousands of characters of coded messages per second. The mathematician Alan Turing, regarded by some as the father of modern computing, was closely involved in the design of this and other decryption machines. At the same time, American scientists John Mauchly and J. Presper Eckert were working on a yet more powerful computer at the University of Pennsylvania. The Electronic Numerical Integrator and Computer (ENIAC) was, once again, built specifically for the war: its original purpose was to make complicated artillery calculations.[24] Such machines would probably have been created anyway, in the fullness of time, but the urgency of the war, and the willingness of governments to provide much needed funding, vastly accelerated their development.

The sheer volume and pace of scientific experiment during the war produced all kinds of results, some of which would turn out to have distinctly non-military uses. For example in 1945 an American engineer named Percy Spencer was visiting a lab where cavity magnetrons were being tested, when he noticed that the peanut bar in his pocket had begun to melt. Cavity magnetrons were the central component in Allied air-to-ground radar, which worked by producing microwaves. Curious to find out more, Spencer sent a boy out to buy a packet of corn: when he placed it near the magnetron, the corn began to pop. The next day a further experiment ended up with an egg exploding all over the face of one of the lab technicians. Thus, out of wartime research, one of the greatest innovations in domestic technology was born: today, cavity magnetrons are no longer used in radar sets, but millions of them are produced each year for use in microwave ovens.[25]

Another household innovation was brought about by wartime research into plastics. American scientist Harry Coover was trying to discover a new kind of clear plastic that could be used for precision gunsights when he stumbled upon a group of substances called cyano-acrylates. They were useless for gunsights, because they were so sticky that they ended up being totally impractical. But after the war they were put to good use as the basis of superglue.[26]

It was not only trained scientists and engineers who made such dis-coveries during the war: sometimes innovation came from the most surprising sources. Hedy Lamarr, for example, was best known as a Hollywood actress and pin-up girl – 'the world's most beautiful woman', as she was routinely called by MGM studios. But in 1942 she proved that she was far more than just a pretty face when she and a composer friend came up with a new idea for the US Navy's guided torpedo sys-tems. The radio transmissions that controlled the torpedoes could be jammed – but if these transmissions could be made to continually hop from one frequency to another, jamming them would be impossible. Her idea was not taken up by the American authorities, who told her that she could better serve the war effort by entertaining the troops – but it later became the basis of the 'spread spectrum' technology used by the vast majority of today's GPS, Bluetooth, wireless systems and mobile phones.[27]

The list of new ideas and new technologies that came out of the war is seemingly endless. Radio wave research not only produced the chain of radar stations that saved Britain from German attack in 1940 but also led to huge leaps forward in aircraft navigation, guided missiles and stealth technology. Nuclear research created new isotopes that could be used in medicine for radiotherapy. Perhaps one of the most important developments was the way that the war had suddenly made physics so glamorous, opening doors for physicists to move into other areas of sci-ence, such as biology. One such pair was Maurice Wilkins, a physicist from New Zealand who had worked on radar research during the war, and Francis Crick, who had worked on the design of magnetic mines. Their switch to biological research after the war bore fruit when, eight years later, they were amongst the small group of researchers who revealed the structure of DNA.

That so many of these scientific and technological innovations took place in Britain and the United States is also partly thanks to the war.

The USA in particular was probably the only nation in the developed world that was both relatively unaffected by the war and had the resources to fund the sort of detailed, large-scale research needed to produce quick results. Since it was almost entirely beyond the reach of an invasion force, or even of German or Japanese bombers, it was a far better venue for sensitive research than anywhere in Europe or Asia, and so scientists and technicians flocked from all over the world to join American scientific institutions. Many of these people stayed after the war was over. While other countries were expending their resources on rebuilding damaged infrastructure, the USA could afford to continue investing massively in scientific research and technological development. That America continues to fund and produce more innovation than almost anywhere else, even today, is at least partly due to the way it stole a march on the rest of the world during and after the war years.

But it was not only in Britain and America that the scientific developments of the war inspired hopes of a new world of plenty for all. In the Soviet Union wartime research led to advances in antibiotics, rocket research and nuclear technology that sometimes put the West in the shade. Prominent Soviet officials, including the premier, Nikolai Bulganin, were so inspired that they began talking of 'a new scientific-technical and industrial revolution, far surpassing in its significance the industrial revolutions connected with the appearance of steam and electricity'.[28] From the mid-fifties onwards, the Soviet popular press began to present fantastic visions of progress in industry, medicine and agriculture – not as utopian dreams but as current events.[29]

There seemed to be no bounds to scientific potential in the postwar world. Long before the USSR put the first man into space Soviet scientists were predicting the exploration of the solar system and beyond in 'photon rockets' whose speed they imagined would 'come close to that of light'.[30] In Germany, newspaper stories shortly after the war claimed that radiation would soon be able to preserve food, cure mental illness and even reverse the ageing process. As early as 1946, the *Neue Berliner Illustrierte* ran a story predicting the advent of spacecraft capable of taking a man to the moon in just three hours and twenty-seven minutes.[31] Meanwhile, Indian newspapers painted dreams of express trains that would run from Bombay to Calcutta in only an hour, of the conversion of deserts into oases and the North Pole into a holiday resort, and even the creation of new forms of life.[32]

It is important to remember that these visions were conjured up not by scientists but by journalists and politicians, as well as ordinary people, many of whom were simply carried away by the general sense of optimism that came out of the end of the war. Most scientists did what they could to rein in this optimism, especially when it came to the more absurd predictions about the future. Albert Einstein, for example, warned the world in November 1945 that no practical benefits from nuclear power would be seen 'for a long time', while the Russian-American physicist George Gamow poured cold water on the idea of atomic cars or aeroplanes on the grounds that they would be completely impractical: the nuclear reactors needed to power such vehicles would have to be huge, and encased in many tons of lead to absorb the radiation. 'Don't expect a pellet of uranium 235 to drive your car for a year,' warned Otto Frisch, who had worked at Los Alamos on the first atom bombs. 'A few minutes' ride in this car would be enough to kill you.'[33]

If their message did not always get through it was partly because the scientists themselves had become part of the myth. The American press often referred to them as 'Titans' and 'gods', the creators of the new world into which mankind was being born. The atomic scientists in particular were often compared to Prometheus, the Titan who, according to Greek legend, gave fire to mankind. (This superhuman quality is still often associated with them today: for example, a Pulitzer Prize-winning biography of Robert Oppenheimer in 2005 called him the 'American Prometheus'.[34]) These men were venerated not only in America but throughout the world, both because of the wonders they had achieved and because the world had an unquenchable thirst for heroes after the war. After all the years of terror and uncertainty people everywhere wanted desperately to believe in the birth of something new and wonderful. As the men who would bring this new world into being, scientists would be venerated, whether they wanted to be or not.

It was in this atmosphere that Eugene Rabinowitch launched his *Bulletin of the Atomic Scientists*, a journal that consistently highlighted the threat of nuclear doom over nuclear Utopia, and which portrayed scientists not as gods but as ordinary, concerned human beings who were just as much at the mercy of governments and world forces as everyone else.

Leafing through the pages of this journal today reveals just about every major issue that concerned the scientists of the 1940s and 50s, and which, through them, found its way into the consciousness of the public at large. The breakthroughs of the war years were justly celebrated, but the question was also asked whether they had come at a cost. So many scientists had been taken out of their usual jobs to work on the war effort that just as many discoveries might well have been delayed by the war as had been accelerated by it. William Shockley, for example, who is regarded by many as the founding father of Silicon Valley, abandoned his Nobel Prize-winning research on semiconductors for several years in order to work on anti-submarine warfare. In the pages of the *Bulletin*, Robert Oppenheimer insisted the war had 'a temporarily disastrous effect on the prosecution of pure science'.[35]

The journal also criticized the utilitarian way that society always praised the revolutionary technologies that were now transforming people's lives, but remained suspicious of pure science conceived in ivory towers. In an editorial in 1951, Rabinowitch claimed that the world seemed to regard science as 'a magic bird whose golden eggs everybody wants, but whose free flight into regions inaccessible to most makes it a suspect creature'. He argued passionately that scientists should be left alone to work on obscure, ethereal ideas – regardless of whether they had any obvious immediate applications for society – otherwise, 'after a while there will be no more golden eggs'.[36] Other scientists agreed. In later life, Ernst Chain was adamant that he would never have been able to make his initial breakthroughs with penicillin in the goal-obsessed atmosphere that was inspired by the war, and which continued long afterwards. What scientists most longed for was freedom.[37]

The journal criticized the politicization of science in America, where budgets were more or less controlled by the military. And it criticized the politicization of science in the Soviet Union, where bogus ideas like Trofim Lysenko's warped view of genetics were propagated for no better reason than that they chimed with Stalinist theory. It argued for the continuing collaboration of scientists across this Cold War divide, and championed the Pugwash Conferences on Science and World Affairs (where, incidentally, Russian-speaking Rabinowitch would often have to act as the mediator between Soviet and Western scientists).

But, most of all, the *Bulletin* agonized over the way that science should interact with society as a whole. Should scientists be held responsible for the inventions they produced? Should they involve themselves in helping to mould a new society, based on scientific principles? Had humanity now reached a point where it was no longer able to cope with the enormity of scientific discovery without the creation of a world body, indeed a world government, to oversee it?[38]

Permeating these ideas was the agonizing suspicion that scientists had unwittingly unleashed forces that mankind was not yet ready for, and which might have been better left undiscovered. As Robert Oppenheimer famously observed, perhaps with a sense of guilt over the way he himself had swaggered after the atom bomb test at Alamogordo, 'In some sort of crude sense which no vulgarity, no humor, no overstatement can quite extinguish, the physicists have known sin; and this is a knowledge which they cannot lose.'[39] In the years immediately following the war a profusion of scientists publicly repented of their work on the atomic bomb project, and bemoaned the fact that their new-found celebrity was partly due to their having been 'brilliant collaborators with death'.[40] The aim of this new 'scientists movement', of which Eugene Rabinowitch and his journal were a major part, was to push the world into creating a new and better society – not a technological Utopia of anti-ageing pills and nuclear cars, but a more conventional social Utopia of international cooperation and understanding.

They failed. Nevertheless their efforts did afford three important benefits for the development of the postwar world.

Firstly, they provided the West in general, and America in particular, with a much-needed voice of conscience. The Allies had not always behaved well during the war, no matter how good their original intentions had been, and it was important for the health of society that this was acknowledged in some way. For various reasons, mainstream society appeared to feel no moral outrage or guilt at what the Allies had done, preferring to remember the war in purely triumphalist terms. Eugene Rabinowitch's scientists movement at least provided an outlet for those who were ready to confront some of the darker episodes of the Allied war effort.[41]

Secondly, they did more than anyone else to preserve the reputation of science and scientists for the rest of the century. It is human nature to expect our heroes to be flawless, and to despise them once we discover that they are not. By voluntarily stepping down from the pedestal on which the world had placed them in 1945, and confessing their 'sins' in public, they won far greater admiration than they would have done had they merely basked in their own temporary glory. Men like Rabinowitch worked tirelessly to demonstrate that science and society were inextricably linked, and had a responsibility to one another that was far more important than any idle dreams of Utopia.

And finally, they established once and for all the necessity of scientists to consider the moral implications of what they were doing. The Second World War, more than any other in modern history, was a moral war, in that it united almost everyone in a general understanding of what was right and what was wrong. The world that emerged from the war contained the seeds of a new morality, and a new spirituality, that was shared by people across the globe. Eugene Rabinowitch, and the movement of which he was a part, ensured that science and scientists would remain deeply attached to this new moral sense, which had been temporarily lost in the madness of the war.

7. Planned Utopias

The scientific and technological innovations that took place during the war would never have happened without government involvement. The atomic bomb project was a perfect example of well-directed state power: the American government had set themselves a goal, poured money and expertise into reaching it, and had ended up transforming the world. There were many other instances that were almost as impressive. In Britain, for example, the wartime government had imposed the world's most comprehensive system of food rationing: this had not only conserved vital food supplies during the war but also ensured that everyone, rich or poor, received a scientifically balanced diet. Despite terrible shortages of most foodstuffs, infant mortality rates actually declined in wartime Britain, as did deaths in the wider population from a variety of diseases.[1]

Such successes, bolstered by the great victory of the war itself, immediately raised the question – if central planning by the state could bring triumph in war, could it not also bring triumph in peace? If the old laissez-faire economics of the 1920s and 30s had led to collapse, depression and ultimately to the war itself, was it not time now for the state to step in and make sure that similar catastrophes would never happen again? And why stop at economic reform? Could the state – *should* the state – use its power to make society fairer, more equal, better for everyone?

In the idealistic atmosphere of 1945, the clamour for greater government involvement in society was impossible to ignore. In war-torn Europe it was not only Communists who pushed for state-led reform, but also many conservatives and Christian Democrats. In other parts of the world the calls came equally from American New Dealers, from Asian and African nationalists, and from Latin America's right-wing populists. Experts of all political persuasions likewise wished to harness the power of the state, from scientists like Britain's J. D. Bernal and America's Edward Teller to economists like John Maynard Keynes and Jean Monnet. All of these people believed passionately in the power of the state to transform our lives for the better.

And yet, as the war had demonstrated, there were just as many dangers in state solutions as there were benefits. Had not the belief in a strong centralized state also been one of the foundation stones of Nazism, Stalinism and Japanese militarism? Those who pursued state solutions to the world's problems could sometimes be quite fanatical – as could those who opposed them. In the aftermath of the war, the old arguments between those who believed in the sanctity of the individual and those who believed in the transformative power of the collective were resurrected. But it was the centralizers who now won out more than they ever had before – sometimes with quite startling results.

One should always beware of visions of Utopia – not because paradise-on-earth is impossible, but because the single-minded pursuit of that paradise represents, for society, a kind of death. 'The whole is the false', as the German philosopher Theodor Adorno wrote in 1944. In other words, any system that believes itself to be the single answer to all our problems can only do so by denying all the myriad other answers and possibilities – including all the other Utopias – that also exist alongside it.[2]

One man who spent a lifetime struggling against various totalitarian dogmas was the Italian architect Giancarlo De Carlo, and the story of his life provides a lesson in how difficult it was to resist grand utopian plans during the turbulent years in the middle of the twentieth century.

De Carlo was born in Genoa in 1919, and grew up in a world dominated by ideological conflict. He was barely a toddler when Mussolini seized control of Italy, and though he went away to live with his grandparents in Tunisia for several years, he could never escape the polarized atmosphere that hung over the Italian community, and indeed Europe as a whole. By the time he was an adult he was well versed in the Fascist obsession with greatness, its fetishization of violence and its fanatical belief in the strong over the weak. De Carlo found these ideas abhorrent, and surrounded himself with people who felt likewise. Some of these acquaintances had their own ideologies – socialism, anarchism, communism – and could also sometimes be quite fanatical; but in De Carlo's mind none of them were anything like as dangerous as those who held the reins of power.[3]

When the war broke out in 1939, De Carlo was studying for a degree in structural engineering, but was gradually becoming more fascinated by a related discipline – that of architecture. Some of his friends were architects, and he found himself increasingly inspired by the ideas they discussed with him. They introduced him to the writings of Le Corbusier, which he found intoxicating – the sense of hope they exuded, the belief in a better life for all, and especially the unshakeable faith that one could change the world just by changing people's environments. 'I was looking for an activity that would allow me to ... tak[e] part in the transformation of society through creative activity,' he explained in later life. 'I realized that architecture could offer that opportunity.'[4] He resolved to start a course in architecture just as soon as he had completed his engineering degree.

Unfortunately, the Fascist authorities had other ideas: having allowed him to finish one degree without being called up for war service, they were not about to allow him to start another. On the day after he enrolled for his architecture course he was summoned to start training for a post in the navy. Thus, in 1943, he was sent to Greece, where he found himself fighting for a cause that he did not believe in, in support of a government that he actively opposed.

De Carlo served four months in naval convoys, sleeping on deck and always expecting to be attacked by British planes. Unlike the ugly fighting that was taking place on the Greek mainland, the war at sea was relatively straightforward, as were his duties on the ship. Nevertheless, there was something deeply disturbing about seeing the Nazi flag flying over the Acropolis. As soon as he was posted back to Milan he decided it was time to take a much more active role against fascism. Still in uniform, he joined a Resistance group called the Movimento di Unità Proletaria, and began delivering anti-Fascist leaflets around local factories. Had he been caught he would immediately have been court-martialled and probably executed. But he was naive and oblivious to the risks – to him it seemed almost like a game.

After Mussolini fell, and the Germans took control of Italy, the game suddenly became more serious. He and a few others fled to the hills above Lake Como. They hoped they might forge a massive resistance along with other former military men, but 'contrary to what was said afterwards there were very few of us'.[5] The partisan war had begun.

As they slowly gathered recruits, De Carlo often found himself with time on his hands. He had taken with him two books – Alfred Roth's *Die Neue Architektur* and Le Corbusier's *Oeuvre Complète* – and he would spend hours sketching elevations and details from the photographs inside. Sometimes he would gather together new recruits in an abandoned farmhouse and, after explaining the guerrilla war situation to them, give lectures on architecture and the possibilities that it offered to society. But when the National Liberation Committee (CLN) learned of this, he was told to stop. The CLN was dominated by Communists, and wanted him and his comrades to focus more narrowly on winning the war against Germany and on solidarity with the Soviet people.

Before long, De Carlo was ordered back to Milan to help train and organize an urban resistance. To avoid the attentions of collaborators and spies he and his future wife, Giuliana, were forced to move home eight times in just a few months. In the desperate atmosphere of the time they found it impossible not to be seduced by the polarizing nature of

Giancarlo De Carlo at work in the 1950s.

the war, which made everything a battle of right or wrong, good or evil. De Carlo found himself becoming every bit as single minded as the Communists who commanded him, or the Fascists he opposed. 'One can reach a level of fanaticism, of isolation, to the point that you make the greatest stupidities and imagine you commit them as acts of extreme virtue,' he admitted in later life. 'It leads you to believe you can reorganize society best only by getting rid of your enemies. We didn't in fact, get rid of anybody; but we did engage in sabotage.'[6]

The City is Dead; Long Live the City

By the end of the war, the world that De Carlo had fought for was in tatters. Up to a third of Italy's road network had been made unusable, and 13,000 bridges were damaged or destroyed. The state of the nation's cities was quite shocking: hundreds of thousands of houses and apartment blocks had been reduced to ruins during the fighting, both by shelling and by aerial bombardment. In war-torn cities like Milan, where De Carlo ended the war, or Turin, or Bologna, people were forced to live in ruins and cellars. In Naples hundreds of desperate women and children had taken to living in caves.[7]

The situation in the rest of Europe was as bad or even worse. In Britain, five years of bombs and V-weapons had destroyed 202,000 houses, and rendered a further 255,000 uninhabitable. France had suffered even more – some 460,000 buildings gone and a further 1.9 million damaged. Germany, meanwhile, had lost 3.6 million apartments, or a fifth of all dwellings in the country. In the Soviet Union not only had many of the major cities been laid waste – Kharkov, Kiev, Odessa, Minsk – but also 1,700 smaller towns and 70,000 villages.[8] Perhaps worst of all was the situation in Poland, which had suffered huge destruction both from the advancing Soviets and from the scorched-earth policy of the retreating Nazis. In the aftermath of the war the country was dismembered and then reassembled with parts of devastated Germany. Nobody knew how to estimate the number of houses or cities destroyed, because it was not even clear which houses or cities to include in the calculations.

Such destruction, which was as bad in Asia as it was in Europe, took an enormous toll on the world's population. It was compounded by the massive displacement of populations that took place during the war. In

1945 there were around 9 million homeless people in Japan, 20 million in Germany and 25 million in the USSR. Some estimates for China, although they can never be much better than guesses, put the figure as high as 100 million.[9] All of this was only made worse after 1945 when worldwide populations suddenly began to boom, and when rural populations once again took up their long-term flight from the countryside into the cities. A lack of urban housing was therefore a truly global problem in the wake of the war.[10]

One might imagine that this vast landscape of destruction and homelessness was a cause for despair amongst architects and city planners, but actually the opposite was true. Many of them had been waiting for an opportunity like this for years. Architects like Sigfried Giedion and Le Corbusier, for example, had been calling for the world's cities to be torn down and rebuilt along modern, functional lines ever since 1933. They had been ignored by those in government because such a wholesale wiping of the slate was politically unthinkable; but with so many cities now in ruins, a complete redesign suddenly seemed possible. In 1945 *anything* seemed possible.[11]

Rather than mourning the devastation of their cities, therefore, many architects and planners saw it as the opportunity they had all been waiting for. 'Urban planning is often born of the canon,' wrote one French intellectual as he contemplated the ruins of Brest and Lorient: now, at last, these notoriously squalid French coastal towns could be rebuilt as grand ports worthy of the twentieth century.[12] Germany's Paul Schmitthenner and Konstanty Gutschow felt the same way about Hamburg and Lübeck, and even went so far as to call their bombing a 'blessing' – albeit one that was heavily disguised.[13] In Warsaw, which was by far the most devastated city in Europe, architects like Stanisław Jankowski enthusiastically joined the Biuro Odbudowy Stolicy (Capital Reconstruction Office), knowing that only in this place, in this time, would they have 'a chance to fulfil their most magnificent dreams!'[14]

Perhaps the most optimistic country of all was Britain. 'The Blitz has been a planner's windfall,' announced one British consultant in 1944. 'Not only did it do a certain amount of much-needed demolition for us, but – more important – it made people in all walks of life realise that reconstruction was necessary.'[15] Other British planners wrote enthusiastically of the chance to 'make a fresh start' of Birmingham, to make Durham a 'City Beautiful' and to turn York into a 'City of our Dreams'.[16] Exeter, according to its planner Thomas Sharp, was a 'phoenix' ready to 'rise renewed from its own ashes'.[17] Plymouth could now be redesigned as a city 'worthy of her glorious past and her present heroism'.[18]

So prevalent was this attitude in Britain, and so determined was everyone to 'plan boldly' for the future, that it left some architects in other parts of the world almost envious. 'If the Blitz did it,' wrote the American housing expert Catherine Bauer in 1944, '. . . then that explains the secret guilty regret deep within many American liberals that we missed the experience.'[19] There was a strong feeling in the USA at the end of the war that, while European cities at last had an opportunity to clear away their slums and to modernize, American cities would be left behind. In an attempt to capture a bit of this modernizing zeal for themselves, architects like Walter Gropius and Martin Wagner, who had fled to America before the war, made direct comparisons between the bombs that were raining down on European cities and the 'blight' that plagued their American counterparts.[20] American industry bodies like the National Association of Real Estate Boards followed suit: 'Every disintegrating building,' read one brochure at the end of the war, 'is just as truly a blockbuster as a four thousand pound bomb that tumbles from a four-engined bomber. The effect is exactly the same.'[21]

Thus the end of the Second World War gave rise to a new atmosphere almost everywhere, even in those parts of the world that had not been physically damaged. The old world, with its crumbling buildings and dysfunctional cities, had to be swept away.

The twenty-five years after 1945 would see the most radical rebuilding in the history of the world's cities. But before this new world began to rise from the ashes of the old, there was a great deal of debate about what it should look like.

The one thing that almost everyone agreed on was that it should not be left to the free market. Private landlords, they pointed out, had no incentive to create spacious, healthy environments for their tenants: quite the opposite, in fact – in order to maximize their profits they were motivated to crowd as many bodies as possible into their properties, and to build on every inch of green space available. According to architects like Le Corbusier, one of the most influential planners of the era, governments that allowed such landlords to act unchecked were effectively failing the people who had elected them. 'A butcher would be condemned for the sale of rotten meat,' he claimed in 1943, 'but the building codes allow rotten dwellings to be forced on the poor. For the enrichment of a few selfish people, we tolerate appalling mortality rates and diseases of every kind, which impose crushing burdens on the entire community.'[22]

Since the state was already obliged to organize communal schemes for things like infrastructure, sewerage and main roads, which private landlords were both unwilling and incapable of providing on their own, many architects argued that it made sense for the state to take control of other aspects of city development as well. In Europe, the Congrès Internationaux d'Architecture Moderne (CIAM) had long been calling for the 'scientific planning' not only of cities but of whole regions, with a carefully designed balance between dwelling places, workplaces and places of leisure, and an efficient transport network between them all.[23] On the other side of the Atlantic the Regional Planning Association of America (RPAA) had also championed greater involvement by the state. One of its leading lights, the architecture critic Lewis Mumford, called for 'regional planning on a grand scale', and even made mention of the creation of 'a world order'. The proper planning of cities in particular, he claimed, was 'perhaps the most pressing task of our civilization: the issues of war and peace, socialization or disorganization, culture or barbarism, rest in good part on our success in handling this problem'.[24]

None of these thoughts were new in 1945: they were arguments that architects had been making for years, and certainly long before the war. The only real difference was that governments were now beginning to take notice. The war had created a new atmosphere in the world: people everywhere were demanding social change, including changes to their physical environments. And, increasingly, they looked to their governments to provide it.

Broadly speaking, there were three schools of thought regarding the best way to plan the cities of the future, all of them based on prewar ideas. The first was inspired by the utopian schemes of Ebenezer Howard, a British idealist who suggested that the evils of overcrowding could be reversed only by rehousing the working classes in new 'Garden Cities'. These were to be towns with a population not greater than about 30,000, planned in every detail so as to combine the benefits of the city with the beauty and fresh air of the countryside. According to Howard's vision, people would live in cottage-style houses on land that was

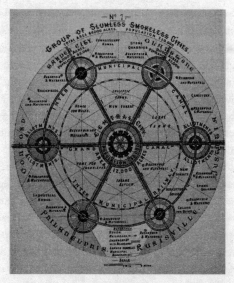

Ebenezer Howard's diagram of the ideal garden city: a central municipality separated from a handful of satellite towns by green-belt land.

communally owned and collectively managed for the good of all. He envisaged hundreds of such towns, making up a society of 'happy people', freed from the cramped and unhealthy conditions of the slum, and living in a state of 'concert and cooperation' with one another and with nature. 'Town and country *must be married*, and out of this joyous union will spring a new hope, a new life, a new civilization.' Howard's vision started a worldwide movement, and would become one of the greatest influences on city planning after 1945.[25]

If the solution to overcrowded cities was to disperse the population into smaller units, then there were some architects who believed that Howard's ideas did not go far enough. This second school of thought wanted to take the idea of dispersal to its logical conclusion and abolish cities altogether. The American architect Frank Lloyd Wright, for example, envisaged a world in which city centres would disappear, and the entire population would disperse across the nation in an endless and idyllic 'festival of life'.[26] In his prewar book *The Disappearing City* he had envisaged a time when every family would be given an acre of land to call their own, and could do with it what they wanted – farm it and become self-sufficient, turn it into a garden, or into a wilderness. While Howard had dreamed of community living, Wright elevated the self-determination of the individual above all other values. He called his model 'Broadacre City', and repeatedly said that it would exist 'everywhere and nowhere' (thus tying his idea quite consciously to the Greek word for 'nowhere' – 'Utopia'). Wright's urge to dissolve cities and disperse the population won many supporters in America in the new, nuclear age: if the population was dispersed, the logic went, then Soviet missiles would have nothing substantial to aim at.[27]

The final school of thought, and by far the most influential on a global scale, was that championed by the modernist CIAM, whose ideas were probably the boldest of them all. For CIAM, the concentration of people in cities was not the problem: the real issue was that the world had an outdated idea of what a city actually *was*. In Europe, in particular, cities were still laid out on medieval street plans, with narrow thoroughfares and crowded buildings that were totally unsuited to a modern age. The only way to change this situation, according to CIAM's vice-president, José Luis Sert, was through 'drastic measures, whose application will change the entire structure of cities'.[28] Traditional streets should be abolished, so that pedestrians could be kept separate from the noise and danger of speeding vehicles. Traditional buildings should also be replaced: instead of living in small, cramped houses and apartment blocks surrounded by traffic and noise, city dwellers should demand tall buildings, aligned with the sun and spaced apart from one another in landscaped parks. For Sert's fellow modernist Sigfried Giedion this was not just a matter of design, but of 'human rights'.[29]

There were, of course, other variants of these ideas around the world. In Communist Europe the idea of a specifically socialist city was discussed, but the models they proposed often ended up bearing a striking resemblance to those in the West. For example, the idea of the garden city, much derided by Communist architects, was actually embraced by many Soviet planners: had not Marx and Engels themselves advocated the 'abolition of the distinction between town and country'?[30] In postwar East Germany, where the government decided that there was no such thing as an ideal socialist town, planners adopted 'sixteen principles' of urban design – most of which were essentially the same as the principles of CIAM.[31] The Stalinist obsession with constructing grand archways and triumphal routes gave the impression that the city was always about to *arrive* at something – the socialist Utopia which, like the modernist Utopia, was always just around the corner.[32]

What all these architectural movements shared was an almost religious belief in central planning – and each group saw themselves as the high priests who would lead mankind to the Promised Land. Architecture, they claimed, was 'the essential commanding art'; it was the 'key to everything', and should therefore be 'a guide to order in every other department of activity'.[33] Even Frank Lloyd Wright, who hated the idea of big government, painted a world that was ordered according to certain universal rules.[34] In eastern Europe, meanwhile, Communist planners deliberately rebuilt their cities with features that were mere reproductions of features in Russia – identical buildings, huge central squares, triumphal main avenues. This was central planning at its most absurd, as if loyalty to the Soviet dream could be ensured simply by reconstructing the world to look more like Moscow.

In all cases, East and West, it was not only the built environment that these architects and planners wished to change, but society as a whole. They were never coy about expressing this. The Polish modernist architect Szymon Syrkus claimed that architecture played 'the supreme social role', and that its most important characteristic was that it 'changes the social pattern'.[35] Modernist architects like him wanted nothing less than to transform society by forcing people to live in a more rational, communal and egalitarian way. The garden city movement likewise wanted to transform society by creating ideal communities that were obliged to cooperate with one another by the very structure of the world in which they lived. Through the application of their visionary plans they believed they could not only save society from ruin, but also bring about a new Renaissance. 'Dignity, action, health, serenity, joy in living,' wrote Le Corbusier, 'all these can be part of our lives', if we only followed the plan.[36]

Utopia Meets Reality

De Carlo followed many of these ideas and debates avidly by reading about them in the architectural press. To him, they represented just a few of the myriad possibilities that had been opened up by the end of the war. He himself had blossomed in the new atmosphere, free from the threat of violence and the dictates of fascism. He had begun writing books and articles for architecture magazines. He had enrolled in the Venice School of Architecture. He was even accepted as a member of the Congrès Internationaux d'Architecture Moderne, the world's leading voice on urban planning. It seemed like a magical time.

And yet he also began to notice an undercurrent of something slightly more worrying: 'I remember those years as a time of great energy and curiosity; I was living through continuous discovery and invention. But I was also sad, for I could see all the old forms returning. Politicians were reconstructing the world exactly as it had been before.'[37]

In De Carlo's mind it was not only the ruling Christian Democrats who were guilty of this, but also the Communists, who stuck perpetually to the Soviet party line rather than embracing the myriad other possibilities for a better society that now lay open. The old black-and-white mindset of the war years was returning as the black-and-white mindset of the Cold War.

Just as disturbingly from De Carlo's point of view, a similar rift seemed to be opening up in the world of architecture and city planning. The division was not so much between East and West as between disciples of the different prewar schools of thought: the modernists of CIAM (and its eastern European spin-offs), the garden city movement, and the 'organic' school of architects like Frank Lloyd Wright. De Carlo, who in the aftermath of the war had written extensively about all these movements, saw no reason why they might not find some common ground. Each of them, he said years later, was born out of the same message of liberty.

Particularly dogmatic was the CIAM. De Carlo had always felt that there was something 'claustrophobic' about the way Le Corbusier's followers insisted that their idea of the city was universal and unquestionable – 'the omniscient Corbusian method', as he scathingly called it.[38] He watched in dismay as, in the postwar building boom, inner-city districts around the world started to be pulled down and replaced with modernist tower blocks, built according to Le Corbusier's principles. Everything was standardized, from the shapes of people's windows and the size of their rooms, to the compartmentalization of cities into different 'zones'. This standardization also had its counterpart in eastern Europe, where it was elevated to a virtue, because it represented a form of equality. In the Eastern Bloc, centrally directed production techniques ensured that identical, monotonous housing estates were built everywhere from Vilnius to Tashkent.

High-density postwar housing in Poland. This single block, containing over a thousand apartments, is just one of dozens in the Zaspa district of Gdansk. After 1945, similar developments sprang up all over the world.

De Carlo suspected that this kind of uniformity was being pursued, both in the East and in the West, because it suited the architects, the builders, the business interests and the governments who financed it all – everyone, that is, except the people who had to live in the cities that were being created. Instead of enhancing the lives and communities of its inhabitants, planners seemed concerned only with the efficiency of design, efficiency of transport, efficiency of cost.

In the 1950s, modernism reached its zenith with the design of two new cities built entirely according to modernist principles: Le Corbusier's plan for Chandigarh in India, and the new Brazilian capital, Brasília, designed by Lúcio Costa and Oscar Niemeyer. Though both contained inspiring set-piece monuments, De Carlo felt there was something soulless about them. 'Questions of ideal cities,' he wrote, 'are of much less concern than questions of real cities – impure, complicated, but real.' He called Chandigarh 'the last great Enlightenment utopia', and worried about the way that the city was explicitly designed to delete the personal histories of the people who moved there and remake them as model citizens.[39]

Eventually, De Carlo began comparing CIAM to the Communist

Party – an organization that had similarly lost touch with the concerns of real people by wrapping itself in dogma.[40] In the mid-1950s he launched a series of scathing attacks on CIAM, calling it a 'self-congratulatory society with its own consecrated rites, high priests and reasons of state', immobilized by a 'cult of rules and a willing enslavement to their despotic discipline'. He urged his fellow modernists to choose between Utopia and reality, between 'drawing-board architecture' and real architecture that is 'consumed daily by people's lives'.[41]

Most importantly, he attacked the results of modernism on the ground: 'As far as Italy is concerned,' De Carlo wrote in 1957, 'the success of the language of modern architecture has not brought positive results . . . Under its broad aegis, urban communities are being summarily destroyed and replaced with arid and inhuman new districts and houses that in a few years become decrepit slums.'[42] Such attacks, along with those of other like-minded architects, eventually led to the disbanding of CIAM at the end of the decade.

Since then, many of De Carlo's criticisms have been borne out. In America, the architecture critic Jane Jacobs wrote a devastating critique of the way that government-funded slum clearance schemes had created a modernist nightmare. In her classic book, *The Death and Life of Great American Cities*, Jacobs demonstrated how much of the postwar rebuilding had led to cities devoid of community life and plagued by antisocial behaviour. Her findings were backed up in a further study by Oscar Newman, who used statistical evidence to show how the design of many modernist housing estates had not only failed to enhance the lives of their residents but also led to a massive increase in inner-city crime.[43]

Other studies from around the world appeared to back up these findings. For example, a UN study of urbanization in Venezuela showed how areas where squatters had erected their own housing actually engendered much more stable social structures than large modernist housing estates, where tenants occasionally murdered rent collectors. Studies from the Netherlands, Finland, Russia, China, South Africa and Puerto Rico showed similar results. Far from leading to Utopia, many of the modernist city districts that were created in the wake of the Second World War were propagating a new sense of urban alienation.[44]

And what of the other utopian ideas for city planning? How did they work out?

In Britain it was the garden city model which most gripped the post-war planners. Foremost amongst them was Patrick Abercrombie, whose Greater London Plan proposed removing more than a million people from the capital and rehousing them in leafy new towns outside the metropolis. In the brave new world of 1945, these new towns – places like Harlow and Stevenage – would serve the dual purpose of providing good-quality housing and producing, in the words of the new planning minister, 'a new type of citizen – a healthy, self-respecting, dignified person with a sense of beauty, culture, and civic pride'.[45]

Over the next thirty years twenty-eight planned communities were set up all around Britain. But if their planners believed they were building Utopia they were sorely mistaken. None of these towns was built according to the original garden city principles: most of them ended up being too big, and sprawled into a seemingly endless landscape of identical houses. Many were built so close to existing major cities that they became mere dormitory suburbs. By the late 1950s there were already studies highlighting the way that some of these new towns were becoming 'dead communities', and home to a new sense of alienation and depression known as 'new town blues'.[46]

In the USA, meanwhile, the ideal of communal ownership, so dear to the original founders of the garden city movement, was almost entirely ignored in favour of private ownership: each homeowner ensconced himself in his own private plot, amidst thousands of similar private plots, like a watered-down version of Frank Lloyd Wright's 'Broadacre City'. By the 1960s and 70s, American suburbia had become a low-density, low-grade 'subtopia' from which, in the words of Lewis Mumford, 'escape is impossible'.[47]

Thirty years after the end of the Second World War the profession of city planning fell into disrepute – ironically, just at the time when it was starting to learn the lessons of the past and finally establishing a scientific basis for itself. Governments everywhere drew back from the urban planning role that they had embraced so deeply: in the 1980s they began to grant much greater autonomy to private developers, trusting once more to the marketplace. High-profile architects also withdrew from involving themselves with grand plans that took into account entire districts or cities, preferring instead to concentrate all their artistic energies on single, autonomous buildings.

Giancarlo De Carlo watched all of this happen with dismay. Looking

Postwar 'subtopia': in the late 1940s and 50s identikit housing, such as this development in Levittown, Pennsylvania, sprawled across the USA.

back on his life in the 1990s, he lamented the 'hysterical' way that architects, and society in general, tended to swing from one extreme to the other, discarding their successes along with their failures according to the dogma of the day, and never learning their lesson:

'For a few years all architects agreed that one could not organize and give form to a space . . . without first deciding the organization and morphology of all the spaces of the neighbourhood, the city, the region, the nation, the whole world . . . A few years later, the terms of the question were stood on their head and architects began to say that the organization and form of the region on the city cannot be their concern . . . Each time, therefore, what was done earlier is thrown away.'[48]

The history of postwar planning is full of triumphs as well as disasters. If the British new towns were not always successful, Scandinavian ones were more so – Vällingby outside Stockholm, for example, or Tapiola Garden City outside Helsinki. While some government-funded housing estates proved disastrous, others became pleasant and popular places to live, such as the Ina Casa estates in Italy. And while modernist ideas for the city could be ugly and alienating, they at least opened up hopes for a better future. In his later years, De Carlo could not help missing the sense of communal purpose that had been unleashed by the idealists who planned the world's postwar cities, along with the passion and debate that their visions of Utopia had inspired. 'Yes, my loneliness has grown,' he told an interviewer towards the end of his life. Before adding, 'No, not just mine; everyone's loneliness has grown.'[49]

The Centrality of the Plan

In the aftermath of the war, the idea of central planning by the state was endorsed by much of the world. It is true that architects were amongst the loudest advocates for big, centralized schemes. And it is true that the plans they came up with are probably still the most tangible examples of how such government intervention changed the world we live in. But their efforts were only one part of a much larger belief in the role of the state, which gripped the world in the years after the Second World War.

Throughout postwar Europe, on both sides of the Iron Curtain, many industries were nationalized, especially coal, steel, utilities and, in some nations, banking and insurance. By May 1946 one-fifth of France's total industrial capacity was already in state ownership. By the end of the following year, three-quarters of Czechoslovakia's industries had also been nationalized – this, remember, was *before* the country was taken over by the Communists.[50] In Poland, Hungary and Romania, meanwhile, all major industry and finance became state controlled, and even the land itself was collectivized. These measures were enacted partly for ideological reasons and partly in retribution against those industrialists and financiers who had collaborated with the Nazis. But it was also about control: if a government were to plan for the future, the logic went, it needed control over what the country was producing.

The postwar period also saw the introduction of much greater state involvement in other areas of European life, such as state-funded education, subsidized public transport and support for art and culture, as well as the introduction of comprehensive social security systems and the provision of public health care. This was social planning on a huge scale, and was a direct counterpart to the economic planning that the state was simultaneously involved in. In 1945 there was a universal belief that those who were born poor should have the opportunity to rise up in society; and that those who fell on hard times – through unemployment, sickness or old age – should have a safety net to catch them. All this was to be paid for by a massive and unprecedented re-distribution of income from the rich to the poor – in western Europe through taxes, and in eastern Europe through direct appropriation.

Similar attempts at economic and social planning occurred in other parts of the world as well. In Japan, postwar planners completely re-focused the economy towards the new technologies that were amongst the 'many valuable lessons and souvenirs' bequeathed by the war.[51] In China, the new Communist regime followed a similar line to their Soviet and eastern European counterparts, and instituted a series of Five Year Plans. In post-independence India too there was a series of Five Year Plans, which aimed at nothing less than 'a new social order free from exploitation and poverty, unemployment and social injustice'.[52] Meanwhile in colonial Africa there was a growing acceptance that pro-gress would have to be centrally directed if African nations were ever to achieve true economic and political independence. Even in the USA, where there was a traditional distrust of the state, central planning expanded after the war – from the 'New Deal' to the 'Fair Deal' to Lyndon Johnson's 'Great Society' in the mid-1960s. Finally, the belief in central planning extended beyond the national to the international, with a variety of global institutions being set up in 1944 and 1945 to regulate the world economy, world law and even world government, with varying success.

These plans all differed in their intentions as well as in their imple-mentation, but they all shared a belief that institutions staffed by experts should take the central role in organizing the life of both the nation and the world. The Second World War – with all its administrative as well as military successes, with the atmosphere of collaboration that it had produced, and the compulsion never to repeat the mistakes of the past – was directly responsible for this.

However, it would be wrong to imagine that all these plans and take-overs were adopted without opposition. Just as Giancarlo De Carlo opposed the dogma of modernist urban planning in the wake of the war, there were plenty of people who similarly opposed the dogma of planned economies and societies.

Chief amongst them was the liberal economist and philosopher Fried-rich Hayek, who regarded the growth of government power with alarm. Hayek fervently believed that socialists – not to mention

Communists – had learned precisely the wrong lessons from the war. The desire to eradicate inequality and discontent was admirable, he argued, but centralizing more and more power in the hands of governments was the wrong way to go about it. Where others saw social progress, Hayek saw only the erosion of fundamental civil liberties. When governments seized power like this, in the long run it made little difference if they were totalitarian or democratic: all big government was, he said, 'the road to serfdom'.[53]

Hayek was not alone. In 1947 he and a group of like-minded thinkers founded the Mont Pelerin Society, whose members championed free speech, political freedom and, above all, free-market economics. Amongst its members were some of the most influential economists of the twentieth century – Wilhelm Röpke, Milton Friedman, George Stigler, Frank Knight, Lionel Robbins, Ludwig von Mises and many others who championed the idea of free markets as the only sure route to liberty. Thus, even at the high point of government interventionism, the seeds of revolt against planned economies were being sown.[54]

The influence of such thinkers would only grow over the rest of the century. In the 1960s and 70s, at around the same time that urban planning was falling into disrepute, the West's growing disillusionment with economic and social planning gave liberal economists much more influence over government policies. By the 1980s, they had already begun to dismantle the postwar system of government interventionism: market regulation was relaxed throughout the West, exchange-rate controls were abandoned and industries everywhere were de-nationalized. By the 1990s, even the former Communist countries of eastern Europe had adopted the free market as their central creed, much to the delight of liberal philosophers everywhere.

In some ways, this was the same swing from one dogma to another that Giancarlo De Carlo had watched take over the world of architecture, and many people viewed it with similar dismay. Regardless of whether central planning is the best way to organize society or not, many ordinary people valued it because it guaranteed their jobs, redistributed income and brought a sense of social justice to a world that, in the 1940s, had only recently seen depression and massive inequality leading to world war. For all its later disasters, government-planned urban regeneration schemes did provide people with minimum standards in the places they lived. For all their inefficiencies, nationalized industries at least sought to harness resources for the good of the whole community. Today, government health-care systems and pension schemes are still some of the most cherished forms of social planning, especially in Europe, because of what they represent: an attempt to bring fairness and equality to everyone, regardless of wealth, class, race, or any other form of social status.

As we shall see in the next chapter, this drive for equality and fairness was yet another utopian idea nurtured by the Second World War. It too would bring about some extraordinary innovations in the wake of the war – but also some crushing disappointments.

8. Equality and Diversity

Before the war Françoise Leclercq led what many would consider to be a privileged life. She was well off. She lived in a 'huge apartment' in Paris just a few minutes' walk from the Louvre. As a French citizen she was part of an imperial culture that claimed control over large parts of the globe. But as a middle-class woman she was also excluded from many important parts of society. In the 1930s, according to French law, she had no right to vote. She had received only a 'modest education' and was certainly not expected to work. 'Until the start of the Second World War,' she later confessed, 'my horizons were a little narrow, confined to the four walls of my house and my four children.'[1]

The war changed all of this suddenly and dramatically. When the Nazis entered Paris in 1940 she was swept away by an overwhelming sense of national shame. She witnessed foreign soldiers marching down her streets and Swastika flags being raised in their honour. She saw notices pasted up on the walls displaying the names of men who had been shot, and was horrified by the announcement that all Jews would now be made to wear yellow stars. Her first act of defiance against the Nazi regime was in support of these, the most vulnerable people in Paris: gathering up all her gold jewellery, she took it to Cartier to be made into her very own gold star, which she wore around her neck for the rest of the war. It was, she admitted, a rather ineffectual thing to do – a 'childish protest' – but as a Catholic Frenchwoman she wanted to show her solidarity with her Jewish compatriots.

At first, despite her feelings of outrage, it never crossed her mind to act more decisively than this. Without support, without a network of people, it was impossible to defy the occupying regime in any meaningful way: as she put it later, 'to be a resister, one must first meet the Resistance'.

Françoise was given this opportunity at the beginning of 1941, quite by chance, thanks to a gall-bladder operation. As she was preparing to go into hospital she learned that her surgeon happened to be an open critic of the new regime – in fact, according to rumour, perhaps a little more than a mere critic. In an act of spontaneity, she decided to take a chance: once she had recovered from her operation she approached this surgeon and offered him the use of her apartment – just in case he wanted to meet with any friends in secret. It was a conversation that ended up changing her life, because her surgeon's friends turned out to be Pierre Villon, Colonel Henri Rol-Tanguy, Laurent Casanova and others whose names would one day become famous throughout France. Over the following months and years, Françoise's apartment became the venue for countless liaisons between some of the most prominent members of the Resistance, and her living room gradually filled up with illegal pamphlets, Resistance newspapers and maps of the Paris sewers.

As the war progressed, Françoise started to become restless. It was all very well playing host to the resistance of others, but watching all this take place in her home had given her the urge to join in more actively. So she approached one of the Resistance leaders, Pierre Villon, and told him 'that I was happy to help the Resistance, but that I'd like to do more'. In the coming weeks she was given a place on the steering committee of a new clandestine organization, the Union of French Women (l'Union des femmes françaises, or UFF). She wrote an appeal to French Catholic women to unite behind the Resistance and 'fight Hitlerite Germany', which was broadcast on BBC radio. On one occasion she was even sent on a mission to collect machine guns from a contact on the outskirts of Paris. She embraced this new lifestyle wholeheartedly, and even allowed her fifteen-year-old daughter to take part in Resistance activities.

The experience of the Second World War profoundly changed Françoise's outlook on life. It exposed her to danger as never before, but it also gave her a freedom she had never previously experienced, and a sense that she was doing something important, worthwhile. She became used to working, campaigning and standing up for herself and for others. She also learned the value of being part of a group that worked together towards a common goal.

After 1945, Françoise Leclercq did not return to her old life. She no longer felt satisfied with the traditional roles that French society had always imposed upon women like her: so she continued as a member of the UFF and began to campaign for women's rights – the right to work, to receive equal pay, to take maternity leave. She also campaigned for the rights of workers and peasants throughout France, for better health care, and for restitution for the victims of fascism. Nor did she stop there: when France's colonies began to demand independence, she campaigned on this too. In 1946 she led a delegation of women to the Colonies Ministry to demand an end to French military intervention in what would one day become Vietnam.[2] 'I believe that our struggle for the liberation of France made us sensitive to the struggles of the people,' she later claimed, as well as 'to women's struggles for independence in oppressed countries'. And thus she translated the lessons she had learned during her own personal liberation, and the liberation of her country, into a universal struggle that involved all mankind. Thanks to the Second World War, her horizons had expanded far beyond her own four walls.

Women's Equality

The Second World War was an awakening for women all around the world. Wherever there was fighting, women not only supported their menfolk but also often fought alongside them. In France, as well as serving on committees, as Françoise Leclercq did, they were also liaison agents, arms smugglers, explosives experts, spies, propagandists, fighters, assassins. It was organizations staffed and headed by women that rescued Jewish children by transporting them to Switzerland or remote areas of the Haute-Loire.[3] The co-founder of the Combat movement was the feminist campaigner Berthie Albrecht; and the Libération-Sud movement was co-founded by Lucie Aubrac, who famously rescued her husband from the Gestapo in a vicious gun battle, despite being pregnant at the time. Women in the Resistance carried out all of the same roles as men, and when they were caught, they often suffered exactly the same fate – torture, imprisonment, execution.[4]

This pattern was reproduced across occupied Europe, where the participation of women was far greater even than in France. In Italy, according to official figures, more than 25 per cent of Resistance members were women, including 35,000 who took an active combat role.[5] In Poland there were 40,000 women members of the clandestine Home Army, and in Yugoslavia up to 100,000 women became soldiers in Tito's National Liberation Army.[6] In Asia too, women played a huge part in the Huk resistance against Japanese rule in the Philippines, as well as in

Indonesian defiance against both the Japanese and the Dutch.[7] Amongst the major Allied nations, hundreds of thousands of women were employed as nurses, naval auxiliaries and air force auxiliaries; and Soviet forces included more than half a million women who saw active service at the front.[8]

But war is not only about fighting, and women proved themselves in many other ways. In France, with 1.5 million French soldiers in captivity, women began to run not only the nation's households but also many of its farms and small businesses. French factories thronged with women, and in 1942 there were so many women working for the French railways that the Prefect of Toulouse complained that female clerks were beginning to outnumber male ones.[9] The same was true in many countries: millions of women who had never worked before became land girls and office girls and factory workers in every kind of industry. In the USA a new image of female strength was glamorized in wartime propaganda: 'Rosie the Riveter', who built the aircraft and the Liberty ships that kept the country fighting.

Because of the war, the myth of the passive, home-bound woman was undermined almost everywhere. According to the former Resistance fighter Denise Breton, the atmosphere of hope and transformation generated by the end of the war in France created a 'new woman', accustomed to standing up for her rights and determined to change the world. Others, like René Cerf-Ferrière, claimed it had also created a new kind of man, particularly in Resistance circles: 'The partnership with women changed the mentality of men in the Resistance,' he wrote. 'They showed themselves to be our equals.'[10] At the same time, the myth of the heroic man was also undermined – particularly in those parts of the world where men had failed to live up to the stereotype. 'Among the many defeats at the end of this war,' wrote one Berlin woman in 1945, 'is the defeat of the male sex.'[11] Some women in wartime France appear to have felt the same way. Marguerite Gonnet, mother of nine, was arrested in 1942 for leading a Resistance cell in the Isère. When asked by the military tribunal why she had taken up arms, she replied, 'Quite simply, colonel, because the men had dropped them.'[12]

In such an atmosphere it is not surprising that women felt a new confidence after the war, or that so many brand-new women's organizations started up around the world. In Egypt there was the newly formed Bint El-Nil (Daughter of the Nile), which campaigned for changes to the law

J. Howard Miller's famous wartime poster calling American women to the factories.

that made women subordinate to their husbands and fathers: in 1951 a group of around 1,500 even stormed the parliament building.[13] In Indonesia there was Gerwis, another brand-new women's organization which coordinated boycotts and mass demonstrations for all kinds of causes, including an end to polygamy.[14] Meanwhile, the Federation of Brazilian Women, started up in 1949, campaigned not only for equal pay but also for the right to clean water, adequate food and housing.[15] Back in France, Françoise Leclercq's UFF was soon joined by a new international movement: the Women's International Democratic Federation (WIDF), formed in Paris in 1945 by women from forty countries, would grow to become one of the most influential women's organizations of the postwar world.[16]

On the back of all this activity, and the occasionally dramatic transformations in public opinion that came with it, women began to win all kinds of new rights for themselves. Foremost amongst them was the right to vote. In many parts of Europe this right had already been won in the aftermath of the First World War, but in France women were not granted the vote until 1944. The role played by women in the Resistance was used as justification: if women could fight alongside men, the argument went, then they should at least have a say in whether their nation went to war in the first place.[17]

Shortly after French women were granted the vote, full suffrage was also extended to women in Italy and Yugoslavia (1945), Malta (1947), Belgium (1948) and Greece (1952). If there is any doubt that these advances resulted directly from the Second World War, consider that women from neutral Switzerland did not win full suffrage until 1971, and women in neutral Portugal had to wait until 1976. In Asia the story was the same: Chinese, Japanese, Korean, Vietnamese and Indonesian women also won full voting rights in the 1940s. Meanwhile, the only Latin American and Caribbean countries to grant universal suffrage *before* the war were Brazil, Uruguay and Cuba – but during and after the war almost all the others quickly followed suit (Paraguay was the last, holding out until 1961).[18]

The rights of women were also finally recognized on an international level in 1945 by the United Nations. The UN Charter opens with a declaration of intent not only to save the world from future wars but also to promote 'the equal rights of men and women and of nations large and small'. By 1946 a UN Commission on the Status of Women had already been set up, which would play a significant role in the drafting of the Universal Declaration of Human Rights. This landmark document, published in 1948, finally spelled out how 'all members of the human family' should be afforded the same rights, dignity and worth.

On the face of it, therefore, the stage appeared to be set for a new era in which women who had grown up without fundamental rights – women like Françoise Leclercq – might at last begin to take their rightful place in the economic, political and social life of the world. The hopes that were expressed by many women, in France and across the world, were unashamedly utopian. Even Simone de Beauvoir, whose savage criticism of French patriarchy pulled no punches, allowed herself to dream of a time in the not-too-distant future when men and women 'would see each other as equals' and 'unequivocally affirm their brotherhood'.[19]

Unfortunately, this was where the progress towards equality ground to a halt. Nowhere was this more apparent than in France. Given the huge transformations that took place there as a result of the war, it is tempting to portray the French as a nation of firebrands – but in reality the forces of conservatism were every bit as strong as the forces of revolution. It was all very well for Resistance members to champion women's rights, but much of the rest of French society, which had merely kept its collective head down during the occupation, wanted only for the world to return to the way it had been before the war. When French prisoners of war returned home in 1945 they expected to resume their positions at the head of the family, regardless of how well their wives had run things in their absence. Women too were often relieved to be able to return to the traditional roles they had grown up with rather than struggling to invent new functions for themselves in public life. They were tired of conflict and wanted only to lead a 'normal' life.[20]

Nor is it strictly true to suggest that the majority of men in the Resistance regarded their female counterparts as equals. Jeanne Bohec, an experienced female explosives expert in Saint-Marcel, complained that she was quickly sidelined as soon as young men began to join the Forces Françaises de l'Intérieur (FFI). She wanted to take part in the liberation, but 'I was told politely to forget about it. A woman isn't supposed to fight when so many men are available. Yet I surely knew how to use a submachine gun better than lots of the FFI volunteers who had just got hold of these arms.'[21] In Italy, female partisans were often banned from taking part in the triumphal march-pasts after the liberation – those who did were often branded 'whores'.[22]

As the war drew to an end, the pressure for women to return to traditional roles was often irresistible. Churches, governments, schools and even the brand-new women's magazines like *Elle* and *Marie-France* that first appeared on the market after the war all exhorted women to return to the home. In August 1946 one woman wrote to *Elle* explaining her desire to take a job against her fiancé's wishes. The magazine told her bluntly, 'Your fiancé is right. The place of the married woman is at home,' before going on to suggest that if she was unwilling to bow to her fiancé's wishes, then perhaps she did not truly love him after all. 'Woman must create happiness,' claimed another magazine. 'She will do this best in her home. The home and only the home is her true professional milieu.' At school, girls were taught with textbooks that told them explicitly that 'true happiness lies in the home' and that a woman's 'absence from the home weakens family life'. The government, meanwhile, exhorted women to get back not only indoors but into the bedroom: an increased birth rate was announced as a national priority, and all kinds of benefits, including tax breaks and extra rations, were announced for mothers. De Gaulle himself proclaimed that he wanted 12 million more babies to help with the reconstruction of France. According to Robert Prigent, the minister of population and public health immediately after the war, women's true fulfilment lay in 'accepting their feminine nature' and devoting themselves to their homes and their children.[23]

By the end of the 1940s it was becoming plain that the fledgling feminist movement, so vibrant in 1945, had stalled. As early as 1947, the much-vaunted equality laws of the previous year were already being routinely ignored: it was easy to justify paying women less than men when the most menial jobs in society were effectively reserved for women.[24] Further reforms also failed to materialize: it would be another twenty years before married women in France would be legally allowed to take a job or open a bank account without the permission of their husbands, and forty years before they would win equal rights over their children.[25] If the sixty-one women who had been elected to the French parliament in 1946 hoped to blaze a trail for others to follow, then they too were to be sorely disappointed: their number dropped sharply during the 1950s and continued to decline. By the end of the 1960s there were only thirteen women members left: eight in the National Assembly and five in the Senate.[26] For all their enthusiasm at the end of the war, French women made little progress in closing the pay gap, the education gap, or the representation gap after 1946, causing some former Resistance fighters to ask whether women had ever been 'liberated' at all.[27]

The same pattern – of immediate progress for women after the war, followed by a long period of stagnation until at least the 1960s – occurred all over the world. The war undoubtedly provided a platform for radical change; but once the chaos of the postwar world began to settle down, old interests began to reassert themselves, and in some cases even reversed the process.

In Egypt, for example, despite the strides women had made towards overturning the Personal Status Law, the movement faltered once the Arab Republic of Egypt was declared in 1952. Egyptian women would

THE WOMEN OF WORLD WAR II

Progress? This monument to 'The Women of World War II', unveiled in London's Whitehall in 2005, finally recognized the role of Britain's women during the war; but it also unconsciously revealed official attitudes towards women by depicting only their clothing. Women themselves are entirely absent.

have to wait until 1979 before the law on their subordinate status was reformed. The campaign of Indonesian women to bring an end to polygamy effectively came to an end when the father of the nation, President Sukarno, himself took a second wife in 1954. In Brazil the campaign by the Federation of Women for better living conditions in the favelas also foundered. In all three countries women's movements were banned in the 1950s and 60s, and did not re-emerge for at least the next fifteen or twenty years.[28]

Likewise, the campaign for equal pay failed almost everywhere. In the USA an Equal Pay Act was not signed into law until 1963, and women in Australia only won the right to equal pay after 1969, when trade unions took a test case to court. In Britain, a similar act did not come into force until 1975. The International Labour Organization drew up the Equal Remuneration Convention as early as 1951, but much of the developed world did not get round to ratifying it until the 1960s and 70s.[29] As a consequence, the global pay gap between men and women did not narrow to any extent until the 1970s. Today, serious disparities remain almost everywhere: in 2015 the World Economic Forum estimated that the pay gap might not finally close until well into the twenty-second century.[30]

Even the campaign for women's suffrage was not entirely successful after the war. As already mentioned, women in Switzerland and Portugal could not vote on equal terms with men until the 1970s. Women in the Middle East had to wait even longer. Bahrain, for example, extended the franchise to women only in 2002, Oman in 2003 and Kuwait, which actually *removed* women's right to vote in 1999, reinstated it in 2005. Saudi Arabia did not have any elections at all until 2005 – but women were not allowed to vote in them until 2015.[31]

Today, despite decades of campaigning by millions of men and women across the world; despite a UN Convention on the Political Rights of Women (which came into force in 1954) and a Convention on the Elimination of All Forms of Discrimination Against Women (1981); despite numerous worldwide conferences under the auspices of organizations as diverse as the WIDF and the UN; despite a Development Fund for Women, a Council of Women World Leaders, a Women's World Wide Web; despite dozens of other international organizations, in many parts of the world the dream of equal rights and equal opportunities seems just as far away as ever. As feminists have been saying

ever since the 1940s, abstract equality means nothing: '[T]o turn freedom into reality, women must also have the health, education and
money they need to make use of their rights.'[32]

Women as 'Other'

So what went wrong? If the appetite for change was so strong in 1945,
why did it take a further twenty-five years before most meaningful
changes even began?

Part of the reason lay in the conservative tendencies of normal human
nature. The 1940s were a time of enormous flux for everyone: not only
had the war caused enormous social and economic upheavals, but scientific and technological advances were transforming our understanding
of the world around us. For many people these changes were already
too much to take in: the idea of also altering the very nature of the relationship between men and women was just a step too far. In most
cultures around the world, and certainly in the West, women represented those aspects of society where the idea of stability was at its most
precious – the home, the family, the marital bed. Many men – and
indeed women – who were willing to face revolution in the world at
large, were not prepared to face similar change at home. Even Eleanor
Roosevelt, champion of minority rights and co-drafter of the Universal
Declaration on Human Rights, held back when it came to the place of
women in society. Whatever a woman's other responsibilities, she
declared, their first loyalty must always be 'to their homes, their husbands and their children'.[33]

Another reason why progress faltered was purely political. It is significant that the process of change stopped at around the same time that
the Cold War began. Many of the most active women's organizations
were left wing, and a number of them were dominated by Communists.
This was particularly the case in France, where the majority of women
in parliament were Communists, as were the largest proportion of
women in local politics. The founders of the Union des Femmes Françaises were all Communists, and its vice-president after the war was
Jeannette Vermeersch, the wife of Maurice Thorez, the leader of the
French Communist Party. This did not matter in 1945 and 1946, when a
spirit of collaboration still existed between the West and the Soviet

Union, but in the atmosphere of distrust that grew up at the start of the Cold War it was easy to dismiss such women as Soviet puppets, no matter how worthwhile the work they did.

In Brazil, Indonesia and elsewhere women's organizations were banned for precisely this reason. In America, too, the most outspoken advocates for women's rights were also silenced because of their leftist tendencies. The Congress of American Women, for example, which fought vociferously for child care, equal pay and an end to racism, was forced to disband in 1950 because it was branded 'Communist' by the House Un-American Activities Committee. The union with the greatest number of women members, the United Electrical, Radio and Machine Workers of America, was also persecuted because of its links to communism, rendering their long-running campaign for equal rights largely impotent.[34] Once tarnished in this way, it was often difficult for individual women or their organizations to reclaim their credibility. For example, despite being probably the most influential international women's organization of the postwar period, the WIDF has been virtually ignored by Western historians – even feminist historians – largely because of the way it was smeared as a Communist front organization during the 1950s.[35]

Given the enthusiasm that the Communists showed for greater equality between the sexes, one might assume that women in Communist countries might be better off than their Western counterparts – but in reality Soviet women were also marginalized, overlooked for promotion at work, expected to do all the most menial jobs and subject to deeply sexist attitudes. Those who married were still expected to do all the housework, even if they also had a job, and even if their husbands were unemployed.[36] Even those who had taken part in the fighting were not given the respect they deserved, but were branded instead as loose women. As one former Soviet nurse remembered, 'A man returned from the war and there he was, a hero . . . But if it was a girl, then immediately people looked askance: "We know what you did there!"'[37] The inequalities that persisted between men and women, both in the East and in the West, clearly ran deeper than mere politics.

It was with this in mind that Simone de Beauvoir embarked on a study of femininity at the end of the 1940s. According to de Beauvoir, the real problem that women faced was far more fundamental than history, or politics, or psychology, or even biology: the source of their subordination lay in the very definition of 'woman' itself. Men, she observed, were not compelled to define themselves as 'men' – they were free to experiment, to live active lives, inventing themselves as they went along. Women, by contrast, were always defined before they had even begun. They were 'mothers' or 'wives', 'virgins' or 'whores', sometimes threatening, often mysterious, but always outside the core of society, which was exclusively male.

In her ground-breaking book *The Second Sex* she defined for the first time the existential differences between men and women. The sexes might tell themselves that they were two halves of one Platonic whole, she wrote, but this was quite patently untrue:

> The terms *masculine* and *feminine* are used symmetrically only as a matter of form, as on legal papers. In actuality the relation of the two sexes is not quite like that of two electrical poles, for man represents both the positive and the neutral, as is indicated by the common use of *man* to designate human beings in general; whereas woman represents only the negative, defined by limiting criteria, without reciprocity . . . Thus humanity is male and man defines woman not in herself but as relative to him . . . she is the incidental, the inessential as opposed to the essential. He is the Subject, he is the Absolute – she is the Other.[38]

This designation of woman as 'Other' was not a million miles away from imagining her as an enemy, even a kind of 'monster'; but unlike with other monsters men were not free to reject her entirely, because they both desired and needed her, not least for the propagation of the species. Therefore, in order to explain and contain her 'Otherness', men had created a series of myths around femininity. They had made her 'exotic', with all the connotations of desirability and inferiority that word implied; and they had made her dependent upon them, just as slaves were dependent upon their masters.

Men convinced themselves that they benefited from women's subordination, because it gave them everything they thought they wanted: a maid in the living room, a cook in the kitchen and a whore in the bedroom. But by maintaining the relationship of master and slave in this way they were only really hiding from their own inadequacies and fears. Furthermore they denied themselves the possibility of a more fulfilling relationship as life partners – the kind of relationship that many men and women had enjoyed during the war when they were fighting together in the Resistance as equals.

Meanwhile, women were also often complicit in their subordination, since it saved them from the burden of responsibility that came with making their own choices in life. In the case of the middle and upper classes, it allowed them to live a life of indolence and luxury. But in reality this kind of life was nothing but a gilded cage, which deprived them of any opportunity to spread their wings and experience what it really meant to be alive. This was the kind of comfortable monotony that Françoise Leclercq had broken free from when she took the decision to involve herself first in the Resistance, and later in the women's movement. For de Beauvoir it was only by striving in this way that women would ever be able to make their lives meaningful. Marriage, motherhood, even a job outside the home were no substitute: 'there is no other way out for woman,' she wrote, 'than to work for her liberation'.[39]

Simone de Beauvoir's book, like the women's movement in general, would not be taken seriously by the French establishment for the next twenty years. It was denigrated in the French press, even by fellow existentialists like Albert Camus, who accused its author of making the French male look ridiculous. Because of its frankness about sexual matters, the Vatican even went so far as to put it on their list of heretical books. Nevertheless, it was read – not only in France but also in America and Britain. Throughout the 1950s there was no other book that women who wanted to think about their status in the world could turn to. In future years it would become an inspiration for a new wave of feminists like America's Betty Friedan and Kate Millett, and Australia's Germaine Greer. According to the Norwegian feminist Toril Moi, de Beauvoir's insights are the very foundation of all contemporary feminism – whether contemporary feminists acknowledge it or not.[40]

But they were also a product of their time. *The Second Sex* was written in the aftermath of the greatest war in history, when much of Europe had struggled to liberate itself from other forms of oppression and tyranny, and when humankind was dreaming of greater equality and justice. These undercurrents are all present in the women's movement that Simone de Beauvoir both described and helped to found.

The Problem of Minorities

The struggle for equality, with its early victories and subsequent disappointments, is not a subject that only concerns women. Equality is not something that can be handed out in ribboned packages to those we deem worthy – it either exists or it doesn't, and where it exists it is indivisible. The treatment of women is a good barometer for how all marginalized groups are treated: the greater the opportunities for women, the greater also the opportunities for ethnic, religious, sexual and other minorities. Indeed, recent international studies show a clear correlation between gender equality and the fulfilment of social and economic rights for us all. What happened to women after the war therefore concerned not only women but everyone.[41]

There are certainly striking parallels between the situation of women after the war and other marginalized groups. At around the same time that Simone de Beauvoir was writing about women as 'the Other', her partner Jean-Paul Sartre was writing about French Jews in exactly the same terms.[42] Across the Atlantic, the mixed-race writer Anatole Broyard wrote passionately about how black people had also been made 'Other'; meanwhile, the black rights activists W. E. B. Du Bois was writing about how Africa – and black people in general – had not only been assigned an inferior role in world history, but often excluded from that history altogether.[43]

Simone de Beauvoir repeatedly acknowledged both of these parallels in 1949.[44] She found the similarities between women and black people in the USA especially poignant:

> Both are being emancipated from a like paternalism, and the former master class wishes to 'keep them in their place' – that is, the place chosen for them. In both cases the former masters lavish more or less sincere eulogies, either on the virtues of 'the good Negro' with his dormant, childish, merry soul – the submissive Negro – or on the merits of the woman who is 'truly feminine' – that is, frivolous, infantile, irresponsible – the submissive woman. In both cases the dominant class bases its argument on a state of affairs that it has itself created.[45]

After the war was over, black people in America were not nearly as submissive as they had been in the past. The war had opened up all kinds of new horizons – not only for the hundreds of thousands of black servicemen who travelled abroad but also for the 1.5 million or so black people who left the American South during the 1940s in pursuit of new jobs and new opportunities.[46] Their participation in the workforce grew massively: during the course of the war, the number of black workers employed in American manufacturing leapt from 500,000 to 1.2 million.[47] Their membership of unions and other political groups also ballooned: the National Association for the Advancement of Colored People (NAACP), for example, grew from just 50,000 members at the start of the war to 450,000 at the war's end. 'I do not believe that Negroes will stand idly by and see their newly opened doors of economic opportunity closed in their faces,' wrote one black news columnist in 1945, especially after having fought in a war 'for democracy against fascism'.[48]

President Truman addresses the NAACP convention at the Lincoln Memorial in 1947. This event would be echoed, far more triumphantly, when Martin Luther King, Jr addressed a quarter of a million black Americans at the same spot, sixteen years later.

Much like women in France, African-Americans won all kinds of rights in the wake of the war. In 1946, the Supreme Court ruled against racial segregation on buses and trains that crossed state boundaries, in 1948 President Truman decreed an end to segregation in the military and a series of anti-racist measures on housing, education and employment opportunities also occurred around this time. However, almost all these changes came as a result of court rulings or executive orders by the president rather than by consensus: indeed, Truman's entire civil rights agenda was voted down by Congress. No matter how enthusiastic the black population might have been for change, it was rarely granted without strong opposition from the white majority.

A similar course can be charted for the status of gay men and women, who enjoyed a period of relative tolerance after the war, particularly in Europe and North America. In Europe, they tried to capitalize on this by forming gay organizations like the Dutch Cultuur en Ontspanningscentrum (commonly known as the COC) or the Danish League of 1948, which eventually banded together with various other groups to form the International Committee for Sexual Equality.[49] In America, gay men and women in the military had also experienced a period of relative tolerance during the war itself. According to historian Allan Bérubé, this amounted to a minor sexual revolution, and many returning gay GIs felt confident enough to declare, 'I'm not going back to what I left.' Such people faced renewed repression in the late 1940s and 50s, particularly during the so-called 'Lavender Scare' of the McCarthy era. Nevertheless, much like the women's movement and the black civil rights movement, the homophile movement that emerged from the Second World War laid the groundwork for the gay rights movements of later decades.[50]

The drive towards equality was even reflected on an international scale in the way that colonial people were treated after 1945. Half a dozen Asian nations won their political independence as a direct consequence of the Second World War. They were followed by the nations of Africa, whose path to freedom was likewise influenced by the events of the war and its aftermath. As each of these nations took their place in international forums like the UN General Assembly they were welcomed for the first time as equal members. Such progress was not easily achieved. Nations like Indonesia or Algeria had to fight tooth and nail for the right to be recognized as sovereign states, and were resisted every step of the way by the same Europeans that had spent the war clamouring for their own right to self-determination.

The Problem of Identity

In the aftermath of the war, many groups were made conscious, sometimes for the first time, of what it meant to be 'the Other'. Women, ethnic minorities, colonial peoples, homosexuals, the impoverished, political outsiders – in each case their humanity might have been 'universally' recognized, but they would continue to be denied the full benefits of that humanity. As 'the Other', they were defined by their difference from the human 'norm' – and yet that norm was not of their choosing, nor could they influence it.

In 1945 each of these groups were forced to choose how they would react to this knowledge. They could try to assimilate themselves within the mainstream, and gain equality that way – and yet, to do so would be to deny the very traits that made them who they were. A black man could never be the same as a white man, because he carried with him an internal history that most white people had no notion of. A former count in eastern Europe, stripped of his title and his lands, might try to live as a Communist – but at heart he would still be an aristocrat. Besides, assimilation was only truly possible where both the majority and the minority agreed to let it happen. The experience of the Jews showed that it made no difference how 'Jewish' a person was or wasn't: all that had mattered during the Holocaust was what the Nazis believed him or her to be.

A second path such groups might choose was to embrace their difference from the norm, celebrate it – declare, as the Gay Pride movement did in the 1980s, that 'I am what I am', regardless of what the world thought about it. But to do this automatically implies an acceptance of being 'the Other'. In effect, it makes any minority complicit in its own marginalization. Differences with the mainstream become entrenched, and the danger always remains that this will lead to greater prejudice on both sides. Few groups chose this path in the aftermath of the war, precisely because it would have made them so vulnerable: the example of what had happened to Jews during the war was a warning to everyone not to stand out.

A more extreme option was to separate oneself off completely – to set up an alternative community in which the 'minority' is the majority, and can choose for itself what is and is not the norm. Some small groups tried to do this in the aftermath of the war, usually with disastrous consequences: in the south of Italy, for example, a handful of disgruntled communities set up 'peasant republics', which were forcefully put down by the central government.[51] On a national scale separation like this could be more effective: eastern Europe succeeded in expelling almost all of its ethnic German populations into Germany, Muslims were likewise ejected from India and Hindus from Pakistan, and the nationalist Chinese preferred to exile themselves to Taiwan rather than submit to communism on the mainland. But such events were never achieved without a great deal of bloodshed, and only shifted the focus of prejudice from a local level to a national or international one. Once again, the Jews are probably the best example of this: if Zionist Jews believed that they could abolish prejudice by creating their own state in 1948, they were sorely mistaken – the state of Israel has since become a national 'Other' for much of the world, and has simultaneously created its own 'Others', both internally and within the region.

The only other option was to work together with other groups, including those in power and those who had oppressed others in the past, and try to achieve some kind of consensus. This was the approach that the United Nations took with its Universal Declaration of Human Rights. It was also the approach favoured by prominent philosophers and sociologists like Simone de Beauvoir and W. E. B. Du Bois, who believed that differences between individuals and groups were inevitable and universal, and that the only hope for greater equality was for all individuals and all groups to recognize their responsibilities towards one another. But this approach also had its drawbacks, as became evident when the following decades failed to produce any significant progress towards equality. It was in reaction to this lack of progress that a more militant civil rights movement, women's rights movement and gay rights movement started up in the 1960s. By this time a new generation of activists had grown up, less interested in consensus and more interested in results.

These were the kinds of dilemmas faced by marginalized groups in the immediate aftermath of the war – to assimilate or fragment, to trust in consensus or to seize one's own destiny unilaterally, regardless of the consequences. Whatever path one chose, equality – *true* equality, in the utopian sense – was, and remains, impossible.

But these dilemmas also point the way to one of the most important characteristics of the age: the conflict between the urge to draw together as one, and the urge to fragment into different and ever smaller groups. This was the single quandary that, more than any other, defined the postwar era. We shall see it again in the way the United Nations was set up both to represent a world consensus and to provide a forum for individual nations to fight for their own particular and selfish agendas. We shall also see it within nations, where the urge for national unity often conflicted with a wide variety of self-destructive forces. But perhaps most poignant was the way it manifested in individuals. As we shall see next, the conflict between the urge to belong and the urge to be free from all constraints was one of the most urgent philosophical dilemmas of the postwar age.

9. Freedom and Belonging

Unlike many of the individuals whose lives I describe in this book, Hans Bjerkholt was not a young man in 1945. He was already well past the age of fifty, and largely set in his ways. The changes that were wrought upon him by the war and its aftermath were therefore all the more remarkable, because over the course of the next five years he would turn his back on everything he had once believed, and launch himself upon a new quest for world unity.[1]

Hans Bjerkholt was born in a rural part of south-east Norway where, by his own account, he had an idyllic childhood. He grew up on a farm, and spent his days feeding the chickens, tending to the horses with his father and playing hide-and-seek in the barn with his many brothers and sisters. During the long summer days he and his siblings would spend hours in the woods, or go swimming or fishing in the lake, before descending upon his mother's kitchen to be fed with home-made bread, fresh butter, bacon, eggs and milk straight from the cows.

All this came to a sudden end when he was ten years old. His father had lent a large amount of money to some businessmen who subsequently declared themselves bankrupt, and the family had no choice but to sell the farm. Weeping, they packed up their belongings and moved to the nearby town of Sarpsborg, where they found themselves a tiny apartment – two small rooms and a kitchen for a family of twelve.

Hans's oldest brother found a job as a chauffeur, his sister as a waitress, and his father went to work in a paper factory – a soulless place full of 'grey-faced, weary workers'. Slowly they managed to get themselves back on their feet, but one day misfortune struck a second time: Hans's father had a serious accident at work, which hospitalized him for a year and a half. The factory owners refused to accept liability, leaving the family to pay the expensive hospital bills. And so the teenaged Hans was also now obliged to take work – in the very same factory where his father had been injured.

Deprived of his birthright, financially ruined by the unscrupulous factory owners, Hans couldn't help feeling as though his life had collapsed. As a child on the farm he had felt free and alive, 'as if the whole world belonged to me'. But now he and his family had become mere cogs in a vast machine that did not care about them, and which had stripped them of their human dignity. 'I felt miserable and physically ill in the factory and the whole social system made me boil with rage.'

So began a lifetime of militant activism. He joined the union and became one of its foremost representatives. Later he became one of the founder members of the Norwegian Communist Party, and represented his country at Comintern conferences in Moscow. Fuelled by the injustices that had been done to him and his family, his guiding principles were a perpetual 'mistrust against management' and a hatred for the capitalist system that ruled not only Norway but also the vast majority of the world. He longed for the time when communism would triumph everywhere, and class injustice would become a thing of the past.

Bjerkholt never imagined that he would begin to lose his faith in communism, but when the Second World War broke out it gave him a new perspective on life. For one thing, some of his communist comrades had not behaved well at the start of the war, when they had argued for collaboration with the Nazis (on the grounds that the Soviets still had a pact with the Germans at this point). More importantly, however, the war introduced him to a new spirit of cooperation which he had never experienced before. When the Germans invaded Norway he found himself working together with all kinds of other groups towards a common goal that had little to do with the workers' struggle: Norwegians of every political persuasion were fighting together for their very freedom. In 1942 he was arrested and thrown into a prison camp, where he was immediately impressed by the atmosphere of unity, especially between the Communists and the Social Democrats. During his thirty-seven months of incarceration he came to an awareness that this unity was not merely a phenomenon in his prison camp – it spread throughout Norwegian society as a whole, and even into the wider world, where the British, the French, the Americans and the Soviets were also working together to defeat Nazism.

When the war ended, he hoped fervently that this spirit of cooperation might continue. He embarked on a series of talks with the socialists with the idea of creating some kind of united front on behalf of the common man. 'The great idea for our age is the idea of teamwork,' he wrote later, 'the teamwork of all progressive forces for one great aim.'

The experience of the war had given him a taste of working with people, rather than against them, and he desperately wished for some way for the different parties, the different classes and the different nations of the world to join together into 'one great uniting force'. But it did not take long before the old class divisions began to express themselves once again, and talks between the Communists and the socialists broke down. On an international scale, relations between East and West also collapsed, 'thus showing our hopes to have been illusions'.

It was at this point that his son gave him a book for Christmas that would change his life. The book was about a new ideological movement called 'Moral Re-Armament' (MRA), which had been started just before the war by a Protestant evangelist but which was now attracting

Hans Bjerkholt, convert from communism to Moral Re-Armament.

followers from all faiths and all walks of life. This movement advocated a different approach to human relationships based upon four moral absolutes: absolute honesty, absolute purity, absolute unselfishness and absolute love. Adherents were advised to sit and meditate for an hour or so each morning, listen out for the voice of God and act according to their conscience. It was a simple idea that appealed to Bjerkholt's strong sense of moral responsibility.

Curious to find out more, Bjerkholt travelled to the movement's conference centre in Caux, Switzerland, where he was immediately struck by the peaceful and consensual atmosphere. He could not help contrasting it to the many Communist Party conferences he had attended, which had always been riven with infighting and factionalism. 'At Caux I felt an amazing unity based on love and understanding strong enough to break down all barriers of class, creed and colour. There were no factions in Caux; and even Communists and socialists found unity.' Here he met delegates from Italy, France and even the recently defeated Germany, all of whom appeared to be relating to one another in a spirit of mutual respect and reconciliation. One French Marxist even stood up and made a formal apology to the German delegates for his former hatred of them – a gesture that Bjerkholt found astonishing, but also very moving.

By the time he returned to Norway he was a changed man. He immediately made a solemn declaration in which he pledged himself to the cause of Moral Re-Armament and promised to introduce its principles into the Communist movement in Norway. 'I accepted MRA with all my heart,' he later wrote. 'I had to accept the challenge of absolute moral standards, and give up my own self-will entirely.' This, he believed, was the only way both to find freedom 'from himself', and to help lay the foundations for the classless society he had always dreamed of. If all men could relate to one another in the way he had witnessed at Caux, then all the world's ills might be cured.

When the Norwegian Communist Party learned of his conversion, they quickly ostracized him. In the end he was left with little choice but to leave the party, but he insisted that he never regretted this choice. 'Marxism is a milestone in the road,' he later told an Italian audience, 'but it is not the decisive answer for the new ideological era. The new way for our time is the philosophy of Moral Re-Armament.' It was only through MRA, with its spirit of consensus and 'absolute love', that mankind would ever be able to achieve its true aims. 'No class and no group can alone and without the assistance of other groups produce the new world we want. We must first create the new men within ourselves, and then fight along with all others to bring the new world to birth.'

The way he told it, Hans Bjerkholt's life was a story of paradise lost and paradise regained – or, at least, *almost* regained. Bjerkholt never lived to see the unified world he dreamed of, or the classless society that he had fought for throughout his life – although Norway's version of social democracy is probably as close as any nation has ever managed. He joined MRA at a time when it was a growing force in the world, and contributed to its rapid expansion during the 1950s and 60s, but by the time he died in 1983 the movement's influence had long since begun to dwindle again. Today its name is 'Initiatives of Change', and it has become just another non-governmental organization amongst many. It continues to preach the same virtues that inspired Hans Bjerkholt in the years after the war – the virtues of tolerance, unselfishness and acting according to one's conscience – but the missionary zeal that once propelled it to prominence all over the world is now a thing of the past.[2]

Everyone needs something to believe in. It is one of the tragedies of modernity that the more affluent our societies become, and the freer we are to choose our own way of life, the more alienated we tend to be from those aspects of our lives that we hold most dear – our sense of self, our sense of community, our links to nature, our familiarity with the divine. Ever since the nineteenth century, sociologists and political thinkers have been charting the long, slow death of mainstream religion and the corresponding descent of humanity into atomization, isolation and the banality of consumerism. Our communal obsession with creating and accumulating wealth, they argue, might have lifted much of the world out of poverty, but along the way it has also reduced mankind to what the father of sociology, Max Weber, called a great 'nothingness' trapped inside a 'steel-hard casing' of materialism, devoid of the very values that make us human.[3]

For all of its violence and inhumanity, the Second World War gave the world a moment of glorious respite from this decline. I have written elsewhere about the destructive elements of the war, about the long-term splits it caused between ethnic, religious and political groups, and about the cruelty it spawned, which continued long after 1945.[4] But on a broader, more abstract level, the Second World War did something that no other event in modern times has ever been able to do to quite the same degree: it united individuals, communities, nations and even whole groups of nations in a single cause. Tens of millions were undoubtedly cast adrift by the war, but hundreds of millions were given a new sense of belonging unlike anything they had ever known. If God is society, as Émile Durkheim famously asserted, then in this sense at least the Second World War was a divine event.[5]

The collective effort that went into the war is unparalleled in modern history. Well over 100 million men and women were mobilized between 1937 and 1945. Around 70 million of these fought on the Allied side – more than all the forces on all sides of the First World War *combined*.[6] This does not include the many tens of millions who served on the home front in factories and land armies, or the tens of millions of civilians who gave their time, their savings and their lives in support of the war effort. Whether they were directly involved in the war or not, almost everyone on the planet was emotionally invested in it to some degree: most people wanted it won by their side; all people wanted it over.

This unity of purpose gave meaning to people's lives in a way that cut across all the traditional divides of race, nationality, politics, religion, class and income. Americans cooperated with Communist apparatchiks, trade unions with employers, Christians with Jews, Hindus with Muslims, blacks with whites, rich with poor. In the armed forces people of all kinds and classes served together, celebrated their victories together, died together and mourned together. Even amongst those who did not fight there was a greater sense of equality and shared sacrifice, brought about by rationing and universal shortages. This does not mean to say that the differences between rival groups disappeared – far from it, tensions between groups remained just beneath the surface, and even erupted from time to time – but because almost everyone had invested so much energy and emotion in the greater conflict, they were generally able to rise above their differences. Amongst all the personal and local storms that built and dispersed during this time, at a global level at least the war always remained a fixed point, a pole star by which everyone might navigate.

Like all universal ideas, this idea of the war was necessarily full of paradoxes. It involved a violent division of humanity, and yet it was fought in the name of peace and unity. It involved compulsory labour, conscription to the armed forces, rationing, restricted travel and increased regulation of virtually every area of people's lives – and yet almost everyone, whatever side they fought on, considered it to be a struggle for freedom. It brought widespread revolutionary change, and yet it spoke to people's desires for a new future and a new stability. Whatever the brutal facts of the war, as an abstract idea it promised all kinds of paradise to all kinds of people: as long as the war continued, the whole world could believe in its ideals, no matter how paradoxical they appeared.

All this came to an end in the summer of 1945. Europe and Asia were liberated. Prisoners were set free from concentration camps. Soldiers were demobilized, factory workers dismissed and forced agricultural labourers allowed to go home. As restrictions on freedom of speech were relaxed everywhere, even in countries like the Soviet Union, people began to ask what they were going to do next. What should they fight for, now that the fighting was over? Should they try to rebuild what they had lost, or should they build something new? Should they demand yet more changes in their communities, or should they instead try to recover some sense of stability? Should they look out for themselves, or for their communities, or for their nations, class, race, or some other, still greater good – the whole of humanity, perhaps? In the absence of war, what was the point of life? What did 'freedom' actually mean?

Today, when we look back at VE Day and VJ Day, we remember only the joy of victory and the relief that the whole world felt at the end of hostilities – but actually, beneath all the celebrations, there was also an undercurrent of something very different. Of course, most people understood that the end of the war had brought a new kind of uncertainty to life, but their feelings often went deeper than mere uncertainty. When reading through diaries, letters and oral testimonies from the end of the war, it is remarkable how often people asked the same question: 'Why am I not really happy?'[7] For those who had lost family and friends there was an obvious answer to this question; but for others, the emptiness they felt was much more difficult to define. They complained that they 'had no anchor in life', or that 'the end of the war took away the purpose' of living.[8] 'When the war ended I was surprised that I wasn't all that elated,' remembered one British intelligence officer, years later. 'I just felt a slightly lost feeling . . . What you'd known for an awfully long time had vanished, and there seemed to be nothing to take its place . . . It was all gone.'[9]

The war had filled people's lives for so long that many of them began to miss it. Compared to the drama of the war years, life afterwards looked mundane, and its continuing hardships no longer seemed to have purpose. Nostalgia for the war – which is still common today, particularly in the victorious nations – was born from this feeling of emptiness. As they looked back on the war, people began to imagine it as an age of heroes when, despite the violence, everyone at least knew what was right and what was wrong. The Soviet author Emmanuil Kazakevich tells the story of a scene he witnessed in his local bar on the fifth anniversary of VE Day in 1950. 'Two invalids and a plumber . . . were drinking beer and reminiscing about the war. One of them wept and said: If there were another war, I would go . . .'[10]

Freedom

Unsurprisingly, the philosophical creed that most captured the spirit of the immediate postwar period was existentialism. For the French philosopher Jean-Paul Sartre the ambivalent atmosphere that was thrown up by the war's ending was only to be expected, although he would never have approved of the nostalgia it provoked. Sartre had witnessed the liberation of Paris in August 1944, in which his fellow citizens had taken to the streets, sometimes armed with revolvers, sometimes not armed at all, 'intoxicated with the feeling of freedom and the lightness of their movements'. According to his description of the liberation a year later, the violence had taken place in an atmosphere of spontaneous festivity, as if it were a 'rehearsal for the apocalypse'. It was, he said, an 'explosion of freedom' in which ordinary people had celebrated not only 'freedom for themselves and for each Frenchman', but 'the power of human beings' in general: 'All Paris felt during that week in August that man still had a chance, that he could still win out against the machine.' And yet this atmosphere of festivity had also been accompanied by an overwhelming sensation of fear. Other towns and cities, like Warsaw in Poland, had been razed to the ground for defiance like this. By choosing to take part in their liberation, the people of Paris had embraced not only their freedom, but also the possible consequences that came with it.[11]

Looking back on these events, Sartre was struck by the universality of both the yearning for freedom he had witnessed and the unbearable fear that accompanied it. In the summer of 1945, when the wider war was finally over, Parisians were still 'dressed up in their Sunday best', but were also still unbearably anxious about what the future might hold. It was significant, he wrote, 'that the anniversary of the Parisian uprising should fall so close to the first appearance of the atomic bomb'. Just as the people of Paris had faced a choice in 1944 over whether to take part in their liberty or to leave it in the hands of others, so now all of humanity was faced with an even greater choice between total freedom (with all the awesome responsibility that implied) and submission to a new, nuclear inhumanity. In the face of such a choice, it was only natural that people were full of anguish.

In the context of the Second World War and its aftermath, people everywhere had been forced to contemplate the notion of freedom with a new sense of urgency. During the war the word 'freedom' had been used to signify all kinds of things, from human rights like 'freedom of speech' and 'freedom of worship' to the liberation of mankind from various oppressive forces – Nazism, Stalinism, imperialism, poverty and so on. For Sartre, however, true freedom was something much deeper – a fundamental human condition that all of us were 'condemned' to whether we liked it or not. According to his philosophy, since all human beings are born without any preconceived notion of what being 'human' means, we are all free to make of life whatever we will: 'man first of all exists, encounters himself, surges up in the world – and defines himself afterwards'.[12] Even those born into repressive societies always have choices – to comply or to resist, to speak out or to be silent, to live or to die. But in this freedom is also the realization that we are all fundamentally alone, and that we are thus entirely responsible for every action we take, along with all of its consequences. There is no guidance from God; there is no template for human action – all we can do is invent ourselves as we go along. In one of his wartime essays Sartre used the metaphor of a Resistance fighter, sitting 'alone and naked' in the torturer's chair trying to decide whether to reveal the names of his comrades. In such circumstances – as in all of life – the freedom to choose how we are going to act is not a gift, but a terrible burden.[13]

In essence, there was nothing especially new about Sartre's concept of freedom: philosophers like Søren Kierkegaard and Friedrich Nietzsche had explored similar thoughts in the nineteenth century, as had Martin

Heidegger in the 1920s. But the context of the war's end brought new meaning to such ideas, as people everywhere, coming face to face at last with their own freedom, were forced to contemplate how they had acted during the war, and how they would greet the huge new vistas of the postwar world. The massive international popularity that Sartre's brand of existentialism enjoyed after 1945 is at least partly attributable to the new sense of angst that people experienced all over the world in the wake of the war.[14]

But Sartre was by no means the only intellectual to spend the war considering the agony of freedom: other thinkers were formulating broadly similar ideas from entirely different perspectives. One of the most influential was Erich Fromm, a German-Jewish social psychologist who had left Germany shortly after Hitler came to power. In 1942 he published his first work in English, a book entirely dedicated to the problem of freedom and the terrifying sense of dread that almost always accompanies it. *The Fear of Freedom* was meant as a critique of the conditions which had first given rise to Nazism; but it also addressed the problems that lay at the heart of capitalist democracies like Britain and America, where people who considered themselves 'free' often gave themselves up to other forms of tyranny without even realizing it.

For Fromm, the 'fear of freedom' arises not from existential causes, but from purely psychoanalytic ones. All human beings begin life in a state of union and harmony within the wombs of their mothers. All human beings are forced to progress towards greater separation as they are born, weaned and gradually grow through childhood and adolescence to the crushing realization that the harmony, union and safety they had once known is gone for ever. In essence, Hans Bjerkholt's traumatic journey from the paradise of his mother's farmhouse kitchen to the impersonal adult world of the factory represents the story of us all. We must all leave our childhood behind, and as adults we are all fundamentally alone. Our freedom, according to Fromm, not only makes us feel unbearably vulnerable but also presents us with the reality of our own insignificance in comparison to the vastness of the universe. In the face of all that is not 'us', he says, we are mere particles of dust, and our individual lives are meaningless.[15]

Like Sartre, Fromm believed that we can react to the terrifying realization of our freedom in one of two ways: either we can face up to it, and embrace our freedom, along with all the angst and responsibility that that entails; or we can recoil from it in fear and abandon our responsibility to some other 'higher' power – God, Fate, society, orders from our superior officers, our nation, our class, our family. Unfortunately, of the two scenarios, the latter is much more common: as Fromm says, 'nothing is more difficult for the average man to bear than the feeling of not being identified with a larger group'.[16] The majority of us will therefore clutch at any ideology that gives us a sense of belonging, whether it involves religion, a slavish adherence to the norms of society or the more malign devotion to a totalitarian regime – because anything is easier to bear than the responsibility and agony of freedom.

In his analysis of Nazi society, Fromm described the desperate urge for Germans to immerse themselves in a collective illusion of power and eternity. Nazism, Fromm claimed, was simply an extreme form of the longings that exist inside all of us. Deep within us all is a core memory from our childhoods when we were able to believe, like Hans Bjerkholt, that 'the whole world belonged to me'. To one degree or another, we all have the desire to consume others or be consumed by them, so that we can be at one with them, just as we were once at one with our mothers. To those who are terrified of facing the vastness of their aloneness, even mass slavery or mass sadism can be made to appear necessary, perhaps even beautiful.

However, he also warned that submission to authoritarianism was not the only way that mankind fled from the emptiness of the human condition. Just because the Allies purported to be fighting in the name of 'freedom' did not mean that men and women in America or Britain were any more 'free' than men and women in Germany. Blind conformity to the expectations of our peers, our employers or our nations was every bit as dangerous as submission to a totalitarian ideology – if not more so, because, unlike Nazism, these dangers had been completely internalized. 'We are fascinated by the growth of freedom from powers *outside* ourselves,' he warned, 'and are blinded to the fact of *inner* restraints, compulsions and fears, which tend to undermine the meaning of the victories freedom has won against its traditional enemies.' The war against Hitler was therefore only one aspect of a much greater battle to free the human soul from the many other shackles that we have forged for ourselves.[17]

In the end, despite various differences between their philosophies, both Sartre and Fromm believed that the idea of freedom held a 'twofold meaning for modern man'.[18] It simultaneously lured us and repelled us: on the one hand it offered the infinite promise of self-invention and self-realization; but on the other hand it doomed us to a life of total responsibility and total aloneness. Both men believed that the only true path for mankind was to turn towards the awesome burden of freedom and embrace it, with all the angst that implied. The alternative was to turn away in what Sartre called 'bad faith', and submit ourselves to new rules, new ideologies and new tyrannies which Fromm believed would only end up imprisoning us all over again.

In a world that was at that very moment in the process of both re-inventing itself and confronting its new-found freedom, this message stood as a stark warning. The end of the war had presented humanity with an unparalleled opportunity to seize its freedom wholeheartedly, and on a global scale; but both Fromm and Sartre understood that to grasp this opportunity would require a leap of faith unlike anything that man had ever before been required to do, even during the perils of the wartime. Whether we rose to this challenge or shrank from it would determine the very nature of the world that was at that moment rising from the ashes of the Second World War.[19]

Explosion of Social Capital

Hans Bjerkholt was not the only person whose beliefs had been profoundly shaken by the war and its aftermath, or who found solace in a new system of belief in the following years. The postwar period saw thousands upon thousands of similar converts to Moral Re-Armament who, like Bjerkholt, saw in it the chance of 'this world, this vast world, becoming a family', of 'a new world based on new men', of 'an end to the divisions between classes and nations', and above all an opportunity to save themselves from 'empty hands and an empty heart'.[20] At its peak, MRA had offices on three continents and over a thousand full-time volunteers – it was a truly worldwide movement.[21]

Nor was Moral Re-Armament the only movement that offered the opportunity for such salvation. The end of the war saw an explosion of all kinds of ideologies all over the world – some old, some new – which sought to continue the spirit of communal purpose born in the war. On a global level there was renewed interest in political movements like world federalism, communism and social democracy, each of which believed itself to be the force that might not only unite mankind once and for all but also heal its spiritual and political wounds. At a regional level there were other panaceas, some of which burst fully formed from the war, and others which would develop over time, such as the desire for 'ever closer union' in Europe, the 'spirit of Bandung' in Asia and Africa, or the idealized vision of the 'American way of life'. Nations similarly chased their own rainbows of 'brotherhood and unity' (Yugoslavia), 'unity in diversity' (Indonesia), 'spiritual unity' (Argentina), and all kinds of other 'unities' from Stalin's 'ideology of friendship' to the appeal in 1945 by South Africa's Jan Smuts for the 'total mobilization of the human spirit'.[22] All of these postwar movements were partly directed from above, sometimes quite cynically by politicians whose only real agenda was to increase their own hold on power. But they were also overwhelmingly supported from below by millions upon millions of ordinary individuals whose first instinct was to build on the sense of mission that they had first experienced during the war.

A crude measure of this postwar urge to believe in something greater than oneself can be seen in the revival of religious belief after 1945, particularly in Europe, where all the traditional sociological models had predicted that the march of 'modernity' would produce nothing but decline. Religious statistics are notoriously difficult to pin down, but all the indications are that Christian beliefs in Europe underwent something of a recovery, at least until the mid-1950s.[23] In Germany, for example, the Catholic Church emerged from the war as a 'victor among ruins': churches everywhere recorded a huge influx of new members, and were soon overflowing with people eager for some kind of stability.[24] In Poland, admissions to seminaries rose threefold between 1945 and 1951, while in Italy the number of priests in the more religious orders also rose strongly.[25] Five times the number of pilgrims came to Rome in the jubilee year of 1950 as did in the previous jubilee year of 1925.[26] Meanwhile, in Britain, the modest recovery in the Protestant faith after the war was accompanied by a much more dramatic rise in Catholicism: according to statistics compiled by the Latin Mass Society of England and Wales, the number of marriages, baptisms and receptions into the Catholic Church all rose by about 60 per cent in the ten or so years immediately following the war, and did not decline again until the 1960s and 70s.[27]

Another crude measure of the desire to believe and to belong can be found in the sudden and massive growth of the Communist Party around the world. At around the same time that Hans Bjerkholt was turning away from communism, millions of others were discovering it for the first time. Once again, some of the most dramatic increases occurred in Europe. Within three years of the end of the war, over 900,000 Frenchmen had joined the Communist Party, as had more than 1 million Romanians, 1.4 million Czechoslovakians, and 2.25 million Italians. In postwar Hungary, Communist Party membership rose from only 3,000 to 500,000 in a single year (1945). This massive expansion of support was also reflected in China, where, in the eyes of one Western observer, the rise of communism after the war finally 'knitted the nation into one'; in Latin America, where Communist Party membership more than quintupled between 1939 and 1947; and even in the Soviet Union itself, where the Communist Party grew by almost 50 per cent between 1941 and 1945, even after all the huge losses of the war.[28] The overwhelming majority of these new Communists were people who wanted to be part of what they saw as the tide of history, which they believed was sweeping the world inexorably towards greater fairness and equality for all. There was something mystical, perhaps even messianic about this rapid expansion. As the Lithuanian-French philosopher Emmanuel Levinas commented in 1957, 'The uninterrupted growth of the Communist Party, its conquest of the world, which was more rapid than the spread of Christianity or Islam, its catholic range, the faith, heroism and purity of its youth . . . have accustomed us to hearing in this movement the very footsteps of Destiny.'[29]

It was not only those who sought radical change in the wake of the war who garnered increased support: political engagement of *all* kinds increased, everywhere, regardless of how radical or conservative the individual parties were. In eastern Europe, for example, it was not the Communists who received the greatest surge in political support, but those parties that appealed to the timeless emotional attachment of people to their land, such as the Smallholders Party in Hungary or the Peasants Party in Romania, both of which held power for a time before being ousted and repressed by the Communists. In western Europe, meanwhile, the surge in support for communism and socialism was matched by a similar surge in support for Christian Democracy, a fairly conservative political movement which came to dominate the political landscape in mainland Europe for the next thirty years. In Latin America the massive populist movements that characterized political life across the continent in 1945 gave way to a deeply felt conservative backlash just a few years later. It is instructive that one of the most rapidly growing political organizations in North Africa and the Middle East was the Muslim Brotherhood – a movement that simultaneously advocated revolution and the promotion of conservative Muslim values.

Another way in which people sought a sense of mission and belonging was through joining workplace organizations, particularly trade unions. These organizations grew massively after the war, all over the world. In Latin America, union membership shot up during this time: typical examples were Brazil and Colombia, where union membership more than doubled between 1940 and 1947, and Argentina, where it almost quadrupled in just four years (from 532,000 in 1945 to nearly 2 million in 1949).[30] In Africa new unions sprang up everywhere, and the stream of new members rapidly turned into a torrent and then a flood. In Ghana alone, for example, the number of unions rose from fourteen to forty-one between 1946 and 1949, and the number of fully paid-up members rose sixfold.[31] Other African countries saw a similar rise in union membership, and indeed union militancy: the late 1940s saw massive strikes in South Africa, Southern Rhodesia, Kenya, Tanganyika, Cameroon, Nigeria and throughout French West Africa. This pattern of growth also happened in Asia, Europe and the Middle East, as workers everywhere gathered into groups, organized themselves into federations and, eventually, joined in the larger nationalist and internationalist movements. Of course, this often made both political and economic sense, but it also gave ordinary workers everywhere a new sense of mission, of community, of belonging.

The list of organizations that blossomed after the war could go on and on – from social and cultural groups, to business networks to charitable organizations. There has never been a worldwide historical survey of what has come to be known as 'social capital', but anecdotal evidence suggests that the same broad patterns can be found in most parts of the world: communal involvement in social groups of all kinds appears to have increased significantly during the war and its aftermath.

Data from the USA, where there *has* been a comprehensive survey, would seem to confirm this. In the year 2000, the American sociologist Robert D. Putnam completed a ground-breaking study of all kinds of community involvement over the course of the century, from formal participation in political groups to informal socializing at dinner parties and poker games. According to his findings, average church attendance in America ballooned in the ten years after the war from around 37 per cent of the adult population to around 47 per cent. Union membership hit its peak soon after the war and did not seriously decline for the next thirty years; and membership of professional organizations such as the American Bar Association or the American Institute of Architects followed a similar pattern. Community organizations like Rotary clubs, Boy Scouts and Girl Guides and parent–teacher associations saw a surge in membership after the war of between 60 and 190 per cent. More Americans joined bowling clubs and played card games together in the 1940s and 50s than at any other time in history. Even charitable giving saw a rise of between 35 and 40 per cent immediately after the war, and its level did not decline again until after the mid-1960s. According to Putnam, 'in virtually every case one can detect the same postwar acceleration in membership growth between the 1940s and the 1960s'. In short, 'The two decades following 1945 witnessed one of the most vital periods of community involvement in American history'.[32]

It must be stressed that none of these trends can be exclusively credited to the spiritual influence of the war. For example part of the growth in membership of certain American civic groups resulted from increasing levels of education and prosperity in the USA during the 1940s and 50s. Likewise, the rise in Catholicism in Britain after the war was partly due to postwar immigration and the increase in union membership in Latin America was partly due to increased industrialization and urbanization. But many of these secondary causes were themselves effects of the Second World War: in other words, all this tells us is that the spiritual and material effects of the war were working in tandem. Until a comprehensive worldwide study of social capital in the aftermath of the war becomes available, it seems safe to assume that the growth in community involvement that seems to have taken place simultaneously in most parts of the world was largely attributable to what has come to be known as the 'spirit of the war'. In other words, those who had experienced the communal triumphs and sacrifices of the war years were more likely to value being a part of something greater than themselves.

According to Robert Putnam, this growth in community involvement came to an end in America at much the same time that MRA went into decline, from the beginning of the 1970s. Since then the collapse in the membership of all civic groups has been dramatic, and in some cases catastrophic. There are many reasons for this, including the growth of TV and computer use, increased pressures on everyone's time and the greater isolation caused by suburban sprawl. But the single biggest factor has been 'generational change'. In other words, as the men and women who had experienced the war grew old and died, so too did America's commitment to community life across the country.[33]

When looking back on the late 1940s and 50s it is easy to fall victim to the same sense of nostalgia that sometimes grips us when looking back at the war. We might envy the greater sense of community experienced by people who lived during this period, but at the same time forget that this almost always came at a cost. The 1950s was an era not only of belonging but also of fear, when people of all kinds and all nations looked around them for someone to blame for their insecurities, and found myriad terrifying reasons to run away from the very thing that they had spent the war years fighting for – freedom.

This is what makes the story of Hans Bjerkholt so compellingly ambiguous. On the one hand, he was determined to embrace the responsibilities of freedom: he acknowledged unequivocally the painful truth that one cannot possibly dream about changing the world without first being willing to live up to one's own principles. As Jean-Paul Sartre observed, 'nothing can be better for us unless it is better for all'. And yet the language Bjerkholt used was not the language of freedom at all, but of enslavement: 'giv[ing] up my own self-will entirely'.[34] He longed not only to embrace his individuality but also to subsume himself in the MRA movement, and through that in humanity as a whole. In other words, what he really wanted was both freedom *and* belonging, a perfect synthesis of his own individual destiny and the communal needs of humanity. 'This will be the greatest and most radical revolution in the whole history of mankind,' he wrote hopefully at the beginning of the 1950s. 'It will give every man the kind of world he is longing for.'[35] Such an idea is the very definition of Utopia.

It is for this reason that many people have dismissed MRA as a millenarian cult. Contemporary journalists questioned its funding, its motives and its 'over-simplification of infinitely complex problems'.[36] Conventional Christian clergymen denounced its 'megalomaniacal self-confidence' and its 'fanaticism', which undermined rather than promoted personal moral responsibility.[37] Sociologists claimed that its emphasis on a *personal* rather than a shared communion with God reflected the very atomization of society that it purported to be trying to heal.[38] Psychologists, likewise, interpreted it as a cult.[39] In reply, MRA's followers were unrepentant. In the wake of the greatest war in history, surely an ideology that cut through all the complexity of who did what to whom was exactly what we needed? It was the adherence to conventional ideas and doctrines that had brought us to war in the first place. And besides, what was wrong with trying to fill the emptiness in our lives? What use was freedom, if it did not also bring us meaning?

All of the visions of Utopia I have discussed so far have been attempts by individuals, and the societies in which they lived, to find some kind of meaning arising from the end of the war. Each of them tried to find universal principles upon which a new kind of society could be built; but in doing so each of them ended up coming face to face with the impossibility of ever achieving their dreams.

Eugene Rabinowitch's desire to promote rational, scientific thinking in relation to the challenges of the nuclear age was his attempt to stand in the way of those irrational human impulses that had led to war. And yet the mythological way that the public, and even some of his fellow atomic scientists, thought about the atom bomb undermined the very message that people like him were trying to promote.

Giancarlo De Carlo likewise devoted his life to making the world a better place after the war. He was simultaneously inspired by the promise of creating new cities that would work for the good of all, and repelled by the way that such promises seemed to trample on the needs of individuals – he would spend the rest of his life trying to reconcile these two opposing impulses.

Meanwhile, Françoise Leclercq saw her life transformed by her experience of the war. Afterwards, she made it her mission to promote a greater equality for women, for the poor, and for people of different nationalities and faiths. And yet at the heart of her actions was a paradox: by singling out these groups she was necessarily acknowledging their difference, their 'Otherness', their inequality.

All of these people were, like Hans Bjerkholt, trying their best to reject fear and embrace freedom. That none of them fully succeeded should not be disappointing: Utopia is, by its very nature, impossible.

All were motivated by a belief that it is better to try and fail than never to try at all, and that if they were indeed doomed to fail, they would at least try to fail well. In the process they each found themselves supported by communities of like-minded people who gave them, if not the realization of their dreams, at least a sense of belonging.

To a degree, the remainder of this book is about what the people of all nations reached for in order to fill the void that 'freedom' presented to them at the end of the war. In the following chapters I will leave it to the reader to decide whether the various protagonists were rushing towards freedom or away from it (or, indeed, tearing themselves apart by trying to fulfil both urges simultaneously). For the moment I wish only to observe that few people can tolerate a spiritual vacuum for long. After the war was over, the one thing that almost everyone craved was a sense of belonging; and whether it manifested itself positively or negatively, it was this urge above all others that most characterized the spirit of the age.

PART III

One World

PART II

One World

10. World Economy

In our collective memory, the Second World War was a time of high drama. It was full of vast battles, where people were killed with guns and shells and bombs and all the other machinery of violence. In our mental images of blood and smoke there is an immediacy that is hard to ignore; but in reality there were many other facets to the Second World War that, while less immediately dramatic, could be no less deadly. As the first truly 'total' war, it manifested itself in terms that were not only military but also economic.

One of those who witnessed the economic side of the war was a young Indian artist named Chittaprosad Bhattacharya. At the outbreak of the war, Chittaprosad was in his early twenties, and was busy struggling to find an artistic style that felt meaningful. He had toyed with Indian traditionalist art and modernist art, but had never managed to find a way to connect his paintings to the realities of Indian life as he saw it all around him. What he wanted to express, he said, seemed always to be 'just around the corner'; but whenever he thought he had found it, 'it turned out again and again to be a myth'.[1]

The war changed everything. Suddenly Chittaprosad's home province became a hive of activity. Government money began to pour into Bengal, especially to the city of Calcutta, which quickly became one of the centres of India's war production. The army started recruiting, and moving resources to the borders of India to protect it from outside invasion. Political activity – already very strong in India – began to increase everywhere. People were pro-war, or anti-war, or simply demanded that the British 'quit India'.

For Chittaprosad this change seemed suddenly to have brought the world into focus. He shared the indignation of millions of Indians at the way the British authorities had taken the country to war without even consulting its people; nevertheless, for the moment at least, the new threat of a fascist Japanese power seemed to outweigh everything else. Inspired by some peasant friends, Chittaprosad joined the Communist Party and immediately began painting propaganda posters in support of

Chittaprosad a few years after the war.

the war effort. He composed songs about the 'people's war' and began to tour the border areas of India and Burma with his anti-Fascist paintings. He felt as though he had been born into a 'new life'.[2]

This 'new life' was confirmed, once and for all, in the middle of 1942, when the Japanese invasion finally reached the fringes of India. Chittaprosad lived in the district of Chittagong, India's last outpost in the east of the country, and he saw at first hand the plight of the tens of thousands of Burmese refugees who now came flooding across the border. In panic, the British authorities began requisitioning rice stocks, and seized or sank all the village boats in order to deny them to the advancing Japanese. No thought was given to the fact that these boats were 'the only means of livelihood or of communication for the vast majority of the village-folks all over the district'. For the first time Chittaprosad witnessed a phenomenon he had never seen before: 'a black market, particularly in food' which quickly 'began to raise its monstrous head'. All of a sudden he felt as though he were 'on a sinking ship'.[3]

Over the course of the following year, Chittaprosad watched the price of rice double, and then double again. By the end of 1943 there were reports of rice being sold in Chittagong for 80 rupees per maund – more than ten times the price before the crisis started.[4] When a cyclone hit the rice-growing areas of western Bengal, the crisis spread out of the border areas and across the whole province. Suddenly rice seemed to be scarce everywhere. Those who had food began to hoard it, driving the price still higher, until only those with substantial savings, or something to sell, could afford it. The Bengali people were beginning to starve.

To say that the government response to this situation was inadequate would be an understatement. Bengal had its own autonomous provincial government before and during the war, which had various powers to impose economic controls on its people. Had it set up a comprehensive system of rationing and price controls at the beginning of the war, like so many other governments around the world had done, the coming crisis might have been averted. Instead, limited price controls were introduced but then abandoned again, with disastrous consequences. Rationing was not introduced until as late as 1944, but even then only in Calcutta, which simply had the effect of sucking yet more food away from the starving countryside.[5]

The reaction of the central Indian government was not much better. When Bengali ministers made muted efforts to highlight the food crisis in their province, central government turned a deaf ear – indeed, it insisted that Bengal continue exporting food to Ceylon, which was also suffering problems of food supply.[6] Perhaps if the central Indian government had set up a supply centre in the same way that the Allies had done in the Middle East, it might have been more attuned to the series of bottlenecks that were beginning to strangle the north-east of the country. But a dedicated Food Department was set up only at the very end of 1942, by which time the conditions for famine had already established themselves. In the meantime, the government committed itself to a policy of 'unrestricted free trade', which, in the context of a world war, proved utterly disastrous.[7] 'It may be bitter, but it must be faced,' wrote one angry journalist in 1944:

Central Government ignored the major problem of food distribution in India until it was too late, and in the face of the threat of invasion, feeding the army, and the sealing of India from the world market, thought fit to leave India's food to blind chance and *laissez faire* at a time when such inaction was not only careless but criminal.[8]

However, the ultimate responsibility for what happened next must lie with the British imperial government in London, whose long-term neglect of Bengal's economic needs had left it ill equipped to cope with the strains of total war. Between 1940 and 1942 the British were too concerned with their own survival to worry about economic events in distant parts of the empire. In 1943, when the extent of the food crisis in Bengal became international news, Churchill and his government still steadfastly resisted taking any action to help. Despite a series of urgent requests for emergency food relief, and offers of help from other parts of the British Commonwealth, both Churchill and the Allied Joint Chiefs of Staff insisted that they could not spare the shipping. Even when Canada offered to supply 100,000 tons of wheat to Bengal, London turned it down. The people of Bengal would be left to starve on their own.[9]

Chittaprosad witnessed the consequences of these events close up. He saw the impact of the British army in east Bengal, which commandeered good agricultural land for building roads, camps, aerodromes and training grounds. He saw the corruption of local officials and 'pot-bellied mahajans' (money lenders), who conspired to keep food prices high, and he shared the 'hatred and bitterness' that those around him felt for national politicians, whose hypocrisy, indifference and relative wealth was 'an insult to the hungry thousands'.[10] But most of all he saw a universal hatred for the British, whose apathy had only fuelled the crisis. It was this 'alien government' that he blamed for a total collapse of national morale during the famine, and the death of 'civilized social instincts' throughout Bengal.

Over the coming months he began to draw pictures of skeletal beggars, of corpses in the street, of flocks of vultures circling over the whole of Bengal. He wrote accounts of the famine in the Communist Party newspapers, and in November 1943 he embarked on a walking tour of Midnapur, one of the worst-affected districts, in order to document what was happening to his country. He described it as a land of 'vultures and robbers', strewn with the bones and the skulls of those who had died. On his journey he met women who were forced to prostitute themselves as the only way to buy food, and destitute families who had sold their farms and all their possessions in exchange for rice. After one particularly bleak walk through an empty countryside, he described a landscape that appeared devoid of all life. 'I began to doubt if we would come across any living creature even if we went to the ends of the earth,'

Chittaprosad's portrayal of a starving man with his child during the Bengal famine: 'He has lost his land and his wife has left him. There is very little left that he could call his own in the world.'

he wrote. 'As far as my eyes could reach, I found no trace of human habitation anywhere. All around there were only barren fields, stretching away to the distant horizon.' This was a kind of Armageddon brought about not by bombs or shells, but by slow economic suffocation. The experience was so profoundly depressing that he began to feel as if he 'had lost faith in life itself'.[11]

The Bengal famine of 1943–44, and the global war that underlay it, would haunt Chittaprosad for the rest of his days. It was this time, more than any other, which defined him as an artist. 'If anyone is in a position to learn anything from life, it is against the background of death,' he later claimed. 'At an hour when the very existence of humanity and civilization is threatened by out-bursts of forces of brutality and destruction and death, an artist either lays down his brush and picks up a gun or walks out of the human-world and joins the devil . . . I could not lay down my brush, just because I could not find a gun to pick up to hold it against the fascist hordes. And I could not find a gun because, you see, the British rulers were "managing things" for us in spite of our eager willingness and unquestionable ability to look after ourselves . . .'

In the context of colonialism, total war and economic devastation, art was the only defence Chittaprosad was granted. 'I was forced by circumstances to turn my brush into as sharp a weapon as I could make it.'[12]

The Economic Effects of the War

The Bengal famine was one of the most devastating events of the Second World War. In the space of just over a year, more people died in this one province than were killed during the liberation of the whole of western Europe – and all without a single bullet being fired. Official estimates at the end of the war put the final death toll at around 1.5 million, but later academic reports consider a figure of 3 million deaths to be more realistic – all of them directly attributable to the famine.[13] Moreover, this was just one example of a phenomenon that occurred all over the world. A similar famine happened the same year in China, where up to 2 million peasants in Henan province are thought to have died; a similar number are also thought to have died in Tonkin, in French Indochina.[14] Millions more died in local famines in the Philippines, the Dutch East Indies, Japan, Russia, Ukraine, Poland, Greece, the Netherlands, and even parts of Africa. According to some historians, around 20 million people died during the war not through violence, but through hunger.[15]

What makes these deaths seem doubly tragic is the fact that, even in Bengal, there was no insurmountable shortage of food. According to economist Amartya Sen there was probably enough food to go around – it's just that those who possessed food supplies were not willing to sell them at a price the poor could afford.[16] On a global scale too the problem was one not of supply but of distribution. Throughout Europe, much of the transport network had been destroyed by the war, and that which remained was reserved largely for military use: the distribution of food around the continent therefore suffered accordingly. The same was true in much of the rest of the world. Tens of millions of tons of shipping was destroyed during the war – some 11.7 million tons in the British Merchant Navy alone – and the Japanese merchant fleet was all but wiped out.[17] So much of the remaining shipping capacity was reserved for military purposes that it became impossible to prevent surpluses of food building up in some nations, and shortages in others. So, for example, while sugar was rationed in the United States, huge stocks of it were building up in the West Indies. And while people starved in much of Asia and eastern Europe, Argentina was burning corn for fuel.[18]

So serious were these supply bottlenecks that governments everywhere were forced to resort to severe controls on the distribution of food. They took charge of the supply chain, imposed price restrictions and introduced systems of rationing. Entire new industries started up, often with government support, in order to maximize shipping space. Meat was deboned, preserved and tinned; eggs were dried and powdered; milk was condensed. Priority was given to high-energy foods like potatoes at the expense of rice and wheat, or to protein-rich foods like cheese in preference to butter. When centralized actions like this were done well, as in Britain, they could be extraordinarily effective. But when they were mismanaged, as they were in Bengal – or exploitative, as they were in much of colonial Africa as well as occupied Europe and Asia – they could cause terrible suffering.

It was not only the trade in food that was disrupted by the Second World War: between 1939 and 1945 the whole global economy was turned upside down. Trade patterns that had been built up over decades broke down almost overnight, often to be replaced with new, unfamiliar arrangements. So, for example, many countries in francophone Africa lost up to two-thirds of their export market when the war cut them off from France while other countries, like the Belgian Congo, doubled the value of their major exports by forming new trading partnerships with Britain, South Africa and the USA.[19] A similar transformation occurred in Latin America and the Caribbean: when traditional ties with Europe were virtually severed, the whole region became much more dependent on trade with the USA – a dependency that would remain for decades to come.[20]

Alongside the changes in international trade came equally dramatic changes in employment. As millions of people were recruited into the world's armies and its vital war industries, levels of employment rose almost everywhere. Wages also rose, as various industries competed to attract workers. Such changes might have delighted ordinary workers in the short term, but they could prove disastrous for some traditional industries. Why should people in Tonga carry on working in the copra industry when they could earn much better money renting bicycles to American soldiers stationed on the island? And why should agricultural labourers in Iceland bother to work long hours on farms when they could double their income working in the new Allied military bases?[21]

In order to keep essential industries running, nations all over the world resorted to conscripting labour. In countries like Britain, Australia and the USA, where a series of Women's Land Armies were set up in order to keep farms working, conscription was more or less accepted as a necessary sacrifice for the war. But in many African countries, conscription was often fiercely resented as yet another form of colonial exploitation. In Tanganyika, for example, plantation workers were housed in guarded compounds to stop them deserting, and the government authorized the use of corporal punishment for those who refused to work. In Nigeria, more than 100,000 peasants were forced to leave their land in order to work in the tin mines; and in Rhodesia white settlers manipulated government opinion in order to conscript tens of thousands of agricultural labourers at knock-down wages.[22] In French West Africa, the universal resentment of forced labour, which had existed before the war but increased substantially during it, was one of the principal drivers of reform in the immediate postwar years.[23]

But perhaps the most widespread and destructive economic consequence of the war was that of inflation. With so much government spending across the world, there were now more people with more money in their pockets. At the same time, because of the war, goods of all kinds were now scarcer than ever. With more money chasing fewer and fewer goods, prices everywhere quickly began to rise. Of course, massive price increases were not necessarily a problem for those whose wages rose in line with inflation – but for some of those struggling in low-paid jobs the effects proved disastrous as their ability to buy goods and services steadily declined, their savings became worthless and, in the worst cases such as in Bengal, they began to starve.

The only way to fight this kind of inflation during the war was to

Rise in the cost of living index due to the war (1937=100)

Nation	mid-1937	mid-1945	1947	Summary
North America				
USA	100	128	156	Stable
Canada	100	120	137	
Latin America				
Argentina	100	135	185	Mostly stable
Bolivia	100	496	650	
Brazil	100	197	——	
Mexico	100	247	354	
Venezuela	100	141	171	
Australasia				
Australia	100	129	136	Stable
New Zealand	100	123	126	
Asia				
India	100	——	260	Sharp increase in
Malaya	100	——	270	most devastated
Indonesia	100	——	1600	nations
Philippines	100	——	400	
Japan	100	250	15,000	
China (Chungking)	100	207,400	——	
Middle East				
Egypt	100	287	280	Sharp increase
Iran	100	779	688	during war,
Lebanon	100 (in 1939)	607	505	followed by
Turkey	100 (in 1938)	354	344	postwar deflation
Africa				
South Africa	100	137	146	Relatively stable in
Kenya	100 (in 1939)	——	198	south, but sharp
Algeria	100 (in 1938)	539	2,160 (in 1949)	increases in war-torn areas of North Africa
Europe				
UK	100	132	132	Stability in UK,
France	100	400	1,200	Scandinavia and
Italy	100	——	5,000	neutral countries;
Poland	100	——	15,000	massive inflation
Romania	100	3,800	160,000	in the most war-torn countries

exercise draconian control of the supply chain and institute a system of fixed prices. This worked well in Britain, where the government had the resources to put such controls in place and where the populace were more or less united in supporting them, but in many other parts of the world it was simply impossible (see table).[24] In occupied Europe, for example, there was almost no popular support for rationing, and so the black market flourished. Thus, while the cost of living in Britain rose by only about 30 per cent during the course of the war, in France it quadrupled, and continued to rise steeply for years afterwards.[25] In much of the developing world, meanwhile, there simply weren't the administrative structures or the resources to impose such strict and complicated systems of control. Thus, the cost of living almost doubled in Brazil, almost trebled in Egypt and increased almost eightfold in Iran.[26] Sometimes, at a local level, the rise in prices could be even more staggering: in the Chinese cities of Quanzhou and Shanghai, for example, rice became between 200 and 240 times more expensive over the course of the war, and then accelerated still further during the civil war that followed.[27]

In many countries, particularly in the devastated regions of Europe, people lost faith in money altogether, preferring to barter food or cigarettes instead. In Poland, Romania and Hungary, money became so worthless that people did not even bother to pick up banknotes that had been dropped in the street. Hungary in particular suffered probably the greatest hyperinflation the world has ever seen – far greater even than the German hyperinflation that occurred after the First World War – with prices tripling from one day to the next. Over the course of a year after the end of the war, the price of a loaf of bread rose from 6 pengős to almost 6 billion pengős. Banknotes were issued with numbers on them that only mathematicians and astronomers had previously heard of. 'Hungarians were multibillionaires,' remembers one man sardonically.[28] While hyperinflation like this was partly a result of deliberate government policy, that policy was largely dictated by the conditions inherited from the war. Hungary might be an extreme example, but inflation rose at alarming rates in all the war-torn regions of the world, and even in many regions that were geographically distant from the war.[29]

The world has never since recovered. Inflation today is a normal part of everyday life in a way that it never was in the eighteenth or nineteenth centuries, when prices all around the world remained relatively stable. It was the two world wars – and particularly, in much of the world, the Second World War – that created this new normality.[30]

Winners and Losers

So great were the economic changes unleashed by the war that there were bound to be winners and losers – not only amongst individuals but also amongst different groups as well as amongst nations. At the height of the Bengal famine, when millions of people were starving, there were nevertheless many who made themselves rich, particularly the 'pot-bellied mahajans' that Chittaprosad so despised. Food speculators are mentioned in virtually every report of the famine, including the official inquiry, and almost always with opprobrium. In the words of one British journalist, 'Money flowed into the Stock Exchange; rice became a commodity of scarcity in value; and the sharks of Big Business made their daily thousands by trading in the people's life-blood – their staple food.'[31]

All around the world, similar fortunes were being made and lost – inspiring similar moral judgements. In the context of so much misery and death it was difficult for many to accept the idea that some people might be profiting by the war. Thus, in Europe there was much criticism of industrialists who had collaborated with Nazis and Fascists, as well as farmers who had profited from the desperation of city folk who had been forced to make regular trips to the countryside to barter their jewellery for food.[32] In parts of Africa there was increasing resentment of Europeans who had used the war as an excuse to exploit black labour, as well as the Asian merchant classes who had made themselves rich by speculating in food and other essential products. Such resentments would return to haunt nations like Tanganyika, Kenya and Uganda in later years.[33] In Bengal, meanwhile, while everyone blamed the British for what had happened, they also blamed one another. The Muslim League accused Hindu retailers of deliberately withholding rice from other communities while Hindus accused Muslim wholesalers of abusing their monopoly of government procurement. None of this boded well for the future of inter-faith relations in Bengal.[34]

On an international scale, there were also winners and losers. The biggest winner was undoubtedly the USA, whose obvious wealth sometimes inspired as much resentment as its contribution to the Allied victory inspired gratitude. America's role as the main supplier to all the Allied nations saw it vastly enriched by the war. Between 1939 and 1945, America's economy almost doubled in size, and by the end of the war the country accounted for around a half of the world's *total* production.[35] Furthermore, the USA also now controlled the world's shipping: while most of its competitors had suffered massive losses to their merchant fleets during the war, America's had more than quadrupled in size, and by 1947 the USA had more merchant shipping than the rest of the world put together. It was, therefore, America that decided what to ship and where to ship it.[36] In such a world, Americans found themselves better off than they had ever been: on average, their personal wealth in 1945 was almost 80 per cent higher than in 1939.[37]

Other winners from the war included Canada, Australia and South Africa, as well as some of the neutral countries like Sweden and Switzerland: by staying out of the fight, or by being far away from the destruction, these nations managed to sustain unprecedented levels of growth, and emerged from the conflict significantly richer than they had ever been.[38] South Africa, for example, paid off its entire national debt while Canada not only paid off its debts but also bought up foreign assets, increased its gold supplies and accumulated massive trade balances with other countries.[39] Many smaller nations also profited from the war. Iceland, for example, managed to wipe out its massive prewar debt problems thanks to American military spending on the island.[40] Iraq, Iran, Egypt and Palestine also ended the war with large budget surpluses, purely because of British military spending in the Middle East.[41] India had also managed to accumulate massive sterling balances during the war, despite simultaneously buying up British assets throughout the country. While Bengal had suffered, India as a whole had not done too badly.[42]

The biggest losers in this economic war included not only Germany and Japan but also those countries they occupied and those who had bankrupted themselves in order to beat them. The USSR had certainly become a military giant, but its economy lay in tatters: a quarter of its entire national wealth had been lost, and agricultural production was so badly disrupted that it did not return to prewar levels until 1955.[43] The economies of France, the Netherlands and Greece halved in size during the war, as did those of the Philippines, South Korea and Taiwan – but while Europe's economies bounced back quickly, helped in part by

American financial aid, most Asian economies did not return to their prewar levels until the mid-1950s.[44]

Britain, meanwhile, had been forced to sell off almost a quarter of its total foreign assets, run massive foreign exchange deficits and beg for billions of US dollars in Lend-Lease aid. Even after the war was over, the British government was obliged to ask the USA for a further loan of $3.7 billion – a debt that was not finally paid off until the end of 2006.[45]

Britain's new reliance on America was symptomatic of a dramatic change in their relationship, and perhaps one of the greatest long-term consequences of the war. In 1939 these two countries had enjoyed similar standards of living, with GDP per capita almost on a par. But as America's standard of living grew during the war, Britain's stagnated. Almost every other developed nation suffered a similar fall in its living standard compared to that of the USA, but over the decades almost all of them recovered, and by the 1970s and 80s had at the very least regained the same positions they had held before the war. But Britain's relative loss was permanent. The war had cost the country its wealth, its empire, some of its traditional markets, and the dominant status of its currency – and when its manufacturing strength also began to decline, the difference became simply too great to make up again. While the USA was easily the biggest winner of the war, Britain was probably the biggest long-term loser.[46]

A final important point to make about the war's economic winners and losers concerns the gap between rich and poor. In some parts of the world – places like Bengal – the war unquestionably punished the poor far more than it did the rich. But in most places, especially in the developed world, the war actually ended up being something of a leveller. The rich not only lost vast amounts of their wealth to the general destruction, but the political climate during and after the war also forced them to accept higher taxes, greater controls on their ability to charge rents, and even the nationalization of their businesses. Throughout eastern Europe and China, the Communist parties instituted massive programmes of land reform, which saw the transformation of some nations from a feudal economy for the first time. And while city dwellers might have resented the black-market price of food, for peasants and farmers this produced a much-needed return of wealth from the city to the countryside. Thus the war massively reduced inequality between rich and poor, city and country. Indeed, some economists have gone so far as to say that the war 'erased the past and enabled society to begin anew with a clean slate'.[47]

The Vision of a Controlled World Economy

In 1944, economists everywhere agreed that some kind of radical action had to be taken to regulate the global economy. The war had left the entire system extremely unstable, and there was a universal fear that the boom years of the war might be followed in 1945 by another world-wide depression. Everyone was afraid of returning to the toxic era of the 1930s, when the disasters of laissez-faire economics had been compounded by a descent into narrow nationalism.

If the war had taught the world anything it was not only that centrally controlled economies could achieve wonders if they were well directed, but also that *nothing* could be achieved without cooperation between allies. As America's chief economist, Harry Dexter White, pointed out in 1944, universal peace and prosperity would never materialize 'if military warfare is followed by economic warfare – if each country, to the disregard of the interest of other countries, battles solely for its own short-range economic interests'. International cooperation was, therefore, one of the indispensable 'foundation stones for a secure peace'.[48]

It was with these thoughts in mind that White, along with Britain's John Maynard Keynes and dozens of other leading economists, attended a conference at the American holiday resort of Bretton Woods in 1944. Their purpose was to set up a series of global institutions that would regulate the world's economy after the war, and help to prevent it from sliding back into crisis and depression. The measures they came up with were not merely practical: there was also a strong moral tone to the proceedings, which were accompanied by a sense of urgency that would be unthinkable today. The fact that forty-four Allied nations were able to set up these institutions in just a few *weeks* is a testament to how desperately important they all believed it was to reach agreement.

The institutions that were created that summer would be the foundation of the world economy for the next thirty years, and even today continue to exert a huge influence. The first and foremost of them was the International Monetary Fund. The main purpose of the IMF was to regulate the flow of money around the world through a system of fixed exchange rates, thus preventing the economic free-for-all that had caused such chaos in the 1930s. It would also provide a pool of funds from which member nations could draw if they were ever struggling with a large balance-of-payments deficit. Finally, it would provide economic direction to those who needed it – a function that it still performs today.

To say that the IMF was a radical idea is an understatement. Never before had the nations of the world so comprehensively overhauled the entire structure of the international monetary system. After Bretton Woods, nations would no longer be able simply to revalue or devalue their currencies at will; nor would they be subject entirely to the whims of the market. The IMF would set exchange rates, which could not be changed substantially without its approval – in other words, the whole world was ceding economic sovereignty to this new international institution.[49] All currencies would be pegged to the US dollar, which had replaced the British pound sterling as the world's international currency – further proof, if any were needed, of how America had displaced Britain in the world economy.

Even at the time of its inception this institution was fraught with controversy. Keynes wanted creditor nations to take as much responsibility as debtor nations for any imbalances between them while White took the much more moralistic view that debtors should be solely responsible for repaying their debts. (Unsurprisingly, given that Britain was now one of the world's most indebted nations while America was its greatest creditor.) In the end, as usual, the American view won the day.[50]

For the rest of the world, meanwhile, the most important thing was to obtain as much influence in the new institution as possible. The higher the contribution, or quota, a nation paid into the IMF, the greater say it had over how the fund was run. Quota size was in theory based on the strength of a nation's economy – but once again, it was the Americans who controlled the calculations. Unbeknown to the participants, the top five economies in the IMF would end up having enormous political as well as economic significance, since these countries would also end up occupying the five permanent seats on the United Nations Security Council.[51]

A second global institution set up during the same conference was the International Bank for Reconstruction and Development – the core body of what is today more commonly known as the World Bank. The original purpose of the bank was to provide loans to countries in Europe and Asia for reconstruction after the war – the rebuilding of war-damaged ports or railway lines, for example – but it also had ambitions to promote 'development of the economically backward areas of the world'.[52] In the decades since the war, development has gradually expanded to become the Bank's primary purpose.

The final major economic organization suggested at the Bretton Woods conference was an International Trade Organization, whose purpose would be to reduce trade barriers between nations. This was supposed to be set up a few years later in 1948, but over the course of those few years the world's memory of the war faded a little, as did its sense of urgency and its spirit of cooperation. The ITO was never ratified by the US Congress, which was no longer willing to sacrifice even minor American interests for the sake of the greater good. As a consequence, the world had to make do with the more limited General Agreement on Tariffs and Trade (GATT), and wait for it to grow slowly over the next five decades.[53]

Money, development and trade. The international management of these three things was supposed to be the foundation upon which the postwar economy would be built, and a bright new world created. By managing the flows of money around the world, by funding big reconstruction and development projects, and by greasing the wheels of trade, everyone was supposed to benefit. As President Roosevelt said to the US Congress in February 1945, these were all part of a consistent vision of 'a world in which plain people in all countries can work at tasks which they do well, exchange in peace the products of their labor, and work out their several destinies in security and peace'.[54] The Bretton Woods agreements in particular were hailed as a breakthrough in 'constructive internationalism'.[55]

Unfortunately, none of these global institutions were capable of ushering in such a bright new world, no matter how high their aspirations. The political and economic inequalities that had to be overcome were simply too great, and the damage inflicted by the war too massive. The World Bank's funds of $10 billion, for example, were a mere drop in the ocean compared to what was needed to reconstruct the whole of Europe and Asia. In the end both the IMF and the World Bank were rendered virtually irrelevant in Europe when the USA granted almost $13 billion in direct aid to the continent under the Marshall Plan.

The IMF was also unable to impose its rules upon those who were determined to ignore them, particularly when those countries were powerful ones. As India's delegate complained at the Bretton Woods conference, expecting the IMF to rein in countries like Britain or America was like 'sending out a jelly fish to tackle a whale'.[56] When the Fund officially became active in 1947, almost every member immediately invoked their right not to allow their currency to become fully convertible for the first five years. Most European countries did not allow their currencies to be convertible until 1958, and did not fully comply with IMF rules until as late as 1961.[57] For all its supposed power as the arbiter of the world's currencies, the IMF was beginning to look a little ineffectual.

At the same time, postwar trade negotiations also seemed to be failing. Not only did the USA pull out of trade talks in 1948, but Britain refused to make more than minimal reductions in the preferential treatment it gave to Commonwealth countries. It would be years before trade talks would significantly reduce trade barriers, and it was not until 1995 that the world finally saw an international body with legal powers over trade policy that was first imagined at Bretton Woods – the World Trade Organization.

Finally, and crucially, there were political differences between many of the world's nations that could not be overcome, no matter how good or bad their intentions. Like it or not, everyone knew that they were dependent upon the USA, which was bankrolling the majority of postwar reconstruction and development. If Britain found this dependency hard to swallow, then the Soviet Union and its satellite states could not countenance it at all. Despite signing the Bretton Woods agreements in 1944, the Soviet Union never officially ratified them, opening up a political and economic divide between East and West that would only expand over the coming decades.

The world's poorer nations, meanwhile, very quickly began to regard the Bretton Woods institutions as something of a rich man's club. Up until 2012, every president of the World Bank was American, and every president of the IMF has been a European. Furthermore, the executive boards of both institutions are also dominated by Americans and Europeans. In the light of this, it is perhaps unsurprising that, in the immediate postwar years, the reconstruction of Europe was always favoured over the reconstruction of Asia. In later years the IMF would be accused of surrounding its loans to the developing world with punitive conditions that seemed to suit nobody but the creditor nations of the West, such as the lowering of trade barriers and the cutting of government spending. To the smaller nations, this has often felt like the developed world infringing on their national sovereignty. As Tanzanian president Julius Nyerere famously asked in 1981, 'Who elected the IMF to be the ministry of finance for every country in the world?'[58]

What emerged from the war, therefore, was not exactly a new epoch of greater economic harmony, but a system that also enshrined the differences between the capitalist West and the Communist East, and between the wealthy North and the developing South. Though the Bretton Woods system has since been mythologized as 'the longest period of stability and economic growth in history', particularly since the world economic crisis of 2008, it was never perfect, and never even entirely fair.[59]

But there are many who argue that, flawed as the Bretton Woods system was, it was better than the alternative. Since the system collapsed in the 1970s, the world economy – just like the national economies of many Western nations – has been subjected to very little regulation at all. It has endured repeated cycles of economic boom and bust, and the gap between rich and poor has once again grown to levels not seen since before the war. Today, some of the world's most influential economists are again arguing for a new era of international cooperation in order to curb the excesses of the free market. This is the only way, they say, that we can avoid in future the sort of massive inequality that produced famine in Bengal in 1943.[60]

One might wonder how ordinary Bengalis regarded these developments in the world economy. Did they welcome the new era of global finance, global trade and global investment? Or did they rail against the injustices in the way that the new world order was being set up? Did they envisage a brighter future for Bengal after the war was over? And if so, how did they reconcile themselves to the fact that, for them, there would be no Marshall Plan, as there was in Europe; that there would be no aid from the United Nations Relief and Rehabilitation Administration, as there was in China; and that there would be no end to the exploitation of the province which had begun under the British, and which after 1947 would continue under the Pakistanis?[61]

Chittaprosad, for one, had no illusions about a world of plenty and prosperity for all. His paint brush, once sharpened to highlight the economic injustices of the war and the famine, continued to be employed in exposing the hypocrisy of the rich in their dealings with the poor. In the immediate postwar years he continued to draw propaganda posters targeting the British, but as the world's balance of power changed he began to concentrate more on the Americans. In one cartoon he depicted the Indian prime minister, Jawaharlal Nehru, exploiting the nation's poor in order to extract dollar aid from what looks like the barrel of an American gun. In another he characterized India as a freed slave, beating away the predatory intentions of Uncle Sam, who has a hatful of dollars and a pocket stuffed with atomic bombs.[62]

Chittaprosad lived the rest of his life, like the subjects he painted, in a condition of dire poverty. Though he eventually became disillusioned with the Communist Party, he never gave up his socialist ideals, and the struggles and triumphs of India's poor and starving would remain a

Chittaprosad's bitterness at a world economy dominated by the USA is shown in this 1952 drawing of Nehru accepting money from the barrel of an American gun. India's poor are held fast as they reach for Communist help.

constant theme of his art. In later years he also drew and painted pictures for the peace movement. But while he achieved some fame as a political artist, the challenging subjects he insisted on painting never entirely captured the imagination of those outside the art world. When he died in Calcutta in November 1978, his death went entirely unsung.[63]

Despite his untimely death, Chittaprosad lived long enough to see the transformation of his native Bengal, although that transformation was never the economic one that he and so many of his fellow Bengalis longed for. Their hopes for a bright future of benign government planning, development and economic and social progress were very quickly dashed. The decades after the war were characterized by repeated political upheavals, natural disasters and the return of famine. In 1947 Bengal was split between India and the new state of Pakistan. When the eastern parts of the province finally became an independent country as Bangladesh in the 1970s, after a prolonged period of repression and bloody civil war, it was still one of the poorest regions in the world.

Since Chittaprosad's death, Bangladesh has become one of the world's greatest recipients of aid and development loans – but even the World Bank admits that decades of financing development projects has done little to address the problem of inequality. More than a quarter of World Bank lending to Bangladesh until the 1990s was aimed at tackling food security and rural poverty, but most of this money instead ended up in the hands of large landowners at the expense of small farmers, who were often driven further into hardship and debt.[64]

At the time of writing, according to the UN Conference on Trade and Development, Bangladesh remains one of the world's least developed countries. Over 30 per cent of the population still live below the poverty line, and more than 15 per cent continue to be malnourished. These parts of Chittaprosad's 'Hungry Bengal' continue to struggle to this day.[65]

11. World Government

'I was trained to kill. Not only other soldiers, but people in cities . . . women, children, old folks . . .'[1] This was how former US bomber pilot Garry Davis summed up his experience of the Second World War. It was a regret he first suffered in 1944, and one that continued to haunt him for the rest of his life: 'I felt morally degraded as a human being. My profession [before the war] was acting. On stage, facing an audience, I was joyful, fulfilled and felt worthy of life itself. My relation to my audience was one of mutual respect, appreciation, even love . . . But as a wartime pilot I had lost my humanity, my soul, if you will. I had become a mere killer of fellow humans . . . "Win the war against the Nazis" was my sole unthinking motive in life . . . No longer was I only a happy entertainer. I felt debased, used, humiliated.'[2]

It is not uncommon for former soldiers to feel cut adrift once they return to civilian life, particularly after experiencing the intense highs and lows of active combat. In 1945 there were tens of millions of fighting men around the world who felt a similar sense of dislocation. Some of them expressed it, as Davis did, in resentment for the way the war had changed them; others struggled to contain their aggression, to conceal their anxiety, or to come to terms with the sudden lack of urgency or focus that characterized peacetime life. It was not only ex-servicemen who felt this way: civilians across the world had shared in the horrors and triumphs of the fighting, and in the wake of the war they also shared a sense of indefinable unease.

What made Garry Davis exceptional was how he chose to cope with these feelings. For two and a half years he drifted aimlessly in New York, plagued not only by memories of his brother and friends who had been killed during the war but also by a sense of personal responsibility for the things he had done, and by a nagging suspicion that the world had learned nothing from all the years of destruction. When he was no longer able to tolerate these thoughts, he decided to take action: he would make a stand for world peace. So he returned to Europe, to the 'scene of the crime', as it were, and on 25 May 1948 he renounced his

American citizenship. It was the first act of defiance in a personal crusade that would end up lasting a lifetime.[3]

Davis had nothing particularly against the country of his birth: his gripe was with the very idea of 'nationality' itself. In his eyes, renouncing his citizenship was not a negative act, but a positive one – the first step to becoming a 'citizen of the entire world' whose primary allegiances were not to any state, but to mankind as a whole. 'The roots of war,' he later explained, 'seemed to me to be inherent in the nation-state . . . To eliminate war . . . one would first have to eliminate nations.' If he could convince enough people to follow in his footsteps and declare themselves world citizens, he reasoned, there would no longer be any need for nation-states, and international war would become a thing of the past.[4]

For the next sixty-five years Davis embarked upon one publicity stunt after another, each designed to draw attention to the inconsistencies and absurdities of national distinctions. Having renounced his citizenship in France, he presented the French authorities with something of a conundrum: since he was not a French citizen, they wanted to deport him – but since he was no longer an American citizen either, they technically had nowhere to deport him to. When the French authorities went ahead with a deportation order regardless, Davis went out and deliberately shoplifted ladies' underwear from a Paris department store with the express purpose of getting himself arrested – that way he would be legally required to remain in the country. On another occasion, in London, he tried to walk into Buckingham Palace with the vague notion of petitioning the queen. He was arrested and shipped back to America for his trouble.

Despite his passionate commitment to world peace, Davis seemed to possess a rare talent for attracting abuse. The American novelist Paul Gallico characterized him and others who renounced US citizenship as stupid young men with 'bleeding hearts' whose exploits played into the hands of 'a gang of brutes' in central and eastern Europe.[5] The Soviets dismissed Davis as 'a maniac exporting world government from America along with powdered eggs and detective stories', whose real agenda was 'to soften Europe for American colonization'.[6] Meanwhile, the president of the United Nations General Assembly, the Australian statesman Herbert Evatt, saw him as a hopeless idealist, out of touch with the realities of international diplomacy.[7]

'World citizen' Garry Davis, carried aloft on the shoulders of his supporters after a speech at the Vélodrome d'Hiver in Paris, 1948.

Nevertheless, there was no denying Davis's enormous popular appeal. In the late 1940s he inspired hundreds of 'world citizen' clubs all over Europe, America and North Africa, and gave speeches to crowds of up to 20,000. He won the support of numerous intellectuals, including the novelist Albert Camus, the philosopher Jean-Paul Sartre, Nobel Peace laureate Albert Schweitzer, concert violinist Yehudi Menuhin and the twentieth century's most famous scientist, Albert Einstein. According to various newspapers, he was 'a dreamer of beautiful dreams' and 'a pioneer who is ahead of his time', who expressed 'a deep emotional need felt by millions of people'. In later life, the *Times of India* compared him to Socrates, Galileo, Joan of Arc and Beethoven. Australia's *The World's News* called him 'a symbol of the thousands of little men in the world who are trying to lift themselves out of the mental trough in which wars are bred'. Regardless of whether Davis was right or wrong, according to the *New Yorker* magazine, he was certainly 'in step with the universe'.[8]

During his lifelong campaign against the concept of nationality, he saw the inside of a dozen jails in as many states, usually for ignoring

national visa restrictions. He started a register of 'world citizens' which
drew almost a million members. He set up his own 'world currency'
and even a 'world government', based in Washington, DC. Since every
nation required him to have papers in order to travel, he printed his own
home-made 'world passport', and issued similar passports to anyone who
asked for one. Part of his enduring appeal was his determination not
merely to talk about world federation, but always to put his words into
actions. The personal sacrifices he made were substantial; and although
even he himself admitted to being hopelessly naive, especially when he
first started out, his dedication to his cause was never in doubt. As he put
it, 'I wanted a crusade, not a meeting. I wanted total commitment, not a
membership card and a lapel button.' At the time of his death in 2013, he
was still campaigning for an end to nations and an end to war.[9]

Davis's popularity was symptomatic of a huge shift in the tides of global
feeling. We have already seen how the Second World War engendered a
new longing for freedom, for equality, for a sense of purpose and a sense
of belonging. We have also seen how the world's faith in scientific
rationalism and centralism had grown as a result of the war. What Davis
appeared to be advocating was a perfect synthesis of all these things. His
insistence on being able to travel without documents was symbolic of
the sense of freedom that everyone wanted after the war. His invocations of a brotherhood of man invited a sense of belonging – not to a
nation, but to a more universal group that included the whole of humanity. His wish to become a 'citizen of the world' implied a sense of
equality between all people: the defining characteristic of a world citizen was not one's race, nationality, religion, class or gender, but one's
humanity. In Davis's world, there would be no need for war since there
would no longer be nations to fight for. At a communal level there
would be no more heroes, no more monsters and no more martyrs.

Davis felt strongly that the only rational way to organize such a world
was to give every human being an equal say in choosing a world government, which should be federal in structure, so as to balance the
desires of each region against the needs of the whole. He was always
vague about what such a government would actually look like, but in
his memoirs he said that he imagined it along the same lines as the
American system: in other words, a United States of the World.[10]

There were all kinds of advantages to such a system. To begin with it was one that Americans were already familiar with. As the driving force behind most international change after the war, it was essential that America should take a leading role in any new world organization, rather than withdrawing into isolation as it had done in the 1920s and 30s. Secondly, it offered a clean break from the old world system – the prewar League of Nations – which had never included the USA and whose failure to prevent the world descending into catastrophe had discredited it in almost everyone's eyes. A federal world government would also mean the centralization of power in the hands of an elected elite. For Davis this meant the rational organization of world society by a body whose only loyalty was to humanity as a whole, and which would incorporate scientists as well as spiritual leaders.[11]

Garry Davis's flamboyant publicity stunts and protests made all these points in a rather chaotic way – but there were plenty of others who were willing to place such ideas within a proper intellectual and ideological framework.

The first book to popularize the idea of a new world government, especially with Americans, was Wendell Willkie's 1943 international bestseller, *One World*. Willkie was a Republican statesman and former candidate for the US presidency who had been sent by Roosevelt on a fact-finding mission around the world during the war. His book, which outlined his findings on this trip, described the universal desire for change that he had discovered along the way. 'The whole world,' he wrote, was 'in an eager, demanding, hungry, ambitious mood ready for incredible sacrifices if only they could see some hope that those sacrifices would prove worth while.'[12] Willkie was adamant that these hopes must be fulfilled if the world was ever to find peace in the future; and, furthermore, that America must lead the way:

> America must choose one of three courses after this war: narrow nationalism, which inevitably means the ultimate loss of our own liberty; international imperialism, which means the sacrifice of some other nation's liberty; or the creation of a world in which there shall be an equality of opportunity for every race and every nation. I am convinced the American people will choose, by overwhelming majority, the last of these three courses.[13]

One World went straight to the top of the *New York Times* bestseller list in May 1943, and remained there for four months, eventually selling

2 million copies. It has been credited with sweeping away the traditional isolationism, particularly by the Republican Party, that had in the past prevented America from taking an active part in world affairs.[14]

Two years later, at the very end of the war, came another influential book by writer and publisher Emery Reves, which ended up being translated into twenty-five languages and which sold 800,000 copies worldwide. Reves was a Hungarian Jew who had been educated in Berlin, Zurich and Paris, and who finally settled in the USA. Like many others of his generation he had been personally affected by the war, and he had lost his mother in the Holocaust.[15]

In a tightly argued treatise, Reves claimed that the Second World War was merely 'the symptom of disease': winning the war would be meaningless if the world failed to follow it up by treating its underlying causes. Like Garry Davis, Reves believed that the root of all modern conflict was mankind's emotional attachment to our nation-states.

> Nationalism is a herd instinct. It is one of many manifestations of that tribal instinct which is one of the deepest and most constant characteristics of man as a social creature. It is a collective inferiority complex, that gives comforting reactions to individual fear, loneliness, weakness, inability, insecurity, helplessness, seeking refuge in exaggerated consciousness and pride of belonging to a certain group of people.[16]

As long as nations existed, said Reves, they would always rub up against other groups with similar fears and insecurities, and conflict would be the inevitable result. The only way to solve this problem was to stop dividing ourselves into frightened, mutually exclusive groups and integrate all nations 'into one unified, higher sovereignty, capable of creating a legal order within which all peoples may enjoy equal security, equal obligations and equal rights under law'. In other words, what was needed was a federal world government.[17]

All across the West, other people were coming to the same conclusions. In America, twenty prominent figures, including Albert Einstein, Thomas Mann and three senators, wrote an open letter to the American people urging them to read Reves's book, 'which expresses clearly and simply what so many of us have been thinking'; their letter was published in the *New York Times*, the *Washington Post* and fifty other newspapers.[18] Meanwhile, a group of prominent academics at the

The logo of the World Citizens Association, one of many organizations around the world that promoted global federalism.

University of Chicago were already drafting what they hoped might form the basis of a world constitution.[19] In Britain, in 1947, the Labour MP Henry Usborne founded the All Party Parliamentary Group for World Governance, which at its peak had over 200 members from both houses of parliament. At the same time, the former French Resistance leader Robert Sarrazac was founding Le Front Humain des Citoyens du Monde. It was Sarrazac's group which eventually took up Garry Davis's cause and promoted him as the face of the movement.[20]

While such groups were most prominent in Europe and North America, grass-roots organizations calling for world government also sprang up in Argentina, Australia, New Zealand, India, Pakistan, the Philippines, Japan and Turkey. In 1947, more than fifty of these organizations from twenty-four countries came together at Montreux in Switzerland and made the decision to merge as a World Federalist Movement. Their manifesto stated that 'mankind can free itself forever from war only through the establishment of a world federal government'. This organization is still active today, and has links to like-minded groups in every corner of the globe.[21]

It is important to reiterate that it was not only idealism that motivated this movement: there was also a desperate fear of what might happen if the world did *not* find a remedy to its problems. In the words of Frank Buchman, founder of the global Moral Re-Armament movement, 'All the world wants an answer. We have reached the moment when, unless we find an answer and bring it quickly to the world, not just one nation, but all nations will be overwhelmed.'[22]

Foremost in people's minds was the threat of a new, even more devastating conflict. Even before the advent of the atom bomb, statesmen like South Africa's Jan Smuts were warning, 'A third world war may well prove beyond the limits of what civilized society can endure, perhaps even beyond the limits of our continued existence as a human world.'[23] But after Hiroshima, such opinions became even more urgent and intense. The idealism of Wendell Willkie's *One World* was giving way to a new message encapsulated in the title of another bestselling book, published in 1945, about the insecurities of the atomic age: *One World or None*.[24]

The United Nations

It was into this atmosphere of passionate idealism, mixed with subconscious dread, that the United Nations was born. At first glance, the UN seemed to share many of the same ideals of people like Garry Davis and Emery Reves. It had the appearance of a kind of world government, with representatives of fifty-one different countries who seemed united in their desire 'to save succeeding generations from the scourge of war'. By signing the UN Charter, these nations solemnly promised 'to practise tolerance and live together in peace with one another as good neighbours'. It all sounded very noble.[25]

In the early days of the UN, people across the globe desperately wanted to believe in it as the solution to all the world's problems. Many of the UN's early recruits had fought for the Allies or in underground resistance movements, and regarded the chance of working for peace as 'a dream fulfilled'.[26] In Europe the new organization was hailed by some newspapers as 'the great historical act . . . which gives to the world a profound hope' that it might 'henceforth life in peace'.[27] In Asia it was praised as a 'great coalition for peace' and a 'utopian garden' (albeit one that was broken up by the occasional 'hard rocks of reality').[28] Some African intellectuals also allowed themselves to believe in it as a beacon of hope for a better world. 'Never before,' said the Nigerian campaigner Eyo Ita, 'has the human race seen a greater and better opportunity for a world community of free and equal peoples.'[29]

There was similar enthusiasm even in the traditionally isolationist United States of America, where both Republicans and Democrats tripped over themselves to praise the new organization. Secretary of State Cordell Hull claimed that the UN held the key to 'the fulfillment of humanity's highest aspirations and the very survival of our civilization'.[30] Other prominent politicians called the UN Charter the 'most hopeful and important document in the history of world statesmanship', whose principles would lead us 'towards a golden age of freedom, justice, peace and social well-being'.[31] Such superlatives were reflected in the American population as a whole. In a Gallup poll conducted in July 1945, those in favour of the UN Charter outnumbered those against it by twenty to one.[32]

Looking back, we still often romanticize the spirit that brought forth the United Nations, just as we continue to romanticize the exploits of eccentric idealists like Garry Davis. Today's UN continues to celebrate the moment when the San Francisco conference voted on the new UN Charter and 'every delegate rose and remained standing . . . and the hall resounded to a mighty ovation'.[33] Modern-day politicians still praise not only the 'ideals of the Charter' but also the 'pioneers' who built the organization 'out of the ashes of war and genocide'.[34] Even historians tend to get a little teary eyed when looking back at the 'visionaries and heroes' who set up the organization.[35]

Unfortunately, the heroes of peace are no more able to live up to such idealization than the heroes of war. The motives of those who created the United Nations were not nearly as pure as they liked to think they were, and the systems they put in place were often directed just as much at selfish, nationalist aims as they were at noble, universalist ones. Just a brief glance at the verbatim transcripts of the debates that took place in San Francisco is enough to reveal that Utopia was never on the cards.[36] Indeed, there were certain aspects of the United Nations system that seemed calculated to disappoint almost everyone.

To begin with, the new organization did nothing at all to tackle the one problem that idealists like Davis and Reves had identified as the root cause of war: nationalism. In fact, if anything, it enshrined nationalism as the single most important political philosophy governing our lives: the very name of the organization underlined that it did not represent the world's *people*, but the world's *nations*.

Furthermore, the charter made it clear that some of these nations were to be more equal than others. Although there were originally fifty-one members of the UN, the five most powerful nations – the United States, the USSR, Britain, France and China – were to have special privileges and responsibilities. Unlike everyone else, these five were to be granted a permanent seat at the UN Security Council, which was regarded as the heart and brain of the new organization. Not only that, but, unlike all the other members, these five would also have the right to veto proposals that they did not agree with.

These arrangements made perfect sense to the Big Five themselves – after all, they were the ones who had done most of the fighting during the war, and they were the ones who would inevitably be called on to provide resources to prevent any future wars from breaking out. But as Colombia's future prime minister Alberto Lleras Camargo pointed out, while only the great powers were strong enough to secure peace, equally 'it is only the great powers which can menace the peace and security of the world'.[37] When the Big Five veto was debated at San Francisco in 1945 it caused a storm of protest amongst the world's smaller nations. Egypt's foreign minister was one of many who objected to the fact that countries such as Britain or the Soviet Union would effectively be able to 'sit both as judge and jury' in any matter that affected themselves.[38] Nations from all corners of the globe denounced the veto as 'immoral' and 'unfair and indefensible', and declared that the 'wings of power' needed to be 'trimmed'. But in the end the Big Five were able to bully enough delegates into toeing their line, and they were granted both their permanent seats in the Security Council and their extensive powers of veto.[39]

A final issue that worried the idealists of 1945 was the way that the UN Charter expressly forbade its member countries from intervening 'in matters which are essentially within the domestic jurisdiction of any state'.[40] On the surface this seems like a reasonable way of preventing nations from undermining their neighbours from within, as Hitler had done in the run-up to the war; but it also meant that any nation could repress its citizens without fear of outside interference. Moreover, it went against the fundamental principle of one law for all; instead it endorsed the idea that different nations would be subject to different political systems, different laws and different levels of freedom. Thus the Soviets were allowed to justify their suppression of the Baltic States as an 'internal' matter; and European powers could reject calls for them to let go of their empires on the grounds that this was nobody's business but their own.

The sanctity of national sovereignty over internal matters was to have immediate and devastating consequences. National minorities, whose rights had always been guaranteed under the prewar League of Nations system, were now effectively abandoned to the mercies of those who governed them. Thus, when millions upon millions of Germans and other minorities were brutally expelled from their homelands across eastern Europe between 1945 and 1947, the United Nations did nothing to intervene. This set a precedent that has caused untold misery ever since: without a mandate to step in on its own authority, the UN has stood by while genocides were carried out in countries like Cambodia, Rwanda, Yugoslavia and Sudan.[41]

There were many who had already begun to feel disillusioned with the UN even before the ink had dried on its charter. According to the Canadian diplomat Escott Reid, the entire Canadian delegation came away from San Francisco full of 'deep pessimism about the future of the United Nations'.[42] The American diplomat George Kennan was sure that the ambiguous wording of the charter would inevitably lead to future quarrels; while the British diplomat Gladwyn Jebb worried that the conference had aimed too high for 'this wicked world'.[43] Meanwhile, members of the smaller nations came away from the conference feeling desperately short-changed. Perhaps the most disappointed of all were those countries and colonies that were not even represented at the conference. 'Today we are on the brink of another era,' lamented one Nigerian newspaper, but far from setting Africa free from the empires that ruled it, the UN Charter seemed designed only 'to deny the colonial peoples parity of treatment in the new world order'.[44]

For idealists like Garry Davis and Emery Reves, the creation of the United Nations was the ultimate expression of all that was wrong with the world. Reves in particular railed against the 'fallacies' that he believed were inherent in the UN system. He guessed from the start that narrow national interests would always trump any initiative for the common good; and that the passion for 'self-determination' would only mean the breaking up of the old empires 'into smaller and ever smaller units, each sovereign in its own corner'. But most of all, he scoffed at the hypocrisy of a system that was so obviously weighted in favour of the mighty. Nations like America or the USSR, he predicted, would almost always get their way, because 'All great powers behave like gangsters. And all small nations behave like prostitutes.'[45]

Garry Davis, meanwhile, was a little more hands-on in his criticism. One of his most high-profile publicity stunts in 1948 involved smuggling himself into the UN General Assembly meeting and heckling the delegates. He declared that 'the people of the world' were not represented by the UN, and called on them 'no longer to deceive us by this illusion of political authority'. Far from promoting world peace, he said, 'The sovereign states you represent divide us and lead us to the abyss of Total War.' Davis's reward for this outburst – as would be the case throughout so much of his life – was to be forcibly removed from the building and locked up for the rest of the evening.[46]

It is easy to detect a feeling of betrayal in Davis's words. Both he and the committee of French intellectuals who supported him – and indeed the millions of people around the world who followed Davis's exploits in the newspapers – had made huge sacrifices over the previous years, and found the uncertainties of the postwar world almost unbearable. They had fought the Second World War in the service of an ideal; in return, all they had been given was a compromise.

Some Quiet Successes

In hindsight, it is hard to see how the United Nations could have been constituted any differently – or, at least, any better. The idea that the people of the world would give up nationalism for a dream of shared humanity was never more than wishful thinking: having fought for their countries during the war, most people were unlikely to follow Garry Davis's lead and abandon their nationality now that the war was over. The idea that the world's most powerful nations would ever abdicate their sovereignty to a higher body was also wishful thinking. But perhaps the most wishful of all was the idea that the Communist East and capitalist West could continue to cooperate without a mutual enemy to unite them. The destruction of capitalism was enshrined in the Communist Manifesto, as was the inevitability of a capitalist reaction. If there were to be one world, there would be room for only one system.

And so the compromises were made, and the UN limped its way

through the rest of the twentieth century. In the years that followed, almost all the doubts of 1945 were borne out. Most of the Big Five indeed used the protection of the veto to embark on their own wars, much to the impotent rage of the vast majority of UN members. Thus the British and the French invaded Suez in 1956, the Soviets invaded Hungary, Czechoslovakia and Afghanistan (1956, 1968 and 1979), and the Americans embarked on a series of dubious adventures in central America in the 1980s. The pattern has continued into the twenty-first century with the American-led invasion of Iraq (2003), the Russian invasion of Georgia (2008) and the Russian annexation of Crimea (2014), all of which were carried out without Security Council approval, and without Security Council reprimand. When push comes to shove, the Big Five have proven themselves more or less free to start wars whenever they want.[47]

As have their allies. Another feature of the Security Council veto is the way that it has consistently been used in order to prevent sanctions against any nation that is under the protection of one of the great powers. Thus the Soviet Union always protected Cuba, China still protects North Korea, and America steadfastly prevents any sanctions against Israel. Regardless of the rights or wrongs of each case, this has produced a system of double standards whereby some nations get punished for threatening the peace while others seem able to do so at will.

And yet, just because the UN has not been able to produce universal and permanent peace, this does not mean we should dismiss it entirely. Away from the great-power interests it has had some impressive successes. For example it helped smooth the path to independence in Indonesia and many African states. At varying stages it has managed to maintain precarious armistice agreements on the Indian subcontinent, in the Middle East and on Cyprus. It retaliated strongly to Communist aggression in Korea in the 1950s, and in the 1990s it forced Saddam Hussein's troops to withdraw from Kuwait.

Even the five permanent members' power of veto has not been exclusively a bad thing. At the very least it has provided a pressure valve that has allowed the great powers to remain engaged with the international process, rather than walking away from the negotiating table as happened so often in the League of Nations. Thus, if the organization has not always been successful in preventing *small* wars, it has at least played a role in preventing another *world* war.

In other spheres of life it has had some estimable successes. After the Second World War, and throughout the twentieth century, it cared for millions upon millions of refugees – feeding them, clothing them, finding them new homes and fulfilling their psychological needs. UN agencies have helped to wipe out smallpox throughout the world, raise labour standards, extend education and improve the rights of women everywhere. Every time we telephone abroad, or post an international letter, or fly to another country we are making use of international agreements that have been brokered and regulated by agencies of the United Nations. The list goes on. These things might seem less impressive than the attempt to achieve world peace, but they are every bit a part of the same urge to build a more united world that so inspired idealists like Garry Davis and Emery Reves.

Today, the most striking thing about the United Nations is how anachronistic it all seems, particularly the structure of its Security Council. Even in 1945 it was plain that Britain and France would never again be as influential as they once were: nowadays they are no different from dozens of other nations. Today's Russia is a mere shadow of the former Soviet Union, and while China wields huge economic power, it has still not achieved the rank of political superpower. Only the United States has managed to maintain a status similar to the one it enjoyed when the United Nations was first formed. In the meantime, economic giants like Germany and Japan and emerging powers like India and Brazil are obliged to defer to a system that does not recognize their true worth. The 'one world' that we chose for ourselves in 1945 preserved in aspic the power configurations of the end of the Second World War. For better or worse, this is still the system that we are obliged to work within today.

Even the UN's staunchest supporters understand that this is an absurd system. As one international lawyer put it:

If someone would come to you and say, 'Look, we want to have an organization which is going to govern the world. But . . . it doesn't have a budget of its own; it doesn't have any enforcement power of its own; it's got to be a beggar to rely upon its member states for either military support or financial support; it's got to have a charter which is a compromise, with contradictory principles in order to get people to accept it; and it's got to deal with all kinds of languages at the same time in the staff that are going to represent it. Do you think it will work?' You'd say to me, 'Are you kidding?' I would say it's a miracle that it's able to do as much as it does. I'm a strong supporter of the United Nations simply because we have nothing better. But you have to improve it.[48]

The man who spoke these words is a Hungarian American who has worked within the UN system for half a century. It is his story that we turn to next.

12. World Law

Benjamin Ferencz did not have a good war.[1] When the Japanese bombed Pearl Harbor at the end of 1941 he immediately volunteered to serve his country, but it seemed that he and the US Army had very different opinions about what sort of contribution he might make. As a Harvard law student who already spoke several languages, Ferencz believed he might be useful in military intelligence. But the army was not interested in his brain – they just wanted to make up numbers. So, after finishing his law degree, Ferencz was drafted as a private in the artillery.

Over the next two years he learned all the tricks of the army. He discovered how to cheat the system, how to avoid following dangerous or illegal orders ('of which there were many'), how to outsmart the bullies amongst his superior officers – and, eventually, how to fight the Germans. He took part in the Normandy landings, the Battle of the Bulge and the breach of the Siegfried Line. He and his artillery unit shot down enemy planes, and bombarded enemy troops. And he hated every minute of it.

It was not until December 1944, after Ferencz had fought his way to the borders of Germany, that someone in the army hierarchy realized that his talents might be better employed elsewhere. They had been receiving disturbing reports from Germany that required investigation – stories of Allied airmen being beaten to death and prisoners being abused, and rumours of much, much worse. What they needed now was an expert in war crimes. Somehow they discovered that Ferencz was exactly such an expert: as part of a research project for one of his professors he had read and summarized virtually every book on the subject in the Harvard library. So they immediately transferred him out of the artillery: from now on Ferencz would be part of Third Army's legal section, as a war-crimes investigator.

At first, he took to his new job with enthusiasm. At least, he reasoned, he would finally be away from the horrors of the battlefield. He was given his own vehicle, and the authority to go anywhere he needed and ask any question he liked. He entertained romantic notions of

Ben Ferencz in France, 1944, while he was still a corporal in the 115th AAA Gun Battalion of the US Army.

himself as a man who could ride into town and set the moral balance straight, like a legal version of the Lone Ranger. He even painted the words IMMER ALLEIN – 'always alone' – on the front of his jeep.

But nothing could prepare him for the sights he was about to see. In the spring of 1945, after exploring a few individual murder cases, Ferencz was called in to investigate the concentration camps that the US Army was beginning to discover as it advanced into Germany and Austria: Ohrdruf, Buchenwald, Mauthausen, Dachau, to name but a few. From the moment Ferencz first set foot in one of these places it was obvious that he was witnessing atrocity on an unprecedented scale. 'They were all basically similar: dead bodies strewn across the camp grounds, piles of skin and bones, cadavers piled up like cordwood before the burning crematoria, helpless skeletons with diarrhoea, dysentery, typhus, TB, pneumonia, and other ailments, retching in their louse ridden bunks or on the ground with only their pathetic eyes pleading for help.' In the course of his duties Ferencz visited at least half a dozen of these places, and the sights he came across would haunt him for the rest of his life.

Neither could his legal background prepare him for the realities of retribution in the chaotic aftermath of the liberation. When Ferencz arrived at the Ebensee concentration camp, for example, he caught some of the inmates taking their revenge on one of their former SS guards. They beat the man mercilessly, and tied him to one of the metal trays used to slide bodies into the crematorium. And then they roasted him alive. 'I watched it happen and did nothing. It was not my duty to stop it, even if I could have, and frankly, I was not inclined to try.' But the sight seared itself on his memory.

Later, during the military trials at Dachau, he witnessed how some of the defendants were given just a minute or two to explain themselves before being sentenced to death. 'As a lawyer, that didn't impress me very much. At least, not in a very positive way. Did I think it was unjust? Not really. They were in the camp, they saw what happened . . . But I was sort of disgusted.'

For almost a year, experiences like this were the stuff of his daily life. By December 1945 he had had enough. Instead of waiting to be demobilized, he went absent without leave, and then stowed away on a troop ship bound for America. Nobody in the army seemed particularly to care. When he arrived in the USA there were no records of what he had done or where he had been, so he was honourably discharged and allowed to go home. 'The three years I spent in the Army in World War Two was the most miserable experience of my life,' he later confessed. All he wanted to do was to return to being a civilian lawyer and try to forget all he had seen.

The Path to Nuremberg and Tokyo

The kind of revenge witnessed by Ben Ferencz at Ebensee was commonplace in the immediate aftermath of the war. Embittered by years of cruelty, many people across Europe and Asia took advantage of the temporary power vacuum to enact their own forms of justice. In Czechoslovakia, captured SS men were hung from the lamp posts. In Poland, suspected Nazis were buried in liquid manure, beaten to death by former concentration camp inmates, or forced to exhume mass graves with their bare hands.[2] In France, the Resistance summarily executed around

9,000 collaborators during and after the liberation; while in Italy up to 20,000 Fascists met the same fate.[3]

In the vast majority of such cases, those who committed revenge saw no reason to involve the law. The guilt of corrupt policemen and violent militiamen was well known: why should they be given a fair trial when they themselves had denied that same luxury to their own victims? Even lawyers could see a savage kind of justice in this. One French barrister, for example, questioned the value of setting up trials for a group of Fascist thugs who admitted to having ripped out the eyes of their prisoners, 'put bugs in the holes and sewn up the sockets'. With people like this, he mused, 'It may have been better to shoot them immediately.'[4]

Sometimes whole groups, even whole populations, were targeted with vengeance. In Yugoslavia some 70,000 collaborationist troops and civilians were lined up in front of trenches and shot, or were tied together and thrown over precipices. While a rudimentary form of selection was employed, none of these people were given any opportunity to defend themselves in a legal sense.[5] At the same time, all across eastern Europe, people with German ancestry were being banished from their communities. Between 1945 and 1948 some 12 to 14 million people were expelled into Germany, with such cruelty that at least half a million are believed to have died along the way.[6] Once again, the legality of such measures was barely considered. 'The whole German nation is responsible for Hitler,' announced the future justice minister of Czechoslovakia in 1945, 'and the whole nation must bear the punishment.'[7]

Similar scenes occurred in parts of Asia. In Hong Kong, Japanese soldiers were pulled from trams and beaten to death in the street; collaborators and informers were hunted down by vigilantes, tried by kangaroo courts and shot in the back of the head; and when the Kempeitai executioner from Stanley jail was discovered trying to escape on a ferry, he was trussed up by a group of Chinese labourers and thrown into the harbour to drown.[8] In Burma, agents of the US Counter-Intelligence Corps had no qualms about executing collaborators, while in Manchuria as many as 3,000 suspected Japanese war criminals are thought to have been summarily executed by the Soviets.[9] In Malaya, meanwhile, Communist guerrillas carried out a postwar 'reign of terror' in which they frequently killed suspected collaborators and women who had slept with Japanese officials. According to eyewitnesses, simple execution was not enough: victims were often bayoneted, beaten or tortured to death. Eyes would be gouged out, genitals cut off, bodies disembowelled. 'There were no longer any proper laws,' claims one Malay historian, 'and human lives no longer had any value.'[10]

The problem with summary justice like this was threefold: it was cruel, there was rarely much discrimination between the innocent and the guilty and – perhaps most importantly – it was often indistinguishable from the atrocities carried out by the Nazis or the Japanese military themselves. 'We are repeating some of the heinous procedures carried out by the Gestapo,' lamented one French Resistance newspaper after the liberation. 'What was the point in triumphing over the Barbarians if only to imitate them and become like them?'[11]

The Western Allies also carried out plenty of summary executions, both in Europe and in Asia. But this was certainly not how they wanted their justice to be remembered. They wanted to imagine themselves as righteous heroes, and architects of a fairer, safer world; and they wanted others to see them in this way too. More importantly, they knew that if a lasting peace were to be established, it would be essential to demonstrate to everyone that the era of indiscriminate violence and atrocity had come to an end: the new world, in which all good men and women would be free from fear, must be one governed by the rule of law.

It was with this in mind that the Allies approached the problem of what to do with German and Japanese leaders once the war was over. Many in the Allied establishment, including very senior figures like Winston Churchill, favoured simple, summary executions. But in the end it was decided that to put them on trial would send the stronger message. Dozens of military tribunals were set up across Europe and Asia, but two especially were designed to serve as beacons of justice – the first at Nuremberg and the second in Tokyo. In these two trials the very highest leaders of each regime would be put in the dock, in order that their crimes might be recorded for posterity. The idea was not only to provide the world with a symbolic example of how justice should be conducted in the future, but also to establish before the whole world the guilt of those who had planned and executed war and atrocity.

However, proceeding in this way provided the Allies with a very real dilemma. On the one hand they wanted to demonstrate their own moral rectitude: thus the defendants must be treated with dignity, given resources to mount a proper defence and be allowed a voice in court. But on the other hand it was essential that the vast majority, if not all, be found guilty. The whole world knew these men to be guilty of something, even if they did not necessarily have the terminology to describe their crimes precisely. If any were allowed to walk free because of a legal technicality, the Allies would never be able to claim that justice had been served.

A great deal of thought was therefore put into how the trials were to be conducted. Meeting in London in the summer of 1945, representatives from Britain, America, the Soviet Union and France drew up a charter describing the laws and procedures that would be used. First and foremost, they made it clear from the start that the 'only following orders' defence would not be allowed. 'There comes a point where a man must refuse to answer to his leader if he is also to answer to his conscience,' explained the British prosecutor, Sir Hartley Shawcross, in the opening stages of the Nuremberg trials. 'Even the common soldier, serving in the ranks of his army, is not called upon to obey illegal orders.'[12] Conversely, commanders were also to be held responsible for their men. Thus, if any army were allowed to run riot through a civilian population, its leaders must be held personally responsible – even if they had not themselves ordered the atrocities or even sanctioned them. This precedent was set at one of the earliest trials, in Manila, when the commander of the Japanese army in the Philippines was – controversially – found guilty for the barbaric actions of his army.[13] Finally, to ensure that as many as possible of the Nazi and Japanese military were held to account, the Allies also added a charge of conspiracy. If they could prove that a conspiracy between the leaders had taken place – to start an illegal war, or to commit atrocities – then they could each be found individually guilty of crimes that had been committed collectively. These principles, which were first formalized in 1945, have since become the bedrock of international criminal law, and remain in force to this day.

The crimes of the defendants at Nuremberg and Tokyo would fall into three broad categories. The first, and least contentious, was conventional war crimes: the murder of prisoners, the killing of hostages, the wanton destruction of cities and so on. Such acts were already established as criminal by the prewar Geneva and Hague Conventions, which formed the basis of the international law that students like Ben Ferencz had studied before and during the war.

However, the sheer scale of some of the atrocities was so unprecedented that it seemed to cry out for an entirely new category of crime. So the Allies coined the term 'crimes against humanity', which would come to be defined as any crime that involved the systematic degradation of human beings on a wide scale: mass persecution, mass slavery, mass deportation, mass murder. It was also around this time that the word 'genocide' was first used to describe the attempt to destroy entire ethnic, racial or national groups. Unfortunately, the introduction of such terms caused outrage amongst jurists everywhere. Even Allied lawyers and judges accused the authorities of making up new laws and applying them retrospectively. The US Supreme Court judge Harlan Fiske Stone went so far as to call it a 'high-grade lynching party'.[14]

But perhaps most controversial was the third 'Class A' category: 'crimes against peace'. According to the London Charter, any leader who planned, prepared or initiated an aggressive war was by definition a war criminal. In fact, starting a war without the justification of self-defence was not merely a crime: the Nuremberg Tribunal considered it 'the supreme international crime' because 'it contains within itself the accumulated evil of the whole'.[15] Needless to say, this made many in the Allied military establishment extremely nervous – not only because this new law would be applied retrospectively, but also because it called into question the concept of war as a normal part of human behaviour. From now on war, if waged without provocation, would no longer be considered noble or glorious – quite the opposite. Indeed, the international community appeared to be making steps towards banning war altogether. As one American general commented at the time, 'the US had better not lose the next war, or our generals and admirals would all be shot at sunrise'.[16]

Thus, when the Nuremberg trials began on 20 November 1945 they were already mired in controversy. During the following year twenty-one of Germany's most senior Nazis were made to explain their actions before the world. The case against them was overwhelming: millions of documents had been gathered, along with photographs and films made by Nazi camera crews, and eyewitness testimonies not only from victims but also from SS officers who frankly admitted to taking part in the mass killings. All of this was watched by the world's press, which covered the trials in close detail. In the end, eleven of the defendants were sentenced to death, seven were given prison terms

David Low's poignant cartoon of the Nuremberg verdict, 1 October 1946.

between ten years and life and three were acquitted owing to lack of evidence.

The Tokyo trials began some five months later, at the end of April 1946, and were even more controversial. Not only were the Allies accused of inventing new crimes after the fact, but they were also criticized for *whom* they were trying. Out of everyone in the Japanese establishment, the only person to have been involved in the war from start to finish was the emperor – and yet he was the one man who had been exempted from trial. The French judge was so angered by this glaring omission that he wrote a dissenting opinion after the trial, stating that since the emperor was the 'principal author' of Japan's aggressive attempt to rule the whole of Asia, all of the other defendants 'could only be considered accomplices'.[17] In the end, out of the twenty-five military and political leaders who saw the trial through, seven were condemned to death, and eighteen were given varying prison sentences.

It is easy to criticize the principles by which the war-crimes trials were conducted. The Allies were quite obviously handing out 'victor's justice', and were themselves guilty of war crimes. Churchill and his bomber chiefs had certainly been guilty of 'the wanton destruction of cities', and presidents Roosevelt and Truman were equally guilty for authorizing the fire-bombing of Tokyo and the nuclear attacks on Hiroshima and Nagasaki. These things were clearly contrary to international law even before the war began. It seemed particularly absurd that the Soviets might judge the Nazi leaders for waging aggressive war on Poland, when the Soviets themselves had attacked Poland almost simultaneously in 1939, equally without provocation.

Even the Allied prosecutors recognized the double standards by which Germany and Japan were being judged. As the American prosecutor at Nuremberg, Robert Jackson, reported to President Truman in 1945, the Allies

> have done or are doing some of the very things we are prosecuting Germans for. The French are so violating the Geneva Convention in the treatment of prisoners of war that our command is taking back prisoners sent to them. We are prosecuting plunder and our Allies are practicing it. We say aggressive war is a crime and one of our allies asserts sovereignty over the Baltic States based on no title except conquest.[18]

And yet what was the alternative? There was never any possibility that more than a few of the Nuremberg and Tokyo defendants would be acquitted. Victor's justice was the only realistic alternative to summary justice, which would not only have sent out the wrong message after the war, but would also have denied jurists the opportunity to establish some of the most important principles of international law.

For all their legal imperfections, the trials certainly fulfilled an important function. They were designed from the very beginning to be a spectacle, so that people all over the world might have the satisfaction of seeing justice done. Photographs of the defendants in the dock appeared in newspapers all over the world, alongside reports of their deeds. The trials featured on newsreels, and on radio programmes, particularly in Germany, where the Nuremberg trials were broadcast twice a day throughout 1946. The documents and films that had formed part of the evidence have been used in German schools, and across the world, ever since. While arguments still rage about their legality, they provided the world with a lasting record of some of the worst crimes in our communal history.

It is important to remember, however, that all this has come at a cost. There are infinite gradations of both guilt and innocence in the Holocaust which the trial of the leaders alone could never have addressed. The symbolic nature of the trials embedded the myths of monsters and martyrs in our global consciousness once and for all; and though this might have been necessary to create a sense of justice after the war, it came with a loss of nuance that historians have been trying to claw back ever since.

Justice After the International Military Tribunals

Benjamin Ferencz also found himself caught up in the Nuremberg trials. He had not been back in America for long when the military establishment sought him out once again. The Allies were planning to carry out a new set of trials at Nuremberg – this time prosecuting members of various professions who had abused their authority to commit atrocities. There was to be a trial of the Nazi doctors, for example, who had carried out human experiments at Auschwitz and other concentration camps. There was to be a judges' trial, a trial of German industrialists, and so on. To conduct these trials, investigators who not only knew the law, but also had experience of working in Germany, were desperately needed.

Early in 1946 Ferencz was summoned to an interview in Washington, where he was asked if he would consider going back to Europe. He was understandably reluctant to return to such a dark period of his life, but those in the War Department did whatever they could to persuade him. 'Benny,' one of them begged him, 'you've been there, you've seen it – you've got to go back.' After a lot of thought, he eventually agreed, but only on the condition that he be allowed to go as a civilian. He never wanted to be forced to follow military rules again.[19]

So it was that he found himself travelling back across the Atlantic, this time to Nuremberg and Berlin. For the rest of 1946 he immersed himself once again in the task of gathering evidence about Nazi war crimes. It was an exhausting job, which would only be made more exhausting the following year when he and his researchers discovered a huge cache of secret Gestapo files in Berlin. These files outlined in detail the actions of the SS Einsatzgruppen in eastern Europe, who had systematically rounded up Jews and other unwanted groups and shot them.

So compelling was this new cache of evidence that Ferencz believed they justified a trial of their own. But when he showed what he had found to his superiors, they hesitated. Allied prosecutors were overstretched, and political support for the trials was already beginning to wane. In desperation, and perhaps also with a spark of ambition, Ferencz suggested that he take on the extra work himself. He could construct his own trial, alongside all the other work he was already doing. And so it was that Ferencz became appointed as chief prosecutor in what the Associated Press would soon be calling 'the biggest murder trial in history'. He was still only twenty-seven years old.

Deciding how to proceed was far from simple. The scale of the crimes he had uncovered was immense, involving the murder of over a million people. It was simply impossible to try everyone who had taken part in this horrific enterprise, so he decided to concentrate all his efforts on a small sample of 'the highest ranking officers and the most educated killers we could lay our hands on'. He would indict twenty-four men, of whom twenty-two would eventually be tried.

When the Einsatzgruppen trial began on 29 September 1947, Ferencz's opening statement made it clear that this was a case with massive implications. 'Vengeance is not our goal,' he said, 'nor do we seek merely a just retribution.' What was at stake was something far greater: 'man's right to live in peace and dignity, regardless of his race or creed'. The trial, he claimed, was therefore nothing less than 'a plea of humanity to law'. The very conscience of mankind demanded that the architects of mass murder be not only found guilty but also given exemplary punishments. 'If these men be immune,' he concluded, 'then law has lost its meaning and man must live in fear.'[20]

Over the course of the next six months, Ferencz presented nearly two hundred documents showing the systematic murder of Jews across eastern Europe in sickening and overwhelming detail. When the trial finally came to an end in April 1948, the judges acknowledged that the revelation of these things was important not only for Germany but also for 'all mankind', and that 'the entire world itself is concerned with the adjudications'. All of the defendants were found guilty. Fourteen of them were sentenced to death.[21]

Ben Ferencz never quite came to terms with what he and the other prosecutors had achieved at Nuremberg. On the one hand, he knew that it was a good thing that the law had at last been followed. But on the

The Einsatzgruppen Case, September 1947, one of thirteen trials prosecuted in Nuremberg. Twenty-seven-year-old Ferencz, who fought to have the trial put on the agenda and became its chief prosecutor, is seated at the table on the left.

other hand he could not help reflecting on all those other killers – the 'lucky bastards', as he called them – who had escaped any kind of punishment at all. The Holocaust had been carried out by thousands: he had only brought a couple of dozen to justice.[22]

Furthermore, he was shocked when all but four of the death sentences handed down in his trial were commuted by the military governor of Germany, John J. McCloy. He knew that justice must be tempered with mercy, but it seemed to him that this decision 'showed more mercy than justice'. Years later, despite his lifelong commitment to upholding the values of the law in all circumstances, he confessed to asking himself if summary justice might not have been a better solution after all. 'Being a lawman, I couldn't accept it, but I often wondered . . .'[23]

Ben Ferencz's disappointment at the results of the Nuremberg trials was shared by many. The trials were supposed to have been the focal point of something much greater – a wholesale purge not just of war criminals but of Nazis and Fascists in general, all across Europe. But in the end this never really happened. Not only did the war-crimes trials grad-ually grind to a halt at the end of the 1940s, but also the de-Nazification process as a whole. As the passions of the war faded, and the demands of a new Cold War began to take over, the will to carry on prosecuting people slowly ebbed away.

At the end of the war, there had been 8 million registered members of the Nazi Party in Germany. Out of all the Allies, it was the Americans who were the most determined to pursue them and their helpers. In the American zone alone they screened over 13 million Germans, and found 3.4 million people who seemed to have some kind of case to answer. But not even the Americans had the resources to try this many: in the end over 70 per cent of them were granted amnesties before they even went to trial.[24] The other major Allies were far less zealous. Of the 207,259 people tried for specifically Nazi or militaristic activities after the war, less than 10 per cent were tried by the Soviets, 8 per cent by the French and only 1 per cent by the British.[25] In the end, nobody was impressed with the results.

Throughout western Europe the story was broadly the same: as the war receded into the past, war criminals were treated more leniently, traitors were more easily excused, collaborators were allowed to return to their old jobs. Italy provides a stark example. In contrast to the 15,000 or 20,000 Fascists who were executed by partisans in the last days of the war, the Italian courts only managed to hand out ninety-two death sen-tences. Even those who went to jail did not do so for very long: in 1946 almost all jail sentences for collaborators were cancelled under a general amnesty. In Belgium 2,940 death sentences were handed out, but all except 242 were commuted, while the courts in Austria produced only forty-three death sentences, of which only thirty were carried out.[26] Justice was sometimes harsher in eastern Europe, but in countries like Romania and Hungary accusations of collaboration and fascism were also used by the Communists as a method of removing their political enemies. Real collaborators and real Fascists were often rehabilitated, absolved and allowed back into their old jobs.[27]

This phenomenon was even more pronounced in Japan. Unfortu-nately, the Tokyo trials turned out to be little more than a symbolic gesture. Not only was Emperor Hirohito given immunity from prosecution but also around a hundred other 'Class A' war-crimes sus-pects arrested in 1945 were all eventually released without trial.[28] In the final count, only around 5,700 Japanese were ever indicted for war crimes in tribunals around Asia, of which only 984 were condemned to death and 475 given life sentences. The rest were either given more minor sentences (2,946), acquitted (1,027) or released without trial (279).[29] Within Japan itself the purge that was supposed to rid society of Fascists and warmongers, though sincere at first, was rapidly reversed in the late 1940s.[30]

In the rest of Asia, meanwhile, the whole concept of 'collaboration' with the Japanese was quietly ignored. From a nationalist point of view, how was collaborating with the Japanese any different from collaborating with the British or the French or the Dutch? In a region that was struggling to free itself from centuries of colonial rule, collaboration with the Japanese could even be painted as something heroic. In India, for example, when the British tried to charge a handful of Indian collaborators with treason, it caused such outrage that they were eventually forced to drop all future trials, not only in India but also in neighbouring Burma. It made no difference that some of these men committed violent atrocities: in its enthusiasm for independence, Indian public opinion was willing to regard them as heroes rather than monsters.[31]

There were many reasons why the pursuit of justice was gradually abandoned in the postwar years. To begin with, it was costly, and in a world that was struggling to feed and house its people there were plenty of other things that politicians preferred to spend money on. Consequently, apart from in Communist countries, of all the categories of people who were tried after the war businessmen seem to have been let off most lightly. If the economies of Asia and western Europe were to get back on their feet, it made no sense to pursue these people, no matter how guilty some of them undoubtedly were.

Secondly, the trials were politically divisive. Many parts of Europe and Asia hovered on the brink of civil war in the late 1940s. Tensions between different ethnic or political groups were so strong that many nations found themselves embroiled in violence all over again: Greece, Poland, Ukraine, the Baltic States, Algeria and Malaya are just a handful of examples, but low-level violence left over from the war continued almost everywhere. For the sake of social cohesion, many nations made a deliberate and conscious decision to stop pursuing collaborators and war criminals and tell themselves that justice had been served. It was safer simply to draw a line under the matter.

But above all, it was the needs of the Cold War that brought an end to the trials. By 1948 the West had a new enemy in the form of communism. If defeating the Communists meant rehabilitating former Fascists and collaborators, then that was deemed a price worth paying. In the Communist East, meanwhile, a subtle rebranding of the term 'fascism' took place so that it also began to include capitalists and businessmen and Western politicians, so leaving the door open for *actual* Fascists to change their allegiances and join the Communist Party.

Thus was the flame of justice eventually snuffed out by the sheer weight of the political and economic issues pressing down upon it. The question of war guilt was never properly laid to rest: it was merely buried. It has lurked deep within our collective subconscious ever since, only surfacing occasionally in our myths about Second World War monsters and martyrs.

The Quest for World Criminal Law

This new, Cold War cynicism was not immediately apparent at a global level. In the United Nations, on the surface at least, there appeared to be widespread support for a new vision of the world in which the pursuit of aggressive war would be proscribed, and those who transgressed would be pursued by the courts. Not only did the United Nations Charter promise to 'save succeeding generations from the scourge of war', but in 1948 the UN also drew up the Universal Declaration of Human Rights. This proclaimed for the first time the 'inalienable rights of all members of the human family', regardless of race, colour, sex, class, politics, religion, language, nationality, or any other distinction of any kind. It was adopted almost unanimously (although a few nations, mostly Communist ones, abstained) and has since formed the basis for human rights legislation all over the world. At the same time, the UN also drew up a Genocide Convention, which outlawed any kind of attempt to destroy national, racial or religious groups. This was immediately signed by forty-one countries, and has since been ratified by 147 in total.[32] The horrors of the war had been so shocking that the nations of the world appeared united in their wish to condemn them.

Unfortunately, however, condemnation was often where they stopped. It was all very well making a declaration about human rights, but who was going to enforce it? The very term 'human rights' implied that those who violated them would be tried and punished by a court that represented all mankind. But once the Nuremberg and Tokyo tribunals were finished, no such court existed. Various plans were drawn up to create one, but whatever urgency there was regarding this issue at the end of the war soon dissolved. The stumbling block was, once again, the problem of national sovereignty. Few nations were willing to allow their own citizens to be tried by outsiders. And even fewer were willing to lay themselves open to potential condemnation by their rivals – especially the two superpowers, who each feared that the other would use such a court merely to embarrass them. As a consequence, the world was left with the absurd system whereby the only authorities capable of safeguarding human rights were national governments, even in cases where those same national governments were responsible for abusing their people's rights in the first place.

Similar problems arose when it came to outlawing 'wars of aggression'. In theory, everyone was willing to agree that this was a crime. But how exactly did one define 'aggression'? The United Nations spent almost thirty years trying to do exactly that. Some people argued that whoever fired the first shots was always the aggressor. Others argued that there were lots of scenarios that might justify firing the first shots – when coming to the aid of an ally, for example, or when pre-empting someone else's attack. Still others argued about whether 'aggression' was necessarily military – was not the economic attack on a country, through blockades or sanctions or unfair trade deals, also a form of aggression? Arguments like these went back and forth in the United Nations for decades before the General Assembly finally produced a definition in 1974 – but, even then, what they came up with was so broad as to be virtually pointless. An 'act of aggression', stated General Assembly Resolution 3314, could be a military invasion, bombardment or blockade, or a variety of other acts – but in the final analysis, it would be up to the Security Council to decide if an act of aggression had in fact taken place.

As the final arbiter of what was and wasn't aggression, what was and wasn't war, and what did or didn't require action, the UN Security Council remained the supreme body in all international relations. But the Security Council was so riven with internal fractures, and so paralysed by its need for unanimity amongst the five permanent members, that it was often completely incapable of doing anything to prevent continued atrocities, genocides and crimes against peace throughout the world.

Ben Ferencz watched this lack of progress from the sidelines. After the Nuremberg trials finally wound themselves up at the end of the 1940s he spent the next thirty years trying to get restitution for people whose lives and livelihoods had been destroyed by the Nazis. He stayed on in Germany for a few years before returning to the United States, where he continued to fight cases on behalf of those affected by the war. Despite his many successes, however, he could not help feeling that something was missing. In those terrible and hopeful days at Nuremberg he had dreamed not only of punishment for the perpetrators and restitution for the victims, but also of building 'a world free of Holocausts'. What use was restitution when war and atrocity continued all around the world unchallenged?

So in 1970 he gave up his practice and decided 'to devote the rest of my life to the quest for world peace'. He started attending meetings and conferences at the United Nations, and studying the intricacies of international law. He began lobbying diplomats and writing articles criticizing how slowly the UN was moving. Most importantly, he also began campaigning for the institution of an International Criminal Court, in the hope that the legacy of Nuremberg might somehow be revived.

His campaign would last for the next twenty years, during which time he found many allies amongst the international legal community. But their collective efforts foundered again and again. The various UN committees devoted to problems of world peace appeared, in Ferencz's understanding, to be little more than exercises in frustration: 'They talk, they talk, they talk, and they crawl forward out of the slime slowly.' Meanwhile, the Cold War superpowers rarely gave any ground, almost as a matter of principle. Ferencz was particularly disgusted by the behaviour of his own government, which he believed had a responsibility to set an example to the rest of the world. 'It took the United States forty years to ratify the Genocide Convention, which *we* sponsored,' he once explained to a UN audience, angrily. 'Forty years!'[33]

It was not until the Cold War had come to an end, and two new genocides had occurred in Yugoslavia and Rwanda in the 1990s, that the international community finally stirred itself into action. An ad hoc tribunal was created, much like the Nuremberg and Tokyo tribunals, and discussions opened up once again about the possibility of creating a permanent International Criminal Court. Within just a few years, these discussions finally bore fruit. The International Criminal Court finally came into being on 1 July 2002, some fifty-seven years after the Second World War had first highlighted the world's need for such an institution.

For Ferencz, this was something of a hollow victory. 'A court coming after the event is a confession of failure,' he later said. 'The idea is to prevent the crime, not to allow it to happen and then hold some people accountable.' It also saddened him that many of the United Nations' most powerful member states, including China, India, Israel and the US, still refused to accept the authority of this court. Nevertheless, he refused to be disheartened. The international system of law, he claimed, was still in its infancy, and we should not be surprised if things move slowly. 'We are seeing here prototypes – a process which has never existed in human history.' If it did not look very impressive yet, this would come with time. The most important thing was that 'we have started to *move*'.

The Second World War, and the Nuremberg trials that followed it, changed Ben Ferencz's life for ever. It was in these years that he first understood the true value of the law, and the role that war played in undermining that law, degrading the human spirit, negating human rights. 'I learned that there never has been, and never will be, a war without atrocities. The only way to prevent such cruel crimes was to prevent war itself.'

At the time of writing, he was still campaigning for practical ways to heal the wounds of 1945, and promoting a future where the crime of international aggression might at last be curtailed by the power of universal law.

As Ben Ferencz's story shows, one of the greatest legacies of the Second World War was a universal and lasting desire to curtail some of mankind's worst instincts, and to create a system that would promote harmony and unity amongst mankind. It is largely because of the war that we have some of our most important global institutions – the World Bank, the International Monetary Fund, the International Criminal Court, the United Nations itself. For all their failings, these institutions represent an ideal: if there was any benefit to the war at all, then this was surely it, that it created the desire and the will to change things.

But just like all other visions of Utopia that emerged in 1945, the idea of 'One World' ended up being just a dream. One of the great ironies of 1945 was that, at the same time as creating the desire for unity, the legacy of the war also created obstacles that would ensure such unity would remain forever impossible. Traumatized peoples were not ready to forgive one another for the wounds that had been inflicted upon them. Nations were unwilling to give up sovereignty to any higher authority when they had fought so hard to secure that sovereignty in the first place. But more than anything else, it would be the rivalry between the two superpowers, both of them born out of the ashes of the Second World War, that would frame international relations for most of the rest of the century.

PART IV

Two Superpowers

13. USA

Cord Meyer was a model American. When the USA went to war, so did Meyer, who hurried to finish his university degree early so that he could enlist in the Marine Corps. Meyer was young, intelligent, full of enthusiasm and keen to devote himself to a cause. America, he believed, had a responsibility to fight against fascism, and it was only right that American troops were taking their place at the forefront of the conflict. On the day that he headed off to war, he wrote in his journal about the feelings that gripped him: 'It seemed that we, the young and the strong, were going out as the champions and defenders of the people in the fields and everywhere in this wide country to fight for our heritage against the inhuman invader.' In his heart he knew that such feelings were not entirely real, that they were merely the expression of a timeless ideal, but still he could not help himself from being carried along by them.[1]

It was not long before the violent realities of war caught up with him. In July 1944, during the battle for Guam, Meyer was sheltering in a foxhole when a Japanese hand grenade landed beside him. The explosion blew out his left eye, and wounded him so severely that the battalion doctor listed him as 'killed in action'. Unfortunately a telegram to this effect was sent out to his distraught parents, who only learned several days later that their son had in fact been saved by a timely blood transfusion. Meyer was loaded onto a hospital ship and returned across the Pacific to America, where he was awarded the Purple Heart and Bronze Star and fitted with a glass eye. So ended Meyer's first adventure in the service of a higher cause. He was twenty-four years old.

At the end of the war, Meyer was invited to join the US delegation to the United Nations Conference at San Francisco. The official delegate, Harold Stassen, thought it would look good to have a decorated war veteran on his team; so Meyer grabbed the chance with both hands. San Francisco, he believed, was a unique opportunity to create 'a peaceful world order . . . from the ruins of the war', and he was eager to play whatever part he could in this historic undertaking. But it did not take long before disillusionment set in:

'Sick of destruction, suffering and death, I watched with growing concern as the structure of the United Nations began to take shape. There was much high-flown oratory concerning the need for peace . . . But it soon became evident that neither the United States nor the Soviet Union was willing to make that real sacrifice of proud national independence and power without which peace could only be a brief armed truce before another world conflict. The victory won at such cost on the battlefield was squandered at the conference table . . . I left San Francisco with the conviction that World War III was inevitable, if the U. N. was not substantially strengthened in the near future.'[2]

It was these concerns that reawakened Meyer's sense of mission. If the United Nations was not fit for purpose, he would campaign for it to be bolstered. And so Meyer devoted himself once again to a cause – this time 'to build a more just and peaceful world'.[3] He started to write articles on the shortcomings of the UN, and how it could be strengthened. He joined the movement for world government, and founded one of its most important organizations, the United World Federalists. For the next two years he toured the United States tirelessly, lobbying, fundraising and lecturing on the dangers of a new arms race with the Soviet Union.

Meyer's greatest fear during this time was the destructive power of the atom bomb, which he imagined reducing the world to a new Dark Age. He believed passionately that, as the only nation to possess the bomb, America had a duty to lead the world away from the possibility of a new catastrophe. 'Those who have the power have also the responsibility,' he wrote. America must wholeheartedly endorse the principle of world government 'in good faith and without the threat of coercion'. Only then might the Soviet Union be inspired to respond in kind.[4]

Once again, Meyer was destined to be disappointed. No matter how much passion and energy he poured into his argument, it became increasingly obvious that the US government was never going to embrace his crusade, and neither were the American people. The Soviet Union did not seem to show any signs of endorsing it either: indeed, Meyer himself had been personally attacked in the Soviet media for being 'the fig leaf of American imperialism'.[5] By the autumn of 1949 he was beginning to suffer a crisis of confidence. He felt 'barren' and 'sterile', and had begun to doubt the 'inhuman fanaticism' of his own arguments. 'My repetitive warnings of approaching nuclear doom echoed hollowly in my head, and I came to dislike the sound of my own

A young Cord Meyer visits Albert Einstein in 1948 to discuss the USSR's attitude towards world federalism.

voice as I promised a federalist salvation in which I no longer had real confidence.' Disillusioned, burnt out, he resigned as president of the United World Federalists and withdrew from public life.[6]

Over the next eighteen months, his mood changed once again. He spent his time mulling over the darkening relations between America and the Soviet Union, and considering the nature of Stalinist communism. He had had some experience with Communists, who had tried to infiltrate and subvert the American Veterans Committee – another of Meyer's causes – and he had acquired an uneasy appreciation of how determined they could be. By the early 1950s he was convinced that it was communism, rather than 'proud national independence', that now posed the greatest threat to world peace. With a hint of bitterness he claimed that, in hindsight, it had never mattered how much 'good faith' America displayed: the Communist leadership would stop at nothing until they dominated the rest of the world. And so, in 1951, he took the decision to 'enlist' in a brand-new crusade: he joined the CIA, and devoted himself to the fight against communism. Unlike the other causes that had inspired him, this one was destined to last the rest of his professional life.[7]

In decades to come, Meyer's conversion from one-world peacenik to committed cold warrior would be characterized by some as a betrayal of his original liberal values: 'He got cold warized,' said one former friend.[8] Meyer himself preferred to think of it as a journey from idealism to realism. He never gave up on his hopes for world peace, or his dream of a genuine, democratic system of international cooperation. But his first priority was the protection of America, and by extension the rest of the world, from the threat of Soviet communism. 'I came only gradually and reluctantly to the conclusion that Americans faced a formidable adversary in the Soviet Union,' he wrote almost twenty years after first joining the CIA. 'What I know now I didn't know to begin with. I had to learn it the hard way.'[9]

American Dreams and Soviet Betrayals

There has always been a utopian streak in American society. The nation that was born in the idealism of the Pilgrim Fathers, that was founded on the truth that all men are created equal, that throughout its history has characterized itself as a 'new world' of liberty, of aspiration and of justice, went to war in 1941 not for economic or territorial gain, but to uphold a dream. America was the land of the free. So when the Japanese bombed Pearl Harbor, in the American mind they attacked not only a nation, but freedom itself.

In the two decades before this 'day of infamy', American foreign policy had been dominated by the illusion that America could pursue its dreams of liberty and happiness in isolation, unencumbered by foreign entanglements; but the coming of war demolished this belief so completely that it has never since been restored. Even former isolationists like Republican Senator Arthur Vandenberg were driven to the conclusion that American liberty could never really be safe while tyranny and injustice were allowed to flourish in other parts of the world. 'Pearl Harbor,' said Vandenberg after the war, 'drove most of us to the conclusion that world peace is indivisible.'[10] When America took up arms, therefore, it did so with the intention of carrying the gift of liberty to all corners of the globe. Roosevelt's four freedoms – freedom of speech, freedom of worship, freedom from want and freedom from fear – were not merely a mantra: they would become a manifesto, enshrined first in the Atlantic Charter and later in the charter of the United Nations itself.

By 1945, when the war was won and America was flushed with victory, this utopian dream seemed, for a moment at least, almost achievable. America stood at the 'summit of the world', with the 'greatest strength and the greatest power which man has ever reached'.[11] All of its enemies lay defeated, and its allies had come together, under American leadership, to create a series of world institutions whose stated purpose was to eradicate war through the promotion of civil rights, human rights, economic reform and democratic freedom.

In the dying days of the war many Americans still hoped and believed that the USSR, with the help of the new international institutions, would also embrace these ideals. Cord Meyer was not alone in his conviction that the Soviets would inevitably see the value of this American dream, if only they were treated with tolerance and understanding. Much of the press were so used to praising 'our gallant allies' that they did not take kindly to diplomats who expressed doubts about the Soviets.[12] Most politicians, whether Republican or Democrat, were similarly willing to give the USSR the benefit of the doubt. 'We do not need to fear Russia,' Wendell Willkie had told America during the war. 'We need to learn to work with her.'[13] The Secretary of War, Henry Stimson, went so far as to advocate the sharing of atomic secrets with the Soviets. 'The chief lesson I have learned in a long life,' he wrote to Truman in September 1945, 'is that the only way you can make a man trustworthy is to trust him.'[14] There is a measure of idealism in such words, and of naivety, but also a touch of arrogance. Men like Meyer and Stimson simply assumed that other nations must want the same things as America, and were genuinely surprised – and upset – when this turned out not to be the case.

Unfortunately, the Soviets did little to inspire trust. By the time the war ended they had already won a reputation for being extremely difficult to work with. Their foreign minister, Vyacheslav Molotov, was known as 'Stone Arse' by his fellow Soviets because of his dogged ability to sit for hours at the conference table without budging; while his subordinate, Andrei Gromyko, would soon be characterized in the American press as 'Mr Nyet'.[15] American officials in Vienna and Berlin found it almost impossible to come to any kind of understanding with their Soviet counterparts, and marvelled at their ability to 'find technical reasons at will to justify the violation of understandings'.[16]

Despite all their wealth, their military might, their atomic supremacy and their political dominance, it was difficult for America not to appear strangely powerless in the face of such intransigence. After the Big Three conference at Yalta, for example, rumours spread in Washington that 'President Roosevelt had given in to Stalin on almost every issue' – a rumour that his aides strenuously denied.[17] At the Bretton Woods conference, where the Soviets openly pursued a policy of 'contracting into all benefits but out of all duties and obligations', delegates from all over the world were incensed at the way that the British and Americans repeatedly backed down whenever the Soviets dug their heels in. One of them, the Belgian delegate Georges Theunis, could not help himself from shouting at British economists: 'It's a disgrace. The Americans give way to the Russians every time. And you too, you British, are just as bad. You are on your knees to them. You wait. You'll see what a harvest you'll reap.'[18]

The first American officials to appreciate what kind of threat the Soviets posed to the world were the diplomats who staffed American embassies in Russia and eastern Europe. According to the American ambassador in Poland, Arthur Bliss Lane, the Soviets never intended to keep the promises they made at Yalta and Potsdam to hold 'free and unfettered elections' in the country: his communiqués home from Warsaw are full of references to 'fictitious elections', 'terroristic activities' and 'Soviet acts against freedom of speech and other human liberties'.[19] The American ambassador to Moscow, Averell Harriman, was even more blunt. 'Stalin is breaking his agreements,' he warned the president during a trip home to Washington in April 1945. He even went so far as to predict a new 'barbarian invasion' of Europe.[20]

Assessments by diplomats in other parts of eastern Europe were broadly similar. In Romania, British and American members of the Allied Control Commission complained that they were 'penned up with a closeness approaching internment', while the Soviets directly involved themselves in breaking up the Romanian government and replacing it with Communist puppets.[21] In Bulgaria, American diplomats complained of being 'powerless' to stop the Soviet-backed terror; they had no voice, were denied any meaningful access to information, and had to stand aside while a Soviet-backed state police was used to 'terrorize and control the population'.[22] Meanwhile the Czech foreign minister, Jan Masaryk, admitted to his American counterparts that he was close to despair over the way the Soviets constantly bullied him into submission: 'You can be on your knees and this is not enough for the Russians.'[23]

Barely a day seemed to go by without new stories of civil rights and human rights violations by the Soviets: the rape of millions of German women by the Red Army, the wholesale looting of eastern European property, the formation of secret police forces, the persecution of Catholic priests, the intimidation of opposition politicians, the execution of former Resistance leaders, the mass deportation of civilians – all of these subjects were commented on repeatedly by horrified American officials, and covered increasingly in the American press.

It was soon obvious that anyone who stood up for freedom and democracy in eastern Europe was a target. The leader of the Bulgarian opposition, Nikola Petkov, was arrested on trumped up charges and executed. The leader of the Polish opposition, Stanisław Mikołajczyk, eventually fled in fear of his life; as did the prime minister of Hungary, Ferenc Nagy; and the prime minister of Romania, Nicolae Rădescu. Jan Masaryk's career came to an abrupt end in 1948 when he mysteriously 'fell' from a window in the Czech Foreign Ministry. These were the kinds of events that ordinary Americans believed they had brought to an end in Europe. The idea that they were happening all over again was intolerable.

But by far the most disturbing idea was that Soviet influence, and indeed Soviet subversion, had begun to destabilize the USA itself. In 1945 came the first of a series of spy scandals that would rock North America. When a cipher clerk named Igor Gouzenko defected from the Soviet embassy in Ottawa, he revealed the names of no fewer than twenty Canadians and three Britons who had been spying for the USSR, many of them government employees. Rumours soon began to circulate of similar spy rings within the US establishment, some of which would turn out to be all too true. In July 1948, a former Soviet go-between named

Elizabeth Bentley appeared before the House Un-American Activities Committee and publicly named thirty-two people as spies. The names included several from the Roosevelt administration, including the man who had masterminded the Bretton Woods conference on the new international economy – Harry Dexter White. Shortly afterwards, a former Communist called Whittaker Chambers revealed several other highly placed Soviet spies – including Alger Hiss, who had played a leading role in both the setting up of the United Nations and the Big Three conference at Yalta. More scandals followed. In 1950, Julius and Ethel Rosenberg were indicted for stealing atomic secrets and passing them to the Soviets. For a while it seemed as though there were spies everywhere.

For the vast majority of Americans, especially those like Cord Meyer who had always wanted to believe the best about the Soviets, this was one betrayal too far. As Meyer asked himself after the Alger Hiss trial, 'Where did suspicion end?'[24] Others resorted to calling the Soviets names: 'Russians are Colossal Liars, Swindlers' ran the headline to a full-page advert in the *New York Herald Tribune*.[25] Bill Mauldin, whose wartime cartoons in *Stars and Stripes* had symbolized the opinions and thoughts of millions of ordinary American soldiers, summed up the pervading sense of bitterness. 'I thought maybe they just didn't understand how we feel,' he told an interviewer, years later. 'If you've been an ally with somebody in war, you feel very strongly toward them. The Russians had this immense reservoir of goodwill in this country. But they weren't interested in being a friend. They just wanted to kick the crap out of us any way they could.'[26]

This sense of betrayal would remain for the rest of the century, and into the next. Even historians have sometimes felt compelled to comment on it. 'Never did one country steal so many political, diplomatic, scientific, and military secrets from another,' wrote one American historian in 2003. 'It was analogous, in espionage terms, to the looting of European artworks by the Nazis. Except that in the friendly, cooperative spirit of the times, we invited them in.'[27]

The American Reaction

As these events unfolded, Americans were forced to begin asking themselves some uncomfortable questions. If America was the most powerful nation on earth, why did it seem so impotent in the face of Soviet provocations? And more importantly, why did it seem unable to stop the steady march of communism? In the years immediately following the Second World War a swathe of eastern and central European countries fell to Communist rule. In China, too, a civil war eventually led to the victory of Mao Zedong's Red Army, so that by the end of 1949 a fifth of the world's population were living under Communist governments – more than half a billion people in total.[28] What use was all of America's power and wealth if it could not save the world from what it could only see as oppression and tyranny? And what use was its monopoly of the atom bomb if it could not use the threat of that weapon to further its aims?

None of this squared with America's heroic view of itself after the Second World War, or with what one political scientist of the time called 'the illusion of American omnipotence'.[29] Rather than come to terms with the disappointing reality that even the USA's power was limited, many preferred to believe that the frustration of American hopes and ambitions had been caused by some kind of government ineptitude – or worse, a stab in the back. They began to imagine that the various spy scandals were merely the symptom of something much deeper – the corruption of American society from within. This was particularly the case with the Republicans, who used the issue as a stick to beat their Democratic rivals. In the congressional elections at the end of 1946 the Republicans accused the Democrats of allowing 'the infiltration of alien-minded radicals' into government, of ignoring 'the imminent danger of Communism' and of failing to rid the labour unions of Reds. One Republican candidate in Indiana went so far as to claim that 70,000 known Communists were on the government payroll – an absurd suggestion that would be echoed by Senator Joe McCarthy's similar but more infamous allegations four years later.[30]

And yet this idea also brought America face to face with some difficult issues. If the nation was indeed riddled with Communists, then why was this so? Was the American dream not enough? Why would any true American wish to betray his country for the sake of a totalitarian state that was so nakedly opposed to American values?

Such questions hint at a set of problems that had plagued American society throughout the 1930s, and which re-emerged, along with some brand-new ones, once the war was over. Most historians of the Cold

War are so focused on the international situation in the aftermath of the war that they forget to look at what was going on within the confines of the USA. America might 'bestride the world like a colossus', as one commentator in *Nation* put it, but ordinary Americans did not feel very powerful.[31] In fact, America in 1945 and 1946 was a society under enormous strain. The demobilization of millions of men from the armed forces, the mass dismissal of women from the workplace, the conversion of the economy from a wartime to a peacetime footing – all of these things created tensions that were difficult to contain. In addition, the political rivalries that had been held in abeyance during the war were also beginning to re-emerge.

Americans had been promised a golden age of prosperity and harmony once the war was over. Instead they got continued rationing, growing inflation and housing shortages. In the autumn of 1945, tens of thousands of women queued outside clothing stores to buy nylons, and then rioted when the stores ran out. At the same time, industrial action threatened nearly every major industry: in 1946 a record 4.6 million workers engaged in nearly 5,000 strikes. Divorce rates soared in the year after the war, particularly amongst returning GIs and their brides, as did rates of venereal disease (two facts that were not always entirely unrelated). Black GIs came out of the army determined to fight against segregation, beginning a struggle that would eventually bring civil rights to the heart of American politics. Without the uniting force of the war to hold society together, many of the old divisions began to open up all over again – between workers and bosses, rich and poor, black and white, men and women, the middle class and the working class, not to mention the return of age-old tensions between hyphenated Americans of every ethnic background.[32]

One of the many ingredients in this cocktail of national frustrations was indeed an increase in Communist activities. By the end of the war the American Communist Party had 63,000 members; and within the Congress of Industrial Organizations, Communists controlled unions with a total membership of 1.37 million.[33] For those who were willing to look, there were people with links to communism in just about every area of public life, including the media, education, industry and even in government. As Cord Meyer and others testified, this was certainly a problem, and some of the methods employed by American Communists could be quite ruthless. But it was only ever a small problem. Even at the time there were plenty of Americans who realized that focusing on this issue to the exclusion of all others was simply an excuse to avoid looking at some of the other deep divisions in American society.[34]

Communism was indeed what just about everyone focused on – not just seasoned Red-baiters like Republican ex-Congressman Hamilton Fish and the head of the FBI, J. Edgar Hoover, but figures from every sphere of public life. This included politicians from both houses and both parties; it included military leaders like George Marshall and Admiral Leahy, business leaders like Francis P. Matthews of the US Chamber of Commerce, and even union leaders like George Meany and William Green of the American Federation of Labor. The Protestant theologian Reinhold Niebuhr denounced communism in his writings, the Catholic radio show host Fulton J. Sheen denounced communism on the air waves, and the American Jewish Committee launched a massive campaign to purge Communists from Jewish groups of every kind.[35] Even President Truman felt compelled to speak out publicly against communism, despite admitting in private that he thought the whole issue a mere 'bugaboo'.[36] Meanwhile the press not only commented on public paranoia, but stoked it with everything they had. The Randolph Hearst-owned press led the way, with headlines like 'Red Tidal Wave Menaces Christian Civilization', which appeared just days after the war in Europe was over.[37] By the late 1940s, the headlines had become more specific and more sinister: 'Red Fascism in the United States Today', 'Communists Penetrate Wall Street' and even 'The Reds Are After Your Child'.[38]

One of the striking things about the language that was routinely used to describe the Communist threat, both at home and abroad, was its similarity to the language that had previously been used to describe the Nazi threat. 'Red Fascism' was a phrase regularly used by newspapers, politicians and the FBI, as though the ideologies of Stalin and Hitler were interchangeable. In the same way, Nazism and communism were often conflated into the single term 'totalitarianism' – a conflation that is still regularly made today.[39] Stalin was sometimes called 'the Russian Hitler', and politicians spoke of the dangers of 'appeasing' him, just as the British had tried to appease Hitler in 1938: 'Remember Munich!' H. V. Kaltenborn warned his radio listeners in March 1946.[40] Communist propaganda was compared to Goebbels's propaganda; Soviet gulags were compared to Nazi concentration camps; the NKVD were compared to the Gestapo. According to the American ambassador to Poland, Arthur Bliss Lane, 'the same terror of a knock at the door in the dead of night exists today as it did during the Nazi occupation'. Such suppression and terror, he told a radio audience in 1947, were just as horrible 'whether they are permitted under the emblem of the Swastika or under the emblem of the Hammer and Sickle'.[41] One future US congressman even compared Marx's *Communist Manifesto* to *Mein Kampf.*[42] The comparison between the Soviets and the Nazis was made everywhere, by everyone, even the president. 'There isn't any difference between the totalitarian Russian government and the Hitler government,' Truman told a news conference in March 1950. 'They are all alike. They are police state governments.'[43]

Thus, fear of the Soviets was dressed up in the clothes of the conflict that America had only recently left behind, and the American people were encouraged to believe that they were running a replay of the 1930s all over again. In some ways, fear of the Soviets was not really about the Soviets at all, but a manifestation of something slightly deeper – an anxiety not to repeat the mistakes of the past that had led to war. It is this anxiety that has itself been repeated, as if in a loop, in the invocations of Hitler that have accompanied almost every subsequent American conflict from Korea to 9/11.

McCarthyism

The consequences of this atmosphere of fear and paranoia would be profound, both domestically and internationally. In March 1947, in an attempt to silence those who thought him soft on communism, President Truman issued an executive order declaring that all civilian government employees would be obliged to undergo a loyalty investigation. Out of all the many anti-Communist measures that would be launched during this time – the restrictions on trade union power embodied in the Taft-Hartley Act, the Hollywood blacklists, the prosecution of Communist leaders under the Smith Act, to name but a few – Truman's loyalty programme would be by far the most pervasive. Over the next nine years more than 5 million civil servants would be screened, and more than 25,000 subjected to a full FBI field investigation. None of these investigations turned up a single spy, although they

"Fire!"

Fear trumps freedom: a hysterical America attempts to extinguish the flame of liberty during the 'Red Scare' in 1949.

did lead to 12,000 resignations and about 2,700 dismissals, causing a great deal of misery along the way. It was perhaps the greatest assault on privacy and civil liberty in American history.[44]

Cord Meyer found himself on the receiving end of a full-blown loyalty investigation shortly after he joined the CIA, and later described how upsetting the process was. He had been accused of consorting with known Communists, associating himself with Communist-front organizations and expressing anti-American views. Typical of the charges against him was that an FBI agent had once overheard some suspected

Communists wondering aloud about whether they might be able to convince Meyer to join them. Despite his indignation, Meyer had to treat
such hearsay with the utmost seriousness. From the beginning, the onus
was on him to prove his innocence. He was never allowed to know who
had accused him. He was not even allowed to be present at his trial.

Meyer was suspended from work for three months without pay, during which time he was obliged to write a detailed autobiography
justifying his upbringing, his education and his political beliefs, and
back it all up with documentation. He lost sleep, he lost a good deal of
money, but worst of all he lost friends: several people he had known and
liked deliberately shunned him, afraid that they might be tarred with
the same brush. 'In the poisonous atmosphere of those times, it took
genuine courage to associate with someone suspected of being a security risk.'[45]

In the end Meyer was lucky – he was not only exonerated but also
investigated only once. There were many other government employees,
particularly those with more leftist views, who found themselves scru-
tinized repeatedly by the FBI, by government loyalty boards, by the
House Un-American Activities Committee and by Senator McCarthy's
Permanent Subcommittee on Investigations.[46] Perhaps the worst ordeal
was to be dragged before the TV cameras to be interrogated by
McCarthy – a spectacle that seared itself so deeply into the American
consciousness that the brutal badgering of suspected Communists has
ever since been known as 'McCarthyism'. Meyer often wondered why
he himself had been spared this indignity, and came to the conclusion
that he had probably been saved by his Purple Heart and Bronze Star.
McCarthy, like any bully, 'didn't want to confront a Marine officer who
had seen more action than he had'.[47]

It is impossible to assess the damage done to the lives of the tens of thousands of individuals who, like Meyer, were subjected to such processes.
Many were so traumatized by the way their personal lives had been raked
over that they were reluctant ever to put their true feelings on paper again,
but those who did described their ordeal as 'exhausting', 'soul-searing' or
even 'hell'.[48] One African-American lawyer who was denied government
work described how the investigation process affected her:

> One feels frightened, insecure, exposed. One thinks of all the personal
> errors, the deep secrets of one's life, unrelated to political activities. One is

apprehensive that all the details of one's intimate life will be spread on the record to be read, sifted, weighed, evaluated, and judged by strangers.[49]

Those on the left have argued that this was all a good excuse for the Republicans to impose conservative values upon a generation. The true cost, they assert, was measured not in people traumatized and careers destroyed, but 'in assumptions unchallenged, in questions unasked, in problems ignored for a decade'. The campaign against communism silenced the voice of the American left for a generation. Liberals were forced to follow a more conservative line or immediately bring themselves under suspicion: indeed, in many people's minds terms such as 'socialist' or 'liberal' soon became synonymous with 'Communist'. Questions of class and of race were sidelined before the all-encompassing Red threat, as were questions of women's roles in society. For the whole of the 1950s and early 1960s, almost anyone who stepped outside their traditional roles in society automatically opened themselves up to charges of dangerous radicalism.[50]

In reality, however, the way these measures were carried out did not always suit Republicans either. While some cited the need to ensure America's security against the threat of world communism as justification, the spectacle of governments meddling in the private lives of individuals, and dictating to them how to live, did not sit well with a Republican belief in individual freedom. Republicans are quick to point out that some of the most repressive aspects of the Red Scare, such as the loyalty programme, were instigated by Democrats.

Regardless of whom one sides with, the rightward shift in values that occurred during this time represented a major change in American society that would affect its outlook on the world for at least the next twenty years.

The Truman Doctrine

The second great change inspired by the threat of communism occurred on an international level. Far from being a hotbed of spies, the US State Department was often at the forefront of the American fight against communism. As early as 1946 there was hardly an official left in the State Department who had anything good to say about the USSR.[51]

The prevailing mood was summed up by one of the diplomats at the US embassy in Moscow, whose message to Washington in February 1946 was to become one of the defining moments in the genesis of the Cold War. George Kennan's 'long telegram' portrayed the Soviet leadership as 'cruel', 'wasteful' and 'insecure' to the point of paranoia, especially when it came to its relationship with the United States. The Soviets, he explained, were 'committed fanatically' to destroying America's way of life, sowing disharmony amongst America's people, and undermining America's international authority.[52] The only way to combat the 'malignant parasite' of world communism was to draw a clear line in the sand. The Soviet threat must be contained.

Kennan's telegram caused a sensation in Washington, but only because it summed up for the first time what everyone at the State Department was already thinking. Over the course of the following year, Kennan's ideas would become the new orthodoxy, not only in the State Department but in the rest of government as well.[53]

As time went on, however, a passive policy of containment was no longer considered enough. In many parts of the world there remained the very real threat of local insurgencies bringing Communists to power independently from Moscow. One such insurgency was going on in Greece, where a brutal civil war had been raging on and off ever since the country had been liberated from the Nazis. When the British announced that they could no longer afford to prop up the nationalist Greek government, the State Department decided that it was time to step into the breach and begin taking a much more active role.

Accordingly, in March 1947, President Truman appeared before a joint session of Congress and made a speech that was designed to 'scare the hell out of the American people'.[54] The reason for his speech was ostensibly to ask for the release of $400 million in immediate aid to Greece and Turkey but, as with his announcement of the loyalty programme that same month, Truman was also trying to demonstrate that he was prepared to take a hard line on communism. Though he could not possibly have known it, the principles outlined in his speech would become the cornerstone of American foreign policy for the rest of the century.

During the course of just twenty minutes, Truman invoked all of the values that Americans hold most dear: liberty, justice, good neighbourliness and the determination to stand up for the little guy. He used the words 'free' or 'freedom' no fewer than twenty-four times: if America wished to live in a peaceful world it was not enough to proclaim itself the 'Land of the Free', it must also support the cause of 'freedom-loving peoples' throughout the world. Truman conjured up an image of America as a lone hero, standing up against the forces of 'terror and oppression', just as it had done in the recent world war.

But it was Truman's appeal to American fears that was arguably more effective. The consequences of *not* standing up for Greece, or for other, smaller countries threatened by communism, 'would be disastrous not only for them but for the world'. Echoing the voices of his most senior advisers in the State Department, he invoked the prospect of 'confusion and disorder' spreading throughout the Middle East, bringing with it the 'collapse of free institutions' and the end of 'freedom and independence'. The spectre of the Second World War, both as a lesson and a warning, was present throughout the speech. America had failed to stand up to totalitarianism once before. The cost of supporting Greece in its hour of need was, he said, a sound investment when compared to the $341 billion America had been forced to spend to win the last war.

The crux of his speech came towards the end, when he uttered the words that would set the tone for American foreign policy throughout the Cold War:

> I believe that it must be the policy of the United States to support free peoples who are resisting attempted subjugation by armed minorities or by outside pressures . . . The free peoples of the world look to us for support in maintaining their freedoms. If we falter in our leadership, we may endanger the peace of the world.[55]

Truman's rhetoric had the desired effect: the request for $400 million in aid to Greece and Turkey was granted. But by speaking in such broad terms, he had implied that America was willing to help any and every nation that felt threatened by communism. In the coming weeks State Department officials like Dean Acheson would be at pains to dispel the idea that this represented some kind of blank cheque for the world; nevertheless, the impression remained that America was committed to fighting communism on a worldwide scale, whatever the cost.[56] It is a measure of just how wealthy the USA had become in the wake of the Second World War that Truman was able not only to make such claims but also largely to live up to them. In the coming weeks, the Secretary of State, George Marshall, would announce a further massive aid package to help stave off the threat of communism throughout western Europe: the Marshall Plan would eventually account for \$12.3 billion in European aid. Between 1945 and 1953 alone, America's total global aid bill came to \$44 billion.[57]

In the years to come, even these huge sums would seem like mere drops in the ocean. By the time the Cold War came to an end in 1989, it was estimated that the USA had spent around \$8 trillion in support of the Truman Doctrine. America had provided aid to more than a hundred countries, established mutual defence treaties with more than fifty of them and built large-scale military bases in thirty. It had deployed an average of more than a million military personnel each year across the world in just about every environment, from European cities to remote Pacific islands, from jungle air bases to desert encampments, from aircraft carriers to nuclear submarines and even, eventually, to space rockets. The Truman Doctrine had been used to justify covert CIA operations everywhere from Cuba to Angola to the Philippines, and full-scale war in Korea and Vietnam. It had provided the rationale behind the toppling of governments in Iran, Guatemala and Chile, and the sponsoring of right-wing dictatorships throughout Central and South America. All of this was a far cry from the policy of isolationism that had dominated American thinking before the Second World War. The legacy bequeathed to America by that war, along with Truman's doctrine of active engagement with the world's affairs, left America feeling honour-bound to enter into all of these conflicts.[58]

America continues to feel honour-bound to this day. Even after the Cold War was over, America's obligation to defend the values of liberal democracy led it to intervene in Iraq (1991), Somalia (1992), Haiti (1994), Bosnia (1995) and Kosovo (1999) – not for its own immediate security, but to defend 'freedom', 'democracy' and 'the very fabric of the West'. Even America's second confrontation with Iraq, which built in intensity from the end of the 1990s to 2003, did not start out as part of George W. Bush's 'war on terror', but as an attempt to maintain order in the world. No matter how tired of this burden the American people have become, nor how much America is criticized by those who are less willing to go to war, the legacy of both the Second World War and the Truman Doctrine look set to continue into the future. As one senior foreign policy adviser to the US State Department observed in 2014, 'Superpowers don't get to retire.'[59]

★

In 1947, when Truman delivered his famous speech, all this lay in the future. Ordinary Americans knew only that for all their supposed wealth and power they felt restless, anxious, as if the entire nation were waiting for something terrible to happen. To the Dutch psychoanalyst Abraham Meerloo, who spent time in the country after the war, it seemed that America was in the grip of a pervasive sense of 'vague, ill-defined fear'. He suggested that the reason behind this mood was America's 'hidden feelings of guilt' for the things it had been obliged to do during the war, including the bombing of Hiroshima and Nagasaki. If the nation could not square up to the reality of what it had done, he said, it would continue to be plagued by premonitions of some kind of punishment.[60]

Judging by the amount of anxiety about the atom bomb in America at the time, it is quite plausible that there was an element of hidden guilt in the American psyche. But that is not the whole story. The Second World War had certainly brutalized some of America, and it had traumatized it to a certain degree – but it had also given it a sense of purpose. When Cord Meyer had set out to war after the attack on Pearl Harbor he had felt alive like never before. His feelings had been shared by millions of Americans who delighted in the sense of mission and togetherness that the war had brought them. America might have celebrated when it was all over, and rejoiced that it had emerged victorious – but there was also a part of many people that mourned the end of the war.

The discovery of a new enemy gave Americans the opportunity to put aside any feelings of guilt they may have had for their wartime actions. It also provided a new repository for all the anger and aggression that people had built up over the course of the war years, and a focus of blame for all those who had axes to grind, old and new. The Soviets were an entity upon which Americans could place their anxieties and fears and, since they were an enemy everyone could agree on, they allowed Americans to feel a sense of solidarity once again. But most importantly this new enemy gave America back its sense of purpose: for what use is a knight in shining armour without a dragon to slay? For better or worse, the Second World War – and the Cold War that followed it – established a kind of psychological template: America has been fighting dragons of one sort or another ever since.[61]

14. USSR

In 1949, the dragon proved it could breathe fire. When the Soviet Union tested its first atomic bomb, everything changed: for the first time the world contained not one but two nuclear powers, and the concept of a nuclear war became an actual possibility. In the coming years, America and the Soviet Union would embark on an arms race that would bring the world repeatedly to the brink of Armageddon – most notably over Korea in the 1950s, during the Cuban missile crisis in the 1960s and during the heightened tensions between East and West in the mid-1980s.

During this time, one Soviet nuclear scientist would become emblematic of the country he served. Andrei Sakharov is remembered today as a Russian dissident and Nobel Peace Prize laureate, but as a young man he was better known as the father of the Soviet thermonuclear bomb. It was scientists such as Sakharov who came to represent everything that the USA feared most about the Soviet state, but also what Americans most admired in its people. A towering figure in the history of not only his country but also the world, Sakharov would play a significant role both in the furthering of Soviet power and, in the end, in its downfall.

When the war for Russia broke out Andrei Sakharov was just twenty years old, and part way through a physics degree at Moscow University. Many of his classmates immediately volunteered to join the army, but Sakharov, who was prevented from doing likewise by a heart condition, volunteered instead to do technical work for the war effort. After finishing his degree, he went to work in a munitions factory in Kovrov, first on the factory floor, but later in its laboratories, where he invented machines for testing the quality of its armour-piercing bullets and shells. The conditions were appalling, with children working alongside adults and pregnant women forced to work along with everyone else. Many of them, Sakharov included, shared dormitories that were infested with lice, and lived off little more than millet porridge mixed with American powdered eggs. But like almost everyone in his generation, he accepted all of this. 'We had to fight to win,' he wrote later, whatever the personal sacrifices.[1]

After the war, Sakharov went back to studying, as a graduate student at the prestigious Physics Institute of the Academy of Sciences. But towards the end of 1946, as he was completing his postgraduate degree, he became aware of a change of atmosphere: suddenly the state seemed to be taking a great interest in the work of theoretical physicists. Twice he was offered top-secret work in the Soviet nuclear programme, with a salary to match, and twice he turned it down. Eventually, in the summer of 1948, he was given no choice. By a decision of the Council of Ministers and the Communist Party Central Committee, a special research group was being set up to investigate the possibility of building a hydrogen bomb. Sakharov was to be amongst its members.

As during the war, Sakharov accepted his new role without really questioning it, because he wholeheartedly believed in the need to keep the Soviet Union safe from American aggression. 'I understood, of course, the terrifying, inhuman nature of the weapons we were building. But the recent war had also been an exercise in barbarity; and although I hadn't fought in that conflict, I regarded myself as a soldier in this new scientific war.' Sakharov and his fellow scientists saw their work as 'heroic', and threw themselves into nuclear weapons research with genuine zeal: 'We were possessed by a true war psychology.' Above all, he wrote, 'I felt myself committed to the goal which I assumed was Stalin's as well: after a devastating war, to make the country strong enough to ensure peace.' The USSR had no option but to embrace the arms race, because this was the only way 'to provide for [Soviet] security in the face of American and British nuclear weapons'.[2]

In the coming years, Sakharov would be instrumental in the creation of a succession of ever-bigger weapons: 'Joe 4', the 'Big Bomb', the 'Extra', the 'Tsar Bomb'. In recognition for his devotion, Sakharov was proclaimed a Hero of Socialist Labour three times, awarded the Stalin Prize in 1953 and the Lenin Prize in 1956.

And yet, as time went on, Sakharov's dedication to the Soviet state began to waver. As a young man it had never entered his head to question Marxism as 'the ideology best suited to liberate mankind'. He had never known any other Russia than Communist Russia, and had been brought up to believe that the Soviet state 'represented a breakthrough into the future, a prototype . . . for all other countries to imitate'. But as an adult, and as a scientist, he could not help noticing certain dangerous flaws in the system. He deplored the violence that had taken place

The 'father of the hydrogen bomb': Andrei Sakharov at the Soviet Atomic Energy Institute in 1957.

during the collectivization programme before the war, and refused to join the Communist Party as a result. He openly condemned the way that Trofim Lysenko, whose politicized version of genetics was ridiculed in other parts of the world, had been granted his influential position in the Academy of Sciences. He also championed the banning of nuclear tests in the atmosphere, which produced so much radioactive fall-out that he began to regard them as 'a crime against humanity'. Bit by bit, he was becoming more critical of the system in which he lived.[3]

The defining moment of his later life came in 1968 when, influenced by events both in Russia and abroad, he decided to write down some of his thoughts on the issues of his time. The result was an essay entitled 'Reflections on Progress, Peaceful Coexistence, and Intellectual Freedom', which he published in samizdat, but which was soon picked up by the foreign press. In this essay he outlined his idealistic hopes that the capitalist and socialist systems would gradually cease opposing one another and eventually converge. Such views were heretical in the Soviet Union, but they were welcomed in the West. The essay was first published in the Dutch newspaper *Het Parool* at the beginning of July, followed by the *New York Times* two weeks later. Over the following year more than 18 million copies of his essay were published around the world, making it a truly global publishing event. All of a sudden, Sakharov's name was being mentioned in the same breath as that of Alexander Solzhenitsyn, as well as dissenters in other countries such as Poland's Jan Lipski and Czechoslovakia's Ivan Klíma.[4]

For the rest of Sakharov's life he would become famous not as a scientist but as a dissident. He lost his job over the 'Reflections' affair, but continued to write dissident pamphlets anyway. He signed numerous petitions against the government, and joined public protests against Soviet state actions. In the 1970s he would win the Nobel Peace Prize along with several other awards, much to the irritation of the Soviet authorities, who attacked him and his wife mercilessly in the press. In 1988 the European Community named a human rights prize after him.

Despite all of this, he remained a scientist at heart, and stood by his work as a theoretical physicist. To the end of his life he never expressed any regret for having contributed to nuclear weapons research. The nuclear arms race, he said in 1988, was 'a great tragedy, which reflected the tragic nature of the entire world situation, where in order to preserve the peace, it was necessary to make such terrible and horrible things'. Nevertheless, 'In the final account, the work which we did was justified, as was the work which was done by our colleagues on the opposite side.'[5]

National Trauma

In the aftermath of the Second World War, the USA and the USSR found themselves in a position neither nation could have foreseen just six years earlier. The war had not only propelled them to military greatness but also diminished or destroyed their rivals to such a degree that no other nation was capable of challenging them. The Soviet Union had the greatest continental army the world has ever seen, which completely dominated the Eurasian landmass. The United States had a maritime force that dominated both the Pacific and the Atlantic, an army and air force that dwarfed those of every other Western power, and a monopoly on the atom bomb. In the absence of any comparable rivals, these two powers became something the world had never seen before: they became superpowers.

And yet, in 1945 at least, it would have been absurd to imagine that these two countries were equals. America had emerged from the war almost entirely physically unscathed, with a booming economy that made it easily the richest nation on earth. The Soviet Union, by contrast, was on its knees. Whatever its military power, it was physically, emotionally and economically exhausted, and quite incapable of projecting its influence much beyond the parts of Europe and north-east Asia that it had liberated.

It was not until the Second World War was over that most people in the USSR allowed themselves to take stock of what they had lost. The physical destruction was quite staggering. 'In the army we often spoke of what life would be like after the war,' wrote journalist Boris Galin in 1947. 'We pictured things in rainbow colours. We never imagined the scale of the destruction or the scope of reconstruction required to heal the wounds inflicted by the Germans.'[6] The official statistics give an insight into what people like Galin saw: as well as major cities like Kiev, Minsk, Kharkov and Stalingrad, more than 1,700 towns and 70,000 villages were devastated. Around 32,000 industrial enterprises had been destroyed and 65,000 kilometres of railway tracks torn up.[7]

In the areas invaded by Germany, more than 50 per cent of the urban housing stock had been severely damaged or destroyed, leaving 20 million people homeless. Even in those places that had not been occupied, the housing stock had badly deteriorated: so many resources had been diverted towards winning the war that essential repairs had not been done. In Moscow, for example, 90 per cent of the central heating systems were out of commission, as were almost half of all water and sewerage systems. Urgent repairs were needed on 80 per cent of roofs, 60 per cent of electrical equipment and 54 per cent of gas equipment. When Sakharov lived here after the war, he and his wife and baby had to move between a succession of miserable apartments every month or two – sometimes living in damp basements, sometimes in rooms that were little better than corridors, and once in an unheated house outside Moscow where they had to drape themselves in fur all day just to keep from freezing to death. Sakharov was lucky that the Academy of Sciences eventually provided him with a room: others like him would be living in ruins, basements, sheds and dugouts until well into the 1950s.[8]

Amidst this material devastation, the human losses were so great that they defied comprehension. Estimates of the dead range from 20 million to 27 million, but modern scholarship generally puts the figure at the top of that range.[9] Alongside the dead, there were also the damaged.

Eighteen million men were wounded in the war, and 2.5 million permanently disabled. As in many other countries, the sight of crippled young men begging in markets and railway stations became one of the characteristic features of the age.[10] Some 15 to 18 million people were also displaced by the war, either because they fled eastwards to escape the Germans, or because they had been taken to Germany as forced labour.[11] Almost everyone in the Soviet Union had experienced some kind of loss or bereavement as a direct consequence of the war: 1945 was a year not only of victory but also of mourning.

The psychological consequences of this vast communal experience are impossible to quantify. Countless people suffered flashbacks and nightmares for years to come, from the radio operators who had recurring dreams of parachuting behind enemy lines to the young women who refused to marry or have children because they could not escape the feeling that another war was about to break out. 'I knew in my mind that the war was over,' claimed one former partisan, 'but my whole body, my whole being remembered.' One front-line medic was pursued everywhere she went after the war by the smell of burning flesh. Another was haunted by the smell of blood: 'As soon as summer came I thought that war was about to break out,' claimed Tamara Umnyagina, years later. 'When the sun warmed everything – trees, houses, asphalt – it had a smell, for me everything smelled of blood. Whatever I ate, whatever I drank, I could not escape that smell!'[12]

Sometimes these flashbacks were communal. Mystical rumours of an impending apocalypse became widespread in the dying days of the war, particularly amongst religious people. In one village in Stavropol territory the rumour spread that 'in the next few days the Earth would collide with a comet, which occurrence would announce the end of the world'. The villagers began feverishly to prepare themselves by praying, lighting votive candles before icons, dressing in their best clothes and lying down in the front of their homes with their arms crossed over their chests, prepared to die.[13]

The interesting thing about this particular episode is that it happened early in 1945, before anyone in the Soviet Union yet knew about the atom bomb. In other words, it was not the fear of nuclear apocalypse that was the source of Soviet feelings of impending doom, but something deeper that had been born in their experience of the war.

After the revelation of the atom bomb, feelings like this only increased. But once again, this was not at first because of any specific fear of the bomb itself. What the Soviet people feared above all else was a repeat of the catastrophe they had just experienced: the atom bomb was only a threat because it opened up a new imbalance of power, and therefore made a new war more likely. As Alexander Werth, the *Sunday Times* correspondent in Moscow, explained: 'The news [of Hiroshima] had an acutely depressing effect on everybody. It was clearly realized that this was a New Fact in the world's politics, that the bomb constituted a threat to Russia, and some Russian pessimists I talked to that day dismally remarked that Russia's desperately hard victory over Germany was now "as good as wasted".'[14]

In the months that followed, the country as a whole began to experience a kind of communal flashback to the dark days of 1941. In Moscow, rumours began to circulate that 'the Soviet state is in danger' and 'England and America are threatening a new war'. Some people went so far as to entertain fears that a new world war had already begun. 'I heard,' said a worker in a Moscow factory in 1946, 'that the war is already on in China and Greece, where America and England have intervened. Any day now they will attack the Soviet Union.'[15]

The catastrophe of the war had plainly affected every level of Soviet society, not only on a physical but on a deeply psychological level. Whether it was merited or not, in 1945 the Soviets felt every bit as vulnerable as they had been in 1941, a feeling that was only exacerbated by the advent of the atom bomb. What was needed was a prolonged period of calm – a kind of national convalescence – in order for the Soviet people to feel that the horrors of war were behind them, and that they could rebuild in safety. Unfortunately, this was exactly what they would be denied.

Us and Them

What of the Soviet leadership? How did they react to this set of circumstances? The first thing to make clear is that the Soviet leadership had *never* felt secure. From their days as revolutionaries, being hunted down by the Tsar's secret police, through the turmoil of the Civil War, the Ukrainian famine and the Great Purge – Stalin and his circle had always felt vulnerable, both internally and externally. However, the German invasion in 1941 was perhaps the closest Soviet communism had ever come to total annihilation, and it is not surprising that Communist Party leaders were determined never to allow themselves to be so vulnerable again. Western diplomats like George Kennan spoke disparagingly of their obsession with 'hostile encirclement', and their 'paranoia' about the West, but there were very clear reasons for this paranoia, which was felt by the regime and the Soviet people alike.

The victory in 1945 offered the Soviets an unprecedented chance to protect their borders from any future attack, and they grabbed it with both hands. Lands that had once been part of the Russian Empire – Karelia, the Baltic States, western Ukraine, Moldova – were reclaimed as Soviet territory. Lands that had provided Germany with a launch pad for its invasion – Poland, Hungary, Romania and Bulgaria – were occupied and subjected to Soviet influence. Potentially hostile governments were removed and replaced with Communist governments; societies were restructured along Communist lines and, in the case of those countries that had actively fought against the USSR, reparations were exacted.

The Soviets believed they had a right to take such action – both historically and morally. The Red Army had captured the territories of eastern Europe with Soviet blood, and the political leadership saw no reason to withdraw its troops without first ensuring the future loyalty of these countries. It must also be stressed that Soviet ideologues genuinely believed that they were *liberating* these countries, which had been oppressed by feudal systems for centuries. But most importantly, the Soviet state felt it had a responsibility to build a buffer zone between its own territory and those of its potential enemies. 'We had to consolidate our conquests,' said the Soviet foreign minister, Vyacheslav Molotov, years later. The subjugation of eastern Europe was therefore not primarily about the spread of communism, or about old-fashioned imperialism, but about protecting the motherland from future attack.[16]

When the West objected, it was difficult for the Soviets to take their objections at face value. As far as Stalin was concerned, he was not doing anything in eastern Europe that Truman and Churchill were not also doing in western Europe. 'This war is not as in the past,' he famously told the Yugoslavian Communist Milovan Djilas in 1944: 'whoever occupies a territory also imposes on it his own social system. Everyone imposes his own system as far as his army can reach. It cannot be otherwise.'[17]

This carving up of Europe into Soviet and Western 'spheres of influence' was not something that Stalin imposed unilaterally – in fact, it was a situation that Britain and America had themselves endorsed. When Churchill had met Stalin in Moscow in October 1944 he had explicitly agreed to leave Bulgaria and Romania to the Soviets in return for British control in Greece. Stalin scrupulously kept his side of the bargain (regardless of what Truman would later imply in his Truman Doctrine speech): what right, then, did Churchill have to complain if British officials were prevented from influencing events in Bucharest? Furthermore, both Britain and America had signed the armistice agreements with Bulgaria, Romania and Hungary, in which, once again, it was explicitly stated that each country would be administered by the Soviets for the duration of the war.[18] As far as the Soviets were concerned, events in these parts of the world were none of the West's business.

From a Soviet point of view, the hypocrisy of Western statesmen was quite shameless. In the Atlantic Charter they harped on about the 'right of all peoples to choose the forms of government under which they will live', and yet they supported colonialism in Asia and Africa. They complained about the abuse of human rights in eastern Europe, and yet wilfully failed to prosecute Fascists and war criminals in western Europe. They spoke out against the 'enslavement' of eastern European populations, but remained silent about the continued subjugation of black Americans in the southern United States. They spoke about the Communists rigging elections, and yet stood aside when right-wingers in countries like Greece, Paraguay or the Dominican Republic – countries directly within a British or American 'sphere of influence' – did similarly. In 1948 the Americans used a great deal of money and influence to ensure that the Italian elections threw up the 'correct' result – how was this any better than Soviet efforts to rig Hungarian or Polish elections?[19]

While the Soviets did everything they could to expand their borders, shore up their defences and bolster themselves against a hostile world, America seemed hell-bent on exposing Soviet vulnerabilities. In the first United Nations conference in San Francisco, America made a great show of denying Soviet requests for Poland to be given membership, while pushing through the membership of Argentina – a country that the Soviets believed had spent most of the war 'assisting the Fascists who are our enemies'. This demonstration of America's overwhelming dominance of world diplomacy seemed heavy-handed even to some of its allies. Over the next seven years the USSR felt obliged to use its veto fifty-nine times – not merely for the sake of being obstructive, as much of the Western press suggested, but because America insisted on introducing resolutions that were against vital Soviet interests. Diplomatically, the veto was the only power that the Soviets had to protect themselves.[20]

America also subjected the USSR to what the Soviets regarded as a series of economic attacks. In 1945, almost as soon as the guns fell silent in Europe, America abruptly cut off all Lend-Lease aid to the Soviet Union. In 1946 it suspended all reparations payments from the American Zone of Germany. In 1947 it announced the Truman Doctrine, followed by the Marshall Plan. The $12 billion that would flow into Europe over the coming years came with strict capitalist strings attached, and was something that the starving, impoverished Soviets could not possibly compete with. It came as no surprise, not even to the Americans, when the Soviet culture minister, Andrei Zhdanov, called the Marshall Plan 'the American plan to enslave Europe'.[21]

Just as worryingly, the USA seemed determined whenever possible to display its military superiority. At the end of the war, America had the most powerful air force in the world, in terms of both quality and quantity. 'I would even say that America was invincible,' Nikita Khrushchev declared in his memoirs, before going on to claim that 'the Americans flaunted this fact by sending their planes all over Europe, violating borders and even flying over the territory of the Soviet Union itself, not to mention a country like Czechoslovakia. Not a single day went by when American planes didn't violate Czechoslovak airspace.'[22]

Finally, and perhaps most damagingly of all, America had a monopoly on the atom bomb. Of all the long list of American advantages in 1945, it was this that most disconcerted the Soviets. No one in the Soviet establishment had ever before appreciated how powerful an atom bomb could be – not only in physical terms, but also in foreign policy terms. Stalin was immediately impressed with the way that the bomb had been used to bring about both the end of the war and Japan's unconditional surrender. Such raw power gave America a strategic advantage over the rest of the world. That this new power affected the USSR was unquestioned. Indeed, there was a general assumption that the bombs on Hiroshima and Nagasaki were 'not aimed at Japan but rather at the Soviet Union'.[23]

As the British ambassador in Moscow explained in December 1945, the timing of Hiroshima and Nagasaki could not have been worse. After all the years of struggle, the victory in Europe had encouraged the

Nuclear diplomacy: a Soviet cartoon depicting America's domination of the oil-rich states around the Persian Gulf.

Soviets to believe that national security was at last within their reach – and more, that the permanence of the Soviet system was at last guaranteed. 'Then plump came the atomic bomb. At a blow the balance which had now seemed set and steady was rudely shaken. Russia was balked by the West when everything seemed to be within her grasp.'[24]

The Soviet response to this was to go on the attack. According to the former Comintern agent George Andreychin, the main reason why the Soviets became so aggressive after September 1945 was because the advent of the atom bomb had exposed their relative weakness – and, as even Stalin's own circle later acknowledged, weakness was the one thing that Stalin always wanted to hide.[25] Over the coming years, both Molotov and Stalin put on a great show of not being intimidated by the Americans, and deliberately played down the effectiveness of nuclear weapons. 'Atom bombs are intended for intimidating the weak-nerved,' Stalin told Western journalists in the autumn of 1946, 'but they cannot decide the outcome of a war, since atom bombs are by no means sufficient for this purpose.'[26]

It was in this context, surrounded by bluster and bravado, that the Soviets launched a new, accelerated programme to acquire an atomic bomb of their own. There is no record of any government debate over whether this undertaking was justified or not – it was simply assumed that if America had the bomb then the USSR must have it too. And yet this decision would have massive repercussions for the whole world. The entire geopolitical atmosphere of the next fifty years – the proxy wars in Asia and Africa, the revolutions and counter-revolutions in the developing world, the nuclear peace in Europe – was born, or at least partly born, in this moment.

By beginning an arms race with America, Stalin was laying the foundations of a policy that his successors would be unable to demolish, and that would eventually cause the collapse of the Soviet Union. Between 1945 and 1946 the Soviet science budget tripled. By 1950, military expenditures accounted for up to a quarter of the USSR's gross national income – and this at a time when the country desperately needed to rebuild.[27] Over the next four decades the Soviet Union would spend a huge but unquantifiable fortune in an economic and technological war they were never likely to win.

Rebirth Forestalled

There is nothing like a war, even a Cold War, to create a sense of 'us' and 'them'. The Soviets therefore embraced their new enemy in 1945. As in the Second World War, 'they' provided a focus for all of society's communal anxieties and fears. As in that war, any measure and any expense could be justified by the need to protect the nation against 'them'. In the short to medium term, 'they' ended up providing a valuable service to the Soviet state.

But who was the great communal 'us' of the Soviet Union? In contrast to the way that people in the West tended to view it, the USSR was not a vast monolith, but a richly varied country, riven with all kinds of splits, much like the USA was. Ever since its creation there had been tensions between the forces of tradition and the forces of modernization, between town and countryside, between the bourgeoisie and the working classes, between the Party and the intelligentsia, between military and civilian; not to mention all the ancient divisions between different regions and republics, and between different ethnic and religious minorities. Before the war, communism had attempted to replace all these divisions with a single unifying ideology, but had done so with such violence and such cruelty that it had only really succeeded in driving these divisions underground; and in the process it had also created new divisions, most notably between people and state.

The Second World War changed all that. It united most of these different groups in a way that no amount of propaganda or coercion had ever previously achieved. In an instant, all the varied categories of 'us' and 'them' were redefined: a single 'us' expanded to include almost everyone in society, because more or less everyone was now united in a common cause; likewise, 'them' became a single, universal enemy – the Nazi invader. During the course of the war this enemy was so demonized, and had taken on such monstrous proportions, that it came to occupy a central part of the Soviet imagination. It also played a vital role in keeping Soviet society unified during these dangerous years.

In 1945, after all the trauma and destruction, there were great hopes that the Soviet Union might be able to salvage something positive from the war. The playwright Konstantin Simonov later remembered how people began to speak 'of liberalization . . . of indulgence . . . of ideological optimism'. According to Andrei Sakharov, 'We all believed – or at least hoped – that the postwar world would be decent and humane. How could it be otherwise?' These things seemed safe to say precisely because of the spirit of unity that still remained after the war.[28]

However, there were strong signs that this sense of unity was already beginning to break down, particularly as the full wreckage of the country's postwar economy became clear. It was not only America that suffered shortages, industrial unrest, ethnic tension and marital breakdown in 1945 – these occurred in the USSR too, but to a much greater degree. When 8.5 million Red Army soldiers were demobilized in the three years after the war, there was no G.I. Bill to ease their transition into civilian society – the Soviet government simply did not have the resources for such a measure. While American workers were striking over pay and conditions, Russian factory workers in Penza were labouring in the open air, knee-deep in snow.[29] While American women were clamouring for nylon stockings, Russians in Tula were making do without shoes, without coats and without underwear.[30] Americans complained about continuing rationing in 1946, but in the Soviet Union people were literally starving. According to the Russian historian Veniamin Zima, 100 million people in the USSR suffered from malnutrition between 1946 and 1948, and around 2 million died from famine. This was due partly to poor weather, partly to government mismanagement – but it was also a direct result of the disruptions to Soviet farms caused by the war.[31]

The contrast between their dreams of a rainbow-coloured future and the reality of postwar life led to waves of discontent across the country. Peasants in the collective farms often refused to work on the grounds that they were being paid too little to live on – and in some cases not being paid at all.[32] Large-scale strikes and demonstrations took place in industrial areas, particularly in the huge defence plants in the Urals and Siberia. In 1945–46 alone, more than half a million people across the Soviet Union sent letters to the Russian Republic's internal affairs commissariat complaining about living conditions. 'So this is what we have come to!' wrote one. 'This is what you call the state's concern for the material needs of the working people . . . !' According to this writer, an atmosphere of revolt was growing, and workers were beginning to ask, 'What did we fight for?'[33]

In some parts of the Soviet Union, full-scale rebellions were already under way. A massive insurgency against Soviet rule had already begun in Ukraine, where some 400,000 people were actively involved in resisting the return of Soviet troops. The uprising, which rapidly became something of a civil war, would continue into the 1950s. Similar insurgencies occurred in the newly annexed republics of Lithuania, Latvia and Estonia, where tens of thousands of people took to the forests to fight against Soviet forces. These doomed enterprises were fuelled by the vain hope that 'England and the United States [would] go to war against the Soviet Union'. In other words, in many parts of the western borderlands, people were actively hoping for a Third World War.[34]

The Soviet authorities clearly could not allow such sentiments to spread. In time-honoured fashion they began to blame all of the country's problems on outsiders. Their denunciations of the West followed the same pattern as American denunciations of communism: Stalin gave interviews to *Pravda* in which he directly compared Churchill to Hitler, his foreign minister Vyacheslav Molotov called America a 'fascisizing' power while other senior members of the party like Andrei Vyshinsky and Georgy Malenkov said that the Americans were 'imitators of the fascist barbarians'.[35] As in America, the Soviet leadership used this new threat both as an excuse and a distraction, and as a way to urge their people to unify behind them once again, just as they had done during the war.

In the meantime, anyone with links to the West was immediately denounced. The witch-hunts began almost as soon as the war was over. The first people to fall foul of these were returning prisoners of war, along with civilians who had been forcibly removed to Germany during the war to work as slave labourers. Such people had spent long periods living in the midst of the enemy, often followed by more time amongst the British or Americans. Though there are no accurate figures of how many returning prisoners of war were sent to the Gulag, it was certainly tens upon tens of thousands; Alexander Solzhenitsyn describes how the labour camps were filled with these people in the aftermath of the war.[36] At the same time 60,000 Communists who had been captured by the Germans during the war found themselves expelled from the party.[37]

Next to be demonized were those national groups who no longer appeared loyal to the Soviet ideal. During the war, several ethnic groups had been deported from their homelands to the Kazakh steppes because of their perceived disloyalty – especially Volga Germans, Chechens, Ingush, Kalmyks and Crimean Tatars. In the aftermath of the war it was the turn of the rebellious populations of the western borderlands. Between 1945 and 1952 more than 108,000 Lithuanians were deported as 'bandits' or 'bandit accomplices', as were 114,000 Ukrainians, 34,000 Moldovans, 43,000 Latvians and 20,000 Estonians. Actions like these sparked a resentment in these countries towards Moscow bordering on hatred, which would only grow over the following decades.[38]

As tensions grew between the Soviet Union and the West, the authorities began waging a violent campaign against what Stalin called the 'admiration of Germans, French, of foreigners, of assholes'.[39] It began in August 1946 with the persecution of the Leningrad intelligentsia, led by the cultural minister Andrei Zhdanov. In essence, this was no different from the purges that had occurred before the war: it was only made halfway respectable by the emphasis on the need to eliminate 'foreign' elements that had infiltrated Soviet society.

This was followed by a series of repressive measures against all forms of art and science. Composers like Shostakovich, Khachaturian and Prokofiev were blacklisted for displaying 'decadent Western influences' in their music. The State Museum of Modern Western Art was closed down, as was Eugen Varga's Institute of the World Economy and World Politics.[40] In January 1947 the philosopher G. F. Aleksandrov was accused of having undervalued the Russian contribution to Western philosophy, and was sacked from his post as the head of agitprop.

At the same time, Soviet officials ran a parallel campaign to promote Russian art, Russian philosophy, and Russian science as superior to that of all other nations. According to Andrei Sakharov, this affected even the all-important nuclear programme, where the experienced German scientists that had been brought to Russia were never really trusted by government officials.[41] Every important discovery had to be a Russian discovery. Journals began to make exaggerated claims about how Russian scientists had invented everything from the aeroplane and the steam engine to the radio and the light bulb. *Real* scientists, like Sakharov, began to make wry jokes about 'Russia, homeland of the elephant'.[42]

All of this was part of an ugly form of nationalism that was one of the major legacies of the war, and which is still visible in Russia today. Western statesmen, and indeed Western historians, have often got into trouble for confusing the terms 'Soviet' and 'Russian' as if they were the same thing. But this is not much different from the way that many Russians came to view themselves in the years after the Second World War. Just as Stalin *was* the state, so Russia *was* the Soviet Union.[43] In the coming years, ethnic Russians increasingly dominated all the top Soviet institutions, from the Army to the Politburo, and Russian was the language of power throughout the Soviet Union. In the long term this would contribute to a growing resentment amongst the other peoples of the Soviet Union – not to mention the people of eastern Europe – that would become one of the causes of the break-up of the Union in 1991. In the meantime, however, nationalism was one of the main forces used by Stalin to justify his persecution of 'foreign elements' in Soviet society.

What exactly constituted a 'foreign element' was not always clear. As time went on Stalin would wage successive campaigns of repression against all kinds of groups, including senior soldiers, Moscow doctors and the Leningrad Communist Party – almost always on the grounds that they were wholly or partly influenced by foreigners. The apogee of this new intolerance came in the campaign against Jews – or 'cosmopolitans' as they were euphemistically called. Between 1948 and 1952 tens of thousands of Soviet Jews were arrested, dismissed from their jobs, thrown out of their universities or evicted from their homes, simply for being Jewish. The official excuse for this persecution was that Jews were Zionists who had links to America and other countries in the West, but even Stalin's closest subordinates admitted that this was 'all pure nonsense'. In reality, as has so often been the case throughout history, Jews were merely a symbol that could be used to represent everything that Stalin feared about the outside world, and which therefore had to be purged from public life.[44]

There are undoubted parallels between the paranoia that gripped America in the 1940s and 50s and that which similarly gripped the USSR. Both countries used the threat of an external enemy to draw a divided society together, and both used repression to punish those who did not conform. If the Soviet mindset reacted in more extreme ways than the American one, this was certainly a reflection of the much, much greater trauma that the Soviet Union had suffered during the recent war, which had almost made their fears of annihilation come true. But the difference in the scale and nature of the repression that occurred in the USSR also owes a great deal to the political system that was in place there. Repression in America was imposed more or less by consensus, and that consensus could easily shift – as indeed it did in the mid-1950s – when the repression was deemed to go too far. In the Soviet Union, by contrast, power was so concentrated in the hands of one man that there were almost no limits to the torments that could be unleashed upon society if Stalin so willed it.

In the end, Stalin's view of what constituted 'us' became so narrow that nobody was entirely safe from persecution, not even those at the centre of power. Stalin murdered several of his closest friends and associates during this time, and had dozens of others tortured or sent to the Gulag. His circle would regularly gather for interminable, alcohol-fuelled dinners, where they were forced by turns to endure various humiliations at Stalin's hands. The future premier, Nikita Khrushchev, remembered these dinners with horror. After one of them, he shared a car home with Nikolai Bulganin, who sank into his seat with visible relief. 'You come to Stalin's table as a friend,' he murmured, 'but you never know if you'll go home by yourself or if you'll be given a ride – to prison!' By the time of Stalin's death in March 1953, there was no group, and no individual, who could consider himself entirely safe from Stalin's distrust.[45]

Sakharov lived on the fringe of these events. He did not witness the horror close up, although he did meet some of those involved, including Stalin's former security chief Lavrentiy Beria, whom he characterized as 'a terrifying human being'.[46] But scientists like Sakharov were largely immune from the daily fear that everyone else in society was forced to endure, because their work was deemed so essential. They were paid better than the vast majority of society, and they were given privileges that were beyond the reach of most people: their own *dachas*, their own cars, and access to literature that was banned everywhere else. An independence of thought that was considered suspicious in the general population was positively encouraged amongst the scientists in the secret installations where the atom bombs were created.

While this might have distanced them from the tribulations of the rest of the population, it did, according to Sakharov, also create a template for the democracy of the future. In his seminal 1968 essay, Sakharov called for the intellectual privileges he and his fellow scientists enjoyed to be extended to society in general. He also suggested that the technocratic elite should govern society along scientific lines, and in a way that prioritized above all else, 'care and concern for human values of a moral, ethical and personal character'.[47]

That Sakharov was immediately stripped of his security clearance as a result of this essay is instructive. In the end, scientists like Sakharov learned what many other people in Soviet society had already long realized – that there was a fundamental and unbridgeable difference between the way they saw the world and the way that the state saw it.

This difference was exemplified in the state's attitude toward the nuclear bomb. Sakharov tells a story about a banquet he attended in 1955, in celebration of a successful bomb test. As the scientist chiefly responsible for the technology behind this particular weapon, he felt it his duty to say a few words; so he rose to his feet and proposed a toast to the hope that the USSR would never have to use nuclear bombs in a real war. According to Sakharov, an embarrassed hush immediately fell over the room. Slowly, ominously, the deputy minister of defence rose to his feet to reply. 'Let me tell a parable,' he said. 'An old man wearing only a shirt was praying before an icon. "Guide me, harden me. Guide me, harden me." His wife, who was lying on the stove, said: "Just pray to be hard, old man, I can guide it in myself." Let's drink to getting hard.' Suitably rebuked, Sakharov drank down his brandy 'and didn't open my mouth again for the rest of the evening'.[48]

In its relentless pursuit of the atom bomb, the Soviet state gained everything they longed for after the Second World War, and lost it at the same time. Their potency, so damaged by the military collapse of 1941, was restored beyond their wildest dreams. But their lack of humanity sowed such seeds of dissent that the state would nevertheless eventually be doomed.

15. World Polarization

The parallels between the collective psychology of the USA in early postwar years and that of the USSR are striking. Both countries had ascended to positions of global power that they were not quite ready for, and had not yet had time to come to terms with. Both countries had been unified by the war in a way that no amount of propaganda or terror, or even New Deal progressivism, had ever previously achieved. But now that the war was over, divisions in both countries were beginning to open up again. The essential ingredient to both American unity and Soviet unity had been the existence of a common enemy – a monster – but now that this monster had been defeated, there was nothing left for either country to unite with the other against. As relations between them began to break down, it seemed only natural for each to replace the old German or Japanese monster with a new American or Soviet one. The hot-war mentality of 'us' and 'them' was, therefore, seamlessly transposed into the Cold War.

The dominance of these two countries in global affairs meant that the rest of the world inevitably found itself sucked into their quarrels. After the experience of the war, it was no longer enough to aim merely for national unity: America began to push for unity in what it was now calling 'the western hemisphere', and even more broadly, 'the West'. Meanwhile the Soviet Union, which had always been internationalist in outlook, began to press its neighbours and allies to form a single, unified 'Communist bloc'. Under pressure from the two superpowers, most other nations had little choice but to take sides.

The Soviet culture minister, Andrei Zhdanov, summed up the new atmosphere in 1947 when he told a conference of European Communist parties that the world would henceforth be divided into 'two camps'. On the one hand, he declared, there was the 'imperialist and anti-democratic camp'. This was led by the USA and its British partner, whose fundamental aim was 'world domination' and 'the smashing of democratic movements'. On the other hand was the Soviet Union and its allies, who must now 'rally their ranks and unite' against the West.

According to Zhdanov, there could be no cooperation between these two camps, which were 'diametrically opposed'.[1]

The Americans, largely speaking, agreed with this point of view, although they put it in very different language. Earlier the same year the American diplomat George Kennan had written a highly influential article in the journal *Foreign Affairs*, in which he stated that 'happy co-existence' between the two superpowers was impossible. America, he wrote, had no choice but to try to 'contain' the Soviet threat. It was therefore high time that Americans started 'accepting the responsibilities of moral and political leadership that history plainly intended them to bear'. The implication – or, at least, this was the way his words were universally interpreted – was that America must be the standard bearer in a new, international crusade against the spread of communism.[2]

But what about the rest of the world? How did they feel about the way that the superpowers were gathering their blocs around them? Some, naturally, accepted this new world order in the spirit of pragmatism. Many countries in western Europe and Asia happily sided with the USA because the Americans were powerful and appeared to offer the best path to re-establishing both security and order in the aftermath of the war. American money also seemed to be the key to rebuilding the shattered infrastructure of these regions. Likewise, most Latin American countries saw little choice but to side with the USA because their economic dependence on their northern neighbour, as well as their geographical proximity, made cooperation the best option. Meanwhile, most of eastern Europe accepted Soviet control because not to do so would have meant a return to all-out war; and Communists everywhere also supported the USSR because they believed this gave them the greatest chance of effecting political change in their own countries.

However, there were many other parts of the world that resented being forced to choose between one side or the other, and who therefore did their best to avoid doing so. They chose all kinds of names for this stance. 'Neutrality' was the legal term for countries like Switzerland, which promised not to involve themselves in any international war, but various others described themselves as 'disengaged', 'uncommitted', 'non-aligned', 'progressively neutral', and so on.[3]

These countries hoped thus to remove themselves from the Cold War, but in the end they merely made themselves vulnerable to a whole raft of other political, economic and moral dilemmas. Did non-alignment mean

Cold War showdown between Andrei Vyshinsky and America's Henry Cabot Lodge, Jr during a UN debate on Korea's future. The response of Britain's Sir Gladwyn Jebb, sandwiched between them, speaks volumes.

that they were obliged to turn down much-needed investment from one side or the other to preserve their impartiality? Did it mean that they could not criticize the misdeeds of the superpowers – and, if they did, would anyone listen? If they refused all military treaties, who would defend them in the event of invasion? Without formal allies, what voice could they have in the world? And, most importantly, what would they do if they ever came under sustained pressure from one side or the other?

The Impossibility of Neutrality

Anthony Curwen knew the pressures of trying to stay neutral. As a British pacifist, he had always abhorred the idea of 'sitting on the end of a gun, and aiming it at a human being and killing them'; so when the whole world went to war in 1939, Curwen chose a different path: he declared himself a conscientious objector. Refusing to take up arms, he joined the Friends Ambulance Unit, a Quaker organization devoted to the principles of pacifism and neutrality. Between 1943 and 1946 Curwen looked after the sick and the injured – first in British hospitals, and later in remote areas of Syria. It was a constructive and entirely neutral war-time job that he later said he found 'very satisfying'.[4]

When the war came to an end, Curwen decided to continue his commitment to pacifism. He stayed on with the Friends Ambulance Unit, who were now sending people out to China to help rebuild the country after its devastating war against the Japanese.

Unfortunately, a new civil conflict had broken out in China, this time between the nationalist Kuomintang government and the Communists. The FAU intended to stay neutral, but this did not stop Curwen feeling quite strongly about the situation. 'When I went to China I was extremely naive politically,' he admitted in later life. 'I remember thinking, how stupid to have a civil war, just after a war when the country is in a state of turmoil. How *stupid* to have a civil war!'

Curwen sailed for Shanghai on 14 March 1946 – his twenty-first birthday. He had no real idea what he was letting himself in for. China was nothing like the world he was used to. After being torn apart by eight years of violence it was now a country full of 'dirt and disorder and destruction and refugees'. He was to be stationed in the town of Zhongmu in east-central China, about thirty miles from the provincial capital of Zhengzhou. Half of the town had been destroyed by Japanese bombing; the other half had been destroyed by the Kuomintang, which had broken the dykes on the Yellow River in 1938 and flooded the whole region in an attempt to hold the Japanese back. 'When we went there,' said Curwen, 'there were no more than half a dozen houses standing.' His first job was to supervise the building of a clinic and a school house using recycled bricks from the broken-down walls of the town. He also set up a variety of cooperatives to help local people get back on their feet. But in the face of the massive postwar chaos, with a civil war raging not far away and hundreds of thousands of penniless refugees returning to the area, he soon began to feel overwhelmed.

One of the greatest obstacles to the process of rebuilding was the attitude of the various officials he came across. Curwen very quickly learned to hate the Kuomintang regime's soldiers and policemen, who were 'ragged, semi-criminal and oppressive': he used to watch the way they kicked people out of their way, or threw them from trains when they did not have a ticket, and his blood would boil. He found the Kuomintang government officials 'totally ineffective', 'totally uncaring' and corrupt to the core. Some were polite, even deferential to foreigners like Curwen, 'but you felt that in their heart they really hated you'.

Even Chinese relief workers were corrupt, and United Nations aid was generally pilfered long before it got to the people it was meant for: 'Of UNRRA [United Nations Relief and Rehabilitation Administration] goods which were sent for the relief of China there was literally nothing that was not for sale. You could buy anything. You could find UNRRA milk powder on any market stall anywhere throughout the country. If you knew your way around you could buy a trawler, which had been sent to build up the fishing industry.'

To Curwen's disgust, the people who ran this black market were the very people who had been entrusted to relieve the plight of China's poorest and most vulnerable.

It was not long before Curwen began to question why he had come to this place at all. His attempts to help out seemed so ineffectual as to be virtually pointless, and he began to regard his relief work as nothing but 'window dressing' for a national tragedy. It seemed to him that the root of China's problems was 'the total uncaringness of the government', its 'complete lack of efficiency' and its violent attitude towards its own people. 'I developed very rapidly a hatred of the regime as it existed.'

Gradually, his belief in maintaining a strict neutrality was beginning to slip. He still knew nothing about communism, and continued to hold the prejudice against it that all British people of his class were brought up with. But his disgust with the Kuomintang was so strong that he began to believe that the only way to save China was to sweep them away – even if to do so meant abandoning his neutrality. 'Having developed a hatred of the nationalist Kuomintang regime, and not knowing anything about the Communists, I hoped for a middle way, but found that the middle of the road was totally impotent . . . There was no central road.'

Curwen's first contact with the Chinese Communists came in the summer of 1948, when they temporarily overran Zhongmu. At first he was extremely nervous about them, but in contrast with almost all the nationalist soldiers he had come across, they appeared polite, honest and well behaved. There were no atrocities in his town, and no looting; quite the opposite, in fact – when a colleague had his pullover stolen, one of the Communist officers made a show of finding the culprit and returning his property. Grain was confiscated from the rich and distributed amongst the poor. His fears returned briefly when the Communists decided to withdraw from the town and he was taken prisoner, but they explained to him that they were only taking him as a witness in case the returning nationalists staged a massacre of the foreigners in Zhongmu and tried to blame it on them.

Over the coming months the battle lines of the civil war moved back and forth, and Curwen had the chance to observe both sides. He found the comparison enlightening: 'I was deeply impressed by the behaviour of Communists as people, as individuals; by the atmosphere of dynamism and enthusiasm that was quite evident all around; by the immense prestige of the Chinese Communist Party, which was undoubtedly deserved, which they won rapidly. What it was like in Peking or Shanghai, I don't know ... But in the countryside and the backlands the Communists won overwhelming support in a very, very short time by their behaviour, by supporting the poor, by all sorts of things like that.'

What impressed him most was the culture of self-criticism that the Communists encouraged. In the areas under Communist rule, the people were expected to examine their behaviour, confess to past misdemeanours and make pledges to reform themselves. This applied as much, if not more, to party leaders, who were expected to lead by example. He remembered one occasion, during a drive to improve women's rights, when the local Communist Party leader stood on stage and admitted to beating his wife. This sort of behaviour, the leader confessed, was entirely unacceptable, and he promised the people a thorough self-examination, in writing. Under the Kuomintang, such honesty, and such determination to change, would have been unthinkable.

When the Communists finally won the civil war in 1949, it brought, in Curwen's eyes, 'a moral renaissance in people, and a revolution in personal relationships'. Far from destroying China, the civil war, and the Communist victory that it had produced, had transformed the country for the better.

It had also transformed him. The strength of his feelings took him by surprise, and challenged everything he had previously believed – not only about staying neutral but also about eschewing violence: 'I can't tell you when I stopped being a pacifist, because I don't know. But at some time or other I realized that it is sometimes necessary to fight ... I couldn't see what possibility there was for the poor, who constituted the majority in the Chinese countryside, without a revolution. And obviously there was no revolution without violence ... So I stopped being a pacifist, and began to criticize my pacifism, and I came to the conclusion that I was wrong.'

Now, whenever Curwen looked back on the Second World War, he deeply regretted having been a conscientious objector. He began to wish he had abandoned his commitment to pacifism earlier, so that he could have actively opposed fascism, and fought Hitler. For all the good he had done with the Friends Ambulance Unit, he still wished he had taken up arms instead.

When he returned to Britain in 1954 he decided that he would never sit on the fence again. He joined the Communist Party, and remained committed to socialism for the rest of his life.

There were many good reasons for trying to stay neutral during the Second World War and its aftermath. Some people were *actively* impartial, because they disagreed with both sides; while others were *passively* impartial, and wanted only to avoid being drawn into what they believed was somebody else's fight. Many people, and many nations, were afraid to get involved in case they chose the wrong side. A few clung to neutrality as a moral ideal. In Curwen's own case, his pacifist stance was a combination of principle and 'pure rebelliousness'. But it made no difference: sooner or later, almost everyone was forced to choose one side or the other; and if they refused to make that choice, then often it was made for them.

Stories like Anthony Curwen's are rare because he at least had the *choice* to avoid taking part in the Second World War. He was fortunate to live in a society that gave him the chance to opt out of fighting during the war – and yet even he had to go before two tribunals to prove that he was acting out of conscience rather than cowardice. In most other countries, the pacifist stand he made would have been absolutely unthinkable – either because the social pressures to conform would have been too overwhelming, or because the societies they lived in simply would not have allowed it. The history of the war is littered with stories of people in occupied nations who tried to keep out of the violence, but who were forced to take one side or the other by their consciences, by their neighbours, or by the various armed forces and militias who ruled the wartime landscape.

It was not only individuals who often failed to maintain a neutral stance during the war: nations fared just as badly. Norway, Denmark, Belgium, the Netherlands and Luxembourg all claimed to be neutral countries before the war – a fact that did nothing to prevent them from being invaded by Germany in 1940. Likewise, Estonia, Latvia and Lithuania – three more neutral countries – were invaded by the Soviet Union. In Southeast Asia, Thailand's claims to neutrality did not save it from being invaded by the Japanese, who wanted to transport their troops across Thai territory. The country's authoritarian government took the hint, and Thailand passed the rest of the war in an uncomfortable alliance with Japan. In Latin America both Argentina and Chile spent the majority of the war protesting their neutrality, but under sustained pressure from the United States were eventually forced to abandon this stance in 1944 and 1945. Nations under colonial rule were never even given the choice: India, Korea, the Middle East and almost the whole of Africa were forced to take one side or another whether they wished to or not.

Only a handful of nations were allowed to keep their neutral status throughout the war, most notably Ireland, Sweden, Switzerland, Spain, Portugal and the Vatican. And yet even these states were frequently coerced into acts that benefited one side or the other. Sweden, for example, was forced to allow trains filled with German troops to cross its territory on the way to the Russian Front; Portugal was pressured into allowing Allied shipping and aircraft to use its overseas ports; and Switzerland, which was entirely surrounded by Axis countries during the war, was forced to drop its trade in armaments to Britain, even while its trade with Germany ballooned.[5]

On the rare occasions when these countries breached their neutrality out of conscience, their true political colours always shone through. Sweden secretly provided bases for the Norwegian Resistance. Spain's Fascist government, like Argentina's, happily tolerated Nazi spies and the Vatican turned a blind eye to the sins of anyone who opposed communism, even when some of those people turned out to be wanted war criminals. In the final reckoning, wartime neutrality was at best only ever an aspiration. At worst, it was an excuse for hypocrisy.[6]

After the harsh lessons of the war, many nations abandoned their pretensions towards neutrality. The Netherlands, which had been a neutral country since 1839, was reborn at the start of the Cold War as one of the founding members of NATO (the North Atlantic Treaty Organization, the military alliance which guaranteed the collective security of western Europe and North America against the Soviet threat). The same was true of Norway, Denmark, Belgium, Luxembourg and Portugal. Turkey, which had also been neutral during the war, declared itself firmly on the side of the West, and became a member of NATO in 1952. Meanwhile formerly neutral Spain entered a direct alliance with the USA.[7] (Conversely, two European nations *became* neutral after the war – Austria (1955) and Finland (1956) – although in each case this was at the behest of the USSR: the Soviets refused to remove their troops from either country otherwise.)

Other parts of the world followed suit. Thailand abandoned its attempt at neutrality and became a founder member of SEATO, the Southeast Asian equivalent of NATO, whose headquarters are in Bangkok. In Latin America, those countries that had been coerced into supporting the USA during the Second World War, such as Chile and Argentina, now deepened their attachment voluntarily with the Rio Treaty of 1947 – perhaps not through love, but at least through a mutual fear of communism. After the start of the Cold War, neutrality became virtually impossible in Latin America. Those nations that did not pay proper lip service to the USA's anti-Communist view of the world either found themselves subjected to enforced regime change, as with Guatemala in 1954, or were harassed so persistently, and so clumsily, by Washington that they were forced into the waiting arms of the Soviet Union – as with Fidel Castro's Cuba in 1961.[8]

Once again, even those nations that maintained their neutral status into the Cold War did not always act in a neutral way. Sweden, for example, was economically integrated into the West, regularly bought arms from Britain and America (but never from the Soviet Union), and even conducted airborne spying missions over the USSR on behalf of NATO.[9] Switzerland, meanwhile, was a deeply conservative state, whose pathological fear of communism led it to make secret pacts with NATO, buy huge quantities of arms from the West and even to flirt with the creation of its own nuclear deterrent.[10] In addition, the Swiss federal police embarked on a grotesque and illegal programme of surveillance upon its own people that was revealed only after the Cold War was over. They were helped by thousands of businessmen, politicians, military men, members of think-tanks and ordinary 'concerned citizens' who gladly spied on their neighbours and reported any left-wing activity to the authorities.[11] Such people were an important part of the national subconscious. Just as Curwen was unable to maintain his neutrality in the face of a corrupt and bankrupt Chinese system, so these 'concerned citizens' were unable to put their distrust of communism aside, no matter how neutral their country professed to be.

The Non-Aligned Movement

If the idea of neutrality often ended up being an illusion both for individuals and for nations, how did it look at an international level? In the postwar era there were two major international organizations that purported to be neutral – or, to be more accurate, 'non-aligned' (since the term 'neutral' had quite a specific legal meaning). These were the United Nations itself, and a group of nations known as the 'Non-Aligned Movement'. Did these international bodies fare any better?

The failings of the UN in this respect are well known. In the 1940s and 50s the organization was dominated by the USA, which provided most of its funding as well as its headquarters, and which could count on the almost unwavering support of the vast majority of its founder members. In these early days it was only the Security Council, and the Soviet veto, that prevented the organization from becoming little more than a tool of American foreign policy.[12]

The Non-Aligned Movement, meanwhile, had different problems. The movement was officially founded in 1961, but its roots go back to the direct aftermath of the Second World War when a variety of Asian nations were on the brink of independence. Having witnessed the destruction caused by the war, India's new prime minister, Jawaharlal Nehru, thought it only sensible 'to keep away from the power politics of groups aligned against one another, which have led in the past to world wars and which may again lead to disasters on an even vaster scale'.[13] More importantly, having fought so long for independence, he saw no reason to subordinate India's foreign policy to someone else's agenda. 'By aligning ourselves with any one power,' he told the Indian parliament in 1951, 'you surrender your opinion, give up the policy you would normally pursue because somebody else wants you to pursue another policy.'[14] As a consequence, India started its new life as an independent nation by following a strictly neutral foreign policy.

This line was also followed by other Asian countries emerging into independence, like Indonesia, whose President Sukarno regarded the

Cold War as just another manifestation of the same old imperialism that his people had just freed themselves from.[15] It spread to the Arab nations, like Egypt, which adopted 'positive neutralism' as 'the only wise policy', and also to African countries, some of whose leaders asserted that 'the whole of the African continent should be a neutral zone'. Egypt's Gamal Abdel Nasser went so far as to call the policy of non-engagement 'the expression of the conscience of mankind', because it was a policy 'against domination and inequality, against militarism, against nuclear experiments, for peace and the independence of nations'. Just as Anthony Curwen embraced communism for the sake of his conscience, so Nasser embraced non-alignment for the sake of his country.[16]

In the fifteen years that followed the end of the Second World War, the Non-Aligned Movement became something of a phenomenon. At the Bandung Conference in 1955, twenty-nine African and Asian nations gathered to express their rejection of great powers meddling in their affairs. The 'spirit of Bandung' quickly ignited the colonial world. In 1961, at the Non-Aligned Movement's founding conference in Belgrade, this spirit spread into Europe and Latin America. By the end of the century the movement had 114 members, which included 37 Asian countries, over 20 Latin American countries, and every single African nation. It has continued to expand ever since: several Caribbean nations joined in the 2000s, and Fiji and Azerbaijan were admitted to the group as recently as 2011.[17]

However, there have always been question marks over exactly how 'non-aligned' this organization really is. Despite their collective title, many of the nations involved quite clearly *were* aligned to one power bloc or another. The People's Republic of China was invited to the Bandung Conference despite being a Communist country explicitly allied to the Soviet Union. Six years later, when Cuba became one of the founder members of the movement, it was just six months away from allowing the USSR to build nuclear missile bases on its territory. Cyprus, another founder member, provided military bases for Britain, and Saudi Arabia and Pakistan had strong links to the USA. Several countries in francophone Africa, like Senegal and Gabon, deliberately maintained military links to France. Many of the supposedly non-aligned states have entered into military pacts with the great powers, and many of them still maintain such pacts to this day. All this is explicitly against the principles of the movement, as laid out in its own documents.[18]

Furthermore, the movement itself has much more often adopted anti-American positions than it has anti-Soviet ones. During the 1970s in particular, it tended to side with the Soviet Union on most issues, and blamed the Western powers, and especially the United States, for its economic imperialism, for atrocities in Vietnam and for political and military meddling in Latin America. Leading the charge was Cuba, which had close ties with the USSR, whose stance was shared by increasing numbers of non-aligned nations, many of whom were themselves turning towards Marxist ideas.[19]

In the end, 'non-alignment' turned out to be just as much of an illusion as 'neutrality'. In a world where almost every action was claimed or rejected by one side or the other, it was virtually impossible to steer a middle course. Perhaps the only nation to come close was Burma, which went to the extreme of virtually cutting itself off from the rest of the world, adopting a near-pacifist stance and even withdrawing temporarily from the Non-Aligned Movement in 1979 because of its concerns about the growing biases within the organization.[20] But for any nation that wished to engage with the rest of the world, there was really no choice but to pick sides. The only guide for which side to pick, as Anthony Curwen demonstrated, was to follow your conscience, whichever way it might lead you.

And yet, this is not the whole story. It is very tempting to portray concepts such as 'neutrality' or 'non-alignment' purely as reactions to the superpower blocs that had established themselves in the aftermath of the war, but, of course, the situation was not nearly so simple as that. There were all sorts of other, equally powerful forces at work. Anthony Curwen did not become a Communist as a reaction to the Cold War, but because of the very specific local circumstances he found himself in. Other individuals from different backgrounds and in different circumstances made exactly the opposite choice, and sided with the Chinese nationalists. Likewise, nations did not always look to the international environment when adopting their foreign policies – often it was their own history and their own domestic issues that proved most influential. The Swiss determination to remain neutral after 1945, for example, had less to do with the Cold War than it did with national pride. In the second half of the twentieth century, neutrality became a defining characteristic of Swiss identity, a marker of difference from its neighbours.

Paradoxically, it was this same sense of national pride that led to the secret *abandonment* of Swiss neutrality, as the country's elite fell into the old trap of believing they were far more important to European and world affairs than they really were.[21]

Similar forces were at work in the Non-Aligned Movement. As Jamaica's prime minister Michael Manley pointed out in 1979, 'the Non-Aligned Movement did not begin simply because there were blocs': there were other reasons that seemed far more pressing than the Cold War.[22] In the early days, the movement's main focus was not the USA or the USSR at all, but western European colonialism. 'The ideological conflict is *not*, I repeat, *not* the main problem of our time,' claimed Sukarno at the Belgrade conference. 'In every single case, the cause, the root of international tension, is imperialism and colonialism and the forcible division of nations.'[23] The movement's first priority therefore, particularly for the Asian and African nations that made up most of its members, was the struggle for independence from the old empires of Britain, France, Belgium, Portugal and the Netherlands. The Cold War was only really considered important because it stood in the way of this struggle.

What gave the Non-Aligned Movement its vast energy was the sense of historical injustice endured by Asians, Africans and eventually also Latin Americans, at the hands of white, predominantly European settlers. All the strongest myths of the immediate postwar period were here employed in abundance. The people of Africa and Asia were portrayed as history's victims, but also the heroes of national liberation, who were now rising from the ashes of Europe's crumbling empires. The war, which had destroyed the old world, had also created the opportunity, as Sukarno put it, 'to build the world anew'.[24]

Beneath all the rhetoric about freedom, justice and world peace was the same force that motivated the USA, the Soviet Union and most other parts of the world: nationalism. It was nationalism that had driven all of the movement's independence struggles, and it was nationalism that inspired them to work together to gain a greater voice in the world's affairs. 'In its essence,' Tunisia's first president, Habib Bourguiba, told the Belgrade conference in 1961, 'nationalism has been for all of us former colonized peoples a fight for man's dignity in all its aspects.'[25] Thus the very force that had been so discredited by the Second World War was given new life in the war's aftermath by the emerging nations of the world.

If ever there was a challenge to the hopes and dreams of world federalists to create a single, world system, it was here. Just as the impetus to unite was brought to a rude halt by the Cold War, so the inequalities and injustices inherent in the world system gave a new impetus to those who wanted to break away.

It is these forces of liberation, of nationalism and of fragmentation – unleashed by the Second World War and nurtured by the old world's tragic attempts to hang on to their dying colonial power – that I shall turn to next.

PART V

Two Hundred Nations

16. The Birth of an Asian Nation

What is a nation? Is it defined by the land that a people chooses to call its home? Is it a matter of race, or ethnicity, or genetics? Or is a nation characterized by other, more intangible characteristics – a shared language or religion, or a common cultural heritage? Can a nation define itself by its political beliefs and, if so, does it have the right to impose such beliefs, directly or indirectly, upon its members?

In the wake of the Second World War, dozens of new nations declared themselves, and then immediately began grappling with such questions. Almost without exception, they rapidly discovered that there is no working definition of a nation. A nation is an 'imagined community', that's all – and it changes depending on who is doing the imagining. It is often defined as much by who is *not* part of the nation as by who is; but enemies can change, as can political beliefs, religious beliefs and all other cultural reference points. Borders between countries can also change: when the demarcation line between one nation and the next is determined merely by a line on a map, how can we truly say who is 'us' and who is 'them'?

One of the first new nations to confront this challenge in 1945 was Indonesia, and the process it went through demonstrates the agony of coming face to face with a blank slate. The people who declared their independence in August that year had the freedom to define themselves in any way they wished, but struggled to find anything that united them. The territory they claimed was spread out across 19,000 different islands, some of them no more than sand spits and atolls, others large and densely populated. The people they represented belonged to more than 200 distinct cultural and ethnic groups. They spoke more than thirty different languages and dialects, had different customs, different religions, and vastly differing relationships with modernity. Hindu peasants in Bali had virtually nothing in common with Muslim oil workers in Aceh or Christian plantation workers in Ambon. The urban elite of Jakarta was a world away from the Dayak hunter-gatherers in Kalimantan. Virtually the only link between these people was that they had all been conquered by the Dutch, some of them only very recently. But beyond their common hatred for colonialism, there was no particular reason why they should bond together as a single nation.[1]

And yet bond together they did. The process by which they did so tells us a great deal about what being a new nation meant in the wake of the Second World War, but also about the perils and pitfalls of 'freedom' itself.

Before the Second World War, Indonesia was ruled by the Dutch and went by the name of the 'Netherlands East Indies'. However, during the 1920s and 30s, a small, committed nationalist movement had grown up in the country, particularly on the island of Java. One of its activists was a young teacher and journalist named Trimurti, who joined the Indonesian National Party in 1933. By the beginning of the war she had been in trouble with the Dutch authorities many times. After instructing her elementary class, in her words, 'to refuse to be ruled by another country', she had been banned from teaching. Later, she had spent nine months in prison for distributing subversive leaflets. By the time the Japanese attacked in 1942 she was in prison again, this time for publishing an article written by her husband, a fellow nationalist named Sayuti Melik, which claimed that the Dutch and the Japanese were just as bad as each other. 'The Netherlands and Japan are like the tiger and the crocodile,' the article said. 'Both are dangerous. Indonesians would be better off empowering themselves, to prepare for their own independence.'[2]

When the Japanese army swept across Java many of Trimurti's countrymen celebrated, believing that they were at last being liberated. Trimurti herself was released from prison shortly after their arrival. But in her heart she knew that neither she nor her country was really free: all that had happened was the replacement of one empire with another. Her suspicions were confirmed in August that year, when she was arrested yet again, this time by the Kempeitai.

She immediately discovered that the Dutch and the Japanese were not so similar after all. Under the Dutch, she remembered, 'It wasn't too bad. We knew what to expect, we served our time and were released when it was due. While in prison we were required to work. That was it. Japanese prison was nothing like that.'[3]

This time, her interrogators showed no mercy. They beat her repeatedly until she lay half-paralysed on the floor, and then led her husband

1. The leaders of twenty nations, including six of the world's ten largest economies, gather on the steps of the Château de Bénouville in France in 2014. The occasion? Not a trade conference or political summit, but a commemoration of the Second World War: the 70th anniversary of D-Day.

2. A Spitfire, a Lancaster bomber and a Hurricane fly over Buckingham Palace during the wedding celebrations for Prince William and Kate Middleton. These Second World War aircraft have become as much a symbol of Britain as the royal family themselves.

3. The art of the victim: *Stolen Innocence*, by Kang Duk-kyung. Kang was raped by a Japanese military policeman in 1944 and spent the rest of the war incarcerated in a Japanese military brothel. Her painting depicts a cherry tree, a symbol of Japan, covered in phallic chilli peppers. Beneath its roots are the skulls of the women it has already consumed.

4. The hero gets his girl: Eduardo Kobra's mural of a sailor and a nurse celebrating VJ Day in New York City. It is a reworking of Alfred Eisenstaedt's famous 1945 photograph in *Life* magazine, which gave Americans a fairy-tale ending to their war.

5. The world reborn: in the UN Security Council chamber, Per Krohg's huge mural depicts people climbing out of the hell of the Second World War into a bright new world. Above the President's seat, a phoenix rises from the ashes.

6. The Second World War is often invoked in the name of nationalist rivalries. Here, Italy's *Il Giornale* proclaims Angela Merkel's Germany in 2012 to be the 'Fourth Reich'.

7. The EU as the enemy. In January 2016 Polish news magazine *Wprost* depicts prominent EU politicians as Hitler and his generals. The headline reads, 'Again they want to supervise Poland'.

8. 'Dachau!' Greek nationalist newspaper *Dimokratia* claims that EU austerity measures, as outlined in a 2012 memorandum, are turning Greece into a German concentration camp.

9. Britain's greatest war hero, Winston Churchill, adorns one side of the country's £5 note. Introduced in the summer of 2016, the note's design immediately prompted speculation in the press about how Churchill would have voted in that summer's Brexit referendum.

10. An alternative wartime hero appears on this Italian postage stamp from 2007: Altiero Spinelli, who spent the war years drafting a blueprint for the European Union.

11. Since the 1990s, interest in the Second World War has ballooned in China. Lu Chuan's 2009 blockbuster *Nanjing! Nanjing!* is one of many productions depicting the savage outbreak of war in 1937.

12. Second World War martyrdom and heroism is a staple of Russian TV and cinema. Fedor Bondarchuk's 2013 film *Stalingrad* broke Russian box office records.

13. Martyrdom and salvation as a museum experience. After making their way through the harrowing exhibition in the Holocaust museum at Yad Vashem, visitors are rewarded with this view over the Jerusalem hills. Thus Zionism and the Holocaust become entwined: the Land of Israel is literally the light at the end of the tunnel.

14. Martyrdom by proxy in Latin America. The Holocaust memorial in Montevideo is proof that the Jewish victims of the Second World War are regarded as universal victims. However, there is more going on here than meets the eye. This memorial was erected in 1994 at a time when Uruguay was still mourning atrocities by its own recent dictatorship.

15. The new Second World War Museum in Gdansk, completed in 2017, uses its architecture to impart an unnerving sense of dystopia. On opening, its ground-breaking exhibition was too nuanced for the nationalist government, which criticized it for being 'not Polish enough'.

16. Since 1945, Western Europe has seen a long boom in immigration. In this controversial image, taken during the 2005 German elections, two Muslim immigrants are seen beside an election poster that reads 'Better for our country'.

17. The rise of the radical right in Europe and America since 2008 has prompted countless parallels with the 1930s. During his presidential campaign, America's Donald Trump was regularly compared to Hitler, especially because of the way he demonized immigrants and Muslims. Here, the *Philadelphia Daily News* employs 'Furor' as a pun on 'Führer'.

S. K. Trimurti a few years after the war.

in to see what had been done to her. It turned out they were not really interested in her at all – they merely wanted to force a confession out of her husband, who was accused of setting up an anti-Japanese resistance cell. He took one look at her on the floor and signed the confession. 'It was the first time I saw my husband shed tears.'[4]

What followed was a time of enormous physical and emotional hardship. Trimurti's husband was sent to prison for the remainder of the war; she, meanwhile, was put under house arrest in Semarang. Unable to work, she fed herself and her children by selling off all her possessions one by one until she had virtually nothing left.

She was finally rescued in 1943 by Sukarno, one of Indonesia's most important political leaders, who had known Trimurti since her early activist days. The Japanese had allowed Sukarno to set up a heavily regulated nationalist administration – not because they particularly supported Indonesian independence, but because they hoped to use it as their puppet. Hearing of Trimurti's predicament, Sukarno had specifically requested that she come and work for him in Jakarta.

Over the next two years Trimurti saw her country transformed.

'Almost every day I saw newly conscripted slave labourers in Jakarta dead at the roadside, or in a state of near-death lying in the side-streets,' she later remembered. For the first time, she felt powerless to do anything about it. 'I could not publicize these incidents in a newspaper. At that time there were no independent newspapers capable of describing what was actually going on in the country. All the newspapers were owned by the Japanese, and strictly controlled.'[5] The only thing she could do was to be patient, and wait to see how the war progressed.

Change did eventually come. In 1944, with the tide finally turning against Japan, the military government began to make some concessions. Indonesians were allowed to display their national flag once more, and to sing the national anthem, 'Indonesia Raya'. In 1945, Trimurti was invited to a conference to discuss how best to prepare for independence. The Japanese even started releasing some of their political prisoners, including Trimurti's husband. Then, in August, news filtered through that some kind of miracle bomb had exploded over Japan. A week or so later, Japan announced its unconditional surrender to the Allies. All of a sudden the war was over.

From this point, events began to move fast. Rather than wait to be granted independence, some of the more radical nationalists thought that it would send out a more positive message if they seized it for themselves. Sukarno and the other main political leader, Muhammad Hatta, were quite reluctant to do this, fearing that it might provoke the Japanese, but after some very heated arguments with the youth wing of their movement they finally agreed. So Trimurti's husband typed out a short declaration. And Trimurti herself headed off with another group to help seize control of the Japanese radio station.

On 17 August 1945, two days after the Japanese surrender, the declaration of independence was read out by Sukarno. The short statement was not poetic or flamboyant in any way – it merely stated the facts: colonialism had come to an end, and the Indonesian nation had been born.

Today, S. K. Trimurti is remembered as one of the handful of people who personally witnessed the moment when the declaration was signed. It was a moment of triumph that linked her to the entire nation: after all the many years of arrests, imprisonment and subjugation by foreign powers, she and her countrymen had at last reached out and grasped their freedom.

Merdeka!

Trimurti's story is an inspiring tale of triumph against the odds, and it is tempting to applaud it as an example of peaceful protest winning out over oppression and violence. Unfortunately, the story does not end there. Indonesia in the wake of the war was a country gripped by chaos. Many of the colonial power structures built up by the Dutch over the preceding century had been swept away by the Japanese during the war. Now the Japanese were themselves being swept away, and Sukarno's fledgling national government, while enjoying massive popular support in principle, did not yet have any real power in practice. It would take time to set up a national police force, a national judiciary and a national army – let alone a proper democratic structure that everyone could be happy with. In the meantime there was no one capable of imposing control upon a people who had been made wildly excited by the idea of freedom, and highly volatile by the idea of revenge.

For a while, therefore, the whole nation was plunged into anarchy as all kinds of local militias, warlords, revolutionary youth groups and gangs of criminals stepped into the power vacuum. The one thing that united all these groups was a fear that the Dutch were planning to return and reclaim their colony – but beyond that they had very little in common. Along the north coast of Java, for example, in the area known as the 'Three Regions', gangs of ruffians called 'Fighting Cocks' teamed up with local Communists to institute a wholesale purge of the local power structures. Local officials and village heads were publicly humiliated in front of their communities, and Eurasians and other people suspected of being pro-Dutch were murdered. In central and eastern Java, by contrast, it was Muslim militias who led the way, fighting battles against leftists in the name of their traditional religious values. Along the coasts of Sumatra and Kalimantan there were savage attacks on the Malay sultans who had held sway under both the Dutch and the Japanese. The lords of Aceh were likewise all executed or deposed by left-wing groups. Chinese merchants throughout the archipelago were attacked because they had been collaborators, because they had 'exploited' the people, or merely because they were Chinese: in one area near Jakarta so many Chinese corpses were thrown down wells that local people had trouble getting hold of any fresh water. Meanwhile,

Europeans who had been interred in hellish prison camps since 1942 were advised not to venture out to freedom even though the war was supposedly over. Given the vengeful atmosphere outside, it was safer to stay under Japanese guard.[6]

Trimurti witnessed this chaotic atmosphere at first hand. In October 1945 she was sent to Semarang to help spread the news of *merdeka* – 'freedom', in Indonesian – and found herself immersed in a battle between Indonesian revolutionary youth groups and Japanese soldiers. Shortly afterwards, she and her husband were sent to Tegal during the Three Regions Revolt, where her husband was captured and almost killed by Communist rebels. When she headed off to Yogyakarta to ask Sukarno for reinforcements, she too was arrested as a 'Dutch spy'. She only escaped with her life because she happened to know the rebel leader, who told his men to let her go. This was a long way from the happy ending that she and her fellow nationalists had struggled so hard for.

Such was the situation that greeted the Allies when they finally arrived on the islands in September and October 1945. The British, who were experienced in policing colonial unrest, knew that their first job would be to re-establish order, but they always expected this to be relatively straightforward. They had been assured by the Dutch that they would be welcomed by most people as liberators, and that after a short and orderly transfer of power they would be able to retire gracefully and concentrate their attentions on their own colonies in the region.[7]

The Dutch assumed that they would be able to re-establish their colonial rule over the country without too much trouble, but what they failed to appreciate was how much Indonesia had changed over the past four years. To say that the Second World War had transformed the country would be an understatement. Indonesia might not have seen any of the major battles of the war, but it had experienced a brutal occupation that had left the population bitter and angry. Hundreds of thousands of civilians had been conscripted by the Japanese as forced labourers. Tens of thousands of women had been sexually assaulted by Japanese soldiers. Hunger had struck everywhere: in Java alone, some 2.4 million people are thought to have died of starvation during the war years, and perhaps a further million had starved on the other islands, largely as a consequence of Japanese colonial policies. Having experienced the very depths of exploitation, Indonesians were no longer prepared to be anyone's vassal nation.[8]

The war had changed them in other ways too. After two years of Sukarno and Hatta, Indonesians had got used to the idea of governing themselves: the wartime administration may have been a Japanese puppet, but it was still more than anything the Dutch had ever given them. Alongside their fledgling government, they also had a fledgling army. The Japanese had trained up more than 35,000 Indonesian troops and 900 officers as 'Homeland Defenders'. 'If it weren't for Japanese training, not one of our soldiers would be soldiers,' remembered one Indonesian nationalist years later. 'That was how Japan helped us, they were really cruel but they were the ones who trained the soldiers.'[9]

After years of propaganda about 'Asia for the Asians', Indonesians were no longer inclined to pay lip service to the myth of European superiority. They had demonstrated that they no longer wanted the Dutch, and believed themselves fully capable of running their own affairs. If the Dutch thought they could simply walk into the country and take back control unopposed, they had another thing coming.

The first major sign that life would not be returning to normal any time soon occurred in Surabaya. On 13 September 1945 a small group of Allied officers had landed in the city to begin negotiations with the Japanese. A few days later, some Dutch and Eurasian men celebrated their arrival by raising the Dutch flag outside the hotel where they were staying. Incensed, a group of schoolboys and local toughs gathered, and one of them climbed up and tore the blue stripe off the Dutch flag, so that it looked instead like the red and white Indonesian nationalist banner. A huge brawl broke out that had to be broken up by Japanese soldiers, but not before one Dutchman sustained fatal injuries.[10]

In the following days, tensions escalated throughout the city. Crowds of freedom fighters, local gangsters and idealistic students took to the streets, attacking Chinese shopkeepers, Europeans, Eurasians and anyone suspected of being pro-Dutch. Several thousand Europeans and Eurasians were rounded up and taken to Kalisosok prison. Meanwhile, confrontations with Japanese soldiers also began to escalate. The Kempeitai headquarters was besieged and Japanese stores were looted for their weapons and supplies. All of a sudden, Indonesian fighters found themselves in possession of an arsenal.[11]

By the time the British arrived in numbers, on 25 October, a rag-tag army of Indonesian youths and former Home Guard members had formed that was well armed and fully prepared to defend the city against a return of the Dutch. 'We who revolt,' announced Sutomo, one of their leaders, 'would rather see Indonesia drowned in blood and sunk to the bottom of the sea than colonized once more!' A rumour began to spread that the British forces, who were mostly Indians and Nepalese Gurkhas, were actually Dutchmen with blacked-up faces.[12]

The British, who had been expecting a routine peace-keeping operation, struggled to calm things down. Skirmishes broke out all over town, culminating in a massive attack by local fighters on British positions. Hundreds of Indian soldiers were killed by the Indonesians, and hundreds more taken prisoner. In desperation, the British asked Sukarno and Muhammad Hatta to come to the city and broker a ceasefire. They did so, but it was not long before fighting broke out again. Passions had become too inflamed to contain.

When the British commander himself, Brigadier Mallaby, was killed while trying to calm down a mob, the British finally lost their cool. For three weeks in November they attacked Surabaya with a massive bombing and shelling campaign. British soldiers fought from house to house, and as terrified civilians fled into the countryside, British planes strafed them. The city was at last pacified, but in the process large parts of it had been reduced to rubble and ashes. Estimates of the dead vary from about 2,500 to 15,000, a high proportion of them innocent civilians. As much as 90 per cent of the population fled.[13]

The whole episode was an appalling waste of life from start to finish. The Indonesian fighters never stood a chance against the full might of the Allies, and yet they refused to give in until they had been driven out of the city's environs. Their slogan *Merdeka atau mati* – 'Freedom or death' – seemed to be something they took quite literally: there are numerous accounts of young fighters throwing themselves at British tanks in doomed suicide attacks. And yet, for all the senseless waste of life that this involved, the Indonesians had at least shown the world that they would not give up their independence without a fight. The Battle of Surabaya was a symbol that *merdeka* was a cause worth fighting for. Today the battle is still commemorated on 10 November each year, which in Indonesia is known as 'Heroes Day'.[14]

Similar scenes occurred throughout the country in the following months and years. In Jakarta, while the Allies were trying to set up a new civil administration, nightly battles broke out between pro-Dutch vigilantes and Indonesian nationalists. In Sumatra, Bali and Sulawesi thousands of young men and women took to the forests armed only with spears, knives and the hand weapons they had taken from the Japanese. When ordered to surrender the city of Bandung in 1946, nationalist militias set fire to it instead. In the Karo highlands above Medan in Sumatra they followed suit, burning down fifty-three villages and turning the region into a 'sea of fire'.[15]

The years that followed were an exercise in futility. The British pulled out of Indonesia not much more than a year after they had arrived, bloodied, tired and disillusioned by the whole affair. The Dutch administration they left behind them was determined to regain control of their colony by any means necessary. In 1946 they sent death squads into Sulawesi to wage a brutal counter-insurgency campaign, but despite an estimated 6,000 people being executed, the republicans refused to be pacified. Between 1947 and 1949 the Dutch launched a series of 'police actions', ostensibly in the name of restoring order, but also to re-establish their own hold on power. They succeeded in conquering large regions of Java and Sumatra, but only at the expense of driving vast numbers of people away. These events were just as devastating as anything that happened during the Second World War: between 45,000 and 100,000 Indonesian fighters were killed and at least 25,000 civilians were caught in the crossfire. In Sumatra and Java alone, more than 7 million people were displaced.[16]

By 1949 it was becoming clear even to the Dutch that such wastefulness was unsustainable. No matter how much they fought, they could not defeat a movement that both refused to be cowed and was supported by a large proportion of the population. Nor could they afford to ignore world opinion. Australia had long been vocal about Indonesian independence, followed by India and other nations; but it was the intervention of the USA that finally defeated Dutch ambitions. When America threatened to withdraw Marshall Aid from the Netherlands, the Dutch finally decided to cut their losses and leave. In December that year, more than four years after it had first declared independence, Indonesia was a free and sovereign nation.[17]

The End of Empire

Unfortunately, Indonesia was not the only Asian nation that had to fight for its independence after 1945, and the Dutch were not the only Western power to block their ears to the cries of '*merdeka!*' In the wake of the Second World War, similar events took place all over the continent. The age of European colonialism, which had defined Asia for the past two hundred years, was at last coming to an end.

The country whose experience was closest to Indonesia's was the French colony of Indochina, comprising Vietnam, Cambodia and Laos. Like the Dutch East Indies, French Indochina had been invaded by Japan near the beginning of the Second World War. Both countries had had their European overlords interned. And both countries had been granted a measure of independence in the dying days of the war. The Japanese had set up puppet administrations in Vietnam (under the emperor Bao Dai), in Cambodia (under King Norodom Sihanouk) and in Laos (under the Lao Issarak, or 'Free Lao' movement). In each case these puppets had been encouraged to sever all ties to France and had been promised full independence at some point in the future.[18]

Of the three nations in Indochina, Vietnam embraced the idea of independence most passionately. During the war a resistance movement had formed called the Viet Minh (Vietnamese Independence League), whose leader was the Communist nationalist Ho Chi Minh. Two weeks after Sukarno had declared the independence of Indonesia, Ho appeared before a crowd of 300,000 people in Hanoi to do the same for Vietnam. In an eloquent speech, which quoted from both the US Declaration of Independence and the French Declaration of the Rights of Man, he announced that 'the entire Vietnamese people' were prepared 'to sacrifice their lives and property in order to safeguard their independence and liberty'.[19]

Much like the Dutch in Indonesia, the French were not prepared to relinquish their colony without a fight. Their return to Vietnam followed much the same pattern. Once again, it was the British who led the way, this time by fighting a bloody battle against the Viet Minh in Saigon. Once again, the British pulled out as soon as the French had re-established themselves in the country. A series of negotiations and truces were made and broken, culminating in all-out war between the colonizers and the colonized. As with the Dutch in Indonesia, the French possessed superior firepower, superior organization and superior training, but they were still unable to match a mobile army of guerrillas who had a significant proportion of the population backing them. By the time the French finally gave up the fight in 1954, some 90,000 colonial French troops and perhaps as many as 200,000 Vietnamese had been killed.[20]

The legacy of this colonial war was poisonous. It left the country split in half, with the Viet Minh in the north, and a series of authoritarian governments in the south. These two sides would remain at war for the next twenty years. Worse still, their conflict would drag in the superpowers. The one major difference between Indonesia and Vietnam was that the independence movement in Vietnam was made up of self-proclaimed Communists. Since the USA had vowed to contain the spread of communism by any means necessary, it took up the fight more or less where the French left off. But its efforts were not much more successful. The American war in Vietnam would end up being one of the greatest disasters in the history of either nation: by 1975 it had cost more than 58,000 American lives and around 1.3 million Vietnamese ones. If this was the price of 'freedom', it was indeed a high and very bloody one.[21]

The other parts of French Indochina fared slightly better, but not for long. Cambodia and Laos were granted independence in 1953, but both countries would be greatly affected by the civil war in neighbouring Vietnam, which often spilled into their own territories. Both would soon find themselves embroiled in civil wars of their own, and by 1975 both states had fallen to communism. In Cambodia this would have tragic results: in the 1970s the Khmer Rouge under Pol Pot would begin a reign of terror in which ethnic enemies as well as class enemies were systematically slaughtered and starved to death. Nobody knows how many people they killed, but estimates range from 1.6 million to 2 million.[22]

It is impossible to say whether these things would have happened if the French had decided not to try to clutch hold of their dying empire. In all likelihood, some kind of violence and chaos was inevitable, given the atmosphere of ideological fervour that had been unleashed by the war. But the French did not do themselves any favours on the international stage: it was hard to portray themselves as the

guardians of liberty, equality and fraternity while simultaneously flout-
ing the UN charter and denying the people of Indochina the right of
self-determination.

Unlike the French and the Dutch, the British never fell into the trap of
trying to hold on to their Asian colonies. For all their faults, they at least
seemed to understand that the world, and Asia, had changed. Britain
had changed too. It was no longer the power it had once been, and was
forced to rely on financial help from the Americans, who made a point
of insisting that the British let go of their empire.

Over the coming years, Britain divested itself of its Asian colonies
one by one. The first to go was the jewel in the British imperial crown,
India, which became independent in 1947. It is worth noting that one of
the reasons the British were so keen to extricate themselves from the
chaos in Indonesia was that so many of the troops under their command
were Indian. Expecting Indian soldiers to subdue an independence
movement when they themselves were undergoing the same process at
home seemed to be asking for trouble. As it was, some 600 Indian soldiers deserted after the Battle of Surabaya alone: many took Indonesian
wives and stayed on in the city for the rest of their lives.[23]

Burma and Ceylon followed on shortly afterwards, gaining independence in 1948. Malaya did not become independent until 1957, but
only because the British were intent on quelling an uprising by Communist Chinese rebels first; however, they made it quite clear, early on,
that they would hand over complete political control just as soon as the
Communists had been defeated. In 1963 North Borneo and Sarawak also
became independent of Britain, and joined Malaya to become the new
state of Malaysia; as did Singapore, before breaking away to form its own
state in 1965. Brunei, a British protectorate, became fully independent in
1967. For the next thirty years the only colony Britain retained in Asia
was Hong Kong, which was eventually handed over to China in 1997.

None of these colonies was made to suffer a prolonged struggle for
independence. However, this did not mean that they escaped violence.
Much of the same political, ethnic and religious chaos that overtook
Indonesia also occurred in Britain's colonies. Hong Kong and Singapore
saw the lynching of Japanese collaborators in the immediate wake of the
war. Waves of revenge swept over Malaya, followed not only by the
Communist uprising that became known as the 'Malayan Emergency'

but also by the persecution of the country's Chinese minority. Ceylon, modern-day Sri Lanka, suffered a series of riots and general strikes in the run-up to independence, and mounting tension between its Sinhalese people and its Tamil minority afterwards. Burma faced a Communist insurrection just two months after achieving its freedom, and ten months after that another insurrection by the Karen people in the south and south-west of the country, who wanted an independent state of their own. The forces unleashed by the idea of independence were often difficult to contain: everyone agreed on the principle of self-determination, but where did it stop?[24]

It was India that saw the greatest bloodshed of all. Here, it was religious violence that finally tipped the country into chaos. Irreconcilable differences between Hindus and Muslims during and after the war had led the British to consider a partition between the two communities: on independence, the nation would be split into three – a predominantly Hindu state to the south, and a predominantly Muslim state, in two parts, to the north-west and north-east. But during the partition process public order broke down completely. Muslims fled India for the newly created East and West Pakistan (now Pakistan and Bangladesh); Hindus and Sikhs fled in the opposite direction. There were wholesale massacres on both sides. In total, some 15 million people were displaced, and between 200,000 and 2 million people killed – though no one can be sure of the exact numbers because even these are hotly disputed. Families were torn apart and almost 100,000 women were kidnapped and either raped or forced into religious conversion followed by marriage to their abductors. The legacy of bitterness and hatred generated by this humanitarian catastrophe has poisoned relations between India and Pakistan ever since.[25]

The last European colonies in Asia were those of Portugal. It is perhaps no coincidence that the one colonial power that had not been directly involved in the Second World War should be the one that held on to its Asian colonies the longest. East Timor did not declare independence from Portugal until 1975 and Macau was not handed over to China until the end of the century. But even Portuguese colonies did not escape the violence associated with independence. East Timor was independent for only a matter of days before it was invaded by neighbouring Indonesia, and a savage occupation began. The country had to suffer a further twenty-four years of violence and atrocity before finally winning lasting independence.

The New Order

The Second World War did not directly cause most of these events, and yet none of them would have happened without it. It was the war that had weakened the European powers to a point where they could no longer dominate their colonies. It was the war that had also created the right environment for Asian nationalist movements to expand and flourish. And it was the war that armed them, and propelled them into positions of power.

But perhaps the greatest changes brought about by the war were psychological. A whole generation had been introduced to the experience of violence, as well as the idea that radical change could be produced by violent means. The hardships produced by the war – occupation, martial law, inflation, shortages, starvation – left many people feeling that they had nothing left to lose; but the atmosphere of optimism that came with the war's end generated a conviction that, after all the hardship, something new and good must be about to happen.

Underpinning all these hopes and desperations was a belief in the

Chittaprosad's 1950 drawing sums up an attitude common in Asia in the wake of the Second World War.

concept of 'freedom'. This had been the watchword throughout the war, and was now the rallying cry of every politician and resistance fighter in Asia. According to former revolutionaries in Sumatra, *merdeka* was the one word on everyone's lips, 'but what this *merdeka* actually was we didn't know yet, we didn't understand independence'. All they did know was that 'whatever was independent was not colonized'.[26]

Unfortunately, different groups had different definitions of 'freedom'. To religious and ethnic minorities it meant freedom from persecution, but to some of their neighbours it meant freedom from foreigners and outsiders. To Communists like Ho Chi Minh it meant liberation from imperialist and capitalist exploitation, while to the imperialists and capitalists themselves it meant the freedom to re-establish what they had had before the war and start making money again.

In reality, none of these groups were talking about genuine freedom in the existential sense. What they actually wanted was not 'freedom' but a realignment of power: from outsiders to national groups; from capitalists to the common people; from 'them' to 'us'. In the process, the concept of true 'freedom' was lost. Or, worse, it began to be associated with something quite terrifying: unrestricted chaos. As the old imperialism broke down, and nothing seemed to take its place but an atmosphere of violence and turmoil, disillusioned people stopped talking about freedom and began to crave a return to order.

What they did not necessarily appreciate was that this too would come at a price.

The re-establishment of 'order' in Indonesia was twenty years in the making. It began in earnest when Sukarno employed the newly formed National Army of Indonesia to put down the Communist insurrection at Madiun in 1948. In an impassioned radio broadcast, he told the nation that they faced a stark choice: to follow the Communists, 'who will destroy the idea of Indonesian independence', or to follow Sukarno and Hatta, who would bring 'freedom from all oppression'. The uprising was suppressed with great loss of life – some 8,000 around Madiun alone – and tens of thousands of arrests.[27]

As usual, Trimurti found herself caught up in the thick of the action when she was arrested yet again. She was imprisoned as a potential Communist, and for a time she believed she was marked down for execution. The accusation was not true – she had never been a Communist, and was at this point actually a member of the more moderate Labour Party. Nevertheless, the stigma would follow her around for the rest of her life.

The crushing of the Communists at Madiun was significant for several reasons. Firstly, it demonstrated beyond any doubt that Sukarno and Hatta were not themselves Communists, and thus calmed American fears about some of the socialist policies they espoused. The support of the USA would be essential in the diplomatic battle to force the Dutch to leave. Secondly, it demonstrated the growing power of the Indonesian army, which by now was the only institution capable of imposing any kind of order in the country. And last, but not least, it set a template in Indonesian affairs: from now on, the army would be ruthless in suppressing its enemies, particularly when those enemies happened to be Communist.

Over the following years there would be plenty of other uprisings. In 1951, the islands around Ambon tried to secede, as did the Aceh region of northern Sumatra in the following years. A group of dissident colonels tried to set up an alternative state in Sumatra, as did another group of dissidents in Sulawesi. In West Java, radical Muslims refused to accept the idea of Indonesia as a multifaith state, and proclaimed an Islamic state called Darul Islam. They soon won followers in other parts of Indonesia: throughout the 1950s and into the 1960s, Darul Islam waged a terrorist struggle that caused the deaths of more than 40,000 people and the displacement of millions. The legacy of this movement has echoes that are still being felt in Indonesia today.[28]

All of these uprisings were put down by the army, which gradually increased its power. Throughout the 1950s army leaders shamelessly promoted themselves as the 'defenders of national unity', and made it clear to everyone that it was only because of their intervention that there was any kind of law and order at all. In 1957 martial law was declared across the whole country, giving the army the opportunity to act with virtual impunity. Local leaders were dismissed for being corrupt – which, indeed, many of them were – and replaced with army officers. Gradually, the army was taking over.[29]

Sukarno tried to limit the power of the military by promoting the only other force in the country capable of opposing them – the Communist Party of Indonesia (PKI), who had a massive following almost everywhere. But in the Cold War atmosphere of the 1950s and 60s it was a dangerous game to play. In the first place, it alienated the USA, who soon started giving support to right-wing opponents of Sukarno: at the end of the 1950s the CIA were caught red handed supplying weapons, training, and even aircraft to various anti-government rebels.[30] Secondly, it began to offend the army, who resented being played off against an old enemy.

Matters came to a head in 1965, when the Communists kidnapped several army generals and killed them at an air base near Jakarta. The army reacted swiftly and brutally. Declaring the kidnappings an attempted coup, they launched a massive nationwide crackdown on Communists. The PKI chairman, D. N. Aidit, was arrested and executed, as were most of the other Communist leaders. An inflammatory propaganda campaign was launched, in which members of the Women's Movement were accused of taking part in a wild sexual orgy while the kidnapped generals were being tortured and mutilated in front of them by their Communist comrades.

Suddenly, spontaneous attacks on Communists began to break out across the country. It was not only Communists who were attacked but also their friends and families, and indeed anyone with suspiciously left-wing views. The Women's Movement was not, strictly speaking, Communist at all – but because of the slanders that had been made, its members became a particular target. Some of these attacks developed into full-blown massacres. In East Java, Communists were lined up by Islamist youth groups who cut their throats and threw their bodies into the rivers. In Sumatra, plantation workers who had agitated for better working conditions were massacred by the thousand. In Bali, a state of civil war broke out in which entire villages were butchered and then put to the torch.

Orchestrating these events were the army generals, who stood idly by while the massacres took place and who, in some cases, even provided lists of names to local militias. When the killings began to flag, as in Java – or where they spun out of control, as in Bali – army officials eventually took over and carried out the purge in a more orderly fashion: Communists were rounded up and processed at detention facilities before being bussed to the countryside, where they could be executed and piled into mass graves.[31]

The massive purge that swept across Indonesia between 1965 and 1967 was probably the most traumatic event in Indonesia's history. It claimed the lives of at least half a million people. Hundreds of thousands more were arrested: perhaps as many as a million and a half over the next fifteen years. The Communist Party was banned. Newspapers that criticized the military were closed down. Once the army had complete control of the country, Sukarno was gradually eased out of government. His place was taken by the leader of the military purge, Suharto, who gradually consolidated his position until his power was virtually absolute.[32]

For the next thirty years there would be little dissent in Indonesia. Those isolated disturbances that did occur – in Aceh, for instance, or in East Timor – were put down with brutal ferocity. Thus Suharto achieved what twenty years of turmoil and argument had so far failed to achieve: he united the nation. In fact, in some respects he had defined what constituted a new nation in the postwar period: it was not a common language, or a common purpose, or values or ideals that made a united Indonesia – it was authority. Indonesia was quite simply what the army said it was, because there was no one left who was capable of arguing with them.

In some ways this was a relief. Now, at least, there would be some sort of order in public affairs; indeed, Suharto's new regime even called itself the 'New Order'. The concept that had so inspired the nation in 1945 – *merdeka*, or 'freedom' – had been quietly pushed to one side.

17. The Birth of an African Nation

Many of the processes that took place in Asia in 1945 would be repeated in Africa a few years later. Here, too, nationalists seized opportunities that were thrown up by the Second World War, but since Africa's experience of the war was very different from Asia's experience, so too were its pathways towards independence.

No single person's story can possibly represent every facet of the African experience in the aftermath of the Second World War. But one story that contains many of the themes of nationalism that were thrown up during these turbulent years was that of Waruhiu Itote, a Kikuyu tribesman from the foothills of Mount Kenya.

Itote was the son of a farmer.[1] He had a limited education, a fair amount of personal ambition, but also a great sense of restlessness which, before the war, he could not quite put a name to. As a young man in 1939 he went to Nairobi to seek his fortune, but immediately found obstacles being placed in his way. For example he tried to open a small shop with some friends but found it almost impossible to obtain a licence: the merchant class in the city was predominantly Asian, and the ruling Europeans seemed to want to keep it that way. There was a long list of other activities from which he also found himself excluded. As a black African, he was not allowed to enter any of Nairobi's major hotels except as a servant. At railway stations he was obliged to use different lavatories from those used by Asians and Europeans. There were even certain types of beer he was not allowed to drink. Such prohibitions made him angry and resentful, not only because they seemed so pointlessly unjust but also because he had no idea how he could resist or change them.

When the war came, the colonial government tried to get people to join the army. They portrayed the Italians and Germans as 'the worst monsters on earth' who were poised to invade Kenya. Itote eventually joined up, but not so much to fight these monsters as to escape the boredom and difficulty of being unemployed. He enlisted in the King's African Rifles in January 1942, shortly before his twentieth birthday.

After a period of training in neighbouring Tanganyika he was sent across the ocean to Ceylon, and finally to fight in the frontier lands between India and Burma.

During the course of his travels he came into contact with all kinds of people he could never have met at home. His conversations with them opened his eyes to a myriad political and personal possibilities he had never considered before. For example in 1943 he met a British soldier who pointed out that India and Burma were part of the same British Empire that had subjugated his own homeland – why was Itote so keen on fighting to preserve the world of his oppressors? He was embarrassed to admit that he had no adequate answer to this question. While on leave in Calcutta he met educated Indian civilians who told him of the deal that India had struck for independence once the war was over. They asked him what Kenyans had demanded in return for their loyalty, but once again Itote was embarrassed, because as far as he knew Kenyans had not demanded anything.[2] He even met black American GIs for the first time, who spoke eloquently about their longing for civil rights in their own country. One of them, a man named Stephenson, warned him that the British were unlikely to be grateful for Itote's contribution to the war effort. '[T]he whites who are fighting now will be heroes in their own countries forever and amen,' he predicted, 'while you Africans will be heroes for a day and then you'll be forgotten. If you want to be heroes, why don't you fight for your own countries?'[3]

But perhaps his greatest political lesson was learned during the heat of battle. In the jungles of Burma, the white soldiers who fought alongside him put boot polish on their faces in order to look more like Itote: the Japanese snipers had a habit of picking out anyone who stood out from the rest. All of his fellow soldiers – black, white or Asian – were equally afraid of the Japanese, and their fear produced a kind of camaraderie he had never experienced before: 'Among the shells and bullets there [was] no pride, no air of superiority from our European comrades-in-arms. We drank the same tea, used the same water and lavatories, and shared the same jokes. There were no racial insults, no reference to "niggers", "baboons" and so on. The white heat of battle had blistered all that away and left only our common humanity and our common fate, either death or survival.'[4]

War, and its indiscriminate nature, seemed to have turned everything that Itote had grown up with in Africa on its head.

When he returned to Kenya in 1945 it was difficult to readjust to civilian life, and it did not take long before his old resentments were inflamed once more. He tried to start a charcoal business, but was not allowed to sell charcoal in the most profitable markets because these were reserved for Asian businessmen. He got a job on the railways, but had to accept lower pay than the Asians and Europeans in equivalent positions, just because of his colour.

After all he had seen of the world, Itote was no longer prepared to put up with such discrimination. So for the first time in his life he joined a political group: he became a member of the Kenya African Union (KAU), whose leader, Jomo Kenyatta, had spent much of the previous twenty years campaigning for greater civil rights. Kenyatta was a personal hero of Itote's, and would remain so for the rest of his life. But Itote quickly became disillusioned by the KAU in general, which seemed to be dominated by cautious old men who were too afraid to seize the opportunity for change. His frustration was exacerbated by the realization that almost none of these elders, with the exception of Kenyatta himself, had travelled or experienced the war as he had. 'When would they learn that the whole world was not like Kenya,' he lamented; 'indeed that Kenya was one of the last outposts of feudalism, racialism and minority privilege and domination? When would they understand that things *could* be changed *and* within our lifetime?'[5]

At about the same time he also joined the Transport and Allied Workers' Union – a militant trade union which campaigned not only for workers' rights but also for much more sweeping social and political change. The TAWU was led by Fred Kubai, one of the country's greatest firebrands, who was not afraid to use violent means if they achieved his ends. Kubai famously claimed in 1950 that if the people united against the government, they could force independence within just three years. Inspired by this new, radical spirit, Itote took part enthusiastically in demonstrations and strikes, even when the only reward seemed to be police brutality and increased government crackdowns.

The third organization that Itote joined was perhaps the most radical of them all: it was a gang of former soldiers called the Anake a Forti – the Forty Group – so named because 1940 was the year that most of them had joined the British army. In later life, Itote emphasized the political nature of this group, which waged a campaign of intimidation against those who were collaborating with government programmes in the

Kikuyu reserves. But its activities in Nairobi were also straightfor-
wardly criminal. Disillusioned war veterans like Itote, who were often
excluded from more legitimate forms of employment or enterprise, had
turned to theft and extortion because it seemed like the only way to
make a living. Itote himself took to breaking into shops to steal firearms
and money, not only for himself, but also to fund the group's political
activities. In the murky Nairobi underworld, the lines between violence, criminality and politics were becoming increasingly blurred.

As the end of the 1940s approached, the various groups that Itote had
joined all began to merge into a single movement. The militant trade
unions had begun taking over the KAU and ousting its former, more
moderate leadership. At the same time they had begun forging links
with Nairobi's criminal underworld. Itote was himself one of these
links, and he relished his new-found sense of importance.

If there was one moment that cemented his devotion to the cause of
independence, it was probably the day in 1950 when he attended a secret
ceremony and took a formal oath to give his life as a sacrifice to the
nation. Tens of thousands of Kikuyu tribesmen were taking similar
oaths all around the country. According to Itote, this solemn oath gave
all who took it a sense of the 'sacred', and made them feel connected to
something grand and ideological – something that had been distinctly
lacking for Africans like him during the recent world war. 'We were
fighting with the weapons of Truth, Love and Justice,' he wrote in later
years, against 'a veritable arsenal of opponents, disguised as Christianity, Loyalty, Wealth and Power'.[6] The mythological monsters and heroes
were at last stirring into life.

In the summer of 1952, shortly before the state of emergency was
declared, Itote and some others went to visit their symbolic leader, Jomo
Kenyatta, at his farm in Gatundu. Kenyatta was aware that he was about
to be arrested, and warned the assembled group that they too might be
arrested in the coming days, or even killed. 'Everything in this world
has to be paid for,' Itote remembers him saying, 'and we must buy our
freedom with our blood.'[7]

There is something beyond mere respect in Itote's description of his
spiritual leader on that afternoon: Kenyatta's predictions of his own
arrest, his instructions to his disciples to keep the faith and his promise
to stay with them even after death are reminiscent of the Last Supper
before Christ's crucifixion. Later, when the insurgency broke out in

earnest, African fighters would sing Christian hymns in which they substituted the name 'Jomo' for 'Jesus'.[8] For Itote, however, it was nationalism rather than religion that most inspired him. For him, Kenyatta and an independent Kenya were so intertwined that he could not imagine one without the other.[9] Receiving Kenyatta's blessing was therefore the last ritual he needed before moving on to the climactic stage in his struggle.

A few days later, Itote took to the forests of Mount Kenya. He adopted the code name 'General China' and began training groups of willing men in the ways of jungle warfare. At the same time other Burma veterans and violent radicals, like Stanley Mathenge and Dedan Kimathi, also took to the forests.

So began the insurgent movement that would come to be known as the 'Mau Mau'.

Heroes of the War, Heroes of the Revolution

The Mau Mau uprising in Kenya had its roots in a wide variety of long-held resentments, many of them much more serious than the petty racial discrimination that Waruhiu Itote experienced in Nairobi. Most important amongst them was the displacement of black Africans from the land by European settlers; but there was also the introduction of controversial government taxes, restrictions on movement, restrictions on employment, attempted bans on tribal customs like polygamy and female circumcision – not to mention all the internal struggles between tribes, and within tribes, that can cause conflict in any society.[10]

Much like in Indonesia, however, the root of all Kenyan grievances lay in the sense of powerlessness felt by the ordinary people of the country. No matter how hard they protested about land rights, or employment rights, it was difficult for black Africans to be heard, because they had virtually no political representation of any substance. In 1951, despite outnumbering the European population of Kenya by more than 170 to one, only four out of the thirty-seven members on the Legislative Council were African. Unlike their European counterparts, none of these members had been elected: they had been appointed from a list of approved candidates who had been chosen precisely because they were unlikely to cause too much trouble.[11]

As in Asia, African leaders had been campaigning to change this unfair system for years, but the Second World War had brought a new impetus to their claims. On a purely abstract level, concepts like freedom, equality and human dignity had suddenly come rushing to the fore: these were the concepts in whose name the war was being fought, and which Kenyans could not help noticing were in short supply in their own country. It cannot have surprised the British when their African subjects redoubled their demands for the right to choose their own government: this was a fundamental right that the British themselves had endorsed when they drew up the Atlantic Charter in 1941.

Fuelled by the experience of the war, a similar atmosphere of idealism and discontent was growing all across the continent. Between 1939 and 1945 more than 800,000 black Africans were enlisted or conscripted into the Allied armies: half a million from British colonies, perhaps a further 300,000 from French Africa.[12] The return of these men caused problems for colonial governments everywhere. In Tanganyika, for example, veterans were amongst the most disgruntled sections of society – many of them had never wanted to go to war in the first place, but had been arbitrarily impressed into the British army by corrupt African officials with quotas to fill.[13] In postwar Nigeria unemployed veterans took part in a series of angry demonstrations against the colonial government: in 1950 they even started a full-scale revolt in the town of Umuahia.[14] In the Gold Coast, in 1948, veterans demonstrated on the streets in protest against the lack of official recognition for the sacrifices they had made during the war. The violent police reaction, and the five days of rioting that ensued, have been credited with kick-starting the process of independence there.[15]

In francophone Africa, too, returning veterans often played a leading role in starting protests against colonial power. In Belgian Congo, for example, former Allied soldiers regularly expressed bitterness at the irony that stood at the centre of their war – that while they had fought to give the metropolitan power its freedom, they themselves were still not truly free in their own lands.[16] In French Guinea, soldiers began a campaign for equal pay under the banner 'Equal sacrifices = Equal rights'. Military veterans there took the lead in postwar agitation against colonial institutions, as well as in challenging the traditional powers of their own chiefs.[17] Meanwhile in Côte d'Ivoire veterans campaigned to abolish forced labour, and held frequent demonstrations for equality, some of which turned violent. Throughout the country, Ivoirians were calling for a new 'Africa for the Africans'.[18]

It is important to stress that the vast majority of returning soldiers did not swell the ranks of the revolutionaries and political malcontents. In fact, there were whole regions, indeed whole countries, where veterans played almost no role at all in gaining independence – Botswana is a good example.[19] But historians who dismiss the veterans as marginal players in Africa's various independence struggles are missing the larger ideological point. African soldiers had returned to their countries as heroes, and it is not surprising that a mythological sense of that heroism was carried forward into the independence movements that came afterwards. In African communal memory, it does not matter whether the soldiers actively fought for independence or not: what is important is that they had become a symbol of a new-found sense of equality.[20]

This is certainly the way they were seen at the time by some of their cultural and political leaders. As the Ugandan writer Robert Kakembo claimed in 1946, the African soldier had 'proved to Europeans that he is not inferior' – now, at last, he deserved to be treated as such.[21] The French West African senator Victor Biaka Boda likewise pointed out that 'an African dies like a white, and he has the same rights; he is a citizen exactly like the other'.[22] Indeed, in the minds of some veterans, the war had raised Africans *above* their former colonial masters. 'Only the French know what we did for them,' remembered one Ivoirian veteran of the war many years later. 'We liberated them. What greater thing could you do for them?' In such circumstances it was no longer appropriate for Africans to cower before Europeans.[23]

The Civilian Experience

The big difference between Asia and Africa during the Second World War is that the vast majority of Africa was never invaded: African civilians therefore experienced much more continuity during the war than did their Asian counterparts. However, this does not mean that Africans had it easy. The Second World War caused such disruptions to the world economy that civilians everywhere were forced to weather massive changes to their lives in a very short space of time. This would have a huge effect all over Africa.

Once again, Kenya provides a good example of the sort of upheavals that affected ordinary people's lives. The economic changes in this country were enormously disruptive. The wartime boom brought huge profits to businesses, to tribal chiefs and to those who owned land, all of whom suddenly found they could sell their goods and services at inflated wartime prices. The poor, by contrast, suffered terribly. As prices rocketed, food became scarce, and some regions of Kenya, particularly in the Central and Southern Provinces, had to endure famine. Thousands were conscripted to work on European farms and sisal plantations, often for starvation wages. Thousands more migrated to the cities to see if they could find work. Such people lived in a parallel society that quickly began to lose its ties to the land, and had to feel its way instead towards the new and much more uncertain world of wage labour. The war therefore introduced Kenya, quite abruptly, to the same crisis of modernity that had hit other parts of the world earlier in the century.[24]

At the same time, new racial tensions began to develop in the countryside, especially between the European landowners and the African farmers who occupied their land – the 'squatters', as they were known. These tensions also had an economic side to them. Before 1939, most white settlers had been crippled by debt, and were forced to rely on the labour of African squatters to work their land. But the wartime boom, and the arrival of Lend-Lease farm machinery from America, made them rich. As a consequence, many white farmers no longer needed or wanted the squatters on their land. When the annual squatter contracts came up for renewal in 1945 and 1946, they placed new limits on the amount of land that their tenants were allowed to farm, and forced them to sell off their cattle. Those families who refused to accept the new rules, which sometimes reduced their income by as much as three-quarters, were evicted from the land and forcibly 'repatriated' to the Kikuyu reserves. In this way more than 100,000 Kikuyu squatters were uprooted from the lands they had occupied for decades, and which many regarded as their own. These events caused such resentment, and so swelled the ranks of the poor and dispossessed, that some historians have interpreted the emergency that came a few years later not as an independence struggle at all, but as a peasants' revolt.[25]

Meanwhile, Kenya's cities were also transformed by the war. The population of Nairobi rose by more than half between 1939 and 1945, while Mombasa's almost doubled from 55,000 to 100,000.[26] Most of

Nairobi's new inhabitants were pressed together in grim municipal housing estates and overcrowded, crime-infested shanty towns in the east of the city. Here tens of thousands competed for unskilled jobs with minimal wages. These were perfect recruiting grounds for the city's unions and many people, Waruhiu Itote amongst them, joined up.[27]

As class consciousness grew amongst the disadvantaged and dispossessed, a series of general strikes spread across the country. They began in Mombasa in 1947 and soon affected Nairobi and beyond. In Nairobi especially, the strikes quickly became a blend of straightforward trade union demands and much broader calls for an end to colonial rule. By 1950 these acts of defiance had become a template for the more radical action that would characterize the coming insurgency. Thus the Mau Mau rebellion was, as well as a nationalist uprising and a peasant revolt, a straightforward class struggle.[28]

Civil war or nationalist uprising, racial conflict or economic crisis, peasant revolt or urban class struggle, or even crisis of modernity – however one classes the tensions in Kenya, they have to be seen in the light of the massive upheaval caused by the Second World War. All of the ingredients of potential conflict had existed before the war, for sure, but it was the war that brought them all to a head. And it was the failure to deal with these problems in the aftermath of the war that led to the emergency just a few years later.

Although other countries in Africa did not descend into the same kind of violence that was about to hit Kenya, they did share many of the same travails. The exploitation of peasants and farmers, for example, was something that had happened all over the continent during the war. Governments everywhere had set up marketing boards, introduced price controls and subsidized mechanization on the larger farms – anything to keep costs down and production up. Unfortunately, price controls meant that the vast majority of African farmers were unable to take part in the wartime boom: it was only the marketing boards and the foreign owners of large farms who were able to enjoy the vast revenues from cash crops sold on the international markets. To make things worse, many governments had also introduced or expanded conscription in order to secure the labour supplies. In Tanganyika, as in Kenya, tens of thousands of peasants had been forced to work on sisal plantations in a condition of virtual slavery.[29] In Nigeria, 100,000 people were conscripted to work in the tin mines.[30] In French West Africa conscription was also rife. Farmers throughout the region were forced to fulfil impossible quotas at their own expense, and whole communities were subjected to mass relocations against their will.[31] As a consequence of practices like this, which often continued after the war, rural protest broke out all over Africa. In 1946 Sudanese tenant farmers on the Gezira Scheme went on strike in protest at government exploitation. Two years later farmers in the Gold Coast joined merchants and war veterans in a boycott of European-owned businesses. There were also varying levels of revolt by peasants in Tanganyika, Southern Rhodesia, Mozambique and South Africa, to name just a few.[32]

The same was true of urban and industrial protests. It was not only Kenya that saw massive general strikes by workers in the postwar years – similar things happened in other parts of British East Africa as well as in Egypt, Algeria and Morocco and throughout French West Africa. In Senegal, military conscripts who had been forced to work on the railways under conditions that even their generals admitted were 'a sort of state slavery', came close to mutiny in 1946.[33] In South Africa, more than 75,000 miners and steel workers came out on strike in 1946, only to have their protest crushed by a heavy-handed police action that left several dead.[34] In the Nigerian mining town of Enugu, coal miners who struck in 1949 were similarly massacred by police.[35] Varying degrees of violence on both sides often accompanied industrial actions.

One Congolese man summed up African frustrations in an impassioned letter which he sent to the US Army attaché in Kinshasa towards the end of the war: 'We are being treated like a dog who has been on a hunt with his master and is not even given a share of the spoils.'[36] A similar sense of betrayal was being expressed in vernacular newspapers and political speeches all across the continent. The winds of change, which would sweep across all Africa in the late 1950s and 60s, were already beginning to blow in 1945. Those who ignored them, or tried to stand in their way, did so at their peril.

Emergency

The bloodshed that engulfed Kenya in the early 1950s produced some of the most shocking images of the end of empire in Africa. It began with a declaration of a state of emergency by the colonial authorities in October 1952, and the arrest of Jomo Kenyatta and five other prominent political leaders. In retaliation, Mau Mau fighters embarked on a spate of violent murders. The first European to be killed was a reclusive rural storekeeper called Eric Bowker, who was hacked to death as he lay in his bath just a few days after the emergency had been declared. A month later a retired naval officer named Ian Meiklejohn and his wife Dorothy were attacked as they sat down for an after-dinner coffee in their home near the edge of the Aberdares forest; Dorothy survived, but her husband died of multiple slash wounds soon after. The following January the whole country was stunned by the murder of a young family on their farmstead near Kinangop. The head of the family, a well-liked man in his early thirties called Roger Ruck, had been lured out of his house by his own farmhands, only to be hacked down with machetes. Hearing his screams, his young wife Esme ran out and was similarly cut down. Their attackers then entered the house to loot it, and on finding the couple's six-year-old son, Michael, in his bedroom upstairs slashed him to death too. Photographs of the boy's bloodstained room, with his toys scattered across the floor, appeared in newspapers both in Kenya and abroad.[37]

These events, along with thirty or so further attacks over the next six months, sent shivers through the European community in Kenya, who were deeply disturbed by the overtly racial motives that underlay the murders. Unsurprisingly, their own racial fears were quickly brought to the surface. They began to imagine the Mau Mau not as an independence movement but as a kind of primitive cult motivated by little more than a love of violence. Their clergymen began to speak of a 'vile, brutal wickedness of satanic power which has been unleashed in this land', and rumours spread that the Mau Mau initiation ceremony involved the drinking of human blood.[38] Many began to voice fears that the rebels would stop at nothing until Christianity had been destroyed, and all Europeans had been driven out of Kenya. In reaction, some of the settlers began to demand not only the elimination of the 'dark' and 'evil' forces of Mau Mau but also the wholesale extermination of the Kikuyu people.[39]

No matter how terrified the European settlers became, however, and no matter how much publicity the murder of Europeans garnered, the settlers were never the true focus of Mau Mau terror. The vast

majority of the violence was directed not at Europeans at all, but at loyalist Africans. During the course of the emergency only thirty-two settlers
were ever killed by the Mau Mau; this compares to about 1,800 Africans
who were murdered in equally brutal, if less well-reported ways.[40]

The greatest atrocity of the war – the massacre at Lari – demonstrates
this perfectly. In a meticulously planned attack, Mau Mau rebels lured
the local Home Guard away from the area before setting fire to the
houses of loyalist African families and chopping down women and children as they tried to escape through the windows. When the Home
Guard returned to find their communities ablaze they took off after the
rebels in search of revenge. Local people suspected of Mau Mau sympa-
thies were dragged from their homes, and before long a second massacre
was taking place. By dawn the total body count was at least 200, and
possibly as many as 400. A handful of European police officers were
implicated in the second part of the massacre, but from start to finish
this was predominantly an African affair: at Lari, as in other parts of
Kenya, the uprising was as much a civil war as it ever was a war of
independence.[41]

In an effort to bring this chaotic, hate-filled situation under control,
the British authorities resorted to drastic measures. A few token efforts
were made to draw the European settlers into line and stop them baying
for blood. Some of the more racist and sadistic members of the security
forces were disciplined, particularly in the British army. Large forces
were sent to the edges of the forests in an attempt to keep the Mau Mau
rebels more effectively fenced in. But the most effective measure adopted
was the one that the British had pioneered in South Africa more than
fifty years earlier, and which they had used most recently against the
Communists in Greece and the insurgents in Malaya: they cut the rebels
off from the people that supported them. From 1954 they began round-
ing up Kikuyu tribesmen and herding them into closely monitored
military camps and fortified villages. Over the next few years at least
150,000 Kikuyu spent time behind barbed wire, and perhaps as many as
320,000, in a network of camps that has been called, with some justification, 'Britain's gulag'. Brutal though this solution was, it broke the
rebellion. Through a network of informers and collaborators they then
hunted down the remaining rebels in their forest hideouts. By the end of
1956 the uprising was effectively over.[42]

★

Waruhiu Itote played an intimate part in all these events. During the first year of the insurgency his followers grew from a rag-bag of about thirty men to a force of 7,500 fighters.[43] By the middle of the year he was able to run raids on several different Home Guard posts simultaneously. He burned down schools and church buildings in Nyeri county, sabotaged road bridges to prevent people pursuing him and began a murder campaign of loyalists throughout the region. Occasionally – rarely – he attacked settlers' farms and businesses, usually in an attempt to steal guns and money. At the end of April 1953, during one such raid on a sawmill in Chehe, his men came across an Italian woman called Nerena Meloncelli, whom they hacked to death along with her two children.[44] Itote later distanced himself from such attacks, insisting that he had always 'absolutely rejected' the indiscriminate killing of women and children. Nevertheless, he also maintained that some sort of violence had always been necessary: 'our people could never win their independence solely through peaceful means'.[45]

For all his determination to fight, however, Itote was still a man capable of compromise – some may even say betrayal. His capture in January 1954 signalled the beginning of the end for the Mau Mau. Though he never mentions it in his memoirs, Itote gave a great deal of information to his captors during his interrogation – it was through his testimony that the British finally understood the sheer scale of support the Mau Mau had enjoyed amongst the Kikuyu population.[46] At his subsequent trial he was sentenced to death for consorting with terrorists, but this was later commuted to a prison term when he agreed to try to broker a peace deal with his former brothers-in-arms. The peace deal faltered, but Itote's life was saved. He would spend the next nine years in prison.

When he was finally set free in 1962, Kenya was a different place. The insurgency was long over – it had effectively ended in 1956 with the death of the last forest leader, Dedan Kimathi. The country was on the brink of independence, along with much of what was left of Britain's empire in Africa, and Jomo Kenyatta, Itote's mentor and idol, was well on his way to becoming the country's first president. On his homecoming to Nyeri, he was greeted by thousands in a tumultuous reception as a Kikuyu hero. And yet there were many in Kenya who disapproved of such a celebration, and for whom the memory of Mau Mau was still a source of terror.

Itote would devote the rest of his life to a form of reconciliation. In his memoirs, which were quickly recognized as a kind of 'official version' of

Waruhiu Itote, otherwise known as General China, stands in the dock during his trial in 1954.

the way the Mau Mau war had been fought, he emphasized the fact that he had not been fighting for Kikuyu rights, but for 'the common undercoat of blackness' that united all Kenya's people.[47] In 1964 he joined the National Youth Service – a multiethnic institution devoted to turning out young people with high ideals, strong moral values and a sense of patriotism. He spent the next twenty years moulding Kikuyu, Luo, Kamba and Meru youths into *Kenyans*. By the time of his death in 1993 he had himself been transformed from a Kikuyu hero to a kind of national treasure: a 'true son of Kenya', as he was described at his funeral, 'whose high place in the pantheon of Kenya's heroes is permanent and irreplaceable'.[48]

The Elusive Nature of 'Freedom'

Just as Indonesian independence was part of a network of similar movements in Asia, so too was Kenya representative of what happened in the rest of Africa. In the decades after the Second World War, colony after colony in Africa struggled for independence. The first to achieve it, perhaps unsurprisingly, was Libya, which had been an Italian colony before the war. Italy renounced all claims to it in their peace treaty with the Allies, and the country was granted its formal independence in 1951. Tunisia and Morocco were next, gaining their independence from France in 1956. The following year the British colony of the Gold Coast became independent Ghana. Most of the rest fell like dominoes: during the late 1950s and 1960s, over thirty new nation-states were created, and by the 1980s there was not a single European colony left on the continent.

The majority of these countries gained their independence relatively peacefully; but some, like Kenya, suffered a much more violent process. Algeria is a case in point. From the very beginning it was clear that any transition towards independence in Algeria would not be easy. On the day when the Second World War came to an end in Europe, Muslim demonstrators at Sétif raised a nationalist red, white and green flag in the midst of the VE Day festivities. What should have been a celebration rapidly turned into a massacre, as demonstrators and police opened fire upon one another (it is still not entirely clear who fired the first shots). Over the following days around a hundred Europeans were murdered, some of them also raped and mutilated, but in reprisal several thousand Muslims were killed. It was a taste of things to come. Nine years later, while the Mau Mau were terrorizing colonial Kenya, a savage civil war broke out in Algeria that would go on to claim the lives of 700,000 people and uproot millions more. Algerian demands for greater freedom, equality and democracy had degenerated into a bloodbath: the legacy of violence, extremism and political fragmentation was still being felt at the end of the century.[49]

Similarly violent wars of independence occurred in most of those African countries where there was a large population of European settlers: not only in Kenya and Algeria but also in Rwanda and Burundi, Angola and Mozambique and, much later, in Southern Rhodesia. In each case, the European settlers claimed greater privileges to the African population; and in each case, just as in Kenya, a lethal cocktail of racial, ethnic, civil and political violence ensued. The bloodshed in the Portuguese colonies of Angola and Mozambique was particularly bad. After a long campaign of civil disobedience in both countries, war finally broke out in the 1960s resulting in hundreds of thousands of deaths. Following independence, around half a million Portuguese and other Europeans fled, leaving both countries in greater political and ethnic turmoil than ever. Mozambique continued to be torn apart by civil war until well into the 1990s. Angola did not find peace until the beginning of the twenty-first century.[50]

Even those countries that achieved a relatively peaceful transition to independence did not always escape violence afterwards. I hesitate to portray Africa as a place defined by conflict, because such a portrayal does not do justice to the diversity of experience in a continent that has, for decades, suffered little but negative reporting in the world's media. Nevertheless, civil wars, ethnic conflict, military coups and economic disintegration became widespread in Africa after independence. In the 1960s alone, there were forty successful insurrections amongst Africa's newly independent nations.[51] By the end of the century Africa had become a continent of the displaced, home to the largest number of international refugees in the world. It was also one of the least democratic regions of the world: in 1990 there were twenty-five military and nineteen civilian dictatorships in Africa. The dreams of parliamentary democracy that had accompanied the demands for freedom in 1945 were little but a distant memory.[52]

This is not the place to go into all the reasons for African instabilities over the rest of the century, which are as diverse as the continent itself. Suffice it to say that the arbitrary borders drawn by Europeans when they were carving up Africa in the nineteenth century rarely suited the tribal and ethnic boundaries of the people who lived there. Neither was the European notion of the nation-state, bequeathed to Africans after they left, always an appropriate way to organize such a diverse and multi-ethnic continent. European elites made a poor job of preparing Africans for the task of taking over their countries: the limits they imposed upon opportunities for Africans actively prevented them from gaining the experience they needed to govern skilfully. But not all of Africa's problems can be laid at Europe's door: many of the African elites who took over after independence turned out to be just as corrupt and exploitative as the Europeans had been. As the Mau Mau veteran Mohamed Mathu commented bitterly in the 1970s, it was hard to escape the feeling that the people had fought and suffered for their independence, 'just to have Africans step into the shoes of our former European masters'. Kenya today remains a nation racked with political and ethnic turmoil.[53]

★

The dreams of a brave new world – a world characterized by equality and freedom and justice – turned out to be just as illusory in Africa after independence as they were in the rest of the world in 1945. No African nation truly achieved independence – at least, not in the way that their leaders had claimed they would. They might have shaken off direct European rule, but they were still dependent on European trade, and European companies, some of which wielded such vast economic power that they could more or less impose their own trade terms. Thus, many Africans continued to feel exploited long after their supposed liberation from foreign rule. So strong was this sense of economic exploitation that the first president of independent Ghana, Kwame Nkrumah, even coined a new term for it – 'neo-colonialism'.[54]

Nor could African countries truly claim political independence. There are countless examples of outside interference in African politics throughout the second half of the twentieth century, some of them very serious indeed – from the assassination of Congo's first democratically elected prime minister, Patrice Lumumba, in 1961, to British and Israeli support for Idi Amin during and after his 1971 coup in Uganda.[55] More importantly, the Americans and the Soviets began to use Africa as a playground in which to fight their proxy wars – particularly in Angola and Mozambique, but also in smaller ways throughout the continent. After independence, virtually every African nation was obliged to align itself with one foreign power or another: if not with its former colonial masters then at least with one of the new superpowers.

Perhaps most depressingly of all, many African nations have been unable to shake off their psychological dependence on the Western powers. This is perhaps unsurprising, given that almost all of Africa's new leaders had been educated by Europeans, and the institutions they headed had largely been set up by Europeans. But their dependence ran far deeper than that. Europe, and by extension the West as a whole, was adopted by many as a kind of monster, whose malign influence could be seen everywhere. At first, pan-African idealists like Kwame Nkrumah and Julius Nyerere were able to use this idea as a way to unite Africans against a common enemy. Later, corrupt dictators like Robert Mugabe exploited this myth in order to draw attention away from their own appalling mismanagement of their countries. And yet, when things went wrong, it was often Europe and America that Africans turned to: during the Somalian famine in the 1980s, for example, or the Ebola crisis in 2014; or during the twenty-first-century civil wars in Mali and Sierra Leone.

In 2006 the Tanzanian intellectual Godfrey Mwakikagile wrote despairingly about how some Africans, disillusioned by years of poverty, violence and corruption, had begun to look back on their colonial past with a kind of warped nostalgia. He described how one political party in Gabon even campaigned for a return of European rule in the 1990s, because their own African leaders had failed them so badly. People all over the continent, he said, were begging for help, telling Western reporters that 'It's only you white people who can save us.'[56] According to Mwakikagile, large parts of his continent had resigned themselves to a future of handouts from Western donors and global agencies, none of which were working according to an African agenda: 'We have, in a way . . . been reconquered and recolonized; our perpetual dependence on other countries being the most searing indictment against our claim that we are genuinely independent. We hate to admit it, but we know it is true.'[57]

Africans might only console themselves with the thought that, in their longing to find a true sense of independence – indeed, a true sense of themselves – they are essentially no different from anyone else. In the aftermath of the Second World War every nation struggled to redefine itself, and every nation suffered varying degrees of internal conflict as a result. If Africans have suffered more than most then this is only a reflection of where they started from. It is not so easy to shake off domination from those who wish to control you, nor to establish a stable democracy for the first time, to develop the economy, transform society, foster unity between hostile tribes or create relationships with a host of brand-new countries on one's doorstep. To do all of these things at once would be a tall order for any nation.

In our postwar, globalized world, nothing and no one – no matter how much we might desire it – can ever be considered truly independent.

18. Democracy in Latin America

There are moments in many of our lives when, reaching a fork in the road, we realize too late that we have stumbled upon a kind of crisis, that the difference between one path and the other is so great that whatever decision we make will necessarily transform both us and those around us, permanently. For Carlos Delgado Chalbaud, one such moment arrived in the autumn of 1945. The decisions he made, and the fate that befell him, are emblematic of the processes that were taking place all over Latin America in the immediate aftermath of the Second World War.

Delgado was an officer, and a teacher, in the Venezuelan army. Since 1943 he had been the head of studies at the military academy in Caracas. He was well read, loved classical music and spoke several languages, including perfect English and French – but his true area of expertise was military engineering, which he taught with a passion. On the whole he was well liked by his fellow officers, who regarded him as sober, honest, down-to-earth, conservative – in short, a safe pair of hands. But he was also an outsider. Unlike his colleagues, Delgado had grown up in exile, in France, after his father had tried to depose Venezuela's military dictator earlier in the century. From the age of four he had only ever really known Venezuela as a concept – a lost home. He had not been able to return permanently until just before the Second World War, when the atmosphere in the country had first shown signs of change.[1]

Delgado's dilemma was thrust upon him one day in September 1945. He was approached by a friend, who took him aside and told him, quite solemnly, that a large group of army officers were planning a coup d'état. Venezuela at that time was ruled by the last in a line of military dictators, General Isaías Medina Angarita, whose autocratic behaviour had begun to alienate a population hungry for change. A large and vocal opposition had grown up across the country, led by a new political party called Acción Democrática (AD). Now it seemed that the army, too, was turning against the dictatorship. The younger officers in particular were angry at the poor conditions they were forced to endure, and accused Medina of being out of touch with both them and the needs of the nation. Their plan was to overthrow him and install a new, democratic government. They had already secured the cooperation of AD, and wanted Delgado to join their cause.

Delgado was immediately taken aback. He told his friend that he was 'neither mentally nor morally prepared for something of this nature', and begged for forty-eight hours to think about it. He gave his word as a gentleman that he would keep quiet about what he had been told.[2]

Over the next two days he grappled with the pros and cons of joining the conspiracy. Politically, he was inclined to support it. Unlike most of his fellow countrymen, he had grown up with the principles of democracy, which he regarded as the only legitimate political system. However, he was not entirely convinced that the best route to democracy was via a military coup. Besides, he knew better than most what would happen if the plan was thwarted. His life in exile had begun because of a failed coup d'état by his father, and at the age of twenty he himself had sailed across the Atlantic with his father to try again. The attempt had ended in disaster: his father had been killed and Delgado had only narrowly escaped with his life. These memories must have weighed heavily on him during his period of contemplation. To repeat the endeavour was certainly not a decision that could be taken lightly.

Nevertheless, there was an ambitious side to Delgado that could not let an opportunity like this pass. It was plain that the conspiracy was well organized, and that it was likely to enjoy massive popular support. To be at the heart of momentous events, to belong at last to a tight-knit group, to have the chance to succeed where his father had failed – all of these factors must have played a part in his eventual decision, because when the coup took place just a few weeks later Carlos Delgado Chalbaud was one of its leaders.

The insurrection that took place on 18 October 1945 owed a great deal to Delgado. It was he who first set it in motion; he who personally arrested the minister of war and seized control of the military academy in Caracas. He also sent word to the provinces, and informed the leader of Acción Democrática, Rómulo Betancourt, that the revolution was under way.

Over the course of the next twenty-four hours his co-conspirators managed to seize the presidential palace, as well as various ports and barracks in other parts of Venezuela. Naval rebels took control of Puerto Cabello and rebels in the air force seized the main air base at Maracay. None of this was achieved without the spilling of blood: estimates of the dead range from several hundred to 2,500.[3] Medina, meanwhile, took refuge in one of the military barracks that remained loyal to him, at Ambrosio Plaza, but once it became clear that he was surrounded, outnumbered, and about to be strafed by the air force, the dictator surrendered. On 19 October, less than thirty-six hours after the coup had started, it came to a successful close.

That evening Delgado and the other rebel leaders gathered in the presidential palace to form their new 'Revolutionary Government Junta'. In their many discussions over the previous weeks, the conspirators had already agreed that this should consist of seven members – five civilian and two military. The AD leader Rómulo Betancourt, who enjoyed enormous popular support, was unanimously accepted as the acting president, along with three other AD members (or 'Adecos', as they were called) and one independent. When it came to choosing the military members, Delgado seized his opportunity. The most popular military candidates, he claimed, were Captain Mario Vargas (to represent the more junior officers), and his brother Major Julio César Vargas (to represent the more senior). However, since it might be considered nepotistic to have two siblings in the junta at the same time, Delgado thought the latter should give way to another senior officer – and he slyly suggested himself as an alternative. His proposal was accepted.

This historic moment completed a remarkable journey for Delgado. His agonized decision, barely a month old, to join the conspiracy against Medina had borne fruit beyond his wildest dreams. Until the coup, he had been little more than a study master, teaching engineering in the military academy. Now, in the blink of an eye, he had become the most senior member of the armed forces in the new government. He would spend the next three years as the nation's minister of defence.

Venezuela's 'Trienio'

Moments of personal ambition like this are perhaps inevitable amongst revolutionaries. To its credit, however, the new junta – Delgado included – did its best to stay true to the spirit of the revolution they had put in place. Their government, they declared, was only a provisional one. Their primary aim was 'that of convoking the country to general elections, so that through the system of direct, universal and secret suffrage, Venezuelans can elect their representatives, give themselves the Constitution they want, and choose the future president of the republic'. To make sure that none of them could abuse their position, they made a strict rule that once elections had been announced no one in the junta would be allowed to stand for president. The new Venezuela – democratic Venezuela – must not be tainted by the undemocratic way in which they had seized power.[4]

In general, the junta was as good as its word. Less than a month after the coup it named a commission to draw up a new constitution – but rather than stuffing this commission with Adecos or military men, as might have been done in the past, the junta made sure that it represented a range of political opinion, including supporters of the previous regimes. After much debate, this commission granted all citizens the right to vote – women as well as men, the illiterate as well as the literate – and instituted a system of proportional representation. Opposition parties were allowed to form, including Communists, Christian Democrats and even groups associated with General Medina. Just a year after seizing power, the junta held the first in a series of elections, which observers from the USA declared were 'conducted more or less cleanly'. This was followed up just over a year later by a presidential election. A delighted Venezuela was being treated to its first taste of meaningful democracy. This period would last from 1945 to 1948, a three-year experience that has been known ever since as the 'Trienio'.[5]

It was not only on a national scale that the new junta made revolutionary changes: they also applied their principles of democracy and freedom of association at a local level. They held municipal elections in May 1948. They also encouraged the formation of mass organizations of the people, such as labour unions and peasant movements: in the two years after the October coup the government officially recognized 740 unions – 240 more than had been allowed in the whole of the previous decade. Furthermore, much like in the rest of the world, the membership of established unions began to expand massively, sometimes by as much as 500 to 600 per cent. These unions were also allowed to confederate for the first time. By 1948 the newly formed Confederation of Workers of Venezuela boasted about 300,000 members (with perhaps another 50,000 in other unions controlled by the Communists). The equally new Peasant Federation of Venezuela had a further 100,000 members. Considering that the population of Venezuela at the time was just 4.2 million, this represented a huge percentage of the workforce who were actively engaged in public life.[6]

The Trienio government also made revolutionary changes to the economy. Venezuela was a nation built on its oil reserves, but those reserves were largely being exploited by British and North American companies. During the war, a new series of taxes and rules had been introduced to ensure that the profits of the oil industry would be shared equally between these companies and the nation. As a consequence, the Trienio government was now awash with oil money: in 1947 government income from oil was more than six times what it had been before the war.[7]

Suddenly Venezuela was able to embark on many of the grand centralized schemes that other nations were also instituting around this time. In 1946 the government quadrupled its housing budget, and then doubled it again the following year. The previous government had already approved a series of housing projects during the war: these were now expanded across the country. A building boom began in Caracas. By the 1950s, the capital had been transformed from a town of traditional red-tiled single-storey buildings into a city of modernist high-rises.[8]

Alongside the building boom came a boom in learning. The education budget rose from 38 million bolívares in 1945 to 119 million in 1948, with a further 53 million given to the Ministry of Public Works for the construction of dozens of primary and secondary schools. A massive campaign to reduce adult illiteracy was started, and within three years there were 3,600 adult literacy centres across the country.[9]

The nation's health budget was also quadrupled, and medical facilities were extended to many rural areas for the first time. According to Rómulo Betancourt, the Trienio government spent three times as much on sewers and public drinking water supplies as its predecessors had spent in *the whole of the preceding century*. They also embarked on a massive campaign to eradicate malaria. Following the successes with DDT during the war, spraying with the insecticide in Venezuela began in December 1945, eventually eradicating malaria from huge regions of the country.[10]

Last but not least, the army, navy and air force were given new staff, new arms, better training, better food and hygiene, better medical supplies, new libraries, new technical colleges, a new Ships and Shipbuilding Institute, 25 per cent more pilots, 100 per cent more specialists, and a complete overhaul of its cultural and recreational facilities. A year into his stint as defence minister, Carlos Delgado Chalbaud was able to talk confidently of a 'rebirth' in the nation's armed forces.[11]

It is easy, and tempting, to characterize the changes that took place in Venezuela after the October coup in rosy terms. As in Indonesia, the arrival of democracy was undeniably a triumph for the ordinary people of the country. But, as in Indonesia, the pace of reform was so fast and so chaotic that it left those of a more conservative disposition reeling. Businessmen, the Catholic Church and some sections of the military all began to voice worries over the social upheavals that were taking place. Of particular concern were the labour unions, whose frequent strikes regularly brought business to a standstill: in 1947 alone there were fifty-five major strikes, almost fourteen times as many as there had been in 1944.[12] Some traditionalists resented the new-found power of the working classes, and dismissed the new AD-dominated administration as *el gobierno de los alpargatudos* – a government of espadrille-wearing peasants.[13] The Church resented attempts to secularize education and bring it under public control, and promoted an image of the government as an institution of atheists.[14] The opposition parties accused the government of trying to consolidate power for AD, and cited instances of AD supporters intimidating or even attacking their members. In the city of Mérida, for example, there were clashes between the supporters of AD and the main opposition party, Copei, which left five people dead.[15] There were also concerns about corruption and inefficiency, and questions over where the huge amounts of new public money were actually going.[16]

Outside the country, too, there were concerns. The acting president, Betancourt, freely admitted that there were strains between his government and some of Venezuela's neighbours, particularly Nicaragua and the Dominican Republic, whose military dictators were happy to encourage plots against this new, democratic regime. Relations with Argentina's Juan Perón were also, according to Betancourt, 'distant, cold, reticent, and even pugnacious on occasion'.[17] However, he was rather less forthcoming about some of the difficulties he had with the USA, where there was a range of opinions on what he and his government were trying to do. Those in financial circles, for example, reacted with 'shocked surprise' to the announcement of a new tax on American oil companies.[18] Some military observers began to panic about alleged Communist activity within the oil unions, and after the presidential elections in 1948 a group of fifty American businessmen wrote to the US embassy in Caracas to accuse the AD government of collaborating with Communists.[19] On the other hand, anyone with any expertise in Venezuelan affairs knew that there was nothing particularly alarming about the new government: US embassy officials in Caracas likened it to the Labour government in Britain. At one point the acting Secretary of State, Dean Acheson, wrote a fairly stern memo to his colleagues in the Department of War warning them not to exaggerate the threat of communism in the country. The rash of strikes in the oil industry, he said, were nothing to do with the Communists but merely 'the reasonable demands of labor'.[20]

Gradually, however, the atmosphere in Venezuela began to change. As the Cold War set in, and as frustrations within the country mounted, enthusiasm for the new democracy began to sour. As in the United States, paranoia about communism began to increase, and many people began to accuse the government of having Communist leanings. Fringe groups such as the Frente Nacional Anticomunista (Anti-Communist National Front) sprang up and began agitating for the army to oust the AD government. Similar groups began to assert themselves within the Venezuelan military establishment too. In mid-1948 a group formed that called itself the Organización Militar Anticomunista (Anti-Communist Military Organization), which spread rumours that 'the Adecos were communists who wanted to destroy the National Armed Forces'.[21]

Just as in 1945, many of the officers began to complain that the army was not being allowed to perform its rightful role in the life of the nation. Foremost amongst them was the Chief of General Staff, Marcos Pérez Jiménez, whose followers began to accuse the government of everything from corruption to national betrayal. Rumours began to circulate that the government was building up its own political militia to rival the army. Such stories deliberately mimicked the reports of similar militias in eastern Europe that were at that time helping the

Communists to seize power: in this way, even when communism was not mentioned explicitly, its presence was still implied.[22]

Carlos Delgado Chalbaud served as minister of defence throughout this period. For a long time he formed the only real bridge between the radical reformers of government and the discontented elements of the army. He continually negotiated for calm, asserting repeatedly that the army was not a political organization and that it should 'at all times give its full and efficient support to the decisions made by the supreme leadership of the President of the Republic'.[23] But by the summer of 1948 an atmosphere of conspiracy had already become entrenched in the army.

Just as in 1945, Delgado was approached by a group of conspirators and asked if he would join them in a second coup d'état. As on the previous occasion, he tried to stall for time so that he could have a chance to think. Delgado was actually quite sympathetic to the army's frustrations. As military men they were all used to a certain degree of efficiency: orders were given, orders were followed, things got done. Democracy, it turned out, was not always quite like that. But he was also worried that a second coup would be a betrayal of the principles of the first, that this time it would be overthrowing not a dictatorship but a democratically elected government. Furthermore, there would be an element of personal betrayal involved: Rómulo Gallegos, the recently elected president, was a personal friend – Delgado had even shared a house with him for a while in Barcelona while in exile.

This time, however, the conspirators refused to give him any time to think: they told him that he was either with them or against them, and would have to accept the consequences either way. Under pressure, Delgado chose to join the conspiracy.

And so, once again, he found himself embroiled in a coup d'état. Just as before, he was right at the heart of the action. On 24 November 1948 it was Delgado who gave the order for the army to seize control of the government. Unlike the previous coup, this one was almost completely bloodless. Nevertheless, the consequences were profound. The ruling party, Acción Democrática, was immediately declared illegal, and across the country its members were rounded up and arrested – Betancourt later claimed that as many as 10,000 were thrown into prison. A handful of protests, particularly by students and by unions, were violently quashed. Democracy was suspended.[24]

Carlos Delgado Chalbaud in 1949.

Now, in place of an elected government, a military triumvirate took power consisting of Delgado, Marcos Pérez Jiménez and a lieutenant colonel named Luis Felipe Llovera Páez. But as the senior member of the group it was Delgado who became Venezuela's new president.

Latin America After the Second World War

The turbulent nature of Venezuela's politics between 1945 and 1948 reflected the huge internal pressures within the country at the time – between conservatives and radicals, between civilians and the military, business and labour, the clergy and educational reformers, and between competing political parties of every colour. But Venezuela did not exist in a vacuum. Alongside these internal pressures were international forces which pressed against the nation from all sides: not only their immediate neighbours – which included European colonies, repressive dictatorships and other democracies similar to themselves – but also the giant super-power that lay to the north, which exercised enormous influence on the entire hemisphere. In such a context, many of the events in Venezuela were shaped as much by external influences as by internal ones.

The dates of Delgado's two coups are instructive. The first happened in October 1945, just a few weeks after the end of the Second World War, when the wave of hope and expectation that was washing over the rest of the world also washed over Latin America. Delgado himself acknowledged that the October coup had been carried out in the name of 'the grand ideals of liberty, equality and fraternity', and had taken place 'within the modern atmosphere of social justice' that was sweeping the world.[25] The wave of populism, democratic reform and union activism that gripped Venezuela over the next three years were all part of the same phenomenon.

The second coup took place in a completely different atmosphere, in November 1948, at a time when people all over the world were speculating about the start of a new global war in which everyone would once again be forced to pick sides. Governments from Ottawa to Buenos Aires were increasingly gripped by fears of subversion, and were clamping down on all forms of dissent. According to Delgado, the November coup was conducted to restore to Venezuelan society a sense of order, or 'social discipline', as he called it. 'The nation must not return to an atmosphere of public unrest,' he told a Colombian newspaper reporter the following year, 'nor to the exacerbation of political passions, nor should there be speculation about social needs and calamities.' What was important in the atmosphere of 1948 was no longer freedom and equality, but stability.[26]

In this context, the parallels between Venezuela and other Latin American countries are quite striking. At the end of the Second World War, led by a sense that the whole world was being reborn, there was a rush for democracy across the region. It was not only in Venezuela that a dictatorship was overthrown: in Ecuador, a popular uprising in 1944 ousted Carlos Arroyo del Río's repressive regime and led to elections the following year. In Guatemala, another popular rebellion led to the overthrow of Jorge Ubico and established a representative democracy for the first time in the country's history. In Bolivia the unpopular dictator Gualberto Villarroel was lynched during a violent revolt and, in an echo of what had happened to Benito Mussolini in Italy, his body hung from a lamp post. Elections were immediately promised for January 1947. In other countries, democracy was achieved in less violent ways. Peru held its first ever free elections in 1945. The dictators of Argentina, Brazil and Cuba were also convinced to hold free elections during this time. Mexico introduced some limited electoral reform in 1946. Even Anastasio Somoza of Nicaragua and Rafael Leónidas Trujillo of the Dominican Republic, two of the most stubborn and repressive dictators in the whole region, felt obliged at least to pay lip service to the new atmosphere of democracy. According to one annual survey just after the war, 'The years 1944 and 1945 brought more democratic changes in more Latin American countries than perhaps in any single year since the wars of independence' in the nineteenth century.[27]

Alongside this rush for democratic change came all kinds of economic and cultural reforms, also stimulated by the war. As we have seen, Venezuela, with its strategically important oil reserves, ended the war much richer than before, but other countries too found themselves with a massive dollar surplus in 1945, particularly Argentina, Brazil and Cuba.[28] Across the continent investments were being made in huge new infrastructure projects, new schools, new universities, new public housing. As industrialization increased, so did urbanization. New suburbs and new districts were built everywhere, designed by central planners according to the new international style. One or two of them, like Mexico City's university campus, would go on to become UNESCO world heritage sites. In 1947 Le Corbusier was invited to Colombia, where he was asked to oversee the replanning of Bogotá. All of South America buzzed with change.

Within this atmosphere, labour militancy increased everywhere. The massive expansion of unions in Venezuela was repeated elsewhere, and by 1946 there were between 3.5 and 4 million union members across Latin America. Civil and industrial unrest also increased. In Chile, for example, the number of strikes rose more than sevenfold between 1942 and 1946, and eventually involved almost 100,000 workers. In Peru, too, there was a steadily increasing number of strikes between 1945 and 1948. Brazil, meanwhile, saw its biggest wave of strikes for more than twenty-five years: in May 1945, while victory was being proclaimed in Europe, there were more than 300 in Sao Paolo alone, involving 150,000 workers. Union activists everywhere were brimming with confidence.[29]

There is no doubt that all these events in neighbouring countries were mutually reinforcing, as witnessed both by the formation of transcontinental organizations like the Confederación de Trabajadores de

América Latina (Confederation of Latin American Workers), and by the direct pressure exercised by governments on their neighbours. A handful of Latin America's most democratic nations – Uruguay is a good example – were very vocal in their condemnation of any country guilty of human rights abuses.[30] But by far the most powerful champion of democracy in 1945 was the United States. During the war, US agencies had bombarded the region with propaganda portraying the USA as the champion of democracy and purveyor of the good life, and had financed local media to do likewise. In some cases they had intervened directly with Latin American governments to promote greater democracy, even when doing so involved a greater toleration of communism.[31]

When the USA began to change its tune at the start of the Cold War, Latin American governments also played along. Communist parties were banned in one country after another. Brazil declared communism illegal as early as May 1947, Chile in April 1948, Costa Rica in July 1948. In countries where communism was not much of a threat, other left-wing parties were targeted instead – APRA in Peru, for example, which was forced out of local and central government, and repressed in a similar fashion to Acción Democrática in Venezuela. Far from condemning such actions, the US State Department appeared to endorse them more or less wholeheartedly.[32]

What followed was a rolling back of democracy across the region. Venezuela was not the only country to see its first experiment with free elections overturned: there were also military coups in Peru (1948), Cuba (1952), Colombia (1953) and Guatemala (1954). By the mid-1950s, the majority of Latin American republics were ruled once again not by democracy but by dictatorship – and the majority of those dictatorships were military and authoritarian in nature. Further military coups would occur later in the century in Brazil (1964), Uruguay (1973) and Chile (1973), each of them overthrowing a formerly democratic government. By the end of the Cold War, the only Latin American republic to have had an unbroken postwar record of democracy was Costa Rica, perhaps not least because it was the one country in Latin America to disband its entire army at the start of the Cold War. Meanwhile, those countries that had never experienced a true democratic renaissance after the war, such as Nicaragua, El Salvador, Honduras and the Dominican Republic, now saw a retightening of repression. Where once the US State Department had been outspoken in its criticism of such regimes, it now fell strangely silent: in the paranoid atmosphere of the Cold war, democracy did not seem nearly as important as hemispheric unity.[33]

For the most part, the USA did not play a direct role in these events. It did not need to: in the words of the American diplomat Spruille Braden, 'Whatever we refrain from saying and whatever we refrain from doing may constitute intervention, no less than what we do or say.'[34] But as the Cold War intensified, the USA showed itself increasingly willing to play dirty. There is circumstantial evidence that the American military attaché in Venezuela in 1948, Colonel Edward F. Adams, had some kind of role in the November coup: nothing was ever proven at the time, but many historians agree that there was something about his presence amongst the core conspirators that does not sit right.[35] The part played by the USA in the Guatemalan coup in 1954, by contrast, is much more clear-cut. Not only is there ample documentation to prove that the State Department and US business interests were deeply involved in destabilizing the Guatemalan government, but also several members of the CIA have openly admitted to doing so. Spruille Braden, though he no longer worked for the State Department, was once again at the heart of the whole sorry affair.[36]

In the following years, the USA would undermine freedom and democracy in a variety of Latin American nations, not only officially recognizing the regimes of military dictators but also honouring them.[37] It interfered directly in elections, provided secret funding for right-wing groups and spread black propaganda about any groups with even moderately left-wing views.[38] It propped up repressive regimes, provided training to members of death squads and – in extreme cases, such as in Guatemala or Nicaragua – deliberately fomented savage civil wars.[39] All this has been documented, and there is undoubtedly plenty more besides that remains classified in CIA and State Department files. This does not say much for the USA's 1948 promise to foster 'justice, freedom and peace' alongside its neighbours; or its promise to the world, repeatedly made, that it would refrain from intervening in other nations' internal affairs.[40]

The Price of Repression

With hindsight, it is obvious that the USA was acting both illegally and undemocratically. But in the atmosphere of the time it was not so clear-cut. Nobody in the US security establishment sanctioned actions in Latin America in order to undermine democracy: quite the contrary, they believed themselves to be *strengthening* democracy. Throughout the Cold War the true monster was always communism, not dictatorship. The battle to defeat this monster justified almost anything, including promoting regimes with the most appalling human rights records.

Carlos Delgado Chalbaud also believed himself to be acting in the name of democracy. When he became president of Venezuela in 1948 he faced some stern questioning by fellow statesmen in other countries, and by the newspapers and diplomatic establishments of some of Venezuela's neighbours. How could he justify being involved in both a coup to establish democracy and a coup to remove it again? If he had truly believed that Venezuela was becoming unstable, why had he not acted sooner, rather than waiting until after the people had taken part in elections? Fellow Venezuelans like Rómulo Betancourt could not resist pointing out that Delgado seemed to have done very well out of both coups. The governments of Mexico, Cuba, Guatemala and Uruguay all announced that they would suspend recognition of the new military government 'indefinitely'.[41]

But Delgado himself always insisted that he had acted purely out of principle. His only true motivation, he claimed, was to save his nation from the powerful forces that were driving it towards greater discord. In October 1945 he had stepped in to restrain the anti-democratic impulses of Venezuela's traditional oligarchy; and in November 1948 he had stepped in to restrain the revolutionary impulses of 'demagogues' in AD.[42] Thus, in Delgado's mind at least, the two coups were part of the same process. 'Social phenomena are like this,' he told a Colombian newspaper at the end of the decade: 'they form part of a historic chain. The events of October [1945] and November [1948], as we have said before, are vigorous strides in the upward march of the nation.'[43] In the end, all Delgado truly wanted was to guide his country towards a middle way between order and change, between the individual and society, between freedom and belonging; or, as he put it, to find a balance 'between the free, dignified life of the citizen and social discipline'.[44]

His mistake lay in believing that these things might somehow be achieved by force. By taking part in not one but two coups he was effectively endorsing the idea that, ultimately, only the military had the right to decide what was right or wrong for the country. This belief had always been a part of Venezuelan military culture, and indeed the military cultures of many Latin American countries, and it would continue to govern political thinking throughout the continent for the rest of the century. Thus Delgado too was part of a 'historic chain', which included his fellow soldiers, many of his fellow countrymen, Latin American elites in general, and eventually the combined security establishments of the entire western hemisphere.

This idea that the military knows best would have profound implications for Latin America. But it would also have profound personal implications for Delgado himself. Of all the military leaders who governed Latin American states during the twentieth century, Delgado was surely one of the most moderate. From the moment he took power, he insisted that he fully intended to re-establish democracy as soon as possible, once 'a climate of serenity and true harmony' had been restored.[45] 'When the Army assumed the responsibility it had to assume,' he told a press conference shortly after seizing power, 'it was not to act against democratic principles but on the contrary to save the existence of those principles.' Elections were eventually scheduled for 1952.[46]

But other factions within the army, and within the nation as a whole, did not want the military to abdicate control, and as the promise of new elections loomed closer, one of them planned a coup of its own. On 13 November 1950, when Delgado was leaving his home, a group of armed men grabbed him and pushed him into a car. They drove him to a villa in Caracas's new Las Mercedes development, where he was assassinated. To this day it is not clear who was behind the kidnapping, or what their precise intentions were. His killer, a political malcontent called Rafael Simón Urbina, was never able to reveal who, if anyone, had put him up to the job: he was himself killed while in police custody shortly afterwards.

Delgado's death signified an end to Venezuela's brief flirtation with democracy, and a change in the political atmosphere over the whole of Latin America. Venezuela would have to wait until the end of the 1950s for democracy to be restored. In the rest of the continent the persistence of military rule would run longer, and deeper, with tragic consequences for democracy across the region.

Unlike Indonesia or Kenya, Venezuela did not have to invent itself after the Second World War. It was more or less secure in its borders, and suffered few of the deep divides over language, ethnicity and religion that split the other two countries. Venezuela was also different in that it had shaken off colonialism many decades earlier, and had long since established the national sovereignty that Indonesia and Kenya had to fight for so desperately. And yet the Second World War awoke many of the same passions here as it did elsewhere. Venezuela's attempt to make a clean break with its past in 1945 was every bit as revolutionary as Indonesia's or Kenya's: the people of all three countries were essentially pursuing the same thing – greater democracy. The surge of idealism that accompanied the end of the war helped all three countries to embrace new ideas and new institutions – but it also unleashed great unrest, which manifested itself in the massive demonstrations, workers' strikes and increasing violence that plagued them all. Like Indonesia and Kenya, Venezuela eventually had to make a choice between freedom and order, and live with the consequences of that choice.

It its way, Venezuela was forced to confront the challenges of independence after 1945 just as much as Kenya or Indonesia. All three countries experienced varying degrees of outside interference in their affairs – by their old colonial masters, by the new Cold War superpowers, or by both at once. All belonged to the 'global south', and would spend the following years accusing the more developed nations of the global north of exploiting them for profit, often with good reason. Maintaining one's independence in such an environment was a constant battle which none of these nations could truthfully say that it always won.

Finally, crucially, Venezuela was forced to struggle with the same question that faced Kenya and Indonesia after the war: what is a nation? Both the 1945 coup and the 1948 coup were carried out in the name of Venezuela, but what was 'Venezuela'? In a country that shares the same language, religion and ancestry as many of those around it, what was there beyond mere geographical location that could both separate it from its neighbours and bind the nation together? Was there a common culture in the country and, if so, who was it that decided what that culture was? Was it the traditional elites, or the Church, or the people, or the workers – or the army? If these different groups disagreed with one another, sometimes violently, could Venezuela ever truly say that it was a single, unified nation?

There are many important benefits that each of these nations gained from imagining themselves to form a single unified group – a sense of common purpose, a feeling of security from outsiders, a sense of belonging. At times these things can not only be comforting, but also essential for maintaining order in society. But they come at a cost. Just as the dream of world federalism puts limits on national freedoms, so the dreams of nations curtail the freedoms of smaller groups and individuals. No one who identifies with any group and abides by its rules is ever truly free: cooperation requires compromise, which does not always sit easily with those who are fixated on pursuing their own Utopias. S. K. Trimurti, Waruhiu Itote and Carlos Delgado Chalbaud all had to learn that ideals were not enough. Sometimes it was also necessary to seize control, or to swallow one's principles and make a deal.

19. Israel: Nation of Archetypes

'Life is permanent war.' So said Aharon Appelfeld when I interviewed him at his Jerusalem home in 2016, and it quickly became clear that he meant this both literally and metaphorically. 'I was in Europe when the Second World War came. Here in Israel I was a child soldier in the Independence War. Then there was the Sinai War, then the Six-Day War, then the Yom Kippur War – and in all of them I was a soldier.' But he also talked about his struggle to fit into Israeli society, to acquire the language and to come to terms with the many terrors he experienced as a child. 'It doesn't matter where you go or what you do, life is a permanent war.'[1]

Appelfeld got his first taste of war when the German army swept through his corner of central Europe on their way to invading Russia. It was the summer of 1941, and he was just nine years old. He and his family had left their home in Czernowitz in the northern borderlands of Romania to spend the vacation at his grandparents' house in the nearby Carpathian mountains: 'I was sick and was asleep in my bed at noon. Suddenly there was shooting. I called out for my parents. There was more shooting. I jumped out of the window and hid in the cornfield behind the house. While in the field, I heard the Germans torturing my beautiful mother. I heard my mother screaming. I heard the Germans murder my grandmother and my mother.'[2]

In the aftermath of this first wave of killings, he and his father were forced into a ghetto, expelled in cattle trucks to Transnistria and finally force-marched to a makeshift concentration camp in an abandoned collective farm in Ukraine. It was the end of autumn, and for two weeks they marched through mud and torrential rain. 'I was lucky. My father was strong, and he carried me on his shoulders. Most children and old people died along the way.'

At the concentration camp he was separated from his father, who was sent away with all the other men to work. After a few days on his own, surrounded by only the weak and the dying, he understood instinctively that if he stayed here he would never survive. So he took a chance: he slipped under the fence and ran away.

The first place he hid was in the forest. He lived for a while by eating rotting apples and berries, but when the rain became worse, and the nights got longer, he realized that he had to find shelter. He began knocking on doors in the villages, asking for work, until eventually a prostitute took him in. All through that winter he worked as her servant, milking the cow, cleaning her hut, going to the local village to buy food for her and her clients. In the evenings he would watch her drink vodka, service the local peasants and then fight with them when they asked too much of her or refused to pay. 'I had only completed first grade at school. This was grade two.'

When one of her clients accused him of being a Jew, he knew it was time to move on. So he ran away to the forest again, where he found refuge with a gang of thieves: 'They used me to help them steal horses. I was small, so they could put me through the window of a stable and then I would open the doors for them . . . Sometimes they gave me a piece of bread to eat, sometimes sausages, sometimes cheese. Generally they ignored me. I was like the two dogs they had – another small animal.'

But soon the thieves also began to ask questions of him, so he moved on once again. He found some more peasants in the forest to adopt him, 'but they were no better than the criminals'. For two years this short, undernourished child moved from place to place, surviving on little more than his wits and sheer luck. Since being a Jew meant certain death, he learned to pass himself off as a Christian. He was blond, and spoke good Ukrainian, which had been the language used by his family's housemaid before the war. But mostly he just kept quiet and learned to observe the world around him. 'This too was a kind of school. I learned a lot about life. And about human beings. They can be kind at times, but in other moments they can be downright beasts. By the end of the war I could see a man, and know immediately if he was dangerous.'

In 1944, the Red Army swept through Ukraine, and Appelfeld got swept along with them. He persuaded a supply unit to give him work as a kitchen boy, and watched as they made their way from village to village, raping and killing as they went. 'The Russian army was a drunken army, drinking day and night. Cursing and drinking and raping and singing patriotic songs: this was my third grade of school.' He was still only twelve years old.

Eventually, Appelfeld was found by some soldiers of the British army's Jewish Brigade, who took him into Italy, then to Yugoslavia, and finally smuggled him across the Mediterranean to Haifa. He was glad to be amongst Jews again, but this did not mean he felt completely safe. By the time he finally arrived in Palestine in 1946 he had long since lost any faith in the notion of a safe haven. As far as he was concerned, Palestine was just one more station in his flight.

In this new land, there were new wars to be fought. Over the course of the next two years, Palestine became embroiled in a bloody civil war between Arabs and Jews. In 1948, when the Jews declared the independent state of Israel, the new nation was immediately attacked by its neighbours. Far from being granted a new life, it appeared that Appelfeld was merely to experience more of the same: 'In Europe there had been a war with a lot of killing. Now in Israel there was a war with a lot of killing.' He was given a rifle and told to help defend his kibbutz.

There were metaphorical battles to be fought too. Appelfeld was expected to forget his German, which was the language of Jew-killers. He was discouraged from speaking Ukrainian and Russian and Romanian – the languages that had helped him to survive in Europe. Now everything had to be done in Hebrew. He was also expected to change his name. His parents had called him Erwin, a very German name – he now became Aharon. But most of all he was expected to learn a new attitude. 'We had come to Israel, as the saying went, "to build, and to be rebuilt". This was interpreted by most of us as the extinction of memory, a complete personal transformation and a total identification with this narrow strip of land.' In short, Appelfeld was expected to 'efface my past and build a new life on its ruins'.[3]

He went about this in the best way he knew. He studied Hebrew diligently. He started running and climbing and lifting weights. He wanted to become tall and rugged and suntanned, to look like a soldier. But no matter how hard he tried, he remained short, underweight and pale; and for a long while he spoke with a stammer. At night he would dream about being pursued by some huge, nameless evil, or about falling into a deep pit where unseen hands were pulling him down. He told himself over and over to forget the past and blend in with his new home. He felt like he was tiptoeing around the rim of an abyss. 'All my experience in Europe became like a cellar, a dark cellar buried deep inside me.

You do not need to be Freud to understand that such a cellar is a dangerous thing.'

What saved him was learning how to write fiction. When he was in his twenties he studied at the Hebrew University, and gradually came to realize that there was no point in pretending that he was something other than the person that the war had made him. He understood that he would always carry the Diaspora within him – but that, despite all the pressure for him to deny it, there was a richness and a value in his memories that was just as worthwhile as the new life he had also embraced. He began to seek the company of other Holocaust survivors in the cafés of Jerusalem. He began to appreciate the silences that fell between them, which were far more expressive than the ocean of words that seemed to characterize the rest of Israeli society. And he began to write. 'Other people just went crazy, in different forms. I was lucky. I was a writer.'

Appelfeld published his first collection of short stories in 1962. Since then he has written over forty other books, almost all about the effects of the Second World War on the lives of the Jews who survived it. His

Israeli novelist Aharon Appelfeld, sixty years after the war.

stories are peppered with prostitutes and orphans and black-market traders – all of whom are based on different aspects of the people he came across during the war and its aftermath. He has long since given up trying to resist the memories from this time, which seem imprinted on his very soul. Instead, he has learned to accept them for what they are – part of life's beauty, and part of its perpetual war.

Nation of Heroes

The nation that took in Aharon Appelfeld in 1946 had a very particular view of itself. Long before Sartre wrote his thesis on existentialism, Zionist Jews had understood that they stood naked before the universe, and that if they were to survive in a hostile world they must seize responsibility for their own destiny.[4] Driven by a combination of ancestral longing and socialist values, they had come to Palestine determined to carve out a new life for themselves in what they regarded as their ancient homeland. They had drained swamps, and made the desert bloom. They had founded kibbutzim and moshavim – farms and communities based on a collectivist ethos. They had built a new city, Tel Aviv, shining white on the shores of the Mediterranean. Had it not been for the Arabs, with whom they were obliged to share the land, and the British, who controlled this part of the Middle East, their history might have been one of unbridled progress and harmony. So the thinking went.[5]

When the Second World War had broken out, the Yishuv – that is, the Jewish community in Palestine – did not stand by and wait to see what fate had in store for them. They stepped forward and fought on the side of freedom. Jewish paratroopers were sent behind enemy lines in order to render help to partisans and Resistance fighters. Jewish spy rings were set up in Sweden, Spain and Turkey to establish escape routes from Hitler's Europe. Thirty thousand Jews had volunteered to fight alongside the British in Syria, North Africa and Italy. But that did not mean they always passively followed British orders – at the same time special commando units were formed to defy the British immigration bans, which had been in place since before the war, and smuggle shiploads of Jewish refugees to safety.[6]

This determination to take charge of their own destiny continued after the Second World War was over. In 1946, the Jewish 'Resistance

'Life is war': yeshiva students in training, 1947–1948.

Movement' waged an insurgency to drive the British out of Palestine. In 1947, Jewish leaders convinced the United Nations to grant them a homeland. When the Arabs of Palestine rose up in protest, Jewish defence forces drove them out. When the British finally withdrew, the Yishuv did not wait for the UN to keep its promise, but declared its own independence. And when Israel was invaded on the very next day – on four fronts, by Egypt, Jordan, Syria and Lebanon – the new state not only repelled the invaders but also pushed their borders back. These were no effeminate shtetl Jews who, in the words of one Yishuv leader, 'preferred the life of a beaten dog to death with honour'. These were young pioneers, 'New Jews', a nation of heroes.[7]

For years, the whole country was engaged in a single, communal task: the creation of the future. Israel was a new nation in every respect. It had brand-new borders, a new parliament, a new national bank, a new currency, a new Supreme Court and a new citizen army. The state subscribed to all of the values of the postwar world: according to the declaration of independence, Israel would be a nation based on 'freedom, justice and peace'; and it promised 'complete equality of social and political rights to all its inhabitants irrespective of religion, race or sex'.[8]

David Ben-Gurion's first government gave particular emphasis to 'complete civil equality for women . . . and the abolition of all existing discrimination against women as embodied in Turkish and Mandatory laws'.[9] Israel was to be a shining example of the brave new world. Even the country's name was new: until Ben-Gurion had announced its independence no one had been sure whether it would be called Zion, or Judea, or Ivriya, or a variety of other possible names.[10]

In the following years, the whole country became a hive of frantic activity. The list of projects that were planned and begun during this extraordinary time seems impossibly ambitious. Massive new irrigation schemes were set in motion, such as the Yarkon–Negev water pipeline, and the National Water Carrier, which sought to bring water all the way from the Sea of Galilee to the Negev desert. A policy of rapid road and rail development was introduced, including new routes across the Negev to the Red Sea and a road along the Dead Sea's western shore. A vast national afforestation project was begun, providing a chain of national parks across the country. A state airline was founded (El Al), along with a state shipping company (Zim). The building of schools and hospitals was yet another national priority: in the fifteen years after independence Israel more than tripled the number of school places, and quadrupled the number of hospital beds.[11]

The long-established Zionist tradition of building new farms and settlements went into overdrive. In 1950 and 1951, 190 new kibbutz or moshav villages were built in the Israeli countryside – an average of one every four days. These were built not only in Israel's fertile valleys and along the coastal plain, but also in remote parts of the Negev, including Yotvata, and a new experimental farm at Ein Yahav. In addition to the new villages, thirty new towns were founded and a massive new port planned. In established cities, new suburbs sprang up as fast as they could be built. In Jerusalem, for example, entire neighbourhoods like the Katamons, Kiryat Hayovel and Ir Ganim were planned and constructed within just a few years.[12]

In the decades after independence, development took precedence over everything. In order to pay for all the schools and the hospitals and the housing estates – and also the new obsession with science and technology which would eventually build Israel into the region's first nuclear power – compromises had to be made. In 1952 Israel accepted a payment from Germany of DM3,450 million ($865 million) 'as reparation for the material damage suffered by Jews at the hands of the Nazis'. The government tried to present this as a form of historical justice: the people who had tried to exterminate world Jewry were now helping to finance the building of a Jewish state. But to many people it looked like Israel was selling its national honour for cash. Despite violent demonstrations outside the Knesset, the payment was accepted, and the drive toward development continued.[13]

For a while, the state seemed to be involved in every aspect of people's lives. After the turbulent war of 1948 put most of the country's Arabs to flight, 90 per cent of the land was brought under state control – as were the nation's water sources, its electricity suppliers, its oil refineries. A national housing company was set up, called Amidar, to build vast new housing estates, and there was a new national employment agency to help provide new immigrants with jobs. By the mid-1950s the government sector accounted for about 20 per cent of the national economy. A further 20 per cent was owned and run by Israel's trade union organization – the Histadrut. Both organizations were dominated by the same political party – David Ben-Gurion's socialist Mapai.[14]

Running so many major plans and projects simultaneously required a huge amount of both improvisation and ambition. Overworked civil servants complained that they had no time to sleep, yet they also gloried in the excitement of all the activity. As one of them put it, 'Who can sleep at a time like this, who would not do anything to live this time more awake, even more intensively, even closer, more attentive and dedicated?'[15] Government leaders gained a reputation for ignoring the advice of economists and experts who cast doubt on whether various projects were affordable or even possible. For example, when an advisory committee concluded that the government's plans to build a new city around Beersheba were unfeasible, Ben-Gurion simply dismissed the committee and appointed a new one. Within just seven years there were 20,000 Jewish immigrants living in Beersheba. Twelve years after that the city had quadrupled in size to 80,000 to become the biggest settlement in the Negev desert, with its own railway station, hospital and soon even its own university.[16]

Even the nation's novelists were swept up in Israel's heroic idea of itself. The 'Generation of 1948', as they were known, wrote documentary-style stories in which the main protagonist was almost always the 'Sabra' – the native-born soldier-boy who is tough on the

outside but tender on the inside, who has none of the hang-ups and worries of the Diaspora but who is, like the country that reared him, 'born
from the sea'.[17] Their novels were infused with the values of the Zionist
pioneers, the kibbutz, the army and the newborn Israeli state – and the
overwhelming atmosphere is one of togetherness, self-sacrifice and cautious optimism.[18] Heroes die for their country.[19] Novels end with babies
being born.[20] This was a generation with its eyes set on the horizon,
where the fears of the past could be transcended by the hopes of a new,
utopian future.[21]

As Aharon Appelfeld remembers it, there was something reassuring
about this, but also something unbearably stifling. The state looked
after its citizens: it gave them work and housing, it guaranteed pensions
for the old, insurance for the sick and the injured, and maternity leave
for women and, most of all, it gave its people a land that they could call
their own, which it would defend to the last ounce of its strength. But
in return it required commitment. There was little room for individual-
ism in this society, and no tolerance for the passive or the weak. 'Actually,
the country was like an army,' he remembers. 'Everyone knew their
place, and their responsibilities. You should be a hero. You should fight
for your country. You should be a socialist. All kinds of commands. But
only God has the power to say these things. Slowly you become trampled by it.' And behind all the manic activity, in the background, was
the Holocaust. 'Everything was a fight against the past, against Jewish
past, against Jewish fate.' The whole nation, much like Appelfeld himself in those early years, seemed to be tiptoeing around the edge of an
abyss.

The Jewish 'Other'

Unfortunately, people like Aharon Appelfeld were part of the problem.
For the previous ten years, the British had always maintained strict
immigration limits in Palestine. With independence, however, these
limits were suddenly lifted. An open-door policy was made official in
1950 with the 'Law of Return', which granted all Jews, wherever they
were in the world, the right to come to the country as full Israeli citizens. Almost overnight the steady stream of Jewish immigrants became
a flood: in the space of just three and a half years around 685,000 foreign

Jews arrived, more than doubling the country's population. The influx of people was so huge, and so sudden, that the minister of agriculture, Pinhas Lavon, called it 'a bloodless revolution'.[22]

For the Yishuv, this represented a challenge unlike anything it had yet experienced. On the one hand, there was a great deal of sympathy for the immigrants, most of whom were refugees like Appelfeld – not only from war-torn Europe but also from brand-new waves of anti-Semitism in Iraq, Yemen and parts of North Africa. It was important to welcome such people with open arms; after all, wasn't this Israel's whole raison d'être? But on the other, alongside such humanitarian concerns were a collection of much more ambivalent feelings. The reality of receiving hundreds of thousands of newcomers filled many people with alarm: where would they all go? How would they find work? Who would feed and house them? More intangibly, what would the influx of so many foreigners do to the Israeli sense of self? The vast majority of these immigrants were not the 'new' Jews so beloved of Zionist myth; they were 'old' Jews – Jews of the Diaspora, who had never particularly wanted to come here, but who were only arriving now because, as one *Haaretz* reporter scornfully put it, 'they have nowhere else to go'. In a country that was only just beginning to establish some kind of national identity, the 'cloudburst' of newcomers threatened the very existence of the Sabra ideal.[23]

It was perhaps little wonder, then, that immigrants like Aharon Appelfeld faced enormous pressure to conform to the norms of the Yishuv almost as soon as they stepped off the boat. They were expected to learn Hebrew as a matter of urgency. Many, like Appelfeld, were pressured to give up their old identities and change their names to something more fitting to their new environment. More than anything else, they were compelled to embrace the new nation's culture of irrepressible positivity, confidence, assertiveness.

For some of the newcomers, there was something desperately attractive about the thought that the past could be thrown off like an old cloak, that one could become new and strong just by deciding to be so. Many remember their arrival in Israel as a kind of rebirth, claiming that they had been given 'an entirely new identity'; that 'Here began my new life'; that they had been plunged into a 'new reality' that enveloped their 'whole personality'.[24] Aharon Barak, who would one day become president of Israel's Supreme Court, perhaps put the experience most succinctly. He described his arrival in 1947 as a revelation: 'I didn't speak the language, I didn't know the land. But when I took off my old clothes I shed the past, the Diaspora, the ghetto. And when I stood in the Atta store in a khaki shirt, khaki trousers, and sandals, I was a new person. An Israeli.'[25]

But for others, the way their transition into Israeli society was managed seemed unnecessarily harsh. Historian Tom Segev has described in detail how some children orphaned by the Holocaust were treated when they arrived in the country. Those who refused to join in at school or in kibbutzim were often labelled 'corrupt', 'antisocial', 'deviant', 'ungrateful', 'retarded' or 'hysterical'. One child was diagnosed by a psychiatrist as being 'over-attached to his mother'; she had been killed in the war. Another was labelled 'disturbed' because he spoke too much in Polish, while yet another was criticized for his inability to listen properly – he only spoke Hungarian, while those around him spoke exclusively in Hebrew. Aharon Appelfeld experienced similar prejudice because of his fondness for speaking in German. To his new countrymen, German was the language of the monsters who had tried to exterminate world Jewry, but Appelfeld could not bear to give it up, because to him it was the language of the mother he had lost in the war.[26]

Prejudices like these were prevalent throughout Israeli society, and certainly in all of the nation's major institutions. Thus, former Resistance fighters from Europe who joined the Histadrut were reprimanded for speaking in Yiddish rather than Hebrew.[27] Disoriented refugees sent to live in kibbutzim were criticized for being 'shirkers', or for expecting 'special treatment'.[28] And immigrants who were drafted into the army were rarely trusted to take an active part in any fighting, despite the desperate need for fighters. In the 1948 war they were mostly used as support troops, and criticized by their commanders for being 'difficult, stubborn and cowardly men' with a tendency to flee 'at the decisive moment'.[29]

Time and again survivors were asked: Why did you not rebel? Why did European Jews walk meekly to their own deaths? Such questions might have been born out of a genuine wish to understand, but the accusation was implicit: weak, effeminate European Jews had been accomplices in their own extermination. The Yishuv simply could not conceive of such things ever having been possible in wartime Palestine: as David Ben-Gurion put it, 'no one could have slaughtered us in the synagogues; every boy and girl would have shot every German soldier'.[30]

There were other, more brutal questions. 'In almost every contact with the inhabitants of the country,' wrote one survivor, 'the question would come up of how we had remained alive. It was asked again and again and not always in the most delicate way. I had a feeling that I was being blamed for having stayed alive.'[31] Questions like these were born partly out of grief: most people in the Yishuv had loved ones who had been killed in the Holocaust, and they could not help feeling resentful towards those who had survived. But they were also born of prejudice: many Sabras suspected that European Jews who had survived the Holocaust had done so only through some kind of moral compromise. The abiding portrayal of the Holocaust survivor from 1945 is that of 'My Sister on the Beach', a famous story written by Yitzhak Sadeh, the founder of the elite commando unit, the Palmach. In the story, a group of young, strong Palmach fighters rescue a ragged, passive damsel in distress, who cries out that she is not worthy of their heroism. Her flesh has been branded 'For Officers Only'.[32]

Beneath this strange cocktail of humanitarian concern and thinly veiled disgust was an atmosphere of half-acknowledged fear. The Yishuv was terrified that its society of heroes would be infected with what it scathingly called the 'Diaspora mentality' – that is, the effeminate attitudes and passivity that had allowed so many Jews to be annihilated in Europe. Images of infection began to turn up throughout society. Mapai representatives voiced concerns that an influx of so many traumatized people might turn all of Palestine into 'one big madhouse'. Health officials worried about potential epidemics of infectious diseases like typhus or tuberculosis. When an epidemic of polio broke out, rumours began to circulate that the immigrants were responsible: symbolically, polio is a disease whose symptoms include physical weakness and paralysis, the very antithesis of the Sabra ideal.[33]

As more and more immigrants arrived in the country, the language used to describe them became harsher and more uncompromising. Years later, novelist Yehudit Hendel, one of the 'Generation of 1948', described the divisions that rent Israeli society:

> To put it bluntly, there were almost two races in this country. There was one race of people who thought they were gods. These were the ones

who had the honour and privilege of being born in Degania [Israel's first kibbutz], or in the Borochov neighbourhood of Givataim [the stronghold of Israel's labour movement] . . . And there was, we can certainly say, an inferior race. People we saw as inferior who had some kind of flaw, some kind of hunchback, and these were the people who came after the war. I was taught in school that the ugliest, basest thing is not the Exile but the Jew who came from there.[34]

The 'gods' of the Yishuv made few distinctions between different kinds of immigrants, many of whom came not from Europe at all, but from other parts of the Middle East and North Africa, especially after 1949. They were grouped together as a vast communal 'Other', whose presence was a threat to everything the Yishuv held dear. These people were 'unsuitable for Israel', warned the right-wing newspaper *Haboker*. They were 'undermining the health and the psychological and moral balance of the Yishuv', warned the left-wing newspaper *Davar*. Even Ben-Gurion himself, one of the main architects of the mass immigration policy, regarded them as 'a motley crowd, human dust lacking language, education, roots, tradition or national dreams'. The only hope for such people, he believed, was to remould them as 'New Jews', reborn into the correct, Israeli way of life.[35]

The fact that the prime minister himself was calling immigrants 'human dust' hints at a disturbing undercurrent in Israeli society in the late 1940s and early 1950s. Other Mapai officials had not hesitated to call Holocaust survivors 'scum', and the slang term describing them as 'soap' became widespread (after the myth that the Nazis had boiled down the Jewish dead to make soap during the Holocaust).[36] One Israeli veteran of the Second World War, who had witnessed conditions in Europe himself when he had parachuted behind enemy lines, described his dismay at the atmosphere towards Holocaust survivors in postwar Israel:

Everywhere I turned, the question was fired at me: why did the Jews not rebel? Why did they go like lambs to the slaughter? Suddenly I realized that we were ashamed of those who were tortured, shot, burned. There is a kind of general agreement that the Holocaust dead were worthless people. Unconsciously, we have accepted the Nazi view that the Jews were subhuman . . . History is playing a bitter joke on us: have we not ourselves put the six million on trial?[37]

Nation of Victims

It does not take much imagination to see that this contempt for the supposed weakness, passivity and paralysis of Diaspora Jews was related to a fear of the same tendencies that already existed within the Yishuv itself – and this is exactly what psychoanalytic and feminist analyses of the postwar period have argued.[38] For all the myths of their Second World War heroism – of spy rings and rescue operations and paratroopers dropped behind enemy lines – the efforts of the Yishuv had actually been fairly ineffectual during the war. According to Jewish partisan leaders in Europe, many of the thirty or so paratroopers dropped behind enemy lines ended up being more of a burden than a help.[39] The spying effort was not much better – even the Jewish Agency's own spy chiefs were forced to admit that the number of people they saved was 'microscopic'.[40] The various plans to negotiate with the Nazis all came to nothing; the attempts to get the British to allow mass immigration were fruitless; and the Jewish defence forces themselves, the Haganah, failed to smuggle more than a token number of Jews into Palestine during the climactic years of the Holocaust.[41] In reality, the Yishuv had been just as powerless during the war as the Jews of the Diaspora had been. Had Palestinian Jews directly confronted this, it would have been difficult to maintain the illusion that they were a nation of heroes; but until they did so, every Holocaust survivor was an admonition. Some of the survivors themselves were not shy about pointing this out: as one Polish community leader remarked pointedly, 'You danced the hora while we were being burned in the crematoriums.'[42]

For many years, an uneasy conspiracy of silence existed between European immigrants and Israeli Sabras, partly because the immigrants did not want to speak about their painful experiences, and partly because Sabras did not want to hear. But partly also because survivors of the Holocaust had not yet managed to find a voice, particularly in a language that was not yet their own: Aharon Appelfeld, for example, did not start to express himself until the mid-1950s, and did not publish his first collection of stories until 1962. This does not mean that the subject of the Holocaust was buried. Far from it. It remained at the forefront of political consciousness throughout the 1950s.[43] For most Sabras, however, the constant rhetoric about the 'six million' or the 'extermination camps' did not touch their souls. Despite its horror, so far as the Yishuv were concerned, it was still something that had happened to 'them', the Diaspora, rather than 'us'.[44]

If there was one event that changed this, or at the very least symbolized a transformation that was starting to take place in Israeli society, then it was the trial of Adolf Eichmann in 1961. Eichmann was one of the most senior Nazi administrators to be involved in the Holocaust. In a daring mission – one might even say a 'heroic' one – Israeli agents captured him in Argentina and brought him back to Jerusalem to face justice. The documentary evidence against him was overwhelming, so there was never any serious doubt about his guilt. But his trial was not only about finding him guilty: it was also about providing the world – and especially Israeli youth – with an education on what Jews had suffered before they had won the right to their own homeland. 'This is not an ordinary trial, nor only a trial,' stated prime minister Ben-Gurion:

> Here for the first time in Jewish history, historical justice is being done by the sovereign Jewish people. For many generations it was we who suffered, who were tortured, were killed – and we who were judged. Our adversaries and our murderers were also our judges. For the first time Israel is judging the murderers of the Jewish people. It is not an individual that is in the dock at this historic trial and not the Nazi regime alone but anti-Semitism throughout history.[45]

The trial succeeded in unifying the Jewish people like few other events in Israel ever have. As dozens of survivors took the stand and detailed the full extent of the inhumanity they had suffered at the hands of the Nazis – but also their attempts at resistance (since the prosecutors were anxious to show that Holocaust survivors had been heroes too) – the whole country listened in on its transistor radios. Commentators like Hannah Arendt criticized these testimonies for being irrelevant to the specific case of Eichmann, but it was these stories that most gripped the nation. For the first time, Sabras began to regard the Holocaust not as something that had happened to 'them', but something that had happened to 'us'.

In the following decades, while continuing to see itself as a nation of heroes, Israel adopted a parallel identity as a nation of martyrs. The Holocaust was no longer just something that had happened to a different generation on a different continent. Suddenly it had a universal relevance. Thus when a new war broke out in 1967 – the Six-Day War – a fear of annihilation gripped the nation as it had never done before, not only amongst those who had themselves experienced the Holocaust but also amongst the rest of the population. 'People believed we would be exterminated if we lost the war,' claimed one young soldier shortly after it was over. 'We got this idea – or inherited it – from the concentration camps. It's a concrete idea for anyone who has grown up in Israel, even if he personally didn't experience Hitler's persecution, but only heard or read about it. Genocide – it's a feasible notion.'[46]

This sense of shared victimhood was magnified six years later when war broke out once more. In 1973 Israel was taken completely by surprise when Egypt and Syria attacked it on Yom Kippur, the holiest day of the Jewish year. The Yom Kippur War was the first time since 1948 when Israel had not been largely in control of events, and it shook the nation to the core. Once again, a new Holocaust seemed imminent. 'We felt totally isolated,' one colonel later remembered: 'the country was about to be destroyed and no one had stepped forward [to help us] . . . Until then we believed in the pairing of the words *Holocaust* and *heroism* and identified ourselves with the heroism. The war made us realize the meaning of the Holocaust and the limitations of heroism.'[47]

The Arab 'Other'

The problem with creating a culture of heroes and martyrs is that societies cannot believe in such things without also believing in a monster. The fear of a new Holocaust necessarily implies that Israel's enemies are the new Nazis. And since Israel's most immediate enemies are Arab nations, it only takes a small leap of the imagination to start seeing all Arabs – including the Arabs who live inside Israel – as potential murderers. On the face of it, there is nothing new about this: Jews have been comparing Arabs to Nazis since before the Second World War. But before 1945 such comparisons contained nothing of the vitriol and sense of terror that was to come in later years.[48]

One of the many things that divided Israel in the 1940s and 50s was the fact that different sections of society had different enemies. For immigrants who had survived the war in Europe, Nazi Germany was the apogee of evil. For Sephardi Jews, meanwhile, Germany had never really been the enemy: they had fled Iraq or Yemen or Egypt or Morocco in the face of Arab violence and discrimination. But for those Jews who had grown up in Palestine, and who had imbibed Zionist ideology with their mother's milk, there was no real distinction between Nazis and Arabs, or indeed any of the other many enemies they had faced in the world: all were incarnations of the same universal evil of anti-Semitism. As David Ben-Gurion expressed it in 1947, the Holocaust was 'merely a climax to the uninterrupted persecution to which we have been subjected for centuries'. Or, to put it more succinctly, as Ariel Sharon did almost sixty years later, 'We know we can trust no one but ourselves.'[49]

In such an atmosphere, it is perhaps not surprising that Nazis and Arabs have become fused into a single, all-purpose enemy. Israel's history since independence has only served to exacerbate this process. Every time Israel has gone to war with its neighbours – as it has in every decade since it became a nation – it has invoked the memory of the Holocaust. During the 1948 civil war, for example, Ben-Gurion described its Jewish casualties as 'victims of a second Holocaust'.[50] During the 1956 Sinai campaign, Israel's newspapers portrayed Egypt's President Nasser as a potential 'Hitler of the East'.[51] The 1967 and 1973 wars were accompanied by an atmosphere of existential panic reminiscent of the atmosphere during the Holocaust; and the 1982 invasion of Lebanon was justified by prime minister Menachem Begin's claims that 'the alternative to this operation is Treblinka'.[52] At the beginning of the 1990s, when Iraq attacked Israel with Scud missiles during the First Iraq War, the Israeli press was filled with articles comparing Saddam Hussein to Hitler.[53] And in 2006 the prime minister, Benjamin Netanyahu, once again tried to convince Jews throughout the world that a new Holocaust was imminent: 'It's 1938 and Iran is Germany,' he said.[54]

Israel is no longer the nation of heroes it once aspired to be. Instead it has become a perpetual victim, the 'Jew amongst nations', destined always to be the focus of the world's hatred in general and Arab hatred in particular. Any danger (and Israel indeed faces many dangers) is automatically interpreted as an *existential* danger. Any criticism (and Israel is undeniably the subject of utterly disproportionate criticism) is immediately reimagined as persecution.

Such a world view has serious consequences, not only for the nation's sense of well-being but also for the geopolitical stability of the whole region. Since Israel is the last refuge for the world's Jews, running and hiding is not an option; and in any case, their history has taught them that running and hiding does not work. In the minds of many Israelis, therefore, the only course of action open to them is to stand and fight, with every means at their disposal.

Herein lies Israel's greatest fear of all, and one which few dare even acknowledge. If life is indeed a perpetual war, as Aharon Appelfeld suggests, then it will almost inevitably involve committing atrocities at some level. An existential war cannot be fought half-heartedly. When a nation faces not only defeat but annihilation, it must be prepared to do anything.

Nation of Monsters

In 1948, at the very moment when the Jewish people were planning their brave new society and aspiring to become a beacon of justice and hope for the world, Jewish troops had already begun entering Arab villages, terrorizing the civilian populations who lived there and driving them away. This was done for good reason: any Arab populations that existed close to Jewish settlements were automatically a threat. Neither was it anything special: many other nations were doing exactly the same thing, at exactly the same time, to ethnic minorities that were considered hostile – all across eastern Europe, for example, or in India and Pakistan. But this was hardly the new start in life that the idealists had envisaged.

The official version of this violent chapter in Israel's history is that the Arabs were not formally expelled, but fled of their own accord in order to escape the civil war. But even those who took part in military operations at the time acknowledge that Arabs were purposely driven away, and that an atmosphere of extreme violence and brutality encouraged them to go.[55] Hundreds of villages were cleared, and later razed to the ground. Inevitably, there were atrocities. At Lydda an anti-tank gun was deliberately fired into a mosque where terrified civilians were trying to find shelter from the fighting.[56] There are several instances of cold-blooded massacres, most famously at Deir Yassin, where at least a hundred men, women and children – and some estimates put the number substantially higher – were murdered by Jewish forces.[57] At Dawaymeh, according to the Israeli government's own sources, Jewish troops killed dozens of prisoners, burned Palestinian women alive in their houses and killed Palestinian children by breaking their skulls open.[58]

Since 1948 there have been many, many other crimes. In 1956 Arab civilians were also massacred at Kafr Qasim.[59] After the Six-Day War in 1967, Israeli soldiers sometimes talked about witnessing the unlawful killing of prisoners of war.[60] In 1991, during the First Intifada, *Haaretz* journalist Ari Shavit exposed the routine torture of Arab inmates in Israeli detention camps in Gaza.[61] In 2014, Human Rights Watch accused Israel of war crimes because of its 'indiscriminate' and 'unlawfully disproportionate' shelling of civilian areas in the Gaza Strip.[62] The list could go on and on.

When one catalogues these atrocities one after another, as a generation of historians has done ever since the 1980s, it is easy to see that Israel is not the nation of heroes it believes itself to be; nor is it a nation of victims. Writers like Benny Morris, Avi Shlaim and Ilan Pappé – the 'New Historians', as they are known – have demonstrated quite meticulously that Israel is capable both of defending itself and committing its own atrocities. They have been joined by Jewish academics in the Diaspora, as well as by Palestinian historians, who are understandably keen to dismantle the network of self-serving myths that Israel has built up over the years.[63] But in focusing such attention on Israeli misdeeds, the pendulum has swung the other way. Now a new myth has appeared: Israel is no longer a nation of heroes or victims, but a nation of perpetrators.

Once again, the language that is used to express this new mythology is the language of the Second World War. It is common today to hear claims that Israel is a 'fascist' state, that it is guilty of 'ethnic cleansing' or even 'genocide'. The Arab term for the 1948 expulsions – the *Nakba* ('the catastrophe') – is now frequently portrayed as the Palestinian equivalent of the Holocaust.[64] Since the turn of the millennium, anti-Israel demonstrations have occurred all over the world in which placards have been raised juxtaposing the Israeli flag with the swastika.[65] Even mainstream political parties have started making the link between Israelis and Nazis: in Britain, for example, the Labour Party had to implore its members in 2016 to stop comparing the Israel–Palestine conflict to the Holocaust.[66]

These comparisons are made not only by outsiders but also within Israel itself, where some Jewish intellectuals have been calling their own nation a 'Judeo-Nazi' state ever since the 1980s.[67] Even those who despair of such comparisons admit that, given Jewish history, it has become almost impossible not to make them. In his 1991 exposé of Israel's prison camps, for example, Ari Shavit made it clear that parallels between Israel and Nazi Germany had no historical basis whatsoever – there were no Israeli gas chambers, no medical experiments on human beings, no organized mass killings. 'The problem is that there isn't enough lack of similarity. The lack of similarity is not strong enough to silence once and for all the evil echoes.'[68]

Nation of Splits

Invoking the Holocaust is not the same as understanding it. Aharon Appelfeld, who has spent a lifetime thinking about the emotional consequences of the Second World War, has always rejected the black-and-white view of history that so regularly surfaces in his country. None of the characters in his novels are heroes or martyrs or monsters – just damaged people who 'spend their entire lives wondering how they should live and what they should do'. Israel, he believes, could learn from such people. 'Sometimes it seems to me that in a country so awash with ideology, it's impossible to write literature. Life itself, in all its complexity, is not something we really ponder.'[69]

The international community could also learn from such characters. We too should be careful not to people our imagination with heroes, martyrs and monsters, but acknowledge the complexities of life in our modern, postwar world. Every nation believes itself heroic or martyred on some level, and has a list of other nations it believes to be monsters. Israel is frequently on that list. No other country of equivalent size and importance has generated anywhere near the same number of column inches in the world's newspapers, or has received anything like the same attention on our TVs, radios and computer screens. Political parties all over the world declare their 'Israel policy' in a way that would be unthinkable with regard to any other country: few national parties have an 'Indonesia policy', for example, or a 'Kenya policy' or a 'Venezuela policy'. The Israel/Palestine question is a global problem – and perpetually so – in a way that other geopolitical stand-offs simply are not.[70]

The question we need to ask ourselves is why this should be. I do not wish to belittle any of the crimes and misjudgements committed by Israel, which are many and substantial and are rightly condemned around the world. I do, however, want to put them in context. The expulsion of the Arabs in 1948, which occurred during a brutal civil war, was not nearly as cold blooded as the similar expulsions that were occurring all over Europe at exactly the same time and often with far greater cruelty. Almost 12 million Germans were expelled from various parts of eastern Europe after the Second World War was supposed to be finished. Likewise, almost 1.2 million Poles were expelled from Lithuania, Ukraine and Belarus and almost half a million Ukrainians were expelled from Poland. Hungarians were expelled from Slovakia, Italians were expelled from Croatia, Albanians were expelled from Greece and Turks were expelled from Bulgaria. Meanwhile, the partition of India and Pakistan in 1947 involved 12–15 million refugees on both sides, and probably a million deaths. If all of these other expulsions have been accepted, forgotten or buried – certainly by the international community, if not always by the nations involved – why is it that the Palestinian expulsion remains a global issue to this day?[71]

Israel has committed repeated human rights violations; then again, so have all its Arab neighbours, without causing anything like the same international outrage. Israel has often treated its own Arab Muslim citizens appallingly – but other nations across the world have also demonized and persecuted their Muslim minorities, especially since 2001, without provoking half so much indignation. The greatest crime of which Israel is accused – the occupation of the West Bank and the Gaza Strip – has inspired repeated and growing protest all over the world. And yet many other nations around the world have also fought, occupied and oppressed smaller states since the end of the Second World War, including *every* permanent member of the UN Security Council. If it is right that Israel should be pressured into relinquishing its control of the Palestinian territories, it must also be right that other, more powerful nations should be forced to undergo the same unwavering scrutiny.

The truth is that popular objections towards Israel often say as much about the people who are objecting as they do about Israel itself. Alongside those who know about Israel, and who criticize it for good, sound reasons, are many fellow travellers who have latched on to the subject for reasons that have little to do with Israel at all. For example, some

Americans attack Israel as a way of expressing a more general anger against American foreign policy in the Middle East, particularly its disastrous and costly occupation of Iraq after 2003. In Europe, where much of the criticism of Israel comes from the liberal left, that criticism increases markedly whenever Israel elects a right-wing government. Indeed, for liberal Europeans, anti-Zionism is a good way to express antipathy towards nationalism in general. In Southeast Asia, meanwhile, Muslims who express hatred for Israel very rarely have any idea what Israel is actually like: they are merely using this as a way to demonstrate Islamist solidarity. Mixed in with all of these points of view is a great deal of misinformation, historical nonsense and ancient prejudice against Jews, or Arabs, or both; all of which has the unfortunate consequence of devaluing genuine criticism of Israel and of its neighbours.

In the Middle East itself, hatred of Israel is a convenient way for governments to distract attention from their own internal problems. In the aftermath of the Second World War, people all over this region expected the birth of a brave new world. They rejoiced in throwing off the yoke of colonialism, entertained dreams of Arab unity and found disappointment when the battles they had fought for freedom, for civil rights, for better living conditions and for their own, myriad visions of Utopia had to be refought again and again. In all these countries, just as in Israel, life has been a perpetual war. The Arab–Israeli conflict has been just one war amongst many: there have also been the Iranian Revolution, the Lebanese Civil War, the Iran–Iraq War, the Iraqi invasion of Kuwait, the Arab Spring, the Syrian Civil War, and several civil wars in Yemen, to name but a few.

If Jews and Arabs could only see past their differences, they would realize that they actually have a great deal in common. Both peoples have a long history of being treated as inferiors, neither liked nor respected by the more powerful nations of the world, and certainly not trusted to take responsibility for their own fate. Before the Second World War they were played off against one another by the British; after the Second World War they were played off against one another by the superpowers. All of the nations in the region were forced to fight for their independence, and all have spent much of the postwar period trying to build new institutions and new ways of governing themselves, while simultaneously resisting attempts by the outside world to meddle in their internal affairs.

It is easy for the rest of the world to sit on the sidelines and condemn one side or the other, but we too are part of the problem. By indulging a narrative of heroes and villains, monsters and martyrs, we perpetuate a view of the world where it becomes impossible to be ordinary, flawed, human. We are all obliged to fight, as the characters in Aharon Appelfeld's books, to find some way to struggle through life. This is the case with every nation in the Middle East – perhaps indeed with every nation in the world – but it is particularly the case with Israel, whose history always draws it back to the Second World War.

20. European Nationalism

If a nation is nothing but an imagined community, then what is to stop us from reimagining it? Rather than showing loyalty only to those who live in our own group, or our own country, could we not align ourselves instead with the whole of humanity? In the aftermath of the war, this was the argument of the world federalist movement. Activists like Garry Davis and Cord Meyer, and influential thinkers like Emery Reves and Albert Einstein, suggested that by a mere act of the imagination world peace might at last become a reality. All we had to do was to give up our emotional attachment to nation-states, and start treating all of humanity as a unified whole.

As we have seen, however, few parts of the world took to this new idea. For the superpowers, there seemed no reason to abandon nationalism: it had served them well throughout the war, and brought them victory. In countries like Indonesia, Kenya and Venezuela people actively began to embrace nationalism in 1945 as a new force for freedom and democracy. Meanwhile, in Israel, Zionism was being promoted as the only way to rescue the world's remaining Jews from anti-Semitism. All over the world, the idea of the nation-state seemed to have been strengthened by the war, rather than weakened by it.

If there was one possible exception to this rule, then it was in Europe. This was the only region of the world where substantial numbers of people actively supported the idea of abandoning nationalism as an ideal. People here had witnessed at first hand the devastation that nationalism could wreak if allowed to run out of control; and as a consequence many of them longed for a new ideology that would free them from the endless cycle of wars that had blighted the continent for centuries.

Thus it was in Europe rather than in any other part of the world that this dream first took hold. The idea of what would come to be known as the 'European project' was far more workable than that of world federalism. Unlike its larger cousin, the European project never had to grapple with the idea of including the Soviet Union. It also had the opportunity to start as a small movement – just a handful of countries – and grow over time. It was therefore far more successful than world federalism ever was: over the coming decades it would give rise to the largest, most powerful supranational organization in the world.

One of the main architects of this dream of a federalist Europe was an Italian journalist named Altiero Spinelli. His story is well known in Europe, but since it lies at the heart of what the continent would become in the decades after the war it warrants a brief retelling here.[1]

Spinelli began the Second World War as a political prisoner, interned on the island of Ventotene, twenty-five miles off the coast of Italy. He had been arrested in the late 1920s for conspiring against Mussolini's Fascist regime, and had spent the last twelve years in various prisons and internment camps, with nothing to do but read up on political philosophy and dream up new schemes and agendas for the liberation of mankind.

In 1941 he and a follow prisoner, Ernesto Rossi, began to write a blueprint for a new Europe. In it, they predicted that the war would eventually be won by the Allies, but that if nothing was done to change the political structure of the continent it would be a hollow victory. 'The population . . . does not know exactly what it wants or how to act,' they wrote. 'A thousand bells ring in its ears. With its millions of minds, it cannot orientate itself, and it breaks up in a number of tendencies, currents and factions, all struggling with one another.' Spinelli and Rossi believed that unless the people of Europe had a new cause to unite them after the war, they would inevitably turn back to their old national rivalries and jealousies, and it would be only a matter of time before the whole of Europe would once again be consumed by conflict.[2]

The key to ending this vicious cycle, they wrote, was to give the people something higher to aim for. It was nationalism that had allowed Europe's people to be exploited, divided, conquered and, ultimately, pitted against one another. Indeed, the nation-state was 'the fundamental enemy of freedom'. The only way to end both war and other forms of exploitation, therefore, was for the peoples of Europe to take power away from their individual governments and create a separate, higher body. If this could be brought to happen, war could be made a thing of the past, and the continent might at last become 'a free and united Europe'.[3]

They wrote their manifesto on cigarette papers – writing paper was hard to come by during the war, especially in an internment camp – and

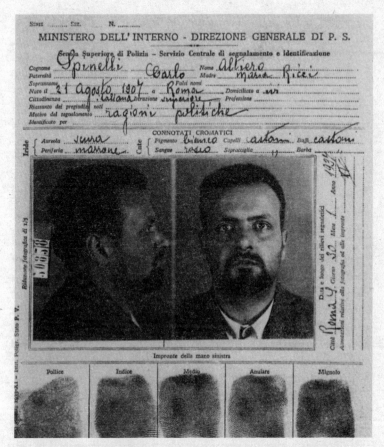

Altiero Spinelli's prison file, 1937, after he was interned for political reasons.

smuggled it to the mainland in a bag belonging to the wife of one of the other prisoners. In 1943, when the Allies invaded southern Italy, Spinelli was at last set free. He immediately set about disseminating his manifesto amongst the Resistance movements both in Italy and in other parts of Europe. But progress was slow. As 1945 arrived, it quickly became clear that his vision of Europe would not come about as he had hoped, spontaneously, in the revolutionary rush of optimism that accompanied the end of the war. Nor would it be implemented methodically by the Allies after a peace conference. The Allies in western Europe were not interested in new political ideas after the war – it was all they could do merely to maintain law and order.

So Spinelli was forced to revise his plans. Instead of creating a new, federal Europe all at once, he and his fellow internationalists would have to do it the hard way, through negotiation and compromise. For the next forty years he would campaign tirelessly as international treaties between nations were fought over, clause by clause. Though he was always a Communist at heart, he had no qualms about working collaboratively with socialists, liberals and Christian Democrats – indeed, he no longer believed in the ideological divide between left and right. For Spinelli, the only true divide was between those who were still devoted to nationalism and those who were willing to put their faith in a supranational state.

The first breakthrough was the creation of the European Coal and Steel Community (ECSC) in 1951. Six years later, in the Treaty of Rome, the European Economic Community (EEC) was created – a common market and customs union between Belgium, France, Italy, Luxembourg, the Netherlands and West Germany. This was gradually expanded to include Denmark, Ireland and the UK in 1973, Greece in 1981 and Portugal and Spain in 1986. The final goal was always supposed to be full integration between states: not only economically but also with a single legislature and a unified foreign policy.

In 1979, for the first time, people all over Europe took part in direct elections to the European Parliament, and Spinelli was elected to represent Central Italy. He used his new position to champion the idea of open borders without passport controls, and was instrumental in persuading the European Parliament to vote for the next step in the process – full European union.

Spinelli died in 1986, just months after the Single European Act was signed at The Hague. He did not live to see the fall of the Berlin Wall, and the subsequent rush by eastern European countries to join the European Union (EU). He never witnessed the Maastricht Treaty, and the creation of the Single European Currency; or the Lisbon Treaty, which strengthened the role of the European Parliament. But he is remembered today as a man who was instrumental in bringing these things about. In 1993, in recognition of his achievements, the largest building in the European Parliament complex in Brussels was named in his honour.

The European dream: Reijn Dirksen's 1950 poster, originally created to promote the Marshall Plan.

The Survival of Nationalism

The European Union is probably the most successful supranational institution in the world, and the only one ever to have wrested significant sovereignty away from its member states. It has the Second World War to thank for this. The destruction and loss of life in Europe was so great that its statesmen became far more open to the ideas of visionaries like Spinelli, and were willing to pool sovereignty in a way that would have been unthinkable in other parts of the world.

On the surface, this merging seems to have been very successful: in 2012 the EU was awarded the Nobel Peace Prize for the way it had transformed Europe 'from a continent of war to a continent of peace'.[4] But there are some obvious problems with this rosy view of postwar history. The first is the idea that Europe remained at peace. Anyone who has lived through the latter half of the twentieth century knows that, far from being at peace, both halves of Europe lived under the almost constant threat of a third world war. Actual conflict was avoided not by the creation of the EU and its forerunners, but by the prospect of mutually assured destruction. There are many historians who argue that it was not the EU that kept the peace in Europe at all, but rather the wider Western defence pact established by the formation of NATO.[5]

The second problem is the idea that all of Europe was united in an ambition to eradicate the nation-state. For all those who applauded the merging of nations, there were plenty of others who found the idea profoundly uncomfortable. They had fought the Second World War not for an internationalist ideal, but to liberate their countries from the Nazis. What mattered to them was their own national independence – in this respect, they were not so different from the people of Indonesia or Kenya after 1945. The thought that they should now voluntarily cede independence, having fought so hard for it, seemed absurd: it would take much more than a manifesto written on cigarette papers to make them turn away from the ideas that had sustained them through the darkest hours of the war.

The truth is that, if the Second World War strengthened the idea of the nation-state around the world, then it had the same effect in Europe. Victorious Britain, much like the superpowers, saw no reason to pool sovereignty with anyone else. It was sceptical of the European dream right from the start: Britain refused to join the ECSC in 1951. The French, who were frantically trying to restore their national pride after the war, were often equally sceptical. They sometimes had to be bullied into cooperation by the Americans, who threatened to withdraw the promise of financial aid if they did not show a more collaborative attitude.[6] Even the Italians did not generally rally to Spinelli's calls. Those on the right continued to regard the nation as their highest ideal; and those on the left regarded internationalism as a condition that would only come to pass once the Communists had won power throughout the continent: Spinelli's vision did not satisfy either of these groups. The story was largely the same elsewhere in Europe.

Altiero Spinelli did not have to wait long before his project encountered its first major setback. In 1954, he and other Europhiles had been arguing for the creation of a collective European army, but, while their plan was agreed in principle, the French parliament refused to ratify it. This happened for a variety of reasons, the most important of which was a dark memory of the Second World War. As Charles de Gaulle remarked sarcastically, 'Since victorious France has an army and defeated Germany has none, let us suppress the French Army.'[7] The French parliament could not countenance anything that might look to the electorate as though they were allowing West Germany to rearm.

In the years since then, there have been many nationalist rejections of European plans and treaties, even in those countries that have embraced the European project most enthusiastically. In 1984 the Danish parliament voted to reject the Single European Act, and eight years later the Danish people also voted to reject the Maastricht Treaty. The British were quick to reject the adoption of a single European currency in the 1990s, amidst claims that the monetary policy behind it was 'a German racket designed to take over the whole of Europe'.[8] In 2005 popular referendums in France and the Netherlands rejected a European constitution. In 2009 the Czech Republic refused to sign the Lisbon Treaty, again because of nationalist fears over German intentions. On each occasion, Europhiles were forced to make significant concessions to the individual countries involved. And, as some of these examples show, the memory of the Second World War was never far from the surface. In 2016 the people of Britain would deliver the ultimate rejection of the European project by voting to leave it altogether.

If nationalism has never gone away in western Europe, in eastern Europe it was never even challenged. Unlike in the West, the Eastern Bloc countries never had the chance to reflect on the excesses of their own nationalism during the war because for many of them the war never really ended: the Nazi occupation was merely replaced in 1945 by Soviet occupation.[9] Thus, Ukraine and the Baltic States continued fighting wars of national liberation well into the 1950s, and passive resistance to the Soviets continued throughout the 1960s, 70s and 80s. Other nationalist uprisings against Soviet power also occurred in East Germany (in 1953), Hungary (1956), Czechoslovakia (1968) and Poland (in the early 1980s).

When the Iron Curtain finally fell in the early 1990s, eastern European countries flocked to join the EU, but this did not mean they wanted to relinquish their nationalism. Quite the opposite: joining the EU was seen by many as an insurance policy against any future attack on their new-found independence from Moscow. As Poland's president, Aleksander Kwaśniewski, put it, membership of the EU would provide 'security to Poland, to every Polish city and village, to each Polish

family'. Latvia's president went so far as to invoke memories of the
Second World War, claiming that joining the EU sounded the death
knell for the Nazi–Soviet pact of 1939.[10]

In such an atmosphere, the internationalist ethos of the European project never properly took root. As in western Europe, the idea that eastern
European nations might have to relinquish some of their new-found sovereignty to a higher body awoke unpleasant memories of the past. One
needs only consider some of the slogans used by Eurosceptics during the
various referendum campaigns to see how fearful some people were
about the European project. 'Yesterday Moscow, tomorrow Brussels,'
warned conservatives in Poland; 'EU = Soviet Union', claimed posters in
Latvia, and in the Czech Republic Eurosceptics crafted an EU symbol
entwined with a hammer and sickle. Alongside memories of the Soviets,
nationalists have also invoked memories of the Nazis. In January 2016,
the Polish news magazine *Wprost* published an issue with a full page
photograph on its cover depicting Angela Merkel as a new Hitler, surrounded on all sides by leading EU figures dressed in Nazi uniforms. For
people who entertain such thoughts, the EU is not a beacon of democracy and freedom, but a reminder of repression and enslavement.[11]

Nationalism Fights Back

In the perennial debate over sovereignty, neither Europhiles nor Eurosceptics always act entirely rationally. Deep collective fears lie beneath
the reasoned arguments of both sides. Europhiles like to present themselves as hopeful, outward looking, welcoming of foreign cultures; but
they are also inwardly terrified of being excluded from a club, of being
forced to compete with one another, perhaps even fight with one
another. The memory of the Second World War so haunts them that
any suggestion that the EU might break up is automatically greeted
with predictions of a return to war 'within a generation'.[12] Eurosceptics,
meanwhile, like to present themselves as libertarians battling for the
rights of individuals, but they are also driven by the anxiety that an
alien group might take away their jobs, their rights, their freedoms, and
that if they give in to the pressure to assimilate they might lose themselves in the undifferentiated mass of the group. There is nothing new
about these fears: they are universal and timeless symptoms of the

human condition. But memories of the Second World War and its aftermath give Europhiles and Eurosceptics alike a focus for these fears, and allow them to make some kind of sense out of them.

Perhaps the starkest demonstration of how the Second World War is used in this way came in the summer of 2016, when the UK held a referendum over whether to remain in the European Union. The referendum came at the end of a twenty-five-year campaign by British nationalists to force the issue of Europe to the top of the political agenda. Throughout this period, nationalists had always celebrated victory in the Second World War as proof that Britain was a nation of heroes, and that Europe was holding them back. This narrative ran directly counter to European myths, which always emphasized the war as a tragedy rather than a triumph. When the time came for Britain to vote on its membership of the European Union, therefore, these two versions of history came up directly against one another.

All of a sudden, the Second World War seemed to be a regular news topic. For example, in an address to the nation, the prime minister, David Cameron, invoked the image of the Second World War cemeteries, and implied that the postwar European peace would come to an end if Britain left the EU.[13] The US president, Barack Obama, who visited Britain during the campaign, also begged the British to vote 'Remain' by referring to a time when Britain and America had 'spilt blood together on the battlefield'.[14] Meanwhile, 'Leave' campaigners invoked the 'spirit of Dunkirk' in 1940, as if the battle to escape the EU were the same as the battle to escape the Nazis. Nigel Farage, the leader of the UK Independence Party (UKIP), even made a habit of playing the theme tune from the war movie *The Great Escape* from his campaign bus.[15]

In this bizarre battle over British cultural memories of the Second World War, all nuance was lost. A perfect example of how absurd things got was the public argument in the press over what Britain's wartime prime minister, Winston Churchill, would have voted had he been alive. 'Leave' campaigners were quick to claim him as their own, saying it was his kind of spirit that would make Britain the 'heroes of Europe' again. 'Remain' campaigners responded by pointing out that Churchill had championed the idea of a 'United States of Europe' in the aftermath of the war. Then 'Leavers' claimed they had 'proof' from the 1950s that Churchill had loathed the idea of European integration, to which 'Remainers' countered that he had publicly backed the EEC in 1962.

Nobody stopped to consider what relevance, if any, this argument had on how Britain should see itself in the twenty-first century.[16]

The final, predictable move came when both sides of the campaign began comparing one another to Nazis. After UKIP unveiled a campaign poster demonizing immigrants, 'Remain' campaigners immediately compared it to Nazi propaganda films of the 1930s. Not to be outdone, prominent 'Leavers' compared their rivals to Hitler's propaganda minister, Josef Goebbels, and their economics experts to Nazi scientists.[17] The former mayor of London, Boris Johnson, was just one of many who turned EU myths of postwar solidarity on their head by claiming that the whole European project was just a modern incarnation of Nazi plans for a united Europe.[18]

Communism also got a mention, though not until after the referendum was over. When EU leaders met together at the island of Ventotene in the wake of the British vote, a venue chosen deliberately to remind them of Altiero Spinelli and his manifesto, the *Daily Telegraph* ran a piece denouncing Spinelli as a Communist who had planned a 'secret' takeover of Europe. No mention was made of the fact that Spinelli was a very unusual kind of Communist – one who had shunned Stalinism right from the beginning, sided with the USA during the Cold War and spent a lifetime championing the rights of the individual. Once again, all nuance had been trampled on.[19]

As a British citizen, I watched these events unfold with growing despair. What upset me most was the atmosphere in which the debate took place. The sensible concerns on both sides about democracy, jobs, the economy and EU bureaucracy were quickly lost in a tsunami of exaggerations, obfuscations and outright lies from both sides. The most famous of these was the claim by the 'Leave' campaign that Brexit would save Britain £350 million per week, which, despite being denounced by the UK Statistics Authority, continued to be writ large across the side of their campaign bus. But the 'Remain' side also made exaggerated and emotional claims – particularly about how a vote to leave would inevitably lead to a new recession. In such an atmosphere, rational debate became virtually impossible.[20]

My fellow historians were not immune to this atmosphere. A group of them – 380 of the most important and well-known historians in the country – wrote an open letter to the nation in which they too invoked the memory of the Second World War. By leaving the European Union, they warned, Britain would encourage other nations to hold the rest of Europe to ransom in pursuit of their own selfish aims. Separatism would inevitably increase – not only national separatism but also regional separatism in places like Scotland and Catalonia – and the whole continent would be destabilized. 'Given the dangers it currently faces, Europe cannot afford this kind of splintering and with it the dangers of national rivalry and insecurity that bedevilled Europe's history before 1945.'[21] For a while, I considered joining this group. I passionately believed that Britain should remain in the EU, despite its obvious flaws, but I held off because the Manichaean tone of their letter went against everything I have always argued for: the message they were pushing was one of the main reasons why the 'Remain' campaign had been widely dubbed 'project fear'.

On 23 June 2016 the UK voted to leave the EU by a margin of around 52 per cent to 48. In the following days I experienced a wide range of emotions: shock, disbelief, disappointment, dread. I had finally succumbed to the fervour that seemed to have gripped everyone else in the country for months, and spent many hours angrily remonstrating with friends and neighbours about how foolish my countrymen were – but since most of my friends and neighbours had also voted to 'Remain', they too were in shock. A profound sense of doom settled over us. I berated myself for not joining the other pro-EU historians – not because I was foolish enough to believe that it would have made any difference, but because I was ashamed at not having strained every sinew in an effort to avert what I saw as a disaster.

It was only after a few days that I was able to pull myself together. I told myself that I had been acting foolishly. As a historian I know that the tides of history rarely turn on a single moment like this one. I also know that it is impossible to predict the future: history is littered with predictions of doom that never came to pass (and, indeed, equally ill-fated predictions of peace and harmony). There was no reason to suppose that the Eurosceptics weren't right: perhaps Britain and Europe might be better off without one another after all. I sat down and did something that I should have done weeks before – I took a pen and paper and tried to compile a list of hard facts about the pros and cons of leaving the EU. I quickly realized that the task was impossible. Without knowing what the future relationship with Europe was going to be, there was no way to gauge whether it was likely to be worse or better than what Britain was throwing away.

So what was it that had prompted me to react so strongly? Was it an exaggerated sense of Britain's importance? Did I really imagine that the whole European edifice might crumble without my country? Or was I merely reacting, belatedly, to the months of division and enmity I had just witnessed, and imagining those schisms writ large?

Increasingly my thoughts drew me back both to 1945 and to the letter written by my fellow pro-EU historians. It eventually dawned on me that Brexit on its own was not the problem: it was what Brexit represented that had made me so anxious. The context of the vote was as important as the vote itself. In the years leading up to the referendum I had witnessed an economic crisis, the rise of radical populism across Europe, a resurgent Russia flexing its geopolitical muscles, and the growing impotence of international institutions like the UN and the EU. Any historian failing to see parallels between these events and those that led to the Second World War would have to be blind. Compared to such developments, the Brexit vote was not really so bad, but since it reversed a policy that had been established in my country for the best part of fifty years, it too looked like a step back towards the past.

Given such a context, it is perhaps little wonder that I reacted badly. For all our attempts at rational detachment, historians are emotional creatures just like anyone else.

The Abuse of History

It is one thing to be affected by events which remind us of the past, but quite another to deliberately invoke the past with the express purpose of influencing the reactions of others. Harnessing the symbols of the Second World War for political purposes is hardly unique to Britain. Throughout this book I have outlined many examples of how the memory of the war has been manipulated to serve dubious ends, but let me give one more example which demonstrates how insidious this process is, and where it is leading us. It is an example that has almost nothing to do with the EU, except to show how irrelevant the EU's aims appear to most nationalists.

In 2008 the Polish government commissioned the building of a brand-new museum devoted to the Second World War. They appointed a history professor to be its director, and briefed him to create an exhibition that put the Polish experience of the war at its heart. They were quite right to do so: despite the fact that Poland was the main battleground of the Second World War in Europe, Polish perspectives have never been given the prominence they deserve in a history that is generally dominated by Soviet, American and British narratives.

The director they appointed, Paweł Machcewicz, was a proud Pole; but first and foremost he was a proud historian. He knew that if the proposed museum was to be meaningful it could not concentrate exclusively on Polish experiences – after all, its subject was a *world* war, not merely a Polish one. So he came up with a concept that was similar to the approach that I myself have tried to take with this book: he would use the experience of Polish civilians during the Second World War as a microcosm of something much greater, and at each point compare and contrast events in Poland with events in other parts of Europe and the world. Polish perspectives would remain central to his exhibition, but he wanted to make sure that visitors from around the world would also be able to come here and recognize their own experience of the war. To achieve this aim, Machcewicz assembled an advisory board of historians not only from Poland but also from institutions in the USA, Russia, Britain, France, Germany and Israel. To their credit, the Polish government wholeheartedly backed his vision.[22]

In 2015, however, a new government was elected. The radical nationalist Law and Justice Party (PiS) had swept to power by portraying Poland as a noble victim besieged by enemies past and present. The new culture minister, Piotr Gliński, wanted the exhibition to reflect his party's world view, with a greater emphasis on the nation's heroism and martyrdom during the war. The museum was, he said, 'not Polish enough'.

In the autumn of 2016, just a few months before the museum was due to open, Gliński announced that it would be merged with an alternative museum devoted to the doomed heroism of Polish troops during the 1939 Battle of Westerplatte. The merger was an obvious ruse: since the Westerplatte Museum barely existed even on paper, it was merely an excuse to create a new institution, so that Gliński might oust Machcewicz and his team, and reverse eight years of their work. In the following days, dozens of historians from around the world, including myself, wrote to Gliński begging him to reconsider. Then the Polish ombudsman questioned the legality of the merger, and it was handed over to the courts.

I visited the exhibition on 22 January 2017, as part of a select group of historians and journalists. Machcewicz and his team wanted to present a preview of their work to us on that day because they were not sure if they would ever get the chance to do so again: the Polish Supreme Court was due to give its verdict on the prospective merger the following day. The whole occasion was almost unbearably poignant. Not only was the exhibition itself quite an emotional experience – it was a more comprehensive antidote to the idea that war is glorious than I have ever seen in a museum – but uncertainty about the exhibition's future only added to the emotion.

The day after I visited, the Supreme Court upheld the government's decision to change the focus of the museum. Paweł Machcewicz lost his job shortly afterwards and later that year the new director began to oversee changes to the main exhibition. Some of these changes involved making the museum 'more Polish'. For example, a film illustrating the long-term consequences of the war was replaced with an animation focusing on a purely Polish experience of the twentieth century.

What this story demonstrates, as much as the argument over Brexit does, is that history matters: as the novelist George Orwell put it in 1949, 'Who controls the past controls the future.' Furthermore, as the foundation stone of postwar European culture, it is the history of the Second World War that matters the most. Politicians throughout the continent know instinctively that whoever controls our understanding of the war wields a powerful political tool.

Historians like Paweł Machcewicz have tried to present the war as a communal experience, a global tragedy that affected different parts of the world in different ways, but which nevertheless affected everybody. It is an inclusive view of history, shared and promoted by institutions like the EU, that allows space for contemplating the reality that nobody comes out of a world war entirely unscathed or unblemished. Radical nationalists, by contrast, want merely to highlight the suffering and heroism of one small slice of the whole, as if their experience is the only one that matters. They place blame exclusively upon outsiders, and promote a mythological narrative which ensures that the untarnished sanctity of the nation can be upheld. In such a world view, the nation is the only group that matters. The bigger picture is happily sacrificed, along with opportunities for reconciliation between former enemies, for the sake of national unity.

What such ideologues often fail to appreciate is that 'national unity' is itself a myth. Poland does not speak with a single voice any more than does Britain, France, or any other nation in Europe. The only thing that allows them to imagine themselves as a single community is a certain amount of flexibility in what defines a Pole, or a Brit, or a Frenchman. Any attempt to impose a single point of view will necessarily lead to conflict.

Herein lies a danger, because if a nation is nothing but an imagined community, then it can be re-imagined – not only as a larger group, like the EU, but also as a succession of smaller groups, splintered off from the whole. As Altiero Spinelli wrote in his Ventotene manifesto, when a thousand bells are ringing in the ears of Europe's people, what is to stop them breaking up into 'tendencies, currents and factions, all struggling with one another'?

Today, as in 1945, it is not only Europe that is dangerously divided, but also nations like Britain and Poland. The Second World War, which once provided the inspiration for the nations of Europe to unite, has now become as much of an inspiration for nationalists and regional separatists – and indeed anyone else with an axe to grind. The postwar European project, after more than seventy years, has at last begun to fragment.

PART VI

Ten Thousand Fragments

21. Trauma

In the last section I explored some of the ideals and dreams that inspired nations to split away from empires and other supranational bodies. This was often a violent process. Many colonies not only had to fight for their independence but also suffered civil conflict afterwards as groups with different ideologies struggled to win control of government. And yet few people who live in these nations today would dispute that the process was worthwhile in the end. Freedom, they say, is worth fighting for.

But what happens when the splitting of one people from another is not something that they have chosen? What if it is carried out against their will? In the wake of the Second World War it was not only empires that broke apart but also nations, communities and families, and this splitting was often something done not *by* them, but *to* them.

One nation that has suffered more than most in this respect is Korea. Colonized by Japan before the Second World War, and ruthlessly exploited during it, Korea was finally liberated by the Allies in 1945. But its deliverance from the Japanese brought it no peace. Instead it was divided by its liberators – the Soviets in the north and the Americans to the south – whose contrasting visions for the country would end up splitting it violently, and permanently, in two.

As a young woman, Choi Myeong-sun witnessed many of these events, and as a consequence suffered splits of her own. Her story is emblematic of what it meant to be powerless in the face of the inhuman forces that exploited and divided her country.

Choi was born in 1926, in a poor suburb of Seoul. Even before the Second World War she grew up in the presence of a nameless dread. When she was eight or nine years old her big sister, who was very beautiful, had suddenly disappeared. For the next two or three years nobody knew what had happened to her, and Choi's mother would frequently spend her days weeping. Then, one day, her sister reappeared. She looked terrible, 'like a beggar . . . nothing but bones'. Nobody told Choi what had happened, but she knew the Japanese police were somehow involved, and she overheard the neighbours saying that it was the fate of any pretty woman 'to endure misfortune'. Over the following months Choi watched her sister waste away from some mysterious illness. She died within a year.[1]

When the Second World War came the rest of the family quickly began to break apart, as Choi later remembered: 'I was particularly close to my second brother, but he was drafted into the military when he was just over twenty. Shortly afterwards my oldest brother moved with his wife and family to Manchuria in search of work, and I was left alone with my parents. I missed my second brother very much, although he wrote to us from Hiroshima. I was gradually getting more and more fed up with our life of poverty.' By January 1945, she and her mother were living alone, with only her mother's income to support them.

One day, an official from the Neighbourhood Community Centre approached Choi and asked her if she would consider working in Japan. If she stayed in Korea, he said, she risked being drafted into the Women's Volunteer Corps – a Japanese programme that forced Korean women to work without pay in essential war industries. But if she went to Japan of her own accord she would be given a good job, with good wages.

Choi thought about this for a few days, and the more she thought about it, the more she liked the idea. She wanted to contribute to the family finances; and if she went to Japan she might even be able to see her brother. She told her mother what the official had said, but her mother begged her not to go. She seemed to be frightened of something, but did not say what it was. In any case, Choi decided to ignore her mother's anxieties. The next day, while her mother was out at work, she packed a bag and reported to the Neighbourhood Community Centre. Twenty-four hours later she found herself on a ship bound for Japan.

The job was not at all what she expected. Choi was not taken to a factory or an office, but to the house of a high-ranking military officer. At first she did not understand what her duties would be, since the family already had a maid and a cook. She was taken to a room, given some food and told to wait. Her function only became clear to her that night, when the officer came to her room and raped her. It turned out that the officer's wife was sick and bedridden: Choi had been brought here purely to satisfy his sexual needs.

Almost every night for the next two months, Choi was forced to undergo the same ordeal. During the day, while the officer was out at work, she would spend long hours with his family. She begged them to let her go, but they ignored her. She appealed directly to the officer's wife, telling her that her husband would love her more without a concubine in the house. 'For two months or so, I kept pestering them, and the wife began to get fed up with me. She became nasty, but I kept on pestering her from morning until night.'

Eventually the officer's wife seemed to relent and told Choi to pack a bag. Overjoyed, she gathered her things and followed the officer's son to a station, where she was handed over to two strange men. She thought that they were taking her to a ship bound for home, but in fact they delivered her to a military brothel. She had been betrayed once again.

For the next five months Choi was forced to endure what she described as a 'living hell'. She was imprisoned in a small cell in what looked like a warehouse, under armed guard. She was forced to service upwards of twenty soldiers a day, and often many more than that, who were allowed to treat her in any way they wished. Her only human contact was with the men she serviced, the guards, and the Japanese woman who occasionally brought her food. Though there were other women working in this brothel, she was never allowed to speak to them: they were all kept in separate rooms, and remained silent on the rare occasions they encountered each other for fear of punishment.

'Because I didn't do as I was told, I was often beaten. I would faint and, when I did so, I was given injections to bring me round . . . I was beaten so often because I would lie with my face covered by my skirt, because I would not suck them off when I was ordered to, because I spoke Korean not Japanese, and so on. I was beaten so much that I seemed to lose my spirit. I just lay like a corpse, with my eyes open but not focused on anything.'

Eventually, the months of continuous abuse took its toll. Her vagina became raw and swollen, and began to smell bad, yet she was still forced to work. A surgeon came to see her, and gave her various pills and injections, but she continued to deteriorate. Eventually she became so sick that the brothel could not use her any more. Finally, she was put on a boat and sent home to Korea.

Choi arrived back in Seoul in July, as penniless as a beggar, and so sick she could barely walk. When she staggered back into her home, her mother wept. She never asked where she had been, but it seemed that she knew everything. She wept frequently, and cried out that both of her daughters had been ruined in the same way. Choi was sent to hospital, where it was discovered that she had been pregnant, but that the baby had died. The reason she was so sick was that the foetus was rotting inside her.

That summer, Korea was liberated from Japan. As her country struggled to get back on its feet, Choi struggled to get back on hers. She married a neighbour, and bore him a son; but her new husband started to beat her, and eventually threw her out of the house, saying he had contracted syphilis from her. Later she married again, and had four more children, but her family circumstances were never happy: 'When I turned thirty, I began to develop restlessness and to become mentally confused. I would suddenly hate my husband, my blood would run hot and cold and I would throw a fit, shouting at him to get away . . . I got scared when I met people, and shuddered when I heard any loud sound. I stayed indoors for thirty years, crawling on my hands and knees.' She dared not speak to anyone about her past, for fear of what they would think of her, and of her children.

By the mid-1980s, Choi Myeong-sun was living with her oldest son, who was now over forty years old. His mental health had suddenly deteriorated, and he was admitted to a psychiatric hospital for tests. Choi, who had only recently learned to walk upright again, was called in to see his doctors. They asked her if she had ever had syphilis: her son, it seemed, had contracted the disease from her in the womb, and the bacteria were now affecting his brain. She dropped her head and wept, unable to speak.

According to psychoanalytic theory, the human mind is simply not equipped to deal with the kind of trauma Choi Myeong-sun was forced to endure. The normal reaction to severe threat is either to run away or to fight, but when we are prevented from doing so – when we are left powerless in the face of possible rape or torture – our minds become flooded with existential fear. The experience upsets the delicate processes by which the mind usually regulates itself. The mental shields which protect us from excessive stimuli in our everyday lives suddenly collapse. The careful way in which we have hitherto made sense of our lives, the way we have balanced our reason against our unconscious desires, or filed away memories of what is good and what is bad – all of it becomes suddenly meaningless in the face of the threat.[2]

Sometimes trauma like this can have severe, long-term effects, particularly if it is prolonged or repeated, as Choi Myeong-sun's was. Survivors lose the ability to distinguish between what is real and what is remembered, what is past and what is present – they suffer flashbacks, in which they experience real sensations as if the trauma is happening all over again. In the worst cases they can suffer profound personality breakdown, and become unable to function at all.

Choi Myeong-sun experienced many of the classic symptoms of what today is commonly known as post-traumatic stress disorder (PTSD). After her return from Japan she didn't speak about what had happened for decades – partly, one suspects, because she could not bear to face the full horror of it, but also because she could not trust anyone else to understand. Her inability to cope with the outside world manifested itself in severe agoraphobia. All of her relationships with other people were poisoned by what she had gone through. She tried to shut off the pain by taking tranquillizers, to which she became addicted, but since that did not work, she also became cruelly aggressive towards herself. She spent years in an abusive relationship with her husband because that was all she thought she deserved, and the psychosomatic symptoms she developed kept her quite literally on her hands and knees for decades. This was a manifestation of what Anna Freud called 'identification with the aggressor': she was punishing herself, just as others had punished her during the war.

Perhaps the most heart-rending part of her story is its coda – the realization that she had passed syphilis on to her son as a baby. In the late 1980s, when she was interviewed by a Korean NGO that was conducting an investigation into wartime sexual slavery, all she could say about her son was 'I am to blame. I have ruined my son's life.' In her own mind, she had done to him what had been done to her – infected him, destroyed his life. She had become the perpetrator.

Trauma and Powerlessness

Choi Myeong-sun might have recovered more easily had the environment she returned to been a stable one, but Korea had undergone its own traumas. Between 1939 and 1945, at least three-quarters of a million Korean men were forcibly conscripted to work in Japanese factories, and a further three-quarters of a million mobilized 'voluntarily'. Choi Myeong-sun's middle brother was one of these. Women were also routinely conscripted for all kinds of work. According to Japanese colonial law, all women between the ages of fourteen and forty-five were obliged to participate in the National Labour Service Corps for two months each year. By the end of the war they were also being forcibly drafted into the longer term 'Volunteer Corps' – the service that Choi Myeong-sun hoped to avoid by going to Japan. The conscription of what were euphemistically termed 'comfort women' was the tip of an iceberg: it was merely the cruellest part of a much wider system of colonial slavery.[3]

Unfortunately, the end of the war, and the end of Japanese rule, did not bring an end to the Korean sense of powerlessness. Unlike the people of Indonesia or Vietnam – or, on the other side of the world, Italy or France – Koreans never had the satisfaction of taking part in their own liberation. Their subjugation to Japanese rule lasted right up until the last moments of the Second World War, at which point another group of outsiders came and took over – the Soviets from the north; the Americans from the south. Koreans themselves seemed to have no control over their own destiny.

In the north, the arrival of the Soviets did not bode well for the future. According to news reports and diplomatic documents of the time, the first wave of Soviet troops were violent and undisciplined: they pillaged their way southwards, stripping all the shops and warehouses bare, dismantling factories and shipping the pieces back to the USSR, attacking local women indiscriminately as they went. Once again, the fate of comfort women seemed to be emblematic. Mun Pilgi, a Korean who had been forced to work in a brothel in Manchuria, described her liberation as just another episode of a long-running trauma: 'Now that the Japanese had gone, the Russians were trying to rape us.' She was forced to flee the Soviets, making her way back to Seoul on foot.[4]

The experience of Koreans in the south of the country was just as demoralizing, and again, the treatment of 'comfort women' spoke volumes. Pak Duri, a Korean woman incarcerated in a sex camp in Formosa (modern-day Taiwan), claimed that she was kept by the Americans for a further three months after her supposed liberation. The only real difference between servicing Japanese soldiers and servicing American ones was the fact that the Americans left bigger tips: if this was 'freedom', then it did not bode well for her country.[5] Sure enough, when US troops arrived in southern Korea in 1945 they did not immediately purge the nation of the Japanese and their collaborators but, for the sake of maintaining law and order, kept things more or less as they were. Collaborators were never brought to justice, and the police force remained entirely unpurged. The cordial, even friendly way that the Americans treated the defeated Japanese was greeted with universal, but largely helpless, outrage.[6]

Historians have often compared the performance of the Soviets and the Americans in their respective zones of Korea. On the whole, the Soviets were brutal but efficient, while the Americans came with good intentions but no clear plan of action, leaving much of their zone in a state of near-chaos. Such comparisons miss a vitally important point, however: what mattered to most Koreans was the fact that they were still being governed by outsiders.

This fact was driven home at the end of 1945 when the Allies announced a plan for the country to be governed as a trusteeship overseen by Britain, China, the Soviet Union and the United States. As soon as this news was released protests broke out on both sides of the 38th parallel. In the north, the moderate and nationalist politicians, who until now had been cooperating with the Soviets, resigned en masse. The Soviets reacted by arresting them all, including one of the most popular leaders in the whole country, Cho Man-sik, whose steadfast integrity had earned him the nickname, 'the Gandhi of Korea'. He was never seen again, and it is rumoured that he was executed at the start of the Korean War. Meanwhile, in the south, there were wild demonstrations and strikes: schools were closed down, as were factories, shops and railways. Some of these protests were violent. For example when the Americans pressured a local politician to endorse the trusteeship plan, he was found dead the next morning: he had been shot in the head in front of his house.[7]

What upset Koreans so much was the way that both superpowers seemed intent on installing their own systems of power and control in the country, just as the Japanese had done decades earlier.

In the north, the Soviets set up a Stalinist, pro-Soviet government under their puppet, Kim Il-sung. All those who resisted this new regime, or who expressed even moderate anti-soviet views, were arrested or removed from their posts. By the end of 1945, many in the north had already succumbed to despair: refugees began streaming southwards at a rate of 6,000 per day. By July 1947, according to *The New York Times*, nearly 2 million had fled to the American zone.[8]

Meanwhile, in the south, the Americans sponsored a conservative coalition of Korean expatriates, right-wing nationalists and wealthy landowners, some of whom had been heavily involved in collaborating with the Japanese. The leader who emerged was a brutal authoritarian, Syngman Rhee, who presided over the wholesale repression of Communists, socialists, left-wingers and moderates alike, and whose reign was marred by repeated massacres of innocent civilians.

By the time the Americans and Soviets finally withdrew their forces in 1948, the country was completely polarized, and remained split across the middle. All attempts to find common ground between the Communist north and the nationalist south had failed, and both provisional governments refused to countenance any kind of power-sharing agreement. Reunification now began to look impossible without the use of force. Thus the stage was set for the Korean War, one of the most brutal conflicts of the second half of the twentieth century.

Civil War

Historians traditionally portray the Korean War as the first open conflict in the new Cold War between the superpowers, and it certainly would not have progressed the way it did without superpower involvement. North Korea employed Soviet advisers right from the beginning, and after the initial stage of the war some 200,000 Chinese Communist soldiers also fought for North Korea. Meanwhile, the South Koreans relied heavily on an unprecedented coalition of fifty-seven other countries, the most important of which was, of course, the USA.[9] In a sense, therefore, the Korean War was a microcosm of the tensions that racked the whole world in the aftermath of 1945. The ideological split that divided Korea was the same as that which divided Europe, and which would continue to divide the whole world for much of the rest of the century. But such an interpretation ignores the fact that it was also a civil war, fought predominantly by Koreans. Neither does it explain the sheer brutality of the violence, which was often directed at civilians rather than soldiers.

The hatreds unleashed during the war were far deeper than can be explained rationally; and they have just as much to do with the Second World War as they do with the Cold War. Many of the officers on both sides had been trained by the Japanese military, and had absorbed its violent nationalist ethos. Some had served as policemen in Korea before 1945, and already had a history of acting violently with impunity. Some had served abroad in the Japanese subjugation of parts of China and Southeast Asia, and had already been involved in atrocities there. Even those who had never been trained by the Japanese still had memories of the Japanese occupation in the back of their minds. In North Korea there was an additional layer of political leaders who had lived in the Soviet Union during the past thirty years, and who had direct experience of Stalinist terror. One way or another, most Koreans had a psychological template of merciless subjugation, and it was partly the fear of falling victim to such subjugation that drove them to act as brutally as they did.

From start to finish the Korean War was characterized by extraordinary cruelty. When the North Koreans first attacked southwards, the South Korean regime reacted by murdering over 100,000 suspected leftists, almost all of them innocent civilians. When the tide turned, and the South Koreans began to march northwards, the North reacted in kind. The most infamous massacre committed by the retreating Communists was at the prison in Taejŏn, where between 5,000 and 7,000 people were executed en masse – but such scenes occurred all across the country. For the Americans, this immediately provoked memories of the Second World War: the *Washington Post* even called one massacre site the 'Red Buchenwald'.[10]

As in the Second World War, women once again found themselves the subject of exploitation. In a chilling echo of the Japanese system, the South Korean army also set up 'special comfort stations' for their troops, where captured North Korean women were subjected to exactly the same forms of sexual slavery that people like Choi Myeong-sun had been forced to experience in 1945. The only substantial difference was that while the Japanese had done these things predominantly to foreign women, Koreans were now perpetrating them upon women of their own nationality.[11]

The Korean War lasted for three years and resulted in the deaths of around 1.25 million people, a large proportion of them civilians. When it finally came to an end in July 1953 the new armistice line was not far off the 38th parallel where the two sides had begun. The war had resolved nothing.

From a psychological point of view, all the war had really done was reinforce the idea that brutality was necessary for survival: in a black-and-white world of perpetrators and victims, both sides had learned that it was better to be a perpetrator.

This too was a legacy of the Second World War and the period of Japanese imperial rule. It is instructive that both North and South Korea were ruled by repressive dictatorships after 1945. Both regimes despised the weakness that had led them to be subjugated by the Japanese, and were determined to punish any behaviour that reminded them of that weakness. The ironies involved in this mindset are painful. During the 1960s and 70s, the military dictator of South Korea, Park Chung-hee, denounced his country's 'slavish mentality' towards strong foreigners, even as he himself subjected his own people to brutal repression. Likewise, in North Korea, Kim Il-sung denounced the people's 'subservient' mentality towards foreigners, while simultaneously demanding that they be subservient to him.

Such attitudes continued to dominate official thinking in South Korea well into the 1980s; in the North they continue to this day. The self-punishment this involves is quite heartbreaking: like Choi Myeong-sun, the nation learned to keep itself crawling on its hands and knees.[12]

Flashbacks

The Korean collective subconscious was deeply scarred by its experience of subjugation to the Japanese. If there are any doubts about this, one need only look at the outbursts of fear and anti-Japanese sentiment that have periodically gripped the nation in the years since the Second World War.

In 1948, for example, when the Americans brought back a handful of Japanese officials to help them to stabilize the South Korean economy, wild rumours immediately began to circulate that 'Japan was being rearmed and would be allowed to reconquer Korea'. All of a sudden, Korean newspapers were full of angry editorials. 'Do our enemies, the Japanese, come again to our land?' asked the *Chosun Ilbo* indignantly. On 24 June, a coalition of twenty-six different political groups issued a joint statement claiming that 'imperialistic elements in Japan, which were the incendiary of World War II' were 'attempting to arm and occupy Korea again'. Politicians like Kim Ku immediately began to call for a 'relentless fight of 30 million Koreans to completely rid Korea of all Japanese exploiters'. Such statements were not just political rhetoric: they also reflected a subconscious fear, irrational but genuine, that Korea might once again fall to Japanese domination.[13]

These fears were stifled by the events of the coming years, but in 1965 they erupted once again with a series of huge anti-Japanese demonstrations on the streets of Seoul. The main trigger this time was the signing of a new treaty with Japan to normalize relations. Japan was a growing power in the region, as was the USA, and there was great resentment that South Korea had recently begun to realign its interests with these two countries.

In the meantime, Korea's renewed subservience towards both the USA and Japan was symbolized by the promotion of a huge new sex industry, catering largely to Japanese tourists and soldiers and sailors from the American military bases. The continued exploitation of Korean women – and by extension of Korea itself – aroused uncomfortable memories of the past.[14]

In more recent years there have been many similar flashbacks to the Second World War. The most powerful of these has been the return of the 'comfort women' issue, which first occurred in the 1990s. South Korea had just emerged from a long period of military dictatorship, and in the new democratic atmosphere, some former comfort women finally felt able to reveal what had happened to them. It was during this time that Choi Myeong-sun first came forward to tell her story.

Once again, these revelations released powerful feelings throughout South Korea. When Japan's prime minister visited the country in 1992, a demonstration took place outside the Japanese embassy in Seoul, in which protesters demanded a Japanese apology. Before long such demonstrations became a weekly occurrence. Every Wednesday for more than twenty years crowds gathered outside the embassy, and former comfort women like Choi Myeong-sun became a living symbol of

Korea's national victimhood. In 2011 a monument was erected in their honour: it was a bronze statue of a young girl on her knees, her fists clenched and her eyes firmly fixed on the Japanese embassy. In response to all this pressure, the Japanese government eventually relented. In December 2015 they agreed to contribute ¥1 billion (around $8 million at the time) towards a new foundation dedicated to healing the psychological wounds of the former comfort women.[15]

In some respects these recent events represented a healthy step forward for South Korea, which was at last confronting some of the things that had been done to its women during the war. The emphasis on healing their psychological wounds was also an acknowledgement of the trauma that they had suffered in the past, and continued to suffer in the present. However, the way the issue was handled by the South Koreans concealed as many facts as it revealed. One need only look at the stories of the comfort women themselves to see that there were many aspects of their traumas that were not being addressed. It was not a Japanese man that first betrayed Choi Myeong-sun to a life of slavery but a Korean man from the Neighbourhood Community Centre. Other women had

'Japanese government! Make an official apology to the Japanese military "Comfort women" victims!' A woman holds up a placard at one of the Wednesday demonstrations outside the Japanese embassy in Seoul. This photo was taken in 2013, more than twenty-one years after the weekly protest rallies first began.

spoken about Soviet rape, or American exploitation, which had continued long after the Second World War was over. All of these women had suffered greatly in later years not only from the initial trauma but also from the stigma placed upon them by South Korean society.

There were other, broader issues too. Feminists pointed out that violence towards women was endemic in South Korean society, and produced shocking statistics on sexual and domestic violence in the country.[16] Other academics drew attention to the repressive nature of Korea's own regimes after the Second World War, which were cruel not just to women but to the whole of society. One scholar went so far as to call the South Korean military dictatorship of the 1960s a 'necropolitical' regime: that is, one that propagated itself by treating its people like objects, squeezing every last ounce of life from them, before discarding them. Its attitude towards comfort women, and the sex trade that contributed so much to Korea's GDP, was the ultimate symbol of this. These things, too, were a legacy of the Second World War.[17]

If Choi Myeong-sun's story, and the story of Korea as a whole, reveals anything, it is how widespread the effects of trauma can be. South Korea is still only in the first stages of confronting its past, particularly when it comes to the terrible things that Koreans did to Koreans in reaction to the powerlessness they experienced during the Japanese occupation. North Korea, which is still under a savagely repressive regime, has not even begun the process.

Split Nations

To a certain degree, Korea's story during and after the war is the story of us all. The Second World War was a global trauma, unleashing vast forces upon the world over which nobody had any control. Many nations during the war were just as powerless over their own fate as Korea. Even the undisputed victors of the war, Britain, the USA and the USSR, were dragged into the violence against their will, and at great cost in both life and treasure. There were, of course, huge differences in experience both between individuals and between nations, but no one was entirely unaffected. The traumas suffered by people like Choi Myeong-sun have become part of our communal experience: whether we are Korean or not, hers is a story that resonates around the world.[18]

In the aftermath of the war a culture of martyrdom grew up in Korea that will be familiar to people of every nation that suffered occupation during the war, and every nation that shook off the shackles of empire in the years that followed. Like most of the rest of the world, Korea hoped for a rebirth in 1945, and a chance to build something new, based on the principles of freedom, equality and progress. Most of all they hoped for unity – not the grand, global unity that was the dream of people like Cord Meyer or Garry Davis, but the simple national unity that would keep the two halves of the country together. Both the North Koreans and the South Koreans did what they could to force the issue, only to find, once again, that it was out of their hands.

Korea was not the only nation to be split apart by outsiders. Vietnam would also spend many years split into two Cold War pieces. Iran suffered the same fate for a few years, before the Soviets were convinced to withdraw. In Europe it was even worse. Here the schism between East and West was expressed on a grand scale by the partition of the whole continent, which would spend more than forty years divided by a metaphorical 'Iron Curtain'. It was expressed on a national scale when Germany was cloven in two, much like Korea was. It was even expressed on a smaller scale in the division of cities like Vienna and Berlin. The wall that separated capitalist West Berlin and Communist East Berlin would become one of the most powerful symbols of the twentieth century.

The collapse of empire produced similar schisms. When the British withdrew from India in 1947 they split it into a predominantly Hindu India to the south, and a predominantly Muslim Pakistan to the north-east and north-west. The fates of tens of millions were therefore decided not so much by an act of self-determination as by the hasty resolutions of British bureaucrats. The geopolitical fault line this created lost none of its volatility in the decades that followed, when India and Pakistan engaged in their own local version of cold war, complete with nuclear weapons.

The splitting of Palestine has produced similarly troubling results. In 1947 the UN drew up a partition plan without the input or the blessing of the Arab population. This was followed by a civil war, in which Israel seized an even larger proportion of the land. The feeling of impotence this engendered in Palestinian Arabs has been at the root of the conflict that still plagues the region today.

The most damaging legacy of the traumatic upheavals caused by the Second World War is the feeling of helpless humiliation they have engendered. This applies to all those who were 'martyred' during and after the war, even those who like to think they have long since recovered. When a community or a nation is violated, and its very existence threatened, it retains a memory of that violation deep within its collective soul. But if the violence and humiliation experienced by a people is prolonged, and if that people is never given a stable environment in which to recover, then the chances that the trauma will ever be resolved fade to nothing.

When considering the societies of any of those nations so violently sundered both during and after the war, one would do well to remember what Choi Myeong-sun told an interviewer from the Korean Council in the early 1990s. 'I look normal on the outside, but I suffer from a nervous disorder,' she said. 'Who would be able to guess what inner agony I suffer with this awful story buried in my heart?'

22. Loss

Evgeniia Kiseleva was once happy. Before the war, when she was not yet twenty-five years old, she had lived in the small mining town of Pervomaisk, in the Luhansk Province of Ukraine. She was married to a handsome man named Gavriil, the foreman of the town's fire brigade, with whom she was very much in love. Every day she would go to work at a food shop, selling fish to the women of the town; and every evening she would come home to her husband. They already had one son, and by the end of 1940 a second was on the way.

For Evgeniia, the war was a trauma from which she would never recover. 'My husband and I lived happily, but when the war began in 1941 it separated us for ever. And my suffering began.'[1] Gavriil left to join the army, and Evgeniia, who was now nursing a newborn baby, moved in with her parents.

It was not long before the vast forces of the Second World War swept over them. Her parents' house was hit by a German shell, killing her mother and severely wounding her father. Her older son was temporarily blinded by an explosion. Evgeniia suddenly found herself responsible for all of them. For the sake of their safety, she was forced to abandon her dead mother in the ruins of the house without burying her. She put her wounded father onto a cart and pushed him to a German field hospital – but before she could find help his leg became badly infected. He ended up dying in front of her. In the following days she dragged her children from shelter to shelter, terrified of the invading soldiers and a veritable apocalypse of 'shells, tanks, mortars, machine guns' and 'holy fear'. When she described the war in later years, she likened it to the 'Last Judgement'.[2]

After the war ended, Evgeniia went off in search of Gavriil. For a while she feared the worst, but it turned out that there was more than one way to lose a husband to the war. When Evgeniia finally tracked him down in 1946 she discovered that, during their long separation, he had taken up with two other women – each of whom he seemed to have married, and each of whom had borne him a child. Their reunion was uncomfortable, to say the least. He reluctantly took Evgeniia back to his new apartment, where she spent an awful, sleepless night, sharing a room with him and one of his new 'wives'. The next day she headed home, defeated. 'I couldn't see the road for tears.'[3]

From that day on, Evgeniia never really found love again. Back in her home town she took up with a war invalid called Dmitrii Tiurichev, a coal miner, but he turned out to be a drunk and a womanizer, and was often brutal to both her and her children. She fought with him on and off for twenty years, before finally leaving him for good in 1966. In all that time she never divorced Gavriil: indeed, when he finally died in 1978, she was still technically married to him.

Her relationships with the rest of her family were never ideal either. Her sons grew up and got married, but she argued incessantly with their wives, and occasionally even got into physical fights with them. Her whole family had problems with alcohol abuse; but then, so did everyone else she knew: she called her era 'the vodka century'.[4]

Towards the end of her life she lived alone, a bitter old lady with nothing for company but the television. Looking back, she blamed the war for what she had become, but not in the same way that Choi Myeong-sun did. What haunted her was not the memory of the trauma she had experienced, but rather the loss of something that she might have been. And in particular she mourned the loss of her first love, Gavriil. 'He was so handsome, and not a bad man in character,' she wrote in her diary after his death. 'He loved me, but the war separated us for ever. If it hadn't been for the war this wouldn't have happened.'[5]

Personal Loss

How does one quantify loss? It is difficult enough to estimate the number of people killed during the war, and historians and demographers often argue about how to pin down more accurate casualty statistics. But every life lost also blights the lives of the bereaved. Each death is like a stone dropped in a pool. One cannot measure the effects of all the anguish, the loneliness and disappointed dreams that rippled out across families and communities, or the way that those ripples collided and combined with the losses felt by other families and communities across a whole nation.

Everyone in Evgeniia Kiseleva's story was affected by the war in some way. Evgeniia herself saw her parents killed before her eyes. She saw her home destroyed, was separated from her husband and was traumatized in many other ways too. There is no way to measure what her life would have been without the war, so her own way of measuring it – in lost love – seems as good as any. It is impossible to tell whether Gavriil would have stayed with her if the war had never happened. Perhaps he would eventually have left her anyway; but, if so, she might have had her parents to comfort her, a home to return to, a more stable community to support her, and a greater choice of men to build new romantic relationships with. When she mourned the death of her marriage, she was simultaneously mourning the loss of all of these things, without which her life had become a mere fragment of its possible self.

Evgeniia's story is emblematic of the fate of millions of Soviet women after the war. One of the main reasons why she was unable to find love again was because so many other marriageable men had been killed. Millions of other women found themselves in similar circumstances. According to Soviet figures, in the decades after the war there were some 20 million more women than men in the country. As a consequence, one third of all Soviet women who came of age in the decade before the war remained unmarried for at least the next twenty years. Evgeniia's disappointments should therefore be seen as part of an epidemic of loneliness that blighted the lives of women all over the western regions of the Soviet Union.[6]

The USSR, in turn, should be seen as merely one piece of a much bigger picture. In large parts of Europe, China, Japan and even in some parts of the USA and Australasia, a generation of young men had been literally decimated by the war. In Germany, according to one witness of the time, 'the most outstanding fact of all was the total absence of men between the ages of 17 and 40'.[7] Those who did come back from the war, like Evgeniia's husband, had often been transformed by it. Women all over the world suffered such loss, and were often left wondering ever after what their lives might have been had the war never happened.

What about the men in Evgeniia's story? At first glance they seem to have come out on top: the lack of other men to rival them means that they can get away with things that would have been unthinkable before the war, whether that means being married to three women at once (as in the case of Gavriil), or openly having affairs with a variety of other women in a small town (as in the case of her second husband). The Communist dream of equality between the sexes, shaky even before the war, was dealt an almighty blow by the realities of life in postwar Soviet society. One could make a similar argument for the way sexual equality in other parts of the world also stalled after the war. A whole generation of men who had been removed from society, placed in an all-male environment and told that they were a special group in the social order were less likely to consider women their equals after the war was over.

But if some men acted badly after the war, one must not dismiss the effects of the things that they had witnessed while they were away. Take, for example, the story of Evgeniia's second husband, Dmitrii. She never mentioned what he had seen and done during his time in the army, but she did say that he was a war invalid, so it is reasonable to assume that some of his experiences had been quite traumatic. According to Soviet figures (unreliable though they are), 15 million other men had also been badly wounded by the war.[8] Many soldiers learned to drink while they were away – the Red Army was by all accounts a drunken army – and millions not only witnessed extreme violence but also took part in it. It is impossible to know whether Dmitrii was always destined to be a sociopath, but the behaviour he exhibited was hardly unusual amongst veterans of the war. Alcoholism, outbursts of anger, the inability to experience intimacy, family breakdown – all of these are well-documented conditions amongst former soldiers who have been subjected to prolonged combat stress.

In other countries these symptoms manifested themselves as a part of what would today be called post-traumatic stress disorder (PTSD). In western Europe alone, over 150,000 British and American soldiers deserted, and 100,000 had to be taken out of battle because they were unable to cope with the stress of combat. These men too had to cope with the loss of what they had once believed themselves to be.[9]

If rates of PTSD from wars later in the century are anything to go by, then the psychological impact of the Second World War is potentially staggering.[10] But there is evidence to suggest that the trauma of war did not present itself in this way at all, especially not in the USSR. In a country where introspection was frowned upon, where the individual was expected to sacrifice himself to the collective, and where mental illness or weakness of any kind was taboo, men did not seek help, only numbness. Soviet veterans – indeed, the people as a whole – never faced up to the enormity of what they had experienced during the Second World War. Instead they buried their experiences in hard work, irony and, above all, like Evgeniia's second husband, in binge drinking.[11]

Demographic Upheavals

If individuals and families were numbed by the violence that had been done to them, then so was Soviet society as a whole. To this day, nobody knows how many people were killed during the war. The official figure given by one of the first Cold War Soviet leaders, Nikita Khrushchev, in 1956 was 20 million; that given by the last, Mikhail Gorbachev, in 1991 was 25 million. Estimates by historians and economists range between 18 and 27 million, although most people agree that, for once, some of the higher figures are actually more likely.[12]

Horrific though these numbers might be, they still do not reflect the full losses experienced by the Soviet Union. Many of those people who had died were people who had yet to meet each other, yet to fall in love, yet to have children of their own. If one factors in the number of babies who were never born because of the war – a calculation that is possible by taking average birth rates from Soviet census data – then the true losses are far greater. One demographer has calculated that if the war had never happened, by 1970 there would have been at least 50 million more people living in the USSR. Thus, even academics are occasionally tempted to mourn what might have been.[13]

Such losses sparked a host of other changes to some of the most intimate aspects of family life. Millions of Soviet children were orphaned by the war. The same was true in the rest of Europe where, according to a report by the Red Cross in 1948, some 13 million children across Europe were growing up without a father. Many children had no male role models in the family at all: they too had had a traditional family life taken from them by the war.[14]

In the Soviet Union, because of housing shortages, the number of extended families living as one household also rose dramatically after 1945. In particular, ageing widows often took to living with their children rather than facing life alone: this is why the *babushka* became such a central figure in Russian families towards the end of the twentieth century.[15] Although Evgeniia lived most of her later life alone, her children and grandchildren often lived in extended households with their in-laws. Right at the end of her life she herself moved in with one of her grandsons for a while, but by this time he too had become an alcoholic, and she was forced to move out again when she was no longer able to cope with him. Thus the changes wrought by the war also affected the lives of children who were not born until decades later, as its effects continued to ripple down the generations.

There were some other, more surprising consequences. After all the turmoil of the war and its aftermath, parents like Evgeniia began to advise their own children not to waste time, but to marry and have children as soon as they could. As a result, the age when people first got married dropped considerably after the war, and continued to drop: in the immediate postwar years the average woman got married at the age of twenty-five, but by the end of the Soviet period she was marrying before she was twenty-two.

In much of the West, the rush to make up for lost time after the war resulted in a similar lowering in the age of marriage, and a sudden rise in the birth rate. Many countries experienced a 'baby boom' after the war, including most of western Europe, North America, Japan, Australia and New Zealand. This sudden spike in the number of births would have huge consequences not only for the families who had them but also for the societies into which they were born. It was this generation that would grow up to become the glut of teenagers and young adults who contributed to the idealism and activism of the 1960s, the abundance of taxpayers who underpinned the growing public sectors of the 1970s, 80s and 90s, and the surfeit of pensioners who threaten to overwhelm health-care and pension systems in the twenty-first century. The demographic upheavals that came at the end of the Second World War had huge consequences throughout the world.[16]

Lost Identities

The war did not affect every part of the Soviet Union equally. East of the Urals, or in the central Asian republics of Kazakhstan and Uzbekistan, life was not so badly disrupted. However the western republics, which saw the brunt of the fighting, were devastated beyond comprehension. Most historians agree that Ukraine, where Evgeniia Kiseleva lived, probably saw the worst of the killing. Once again the figures are uncertain, but if we are to believe the most widespread estimates of between 7 and 8 million deaths, that means that one Ukrainian in every five was lost to the war.[17] Even within Ukraine, different communities were affected to different degrees: in some places very few people were killed; in others whole villages were massacred, leaving the landscape entirely empty of people. As throughout the rest of Europe, Jews suffered disproportionately. Around half of all Ukrainian Jews were killed during the war, and the vast majority of those who survived only did so by fleeing. By 1944, when the Germans had finally been driven out, Ukraine was already like a tapestry with large chunks ripped out of it, and with one or two threads of specific colours entirely removed.

However, the killing did not stop there. Even while the war with the Germans was going on, a separate civil conflict had broken out between Ukrainian partisans and the Polish minority. In an echo of the Holocaust, entire Polish villages were massacred, and over 100,000 more people killed. The Soviet solution to this savage ethnic conflict was to deport around 800,000 Poles from the west of the republic, across the border with Poland. In this way the western half of Ukraine, which had already been emptied of its Jews, was now also emptied of its Poles.[18]

But still Ukraine's tribulations were not over. One of the effects of the Second World War was to reawaken Ukrainian nationalist hopes, again particularly in the west of the republic. Ukrainian partisans here resisted the return of the Soviets, and fought a long but doomed war of independence that lasted well into the 1950s. Hundreds of thousands of people were involved: between 1945 and 1947 alone, more than 55,000 Ukrainian partisans were killed, and well over 100,000 of their family members deported to remote parts of the Soviet empire. Ukraine was therefore cleansed not only ethnically but also politically after the war. Effectively it had suffered not one but four conflicts – a world war, a war of national independence and at least two attempts at wholesale genocide.[19]

When one repeatedly tears pieces from a tapestry, damaging it again and again, at what point does the remnant cease to be the original tapestry at all? By 1945, all of Ukraine's cities had been destroyed, and most of its infrastructure had collapsed; it had new borders, and huge holes in its population; it had lost most of its Jews and almost all of its Poles, and its hopes of nationhood, briefly reawakened by the war, had been ruthlessly crushed.

Many of Ukraine's inhabitants no longer knew whether to identify themselves as Ukrainian. Evgeniia Kiseleva, despite having attended a Ukrainian school as a girl, thought of herself as a Russian. In her later life she not only accepted the dominant Soviet culture but embraced it. After the collapse of both her marriages, and the slow, painful disintegration of her family, the Soviet state was the one part of her life that provided her with any kind of stability at all, giving her a job, a home, a pension and a sense of belonging. It is perhaps a blessing that she did not live to see this, too, fall apart.

When Ukraine won its independence in 1991, millions of people like her were left in an unpleasant kind of limbo. In a post-Soviet world they were neither truly Ukrainian nor truly Russian, and unsure of where to invest their loyalties. This crisis of identity still plagues Ukraine today, which continues to find itself split between those who fear a return to its Soviet past and those who long for it.

And what of the Soviet Union as a whole? By exiling people, crushing independence movements and enforcing the values of the state, the Soviet authorities believed they were making the USSR stronger and more unified. It was not only Ukrainian people who were suppressed: the same happened in many of the other reconquered territories – Lithuania, Latvia, Estonia and Moldova in the western borderlands; Crimea and the Caucasian republics in the south. While this succeeded in the short term, it also sowed the seeds of future unrest: people from each of these regions would remember their treatment in the immediate postwar years with great resentment. By the time of Stalin's death in 1953, the Soviet Union was held together with little more than brute force.

Such a state could never last. Over the coming decades the irrepressible urge for freedom, both personal and national, would continue to undermine Soviet rule. Eventually, like all other European empires before it, the Soviet Union would disintegrate.

23. Outcasts

Mathias Mendel was born in a time before nations. He grew up in Hedwig, a German-speaking village in the foothills of the Carpathian mountains. Though he and his family were German, most of the other people in the region were Slovakian, and his teacher at school spoke nothing but Hungarian: these were the dying days of the Austro-Hungarian Empire, when nationality meant both everything and nothing. In any case, Mathias always took it for granted that this was where both he and his community belonged. German people had lived in this part of Europe for more than 500 years.[1]

After the First World War, when Czechoslovakia became an independent state, little changed in his village. He grew up, and married a woman named Maria, who was half Slovakian. In 1924 they had a daughter called Margit and three years later they had another, whom they named Maria after her mother. Over the next thirteen or fourteen years they would have five more children: four boys (Ernst, Richard, Emil and Willi) and a little girl named Anneliese.

Though they were poor, they were generally happy. They worked their fields, growing potatoes and grain, and owned a few animals. Every spring Mathias would travel to the large aristocratic farm estates in Germany to work, and only return in October after the harvest was done. The wages he earned during these trips abroad was the only money they had.

For the first four decades of the twentieth century, this was how Mathias and his family lived. In all that time none of the big political events significantly altered the timeless rhythms of the village. But then the Second World War came and nothing was the same ever again.

The first thing to change was the atmosphere around nationality. Mathias's community had lived amongst Slovakians for centuries in a spirit of mutual cooperation, but after the Nazis' rise to power there was a new tension in the air. Suddenly the only political issue that seemed to matter was that of ethnicity, and which people had rights to the land. Events came thick and fast. Germany seized the Sudetenland in 1938, and marched into Czechoslovakia a year later. Slovakia declared its independence in 1939, only to have Hungary invade its borderlands. Centuries of tolerance between neighbours rapidly disintegrated.

Mathias stopped working as an agricultural labourer. He spent the war working on road-building schemes, and got a job in a chemical works. In 1944 he was conscripted into the Home Guard to help protect his village: Slovakian partisans, who had risen up against their own regime, were now attacking anyone with links to Germany. It seemed that Slovakians and Germans were no longer friends.

The end came in 1945, when the Red Army arrived from the east. Fearing what was about to hit Slovakia, the German High Command ordered a general evacuation of the entire German-speaking minority.

Before they knew it, the Mendel family was being split up. The first to go were two of the boys, nine-year-old Emil and seven-year-old Willi, who were sent to the Sudetenland with the children's evacuation authority, the Kinderlandverschickung (KLV), to be housed with strangers. The older children went next, with friends and neighbours on a trek westwards towards Germany. Mathias's wife, Maria, who was

Mathias Mendel, shortly after his expulsion from Czechoslovakia.

heavily pregnant once again, took five-year-old Anneliese and went to Austria. She would give birth to her eighth child, Dittmann, while she was still in flight.

Soon Mathias was the only one left. As a member of the Home Guard, he stayed behind for a while to help protect the village, but soon they too were to be evacuated. The unit left for Prague, but before long were captured by the Red Army and interned in a concentration camp previously used for Jews. Eventually Mathias was released, but he was not allowed to return to Hedwig. Instead he was expelled from the country, along with all of the other Germans in Czechoslovakia. He would never see his homeland again.

Mathias would not be reunited with his family until the summer of 1946, when he finally found them in the town of Möckmühl, near Heilbronn in southern Germany. The country they had arrived in was a place in chaos. The Mendel family were just a handful of more than 4 million German refugees who had fled in the face of the Red Army. Most of these people had left eastern parts of the Reich along the old Polish border, but some, like the Mendels, had also fled other nations in central Europe.

There were so many refugees that it was difficult to find anywhere for them all to go. After years of bombing by the Allies, most of the cities in Germany were in ruins: about 3.9 million of the country's 19 million dwellings had been destroyed. Refugees were forced to take shelter in anything that had a roof: bomb shelters, barns, army barracks, factory buildings, even former prison camps. The Mendels were relatively lucky: they found sanctuary with a farmer, who gave them two small rooms and provided Mathias with work. The four older children also managed to find farm work locally.[2]

It was not only families like the Mendels who were looking for somewhere to live at this time: Germany was teeming with all kinds of refugees. The numbers are quite staggering. Alongside the 4 million Germans who had fled from the east there were around 4.8 million more who had fled the cities in order to escape the bombing. Neither was it only German people who had been displaced by the war: the Nazis had forced millions of foreign workers to come to the country, mostly against their will, and at the end of the war some 8 million were still there. Most came from the Soviet Union, Poland and France, but there were also significant numbers from Italy, Greece, Yugoslavia, Czecho-slovakia, Belgium and the Netherlands. The Allied armies, along with the United Nations Relief and Rehabilitation Administration (UNRRA), worked hard to repatriate these people as quickly as pos-sible, but there were hundreds of thousands who refused to go home because they feared what would happen to them when they got there. Many preferred a life of exile to a life under communism.

Thus, despite the best efforts of the Allies, the number of refugees remained stubbornly high. If one includes the 275,000 or so British and American prisoners of war, the total number of displaced persons in Germany in 1945 comes to more than 17 million. With the possible exception of China, which had seen similarly vast internal displacements during the war, at the time this was probably the greatest concentration of refugees and displaced persons the world had ever seen.[3]

To make matters worse, the refugees kept coming. In the wake of the war, people from other parts of Europe continued to pour into Ger-many. Some of these were Jews fleeing renewed anti-Semitism in the east. Some were collaborators, or suspected collaborators, fleeing retri-bution in their own countries. But the vast majority were ethnic Germans who were being chased out of other parts of eastern and cen-tral Europe. As Mathias Mendel had discovered, no nation after the war wanted a German minority living in their country any longer. The community of Hedwig was just one of thousands that would be swept away in the wake of the war.

Between 1945 and 1948 all of Czechoslovakia's 3 million Sudeten Germans were expelled from the Czech borderlands. They were joined by almost the entire population of East Prussia, Silesia and Pomerania – those parts of Germany that had been annexed by Poland and the USSR in 1945. Many of these people had already fled, like the Mendels, during the last days of the war, but over the next three or four years, according to German government figures, a further 4.4 million were forcibly expelled from these areas. Eventually other countries in Europe fol-lowed suit: 1.8 million ethnic Germans were also expelled from Hungary, Romania and Yugoslavia.[4]

These huge expulsions were carried out with great brutality. In Czechoslovakia, German-speaking civilians were literally herded over the border with only those possessions they could carry. In Prague and other cities, Germans were rounded up and forced into detention

Refugees were so numerous in Germany in the aftermath of the war that political parties made direct appeals to them. This poster, produced for a referendum on the Bavarian constitution in 1946, appealed to refugees' hopes for a reunified Germany.

centres pending expulsion, and while they were waiting many of them were subjected to interrogations and torture in order to ascertain what part they had played in the German occupation. Wholesale massacres took place up and down the country, most famously in Ústí nad Labem (formerly known as Aussig), but also in smaller towns like Postoloprty, where, according to both Czech and German records, at least 763 Germans were massacred and buried in mass graves around the town. Similar atrocities against Germans were carried out in Poland, where officers in charge of internment camps deliberately emulated some of the worst behaviour of the Nazis in order to enact revenge upon their civilian inmates. The expulsion of the Germans from around east and central Europe was so brutal that it is thought that at least half a million died during the process.[5]

If one adds all of these people to those who were already displaced in 1945, the total number of refugees who passed through Germany between 1945 and 1950 was around 25 million. Considering that the population of Germany at this time was less than 67 million, this represents a tide of human misery unlike anything Europe has since seen.

The Unmixing of Peoples

The expulsion of the Germans from east and central Europe was just one example of a phenomenon that took place all over the continent in 1945. The world that Mathias Mendel had grown up with – in which Slovakians, Germans and Hungarians had lived side by side without excessive regard for their differences – was fast disappearing.

Hungarians suffered similarly from their country's decision to side with Germany. In the wake of the war, Slovak government officials wanted to eject them from the country – all 600,000 of them. The Allies, having seen what had been done to the Germans, refused to give their permission and, in the end, only 70,000 Hungarians were pushed 'home' across the border as part of a population exchange while another 44,000 were removed from their historic villages and forced to assimilate with Slovak communities in other parts of the country.[6]

Other nations also ejected unwanted populations after the war. Poland, for example, not only expelled its Germans but also removed around 482,000 Ukrainians from the country, mostly from the region of

Galicia in the south-east. When the borders with Ukraine were closed to further expulsions in 1947, the Polish authorities found other ways to remove this minority. Whole villages of Ukrainians were cleared, their communities split up and small groups dispersed amongst Polish villages on the opposite side of the country. If the Ukrainians could not be removed, they could be forced to assimilate: Orthodox and Uniate churches were banned, and those who were caught speaking Ukrainian were punished. To prevent Ukrainians from returning to the places they had once called home, many of their former villages were burned to the ground.[7]

In the end, just about every nation in the eastern half of Europe indulged in similar behaviour. The Soviet republics of Lithuania, Belarus and Ukraine expelled around 1.2 million Poles after 1945, mostly from the borderlands that they had recently acquired from Poland in the various peace agreements. Likewise, a quarter of a million Finns were ejected from western Karelia when this area was ceded to the Soviet Union. Bulgaria forced some 140,000 Turks and Gypsies over the border into Turkey. The list goes on. Romanians expelled Hungarians and vice versa. Yugoslavia expelled Italians from its borderlands, Ukraine expelled Romanians, Greece expelled Albanian Chams. In the wake of the war each of the nations in eastern Europe seemed determined to remove as many foreign influences as possible.[8]

The result was ethnic cleansing on a continental scale. In the course of just a couple of years, the proportion of national minorities in these countries more than halved. The ancient imperial melting-pot that Mathias Mendel had taken for granted when he was growing up was destroyed for ever.[9]

Post-Colonial Expulsions

The reasons behind the various expulsions in Europe were all to do with fear. The Second World War had taught the people of countries like Czechoslovakia that they could not trust the fragments of foreign nations in their midst, because these fragments could be used to drive a wedge into the heart of their state, split it into pieces, dominate it. The Nazis had used the German minority in Czechoslovakia as an excuse to invade in 1938 and 1939, and so it is not surprising that the Czechs and Slovaks reacted by blaming that minority, punishing it and casting it out. Being banished from the land was the price that Mathias Mendel and people like him had to pay for Nazi Germany's expansionist greed.

The nations of Asia and Africa also had fragments of foreign powers in their midst. The Japanese in Korea, the British in India, the Dutch in Indonesia, the French in Algeria – these were all communities of outsiders that had similarly been implicated in a culture of colonization and domination, and as a consequence the indigenous people of these countries also sought to eject them after 1945.

Of course, the reasons why the British were in India were very different from the reasons why Mathias Mendel's family was in Slovakia – they had not grown organically within the country but had deliberately come to dominate it. And the hatred that the Indonesians had for the Dutch was not primarily about ethnicity – it was the culture of imperialism that they wanted to excise. Nevertheless, the end result was the same. These foreign fragments had to be expelled.

The first to be sent home were the Japanese. The Second World War had brought their empire to an end, and as a consequence all Japanese people living abroad were obliged to leave, even those whose families had lived in places like Korea, Manchuria or Formosa (modern-day Taiwan) for two or three generations. More than 6.5 million Japanese people were deported in the four years after the war. Just over half of these were soldiers and other members of the military establishment. But the remaining 3 million were civilians: businessmen, traders, administrators and their families. Like Mathias Mendel, they were forced to abandon their homes and leave all their possessions behind.[10]

The expulsion of these people was both similar to and different from what was going on in Europe. As in Europe, some serious atrocities were committed in the wake of the war in Asia. In Manchuria and North Korea, Japanese civilians were often attacked, tortured, raped and occasionally massacred. A year after the war was over more than half a million expatriate Japanese remained unaccounted for: it is thought that in Manchuria alone around 179,000 Japanese civilians and 66,000 military personnel died in the confusion and the harsh winter that followed the war. But in other parts of the empire the Japanese did not undergo anything like the ordeal experienced by German expellees.

This is partly because their removal was carried out by the Allies, rather than by local people who were keen to take the law into their own hands. But there were other reasons too. The atmosphere around the deportations in Asia was much different from the atmosphere in Europe: there was very little of the toxic ideology about race or ethnic cleansing that occasioned such cruelty towards Germans in Poland and Czechoslovakia. Instead, all the talk was about empire. The Japanese had been defeated, their empire had collapsed, and so it was time for them to go home. On the whole, even the expatriate Japanese themselves recognized this, and went more or less willingly.[11]

The country they returned to, like Germany, was a chaos of destruction. Sixty-six major cities had been heavily bombed during the war. In Tokyo, 65 per cent of all residences had been destroyed, in Osaka 57 per cent and in Nagoya 89 per cent; and Hiroshima and Nagasaki had been flattened by the atomic bombs. Almost a third of Japanese city dwellers were homeless at the end of the war, and they did not take kindly to accepting another 6.5 million people into a country where living standards had collapsed. Unlike German expellees, Japan's repatriates would never receive much sympathy from their countrymen: no matter how bad their suffering, they could never compete with those who had experienced the atom bomb.[12]

As in Europe, the dismantling of Japan's empire worked both ways: if it involved the repatriation of Japanese colonists, it also involved the removal of foreigners from Japan. According to American military government sources at the time, there were around 1.5 million foreigners in Japan, the vast majority of them Koreans, Taiwanese and Chinese. Subsequent scholarship has put the number even higher, at over 2 million. Many of these people had been brought there during the war, and eagerly wanted to return home; but some had been born there, and claimed the right to stay as imperial citizens. In the year after the end of the war around a million returned to their home countries, mostly to Korea. Those who refused to go were also mostly Korean, around 600,000 of them in total.

These people were not regarded well in 1945, and have been subject to harsh discrimination ever since. Unfortunately, the decolonization process contributed to this. When the Japanese formally gave up their right to rule Korea, they simultaneously renounced their responsibilities towards the minority in their midst. As a consequence, Koreans in Japan were denied the right to vote, the right to war pensions, the right to national health insurance and social security, and the right to a passport. To this day, Koreans who have been living in Japan for several generations are not allowed the same rights as Japanese citizens unless they first renounce their Korean identity: they are still, after all this time, regarded by many Japanese people as 'foreigners'. The fact that they were originally brought to the country as subjects of imperial Japan has largely been forgotten.[13]

After the collapse of the Japanese empire in Asia came the long, slow dismantling of the European empires. This too involved the removal of imperial elites, and the mass exodus of Europeans from the colonies they had once ruled. After India and Pakistan gained their independence in 1947, for example, well over 100,000 British people left the subcontinent.[14] The British also left Burma, Malaysia, Singapore and, later, the various colonies in Africa. By the beginning of the 1990s more than 328,000 white people born in these countries had come 'home' to Britain (although the real number of 'returnees' was undoubtedly much higher, since those who had been born in Britain do not show up on the census data).[15] Although all these people proudly regarded themselves as British, a good many of those who returned never wholly felt at home again. In the empire they had been used to a life of privilege; back in Britain they had to fend for themselves, without domestic servants, and in a postwar atmosphere of rationing and austerity. It was a desperately disappointing end to two centuries of colonial adventure.

The dismantling of the Dutch empire had rather more immediate consequences, and rather more traumatic ones. Having fought a savage and unsuccessful war against Indonesian independence, the Dutch had no choice but to leave: some 250,000 to 300,000 Dutch nationals returned at the beginning of the 1950s. These people had a much harder time than their British equivalents. Many of them had spent several years in Japanese internment camps, and then lived through a violent civil war, but when they arrived in the Netherlands they received little sympathy from their Dutch compatriots, who imagined that they had whiled away the war years in comfort and sunshine. As a consequence, Dutch colonists were largely ignored and dismissed by wider society, and continued to suffer greatly in the years to come. Psycho-sociological studies from the end of the twentieth century show that returnees from the Netherlands East Indies demonstrated significantly higher rates of divorce, unemployment and health problems than equivalent groups in mainstream Dutch society.[16]

Similar things can be said about the other colonists who returned to France, Belgium and Portugal in the second half of the twentieth century. After the Algerian War around a million French colonists, or *pieds noirs*, as they were known, fled to France. In the anti-colonial spirit of the 1960s they were never given much sympathy: instead, they were made scapegoats for the failure of the French colonial project. A decade later more than 300,000 Portuguese colonists fled Angola for Portugal, and a similar number fled Mozambique. The country they arrived in was too busy dealing with the aftermath of years of dictatorship to give them much thought.[17]

It is easy to imagine this movement of Europeans back to Europe as a kind of de-fragmentation: the tiny pieces of Europe that had implanted themselves in other nations around the world were being sent back to where they belonged. But many of these people did not feel part of the countries they 'returned' to at all, and found it extremely hard to adjust to a life in Europe. Of course, the circumstances of their return were nothing like those experienced by such people as Mathias Mendel – and one might argue that their culture of exploitation and privilege deserved to end. But their sense of loss cannot be denied: after two centuries of colonialism, a whole way of life had been brought to a close.

The International Response

The period since the Second World War has often been called an age of refugees and exiles. In the years since 1945 one humanitarian crisis has followed another. The collapse of empire, the beginning of the Cold War, internal struggles for power in nations around the world, famine, flood, civil war – all of these things and more have kept the tides of human misery flowing more or less constantly.

In the wake of the war a variety of institutions were set up to deal with this: the already mentioned UNRRA was followed by the International Refugee Organization (IRO) and the United Nations High Commissioner for Refugees (UNHCR), which was created at the beginning of the 1950s. This last institution was only supposed to be temporary: so many nations were worried about the political implications of creating a permanent body that they originally only set it up for a period of three years. But the refugees simply kept coming. The displacements caused by the Second World War turned out not to be a temporary phenomenon, but rather a sign of how the world had changed.[18]

As new emergencies arose, the UNHCR's mandate was renewed and expanded. It coordinated a response to the exodus from Hungary in 1956, and from Algeria in the late 1950s. It dealt with African refugees in the wake of the decolonization of the 1960s, and in the 1970s it looked after refugees from Vietnam, Cambodia and Bangladesh. In the 1980s it helped people fleeing internal conflict in Central America and famine in Ethiopia, and in the 1990s it tried to bring relief to people fleeing ethnic cleansing in Rwanda and Yugoslavia.[19]

In recent years there has been a whole succession of crises to swell the ranks of the world's refugees. To name but a few, there have been major wars in Iraq and Afghanistan, internal unrest in central Africa and the Horn of Africa, huge turmoil caused by the aftermath of the Arab Spring, and, most disastrously of all, a long-running civil war in Syria. According to the UNHCR, in 2014 there were 13.9 million people newly displaced by conflict or persecution – the highest number on record since the Second World War. The total number of refugees and displaced persons worldwide was estimated at 59.5 million – again, an unprecedented figure. The problem is getting worse, not better.[20]

In all this time, one of the nations most generous towards refugees has been Germany. According to its Basic Law, written in 1948, 'Persons persecuted on political grounds shall have the right of asylum' – and for the next forty years this right applied to all asylum seekers, without conditions.[21] Thus West Germany accepted a further 3 million refugees from Communist East Germany before the Berlin Wall was constructed in 1961. After the failed revolution in Hungary in 1956, West Germany was amongst the first to offer asylum to the tens of thousands of refugees pouring across the Hungarian border. During the collapse of communism in eastern Europe, Germany opened its doors to hundreds of thousands of asylum seekers from the east – almost 600,000 between 1988 and 1992 alone. Over the next three years, Germany also played host to 345,000 refugees from the conflict in Yugoslavia. In 1999 there were over 1.2 million refugees and asylum seekers in the country.[22]

In 2015, in response to a new war in Syria, Germany declared an open-door policy for all refugees fleeing the crisis. Over the coming months hundreds of thousands of migrants crossed the Mediterranean, many of them bearing photographs of the German chancellor, Angela Merkel, and telling TV reporters that 'Angela said we could come'. By the end of the year the number of asylum seekers to Germany had quadrupled to just under a million.[23]

Many other European nations have never been so generous, and particularly not during the 2015 refugee crisis. Some built fences along their borders to keep the refugees out. Others pointed out – with some justification – that many of the people streaming into Europe were not refugees at all but economic migrants. Almost every nation criticized Germany for throwing the doors open. They claimed that Germans were merely trying to expiate their historical guilt, that they were guilty of a 'tyrannical display of German virtue', and even 'moral imperialism'.[24]

For Dittmann Mendel, the eighth son of Mathias Mendel, there is a simpler explanation for Germany's refugee policy. He grew up in a community that knew what it meant to be expelled from its homeland. His family had to start again from scratch, build their own house and rely on the goodwill of strangers; and he often heard his parents speaking mournfully with their friends from the old country about the world they had been forced to leave behind. 'There may be more understanding here for the world refugee problem than elsewhere,' he says, 'partly because we ourselves went through this fate.'[25]

24. The Globalization of Peoples

The Second World War did not only bring sorrow and trauma. Nor did it always result in the polarization of peoples. In some nations exactly the opposite process was taking place: the vast displacements caused by the war brought with them the benefits of diversity as communities of refugees became the basis of new minorities.

By no means all those who moved during and after the war were forced to do so: many relocated of their own accord. For these people the idea of displacement from their old lives represented not a loss but an opportunity. The war gave them a chance to see the world, to experience new ideas and gain new skills, and perhaps even to build better lives for themselves. One such person was Sam King, the son of a Caribbean banana farmer, and his story demonstrates one of the biggest social changes brought about by the war: the postwar boom in migration.

Sam King was a teenager when the war broke out, but his father already had his future mapped out for him. As the oldest son, King was expected to take over his father's farm in Priestman's River, Jamaica, when he retired. The prospect did not excite King at all. He had watched the annual battles his father fought against drought and flooding, against the damage wrought by hurricanes, against the Panama disease that attacked his bananas, and the yellowing disease that wiped out his coconuts. He had seen the crops rotting in the fields when international markets suddenly dried up. A life like his father's seemed to offer nothing but hardship. 'I decided . . . that such misfortune would be difficult for me to bear as a farmer and therefore I'd better be looking for a way out.'[1]

The war offered him exactly the opportunity he had been waiting for. One day, when he was eighteen years old, an advertisement appeared in the *Daily Gleaner* calling for volunteers to join the Royal Air Force. His mother said to him, 'Son, the Mother Country is at war. Go! And if you live it will be a good thing.' So he took the RAF examination, which he passed with a good grade. In 1944, he boarded the SS *Cuba* and set sail across the Atlantic.[2]

Over the coming months he would experience much that he had never imagined before. The first was the war itself. 'I knew about war,' he remembered years later, 'but when you actually see it, it's frightening.' When he arrived in Glasgow that November he was shocked to discover how much of the city had been destroyed by bombs. The same was true of every city he passed through, particularly London, which was still under attack from V1 and V2 rockets.

He was also shocked by the cold. The temperature in Britain was just 4°C (39°F) when he arrived: 'I thought I was going to die!' But his drill instructors told him and the other Jamaican recruits to strip and play a game of football: once they had finished running around, and discovered that they were sweating, they realized that life in this country would not be so bad.

The RAF trained King as an aircraft fitter, and put him to work servicing Lancaster bombers. He worked long hours, but he was happy. 'I was privileged to be working with people from Norway to the Sudan. We all had to work together to beat Nazi Germany.' He was seduced by the strong sense of community that this engendered: 'It felt good to be a part of Britain.'[3]

Sam King in his RAF uniform, after he left Jamaica in 1944.

King eagerly seized the opportunities that were presented to him. While he was in Britain he started a correspondence course, so that he could catch up on the schooling he had missed as a boy in Jamaica. He signed up for a carpentry course with the RAF, so that he could learn a new skill. Whenever he was on leave, he spent it working on building sites so that he could earn a little money and save. The future looked brighter than he had ever thought possible.

'The war gave me the chance to move out of my village,' he confessed in an interview towards the end of his life. 'I won't say the war was a good thing, but I took the opportunity. Without the war, my father would have put a ball and chain round my foot. But I had no intention of planting bananas like him.'[4]

Diversity in Western Europe

The population of Britain was transformed between 1939 and 1945. As the Nazis marched across Europe, governments, armies and refugees fled the mainland and set themselves up in Britain. The Norwegian navy sailed to Scotland. Remnants of the French navy were based in Plymouth, and remnants of the Polish air force formed more than a dozen squadrons around London and Lincolnshire. Thousands of Jews also fled to Britain, including Georgina Sand, whose story forms the opening passages of this book. London especially became the headquarters of the Free French, the Free Belgians, the Czech and Polish governments in exile, the Dutch queen and her administration and a whole variety of other official and unofficial European groups. They mingled with men from the British colonies and dominions who came to join the fight, particularly Canadians, Australians, West Africans and men from the Caribbean like Sam King. More than 170,000 Irish people came to Britain to work during the war. Perhaps the largest group to add to this mix were the hundreds of thousands of Americans who were stationed in Britain as members of the US Army and its air force. Britain during the war was a more diverse country than it had ever been.[5]

Almost none of these people were long-term immigrants. They were mostly fighting men and women or refugees from Europe, and the vast majority stayed only for the duration of the war. After 1945, when victory was announced, the Norwegian navy was free to return to the Oslofjord. The Free French returned to France and the various governments-in-exile left to rebuild their respective countries. The massive forces of the US military boarded ships and sailed back across the Atlantic. In 1947 Sam King was also demobilized and sent back to Jamaica.

But if people imagined that Britain would go back to the way it had been before the war, they were wrong. Just as one group of foreigners were leaving, another group were arriving. Tens of thousands of Polish refugees came to Britain in the aftermath of the war and set up homes in west London and elsewhere. These were men who had fought for the British army during the war, but who had no nation to go to because the Soviets had annexed their homeland. Having allowed Stalin to do this, Britain owed them a debt of responsibility. In 1947 the British Parliament passed the Polish Resettlement Act, and well over 100,000 Polish immigrants arrived.[6]

Britain needed these people. The whole country was rebuilding, and there was a huge demand for workers in the aftermath of the war. The new institutions of the Welfare State needed to be staffed, especially the National Health Service, which would grow to become one of the biggest employers in the world. Britain's infrastructure had been badly damaged, especially the housing stock, which urgently needed rebuilding. Job vacancies began to appear everywhere: the need to make up for years of neglect in a variety of industries required more workers than Britain alone could provide.

Much of this shortfall was made up with Irish labour – so much so that Ireland was quickly drained of its own people. Between 1945 and 1971, about a third of the Irish population under the age of thirty left the country looking for work, most of them for Britain. The British government also started recruiting people from other countries. They set up a European Volunteer Worker scheme, followed by an even larger scheme called 'Westward Ho!', which sought to attract up to 100,000 workers from other parts of Europe.[7]

Much the same process was taking place across the continent. Like Britain, other European countries also set up schemes to attract foreign workers. One of the earliest to do so was Belgium, which employed 50,000 displaced persons to work in the coal mines and the steel industry almost as soon as the war was over. France opened an Office National d'Immigration (ONI) to organize the recruitment of workers from nearby countries, and later Germany also started a guest worker scheme through its Federal Labour Administration.

Before long, huge numbers of people were moving from poorer parts of Europe to regions where the jobs were more plentiful. In the fifteen years after the war an average of more than 264,000 Italians left Italy *each year*, most of them looking for work in Germany, Switzerland and France. Likewise hundreds of thousands of Spanish and Portuguese people moved to France, Turks and Yugoslavs moved to Germany, Finns moved to Sweden, and so on.

Therefore, at exactly the same time that eastern Europe was expelling its ethnic minorities and striving to create monocultural nation-states, western Europe was mixing itself up like never before. By the early 1970s the industrial powerhouse nations in north-west Europe had already become home to some 15 million migrants.[8]

Immigration from the Colonies

Sam King had returned home reluctantly. Back on his father's farm, he heard rumours about all the transformations that were taking place in Britain and began to feel restless again. He was not happy in Jamaica. The island had changed since he'd been away. Like many other parts of the world, it was struggling with postwar turbulence, calls for independence, labour strikes and widespread unemployment. A new sense of restlessness was in the air.

King had changed too. Ever since his return, he had found himself drifting. 'I tried to calm my restless mind, looking at various schemes to which I could apply myself, but they all turned out shadowy and vague. I could not see myself making headway socially or financially in Priestman's River, or in Jamaica for that matter . . . I was impatient and eager, I grant you, but I felt that time was running out.'[9]

One day he saw a second advertisement in the *Daily Gleaner*. A troop ship named the *Empire Windrush* was due to dock in Kingston that May, and cheap passage was being offered for anyone who wanted to sail to Britain to find work. He knew immediately what he had to do. He approached his mother and father, who gave him their blessing to go – but with great sadness, because they sensed that if he went back to Britain he would probably never return. His father sold three cows to pay for his fare. And on 24 May 1948, Sam King once again boarded a ship bound for the 'Mother Country', this time as a civilian.

King could not have known it at the time, but the journey he made across the Atlantic in 1948 was part of something more than just a personal milestone: he was in the vanguard of a revolution that would take Britain completely by surprise.

The British government believed it could control immigration after the war. The schemes set up to attract workers from Europe all had strict limits, and strict criteria. The ideal immigrant, as far as the British government was concerned, was someone who would be able to melt invisibly into British society – someone young, healthy in body and mind, middle class, Protestant and, above all, white. It was for this reason that they so actively tried to recruit refugees from the Baltic States through their European Volunteer Worker scheme: they were the people that the government felt would be most likely to fit in.

However, there was one glaring loophole in their plans. Unlike with European workers, there were no barriers for immigrants coming from the British Empire. As 'citizens of the United Kingdom and colonies', people like Sam King enjoyed the automatic right to enter the UK, work, live and even to vote in UK elections. These rights remained to all Commonwealth citizens until the British government started to repeal them in 1962. When they arrived, they enjoyed many advantages over some of their European rivals. They already spoke English, and were familiar with many aspects of British culture: as King put it, 'We were Christians and we played cricket.'[10] Though they had to travel a long way, their journeys were made much easier by the links that their countries already had with Britain – they simply followed the long-established trade routes.

As a consequence of all this immigration, Britain's cities were rapidly transformed from the monocultures they had been in 1939 into the multicultural, multiracial melting pots they are today. By 1971 over 300,000 West Indians had settled in Britain. They were joined by a further 300,000 from India, 140,000 from Pakistan and over 170,000 from Africa. These communities would form the core base for further waves of immigration in years to come.

It was, as the Jamaican-born poet Louise Bennett gleefully put it, 'colonization in reverse'.[11]

Much the same was happening all over western Europe. Alongside the flows of people within the continent would come migrants from much further afield. In the twenty-five years after the Second World War, metropolitan France would become home to not only Italians, Spaniards and Portuguese but also millions of people from its former colonies. Nearly a million *'pieds noirs'* – Frenchmen born in Algeria – fled North Africa in the wake of the Algerian War of Independence that began in 1954. Along with them came some 600,000 native Algerians in search of a better life. Then there were 140,000 Moroccans and 90,000 Tunisians who found work in France through the ONI, and the 250,000 or so French citizens who arrived from overseas departments and territories such as Guadeloupe, Martinique and Réunion. The diversity of today's France is rooted in this postwar period.

The Netherlands also saw the 'return' of 300,000 Dutch nationals from the newly independent Indonesia. They brought 32,000 Moluccans with them, mostly Ambonese Christians who wanted nothing to do with the Indonesian state. They were later joined by around 160,000 people from the other Dutch colonies of Suriname and the Netherlands Antilles. Similar flows of people came from Angola and Mozambique to Portugal, and from the Democratic Republic of Congo to Belgium.[12]

On a global scale, these population movements to Europe became part of a wider trend of migration from the global south to the richer countries of the north. It was not only the populations of former colonies that migrated north to their 'mother countries' in Europe, but also Somalians and Sri Lankans who travelled to the Gulf States to find work, Filipinos and Indonesians who went to Hong Kong or Japan and Mexicans and Puerto Ricans who travelled into the USA. Historians and political scientists often write about the West Indians who came to Britain after the war, but by the mid-1970s there were actually more Caribbean migrants in New York City alone than in the whole of western Europe. Colonial ties were important; but more important were the opportunities that migrants sought.[13]

The transformation that took place in Latin America during the thirty or so years after the Second World War is telling. Before the war, waves of Europeans had migrated to countries like Argentina and Brazil to seek their fortune, much the same as they had migrated to their colonies in Asia and Africa. Once the Second World War was over, this pattern resumed: hundreds of thousands of European refugees and economic migrants once again began to arrive. But as the long economic boom in Europe continued through the 1950s and 60s, the numbers soon began to tail off. Instead, the richer Latin American nations began to rely on migrant labour from within the region: Paraguayans, Chileans and Bolivians came to Argentina; and hundreds of thousands of Colombians flocked to Venezuela to find work on its farms and in its oil fields. Finally, when the whole region fell into a spiral of crippling debt during the 1970s, most of Latin America began to follow the same patterns of migration as the rest of the global south: people fled northwards in search of the opportunities that had never quite materialized in their own countries. It was not only the USA they went to. Argentineans also began migrating to countries like Italy and Spain: it was a kind of economic migration in reverse.[14]

In some ways there was nothing new about any of this. It was simply a progression from something that had already been going on for a century – the movement of the rural poor to the richer cities, only written on an international scale. What *was* new was the volume of people who were migrating, and the rate at which they came; and both of these things had been greatly accelerated by the Second World War. A generation that had been shaken up by the onset of modernity and the global effects of war was much less rooted in their communities than their parents and grandparents had been: like Sam King, they saw an opportunity for a better life and wanted to seize it with both hands. The same urge that drove the independence movements of colonies around the world also drove millions of individuals to strike out on their own and seek their fortune elsewhere.

Not only had the urge to move grown, but so had the opportunity. The global system of trade, economy and international cooperation that was built after 1945 accelerated a trend that might otherwise have taken much longer to develop. The shipping industry boomed in these years; and a new air-travel industry blossomed, built on the foundations of the massive fleets of aircraft that had been constructed for war. Globalization as we know it today really took off in the wake of the Second World War.

In western Europe especially, this started a revolution. It was as if fragments of India or the Caribbean had broken off and embedded themselves in Britain. All of a sudden splinters of North Africa had been transplanted to France, and tiny pieces of Turkey and the Levant scattered across Germany and the Netherlands.

Economists, artists and gastronomists are quick to point out the enormous benefits this revolution has brought to Europe, but there have also undeniably been costs. One of those costs was a growing feeling of alienation in their hosts. It was not only the immigrant populations who suffered from fragmentation: their arrival would also cause fissures to open up in the very communities that they were joining. This too would have profound consequences in the years to come.[15]

The Windrush Generation

Sam King had no idea what he was letting himself in for when he boarded the *Empire Windrush* in 1948. During the war he had been welcomed in Britain as an ally. He had seen very little naked prejudice, and what little he had seen tended to come not from British people but from other outsiders – like the American GIs in Manchester who tried to beat up his friend and take his girl, or the South African officer who tried to have him billeted separately from the white ground crew. On both occasions, British people stepped in to help him.

When he returned in 1948, things were slightly different. Apparently it was one thing to have black men in Britain temporarily to help fight a war, but another thing altogether to have them here in peacetime, perhaps even permanently.

Antipathy towards his arrival began even before he had stepped off the boat, and was voiced at the very top of British society. On hearing that the *Empire Windrush* was carrying 492 West Indian immigrants to London, the minister of labour, George Isaacs, warned Parliament: 'The arrival of these substantial numbers of men under no organized arrangement is bound to result in considerable difficulty and disappointment.'[16] The colonial secretary, Arthur Creech Jones, promised that this was almost certainly a unique event, and that 'a similar mass movement' of Jamaican immigrants was unlikely to happen again.[17] Soon afterwards, eleven Labour MPs wrote to their prime minister asking for new legislation to stop such people coming in future:

The British people fortunately enjoy a profound unity without uni-formity . . . and are blessed by the absence of a colour racial problem. An influx of coloured people domiciled here is likely to impair the har-mony, strength and cohesion of our public and social life and to cause discord and unhappiness among all concerned.[18]

It was not long before the press joined in. For example, on the very day when the *Empire Windrush* docked at Tilbury, a headline in the *Daily Graphic* called their arrival the start of an 'invasion'. People like Sam King were just the vanguard, it warned: a 'huge army of unemployed labourers' was on its way from Jamaica.[19]

It is tempting to dismiss these concerns as racist nonsense: the arrival of 492 men hardly constituted an 'invasion' or a 'mass movement', espe-cially when compared with the hundreds of thousands of white immigrants that were being actively courted by the government at the same time. But while such comments were undoubtedly racist, there was also something else going on. For all their latent prejudice, British officials were genuinely worried about social cohesion after the war, and they feared that black Caribbean workers simply would not be able to fit in. European immigrants at least looked British; black workers, by contrast, would always be visible in a crowd.[20]

The British government's wartime call for unity. Pride in the diversity of people coming to the country's aid did not last long after 1945.

When Sam King arrived in London, he began to find this out for himself. When he stepped off the *Empire Windrush* he was treated well. He was given somewhere to sleep in a disused air-raid shelter in south London, and welcomed by the members of a local church. But over the coming months he began to notice prejudice everywhere, some of it subtle, some of it not so subtle at all. When he went to the labour exchange to sign up as a carpenter, he was told that as a Jamaican his work could not possibly be up to British standards. It was only when he produced a certificate showing that he had been trained by the RAF that they bashfully offered him a choice of jobs. Accommodation was very hard to come by, and signs went up in boarding-house windows saying 'No blacks, no dogs'. When he and his brother applied for a loan to buy their own house he received a letter from the mortgage provider turning their application down and advising them to go back to Jamaica. Later, when he worked for the Post Office, he was frequently subjected to calls of 'Send 'em back!' by white workers, and one of the executives told him openly, 'If I had my way you would not even be a postman in my office.'[21]

King steadfastly refused to let such comments and attitudes hold him back. He always considered himself British, and was proud to be so. He joined the union. He joined the Labour Party. He opened his house up to fellow Jamaicans who could not find anywhere else to stay. He helped set up a credit union for his fellow immigrants, and was the driving force behind Britain's first black newspaper, the *West Indian Gazette*. After race riots hit London's Notting Hill in 1958, he helped his friend and colleague Claudia Jones set up a West Indian carnival in an attempt to show the positive side of Caribbean culture: this would eventually grow into one of Europe's biggest annual street festivals, today's Notting Hill Carnival.

In 1982 King was elected to his local council in Southwark, and a year later he became the borough's first black mayor. He immediately began to receive phone calls from people threatening to cut his throat and burn his house down. A permanent police guard was placed at his home. Though such things angered him, he never let them cloud his judgement: 'Negativism only serves to depress and discourage.'

Before his death in 2016, at the age of ninety, the council he once worked for erected a blue commemorative plaque on his former house in recognition of all he had achieved in his life, and all he had done for his community.[22]

Backlash

The attitudes that Sam King encountered were deeply embedded in British culture. After more than two centuries of colonialism, British people had built up a wide variety of assumptions about the black races, considering them backward, lazy, inferior: so when people like Sam King arrived, who were not only educated but also hardworking, ambitious, erudite and capable, it threw their assumptions into disarray. Some people learned from this experience, including one of Sam King's early tormentors who, on falling on hard times later, turned to him for help; but others were never able to see beyond the colour of King's skin.

If there were few organized anti-immigration movements in Britain during the 1940s and 50s, this was not because of a lack of hostility. British people, much like the British government, spent much of this era in denial: they simply assumed that black and Asian immigrants would soon go home. Ironically, it was the first British attempts to limit immigration that finally exposed the truth. The Commonwealth Immigrants Act of 1962 put severe restrictions on primary immigration, so the people who now arrived were no longer single men and women looking for work, but family members of those who were already in Britain. Sam King's family was a case in point: 'My mother had nine of us,' he later revealed; 'eight of us came to Britain.' This family consolidation was not the action of people who intended to return to Jamaica. King and his ilk were in Britain to stay.[23]

British society now began to realize that they were experiencing a permanent change to their way of life. The Conservative politician Enoch Powell made a series of famous speeches about how British people now felt as though they were living in 'alien territory'.[24] A new, racist party called the National Front was set up, whose agenda included the 'repatriation of all coloured immigrants and their descendants'.[25] Racist marches took place in London, Huddersfield, Bradford, Leicester, Oldham and many other places across the country, often leading to violent clashes with police and with counter-demonstrators.[26]

Similar unrest was seen across Europe. In the 1970s, neo-fascist parties like the Dutch People's Union, and the German People's Union began to spring up everywhere. They were joined by radical right-wing populist parties like the Front National in France, and the Danish and

Norwegian Progress Parties. Regional separatists such as the Northern League in Italy and the Flemish Block in Belgium also jumped on the bandwagon. All of these parties saw a rapid increase in their popularity during the 1970s and 80s, each adopting a xenophobic rejection of immigrants as their central policy. More-mainstream parties also saw an opportunity here. The best example is Austria's Freedom Party, whose transformation in the 1980s from a moderate conservative stance to a stridently anti-immigration one saw its share of the vote rise from around 5 per cent to 33 per cent. In May 2016 the Freedom Party candidate missed out on becoming Austria's president by such a narrow margin that a new election had to be held at the end of the year (which he also narrowly lost).[27]

At the time of writing, the radical right is more powerful in Europe than it has been at any time since the Second World War. Hungary's government, which is dominated by the right-wing Fidesz party, has frequently been criticized by politicians and newspapers around the world for its authoritarianism and demonization of outsiders. The only consolation for critics of Fidesz is that at least they are less extreme than the more openly racist Jobbik party, which won more than 20 per cent of the vote in 2014.[28] Poland's Law and Justice Party, which came to power in 2015, is also a party of the radical right which has been shunned by more moderate groups in the country, and even by some of its former members.[29] In France, support for the Front National has been growing steadily for twenty years, and in Britain the UK Independence Party received 3.8 million votes in the 2015 general election, making it the third most popular party in Britain. All these parties have one thing in common: they are all fiercely opposed to immigration.

In many other rich industrial nations around the world, attitudes towards immigration have followed broadly similar paths. Australia is a good example. After 1945, Australia's first minister for immigration, Arthur Calwell, ran a campaign to 'populate or perish': 'We must fill this country or we will lose it,' he announced. 'We need to protect ourselves from the yellow peril from the north.' In the wake of the Second World War, Asia could still only be conceived of as a threat, so Calwell only ever tried to encourage immigration from Europe, preferably from Britain. This 'White Australia Policy' was not dismantled until the 1960s; but the immigration that came in the following years, predominantly from Asia, was never fully accepted. In the 1990s, politician

Pauline Hanson founded One Nation, a party whose policies closely resembled those of the radical right in Europe and America. She called for a complete halt to immigration, and an end to multiculturalism. 'I believe we are in danger of being swamped by Asians,' she said in her maiden speech to Parliament. Since then, immigration has become one of the most emotive subjects in the country. From 2012 Australia adopted the controversial measure of interning refugees offshore in camps in Micronesia or Papua New Guinea.[30]

Fear and Freedom

So, what are all these people afraid of? One of the most common reasons, and justifications, for xenophobia in industrialized nations is that native people fear for their jobs. Immigrants are regularly blamed for undercutting the traditional labour force and driving down wages. But regardless of whether this is true or not, this does not seem to be most people's main concern. If it were, then one would expect animosity towards foreigners to rise during times of high unemployment, but historical data from western Europe show that there are only tenuous links between xenophobia and employment rates.[31]

The real threat that immigration poses to communities in the developed world seems to be less about jobs than about culture. As Enoch Powell made clear in 1960s Britain, it is a numbers game. When the proportion of black immigrants had reached a quarter or a third of the population in some cities, he called it an 'invasion': 'In all its history, our nation has never known a greater danger.' The people of Britain, he wrote, were being 'displaced, in the only country that is theirs'.[32] In the years to come, similar sentiments were voiced all over Europe, Australasia and North America: it was not their jobs that people feared for, but their communities.

This was part paranoia, part prejudice, but it also contained more than a seed of truth. Communities *were* being eroded. People *were* beginning to feel alienated. Nations *were* being transformed. This was not all the fault of immigrants, of course, but since immigrants were – and are – the most noticeable manifestation of the way developed societies have changed since the end of the Second World War, they have become a potent symbol of alienation.

The figures for immigration in our own century are quite startling. This is particularly the case in the richer Commonwealth countries. In 1947 only 10 per cent of the Australian population had been born overseas, and almost three-quarters of those were British or Irish. By 2015, this proportion had soared to more than 28 per cent, with the biggest growth coming from Asian immigrants.[33] Similar patterns can be found in New Zealand and Canada. In each of these countries, the communities that in the 1940s and 50s had seemed so stable, so uniform – and so white – have been transformed beyond recognition.[34]

Similar proportions of immigrants can now also be found in many countries in Europe. According to the OECD, by 2013 more than 28 per cent of the Swiss population had also been born elsewhere. There the issue of immigration became so politically sensitive that those who wanted to bring back stricter controls managed to force the government to hold a referendum over whether to introduce immigration quotas, which they then won.[35]

At first glance, figures for the rest of Europe do not appear quite so dramatic. In the Netherlands, the foreign-born population in 2013 was only 11.6 per cent, in France it was 12 per cent, in Germany almost 13 per cent and in Austria approaching 17 per cent. But these figures do not take into account the children and grandchildren of immigrants who first came to these countries after the Second World War – people who are often easily identifiable by the colour of their skin. For those who refuse to reconcile themselves to the changes that have already taken place to their societies, these people are a permanent reminder of the way their countries have altered.

Meanwhile, in the USA, more than 13 per cent of the population was born in a foreign country. The fastest growing demographic is people of Hispanic origin: indeed, Spanish is quickly becoming the nation's second language. No wonder that white, Anglo-Saxon Americans feel themselves to be 'strangers in their own land'.[36]

The UK has seen similar changes in its cultural make-up, particularly in its cities. London has a serious claim to be the most diverse city in the world. More than 300 languages are spoken here, and there are at least fifty different non-indigenous communities of 10,000 people or more. Almost one in every five Londoners is black or mixed race. Almost one in five is of Asian origin. In 2013 the mayor of London, Boris Johnson, announced – perhaps misleadingly – that the British capital was actually France's 'sixth biggest city', with more Frenchmen living there than in Bordeaux.[37]

While this makes for an exciting place to live, it does not do much to engender a feeling of belonging. There is such a high turnover of people in London that any sense of community is often only temporary, and must be enjoyed while it lasts before friends and neighbours move on and are replaced. Londoners are used to this now. Those who have lived there all their lives, as have I, have learned to let go of the traditions they grew up with and ride the waves of new ideas that are constantly rolling over the city; but that does not mean that they do so without regret, or without, occasionally, a painful sense of nostalgia for the things they knew in their youth that are now gone for ever.

In recent years, the new front line of immigration has moved from cities like London to small towns like Boston in Lincolnshire, which in 2016 became to some a symbol of everything that was wrong with Britain's immigration policy. In this close-knit community of 60,000 souls, the sudden changes that come with large-scale immigration were much more difficult to cope with. Between 2005 and 2016, almost 7,000 Polish immigrants came to the town, and people quickly began to fear that their community and traditions would be lost. By the time of the Brexit referendum, Boston had become 'the most divided place in England', and was a stronghold for the UK Independence Party. The fear of foreigners here was not really a fear of foreigners at all, but a fear of losing something precious – a sense of belonging.[38]

There are, of course, other explanations for people's fears. It is not only a sense of belonging that has been threatened by large-scale immigration, but also a sense of entitlement. The European cultures whose empires exploited the world did not take kindly to 'colonization in reverse'. Likewise, the peoples that conquered Australasia, South Africa, Canada and the USA in the eighteenth and nineteenth centuries believed that they had a right to oust those who were there before them – but complained when they found their imported cultures challenged in turn.

Perhaps the best example of this behaviour has been in the USA, a nation built entirely upon immigration, but where immigrants are nevertheless routinely demonized by the political establishment. Anti-immigration rhetoric has been growing here since at least the 1980s, but probably reached its height during the 2016 presidential election campaign, when Donald Trump famously accused Mexican immigrants of being 'rapists' and 'drug smugglers', and vowed not only to deport 11 million illegal immigrants back to Latin America, but to build a wall between the USA and Mexico.[39] His campaign slogan, 'Make America Great Again', was interpreted by some Americans as a thinly veiled call to make America white again.[40]

For America's minorities it might be tempting, perhaps even satisfying, to see a kind of historical justice in the way that the tides of immigration have washed over white America, and will doubtless continue to do so despite Trump's rhetoric. But to glory in the misfortunes of the white working class is both unpleasant and misses the nuances of the bigger picture. Many of those who voted for Trump were themselves immigrants, or children of immigrants, who had arrived in the country with nothing and who hoped to prosper through hard work and determination. Such people were once the very embodiment of the American Dream.

But the world has changed irrevocably since the 1940s and 50s, when America truly was a 'great' nation. Mass migration is just one component of a much bigger process of globalization which has been eating away at the prospects of American workers for decades. Now it is not only newcomers that threaten to take away American jobs – the jobs themselves have migrated overseas, where labour is even cheaper than that provided by American immigrants. Mechanization is also revolutionizing the workplace: the technologies that in 1945 promised Americans a life of leisure now threaten to deprive them of their livelihoods.

According to Arlie Russell Hochschild, the people who felt left behind by globalization voted for Trump because they had lost all faith in the more conventional leaders who had allowed the American Dream to wither and die. It was not necessarily that the white working class begrudged immigrants the chance to make good: they were more angry at the fact that they had seen their own status drop so precipitously over the previous years. The opportunities, so plentiful in 1945 and the decades which followed, seemed to have withered to a point where American workers now had to fight as hard as any immigrant just to survive.

Here again, the xenophobia they sometimes displayed was not really xenophobia at all, but resentment of their powerlessness in the face of global forces, and the crushing realization that the future that they once believed was waiting for them no longer existed.[41]

The New 'Other'

As the twenty-first century dawned, all of these fears crystallized into one meta-fear, which has become one of the dominant features of our age. On 11 September 2001, Islamic extremists launched a series of attacks on America, most famously by flying passenger airliners into the twin towers of the World Trade Center in New York. In the following years Islamic terrorists would also bomb commuter trains in Madrid (March 2004), the public transport network in London (July 2005), the international airport in Brussels (March 2016), and launch a string of attacks in France and Germany. All of a sudden it seemed that the rich industrial nations of the developed world had another reason to fear their immigrant populations: now it was not only jobs, communities and historic privilege that were threatened, but Western civilization as a whole. In reality, there is nothing new about this fear. It is the same fear that was once felt towards the Nazis, then transferred to the Communists, and which has been looking for a home ever since the Cold War ended.

The anti-immigration lobby has a vested interest in stirring up this fear wherever possible, because it calls into question our immigration policy since the Second World War. It seems to justify what they have been saying all along: by allowing Muslims into their societies in such numbers ever since the 1940s, Western governments have invited an enemy in.

This is the reason Donald Trump promised to ban the immigration of Muslims during the 2016 US presidential campaign. It is why Hungary refused to take in Muslim refugees from the Syrian War the same year. And it is why Dutch presidential hopeful Geert Wilders called for the 'de-Islamification' of the Netherlands the same year – and thereby took his 'Party for Freedom' to the top of the polls, despite the fact that he was simultaneously facing police charges for inciting racial hatred.[42] Muslims now occupy the same place in the European imagination that Jews did at the beginning of the twentieth century: the actions of a tiny minority have opened the door to the demonization of an entire religion.

Ironically, the only other people to benefit from such thinking are the Islamic terrorists themselves. Since the primary aim of terrorism is to spread fear, extremist groups like al-Qaeda and Islamic State can congratulate themselves on a job well done. Their actions in and after 2001 provoked a reaction beyond their wildest dreams. They triggered a US-led attack on Afghanistan, where many of the terrorists were based, which rapidly became a holy war, and a beacon to disaffected Muslims everywhere. They provoked a second war between the USA and Iraq, which destabilized another region of the Middle East. And along the way a succession of martyrs and heroes were advertised to the world in the mainstream media. The rise and rise of Islamic extremism since the end of the Cold War has been built on an ability to provoke a reaction from the West.

And yet Islamic extremists are also afraid. The reason they want to overthrow Western liberal democracy is because it threatens their traditions, their culture and a way of life they imagine has remained unchanged for centuries. They see the governments of predominantly Muslim countries like Saudi Arabia or Jordan apparently dancing to a Western tune. They see the effects of mass immigration, as workers from all over south Asia flock to the Gulf States in search of work. They see Islamic values being eroded by new, Western traditions and the growth of information technology. They see the ancient privileges reserved for men and for religious leaders slowly ebbing away. And they know that unless they do something dramatic, destructive, gigantic – unless they can create their own global revolution – these changes will inevitably continue.

The same is true for some sections of the new Muslim populations of rich Western nations. These communities came, like Sam King, in search of a better life in the wake of the Second World War. Like Sam King they had to fight for a place in British, or German, or American society, and they resigned themselves to making compromises for the sake of fitting into their adopted home. But things are different for their children and grandchildren. Muslims who were born in, say, France have a sense of entitlement that their parents never quite had: they consider themselves just as French as any of their countrymen, and rightly so. And yet the prejudice against them remains. They feel themselves attacked on two sides: they are simultaneously rejected by society and under pressure to assimilate more fully.

As Jean-Paul Sartre observed in 1944, such people face an impossible choice: if they assimilate completely, they are denying themselves; but if they do not assimilate, they are accepting that they will always have to be the outsider, the 'Other'.[43] It is little wonder that a small percentage have found the internal conflict that this arouses too difficult to face, that they have instead chosen to embrace rejection, nurture it, and turn it back on the societies in which they live.

I started this book by claiming that we are all, in a sense, refugees and immigrants. For some of the people whose lives I have described, this is literally the case. People like Georgina Sand, whose story I opened with, or Aharon Appelfeld, or Sam King left their countries of origin for good and have lived out the rest of their lives abroad. For many more, like Anthony Curwen or Waruhiu Itote, the defining moments of their lives took place in foreign countries during times of war or revolution. But every person in this book experienced massive upheavals in their lives as a direct consequence of the Second World War. Even if they did not travel to other countries, the world they had once known was transformed beyond recognition by the things that they experienced and the times in which they lived. The same can be said of most people who survived the momentous changes of the twentieth century.

The war unleashed forces that changed our world in 1945, and have continued to affect our way of life up to today. First and foremost, it created a great deal of trauma that has haunted people and societies ever since. The war also created the superpowers, and the tensions between East and West that defined the world for the next forty-five years. It swept away the European and Japanese empires, setting hundreds of millions free to choose their own destinies – or at least to try to do so. It produced advances in science and technology, in human rights and international law, in art, architecture, medicine and philosophy. It cleared the way for new political and economic systems and laid down the foundations of the globalization we know today. The upheaval of peoples started by the war threw alien cultures into close proximity, and now the pace of change has grown so fast that fewer and fewer of us can say with absolute certainty who our neighbours will be tomorrow, or whereabouts in the world we ourselves will end our days.

No matter what we may wish, these changes cannot be undone. As the twenty-first century progresses we face a choice. Either we can embrace world change, ride the forces of progress and try to make it work to our advantage; or we can resist change, try to hold it in abeyance so that we can protect what is left of the old ways of life that we value so dearly. If history is anything to go by, I suspect we shall probably take both courses of action simultaneously, satisfying no one completely, but muddling through nevertheless.

There is a third choice: we can kick over the whole system and try to start again from scratch. The world today is full of people promising to do exactly this. They are angry, and disillusioned with the way that the world has changed, and they are looking more than ever for someone to blame. This is not so much a legacy of the Second World War as a return to the same ways of thinking that brought about the war in the first place.

The frustrations that are gripping the world today will be familiar to anyone who has studied the rise to war in the 1930s. Now, as then, large parts of the world are subject to high levels of unemployment, growing poverty and economic stagnation. There is a growing anger at the gap between rich and poor, a growing distrust of outsiders and, above all, a growing fear of what used to be called modernity, but which today has become globalization.

In 1945, these were problems we believed we could solve. Unless we begin to solve them again, the demagogues and revolutionaries will step in to solve them for us, just as they once did in the middle of the twentieth century.

Epilogue

The Second World War was not just another event – it changed everything. As armed forces swept from one end of the globe to the other, consuming whole economies, sacrificing civilians as readily as soldiers, even those caught up in the violence could see that something fundamental was being destroyed. 'You have to understand that a world is dying', observed Ed Murrow, an American war reporter, in 1940; 'old values, the old prejudices, and the old bases of power and prestige are going'. The Allies on both sides of the Atlantic, and on both sides of the Pacific, entered the war against Germany and Japan in the belief that they were fighting to preserve a way of life. In reality they were to become bystanders as that way of life disappeared.[1]

The world that emerged in 1945 was entirely different from the world that had gone to war. On the one hand it was physically scarred and psychologically traumatized: whole cities had been destroyed, whole nations devoured and, in much of Europe and east Asia, whole communities murdered or displaced. Hundreds of millions of people had been exposed to violence on a scale they had never before imagined. On the other hand the world in 1945 was probably more unified than it had ever been. Friendships had been forged in the fires of war, and for a while there was genuine hope that these friendships could be carried forward into peacetime. The end of the war also brought feelings of release that people everywhere would remember for the rest of their lives. These two forces – the fear and the freedom – would be amongst the most important drivers in the creation of the postwar world.

This book has been an attempt to chart how the Second World War, and its material and psychological consequences, have shaped our lives. In the opening chapters I showed how, in an effort to cope with the violence and cruelty they had just witnessed, people everywhere adopted new ways of thinking. They were shown a universe populated with heroes, monsters and martyrs. They imagined the war as a titanic struggle between good and evil. They created a mythology that made sense of the incomprehensible, reassured them that their sacrifices had been worthwhile, and gave them hope that the darkness had been banished for ever.

It was such thinking that allowed the world to recover as quickly as it did. Our heroes continued to act heroically, and took responsibility for imposing order, building new institutions, and nursing shattered nations back to health. Those we considered monsters were destroyed, brought to justice, silenced, tamed, and sometimes even reformed. The victims of the war, wherever possible, retired to tend to their wounds. And everyone, everywhere, began to have faith that a new era had dawned.

Thus a time of ideals was born. In Part II I showed how these ideals inspired dreams of Utopia amongst those who were determined that mankind should learn the lessons of the war. Scientists dreamed of a world not only powered by new technologies – the jets and rockets and computers that had come out of the war – but infused with scientific ways of thinking: rational, enlightened and peaceful. Architects dreamed of radiant new cities rising phoenix-like from the rubble, where everyone would at last have access to light and air and healthy living. Social planners and philosophers saw an opportunity to bring people together, to iron out the differences between them and make the world a fairer, more equal place. It was a future not of fear, but of freedom, that they imagined.

In such an atmosphere it seemed quite natural that every dream should be a universal dream, and that every solution to our ills should be a universal solution. In Part III I showed how postwar politicians, lawyers and economists tried to create a system that would allow the whole world to act together as a single unit. The global institutions they set up in the aftermath of the Second World War were far more inclusive than any other previous institutions, and far more robust; but for some idealists they did not go far enough. These visionaries argued that if all human beings were to have the same freedoms, rights and responsibilities, then all human beings should live under the same system, and have an equal say in how that system was run. They wanted nothing short of a single world government.

It was in ideas like this that the dreams of the postwar era began to fall down. For every person who saw world government as a chance for perpetual peace there was another that imagined it as a form of perpetual enslavement. Of all the mirages that people scrambled towards in the wake of the war, the most unreachable was surely the idea of absolute universality. Thus, at exactly the same time that the world was trying to unite, it also began to fragment.

As I showed in Part IV, one of the greatest legacies of the Second World War was that it produced not a single superpower, but two, and each eyed the other's pretensions towards world domination with increasing suspicion. The Americans knew that if a world government were created there was no guarantee that it would be a democratic government: they were just as determined to stop the world from falling into Stalin's hands as they had been to stop it from falling into Hitler's. The Soviets, meanwhile, were equally committed to stopping the spread of American power, and began to use the same language of heroes, monsters and martyrs that they had adopted during the Second World War to describe their new ideological conflict with the West. This split between East and West would be duplicated all over the globe, as nations everywhere were tempted, coaxed and coerced into taking one side or the other.

It was not only the superpowers who provided a challenge to the idea of world unity. In Part V I showed how dreams of freedom, inspired by the Second World War, produced a resurgence of nationalism everywhere. People in Asia, Africa and the Middle East began to clamour for independence from the European empires that had ruled them for centuries; but their passion for self-determination sometimes resulted in nations breaking up into smaller and smaller units. In many parts of the developing world, authoritarian governments and dictatorships took power in the name of restoring order: if agreement between factions did not arise naturally, sooner or later it would be imposed, often at the expense of freedom.

The only region where nationalism was held in abeyance for a while was in Europe, but even here it burst forth occasionally in flashbacks to the Second World War. The European Union was set up in an attempt to make war between nations in Europe impossible, but in the end this institution would itself inspire dreams of national freedom. At the time of writing the EU has also begun to fragment, and nationalism is once again growing all over the continent.

In Part VI I explored some of the most destructive legacies of the Second World War, which took these divisive tendencies to their logical extreme – splitting nations, splitting communities and families, and creating a sense of trauma and loss which still burrow at the very heart of many societies today. I ended by looking at the ultimate splitting of society into its smallest constituent parts of all – individual human beings, who have been cut free from their own communities, sometimes against their will, and scattered across the globe in search of work, or opportunity, or stability. The globalization of peoples, which was yet another process vastly accelerated by the Second World War, contributed to new tensions in the richer nations, which have also become fragmented and atomized. Greater freedom has not brought greater happiness.

Individuals can also be split. Some of those who suffered severe traumas during the war found themselves unable to reconcile their experiences with who they thought they were and who they wanted to be. They found themselves cut off from the bright new future that everyone else was striving for, condemned instead to a perpetual reliving of the past. Several of the people whose stories I have told in these pages have suffered this fate – not only the victims of the war, like Otto Dov Kulka, Aharon Appelfeld, Evgeniia Kiseleva and Choi Myeong-sun, but also some of its 'monsters', like Yuasa Ken. Even some of the 'heroes' of the war – people like Ben Ferencz or Garry Davis – were unable to leave the war behind them. The things they had seen, and the lessons they learned, would follow them relentlessly for the rest of their lives.

Many of the individuals in this book found themselves split in other ways too, by internal conflicts and dilemmas that were thrown up by the situations in which they found themselves during the war and its aftermath. Both Hans Bjerkholt and Cord Meyer were forced to re-evaluate their commitment to ideas they had believed in passionately before and during the war. Bjerkholt reluctantly abandoned the Communist Party to follow his new-found spirituality, and Meyer abandoned his dream of world unity to begin a new crusade against the Soviet Union. Conversely, Anthony Curwen was driven to embrace communism, and even violent revolution, after having been a pacifist throughout the war. All of these people were forced into making such decisions by circumstances beyond their control. None made their decisions lightly.

In a similar vein, both Eugene Rabinowitch and Andrei Sakharov had to reconcile different beliefs that appeared to contradict one another: they had both worked on nuclear weapons, and yet they were both utterly committed to promoting peace and cooperation between their respective superpowers. Some people had to struggle with such dilemmas repeatedly. Carlos Delgado Chalbaud, for example, had to justify taking part in not one revolution but two – the first to install democracy in Venezuela, and the second to remove it again. Waruhiu Itote also had to make a double transition: firstly from loyal soldier to rebel against the British; secondly from rebel to peacemaker.

Almost every one of these people expressed some kind of alienation – from their countries, from their families or communities, even from themselves. The same splits that were being expressed on a global or a national scale were present on the most intimate scale of all.

This link between the global, the national and the personal is the most important part of this book. The Second World War not only changed our world – it also changed us. It brought us face to face with some of our greatest fears, and traumatized us in ways that we still have not fully acknowledged; some parts of the world have never recovered from the experience. But it also inspired us, and taught us the true value of freedom – not only political and national freedom, and freedom of worship and belief, but also personal freedom and the awesome responsibilities it places upon the individual.

It is for this reason that I have put personal stories at the very heart of this history. Such stories are not only a window to our past, but also a key to understanding why we act the way we do today. Those who think of history as a progressive force, leading us slowly but surely towards a better, more rational world, underestimate man's capacity for irrationality. History is driven as much by our collective emotions as it is by any rational march towards 'progress'. Some of the most powerful forces driving our world were either born during the Second World War, or arose from our reactions to the consequences of that war. It is only by understanding where these collective emotions have come from that we have any hope of preventing ourselves from being swept away by them.

This is not easy. We have wrapped ourselves up in a blanket of myth; and it is only by peeling this away that we can get at the roots of the fear, indignation and self-righteousness that drive so much of our thinking. Again, it is the stories of individuals that can provide us with a key. Towards the beginning of this book I told the story of Leonard Creo, who gladly accepted the medals he was given during the war, and the praise which came with them, and only came gradually to the realization that he had not really done anything heroic, but merely acted as any human being would have done in his situation. 'The army needs heroes,' he told me; 'that's why they give them medals. They've got to get the best out of these slobs.' Society also needs heroes, and it is willing to promote them as role models for the rest of us, even if that means bending or hiding the truth.[2]

If it takes time for our 'heroes' to acknowledge what really happened in the past, then the same is true for our 'monsters'. Often, they never get there. It took years of silent contemplation to force Yuasa Ken to realize that he had committed not only crimes but atrocities in China. When he finally returned to Japan after the war he was astonished to discover that none of those who had collaborated with him in these atrocities acknowledged that they had done anything wrong at all. Sometimes it is simply easier to remember a more convenient version of events than the one that actually took place.

Nations also act like this. How else can one explain the way that nations like Britain or the USA still shy away from acknowledging their lack of mercy during the Second World War, both towards those they vanquished and towards those they liberated? Or the way that nationalist factions in Japan continue to deny crimes that everyone else in the world knows they committed? Why else would the Poles or the French devote so much energy towards remembering their own 'heroic' resistance during the war, and so little towards acknowledging their own cowardice or cruelty? All nations give in to such tendencies, just as all individuals do, and they should remind themselves of this fact when fighting today's battles.

Perhaps the most damaging myths that arose from the Second World War are those of martyrdom. I have spent a great deal of this book exploring suffering: I believe it is vitally important for every nation to acknowledge the traumas it has experienced, because it is only through mourning our losses that we are able to move on. But wounded nations often like to elevate their anguish into something sacred, because to do so allows them to imagine that they had no part in their own suffering, that it was exclusively someone else's doing. Such holy innocence grants them both absolution from past sins and justification for future ones. Rather than examining their loss in order to come to terms with it, they clutch their grief like a weapon, and transform it into holy indignation.

These are the kinds of emotions deliberately stirred up by those who wish to exploit them for their own gain – unscrupulous politicians, media moguls, religious demagogues and so on. They invite us to lose ourselves in the righteous power of the crowd. Those who answer their call and allow themselves to be swept away in communal emotion can gain both a sense of purpose and a sense of belonging, but only at the expense of giving up their freedom. If the Second World War should have taught us anything, it is that freedom, once abdicated, is rarely regained easily.

Unfortunately, embracing freedom is not an easy option either. True freedom requires us to step out of the crowd, even to stand up to it occasionally, and to think for ourselves whenever we can. It obliges us to face our losses squarely and honestly, to understand that we too made mistakes, and played a part in our own suffering. A free person is a person burdened with responsibility and uncomfortable truths.

Once again, personal stories from people who survived the war can provide us with examples of how to walk this lonely path. I began this book with the story of Georgina Sand, and I shall end it with her too. A child refugee from Austria, she was forced to make a new life for herself in Britain. After repeated displacements over a period of ten years, she finally settled down with her husband in London, but she knows that the experience damaged her along the way. 'For many years I didn't talk to anyone about what I'd gone through. My children never knew. Only when I got older, and the children were grown up already did it come back to me, but I didn't want to talk about it. It was too painful.' She knows that her marriage was not always a happy one, that her husband sometimes treated her like the child she was when she first met him, and that she herself passively allowed him to organize their lives, as if she were still as helpless as she had been as a refugee during the war. She also acknowledged that she made mistakes with her children, and that she has passed her own unbearable anxiety on to them. And she has long since reconciled herself to the fact that she will always be an outsider, no matter how long she lives. 'But I'm calmer now,' she told me. 'I appreciate what I've got. The experiences were painful at times. But look, maybe in a way it made me.'

All of the people in this book were forced to come to similar conclusions. The Second World War remained a fixed point in all of their lives, but as the world changed around them they each came to the gradual realization that the ways of thinking they had adopted in order to cope with the war were no longer serving them well. If they wanted to grasp a new future, they had no choice but to face their old fears and resentments, and do whatever they could to let them go.

Unless we too can reconcile ourselves to the traumas and disappointments that have come our way since the war, we will be doomed to repeat the mistakes of the past. If we can't embrace the richness and complexities of life, however painful, we will reach for comforting simplicities instead. We will continue to tell ourselves stories of heroes who can do no wrong, and monsters who are the irredeemable embodiment of evil. We will continue to imagine ourselves as martyrs, whose suffering makes us holy and justifies our every action, no matter how wicked. And no doubt we will continue to couch these myths in the language of the Second World War, just as we have done ever since 1945, as if the decades that separate us from that time never happened.

Acknowledgements

I would like to thank the staff of the many global, national and regional archives and libraries I have consulted during the five years that it took to write this book: they have, without exception, been courteous and helpful, sometimes above and beyond the call of duty. Chief amongst these institutions is the British Library, whose foreign-language collections are second to none, and without which this book would have been impossible. All other institutions are listed in the notes at the end of this book.

I would also like to thank Eleo Gordon, Daniel Crewe, Michael Flamini, and my many editors in other parts of the world who have shown faith in me and my books. And not only the editors, but also the many translators, publicists, marketers, salespeople and others who have been involved in the production of this book. As a former editor myself, I appreciate that publishing is a communal effort, and while authors and editors invariably get the credit, much of the hard work is done by others behind the scenes. Thanks must also go to my agents Simon Trewin and Jay Mandel, whose help and advice have been invaluable.

This book would not have been possible without the help of a variety of people who translated documents for me, guided me through some of my foreign-language research and helped me to get hold of documents that would otherwise have remained inaccessible. In particular I would like to thank Ben Groom, Dave Rickwood, Andrew Walkley, Lisa Sjukur, Tuti Suwidjiningsih, Kenneth Noble, Rie Nakanishi, James Dawes, Jeong Ho-Cheol and Tomoko Smidt-Olsen. I am also greatly indebted to all those who consented to me using their stories and photographs, and particularly those who I interviewed and corresponded with: Georgina Sand, Leonard Creo, Otto Dov Kulka, Nagai Tokusaburou, Ben Ferencz and his son Don, Gabriel Bach, Aharon Appelfeld and Dittmann Mendel. If there are any mistakes or omissions in the preceding pages – and there are bound to be many – they are my fault, and mine alone.

Finally, as is traditional, I would like to thank my wife, Liza and my children, Gabriel and Grace, to whom this book is dedicated. I do this not for tradition's sake, but out of a sense of huge personal debt: for five years they have put up with my repeated absences, neglect of my family duties and prolonged withdrawals from our everyday life into a world that must, to my children at least, seem like ancient history. I hope that one day they will read these pages and come to realize that what has taken me away from them so often has not been an unhealthy preoccupation with the past, but a concern for the present, and a hope that the world might one day come to terms with the anxieties and traumas that have affected us all.

Bibliography

Abercrombie, Patrick, *The Greater London Plan 1944* (London: HMSO, 1945)

Adenauer, Konrad, *Journey to America: Collected Speeches, Statements, Press, Radio and TV Interviews* (Washington, DC: Press Office, German Diplomatic Mission, 1953)

Adenauer, Konrad, *World Indivisible: With Liberty and Justice for All*, trans. Richard and Clara Winston (New York: Harper & Bros, 1955)

Adorno, Theodor, *Minima Moralia*, trans. E. F. N. Jephcott (London: Verso, 2005)

Afontsev, Sergey et al., 'The Urban Household in Russia and the Soviet Union, 1900–2000: Patterns of Family Formation in a Turbulent Century', *History of the Family*, vol. 13, no. 2 (2008)

Aizenberg, Edna, 'Nation and Holocaust Narration: Uruguay's Memorial del Holocausto del Pueblo Judío', in Jeffrey Lesser and Raanan Reín (eds), *Rethinking Jewish-Latin Americans* (Albuquerque: University of New Mexico Press, 2008)

Al-Ali, Nadje, *Secularism, Gender and the State in the Middle East: The Egyptian Women's Movement* (Cambridge University Press, 2009)

Albrecht, Mireille, *Berty* (Paris: Robert Laffont, 1986)

Alexander, Robert J., *Rómulo Betancourt and the Transformation of Venezuela* (New Brunswick, NJ: Transaction Books, 1982)

Alexiyevich, Svetlana, *War's Unwomanly Face*, trans. Keith Hammond and Lyudmila Lezhneva (Moscow: Progress, 1988)

Ali, H. M. Wajid, *India and the Non-Aligned Movement* (New Delhi: Adam Publishers & Distributors, 2004)

Aluit, Alfonso J., *By Sword and Fire: The Destruction of Manila in World War II, 3 February – 3 March 1945* (Manila: National Commission for Culture and the Arts, 1994)

Amir, Ruth, *Who is Afraid of Historical Redress?* (Boston, MA: Academic Studies Press, 2012)

Ammendolia, Ilario, *Occupazione delle Terre in Calabria, 1945–1949* (Rome: Gangemi, 1990)

Anderson, Benedict R. O'G., *Java in a Time of Revolution: Occupation and Resistance, 1944–1946* (Ithaca, NY: Cornell University Press, 1972)

Anderson, David, *Histories of the Hanged* (London: Weidenfeld & Nicolson, 2005)

Anon., '*Historikerstreit*': *Die Dokumentation der Kontroverse um die Einzigartigkeit der nationalsozialistischen Judenvernichtung* (Munich: Piper, 1991)

Anon., *The Seventh Day: Soldiers' Talk About the Six-Day War* (London: André Deutsch, 1970)

Anon., *A Woman in Berlin* (London: Virago, 2006)

Appelfeld, Aharon, *The Story of a Life* (Harmondsworth: Penguin, 2006)

Appelfeld, Aharon, *Table for One* (New Milford, CT: The Toby Press, 2007)

Applebaum, Anne, *Gulag* (London: Allen Lane, 2003)

Arendt, Hannah, *Eichmann in Jerusalem* (Harmondsworth: Penguin, 1994)

Aronson, Ronald and Adrian van den Hoven (eds), *We Have Only This Life to Live: The Selected Essays of Jean-Paul Sartre* (New York Review of Books, 2013)

Arthur, Max, *Forgotten Voices of the Second World War* (London: Ebury Press, 2004)

Atkinson, Rick, *The Guns at Last Light* (London: Little, Brown, 2013)

Attwood, Lynne, *Creating the New Soviet Woman* (Basingstoke: Macmillan, 1999)

Augustine, Dolores L., 'Learning from War: Media Coverage of the Nuclear Age in the Two Germanies', in van Lente (ed.), *The Nuclear Age in Popular Media*

Baert, Patrick, *The Existentialist Moment* (Cambridge: Polity Press, 2015)

Barghoorn, Frederick Charles, *Soviet Russian Nationalism* (New York: Oxford University Press, 1956)

Barnett, Donald L. and Karari Njama, *Mau Mau from Within* (New York: Modern Reader Paperbacks, 1970)

Bartov, Hanoch, *Each Had Six Wings* (Merhavia: Sifriat Poalim, 1954)

Batinić, Jelena, *Women and Yugoslav Partisans* (New York: Cambridge University Press, 2015)

Bauer, Catherine, 'The County of London Plan – American Reactions: Planning is Politics – But are Planners Politicians?', *Architectural Review*, vol. 96, no. 573 (1944)

Bedi, Freda, *Bengal Lamenting* (Lahore: The Lion Press, 1944)

Beevor, Antony, *The Second World War* (London: Weidenfeld & Nicolson, 2012)

Beevor, Antony, *Stalingrad* (London: Viking, 1998)

Bell, Daniel, *The End of Ideology* (New York: The Free Press, 1965)

Bell, P. M. H., *The World Since 1945* (London: Bloomsbury Academic, 2010)

Ben-Gurion, David, *Israel: A Personal History* (New York: Funk & Wagnalls, 1971)

Berger, Ronald J., *The Holocaust, Religion and the Politics of Collective Memory* (New Brunswick, NJ: Transaction Publishers, 2013)

Bergman, Jay, *Meeting the Demands of Reason: The Life and Thought of Andrei Sakharov* (Ithaca, NY: Cornell University Press, 2009)

Berry, Michael, 'Cinematic Representations of the Rape of Nanking', in Peter Li (ed.), *Japanese War Crimes* (New Brunswick, NJ: Transaction Publishers, 2009)

Bérubé, Allan, *Coming Out Under Fire: The History of Gay Men and Women in World War II* (Chapel Hill: University of North Carolina Press, 2010)

Bessel, Richard, *Nazism and War* (London: Weidenfeld & Nicolson, 2004)

Bethell, Leslie and Ian Roxborough (eds), *Latin America Between the Second World War and the Cold War, 1944–1948* (New York: Cambridge University Press, 1992)

Bird, Kai and Martin J. Sherwin, *American Prometheus: The Triumph and Tragedy of J. Robert Oppenheimer* (New York: Random House, 2005)

Bier, Jean-Paul, 'The Holocaust, West Germany and Strategies of Oblivion, 1947–1979', in Anson Rabinbach and Jack Zipes (eds), *Germans and Jews Since the Holocaust* (New York: Holmes & Meier, 1986)

Bohec, Jeanne, *La plastiqueuse à bicyclette* (Paris: Mercure de France, 1975)

Bohlen, Charles E., *Witness to History* (New York: W. W. Norton, 1973)

Bose, Sugata, 'Starvation Amidst Plenty: The Making of Famine in Bengal, Honan and Tonkin, 1942–45', *Modern Asian Studies*, vol. 24, no. 4 (1990)

Bourdrel, Philippe, *L'épuration sauvage* (Paris: Perrin, 2002)

Boyer, Paul, *By the Bomb's Early Light* (Chapel Hill: University of North Carolina Press, 1994)

Bridger, Susan, 'Soviet Rural Women: Employment and Family Life', in Beatrice Farnsworth and Lynne Viola (eds), *Russian Peasant Women* (New York: Oxford University Press, 1992)

Bridgman, P. W., 'Scientists and Social Responsibility', *Bulletin of the Atomic Scientists*, vol. 4, no. 3 (1948)

Brokaw, Tom, *The Greatest Generation* (London: Pimlico, 2002)

Brosse, Thérèse, *War-Handicapped Children* (Paris: UNESCO, 1950)

Browning, Christopher R., *Ordinary Men: Reserve Police Battalion 101 and the Final Solution in Poland* (New York: HarperCollins, 1992)

Broyard, Anatole, 'Portrait of the Inauthentic Negro', *Commentary*, vol. 10, no. 1 (1950)

Bryant, Mark, *World War II in Cartoons* (London: Grub Street, 1989)

Buchman, Frank N. D., *Remaking the World: The Speeches of Frank N. D. Buchman* (London: Blandford, 1947)

Buder, Stanley, *Visionaries and Planners: The Garden City Movement and the Modern Community* (New York: Oxford University Press, 1990)

Bùi Minh Dũng, 'Japan's Role in the Vietnamese Starvation of 1944–45', *Modern Asian Studies*, vol. 29, no. 3 (1995)

Buisson, Patrick, *1940–1945: Années érotiques* (Paris: Albin Michel, 2009)

Burleigh, Michael, *Small Wars, Far Away Places* (London: Macmillan, 2013)

Buruma, Ian, *Year Zero: A History of 1945* (London: Atlantic, 2013)

Butter, Michael, *The Epitome of Evil: Hitler in American Fiction, 1939–2002* (New York: Palgrave Macmillan, 2009)

Byfield, Judith A. et al. (eds), *Africa and World War II* (New York: Cambridge University Press, 2015)

Calhoun, Craig (ed.), *Dictionary of the Social Sciences* (New York: Oxford University Press, 2002)

Cannadine, David (ed.), *Blood, Toil, Tears and Sweat: Winston Churchill's Famous Speeches* (London: Cassell & Co., 1989)

Carton, Evan, 'The Holocaust, French Poststructuralism, the American Literary Academy, and Jewish Identity Politics', in Peter C. Herman (ed.), *Historicizing Theory* (Albany: State University of New York Press, 2004)

Castles, Stephen and Mark J. Miller, *The Age of Migration*, 3rd edn (New York: Palgrave Macmillan, 2003)

Ceplair, Larry, *Anti-Communism in Twentieth-Century America* (Santa Barbara, CA: Praeger, 2011)

Cerf-Ferrière, René, *Le Chemin Clandestin* (Paris: Julliard, 1968)

Chain, Ernst, 'A Short History of the Penicillin Discovery from Fleming's Early Observations in 1929 to the Present Time', in John Parascandola (ed.), *The History of Antibiotics: A Symposium* (Madison, WI: American Institute of the History of Pharmacy, 1980)

Chamberlin, William Charles, *Economic Development of Iceland through World War II* (New York: Columbia University Press, 1947)

Chang Kia-Ngau, *The Inflationary Spiral: The Experience in China, 1939–1950* (Cambridge, MA: Technology Press of the Massachusetts Institute of Technology, 1958)

Chase, William C., *Front Line General: The Commands of Maj. Gen. Wm. C. Chase* (Houston: Pacesetter Press, 1975)

Cheah Boon Kheng, *Red Star Over Malaya*, 3rd edn (Singapore University Press, 2003)

Cheong, Sung-Hwa, *The Politics of Anti-Japanese Sentiment in Korea* (Westport, CT: Greenwood Press, 1991)

Cheyette, Bryan, 'Israel', in John Sturrock (ed.), *The Oxford Guide to Contemporary World Literature* (Oxford University Press, 1996)

Chittaprosad, *Hungry Bengal* (Bombay: no publisher, 1944)

Claudin, Fernando, *The Communist Movement: From Comintern to Cominform* (Harmondsworth: Penguin, 1975)

Clay, Lucius D., *Decision in Germany* (London: William Heinemann, 1950)

Cline, Sharon Elise, '*Féminité à la Française*: Femininity, Social Change and French National Identity, 1945–1970', PhD Thesis, University of Wisconsin–Madison, 2008

Clough, Marshall S., *Mau Mau Memoirs: History, Memory and Politics* (Boulder, CO: Lynne Rienner, 1998)

Coleman, Alice, *Utopia on Trial* (London: Hilary Shipman, 1985)

Collingham, Lizzie, *The Taste of War* (London: Allen Lane, 2011)

Committee to Frame a World Constitution, *The Preliminary Draft of a World Constitution* (University of Chicago Press, 1948)

Connolly, Tracey, 'Emigration from Ireland to Britain During the Second World War', in Andy Bielenberg (ed.), *The Irish Diaspora* (London: Pearson Education, 2000)

Conot, Robert E., *Justice at Nuremberg* (London: Weidenfeld & Nicolson, 1983)

Conway, Ed, *The Summit* (London: Little, Brown, 2014)

Conway, Martin, 'Justice in Postwar Belgium: Popular Passions and Political Realities', in István Deák, Jan T. Gross and Tony Judt (eds), *The Politics of Retribution in Europe* (Princeton University Press, 2000)

Cullather, Nick, *Secret History: The CIA's Classified Account of Its Operations in Guatemala, 1952–1954* (Stanford University Press, 1999)

Currie, Robert, Alan Gilbert and Lee Horsley, *Churches and Churchgoers: Patterns of Church Growth in the British Isles since 1700* (Oxford: Clarendon Press, 1977)

D'Imperio, Ocarina Castillo, *Carlos Delgado Chalbaud* (Caracas: El Nacional, 2006)

Dahl, Hans Fredrik, 'Dealing with the Past in Scandinavia', in Jon Elster (ed.), *Retribution and Reparation in the Transition to Democracy* (New York: Cambridge University Press, 2006)

Danilova, Nataliya, *The Politics of War Commemoration in the UK and Russia* (Basingstoke: Palgrave Macmillan, 2015)

Daves, Joseph H., *The Indonesian Army from Revolusi to Reformasi*, vol. 1: *The Struggle for Independence and the Sukarno Era*; vol. 2: *Soeharto and the New Order* (Self published: printed by CreateSpace, Charleston, 2013)

Davidson, Eugene, *The Death and Life of Germany* (London: Jonathan Cape, 1959)

Davies, Norman, *God's Playground* (New York: Oxford University Press, 2005)

Davies, Norman, *Rising '44* (London: Pan, 2004)

Davis, Garry, *The World is My Country* (New York: G. P. Putnam's Sons, 1961)

Dawidowicz, Lucy, *The War Against the Jews, 1933–1945* (Harmondsworth: Pelican, 1979)

de Beauvoir, Simone, *The Second Sex*, trans. H. M. Parshley (London: Picador, 1988)

de Haan, Francisca, 'Hoffnungen auf eine bessere Welt: Die frühen Jahre der Internationalen Demokratischen Frauenföderation (IDFF/WIDF) (1945–50)', *Feministische Studien*, vol. 27, no. 2 (2009)

Delaney, Edna, 'Placing Irish Postwar Migration to Britain in a Comparative European Perspective, 1945–1981', in Andy Bielenberg (ed.), *The Irish Diaspora* (London: Pearson Education, 2000)

Delbo, Charlotte, *Convoy to Auschwitz: Women of the French Resistance* (Boston, MA: Northeastern University Press, 1997)

Deletant, Dennis, *Communist Terror in Romania* (London: Hurst & Co., 1999)

Della Sala, Vincent, 'Myth and the Postnational Polity: The Case of the European Union', in Gérard Bouchard (ed.), *National Myths* (Oxford: Routledge, 2013)

Diamond, Hanna, *Women and the Second World War in France, 1939–48: Choices and Constraints* (Harlow: Longman, 1999)

Diefendorf, Jeffry M., *In the Wake of War* (New York: Oxford University Press, 1993)

Diefendorf, Jeffry M. (ed.), *Rebuilding Europe's Bombed Cities* (Basingstoke: Macmillan, 1990)

Diner, Hasia R., *We Remember with Reverence and Love: American Jews and the Myth of Silence after the Holocaust, 1945–1962* (New York and London: New York University Press, 2009)

Djilas, Milovan, *Conversations with Stalin*, trans. Michael B. Petrovich (New York: Harcourt Brace Jovanovich, 1962)

Dolgopol, Ustinia and Snehal Paranjape, *Comfort Women: An Unfinished Ordeal: Report of a Mission* (Geneva: International Commission of Jurists, 1994)

Donovan, Robert J., *Conflict and Crisis: The Presidency of Harry S. Truman, 1945–48* (New York: W. W. Norton, 1977)

Douglas, R. M., *The Labour Party, Nationalism and Internationalism, 1939–1951* (London: Routledge, 2004)

Douglas, R. M., *Orderly and Humane: The Expulsion of the Germans After the Second World War* (New Haven, CT: Yale University Press, 2012)

Dower, John W., *Embracing Defeat: Japan in the Wake of World War II* (New York: W. W. Norton, 2000)

Dower, John W., *War Without Mercy: Race and Power in the Pacific War* (New York: Pantheon, 1986)

Driberg, Tom, *The Mystery of Moral Re-Armament: A Study of Frank Buchman and His Movement* (London: Secker & Warburg, 1964)

Du Bois, W. E. B., *The World and Africa/Color and Democracy* (New York: Oxford University Press, 2007)

Duchen, Claire, *Women's Rights and Women's Lives in France, 1944–1968* (London: Routledge, 1994)

Duignan, Peter, *NATO: Its Past, Present, and Future* (Stanford: Hoover Institution Press, 2000)

Dunlap, Thomas R., *DDT: Scientists, Citizens, and Public Policy* (Princeton University Press, 1981)

Dupuy, R. Ernest and Trevor N. Dupuy, *The Harper Encyclopedia of Military History*, 4th edn (New York: HarperCollins, 1993)

Durkheim, Émile, *The Elementary Forms of the Religious Life*, trans. Joseph Ward Swain (London: George Allen and Unwin, 1915)

Düwel, Jörn and Niels Gutschow (eds), *A Blessing in Disguise* (Berlin: Dom, 2013)

Edmondson, Locksley, 'Reparations: Pan-African and Jewish Experiences', in William F. S. Miles (ed.), *Third World Views of the Holocaust: Summary of the International Symposium* (Boston, MA: Northeastern University, 2002)

Einstein, Albert, 'A Reply to the Soviet Scientists', *Bulletin of the Atomic Scientists*, vol. 4, no. 2 (1948)

Eisen, Jonathan (ed.), *The Glasnost Reader* (New York: New American Library, 1990)

Eister, Allan W., *Drawing-Room Conversion: A Sociological Account of the Oxford Group Movement* (Durham, NC: Duke University Press, 1950)

Elkins, Caroline, *Britain's Gulag: The Brutal End of Empire in Kenya* (London: Bodley Head, 2014)

Emanuel, Muriel (ed.), *Contemporary Architects* (Basingstoke: Macmillan, 1980)

Emmons, Caroline S. (ed.), *Cold War and McCarthy Era: People and Perspectives* (Santa Barbara, CA: ABC-Clio, 2010)

English Translation Group, *The Witness of Those Two Days: Hiroshima & Nagasaki August 6 & 9, 1945*, 2 vols (Tokyo: Japan Confederation of A- and H-Bomb Sufferers Organization, 1989)

Entwistle, Basil and John McCook Roots, *Moral Re-Armament: What Is It?* (Los Angeles: Pace, 1967)

Escoda, Jose Ma. Bonifacio M., *Warsaw of Asia: The Rape of Manila* (Quezon City: Giraffe Books, 2000)

Evans, Peter, *Law and Disorder: Scenes from Life in Kenya* (London: Secker & Warburg, 1956)

Evatt, Herbert V., *The Task of Nations* (New York: Duell, Sloan & Pearce, 1949)

Falconi, Carlo, *La Chiesa e le organizzazioni cattoliche in Italia (1945–1955)* (Rome: Einaudi, 1956)

Famine Inquiry Commission, *Report on Bengal* (New Delhi: Government of India, 1945)

Fiddes, Paul S., *Past Event and Present Salvation: The Christian Idea of Atonement* (London: Darton, Longman & Todd, 1989)

Field, John, *Social Capital* (Oxford: Routledge, 2008)

Figes, Orlando, *The Whisperers* (London: Allen Lane, 2007)

Fish, Hamilton, *The Challenge of World Communism* (Milwaukee: Bruce Publishing Co., 1946)

Fishman, Sarah, 'Waiting for the Captive Sons of France: Prisoner of War Wives, 1940–1945', in Margaret Higonnet et al. (eds), *Behind the Lines: Gender and the Two World Wars* (New Haven, CT: Yale University Press, 1987)

Ford, Brian J., *Secret Weapons: Technology, Science and the Race to Win World War II* (Oxford: Osprey, 2011)

Foreign Broadcast Information Service, *East Europe Report* (Arlington, VA: Joint Publications Research Service, 25 June 1985)

Foulkes, S. H., *Introduction to Group-Analytic Psychotherapy* (London: Heinemann, 1948)

Franck, Thomas M., *Nation Against Nation: What Happened to the UN Dream and What the US Can Do About It* (New York: Oxford University Press, 1985)

Frederick, William H., *Visions and Heat: The Making of the Indonesian Revolution* (Athens: Ohio University Press, 1989)

Freeman, Gary P., *Immigrant Labor and Racial Conflict in Industrial Societies: The French and British Experience, 1945–1975* (Princeton University Press, 2015)

Freud, Sigmund, 'Beyond the Pleasure Principle' (1920), reproduced in Salman Akhtar and Mary Kay O'Neil (eds), *On Freud's 'Beyond the Pleasure Principle'* (London: Karnac, 2011)

Freud, Sigmund, *Civilization and its Discontents* (Harmondsworth: Penguin, 2002)

Frey, Eric, *Das Hitler Syndrom* (Frankfurt-am-Main: Eichborn, 2005)

Friedländer, Saul, 'West Germany and the Burden of the Past: The Ongoing Debate', *Jerusalem Quarterly*, vol. 42 (1987)

Friedrich, Jörg, *The Fire: The Bombing of Germany, 1940–1945* (New York: Columbia University Press, 2006)

Friel, Ian, *Maritime History of Britain and Ireland* (London: British Museum Press, 2003)

Frisch, O. R., *Meet the Atoms: A Popular Guide to Modern Physics* (New York: A. A. Wyn, 1947)

Fromm, Erich, *The Fear of Freedom* (Oxford: Routledge Classics, 2001)

Fukuda-Parr, Sakiko, Terra Lawson-Remer and Susan Randolph, *Fulfilling Social and Economic Rights* (New York: Oxford University Press, 2015)

Gaglione, Anthony, *The United Nations Under Trygve Lie, 1945–1953* (Lanham, MD: Scarecrow Press, 2001)

Gamow, George, *Atomic Energy in Cosmic and Human Life* (New York: Macmillan, 1946)

Ganson, Nicholas, *The Soviet Famine of 1946–47 in Global and Historical Perspective* (Basingstoke: Palgrave Macmillan, 2009)

Garland, Caroline (ed.), *Understanding Trauma: A Psychoanalytical Approach* (London: Karnac Books, 2002)

Ghosh, Prodyot, *Chittaprosad: A Doyen of Art-World* (Calcutta: Shilpayan Artists Society, 1995)

Giedion, Sigfried, *Space, Time & Architecture*, 5th edn (Cambridge, MA: Harvard University Press, 2008)

Gilbert, Martin, *Israel: A History* (London: Black Swan, 1999)

Gildea, Robert, *Fighters in the Shadows* (London: Faber & Faber, 2015)

Gill, Graeme, *Symbols and Legitimacy in Soviet Politics* (Cambridge University Press, 2011)

Ginsborg, Paul, 'The Communist Party and the Agrarian Question in Southern Italy, 1943–48', *History Workshop*, vol. 17 (1984)

Gitelman, Zvi, 'Comparative and Competitive Victimization in the Post-Communist Sphere', in Alvin H. Rosenfeld (ed.), *Resurgent Antisemitism: Global Perspectives* (Bloomington: Indiana University Press, 2013)

Glass, Charles, *Deserter* (London: HarperPress, 2013)

Glynn, Paul, *A Song for Nagasaki* (London: Fount Paperbacks, 1990)

Goldberg, Michael, *Why Should Jews Survive?* (New York: Oxford University Press, 1995)

Goldberg, Ronald Allen, *America in the Forties* (Syracuse University Press, 2012)

Goldhagen, Daniel, *Hitler's Willing Executioners: Ordinary Germans and the Holocaust* (London: Little, Brown, 1996)

Gopalaswami, R. A. (ed.), *Census of India, 1951* (Delhi: Government of India Press, 1955)

Greenberg, Gershon, 'Crucifixion and the Holocaust: The Views of Pius XII and the Jews', in Carol Rittner and John K. Roth (eds), *Pope Pius XII and the Holocaust* (London: Continuum, 2002)

Greenough, Paul R., *Prosperity and Misery in Modern Bengal: The Famine of 1943–1944* (New York: Oxford University Press, 1982)

Griffing, Sean M. et al., 'Malaria Control and Elimination, in Venezuela, 1800s–1970s', *Emerging Infectious Diseases*, vol. 20, no. 10 (2014)

Grisard, Dominique, 'Female Terrorists and Vigilant Citizens: Gender, Citizenship and Cold War Direct-Democracy', in Jadwiga E. Pieper Mooney and Fabio Lanza (eds), *De-Centering Cold War History* (Oxford: Routledge, 2013)

Grynberg, Michał (ed.), *Words to Outlive Us: Eyewitness Accounts from the Warsaw Ghetto* (London: Granta, 2003)

Guhan, S., 'The World Bank's Lending in South Asia', in Devesh Kapur, John P. Lewis and Richard Webb (eds), *The World Bank: Its First Half Century* (Washington, DC: Brookings Institution Press, 1997)

Hachiya, Michihiko, *Hiroshima Diary*, ed. and trans. Warner Wells (Chapel Hill: University of North Carolina Press, 1955)

Hager, Kurt, 'Der Sozialismus ist Unbesiegbar', *Einheit*, vol. 40, nos 4–5 (1985)

Hailbronner, Kay, 'Asylum Law Reform in the German Constitution', *American University International Law Review*, vol. 9, no. 4 (1994)

Halberstam, David, *War in a Time of Peace: Bush, Clinton and the Generals* (London: Bloomsbury, 2003)

Ham, Paul, *Hiroshima Nagasaki* (London: Doubleday, 2012)

Harriman, W. Averell and Elie Abel, *Special Envoy to Churchill and Stalin, 1941–1946* (London: Hutchinson, 1976)

Harrison, Mark (ed.), *The Economics of World War II* (Cambridge University Press, 1998)

Hartwell, R. M., *A History of the Mont Pelerin Society* (Indianapolis: Liberty Fund, 1995)

Hasan, Mushirul (ed.), *Nehru's India: Select Speeches* (New Delhi: Oxford University Press, 2007)

Hastings, Max, *All Hell Let Loose: The World at War, 1939–1945* (London: HarperPress, 2011)

Hastings, Max, *Armageddon: The Battle for Germany, 1944–45* (London: Macmillan, 2004)

Hatherley, Owen, *Landscapes of Communism* (London: Allen Lane, 2015)

Hausner, Gideon, *Justice in Jerusalem* (London: Thomas Nelson, 1966)

Hayek, F. A., *The Road to Serfdom* (London: Routledge, 1944)

Haynes, Roslynn D., *From Faust to Strangelove: Representations of the Scientist in Western Literature* (Baltimore: Johns Hopkins University Press, 1994)

Heer, Hannes, *'Hitler war's': die Befreiung der Deutschen von ihrer Vergangenheit* (Berlin: Aufbau, 2008)

Helfand, W. H. et al., 'Wartime Industrial Development of Penicillin in the United States', in John Parascandola (ed.), *The History of Antibiotics: A Symposium* (Madison, WI: American Institute of the History of Pharmacy, 1980)

Hitchcock, William I., *Liberation* (London: Faber & Faber, 2008)

Hixson, Walter L. (ed.), *The American Experience in World War II*, vol. 12: *The United States Transformed: The Lessons and Legacies of the Second World War* (London: Routledge, 2003)

Ho Chi Minh, 'Declaration of Independence of the Democratic Republic of Vietnam', in Gregory Allen Olson (ed.), *Landmark Speeches on the Vietnam War* (College Station: Texas A&M University Press, 2010)

Hochschild, Arlie Russell, *Strangers in Their Own Land* (New York: New Press, 2016)

Hodgson, Godfrey, *America in Our Time* (Garden City, NY: Doubleday, 1976; repr. Princeton University Press, 2005)

Hofmann, Tom, *Benjamin Ferencz: Nuremberg Prosecutor and Peace Advocate* (Jefferson, NC: McFarland, 2014)

Hofstadter, Richard, *Anti-Intellectualism in American Life* (New York: Knopf, 1963)

Holloway, David, *Stalin and the Bomb* (New Haven, CT: Yale University Press, 1994)

Holmes, Colin, *John Bull's Island: Immigration and British Society* (Basingstoke: Macmillan, 1988)

Holtzman, Avner, ' "They Are Different People": Holocaust Survivors as Reflected in the Fiction of the Generation of 1948', *Yad Vashem Studies*, vol. 30 (2002)

Hondius, Dienke, *Return: Holocaust Survivors and Dutch Anti-Semitism* (Westport, CT: Praeger, 2003)

Hopper, Earl and Haim Weinberg (eds), *The Social Unconscious in Persons, Groups and Societies*, vol. 1: *Mainly Theory* (London: Karnac, 2011)

Horne, Alistair, *A Savage War of Peace* (London: Macmillan, 1977)

Howard, Ebenezer, *To-morrow: A Peaceful Path to Real Reform* (London: Swan Sonnenschein, 1898)

Howard, Keith (ed.), *True Stories of the Korean Comfort Women*, trans. Young Joo Lee (London: Cassell, 1995)

Howson, Susan and Donald Moggridge (eds), *The Wartime Diaries of Lionel Robbins and James Meade, 1943–45* (Basingstoke: Macmillan, 1990)

Hutton, J. H. (ed.), *Census of India: Part I Report* (Delhi: Manager of Publications, 1933)

Hyde, David, 'The Nairobi General Strike (1950): From Protest to Insurgency', in Andrew Burton (ed.), *The Urban Experience in Eastern Africa c.1750–2000* (Nairobi: British Institute in Eastern Africa, 2002)

Iliffe, John, *A Modern History of Tanganyika* (Cambridge University Press, 1979)

Independent Commission of Experts – Second World War, *Switzerland, National Socialism and the Second World War: Final Report*, trans. Rosamund Bandi et al. (Zürich: Pendo Verlag, 2002)

International Military Tribunal, *Trials of the Major War Criminals Before the International Military Tribunal* (Nuremberg: International Military Tribunal, 1947–9)

Isaacman, Allen, 'Peasants and Rural Social Protests in Africa', *African Studies Review*, vol. 33, no. 2 (1990)

Israel, Adrienne M., 'Ex-Servicemen at the Crossroads: Protest and Politics in Post-war Ghana', *Journal of Modern African Studies*, vol. 30, no. 2 (1992)

Issawi, Charles, *An Economic History of the Middle East and North Africa* (New York: Columbia University Press, 1982)

Itote, Waruhiu, *'Mau Mau' General* (Nairobi: East African Publishing House, 1967)

Jackson, Ashley, *Botswana, 1939–1945* (Oxford: Clarendon Press, 1999)

Jackson, Ashley, *The British Empire and the Second World War* (London: Hambledon Continuum, 2006)

Jacobs, Jane, *The Death and Life of Great American Cities* (London: Jonathan Cape, 1962)

Jager, Sheila Miyoshi, *Brothers at War: The Unending Conflict in Korea* (New York: W. W. Norton, 2013)

James, Martin W. III, *A Political History of the Civil War in Angola, 1974–1990* (New Brunswick, NJ: Transaction Books, 2011)

Jensen, Olaf and Claus-Christian W. Szejnmann (eds), *Ordinary People as Mass Murderers* (Basingstoke: Palgrave Macmillan, 2008)

Jinwung, Kim, *A History of Korea* (Bloomington: Indiana University Press, 2012)

Johnstone, Patrick, *The Future of the Global Church: History, Trends and Possibilities* (Downers Grove, IL: InterVarsity Press, 2011)

Jones, Emrys, 'Aspects of Urbanization in Venezuela', *Ekistics*, vol. 18, no. 109 (1964)

Jordaan, L. J., *Nachtmerrie over Nederland: Een herinneringsalbum* (Amsterdam: De Groene Amsterdammer, 1945)

Judt, Tony, *Postwar* (London: Pimlico, 2005)

Jungk, Robert, *Brighter Than a Thousand Suns*, trans. James Cleugh (London: Victor Gollancz, 1958)

Kahn, Albert Eugene, *High Treason: The Plot Against the People* (New York: Lear Publishers, 1950)

Kakembo, Robert, *An African Soldier Speaks* (London: Edinburgh House Press, 1946)

Karesh, Sara E. and Mitchell M. Hurvitz, *Encyclopedia of Judaism* (New York: Facts on File, 2006)

Kargon, Robert H. and Arthur P. Molella, *Invented Edens: Techno-Cities of the Twentieth Century* (Cambridge, MA: MIT Press, 2008)

Karpf, Anne, *The War After* (London: Minerva, 1997)

Keen, Sam, *Faces of the Enemy: Reflections of the Hostile Imagination: The Psychology of Enmity* (San Francisco: Harper & Row, 1986)

Kenez, Peter, *Hungary from the Nazis to the Soviets* (New York: Cambridge University Press, 2006)

Kennan, George, *Memoirs, 1925–1950* (Boston, MA: Little, Brown, 1967)

Kennan, George (under the pseudonym 'X'), 'The Sources of Soviet Conduct', *Foreign Affairs*, vol. 25, no. 4 (1947)

Kennedy, Paul, *The Parliament of Man* (London: Allen Lane, 2006)

Kenya Cost of Living Commission, *Cost of Living Commission Report* (Nairobi, 1950)

Kern, Friedrich, *Österreich: Offene Grenze der Menschlichkeit* (Vienna: Bundesministeriums für Inneres, 1959)

Khrushchev, Nikita, *Khrushchev Remembers*, trans. and ed. Strobe Talbott (Boston, MA: Little, Brown, 1970)

Killingray, David, 'African Civilians in the Era of the Second World War, c.1939–1950', in John Laband (ed.), *Daily Lives of Civilians in Wartime Africa* (Westport, CT: Greenwood Press, 2007)

Killingray, David, 'Soldiers, Ex-Servicemen and Politics in the Gold Coast, 1939–50', *Journal of Modern African Studies*, vol. 21, no. 3 (1983)

Killingray, David and Richard Rathbone (eds), *Africa and the Second World War* (Basingstoke: Macmillan, 1986)

Kim, Mikyoung, 'Memorializing Comfort Women: Memory and Human Rights in Korea–Japan Relations', *Asian Politics and Policy*, vol. 6, no. 1 (2014)

King, Sam, *Climbing Up the Rough Side of the Mountain* (Peterborough: Upfront, 1998)

Klein, Ronald D., *The Other Empire: Literary Views of Japan from the Philippines, Singapore, and Malaysia* (Quezon City: University of the Philippines Press, 2008)

Klemperer, Victor, *To the Bitter End: The Diaries of Victor Klemperer, 1942–1945*, trans. Martin Chalmers (London: Weidenfeld & Nicolson, 1999)

Köhler, Joachim and Damian van Melis (eds), *Siegerin in Trümmern: Die Rolle der katholischen Kirche in der deutschen Nachkriegsgesellschaft* (Stuttgart: Verlag W. Kohlhammer, 1998)

Kollek, Teddy, *For Jerusalem* (London: Weidenfeld & Nicolson, 1978)

Kozlova, N. N. and I. I. Sandomirskaia, *Ia tak khochu nazvat' kino: 'Naivnoe pis'mo'. Opyt lingvo-sotsiologicheskogo chteniia* (Moscow: Gnozis, 1996)

Kraus, Jon (ed.), *Trade Unions and the Coming of Democracy in Africa* (New York: Palgrave Macmillan, 2007)

Kristensen, Hans M. and Robert S. Norris, 'Global Nuclear Weapons Inventories, 1945–2013', *Bulletin of the Atomic Scientists*, vol. 69, no. 5 (2013)

Kritz, Reuven, *Hebrew Narrative Fiction of the Struggle for Independence Era* (Kiryat Motzkin: Poreh, 1978)

Krivosheev, G. F. (ed.), *Soviet Casualties and Combat Losses in the Twentieth Century* (London: Greenhill Books, 1997)

Krylova, Anna, *Soviet Women in Combat* (New York: Cambridge University Press, 2010)

Kulka, Otto Dov, *Landscapes of the Metropolis of Death* (London: Allen Lane, 2013)

Kumagai, Naoko, 'The Background to the Japan–Republic of Korea Agreement: Compromises Concerning the Understanding of the Comfort Women Issue', *Asia-Pacific Review*, vol. 23, no. 1 (2016)

Kynaston, David, *Austerity Britain, 1945–51* (London: Bloomsbury, 2007)

Laar, Mart, *War in the Woods: Estonia's Struggle for Survival, 1944–1956*, trans. Tiina Ets (Washington, DC: The Compass Press, 1992)

Lacina, Bethany and Nils Petter Gleditsch, 'Monitoring Trends in Global Combat: A New Dataset of Battle Deaths', *European Journal of Population*, vol. 21, nos 2–3 (2005)

LaFeber, Walter, *America, Russia and the Cold War, 1945–2002* (New York: McGraw-Hill, 2002)

Lane, Arthur Bliss, *I Saw Poland Betrayed* (New York: Bobbs-Merrill, 1948)

Lankov, Andrei, *From Stalin to Kim Il Sung: The Formation of North Korea, 1945–1960* (London: Hurst & Co., 2002)

Lanzona, Vina A., *Amazons of the Huk Rebellion* (Madison: University of Wisconsin Press, 2009)

Lary, Diana, *The Chinese People at War: Human Suffering and Social Transformation, 1937–1945* (New York: Cambridge University Press, 2010)

Lary, Diana and Stephen MacKinnon (eds), *Scars of War: The Impact of Warfare on Modern China* (Vancouver: University of British Columbia Press, 2001)

Laurence, William L., *Dawn Over Zero* (London: Museum Press, 1947)

Lawler, Nancy Ellen, *Soldiers of Misfortune: Ivoirien Tirailleurs of World War II* (Athens: Ohio University Press, 1992)

Lawson, Konrad Mitchell, 'Wartime Atrocities and the Politics of Treason in the Ruins of the Japanese Empire, 1937–1953', PhD thesis, Department of History, Harvard University (2012)

Le Corbusier, *The Athens Charter* (New York: Viking, 1973)

Le Corbusier, *The Radiant City* (London: Faber & Faber, 1967)

Lee, Jin-kyung, *Service Economies: Militarism, Sex Work, and Migrant Labor in South Korea* (Minneapolis: University of Minnesota Press, 2010)

Legge, J. D., *Sukarno: A Political Biography* (London: Allen Lane, 1972)

Lentin, Ronit, *Israel and the Daughters of the Shoah* (New York: Berghahn Books, 2000)

Levinas, Emmanuel, *Difficult Freedom*, trans. Seán Hand (Baltimore: Johns Hopkins University Press, 1990)

Levy, Susan and Alessandra Lemma (eds), *The Perversion of Loss: Psychoanalytic Perspectives on Trauma* (New York: Brunner-Routledge, 2004)

Lewis, Robert A., Richard H. Rowland and Ralph S. Clem, *Nationality and Population Change in Russia and the USSR: An Evaluation of Census Data, 1897–1970* (New York: Praeger, 1976)

Li, Peter (ed.), *Japanese War Crimes* (New Brunswick, NJ: Transaction Books, 2009)

Lifton, Jay Robert, *Death in Life: Survivors of Hiroshima* (Harmondsworth: Pelican, 1971)

Lilley, J. Robert, *Taken by Force: Rape and American GIs during World War II* (Basingstoke: Palgrave Macmillan, 2007)

Linz, Susan J. (ed.), *The Impact of World War II on the Soviet Union* (Totowa, NJ: Rowman and Allanheld, 1985)

Lipscomb, J. F., *White Africans* (London: Faber & Faber, 1955)

Liss, Sheldon B., *Diplomacy and Dependency: Venezuela, the United States, and the Americas* (Salisbury, NC: Documentary, 1978)

Littell, Franklin H., *The Crucifixion of the Jews* (New York: Harper & Row, 1975)

Lloyd, E. M. H., *Food and Inflation in the Middle East, 1940–45* (Stanford University Press, 1956)

Lonsdale, John, 'The Moral Economy of Mau Mau: Wealth, Poverty and Civic Virtue in Kikuyu Political Thought', in Bruce Berman and John

Lonsdale, *Unhappy Valley: Conflict in Kenya & Africa* (London: James Currey, 1992)

Lowe, Keith, *Inferno* (London: Viking, 2007)

Lowe, Keith, *Savage Continent* (London: Viking, 2012)

Lowenthal, David, 'West Indian Emigrants Overseas', in Colin G. Clarke (ed.), *Caribbean Social Relations* (Liverpool: Centre for Latin American Studies, University of Liverpool, 1978)

Lüdtke, Alf, '"Coming to Terms with the Past": Illusions of Remembering, Ways of Forgetting Nazism in West Germany', *Journal of Modern History*, vol. 65, no. 3 (1993)

Lundestad, Geir, *East, West, North, South* (London: Sage, 2014)

Lustiger, Cardinal Jean-Marie, 'The Absence of God? The Presence of God? A Meditation in Three Parts on *Night*', in Harold Bloom (ed.), *Elie Wiesel's Night* (New York: Infobase, 2010)

MacQueen, Norrie, *The Decolonization of Portuguese Africa* (Harlow: Longman, 1997)

Macunovich, Diane J., *Birth Quake: The Baby Boom and its Aftershocks* (University of Chicago Press, 2002)

Maddison, Angus, *The World Economy: Historical Statistics* (Paris: OECD, 2003)

Maharatna, Arup, *The Demography of Famines: An Indian Historical Perspective* (New Delhi: Oxford University Press, 1996)

Mallik, Sanjoy Kumar (ed.), *Chittaprosad: A Retrospective*, 2 vols (New Delhi: Delhi Art Gallery, 2011)

Maloba, Wunyabari O., *Mau Mau and Kenya: An Analysis of a Peasant Revolt* (Bloomington: Indiana University Press, 1993)

Marais, Hein, *South Africa: Limits to Change* (London: Zed Books, 2001)

Marcel, Gabriel (ed.), *Fresh Hope for the World* (London: Longmans, Green & Co., 1960)

Marrus, Michael, *The Holocaust in History* (New York: Penguin, 1989)

Marrus, Michael, *Lessons of the Holocaust* (University of Toronto Press, 2016)

Marx, Karl and Friedrich Engels, *The Communist Manifesto* (Harmondsworth: Penguin, 1985)

Masaaki, Noda, 'One Army Surgeon's Account of Vivisection on Human Subjects in China', trans. Paul Schalow, in Li (ed.), *Japanese War Crimes*

Masaaki, Noda, *Senso to Zaiseki* (Tokyo: Iwanami Shoten, 1998)

Mason, Alpheus Thomas, *Harlan Fiske Stone: Pillar of the Law* (Hamden, CT: Archon Books, 1968)

Masters, Dexter and Katharine Way (eds), *One World or None* (New York: McGraw-Hill, 1946)

Mathu, Mohamed, *The Urban Guerrilla* (Richmond, BC: LSM Information Center, 1974)

Mayne, Richard, *Postwar: The Dawn of Today's Europe* (London: Thames & Hudson, 1983)

Mazower, Mark, *No Enchanted Palace* (Princeton University Press, 2009)

Mazower, Mark (ed.), *After the War Was Over* (Princeton University Press, 2000)

McKean, John, *Giancarlo De Carlo: Layered Places* (Stuttgart and London: Edition Axel Menges, 2004)

Meerloo, A. M., *Aftermath of Peace: Psychological Essays* (New York: International Universities Press, 1946)

Messina, Anthony M., *The Logics and Politics of Post-WWII Migration to Western Europe* (New York: Cambridge University Press, 2007)

Meyer, Cord, *Facing Reality* (New York: Harper & Row, 1980)

Meyer, Cord, *Peace or Anarchy* (Boston, MA: Little, Brown, 1947)

Miller, Arthur G., Amy M. Buddie and Jeffrey Kretschmar, 'Explaining the Holocaust: Does Social Psychology Exonerate the Perpetrators?', in Leonard S. Newman and Ralph Erber (eds), *Understanding Genocide* (New York: Oxford University Press, 2002)

Miller, Francesca, *Latin American Women and the Search for Social Justice* (Hanover, NH: University Press of New England, 1991)

Millett, Allan R., *The War for Korea, 1945–1950: A House Burning* (Lawrence: University Press of Kansas, 2005)

Milward, Alan, *War, Economy and Society, 1939–1945* (Berkeley and Los Angeles: University of California Press, 1977)

Moi, Toril, 'The Adulteress Wife', *London Review of Books*, vol. 32, no. 3 (11 February 2010)

Molotov interview with Felix Chuev, 1 July 1979, in Resis (ed.), *Molotov Remembers*

Moltmann, Jürgen, *The Crucified God*, trans. R. A. Wilson and John Bowden (London: SCM Press, 1974)

Montefiori, Simon Sebag, *Stalin: The Court of the Red Tsar* (London: Weidenfeld & Nicolson, 2003)

Mooney, Jadwiga E. Pieper, 'Fighting Fascism and Forging New Political Activism: The Women's International Democratic Federation (WIDF) in the Cold War', in Jadwiga E. Pieper Mooney and Fabio Lanza (eds), *De-Centering Cold War History* (Oxford: Routledge, 2013)

Moore, Aaron William, *Writing War: Soldiers Record the Japanese Empire* (Cambridge, MA: Harvard University Press, 2013)

Moorehead, Alan, *Eclipse* (London: Granta, 2000)

Moorehead, Caroline, *Village of Secrets* (London: Chatto & Windus, 2014)

Mooren, Trudy T. M., *The Impact of War: Studies on the Psychological Consequences of War and Migration* (Delft: Eburon, 2001)

Moorhouse, Roger, *Berlin at War* (London: Bodley Head, 2010)

Morgan, Philip, *The Fall of Mussolini* (New York: Oxford University Press, 2007)

Morgan, Ted, *Reds: McCarthyism in Twentieth-Century America* (New York: Random House, 2003)

Morrell, J. B., *The City of Our Dreams* (London: St Anthony's Press, 1955)

Morris, Benny, *Righteous Victims* (New York: Vintage, 2001)

Moses, Rafael, 'An Israeli View', in Rafael Moses (ed.), *Persistent Shadows of the Holocaust* (Madison, CT: International Universities Press, 1993)

Mossinsohn, Yigal, *Way of a Man* (Tel Aviv: N. Tversky Publishers, 1953)

Muchai, Karigo, *The Hardcore* (Richmond, BC: LSM Information Center, 1973)

Mukerjee, Madhusree, *Churchill's Secret War* (New York: Basic Books, 2010)

Mumford, Lewis, *The Culture of Cities* (London: Secker & Warburg, 1940)

Mwakikagile, Godfrey, *Africa is in a Mess: What Went Wrong and What Should be Done* (Dar es Salaam: New Africa Press, 2006)

Nagai, Takashi, *The Bells of Nagasaki*, trans. William Johnston (Tokyo: Kodansha International, 1984)

National Front, *For a New Britain: The Manifesto of the National Front* (Croydon: National Front, 1974)

Neval, Daniel A., '*Mit Atombomben bis nach Moskau': gegenseitige Wahrnehmung der Schweiz und des Ostblocks im Kalten Krieg, 1945–1968* (Zürich: Chronos, 2003)

New Zealand Department of External Affairs, *United Nations Conference on International Organization* (Wellington: Department of External Affairs, 1945)

Newman, Oscar, *Defensible Space* (New York: Macmillan, 1972)

Nitzan, Shlomo, *Togetherness* (Tel Aviv: Hakibbutz Hameuchad, 1956)

Nkrumah, Kwame, *Neo-Colonialism: The Last Stage of Imperialism* (London: Nelson, 1965)

Nossack, Hans Erich, *Der Untergang* (Hamburg: Ernst Kabel Verlag, 1981)

Novick, Peter, *The Holocaust in American Life* (New York: Mariner, 2000)

Nwaka, Geoffrey I., 'Rebellion in Umuahia, 1950–1951: Ex-Servicemen and Anti-Colonial Protest in Eastern Nigeria', *Transafrican Journal of History*, vol. 16 (1987)

Ofer, Dalia, *Escaping the Holocaust* (New York: Oxford University Press, 1990)

Ogura, Toyofumi, *Letters from the End of the World*, trans. Kisaburo Murakami and Shigeru Fujii (Tokyo: Kodansha International, 2001)

Olusanya, Gabriel, 'The Role of Ex-Servicemen in Nigerian Politics', *Journal of Modern African Studies*, vol. 6, no. 2 (1968)

Oppenheimer, J. Robert, 'Physics in the Contemporary World', *Bulletin of the Atomic Scientists*, vol. 4, no. 3 (1948)

Osada, Arata (ed.), *Children of the A-Bomb* (New York: Putnam, 1963)

Osborne, Myles (ed.), *The Life and Times of General China* (Princeton, NJ: Marcus Wiener Publishers, 2015)

Ota, Yoko, 'City of Corpses', in Richard H. Minear (ed.), *Hiroshima: Three Witnesses* (Princeton University Press, 1990)

Ovalle-Bahamón, Ricardo E., 'The Wrinkles of Decolonization and Nationness: White Angolans as *Retornados* in Portugal', in Andrea L. Smith (ed.), *Europe's Invisible Migrants* (Amsterdam University Press, 2003)

Overy, Richard, *The Bombing War* (London: Allen Lane, 2013)

Owen, James and Guy Walters (eds), *The Voice of War* (London: Viking, 2004)

Palgi, Yoel, *Into the Inferno*, trans. Phyllis Palgi (New Brunswick, NJ: Rutgers University Press, 2003)

Paperno, Irina, *Stories of the Soviet Experience: Memoirs, Diaries, Dreams* (Ithaca, NY: Cornell University Press, 2009)

Pappé, Ilan, *The Ethnic Cleansing of Palestine* (London: Oneworld, 2007)

Patil, Anjali V., *The UN Veto in World Affairs, 1946–1990* (London: Mansell, 1992)

Patterson, James T., *Grand Expectations: The United States, 1945–1974* (New York: Oxford University Press, 1996)

Payne, Stanley G., *Franco and Hitler* (New Haven, CT: Yale University Press, 2009)

Peach, Ceri, 'Patterns of Afro-Caribbean Migration and Settlement in Great Britain, 1945–1981', in Colin Brock (ed.), *The Caribbean in Europe* (London: Frank Cass, 1986)

Peach, Ceri, 'Postwar Migration to Europe: Reflux, Influx, Refuge', *Social Science Quarterly*, vol. 78, no. 2 (1997)

Pearson, Raymond, *National Minorities in Eastern Europe, 1848–1945* (London: Macmillan, 1983)

Pelle, János, *Az utolsó vérvádak* (Budapest, Pelikán, 1995)

Piccigallo, Philip R., *The Japanese on Trial* (Austin: University of Texas Press, 1979)

Picketty, Thomas, *Capital in the Twenty-First Century*, trans. Arthur Goldhammer (Cambridge, MA: The Belknap Press of Harvard University Press, 2014)

Pilisuk, Marc, *Who Benefits from Global Violence and War: Uncovering a Destructive System* (Westport, CT: Praeger Security International, 2008)

Pilzer, Joshua D., *Hearts of Pine: Songs in the Lives of Three Korean Survivors of the Japanese 'Comfort Women'* (New York: Oxford University Press, 2012)

Pollock, James K., James H. Meisel and Henry L. Bretton, *Germany Under Occupation: Illustrative Materials and Documents* (Ann Arbor: George Wahr Publishing Co., 1949)

Potter, William and Gaukhar Mukhatzhanova, *Nuclear Politics and the Non-Aligned Movement: Principles vs. Pragmatism* (London: Routledge, 2012)

Powell, J. Enoch, *Still to Decide* (London: B. T. Batsford, 1972)

Putnam, Robert D., *Bowling Alone: The Collapse and Revival of American Community* (New York: Simon & Schuster, 2000)

Rabe, Stephen G., *Eisenhower and Latin America: The Foreign Policy of Anti-communism* (Chapel Hill: University of North Carolina Press, 1988)

Rabinowitch, Alexander, 'Founder and Father', *Bulletin of the Atomic Scientists*, vol. 61, no. 1 (2005)

Rabinowitch, Eugene, *The Dawn of a New Age* (University of Chicago Press, 1963)

Rabinowitch, Eugene, 'Five Years After', *Bulletin of the Atomic Scientists*, vol. 7, no. 1 (1951)

Rabinowitch, Eugene, 'The Labors of Sisyphus', *Bulletin of the Atomic Scientists*, vol. 7, no. 10 (1951)

Ramras-Rauch, Gila, *The Arab in Israeli Literature* (London: I. B. Tauris, 1989)

Rees, Laurence, *Their Darkest Hour* (London: Ebury Press, 2008)

Rees, Siân, *Lucie Aubrac* (London: Michael O'Mara, 2015)

Reid, Anthony, *The Indonesian National Revolution, 1945–1950* (Hawthorn: Longman Australia, 1974)

Reid, Anthony, *To Nation by Revolution: Indonesia in the Twentieth Century* (Singapore: NUS Press, 2011)

Reid, Escott, *On Duty: A Canadian at the Making of the United Nations, 1945–1946* (Kent, OH: Kent State University Press, 1983)

Reid, P. R., *The Latter Days at Colditz* (London: Hodder and Stoughton, 1953)

Resis, Albert (ed.), *Molotov Remembers* (Chicago: Ivan R. Dee, 1993)

Reves, Emery, *The Anatomy of Peace* (London: George Allen & Unwin, 1946)

Richardot, Jean, *Journeys for a Better World: A Personal Adventure in War and Peace* (Lanham, MD: University Press of America, 1994)

Roberts, Andrew, *The Storm of War* (London: Allen Lane, 2009)

Roberts, Mary Louise, *What Soldiers Do: Sex and the American GI in World War II France* (Chicago University Press, 2013)

Rodrigues, Luís and Sergiy Glebov, *Military Bases: Historical Perspectives, Contemporary Challenges* (Amsterdam: IOS Press, 2009)

Röling, B. V. A. and C. F. Rüter (eds), *The Tokyo Judgment* (APA-University Press Amsterdam, 1977)

Roosevelt, Eleanor, *My Day: The Best of Eleanor Roosevelt's Acclaimed Newspaper Columns, 1936–1962*, ed. David Emblidge (Boston, MA: Da Capo Press, 2001)

Ruff-O'Herne, Jan, *Fifty Years of Silence* (Sydney: Heinemann Australia, 2008)

Rupp, Leila J., 'The Persistence of Transnational Organizing: The Case of the Homophile Movement', *American Historical Review*, vol. 116, no. 4 (2011)

Rushford, Frank H., *City Beautiful: A Vision of Durham* (Durham County Advertiser, 1944)

Rustin, Michael, 'Why are We More Afraid Than Ever? The Politics of Anxiety After Nine Eleven', in Levy and Lemma (eds), *The Perversion of Loss: Psychoanalytic Perspectives on Trauma*

Ryan, Allan A., *Yamashita's Ghost* (Lawrence: University Press of Kansas, 2012)

Ryang, Sonia, *Koreans in Japan* (London: Routledge, 2000)

Ryckmans, François, *Mémoires noires: Les Congolais racontent le Congo belge, 1940–1960* (Brussels: Éditions Racine, 2010)

Sachs, Jeffrey, *The End of Poverty* (Harmondsworth: Penguin, 2005)

Sack, Daniel, *Moral Re-Armament: The Reinventions of an American Religious Movement* (New York: Palgrave Macmillan, 2009)

Sack, John, *An Eye for an Eye* (New York: Basic Books, 1993)

Sakharov, Andrei, *Memoirs* (London: Hutchinson, 1990)

Sakharov, Andrei, *Progress, Coexistence and Intellectual Freedom*, ed. Harrison E. Salisbury (New York: W. W. Norton, 1968)

Salas, Miguel Tinker, *Venezuela: What Everyone Needs to Know* (New York: Oxford University Press, 2015)

Sand, Shlomo, *The Invention of the Jewish People*, trans. Yael Lotan (London and New York: Verso, 2009)

SarDesai, D. R., *Southeast Asia: Past and Present* (Boulder, CO: Westview Press, 1997)

Sarkar, Nikhil, *A Matter of Conscience: Artists Bear Witness to the Great Bengal Famine of 1943*, trans. Satyabrata Dutta (Calcutta: Punascha, 1994)

Sartre, Jean-Paul, *Anti-Semite and Jew*, trans. George J. Becker (New York: Schocken Books, 1948)

Sartre, Jean-Paul, *Existentialism and Humanism*, trans. Philip Mairet (London: Methuen, 2007)

Sartre, Jean-Paul, 'The Liberation of Paris: An Apocalyptic Week', in Ronald Aronson and Adrian van den Hoven (eds), *We Have Only This Life to Live: The Selected Essays of Jean-Paul Sartre* (New York: New York Review of Books, 2013)

Satoshi, Nakano, 'The Politics of Mourning', in Ikehata Setsuho and Lydia N. Yu Jose (eds), *Philippines–Japan Relations* (Quezon City: Ateneo de Manila University Press, 2003)

Sayer, Derek, *The Coasts of Bohemia* (Princeton University Press, 1998)

Scalapino, Robert and Chong-Sik Lee, *Communism in Korea* (Berkeley: University of California Press, 1972)

Schleh, Eugene P. A., 'The Post-War Careers of Ex-Servicemen in Ghana and Uganda', *Journal of Modern African Studies*, vol. 6, no. 2 (1968)

Schlesinger, Stephen and Stephen Kinzer, *Bitter Fruit: The Story of the American Coup in Guatemala* (Boston, MA: Harvard University Press, 2005)

Schmid, Sonja D., 'Shaping the Soviet Experience of the Atomic Age: Nuclear Topics in *Ogonyok*', in van Lente (ed.), *The Nuclear Age in Popular Media*

Schollmeyer, Josh, 'Minority Report', *Bulletin of the Atomic Scientists*, vol. 61, no. 1 (2005)

Schrijvers, Peter, *Liberators: The Allies and Belgian Society, 1944–1945* (Cambridge University Press, 2009)

Schuler, Kurt and Andrew Rosenberg (eds), *The Bretton Woods Transcripts* (New York: Center for Financial Stability, 2012)

Schweber, Silvan S., *Einstein and Oppenheimer: The Meaning of Genius* (Cambridge, MA: Harvard University Press, 2009)

Scott, Carl-Gustaf, 'The Swedish Midsummer Crisis of 1941: The Crisis that Never Was', *Journal of Contemporary History*, vol. 37, no. 3 (2002)

Sebald, W. G., *On the Natural History of Destruction* (Harmondsworth: Penguin, 2004)

Segal, Hanna, 'From Hiroshima to the Gulf War and After: A Psychoanalytic Perspective', in Anthony Elliott and Stephen Frosh (eds), *Psychoanalysis in Contexts: Paths Between Theory and Modern Culture* (London and New York: Routledge, 1995)

Segev, Tom, *1949: The First Israelis* (New York: Henry Holt, 1986)

Segev, Tom, *The Seventh Million* (New York: Hill & Wang, 1993)

Sen, Amartya, *Poverty and Famines: An Essay on Entitlement and Deprivation* (Oxford: Clarendon Press, 1981)

Sert, José Luis, *Can Our Cities Survive?* (Cambridge, MA: Harvard University Press, 1944)

Service, Robert, *A History of Modern Russia* (Harmondsworth: Penguin, 2003)

Shamir, Moshe, *He Walked Through the Fields* (Merhavia: Sifriat Poalim, 1947)

Shamir, Moshe, *With His Own Hands* (Jerusalem: Israel Universities Press, 1970)

Shapira, Anita, *Israel: A History* (Waltham, MA: Brandeis University Press, 2012)

Sharp, Thomas, *Exeter Phoenix* (London: Architectural Press, 1946)

Shavit, Ari, *My Promised Land* (London: Scribe, 2015)

Shephard, Ben, *The Long Road Home: The Aftermath of the Second World War* (London: Bodley Head, 2010)

Sherwood, Marika, ' "There is No New Deal for the Blackman in San Francisco": African Attempts to Influence the Founding Conference of the United Nations, April–July, 1945', *International Journal of African Historical Studies*, vol. 29, no. 1 (1996)

Shim, Young-Hee, *Sexual Violence and Feminism in Korea* (Seoul: Hanyang University Press, 2004)

Shlapentokh, Vladimir, *A Normal Totalitarian Society* (Armonk, NY: M. E. Sharp, 2001)

Shurkin, Joel, *Broken Genius: The Rise and Fall of William Shockley, Creator of the Electronic Age* (Basingstoke: Macmillan, 2006)

Siklos, Pierre L., *War Finance, Reconstruction, Hyperinflation and Stabilization in Hungary, 1938–48* (Basingstoke: Macmillan, 1991)

Singham, A. W. and Shirley Hune, *Non-Alignment in an Age of Alignments* (London: Zed Books, 1986)

Slade, E. H. (ed.), *Census of Pakistan, 1951* (Karachi: Government of Pakistan, 1951)

Slaughter, Jane, *Women and the Italian Resistance, 1943–1945* (Denver: Arden Press, 1997)

Smith, Robert Ross, *Triumph in the Philippines* (Washington, DC: Office of the Chief of Military History, Department of the Army, 1963)

Snow, Philip, *The Fall of Hong Kong* (New Haven, CT: Yale University Press, 2003)

Soebagijo, I. N., *S. K. Trimurti: Wanita Pengabdi Bangsa* (Jakarta: Gunung Agung, 1982)

Soh, C. Sarah, *The Comfort Women* (University of Chicago Press, 2008)

Solomon, Susan Gross et al. (eds), *Shifting Boundaries of Public Health: Europe in the Twentieth Century* (Rochester, NY: University of Rochester Press, 2008)

Solzhenitsyn, Alexander, *The Gulag Archipelago*, vol. 1 (London: Collins & Harvill, 1974)

Spellman, W. M., *A Concise History of the World Since 1945* (Basingstoke: Palgrave Macmillan, 2006)

Spinelli, Altiero, *Come ho tentato di diventare saggio*, 2 vols (Bologna: Società editrice il Mulino, 1984 and 1987)

Spinelli, Altiero, *From Ventotene to the European Constitution*, ed. Agustín José Menéndez (Oslo: Centre for European Studies, 2007)

Spoerer, Mark, *Zwangsarbeit unter dem Hakenkreuz* (Stuttgart and Munich: Deutsche Verlags-Anstalt, 2001)

Srimanjari, *Through War and Famine: Bengal, 1939–45* (New Delhi: Orient Black-Swan, 2009)

Staněk, Tomáš, *Odsun Němců z Československa, 1945–1947* (Prague: Academia/ Naše vojsko, 1991)

Stange, Mary Zeiss et al. (eds), *Encyclopedia of Women in Today's World*, vol. 1 (Los Angeles: Sage, 2011)

Starman, Hannah, 'Israel's Confrontation with the Holocaust: A Journey of Uncertain Identity', in C. J. A. Stewart et al. (eds), *The Politics of Contesting Identity* (Edinburgh: Politics, University of Edinburgh, 2003)

Statiev, Alexander, *The Soviet Counterinsurgency in the Western Borderlands* (New York: Cambridge University Press, 2010)

Steedly, Mary Margaret, *Rifle Reports: A Story of Indonesian Independence* (Berkeley and Los Angeles: University of California Press, 2013)

Steffen, Katrin and Martin Kohlrausch, 'The Limits and Merits of Internationalism: Experts, the State and the International Community in Poland in the First Half of the Twentieth Century', *European Review of History*, vol. 16, no. 5 (2009)

Steinacher, Gerald, *Nazis on the Run* (New York: Oxford University Press, 2012)

Stephens, Ian, *Monsoon Morning* (London: Ernest Benn, 1966)

Stephenson, Flora and Phoebe Pool, *A Plan for Town and Country* (London: The Pilot Press, 1944)

Stettinius, Edward R., *Roosevelt and the Russians* (Garden City, NY: Doubleday, 1949)

Stiglitz, Joseph E., *Globalization and its Discontents* (London: Allen Lane, 2002)

Stora, Benjamin, *Algeria, 1830–2000: A Short History*, trans. Jane Marie Todd (Ithaca, NY: Cornell University Press, 2001)

Stora, Benjamin and Zakya Daoud, *Ferhat Abbas: une utopie algérienne* (Paris: Denoël, 1995)

Storrs, Landon R. Y., *The Second Red Scare and the Unmaking of the New Deal Left* (Princeton University Press, 2013)

Sukarno, *Toward Freedom and the Dignity of Man: A Collection of Five Speeches by President Sukarno of the Republic of Indonesia* (Jakarta: Department of Foreign Affairs, 1961)

Sutcliffe, Anthony and Roger Smith, *History of Birmingham*, vol. 3: *Birmingham, 1939–1970* (London: Oxford University Press for Birmingham City Council, 1974)

Szczerbiak, Aleks and Paul Taggart (eds), *EU Enlargement and Referendums* (Abingdon: Routledge, 2005)

Szyk, Arthur, *The New Order* (New York: G. P. Putnam's Sons, 1941)

Talbot, Ian and Gurharpal Singh, *The Partition of India* (Cambridge University Press, 2009)

Tanaka, Yuki, '"Comfort Women" in the Dutch East Indies', in Margaret Stetz and Bonnie B. C. Oh (eds), *Legacies of the Comfort Women of World War II* (Armonk, NY: M. E. Sharp, 2001)

Tanner, Jakob, 'Switzerland and the Cold War: A Neutral Country Between the "American Way of Life" and "Geistige Landesverteidigung"', in Joy Charnley and Malcolm Pender (eds), *Switzerland and War* (Bern: Peter Lang, 1999)

Tassin, Kristin S., '"Lift up Your Head, My Brother": Nationalism and the Genesis of the Non-Aligned Movement', *Journal of Third World Studies*, vol. 23, no. 1 (2006)

Tauger, Mark B., 'Entitlement, Shortage and the Bengal Famine of 1943: Another Look', *Journal of Peasant Studies*, vol. 31, no. 1 (2003)

Taylor, Frederick, *Dresden* (London: HarperCollins, 2004)

Taylor, Stan, *The National Front in English Politics* (London: Macmillan, 1982)

Tenney, Jack B., *Red Fascism* (Los Angeles: Federal Printing Co., 1947)

Teplyakov, Yuri, 'Stalin's War Against His Own Troops: The Tragic Fate of Soviet Prisoners of War in German Captivity', *Journal of Historical Review*, vol. 14, no. 4 (1994)

Terami-Wada, Motoe, *The Japanese in the Philippines 1880s–1980s* (Manila: National Historical Commission of the Philippines, 2010)

Terkel, Studs, *'The Good War': An Oral History of World War Two* (London: Hamish Hamilton, 1984)

Tomasevich, Jozo, *War and Revolution in Yugoslavia, 1941–1945* (Stanford University Press, 2001)

Tooze, Adam, *The Wages of Destruction* (Harmondsworth: Penguin, 2007)

Trgo, Fabijan (ed.), *The National Liberation War and Revolution in Yugoslavia (1941–1945): Selected Documents* (Belgrade: Military History Institute of the Yugoslav People's Army, 1982)

Trimurti, S. K., *95 Tahun S. K. Trimurti: Pejuang Indonesia* (Jakarta: Yayasan Bung Karno, 2007)

UN, *The United Nations Conference on International Organization: Selected Documents* (Washington, DC: US Government Printing Office, 1946)

UN Conference on Trade and Development, *The Least Developed Countries Report, 2014* (Geneva: UNCTAD, 2014)

UN Department of Economic Affairs, *Economic Report: Salient Features of the World Economic Situation, 1945–47* (Lake Success, NY: UN, 1948)

UN Department of Economic and Social Affairs, 'World Urbanization Prospects: The 2011 Revision', Working Paper no. ST/ESA/SER.A/322

UN San Francisco Conference, 1945, in UN, *The United Nations Conference on International Organization: Selected Documents* (Washington, DC: US Government Printing Office, 1946)

Union des Femmes Françaises, *Les Femmes dans la Résistance* (Monaco: Éditions du Rocher, 1977)

Urquhart, Brian, *A Life in Peace and War* (London: Weidenfeld & Nicolson, 1987)

US Army Military Government in Korea, *Summation of the United States Military Government Activities in Korea*, no. 33 (Seoul: National Economic Board, 1948)

US Department of State, *Foreign Relations of the United States* (Washington, DC: US Government Printing Office, various years)

USSR Central Statistical Office, *Soviet Census 1959: Preliminary Results* (London: Soviet Booklets, 1959)

Vailland, Geneviève, *Le Travail des Femmes* (Paris: Jeune Patron, 1947)

van Dijk, Cees, *Rebellion Under the Banner of Islam: The Darul Islam in Indonesia* (The Hague: Martinus Nijhoff, 1981)

van Lente, Dick (ed.), *The Nuclear Age in Popular Media: A Transnational History, 1945–1965* (New York: Palgrave Macmillan, 2012)

Varga, Aniko, 'National Bodies: The "Comfort Women" Discourse and Its Controversies in South Korea', *Studies in Ethnicity and Nationalism*, vol. 9, no. 2 (2009)

Venezuela, Junta Militar de Gobierno, *Saludo de la Junta Militar de Gobierno a los Venezolanos con Ocasion del Año Nuevo* (Caracas: Oficina Nacional de Información y Publicaciones, 1950)

Vickers, Adrian, *A History of Modern Indonesia* (New York: Cambridge University Press, 2013)

Vincent, Madeleine, *Femmes: quelle libération?* (Paris: Éditions sociales, 1976)

von Tunzelmann, Alex, *Red Heat* (London: Simon & Schuster, 2011)

Wachanga, Henry Kahinga, *The Swords of Kirinyaga* (Nairobi: East African Literature Bureau, 1975)

Ward, Stephen V. (ed.), *The Garden City* (London: E & FN Spon, 1992)

Watson, James and Patrick Abercrombie, *A Plan for Plymouth* (Plymouth: Underhill, 1943)

Watt, Lori, *When Empire Comes Home: Repatriation and Reintegration in Postwar Japan* (Cambridge, MA: Harvard University Asia Center, 2009)

Waxman, Zoë, 'Testimonies as Sacred Texts: The Sanctification of Holocaust Writing', *Past and Present*, vol. 206, supplement 5 (2010)

Weber, Max, *The Protestant Ethic and the Spirit of Capitalism* (New York: Oxford University Press, 2011)

Webster, Sir Charles and Noble Frankland, *The Strategic Air War Against Germany, 1939–1945* (London: HMSO, 1961)

Weinberg, Werner, *Self-Portrait of a Holocaust Survivor* (Jefferson, NC: McFarland & Co., 1985)

Weiner, Tim, *Enemies: A History of the FBI* (London: Allen Lane, 2012)

Weiner, Tim, *Legacy of Ashes* (London: Allen Lane, 2007)

Weiss, Thomas G., *Global Governance: Why? What? Whither?* (Cambridge: Polity Press, 2013)

Wendt, Gerald, 'What Happened in Science, in Jack Goodman (ed.), *While You Were Gone: A Report on Wartime Life in the United States* (New York: Simon & Schuster, 1946)

Werth, Alexander, *Russia at War* (London: Barrie & Rockliff, 1964)

Westad, Odd Arne, *The Global Cold War* (Cambridge University Press, 2007)

Wettig, Gerhard, *Stalin and the Cold War in Europe* (Lanham, MD: Rowman & Littlefield, 2008)

Whitaker, Arthur P. (ed.), *Inter-American Affairs 1945* (New York: Columbia University Press, 1946)

White, E. B., *The Wild Flag* (Boston, MA: Houghton Mifflin, 1946)

Wieringa, Saskia, *Sexual Politics in Indonesia* (Basingstoke: Palgrave Macmillan, 2002)

Willis, David K., *Klass: How Russians Really Live* (New York: St Martin's Press, 1985)

Willkie, Wendell, *One World* (London: Cassell & Co., 1943)

Wilson, Roland (ed.), *Census of the Commonwealth of Australia, 30 June, 1947* (Canberra: Commonwealth Government Printer, 1947)

Winkler, Heinrich August, *The Age of Catastrophe* (New Haven, CT: Yale University Press, 2015)

Wright, Frank Lloyd, *The Disappearing City* (New York: William Farquhar Payson, 1932)

Wright, Frank Lloyd, *Modern Architecture: Being the Kahn Lectures for 1930* (Princeton University Press, 2008)

Wyman, Mark, *DPs: Europe's Displaced Persons, 1945–1951* (Ithaca, NY: Cornell University Press, 1998)

Wyss, Marco, *Arms Transfers, Neutrality and Britain's Role in the Cold War* (Boston, MA: Brill, 2012)

Yizhar, S., 'The Prisoner', in Robert Alter (ed.), *Modern Hebrew Literature* (West Orange, NJ: Behrman House, 1975)

Yoshiaki, Yoshimi, *Comfort Women*, trans. Suzanne O'Brien (New York: Columbia University Press, 2002)

Young, Arthur N., *China's Wartime Finance and Inflation, 1937–1945* (Cambridge, MA: Harvard University Press, 1965)

Young, Michael and Peter Willmott, *Family and Kinship in East London* (Harmondsworth: Penguin, 2007)

Zdaniewicz, Witold, *Kościół Katolicki w Polsce, 1945–1982* (Poznan: Pallottinum, 1983)

Zertal, Idith, *From Catastrophe to Power: The Holocaust Survivors and the Emergence of Israel* (Berkeley and Los Angeles: University of California Press, 1998)

Ziemann, Benjamin, *Encounters with Modernity: The Catholic Church in West Germany, 1945–1975*, trans. Andrew Evans (New York: Berghahn, 2014)

Zima, V. F., *Golod v SSSR, 1946–1947 godov: Proiskhozhdenie i posledstviia* (Moscow: Institut rossiiskoi istorii RAN, 1996)

Zubkova, Elena, *Russia After the War*, trans. Hugh Ragsdale (Armonk, NY: M. E. Sharpe, 1998)

Zubrzycki, Geneviève, 'Polish Mythology and the Traps of Messianic Martyrology', in Gérard Bouchard (ed.), *National Myths: Constructed Pasts, Contested Presents* (Oxford: Routledge, 2013)

Zucchi, Benedict, *Giancarlo De Carlo* (Oxford: Butterworth Architecture, 1992)

Notes

Introduction

1 Interview with the author 12 September 2015. Georgina Sand is a pseudonym chosen by my interviewee.

2 R. Ernest Dupuy and Trevor N. Dupuy, *The Harper Encyclopedia of Military History*, 4th edn (New York: HarperCollins, 1993), pp. 1083, 1309.

3 K. O. Mbadiwe, quoted in Marika Sherwood, ' "There is No New Deal for the Blackman in San Francisco": African Attempts to Influence the Founding Conference of the United Nations, April–July, 1945', *International Journal of African Historical Studies*, vol. 29, no. 1 (1996), p. 78.

4 Nicaragua's Leonardo Argüello Barreto and Panama's Roberto Jimenez, speaking at the UN's foundation conference, 8th plenary session: see *The United Nations Conference on International Organization: Selected Documents* (Washington, DC: US Government Printing Office, 1946), pp. 385, 388.

5 Wendell Willkie, *One World* (London: Cassell & Co., 1943), pp. 134, 140, 147, 169.

6 Erich Fromm, *The Fear of Freedom* (Oxford: Routledge Classics, 2001), pp. ix and 118. See also S. H. Foulkes, *Introduction to Group-Analytic Psychotherapy* (London: Heinemann, 1948). For subsequent developments on the theme, see Earl Hopper and Haim Weinberg (eds), *The Social Unconscious in Persons, Groups and Societies*, vol. 1: *Mainly Theory* (London: Karnac, 2011), pp. xxiii–lvi.

7 Jean-Paul Sartre, *Existentialism and Humanism*, trans. Philip Mairet (London: Methuen, 2007), pp. 32–3.

Chapter 1 – The End of the World

1 Toyofumi Ogura, *Letters from the End of the World*, trans. Kisaburo Murakami and Shigeru Fujii (Tokyo: Kodansha International, 2001), p. 16.

2 Ibid., pp. 37, 54, 57, 105.

3 Ibid., pp. 55, 162–3.

4 Quoted by Jay Robert Lifton, *Death in Life: Survivors of Hiroshima* (Harmondsworth: Pelican, 1971), pp. 22–3; an alternative translation is given in Yoko Ota, 'City of Corpses', in Richard H. Minear (ed.), *Hiroshima: Three Witnesses* (Princeton University Press, 1990), p. 185; see also p. 211.

5 See for example, English Translation Group, *The Witness of Those Two Days: Hiroshima & Nagasaki August 6 & 9, 1945*, 2 vols (Tokyo: Japan Confederation of A- and H-Bomb Sufferers Organization, 1989), passim, but especially vol. 1, p. 149; Takashi Nagai, *The Bells of Nagasaki*, trans. William Johnston (Tokyo: Kodansha International, 1984), pp. 13, 14; Michihiko Hachiya, *Hiroshima Diary*, ed. and trans. Warner Wells (Chapel Hill: University of North Carolina Press, 1955), p. 54; Paul Ham, *Hiroshima Nagasaki* (London: Doubleday, 2012), p. 322; Arata Osada (ed.), *Children of the A-Bomb* (New York: Putnam, 1963), passim; Lifton, *Death in Life*, pp. 26–31.

6 *L'Osservatore Romano*, 7 August 1945, quoted in Paul Boyer, *By the Bomb's Early Light* (Chapel Hill: University of North Carolina Press, 1994), p. 15.

7 Ota, 'City of Corpses', pp. 165–6.

8 Hans Erich Nossack, *Der Untergang* (Hamburg: Ernst Kabel Verlag, 1981), p. 68.

9 Frederick Taylor, *Dresden* (London: HarperCollins, 2004), p. 328; Victor Klemperer, *To the Bitter End: The Diaries of Victor Klemperer, 1942–1945*, trans. Martin Chalmers (London: Weidenfeld & Nicolson, 1999), diary entry for 22 May 1945, p. 596; General Anderson quoted in Richard Overy, *The Bombing War* (London: Allen Lane, 2013), p. 410.

10 Jörg Friedrich, *The Fire: The Bombing of Germany, 1940–1945* (New York: Columbia University Press, 2006), p. 344.

11 Antony Beevor, *Stalingrad* (London: Viking, 1998), pp. 406–17.

12 Krzysztof Zanussi and Ludwika Zachariasiewicz, quoted in Norman Davies, *Rising '44* (London: Pan, 2004), pp. 476, 492.

13 See http://philippinediaryproject.wordpress.com/1945/02/13 – Diary of Lydia C. Gutierrez, Tuesday, 13 February, 1945 – published as 'Liberation Diary: The Longest Wait', in *Sunday Times Magazine*, 23 April 1967.

14 Ota, 'City of Corpses', p. 148; Nossack, *Der Untergang*, p. 67.

15 Cyrus Sulzberger, 'Europe: The New Dark Continent', *New York Times Magazine*, 18 March 1945, p. SM3.

16 Sir Charles Webster and Noble Frankland, *The Strategic Air War Against Germany, 1939–1945* (London: HMSO, 1961), vol. 4, p. 484; John W. Dower, *Embracing Defeat: Japan in the Wake of World War II* (New York: W. W. Norton,

2000), p. 45; Norman Davies, *God's Playground* (New York: Oxford University Press, 2005), vol. 2, p. 355; Tony Judt, *Postwar* (London: Pimlico, 2005), p. 17; Keith Lowe, *Savage Continent* (London: Viking, 2012), p. 10; Unesco Postwar Educational Survey, 'The Philippines' (1948), p. 8 – document online at http://unesdoc.unesco.org/images/0015/001553/155396eb.pdf.

17 W. G. Sebald, *On the Natural History of Destruction* (Harmondsworth: Penguin, 2004), p. 3; R. Ernest Dupuy and Trevor N. Dupuy, *The Harper Encyclopedia of Military History*, 4th edn (New York: HarperCollins, 1993), p. 1309; Lifton, *Death in Life*, p. 20.

18 Max Hastings, *All Hell Let Loose: The World at War, 1939–1945* (London: HarperPress, 2011), p. 669; Antony Beevor, *The Second World War* (London: Weidenfeld & Nicolson, 2012), p. 781. Dupuy and Dupuy, *Harper Encyclopedia of Military History*, have 50 million (p. 1309), but their numbers for Chinese dead are far too low.

19 For objections to the term see Michael Marrus, *The Holocaust in History* (New York: Penguin, 1989), pp. 3–4.

20 For other, similarly doom-laden terminology see Rick Atkinson, *The Guns at Last Light* (London: Little, Brown, 2013), pp. 631–2; Lucy Dawidowicz, *The War Against the Jews, 1933–1945* (Harmondsworth: Pelican, 1979), p. 18.

21 Max Hastings, *Armageddon: The Battle for Germany, 1944–45* (London: Macmillan, 2004).

22 Daniel Costelle and Isabelle Clarke's six-part documentary *Apocalypse: la deuxième Guerre mondiale* (CC&C, 2009).

23 Atkinson, *The Guns at Last Light*, p. 640; Andrew Roberts, *The Storm of War* (London: Allen Lane, 2009), p. 579; Beevor, *The Second World War*, p. 781.

24 Vladimir Putin, VE Day 60th anniversary speech, 9 May 2005, http://news.bbc.co.uk/1/hi/world/europe/4528999.stm.

25 Hu Jintao, 'Speech at a Meeting Marking the 60th Anniversary of the Victory of the Chinese People's War of Resistance against Japanese Aggression and the World Anti-fascist War', 3 September 2005, www.china.org.cn/english/2005/Sep/140771.htm.

26 Herbert Conert, quoted in Taylor, *Dresden*, p. 396.

27 Dawidowicz, *The War Against the Jews, 1933–1945*, p. 480; Sara E. Karesh and Mitchell M. Hurvitz, *Encyclopedia of Judaism* (New York: Facts on File, 2006), p. 216.

28 For Japanese statistics see John W. Dower, *War Without Mercy: Race and Power in the Pacific War* (New York: Pantheon, 1986), pp. 298–9; for Chi-

nese, see Roberts, *The Storm of War*, p. 267; for French, German and British, see Lowe, *Savage Continent*, pp. 13–16; for Americans see Hastings, *All Hell Let Loose*, p. 670. For total population statistics, see Angus Maddison, *The World Economy: Historical Statistics* (Paris: OECD, 2003), passim.

29 Sigmund Freud, 'Beyond the Pleasure Principle' (1920), reproduced in Salman Akhtar and Mary Kay O'Neil (eds), *On Freud's 'Beyond the Pleasure Principle'* (London: Karnac, 2011); and Sigmund Freud, *Civilization and its Discontents* (Harmondsworth: Penguin, 2002), pp. 56–7.

30 See, for example, Richard Bessel, *Nazism and War* (London: Weidenfeld & Nicolson, 2004), pp. 94–6; and Lowe, *Savage Continent*, pp. 9–10.

31 Ham, *Hiroshima Nagasaki*, p. 225.

32 Nossack, *Der Untergang*, pp. 18–19.

33 Ibid., p. 98; Keith Lowe, *Inferno* (London: Viking, 2007), p. 319.

34 Ogura, *Letters from the End of the World*, p. 16.

35 Ibid., letter 9 (10 May 1946), p. 122.

Chapter 2 – Heroes

1 The following story is taken from two personal interviews with Leonard Creo on 10 August and 29 September 2015.

2 Leonard Creo, medal citation.

3 See, for example, *Stars and Stripes*, 26 and 28 August, 9 September 1944; *Life*, 4 September 1944; *Daily Express*, 28 August 1944. For a discussion of similar images and stories, see Mary Louise Roberts, *What Soldiers Do: Sex and the American GI in World War II France* (Chicago University Press, 2013), pp. 59–73.

4 IWM Docs, 94/8/1, Captain I. B. Mackay, typescript memoir, p. 104.

5 IWM Docs, 06/126/1, Derek L. Henry, typescript memoir, p. 57.

6 For erotic interpretations, see Roberts, *What Soldiers Do*, passim; Patrick Buisson, *1940–1945: Années érotiques* (Paris: Albin Michel, 2009), passim; and Ian Buruma, *Year Zero: A History of 1945* (London: Atlantic, 2013), p. 23.

7 'Paris – the Full Story', *Daily Express*, 28 August 1944; and Alan Moorehead, *Eclipse* (London: Granta, 2000), p. 153.

8 Maria Haayen, quoted in Buruma, *Year Zero*, p. 23.

9 Quoted ibid.

10 P. R. Reid, *The Latter Days at Colditz* (London: Hodder and Stoughton, 1953), pp. 281–2.

11 President William J. Clinton's speech at VE Day commemoration, 8 May 1995, available online at www.presidency.ucsb.edu/ws/index.php?pid= 51328&st=&st1; Studs Terkel, *'The Good War': An Oral History of World War Two* (London: Hamish Hamilton, 1984); Tom Brokaw, *The Greatest Generation* (London: Pimlico, 2002), p. xxx.

12 Hanna Segal, 'From Hiroshima to the Gulf War and After: A Psychoanalytic Perspective', in Anthony Elliott and Stephen Frosh (eds), *Psychoanalysis in Contexts: Paths Between Theory and Modern Culture* (London and New York: Routledge, 1995), p. 194.

13 Clinton's speech at VE Day commemoration, 8 May 1995. See also his D-Day commemoration speech, 6 June 1994, available online at www. presidency.ucsb.edu/ws/?pid=50300.

14 President Jacques Chirac, speech 6 June 2004, available online at http:// georgewbush-whitehouse.archives.gov/news/releases/2004/06/20040606. html.

15 Charles Glass, *Deserter* (London: HarperPress, 2013), pp. xiii, 228.

16 IWM Docs, 6839, Madame A. de Vigneral, typescript diary.

17 IWM Docs, 91/13/1, Major A. J. Forrest, typescript memoir, 'Scenes from a Gunner's War', chapter 7, p. 7.

18 See Roberts, *What Soldiers Do*, p. 281, fn. 49; and Peter Schrijvers, *Liberators: The Allies and Belgian Society, 1944–1945* (Cambridge University Press, 2009), p. 243.

19 J. Robert Lilley, *Taken by Force: Rape and American GIs during World War II* (Basingstoke: Palgrave Macmillan, 2007), pp. 11–12. For statistics on Soviet rape in eastern Europe see Keith Lowe, *Savage Continent* (London: Viking, 2012), p. 55.

20 Nancy Arnot Harjan, quoted in Terkel, *'The Good War'*, p. 560.

21 Yvette Levy, quoted in William I. Hitchcock, *Liberation* (London: Faber & Faber, 2008), p. 307.

22 Aaron William Moore, *Writing War: Soldiers Record the Japanese Empire* (Cambridge, MA: Harvard University Press, 2013), pp. 200, 210–14.

23 Robert Ross Smith, *Triumph in the Philippines* (Washington, DC: Office of the Chief of Military History, Department of the Army, 1963), pp. 306–7. The figure of 100,000 Filipinos is probably too high, but accurate figures have never been established: see Jose Ma. Bonifacio M. Escoda, *Warsaw of Asia: The Rape of Manila* (Quezon City: Giraffe Books, 2000), p. 324.

24 Carmen Guerrero Nakpil, quoted in Alfonso J. Aluit, *By Sword and Fire: The Destruction of Manila in World War II, 3 February – 3 March 1945* (Manila: National Commission for Culture and the Arts, 1994), p. 397.

25 See, for example, President Harry S. Truman's special message to Congress, 19 July 1950; his radio and TV reports to the people on 1 September 1950 and 15 December 1950; his address to the UN General Assembly, 24 October 1950; and his State of the Union address, 8 January 1951: all available online at The American Presidency Project: www.presidency.ucsb.edu.

26 President John F. Kennedy, 'The Vigor We Need', *Sports Illustrated*, 16 July 1962; President Lyndon B. Johnson's remarks on presenting the Congressional Medal of Honor posthumously to Daniel Fernandez, 6 April 1967, available online at www.presidency.ucsb.edu/ws/?pid=28190.

27 Nataliya Danilova, *The Politics of War Commemoration in the UK and Russia* (Basingstoke: Palgrave Macmillan, 2015), pp. 20–21.

28 President Ronald Reagan's speech on 40th anniversary of D-Day, 6 June 1984, available online at www.presidency.ucsb.edu/ws/?pid=40018.

29 President George W. Bush, Remarks to the United Nations General Assembly in New York City, 10 November 2001: speech available online at www.presidency.ucsb.edu/ws/?pid=58802.

30 President George W. Bush, Remarks at a Ceremony Commemorating the 60th Anniversary of Pearl Harbor in Norfolk, Virginia, December 7, 2001: speech available online at www.presidency.ucsb.edu/ws/?pid=63634.

31 Speeches at dinner hosted by the Mexican president, Vincente Fox, in Monterrey, 22 March 2002; welcome to British prime minister, Tony Blair, at Crawford, Texas, 6 April 2002; press conference with President Vladimir Putin, 24 May 2002; speech at Virginia Military Institute, 17 April 2002; speech about 'compassionate conservatism' in San Jose, California, 30 April 2002: all of these speeches are available online at www.presidency.ucsb.edu/ws/.

32 Remarks at a Memorial Day ceremony in Colleville-sur-Mer, 27 May 2002, available online at www.presidency.ucsb.edu/ws/?pid=73018.

33 See, for example, Putin's Victory Day speech, 9 May 2005, http://news.bbc.co.uk/1/hi/world/europe/4528999.stm.

34 See President Hu Jintao's 'Speech at a Meeting Marking the 60th Anniversary of the Victory of the Chinese People's War of Resistance against Japanese Aggression and the World Anti-fascist War', www.china.org.cn/english/2005/Sep/140771.htm.

35 Lowe, *Savage Continent*, pp. 61–3 and passim.

Chapter 3 – Monsters

1 Sigmund Freud, *Civilization and its Discontents* (Harmondsworth: Penguin, 2002), p. 50. See also Hanna Segal, 'From Hiroshima to the Gulf War and After: A Psychoanalytic Perspective', in Anthony Elliott and Stephen Frosh (eds), *Psychoanalysis in Contexts: Paths Between Theory and Modern Culture* (London and New York: Routledge, 1995), p. 194.

2 Mark Bryant, *World War II in Cartoons* (London: Grub Street, 1989), pp. 77, 90, 83, 99, 83; John W. Dower, *War Without Mercy: Race and Power in the Pacific War* (New York: Pantheon, 1986), pp. 192, 196, 242; Roger Moorhouse, *Berlin at War* (London: Bodley Head, 2010), p. 371.

3 'This is the Enemy' images, reproduced in Sam Keen, *Faces of the Enemy: Reflections of the Hostile Imagination: The Psychology of Enmity* (San Francisco: Harper & Row, 1986), pp. 33, 37; L. J. Jordaan, *Nachtmerrie over Nederland: Een herinneringsalbum* (Amsterdam: De Groene Amsterdammer, 1945), n.p.; Dower, *War Without Mercy*, pp. 93, 113.

4 See Nazi anti-Semitic propaganda posters in Belgium and France: IWM PST 8359; IWM PST 6483; IWM PST 8358; IWM PST 3142. See also David Low cartoons 'Rendezvous' and 'He must have been mad', *Evening Standard*, 20 September 1939 and 15 May 1941; Vicky cartoon 'Sabotage in Nederland', *Vrij Nederland*, 24 August 1940; Arthur Szyk, *The New Order* (New York: G. P. Putnam's Sons, 1941), passim; German propaganda postcard and Soviet portraits of Hitler and Himmler in Bryant, *World War II in Cartoons*, pp. 43, 77, 98, 131; Keen, *Faces of the Enemy*, pp. 33, 74, 76, 77, 127.

5 Dower, *War Without Mercy*, pp. 192, 241; chineseposters.net/posters/d25-201.php 'As long as the Japanese dwarves have not been vanquished, the struggle will not stop'; chineseposters.net/posters/pc-1938-005.php 'As the invasion by the Japanese dwarves does not stop for a day . . .'; 'Defeat Japanese imperialism', International Institute of Social History, Landsberger Collection D25/197.

6 Keith Lowe, *Savage Continent* (London: Viking, 2012), p. 118; Bryant, *World War II in Cartoons*, pp. 14, 26, 115; Jordaan, *Nachtmerrie over Nederland*, n.p.

7 Ilya Ehrenburg, writing in *Krasnaya Zvezda*, 13 August 1942; quoted in Alexander Werth, *Russia at War* (London: Barrie & Rockliff, 1964), p. 414.

8 Dower, *War Without Mercy*, pp. 89–91, 242–3.

9 Soviet hydra poster, IWM PST 5295; German flying skeleton poster, IWM PST 3708; British cartoon of Germany as winged demon, *Punch*, 6 November 1939; for Germany as robot, werewolf and Horsemen of Apoc-

alypse, see Jordaan, *Nachtmerrie over Nederland*; for USA as Grim Reaper and Frankenstein, see Bryant, *World War II in Cartoons*, pp. 77, 124. See also Dower, *War Without Mercy*, pp. 244–61.

10 *Collier's* cover, 12 December 1942; *Manga* cover, February 1943.

11 Jordaan, *Nachtmerrie over Nederland*, n.p.; Bryant, *World War II in Cartoons*, p. 85. See also Keen, *Faces of the Enemy*, p. 45.

12 See, for example, Dower, *War Without Mercy*, p. 73.

13 Robert Rasmus, quoted in Studs Terkel, *'The Good War': An Oral History of World War Two* (London: Hamish Hamilton, 1984), pp. 44–5; see also Keen, *Faces of the Enemy*, p. 26.

14 Dower, *War Without Mercy*, pp. 302–5; President William J. Clinton's speech at VE Day commemoration, 8 May 1995, available online at www.presidency.ucsb.edu/ws/index.php?pid=51328&st=&st1.

15 Post-hostility pamphlet quoted in Eugene Davidson, *The Death and Life of Germany* (London: Jonathan Cape, 1959), p. 81.

16 Hans Fredrik Dahl, 'Dealing with the Past in Scandinavia', in Jon Elster (ed.), *Retribution and Reparation in the Transition to Democracy* (New York: Cambridge University Press, 2006), p. 151.

17 Charles de Gaulle, 13 October 1945, quoted in Davidson, *The Death and Life of Germany*, p. 82.

18 Lowe, *Savage Continent*, p. 131; Derek Sayer, *The Coasts of Bohemia* (Princeton University Press, 1998), p. 240; Tomáš Staněk, *Odsun Němců z Československa, 1945–1947* (Prague: Academia/Naše vojsko, 1991), p. 59.

19 Motoe Terami-Wada, *The Japanese in the Philippines 1880s–1980s* (Manila: National Historical Commission of the Philippines, 2010), pp. 118–37. Characterizations in English-language fiction are more generous, but even so frequently return to Japanese wartime atrocities: see Ronald D. Klein, *The Other Empire: Literary Views of Japan from the Philippines, Singapore, and Malaysia* (Quezon City: University of the Philippines Press, 2008), pp. 10–15.

20 Yukawa Morio, quoted in Nakano Satoshi, 'The Politics of Mourning', in Ikehata Setsuho and Lydia N. Yu Jose (eds), *Philippines–Japan Relations* (Quezon City: Ateneo de Manila University Press, 2003), p. 337.

21 Klein, *The Other Empire*, pp. 176–9.

22 Sung-Hwa Cheong, *The Politics of Anti-Japanese Sentiment in Korea* (Westport, CT: Greenwood Press, 1991), pp. 135–43; Kim Jinwung, *A History of Korea* (Bloomington: Indiana University Press, 2012), p. 449.

23 'Japan-Bashers Try to Turn a Trade War into a Race War', *Chicago Tribune*, 23 July 1989; 'The Danger from Japan', *New York Times Magazine*, 28 July

1985; 'Yellow Peril Reinfects America', *Wall Street Journal*, 7 April 1989; see also Dower, *War Without Mercy*, pp. 313–14.

24 Michael Berry, 'Cinematic Representations of the Rape of Nanking', in Peter Li (ed.), *Japanese War Crimes* (New Brunswick, NJ: Transaction Books, 2009), p. 203; http://cinema-scope.com/features/features-a-matter-of-life-and-death-lu-chuan-and-post-zhuxuanlu-cinema-by-shelly-kraicer/. See also Wu Ziniu's *Don't Cry, Nanjing* (1995), Lu Chuan's *City of Life and Death* (2009) and Zhang Yimou's box office smash *The Flowers of War* (2011).

25 See 'China and Japan: Seven Decades of Bitterness', www.bbc.co.uk/news/magazine-25411700; 'China Mulls Holidays Marking Japanese Defeat and Nanjing Massacre', www.bbc.co.uk/news/world-asia-26342884; 'China ratifies national memorial day for Nanjing Massacre victims', http://english.peopledaily.com.cn/90785/8549181.html.

26 'Czech Poll Descends into Anti-German Insults', *Financial Times*, 25 January 2013; 'Nationalistische Kampagne bringt Zeman auf die Burg', *Die Welt*, 26 January 2013; 'Konjunktur für antideutsche Polemik in Europa', *Die Welt*, 27 January 2013.

27 *Dimokratia*, 9 February 2012.

28 *Il Giornale*, 3 August 2012.

29 Eric Frey, *Das Hitler Syndrom* (Frankfurt-am-Main: Eichborn, 2005), pp. 29, 54, 70, 80, 150 and passim.

30 'Congress MP Compares Narendra Modi to Hitler and Pol Pot', *Times of India*, 7 June 2013; 'Kevin's Sister Crusades Against Gays', *The Australian*, 14 July 2011.

31 'The New Furor', *Philadelphia Daily News*, 8 December 2015.

32 Michael Butter, *The Epitome of Evil: Hitler in American Fiction, 1939–2002* (New York: Palgrave Macmillan, 2009), passim.

33 Christopher R. Browning, *Ordinary Men: Reserve Police Battalion 101 and the Final Solution in Poland* (New York: HarperCollins, 1992). Daniel Goldhagen's bestselling *Hitler's Willing Executioners: Ordinary Germans and the Holocaust* (New York: Little, Brown, 1996) was written partly as a reaction to Browning's claims.

34 See, for example, the controversies around the *Historikerstreit* in the 1980s and the 2008 Prague Declaration on European Conscience and Communism: Anon., *'Historikerstreit': Die Dokumentation der Kontroverse um die Einzigartigkeit der nationalsozialistischen Judenvernichtung* (Munich: Piper, 1991), passim; Peter Novick, *The Holocaust in American Life* (New York: Mariner,

2000), pp. 9–10; Zvi Gitelman, 'Comparative and Competitive Victimization in the Post-Communist Sphere', in Alvin H. Rosenfield (ed.), *Resurgent Antisemitism: Global Perspectives* (Bloomington: Indiana University Press, 2013), pp. 227–9.

35 Noda Masaaki, 'One Army Surgeon's Account of Vivisection on Human Subjects in China', trans. Paul Schalow, in Li (ed.), *Japanese War Crimes*, pp. 142–4.

36 Ibid., pp. 150–51.

37 Ibid., p. 148.

38 Laurence Rees, interview with Yuasa in his *Their Darkest Hour* (London: Ebury Press, 2008), p. 214.

39 Masaaki, 'One Army Surgeon's Account', p. 156.

40 Ibid., p. 160.

41 Ibid., p. 135.

42 Hannes Heer, *'Hitler war's': die Befreiung der Deutschen von ihrer Vergangenheit* (Berlin: Aufbau, 2008), passim; Butter, *The Epitome of Evil*, p. 177.

43 For an alternative view, that attempting to 'understand' perpetrators leads towards exoneration, see Arthur G. Miller, Amy M. Buddie and Jeffrey Kretschmar, 'Explaining the Holocaust: Does Social Psychology Exonerate the Perpetrators?', in Leonard S. Newman and Ralph Erber (eds), *Understanding Genocide* (New York: Oxford University Press, 2002), pp. 301–24.

44 For a good introduction to the vast array of evidence linking atrocity to seemingly normal people, see Olaf Jensen and Claus-Christian W. Szejnmann (eds), *Ordinary People as Mass Murderers* (Basingstoke: Palgrave Macmillan, 2008).

Chapter 4 – Martyrs

1 Otto Dov Kulka, *Landscapes of the Metropolis of Death* (London: Allen Lane, 2013), passim.

2 Ibid., pp. 82–3.

3 Ibid., pp. 23, 77.

4 Robert Jay Lifton, *Death in Life: Survivors of Hiroshima* (Harmondsworth: Pelican, 1971), esp. pp. 505–11.

5 Kulka, *Landscapes of the Metropolis of Death*, p. 80.

6 Hasia R. Diner, *We Remember with Reverence and Love: American Jews and the Myth of Silence after the Holocaust, 1945–1962* (New York and London: New York University Press, 2009), passim.

7   Anne Karpf, *The War After* (London: Minerva, 1997), p. 5.

8   See Saul Friedländer, 'West Germany and the Burden of the Past: The Ongoing Debate', *Jerusalem Quarterly*, vol. 42 (1987), p. 16; Shlomo Sand, *The Invention of the Jewish People*, trans. Yael Lotan (London and New York: Verso, 2009), p. 285.

9   Keith Lowe, *Savage Continent* (London: Viking, 2012), pp. 13–16.

10 Andrew Roberts, *The Storm of War* (London: Allen Lane, 2009), p. 267; Diana Lary and Stephen MacKinnon (eds), *Scars of War: The Impact of Warfare on Modern China* (Vancouver: University of British Columbia Press, 2001), p. 6; Antony Beevor, *The Second World War* (London: Weidenfeld & Nicolson, 2012), p. 780.

11 President William J. Clinton's speech at VE Day commemoration, 8 May 1995; available online at www.presidency.ucsb.edu/ws/index.php?pid= 51328&st=&st1.

12 Al Newman of *Newsweek* and US Army report on Buchenwald, quoted in William I. Hitchcock, *Liberation* (London: Faber & Faber, 2008), p. 299.

13 Letter from Lieutenant General Sir Frederick Morgan to the Foreign Office's Under Secretary of State, 14 September 1946, IWM Docs, 02/49/1; see also Ben Shephard, *The Long Road Home: The Aftermath of the Second World War* (London: Bodley Head, 2010), pp. 295–9.

14 Lowe, *Savage Continent*, pp. 193–8.

15 Dienke Hondius, *Return: Holocaust Survivors and Dutch Anti-Semitism* (Westport, CT: Praeger, 2003), passim; Hitchcock, *Liberation*, pp. 271–2; János Pelle, *Az utolsó vérvádak* (Budapest, Pelikán, 1995), pp. 228–9; Shephard, *The Long Road Home*, p. 393.

16 Peter Novick, *The Holocaust in American Life* (New York: Mariner, 2000), pp. 86–90.

17 Leah Goldberg, quoted in Tom Segev, *1949: The First Israelis* (New York: Henry Holt, 1986), p. 138.

18 David Ben-Gurion, quoted in Tom Segev, *The Seventh Million* (New York: Hill & Wang, 1993), pp. 118–19.

19 Gideon Hausner, *Justice in Jerusalem* (London: Thomas Nelson, 1966), pp. 291–2.

20 Jean-Paul Sartre, *Anti-Semite and Jew*, trans. George J. Becker (New York: Schocken Books, 1948), pp. 83, 136; Evan Carton, 'The Holocaust, French Poststructuralism, the American Literary Academy, and Jewish Identity Politics', in Peter C. Herman (ed.), *Historicizing Theory* (Albany: State University of New York Press, 2004), pp. 20–22.

21 Jean-Paul Bier, 'The Holocaust, West Germany and Strategies of Oblivion, 1947–1979', in Anson Rabinbach and Jack Zipes (eds), *Germans and Jews Since the Holocaust* (New York: Holmes & Meier, 1986), pp. 202–3; Alf Lüdtke, ' "Coming to Terms with the Past": Illusions of Remembering, Ways of Forgetting Nazism in West Germany', *Journal of Modern History*, vol. 65, no. 3 (1993), pp. 544–6.

22 Phillip Lopate, quoted in Novick, *The Holocaust in American Life*, pp. 235–6.

23 Elie Wiesel, speech at the 28th Special Session of UN General Assembly, quoted in UN Press Release GA/10330, 24 January 2005 – see www.un.org/News/Press/docs/2005/ga10330.doc.htm.

24 Hannah Arendt, *Eichmann in Jerusalem* (Harmondsworth: Penguin, 1994), pp. 282–5, and reaction in Novick, *The Holocaust in American Life*, pp. 134–7.

25 John Sack, *An Eye for an Eye* (New York: Basic Books, 1993), and reaction in Lowe, *Savage Continent*, p. 182.

26 Christopher R. Browning, *Ordinary Men: Reserve Police Battalion 101 and the Final Solution in Poland* (New York: HarperCollins, 1992); Daniel Goldhagen, *Hitler's Willing Executioners: Ordinary Germans and the Holocaust* (London: Little, Brown, 1996).

27 See, for example, British Chief Rabbi Jonathan Sacks's speech on Holocaust Memorial Day 2013, www.hmd.org.uk/resources/podcast/chief-rabbi-lord-sacks-speech-uk-commemoration-event-holocaust-memorial-day-2013.

28 Alice Herz-Sommer obituary, *Telegraph*, 24 February 2014; Leon Weinstein obituary, *Los Angeles Times*, 4 January 2012; Sonia Weitz obituary, *Boston Globe*, 25 June 2010.

29 Speeches by the Israeli president, Shimon Peres, 27 April 2014; Pope John Paul II, 24 March 2000; and the US president, Barack Obama, 23 April 2012. See http://mfa.gov.il/MFA/AboutIsrael/History/Holocaust/Pages/President-Peres-at-Holocaust-Remembrance-Day-ceremony-at-Yad-Vashem-27-Apr-2014.aspx; www.natcath.org/NCR_Online/documents/YadVashem.htm; www.presidency.ucsb.edu/ws/?pid=100689.

30 Leon Wieseltier, Elie Wiesel, Rt Revd Paul Moore, Jr and Shalmi Barmore, all quoted in Novick, *The Holocaust in American Life*, pp. 201, 211, 236.

31 Zoë Waxman, 'Testimonies as Sacred Texts: The Sanctification of Holocaust Writing', *Past and Present*, vol. 206, supplement 5 (2010), pp. 321–41; Novick, *The Holocaust in American Life*, pp. 201, 211; Michael Goldberg, *Why Should Jews Survive?* (New York: Oxford University Press, 1995), pp. 41–65.

32 Several senior political figures in America, including Barack Obama, have made reference to American troops liberating Auschwitz. While this is *factually* incorrect it is entirely in keeping with current mythological thinking: 'America' represents the hero, and 'Auschwitz' represents the martyr he rescued.

33 Novick, *The Holocaust in American Life*, p. 11.

34 Paul S. Fiddes, *Past Event and Present Salvation: The Christian Idea of Atonement* (London: Darton, Longman & Todd, 1989), p. 218; Jürgen Moltmann, *The Crucified God*, trans. R. A. Wilson and John Bowden (London: SCM Press, 1974), pp. 273–4; Cardinal Jean-Marie Lustiger, 'The Absence of God? The Presence of God? A Meditation in Three Parts on *Night*', in Harold Bloom (ed.), *Elie Wiesel's Night* (New York: Infobase, 2010), pp. 27–37; Franklin H. Littell, *The Crucifixion of the Jews* (New York: Harper & Row, 1975), passim; Gershon Greenberg, 'Crucifixion and the Holocaust: The Views of Pius XII and the Jews', in Carol Rittner and John K. Roth (eds), *Pope Pius XII and the Holocaust* (London: Continuum, 2002), pp. 137–53.

35 For an analysis of the supposed lessons of the Holocaust, see Novick, *The Holocaust in American Life*, pp. 239–63.

36 Kulka, *Landscapes of the Metropolis of Death*, p. 80.

37 Werner Weinberg, *Self-Portrait of a Holocaust Survivor* (Jefferson, NC: McFarland & Co., 1985), p. 152.

38 For an excellent summary of the Polish national martyr myth, see Geneviève Zubrzycki, 'Polish Mythology and the Traps of Messianic Martyrology', in Gérard Bouchard (ed.), *National Myths: Constructed Pasts, Contested Presents* (Oxford: Routledge, 2013), pp. 110–32.

39 28th Special Session of UN General Assembly, quoted in UN Press Release GA/10330, 24 January 2005; see www.un.org/News/Press/docs/2005/ga10330.doc.htm.

40 Thomas Kühne, 'Europe Exploits the Holocaust to Spread Its Message of Tolerance', *Guardian*, 27 January 2011.

41 Edna Aizenberg, 'Nation and Holocaust Narration: Uruguay's Memorial del Holocausto del Pueblo Judío', in Jeffrey Lesser and Raanan Reín (eds), *Rethinking Jewish-Latin Americans* (Albuquerque: University of New Mexico Press, 2008), pp. 207–30.

42 Locksley Edmondson, 'Reparations: Pan-African and Jewish Experiences', in William F. S. Miles (ed.), *Third World View of the Holocaust: Summary of the International Symposium* (Boston, MA: Northeastern University, 2002), p. 4.

43 Novick, *The Holocaust in American Life*, p. 13.

44 Ruth Amir, *Who is Afraid of Historical Redress?* (Boston, MA: Academic Studies Press, 2012), p. 239.

Chapter 5 – The Beginning of the World

1 Takashi Nagai, *The Bells of Nagasaki*, trans. William Johnston (Tokyo: Kodansha International, 1984), p. 82.

2 Ibid., p. 101.

3 Ibid., pp. 48, 60.

4 For Nagai as a cultural icon in Japan in the 1940s and 50s see William Johnston's introduction to Nagai, *The Bells of Nagasaki*, p. xx; Paul Glynn, *A Song for Nagasaki* (London: Fount Paperbacks, 1990), pp. 202–50; and John W. Dower, *Embracing Defeat: Japan in the Wake of World War II* (New York: W. W. Norton, 2000), pp. 197–8.

5 Glynn, *A Song for Nagasaki*, pp. 188–90.

6 Nanbara Shigeru, postwar president of Tokyo Imperial University, address to students, November 1945, quoted in Dower, *Embracing Defeat*, p. 488.

7 Dower, *Embracing Defeat*, pp. 497–500.

8 Ibid., pp. 493–4.

9 'South Korean Court Tells Japanese Company to Pay for Forced Labor', *New York Times*, 30 July 2013; 'Chinese Families Suing Japan Inc. for War Redress in Bigger Numbers', *Japan Times*, 13 May 2014; 'Unfinished Business', *Foreign Policy*, 28 June 2010. See also Dower, *Embracing Defeat*, pp. 531–4.

10 See the story of Tsuji Masanobu in Dower, *Embracing Defeat*, p. 513. See also pp. 464–5 and 508–521.

11 Noda Masaaki, 'One Army Surgeon's Account of Vivisection on Human Subjects in China', in Peter Li (ed.), *Japanese War Crimes* (New Brunswick, NJ: Transaction Books, 2009), pp. 135–8. For a longer exposition on this theme, see Noda Masaaki, *Senso to Zaiseki* (Tokyo: Iwanami Shoten, 1998).

12 See Harry S. Truman, Proclamation 2660, 'Victory in the East', 16 August 1945, www.presidency.ucsb.edu/ws/index.php?pid=12388&st=&st1.

13 Graeme Gill, *Symbols and Legitimacy in Soviet Politics* (Cambridge University Press, 2011), pp. 198–200.

14 Speech by Gustáv Husák at the opening of the 'Czechoslovakia 1985' Exhibition in Moscow, 31 May 1985, quoted in Foreign Broadcast Infor-

mation Service, *East Europe Report JPRS-EPS-85-070* (Arlington, VA: Joint Publications Research Service, 25 June 1985), p. 7; Tito's declaration of Democratic Federal Yugoslavia, 9 March 1945, in Fabijan Trgo (ed.), *The National Liberation War and Revolution in Yugoslavia (1941–1945): Selected Documents* (Belgrade: Military History Institute of the Yugoslav People's Army, 1982), p. 711; Kurt Hager, 'Der Sozialismus ist Unbesiegbar', *Einheit*, vol. 40, nos 4–5 (1985), pp. 313–18.

15 Prokop Murra, 'Order of the Day', Tirana, 9 May 1985, quoted in Joint Publications Research Service, *East Europe Report JPRS-EPS-85-072* (Arlington, VA: Joint Publications Research Service, 1 July 1985), p. 1.

16 Indeed, mourning in East Germany was officially discouraged. See 'Appeal on the 40th Anniversary of the Victory over Hitler Fascism and of the Liberation of the German People', in *Neues Deutschland*, 11 January 1985, p. 1.

17 Nehru's Independence Resolution, 13 December 1946, in Mushirul Hasan (ed.), *Nehru's India: Select Speeches* (New Delhi: Oxford University Press, 2007), p. 32.

18 Sukarno, speech on the birth of Pantja Sila, 1 June 1945, in Sukarno, *Toward Freedom and the Dignity of Man: A Collection of Five Speeches by President Sukarno of the Republic of Indonesia* (Jakarta: Department of Foreign Affairs, 1961), p. 20.

19 Nehru, speech on Indian membership of the British Commonwealth, 16 May 1949, in Hasan (ed.), *Nehru's India*, p. 87.

20 Ferhat Abbas, quoted in Benjamin Stora and Zakya Daoud, *Ferhat Abbas: une utopie algérienne* (Paris: Denoël, 1995), p. 133.

21 Keith Lowe, *Savage Continent* (London: Viking, 2012), passim.

22 See, for example, the Roberto Rossellini film *Germania, Anno Zero* (1948).

23 Speech by Romano Prodi, president of the European Commission, 'The New Europe and Japan', Tokyo, 19 July 2000, europa.eu/rapid/press-release_SPEECH-00-277_en.htm.

24 See the Schuman Declaration: http://europa.eu/about-eu/basic-information/symbols/europe-day/schuman-declaration/index_en.htm.

25 Statement to US Senate Foreign Relations Committee, 9 April 1953, in Konrad Adenauer, *Journey to America: Collected Speeches, Statements, Press, Radio and TV Interviews* (Washington, DC: Press Office German Diplomatic Mission, 1953), p. 51; and Konrad Adenauer, *World Indivisible: With Liberty and Justice for All*, trans. Richard and Clara Winston (New York: Harper & Bros, 1955), p. 6.

26 Vincent Della Sala, 'Myth and the Postnational Polity: The Case of the European Union', in Gérard Bouchard (ed.), *National Myths* (Oxford: Routledge, 2013), p. 161.

27 Speech by UN Secretary-General Ban Ki-moon, Moscow State University, 10 April 2008, https://www.un.org/sg/en/content/sg/statement/2008-04-10/secretary-generals-address-moscow-state-university; UN Under-secretary General for Communications and Public Information Shashi Tharoor, quoted in *World Chronicle*, no. 980 (8 June 2005), p. 2; statements by France's Michel Barnier, and the Netherlands' Max van der Stoel and Bulgaria's Stefan Tavrov in 28th Special Session of UN General Assembly, quoted in UN Press Release GA/10330, 24 January 2005 – see www.un.org/News/Press/docs/2005/ga10330.doc.htm.

28 Jawaharlal Nehru, speech to Indian Constituent Assembly, 16 May 1949, in Hasan (ed.), *Nehru's India*, p. 82.

Chapter 6 – Science

1 For a brief biography of Eugene Rabinowitch, written by his son, see Alexander Rabinowitch, 'Founder and Father', *Bulletin of the Atomic Scientists*, vol. 61, no. 1 (2005), pp. 30–37.

2 Eugene Rabinowitch, quoted in Robert Jungk, *Brighter Than a Thousand Suns*, trans. James Cleugh (London: Victor Gollancz, 1958), p. 183.

3 For the full text of the Franck Report, see ibid., pp. 335–46.

4 Quoted in Josh Schollmeyer, 'Minority Report', *Bulletin of the Atomic Scientists*, vol. 61, no. 1 (2005), p. 39.

5 Rabinowitch, 'Founder and Father', p. 36.

6 Eugene Rabinowitch, 'Five Years After', *Bulletin of the Atomic Scientists*, vol. 7, no. 1 (1951), p. 3.

7 Hans M. Kristensen and Robert S. Norris, 'Global Nuclear Weapons Inventories, 1945–2013', *Bulletin of the Atomic Scientists*, vol. 69, no. 5 (2013), p. 75.

8 Eugene Rabinowitch, *The Dawn of a New Age* (University of Chicago Press, 1963), p. 183.

9 E. B. White, editorial, 18 August 1945, reproduced in E. B. White, *The Wild Flag* (Boston, MA: Houghton Mifflin, 1946), p. 108; 'The Bomb', *Time*, 20 August 1945; William L. Laurence, *Dawn Over Zero* (London: Museum Press, 1947), p. 227.

10 *New York Times*, 29 September 1945.

11 *New York Times*, 26 September 1945.

12 Raymond Gram Swing, *Coronet*, and *New York Herald Tribune*, all quoted in Paul Boyer, *By the Bomb's Early Light* (Chapel Hill: University of North Carolina Press, 1994), pp. 33, 136 and 109.

13 Gerald Wendt, 'What Happened in Science', in Jack Goodman (ed.), *While You Were Gone: A Report on Wartime Life in the United States* (New York: Simon & Schuster, 1946), pp. 253–4.

14 Quoted in Boyer, *By the Bomb's Early Light*, p. 143; see also pp. 145–9.

15 See Jean-Paul Sartre, 'The Liberation of Paris: An Apocalyptic Week', in Ronald Aronson and Adrian van den Hoven (eds), *We Have Only This Life to Live: The Selected Essays of Jean-Paul Sartre* (New York: New York Review of Books, 2013), p. 117; Albert Einstein, 'A Reply to the Soviet Scientists', *Bulletin of the Atomic Scientists*, vol. 4, no. 2 (1948), p. 37; and 'Gen. Spaatz on Atomic Warfare', *Life*, 16 August 1948, p. 104.

16 *Picture Post*, 25 August 1945.

17 See, in the *Illustrated Weekly of India*, Autolycus, 'As I See It', 19 August 1945; 'Journey to the Moon: Atomic Power Might Make Idle Dreams Come True One Day!', 2 September 1945; 'Atomic Power in Industry', 18 November 1945.

18 See the essays by Dolores L. Augustine, Dick van Lente, Hirofumi Utsumi and Sonja D. Schmid in Dick van Lente (ed.), *The Nuclear Age in Popular Media: A Transnational History, 1945–1965* (New York: Palgrave Macmillan, 2012).

19 Roslynn D. Haynes, *From Faust to Strangelove: Representations of the Scientist in Western Literature* (Baltimore: Johns Hopkins University Press, 1994), passim.

20 See the figures of the 2002 International Symposium on Crimes of Bacteriological Warfare quoted in Brian J. Ford, *Secret Weapons: Technology, Science and the Race to Win World War II* (Oxford: Osprey, 2011), p. 173.

21 Ibid., pp. 45–52, 115–61.

22 W. H. Helfand et al., 'Wartime Industrial Development of Penicillin in the United States', in John Parascandola (ed.), *The History of Antibiotics: A Symposium* (Madison, WI: American Institute of the History of Pharmacy, 1980), pp. 40, 50–51.

23 *Straits Times* (Singapore), 20 September 1945 and 9 October 1945; Thomas R. Dunlap, *DDT: Scientists, Citizens, and Public Policy* (Princeton University Press, 1981), pp. 17, 60–63.

24 Ford, *Secret Weapons*, pp. 270–74.

25 Ibid., pp. 250–58; Don Murray, 'Percy Spencer and his Itch to Know', *Reader's Digest* (US), August 1958, p. 114.

26 'Harry Coover, Super Glue's Inventor, Dies at 94', *New York Times*, 27 March 2011.

27 Gary Chapman, 'Hedy Lamarr's Invention Finally Comes of Age', *Los Angeles Times*, 31 January 2000.

28 Nikolai Bulganin, speech to the Central Committee plenum, July 1955, quoted in David Holloway, *Stalin and the Bomb* (New Haven, CT: Yale University Press, 1994), p. 356.

29 Sonja D. Schmid, 'Shaping the Soviet Experience of the Atomic Age: Nuclear Topics in *Ogonyok*', in van Lente (ed.), *The Nuclear Age in Popular Media*, p. 41.

30 Soviet scientist quoted in *Illustrated Weekly of India*, 8 November 1959.

31 *Neue Berliner Illustrierte* and *Stern*, quoted in Dolores L. Augustine, 'Learning from War: Media Coverage of the Nuclear Age in the Two Germanies', in van Lente (ed.), *The Nuclear Age in Popular Media*, p. 89.

32 *Illustrated Weekly of India*, 19 August 1945, 14 July 1946, 3 October 1946.

33 Boyer, *By the Bomb's Early Light*, pp. 115–16; George Gamow, *Atomic Energy in Cosmic and Human Life* (New York: Macmillan, 1946), p. 153; O. R. Frisch, *Meet the Atoms: A Popular Guide to Modern Physics* (New York: A. A. Wyn, 1947), pp. 220–21.

34 Jungk, *Brighter Than a Thousand Suns*, pp. 217–18; Kai Bird and Martin J. Sherwin, *American Prometheus: The Triumph and Tragedy of J. Robert Oppenheimer* (New York: Random House, 2005).

35 Joel Shurkin, *Broken Genius: The Rise and Fall of William Shockley, Creator of the Electronic Age* (Basingstoke: Macmillan, 2006), pp. 65, 95–9; J. Robert Oppenheimer, 'Physics in the Contemporary World', *Bulletin of the Atomic Scientists*, vol. 4, no. 3 (1948), p. 65.

36 Eugene Rabinowitch, 'The Labors of Sisyphus', *Bulletin of the Atomic Scientists*, vol. 7, no. 10 (1951), p. 291.

37 Ernst Chain, 'A Short History of the Penicillin Discovery from Fleming's Early Observations in 1929 to the Present Time', in Parascandola (ed.), *The History of Antibiotics*, pp. 22–3.

38 For discussion of these issues, see in particular P. W. Bridgman, 'Scientists and Social Responsibility', *Bulletin of the Atomic Scientists*, vol. 4, no. 3 (1948), and discussion afterwards, pp. 69–75; but these issues are repeated throughout the first ten years of the journal.

39 Oppenheimer, 'Physics in the Contemporary World', p. 66.

40 Dr Theodor Hauschke, quoted in Jungk, *Brighter Than a Thousand Suns*, p. 231.

41 See Boyer, *By the Bomb's Early Light*, pp. 181–95.

Chapter 7 – Planned Utopias

1 Alan Milward, *War, Economy and Society, 1939–1945* (Berkeley and Los Angeles: University of California Press, 1977), pp. 284–6.

2 Theodor Adorno, *Minima Moralia*, trans. E. F. N. Jephcott (London: Verso, 2005), p. 54.

3 The story of Giancarlo's life is taken mostly from Benedict Zucchi, *Giancarlo De Carlo* (Oxford: Butterworth Architecture, 1992), especially pp. 157–73, and John McKean, *Giancarlo De Carlo: Layered Places* (Stuttgart and London: Edition Axel Menges, 2004), especially pp. 202–4.

4 McKean, *Giancarlo De Carlo*, p. 202.

5 Ibid., p. 202.

6 Ibid., p. 203.

7 Keith Lowe, *Savage Continent* (London: Viking, 2012), p. 10; UN Archives, UNRRA photos 1202, 1204, and S-0800-0016-01-17.

8 Tony Judt, *Postwar* (London: Pimlico, 2005), p. 17.

9 UK National Archives, CAB 21/2110; Lowe, *Savage Continent*, pp. 6–7, 400–401; Judt, *Postwar*, pp. 16–17; John W. Dower, *Embracing Defeat: Japan in the Wake of World War II* (New York: W. W. Norton, 2000), p. 47; Pankaj Mishra, 'Land and Blood', *New Yorker*, 25 November 2013.

10 Between 1945 and 1970 the world's population rose by around 50 per cent, but the population of the world's cities approximately doubled: see UN Department of Economic and Social Affairs, 'World Urbanization Prospects: The 2011 Revision', Working Paper no. ST/ESA/SER.A/322, p. 4.

11 Sigfried Giedion, *Space, Time & Architecture*, 5th edn (Cambridge, MA: Harvard University Press, 2008), pp. 819, 822; Le Corbusier, *The Radiant City* (London: Faber & Faber, 1967), p. 96.

12 Paul Morand, 'Nouveau style', *Voix Française*, 19 March 1943; quoted in Pierre Le Goïc, *Brest en reconstruction* (Presses Universitaires de Rennes, 2001), p. 129.

13 Paul Schmitthenner, quoted in Jörn Düwel and Niels Gutschow (eds), *A Blessing in Disguise* (Berlin: Dom, 2013), p. 163; and Konstanty Gutschow, quoted in Spiegel Online, 'Out of the Ashes: A New Look at Germany's

Postwar Reconstruction', www.spiegel.de/international/germany/out-of-the-ashes-a-new-look-at-germany-s-postwar-reconstruction-a-702856-2.html. See also Jeffry M. Diefendorf, *In the Wake of the War* (New York: Oxford University Press, 1993), pp. 188–9.

14 Stanisław Jankowski, 'Warsaw: Destruction, Secret Town Planning, 1939–1944, and Postwar Reconstruction', in Jeffry M. Diefendorf (ed.), *Rebuilding Europe's Bombed Cities* (Basingstoke: Macmillan, 1990), p. 81.

15 Julian Huxley, foreword to Flora Stephenson and Phoebe Pool, *A Plan for Town and Country* (London: The Pilot Press, 1944), p. 7. See also Patrick Abercrombie, *The Greater London Plan 1944* (London: HMSO, 1945), p. 1.

16 Cabinet Committee on the Reconstruction of Town and Country, quoted in Anthony Sutcliffe and Roger Smith, *History of Birmingham,* vol. 3: *Birmingham, 1939–1970* (London: Oxford University Press for Birmingham City Council, 1974), p. 464; Frank H. Rushford, *City Beautiful: A Vision of Durham* (Durham County Advertiser, 1944); J. B. Morrell, *The City of Our Dreams* (London: St Anthony's Press, 1955).

17 Thomas Sharp, *Exeter Phoenix* (London: Architectural Press, 1946), p. 134.

18 James Watson and Patrick Abercrombie, *A Plan for Plymouth* (Plymouth: Underhill, 1943), p. 11.

19 Catherine Bauer, 'The County of London Plan – American Reactions: Planning is Politics – But are Planners Politicians?', *Architectural Review,* vol. 96, no. 574 (1944), p. 81.

20 Diefendorf, *In the Wake of War,* p. 183.

21 Brochure by the National Association of Real Estate Boards published in 1944, quoted in Friedhelm Fischer, 'German Reconstruction as an International Activity', in Diefendorf (ed.), *Rebuilding Europe's Bombed Cities,* pp. 133–4.

22 Le Corbusier, *The Athens Charter* (New York: Viking, 1973), p. 54.

23 José Luis Sert, *Can Our Cities Survive?* (Cambridge, MA: Harvard University Press, 1944), pp. 246–9.

24 Lewis Mumford, *The Culture of Cities* (London: Secker & Warburg, 1940), pp. 296, 298, 330.

25 Ebenezer Howard, *To-morrow: A Peaceful Path to Real Reform* (London: Swan Sonnenschein, 1898), p. 10. For discussion of Howard's legacy, see Stephen V. Ward (ed.), *The Garden City* (London: E & FN Spon, 1992); and Stanley Buder, *Visionaries and Planners: The Garden City Movement and the Modern Community* (New York: Oxford University Press, 1990).

26 Frank Lloyd Wright, *Modern Architecture: Being the Kahn Lectures for 1930* (Princeton University Press, 2008), p. 112.

27 Frank Lloyd Wright, *The Disappearing City* (New York: William Farquhar Payson, 1932), p. 17; see also Neil Levine's introduction to Wright's *Modern Architecture*, p. xlix. For the debate on the merits of dispersal as a nuclear defence, see *Bulletin of the Atomic Scientists*, vol. 7, no. 9 (1951), pp. 242–4.

28 Sert, *Can Our Cities Survive?*, p. 210.

29 Giedion, *Space, Time & Architecture*, p. 822.

30 Karl Marx and Friedrich Engels, *The Communist Manifesto* (Harmondsworth: Penguin, 1985), p. 105. See also Robert H. Kargon and Arthur P. Molella, *Invented Edens: Techno-Cities of the Twentieth Century* (Cambridge, MA: MIT Press, 2008), p. 27; and Owen Hatherley, *Landscapes of Communism* (London: Allen Lane, 2015), pp. 11, 13.

31 Klaus von Beyme, 'Reconstruction in the German Democratic Republic', in Diefendorf (ed.), *Rebuilding Europe's Bombed Cities*, p. 193.

32 Hatherley, *Landscapes of Communism*, p. 20.

33 Mumford, *The Culture of Cities*, p. 403; Le Corbusier, *The Athens Charter*, pp. 103–4.

34 Wright, *The Disappearing City*, pp. 28, 44.

35 Syrkus, quoted in Katrin Steffen and Martin Kohlrausch, 'The Limits and Merits of Internationalism: Experts, the State and the International Community in Poland in the First Half of the Twentieth Century', *European Review of History*, vol. 16, no. 5 (2009), p. 723.

36 Le Corbusier, *The Radiant City*, p. 118.

37 McKean, *Giancarlo De Carlo*, p. 203.

38 Zucchi, *Giancarlo De Carlo*, p. 158.

39 Giancarlo De Carlo writing in *Casabella Continuità* in 1954, quoted in Zucchi, *Giancarlo De Carlo*, p. 15.

40 Zucchi, *Giancarlo De Carlo*, p. 161.

41 Ibid., pp. 10, 13.

42 Ibid., p. 10.

43 Jane Jacobs, *The Death and Life of Great American Cities* (London: Jonathan Cape, 1962); Oscar Newman, *Defensible Space* (New York: Macmillan, 1972).

44 See Emrys Jones, 'Aspects of Urbanization in Venezuela', *Ekistics*, vol. 18, no. 109 (1964), pp. 420–25; Alice Coleman, *Utopia on Trial* (London: Hilary Shipman, 1985), p. 17.

45 Lewis Silkin, quoted in Buder, *Visionaries and Planners*, p. 186.

46 Michael Young and Peter Willmott, *Family and Kinship in East London* (Harmondsworth: Penguin, 2007), pp. 197–9; Buder, *Visionaries and Planners*, pp. 188–9.

47 Lewis Mumford, quoted in Buder, *Visionaries and Planners*, p. 203.

48 Zucchi, *Giancarlo De Carlo*, p. 169.

49 McKean, *Giancarlo De Carlo*, p. 204.

50 Judt, *Postwar*, pp. 70–71.

51 Advisory Committee to Japan's Ministry of Foreign Affairs, quoted in Dower, *Embracing Defeat*, p. 539. See also note 34 on p. 646.

52 Jawaharlal Nehru, broadcast to the nation, 31 December 1952, quoted in Mushirul Hasan (ed.), *Nehru's India: Selected Speeches* (New Delhi: Oxford University Press, 2007), p. 160.

53 F. A. Hayek, *The Road to Serfdom* (London: Routledge, 1944).

54 R. M. Hartwell, *A History of the Mont Pelerin Society* (Indianapolis: Liberty Fund, 1995), pp. 18–19.

Chapter 8 – Equality and Diversity

1 For Françoise Leclercq's story see her speech to the conference of l'Union des Femmes Françaises on 23 November 1975, reproduced in Union des Femmes Françaises, *Les Femmes dans la Résistance* (Monaco: Éditions du Rocher, 1977), pp. 168–70.

2 Documentary film: *2ème congrès de l'Union des Femmes Françaises*, available in the Cine Archives of the Parti Communiste Français Mouvement Ouvrier et Démocratique, www.cinearchives.org/Catalogue-d-exploitation-494-132-0-0.html.

3 Madeleine Dreyfus of the Oeuvre de Secours aux Enfants and Madeleine Barot of Cimade: see Caroline Moorehead, *Village of Secrets* (London: Chatto & Windus, 2014), passim.

4 Mireille Albrecht, *Berty* (Paris: Robert Laffont, 1986), pp. 169–333; Siân Rees, *Lucie Aubrac* (London: Michael O'Mara, 2015), pp. 135–55; Charlotte Delbo, *Convoy to Auschwitz: Women of the French Resistance* (Boston, MA: Northeastern University Press, 1997), passim.

5 Jane Slaughter, *Women and the Italian Resistance, 1943–1945* (Denver: Arden Press, 1997), pp. 33, 58.

6 Jelena Batinić, *Women and Yugoslav Partisans* (New York: Cambridge University Press, 2015), pp. 260–62.

7 Vina A. Lanzona, *Amazons of the Huk Rebellion* (Madison: University of Wisconsin Press, 2009), pp. 72–5; for Indonesia, see below, chapter 16.

8 Anna Krylova, *Soviet Women in Combat* (New York: Cambridge University Press, 2010), p. 145.

9 Geneviève Vailland, *Le Travail des Femmes* (Paris: Jeune Patron, 1947), p. 9; Hanna Diamond, *Women and the Second World War in France, 1939–48: Choices and Constraints* (Harlow: Longman, 1999), p. 34.

10 Denise Breton, 'La Résistance, étape importante dans l'évolution de la condition féminine', in Union des Femmes Françaises, *Les Femmes dans la Résistance*, pp. 227, 228, 233–4; René Cerf-Ferrière quote: p. 230.

11 Anon., *A Woman in Berlin* (London: Virago, 2006), p. 62.

12 Robert Gildea, *Fighters in the Shadows* (London: Faber & Faber, 2015), p. 131.

13 See Nadje Al-Ali, *Secularism, Gender and the State in the Middle East: The Egyptian Women's Movement* (Cambridge University Press, 2009), pp. 64, 73–4.

14 Saskia Wieringa, *Sexual Politics in Indonesia* (Basingstoke: Palgrave Macmillan, 2002), pp. 115–16, 252–5.

15 Francesca Miller, *Latin American Women and the Search for Social Justice* (Hanover, NH: University Press of New England, 1991), p. 143.

16 See Jadwiga E. Pieper Mooney, 'Fighting Fascism and Forging New Political Activism: The Women's International Democratic Federation (WIDF) in the Cold War', in Jadwiga E. Pieper Mooney and Fabio Lanza (eds), *De-Centering Cold War History* (Oxford: Routledge, 2013), pp. 52–3; and Francisca de Haan, 'Hoffnungen auf eine bessere Welt: die frühen Jahre der Internationalen Demokratischen Frauenföderation (IDFF/WIDF) (1945–50)', *Feministische Studien*, vol. 27, no. 2 (2009), pp. 243–46.

17 René Cerf-Ferrière, *Chemin Clandestin* (Paris: Julliard, 1968), p. 189. See also Diamond, *Women and the Second World War in France, 1939–48*, pp. 179–85, who offers alternative interpretations.

18 Mary Zeiss Stange et al. (eds), *Encyclopedia of Women in Today's World*, vol. 1 (Los Angeles: Sage, 2011), pp. 1529–31.

19 Simone de Beauvoir, *The Second Sex*, trans. H. M. Parshley (London: Picador, 1988), pp. 737, 741.

20 Diamond, *Women and the Second World War in France, 1939–48*, p. 55; Claire Duchen, *Women's Rights and Women's Lives in France, 1944–1968* (London: Routledge, 1994), pp. 64–5; Sarah Fishman, 'Waiting for the Captive Sons of France: Prisoner of War Wives, 1940–1945', in Margaret Higonnet et al. (eds), *Behind the Lines: Gender and the Two World Wars* (New Haven, CT: Yale University Press, 1987), p. 193.

21 Jeanne Bohec, *La plastiqueuse à bicyclette* (Paris: Mercure de France, 1975), p. 186.

22 Philip Morgan, *The Fall of Mussolini* (New York: Oxford University Press, 2007), p. 193.

23 'Merci de nous écrire', *Elle*, 27 August 1946, p. 22; 'L'aide aux mères de famille', *Pour la vie*, no. 34 (1950); quoted in Duchen, *Women's Rights and Women's Lives in France, 1944–1968*, p. 67; Mme Foulon-Lefranc's domestic science manual, *Le Femme au Foyer*, quoted ibid., pp. 66, 68; see also pp. 65, 67, 101–2; Diamond, *Women and the Second World War in France, 1939–48*, pp. 162–3.

24 François Billoux, 'À la Libération, une legislation sociale favourable aux femmes', Union des Femmes Françaises, *Les Femmes dans la Résistance*, p. 251; Diamond, *Women and the Second World War in France, 1939–1948*, pp. 175–6.

25 Sharon Elise Cline, '*Féminité à la Française*: Femininity, Social Change and French National Identity, 1945–1970', PhD Thesis, University of Wisconsin–Madison, 2008, p. 144.

26 Duchen, *Women's Rights and Women's Lives in France, 1944–1968*, p. 54.

27 Madeleine Vincent, *Femmes: quelle liberation?* (Paris: Éditions sociales, 1976), pp. 29–30, 37–8.

28 Al-Ali, *Secularism, Gender and the State in the Middle East*, pp. 73–4; Wieringa, *Sexual Politics in Indonesia*, pp. 115–16, 252–5; Miller, *Latin American Women and the Search for Social Justice*, p. 143.

29 See the ILO website: especially www.ilo.org/dyn/normlex/en/f?p=NO RMLEXPUB:11300:0::NO::P11300_INSTRUMENT_ID:312245.

30 'Gender Pay Gap "May Take 118 Years to Close" – World Economic Forum', BBC News, 19 November 2015, www.bbc.co.uk/news/world-europe-34842471.

31 Stange et al. (eds), *Encyclopedia of Women in Today's World*, vol. 1, pp. 1529–31; 'Women in Saudi Arabia Vote for the First Time', *Washington Post*, 12 December 2015.

32 Toril Moi, 'The Adulteress Wife', *London Review of Books*, vol. 32, no. 3 (11 February 2010), p. 4.

33 'My Day' column, 16 February 1962, in Eleanor Roosevelt, *My Day: The Best of Eleanor Roosevelt's Acclaimed Newspaper Columns, 1936–1962*, ed. David Emblidge (Boston, MA: Da Capo Press, 2001), p. 301.

34 Michella M. Marino, 'Mothers, Spy Queens, and Subversives: Women in the McCarthy Era', in Caroline S. Emmons (ed.), *Cold War and McCarthy Era: People and Perspectives* (Santa Barbara, CA: ABC-Clio, 2010), p. 140.

35 See Mooney, 'Fighting Fascism', pp. 52–3; and de Haan, 'Hoffnungen auf eine bessere Welt', pp. 243–6.

36 Lynne Attwood, *Creating the New Soviet Woman* (Basingstoke: Macmillan, 1999), pp. 114, 150–55, 167; David K. Willis, *Klass: How Russians Really Live* (New York: St Martin's Press, 1985), pp. 155–82; Susan Bridger, 'Soviet Rural Women: Employment and Family Life', in Beatrice Farnsworth and Lynne Viola (eds), *Russian Peasant Women* (New York: Oxford University Press, 1992), pp. 271–93.

37 Valentina Pavlovna Chudayeva, quoted in Svetlana Alexiyevich, *War's Unwomanly Face*, trans. Keith Hammond and Lyudmila Lezhneva (Moscow: Progress, 1988), pp. 189, 244.

38 De Beauvoir, *The Second Sex*, pp. 15–16.

39 Ibid., p. 639.

40 Moi, 'The Adulteress Wife', pp. 3–6.

41 Sakiko Fukuda-Parr, Terra Lawson-Remer and Susan Randolph, *Fulfilling Social and Economic Rights* (New York: Oxford University Press, 2015), p. 146.

42 Jean-Paul Sartre, *Anti-Semite and Jew*, trans. George J. Becker (New York: Schocken Books, 1948), originally published in French in 1946.

43 Anatole Broyard, 'Portrait of the Inauthentic Negro', *Commentary*, vol. 10, no. 1 (1950), pp. 56–64; W. E. B. Du Bois, *The World and Africa/Color and Democracy* (New York: Oxford University Press, 2007), p. 13 – *The World and Africa* was originally published 1947.

44 De Beauvoir, *The Second Sex*, pp. 14, 18, 23, 159, 706–7, 723.

45 Ibid., pp. 23–4.

46 Godfrey Hodgson, *America in Our Time* (Princeton University Press, 2005), p. 58.

47 Ronald Allen Goldberg, *America in the Forties* (Syracuse University Press, 2012), p. 103.

48 Quoted ibid., p. 103.

49 Leila J. Rupp, 'The Persistence of Transnational Organizing: The Case of the Homophile Movement', *American Historical Review*, vol. 116, no. 4 (2011), p. 1019.

50 Allan Bérubé, *Coming Out Under Fire: The History of Gay Men and Women in World War II* (Chapel Hill: University of North Carolina Press, 2010), pp. 228, 244, 257.

51 Paul Ginsborg, 'The Communist Party and the Agrarian Question in Southern Italy, 1943–48', *History Workshop*, vol. 17 (1984), p. 89; Ilario

Ammendolia, *Occupazione delle Terre in Calabria, 1945–1949* (Rome: Gangemi, 1990), pp. 22–8.

Chapter 9 – Freedom and Belonging

1 Hans Bjerkholt's story is taken from three sources: Gabriel Marcel (ed.), *Fresh Hope for the World* (London: Longmans, Green & Co., 1960), pp. 79–91; and two pamphlets written by Bjerkholt, 'The Revolution for Our Time' and 'Perchè ho scelto il Riarmo morale', from the Archives Cantonales Vaudoises in Switzerland, PP746/2.1/71 and PP746/2.1/72.

2 Daniel Sack, *Moral Re-Armament: The Reinventions of an American Religious Movement* (New York: Palgrave Macmillan, 2009), pp. 190, 192.

3 Max Weber, *The Protestant Ethic and the Spirit of Capitalism* (New York: Oxford University Press, 2011), pp. 177–8.

4 Keith Lowe, *Savage Continent* (London: Viking, 2012).

5 Émile Durkheim, *The Elementary Forms of the Religious Life*, trans. Joseph Ward Swain (London: George Allen and Unwin, 1915), pp. 225–6.

6 R. Ernest Dupuy and Trevor N. Dupuy, *The Harper Encyclopedia of Military History*, 4th edn (New York: HarperCollins, 1993), pp. 1083, 1309.

7 Irena Grocher diary, on the liberation of Warsaw, quoted in Michał Grynberg (ed.), *Words to Outlive Us: Eyewitness Accounts from the Warsaw Ghetto* (London: Granta, 2003), p. 404.

8 Major Corrie Halliday, IWM Sound 15620, Reel 32; and Flight Lieutenant Frank Ziegler, quoted in Max Arthur, *Forgotten Voices of the Second World War* (London: Ebury Press, 2004), p. 473.

9 Captain John MacAuslan, IWM Sound 8225, reel 4.

10 Emmanuil Kazakevich, quoted in Elena Zubkova, *Russia After the War*, trans. Hugh Ragsdale (Armonk, NY: M. E. Sharpe, 1998), p. 28.

11 Jean-Paul Sartre, 'The Liberation of Paris: An Apocalyptic Week', in Ronald Aronson and Adrian van den Hoven (eds), *We Have Only This Life to Live: The Selected Essays of Jean Paul Sartre* (New York Review of Books, 2013), pp. 115–18; originally published in *Clarté*, 24 August 1945.

12 Jean-Paul Sartre, *Existentialism and Humanism*, trans. Philip Mairet (London: Methuen, 2007), pp. 30, 38.

13 Jean-Paul Sartre, 'The Republic of Silence', in Aronson and van den Hoven (eds), *We Have Only This Life to Live*, p. 84; originally published in *Les Lettres françaises*, September 1944.

14 For other interpretations of Sartre's sudden and massive popularity see Patrick Baert, *The Existentialist Moment* (Cambridge: Polity Press, 2015), pp. 5–13, 135–49.

15 Erich Fromm, *The Fear of Freedom* (Oxford: Routledge Classics, 2001), p. 17.

16 Ibid., p. 181.

17 Ibid., pp. 90–91, 111, 218.

18 Ibid., p. 232.

19 Ibid., pp. 232–3; Sartre, 'The Liberation of Paris', p. 118.

20 Gabriel Marcel, Damasio Cardoso, Luigi Rossi and Maurice Mercier quoted in Marcel (ed.), *Fresh Hope for the World*, pp. 15, 33, 79, 123.

21 Sack, *Moral Re-Armament*, p. 5.

22 Lowe, *Savage Continent*, p. 64; Mark Mazower, *No Enchanted Palace* (Princeton University Press, 2009), p. 61.

23 Patrick Johnstone, *The Future of the Global Church: History, Trends and Possibilities* (Downers Grove, IL: InterVarsity Press, 2011), p. 99.

24 'Einleitung der Herausgeber', in Joachim Köhler and Damian van Melis (eds), *Siegerin in Trümmern: Die Rolle der katholischen Kirche in der deutschen Nachkriegsgesellschaft* (Stuttgart: Verlag W. Kohlhammer, 1998), p. 11; Benjamin Ziemann, *Encounters with Modernity: The Catholic Church in West Germany, 1945–1975*, trans. Andrew Evans (New York: Berghahn, 2014), pp. 10, 49.

25 Witold Zdaniewicz, *Kościół Katolicki w Polsce, 1945–1982* (Poznan: Pallottinum, 1983), pp. 47–50; Carlo Falconi, *La Chiesa e le organizzazioni cattoliche in Italia (1945–1955)* (Rome: Einaudi, 1956), p. 52.

26 Falconi, *La Chiesa e le organizzazioni cattoliche in Italia (1945–1955)*, p. 133.

27 See www.brin.ac.uk/figures/#ChangingBelief.

28 Anthony Curwen interview, IWM Sound 9810, Reel 9 (and see chapter 15 below); Lowe, *Savage Continent*, pp. 278, 336; Fernando Claudin, *The Communist Movement: From Comintern to Cominform* (Harmondsworth: Penguin, 1975), p. 309; Cynthia S. Kaplan, 'The Impact of World War II on the Party', in Susan J. Linz (ed.), *The Impact of World War II on the Soviet Union* (Totowa, NJ: Rowman and Allanheld, 1985), p. 160.

29 Emmanuel Levinas, 'Freedom of Speech', in Emmanuel Levinas, *Difficult Freedom*, trans. Seán Hand (Baltimore: Johns Hopkins University Press, 1990), p. 205.

30 See the editors' introduction in Leslie Bethell and Ian Roxborough (eds), *Latin America Between the Second World War and the Cold War, 1944–1948* (New York: Cambridge University Press, 1992), p. 13.

31 Jon Kraus, 'Trade Unions, Democratization, and Economic Crises in Ghana', in Jon Kraus (ed.), *Trade Unions and the Coming of Democracy in Africa* (New York: Palgrave Macmillan, 2007), pp. 89–91. For commentary on trade union growth in other African nations, see other essays in the same volume; and David Killingray and Richard Rathbone (eds), *Africa and the Second World War* (Basingstoke: Macmillan, 1986), pp. 15 and 155.

32 Robert D. Putnam, *Bowling Alone: The Collapse and Revival of American Community* (New York: Simon & Schuster, 2000), pp. 71, 81, 84, 103, 112 and Appendix III; and quotes from pp. 54–5, 83.

33 Ibid., pp. 54, 275–6, 283–4. For a summary of criticism against Putnam's approach, see John Field, *Social Capital* (Oxford: Routledge, 2008), pp. 41–3.

34 Bjerkholt in Marcel (ed.), *Fresh Hope for the World*, p. 87.

35 Bjerkholt, 'The Revolution for Our Time'.

36 Tom Driberg, *The Mystery of Moral Re-Armament: A Study of Frank Buchman and His Movement* (London: Secker & Warburg, 1964), p. 299.

37 Dr Hensley Henson, Bishop of Durham and Rt Revd M. J. Browne, Bishop of Galway, quoted ibid., pp. 192–3.

38 Allan W. Eister, *Drawing-Room Conversion: A Sociological Account of the Oxford Group Movement* (Durham, NC: Duke University Press, 1950), pp. 210–16.

39 Basil Entwistle and John McCook Roots, *Moral Re-Armament: What Is It?* (Los Angeles: Pace, 1967).

Chapter 10 – World Economy

1 Chittaprosad, quoted in Prodyot Ghosh, *Chittaprosad: A Doyen of Art-World* (Calcutta: Shilpayan Artists Society, 1995), pp. 3–4.

2 Ibid., p. 7; Nikhil Sarkar, *A Matter of Conscience: Artists Bear Witness to the Great Bengal Famine of 1943*, trans. Satyabrata Dutta (Calcutta: Punascha, 1994), p. 28.

3 Ghosh, *Chittaprosad*, p. 7.

4 Amartya Sen, *Poverty and Famines: An Essay on Entitlement and Deprivation* (Oxford: Clarendon Press, 1981), pp. 55, 69; Srimanjari, *Through War and Famine: Bengal, 1939–45* (New Delhi: Orient BlackSwan, 2009), pp. 158–9. A maund is a measure equivalent to around 82lb or 37kg.

5 Famine Inquiry Commission, *Report on Bengal* (New Delhi: Government of India, 1945), pp. 38–41, 63, 104–5.

6 Bengal exported 185,000 tons of rice in 1942, the year the famine began: see Madhusree Mukerjee, *Churchill's Secret War* (New York: Basic Books, 2010), p. 67.

7 Famine Inquiry Commission, *Report on Bengal*, pp. 105–6; Lizzie Colling-ham, *The Taste of War* (London: Allen Lane, 2011), pp. 145, 152; Ian Stephens, *Monsoon Morning* (London: Ernest Benn, 1966), p. 179.

8 Freda Bedi, *Bengal Lamenting* (Lahore: The Lion Press, 1944), p. 105.

9 Collingham, *The Taste of War*, p. 151.

10 See Chittaprosad's newspaper articles 'Journey Through Midnapore – Den of Rice-Smuggling Mahajans', *People's War*, 16 July 1944, p. 4; 'The Riches Piled Here: An Insult to Hungry Thousands Around', *People's War*, 6 August 1944, p. 4; 'Life Behind the Front Lines', *People's War*, 24 September 1944.

11 Chittaprosad, *Hungry Bengal* (Bombay: no publisher, 1944), pp. 6, 8.

12 Ghosh, *Chittaprosad*, pp. 4–5. See also the similar comments he made in the film *Confession* in 1972, quoted in Sanjoy Kumar Mallik (ed.), *Chittaprosad: A Retrospective*, 2 vols (New Delhi: Delhi Art Gallery, 2011), vol. 2, pp. 489–90.

13 Famine Inquiry Commission, *Report on Bengal*, p. 110; Sen, *Poverty and Famines*, p. 202; Paul R. Greenough, *Prosperity and Misery in Modern Bengal: The Famine of 1943–1944* (New York: Oxford University Press, 1982), p. 140; but see also Arup Maharatna, *The Demography of Famines: An Indian Histor-ical Perspective* (New Delhi: Oxford University Press, 1996), p. 147, who puts the figure at between 1.8 and 2.4 million. For statistics on epidemics, see Srimanjari, *Through War and Famine*, p. 216.

14 Collingham, *The Taste of War*, p. 241; Sugata Bose, 'Starvation Amidst Plenty: The Making of Famine in Bengal, Honan and Tonkin, 1942–45', *Modern Asian Studies*, vol. 24, no. 4 (1990), p. 699; Bùi Minh Dũng, 'Japan's Role in the Vietnamese Starvation of 1944–45', *Modern Asian Studies*, vol. 29, no. 3 (1995), p. 576.

15 Keith Lowe, *Savage Continent* (London: Viking, 2012), pp. 34–40; Colling-ham, *The Taste of War*, p. 1.

16 See Sen, *Poverty and Famines*, passim. For a view which disputes Sen's anal-ysis, see Mark B. Tauger, 'Entitlement, Shortage and the Bengal Famine of 1943: Another Look', *Journal of Peasant Studies*, vol. 31, no. 1 (2003), pp. 45–72.

17 Ian Friel, *Maritime History of Britain and Ireland* (London: British Museum Press, 2003), p. 245; UN Department of Economic Affairs, *Economic Report: Salient Features of the World Economic Situation, 1945–47* (Lake Success, NY: UN, 1948), p. 79.

18 Alan Milward, *War, Economy and Society, 1939–1945* (Berkeley and Los Angeles: University of California Press, 1977), p. 247.

19 UN, *Salient Features of the World Economic Situation, 1945–47*, pp. 108, 113.

20 Milward, *War, Economy and Society, 1939–1945*, pp. 356–7.

21 Ibid., p. 347; William Charles Chamberlin, *Economic Development of Iceland through World War II* (New York: Columbia University Press, 1947), p. 96.

22 David Killingray, 'Labour Mobilization in British Colonial Africa', in David Killingray and Richard Rathbone (eds), *Africa and the Second World War* (Basingstoke: Macmillan, 1986), pp. 70, 82–90. See also John Iliffe, *A Modern History of Tanganyika* (Cambridge University Press, 1979), pp. 351–4.

23 Nancy Ellen Lawler, *Soldiers of Misfortune: Ivoirien Tirailleurs of World War II* (Athens: Ohio University Press, 1992), pp. 208–18.

24 Sources for table: UN, *Salient Features of the World Economic Situation, 1945–47*, pp. 39, 43, 46 (America); 56 (Latin America), 68 (Australasia), 86 (Asia), 100 (Middle East), 116 (Africa), 160, 162, 165, 166 (Europe). For Kenya see Kenya Cost of Living Commission, *Cost of Living Commission Report* (Nairobi, 1950), p. 4. For Algeria see Charles Issawi, *An Economic History of the Middle East and North Africa* (New York: Columbia University Press, 1982), p. 188. For China, see Arthur N. Young, *China's Wartime Finance and Inflation, 1937–1945* (Cambridge, MA: Harvard University Press, 1965), table 52, p. 352.

25 UN, *Salient Features of the World Economic Situation, 1945–47*, pp. 160, 164.

26 Ibid., pp. 160, 164.

27 Collingham, *The Taste of War*, p. 247; Diana Lary, *The Chinese People at War: Human Suffering and Social Transformation, 1937–1945* (New York: Cambridge University Press, 2010), p. 122; Chang Kia-Ngau, *The Inflationary Spiral: The Experience in China, 1939–1950* (Cambridge, MA: Technology Press of the Massachusetts Institute of Technology, 1958), pp. 371–3.

28 Tomasz Pattantyus, 'My Life as a 12-Year-Old Billionaire', *Santa Clarita Valley Signal*, 22 August 2009; available online at www.signalscv.com/archives/17111/.

29 Pierre L. Siklos, *War Finance, Reconstruction, Hyperinflation and Stabilization in Hungary, 1938–48* (Basingstoke: Macmillan, 1991), p. 1.

30 Thomas Picketty, *Capital in the Twenty-First Century*, trans. Arthur Goldhammer (Cambridge, MA: The Belknap Press of Harvard University Press, 2014), pp. 107–9.

31 Bedi, *Bengal Lamenting* (Lahore: The Lion Press, 1944), p. 102.

32 Lowe, *Savage Continent*, pp. 67–8, 157. For an in-depth case study, see Martin Conway, 'Justice in Postwar Belgium: Popular Passions and Polit-

ical Realities', in István Deák, Jan T. Gross and Tony Judt (eds), *The Politics of Retribution in Europe* (Princeton University Press, 2000), pp. 143–7.

33 Iliffe, *A Modern History of Tanganyika*, p. 375; W. M. Spellman, *A Concise History of the World Since 1945* (Basingstoke: Palgrave Macmillan, 2006), pp. 86–7; for Kenya see chapter 17.

34 Srimanjari, *Through War and Famine*, p. 222.

35 The US government nevertheless recognized that this was only a temporary state of affairs, and put a more realistic long-term figure on their share of world GDP at 31 per cent: Kurt Schuler and Andrew Rosenberg (eds), *The Bretton Woods Transcripts* (New York: Center for Financial Stability, 2012), introduction, overview on Commission I. By 1950, US share of world GDP was down to around 27 per cent; see Angus Maddison, *The World Economy: Historical Statistics* (Paris: OECD, 2003), pp. 85, 259.

36 UN, *Salient Features of the World Economic Situation, 1945–47*, p. 224.

37 Maddison, *The World Economy*, p. 88. Alan Milward has a lower estimate of about 60 per cent, based on per capita GNP rather than GDP: *War, Economy and Society, 1939–1945*, p. 331.

38 UN, *Salient Features of the World Economic Situation, 1945–47*, pp. 45, 60, 110–11, 124; Maddison, *The World Economy*, pp. 51, 85.

39 UN, *Salient Features of the World Economic Situation, 1945–47*, pp. 46, 48, 110.

40 Chamberlin, *Economic Development in Iceland through World War II*, p. 99.

41 E. M. H. Lloyd, *Food and Inflation in the Middle East, 1940–45* (Stanford University Press, 1956), p. 190.

42 Milward, *War, Economy and Society, 1939–1945*, p. 349.

43 Mark Harrison, 'The Economics of World War II: An Overview', in Mark Harrison (ed.), *The Economics of World War II* (Cambridge University Press, 1998), table 1.11; Tony Judt, *Postwar* (London: Pimlico, 2007), p. 17; Milward, *War, Economy and Society, 1939–1945*, p. 270.

44 Maddison, *The World Economy*, pp. 50, 56, 172–4.

45 Ibid., p. 50; Milward, *War, Economy and Society, 1939–1945*, pp. 349–50; 'Britain Pays Off Final Instalment of US Loan – After 61 Years', *Independent*, 29 December 2006.

46 Per capita GDP for Britain and the USA were on a par in 1938. After the war Britain was 30 per cent below the level of the USA, and has remained so ever since. See Mark Harrison, 'The Economics of World War II', table 1.10; and Maddison, *The World Economy*, pp. 63–5, 88–9.

47 Picketty, *Capital in the Twenty-First Century*, pp. 275, 397; Lowe, *Savage Continent*, pp. 66–8.

48 White speech quoted in Schuler and Rosenberg (eds), *The Bretton Woods Transcripts*, First meeting, Commission I, 3 July 1944, transcript p. 2.

49 Ed Conway, *The Summit* (London: Little, Brown, 2014), pp. 169–70.

50 Ibid., pp. 210–11, 331.

51 Ibid., pp. 222, 224.

52 Roosevelt's speech to Congress on the Bretton Woods agreements, 12 February 1945. Available online at www.presidency.ucsb.edu/ws/?pid=16588.

53 The GATT agreement would eventually be replaced by the World Trade Organization in 1994. See the 1947 GATT agreement, available at www.wto.org/english/docs_e/legal_e/gatt47_e.pdf.

54 Roosevelt's speech to Congress on the Bretton Woods agreements, 12 February 1945.

55 Lionel Robbins, quoted in Susan Howson and Donald Moggridge (eds), *The Wartime Diaries of Lionel Robbins and James Meade, 1943–45* (Basingstoke: Macmillan, 1990), p. 193.

56 A. D. Shroff, quoted in Schuler and Rosenberg (eds), *The Bretton Woods Transcripts*, Third meeting, Commission I, 10 July 1944, transcript pp. 4–7.

57 Conway, *The Summit*, pp. 356, 371. One early experiment, when America forced Britain to make its currency fully convertible, was such a disaster that it caused a collapse in currency values worldwide.

58 Joseph E. Stiglitz, *Globalization and its Discontents* (London: Allen Lane, 2002), pp. 42–4; Jeffrey Sachs, *The End of Poverty* (Harmondsworth: Penguin, 2005), p. 74; Godfrey Mwakikagile, *Africa is in a Mess: What Went Wrong and What Should be Done* (Dar es Salaam: New Africa Press, 2006), p. 27.

59 Conway, *The Summit*, pp. xix–xx.

60 Picketty, *Capital in the Twenty-First Century*, p. 573.

61 James A. Gillespie, 'Europe, America and the Space of International Health', in Susan Gross Solomon et al. (eds), *Shifting Boundaries of Public Health: Europe in the Twentieth Century* (Rochester, NY: University of Rochester Press, 2008), p. 126.

62 Mallik, *Chittaprosad: A Retrospective*, vol. 1, pp. 46, 50.

63 Ghosh, *Chittaprosad*, pp. 3–4; Sarkar, *A Matter of Conscience*, p. 30. See also 'An Artist, Possessed', *The Hindu*, 7 July 2011.

64 S. Guhan, 'The World Bank's Lending in South Asia', in Devesh Kapur, John P. Lewis and Richard Webb (eds), *The World Bank: Its First Half Century* (Washington, DC: Brookings Institution Press, 1997), pp. 327, 337, 356–8, 380–83.

65 UN Conference on Trade and Development, *The Least Developed Countries Report, 2014* (Geneva: UNCTAD, 2014), pp. 23, 26; available online at http://unctad.org/en/PublicationsLibrary/ldc2014_en.pdf.

Chapter 11 – World Government

1 Garry Davis, personal blog, 10 November 2009, www.worldservice.org/2009_11_01_archive.html.

2 Garry Davis, personal blog, 22 January 2008, www.worldservice.org/2008_01_01_archive.html.

3 Garry Davis, *The World is My Country* (New York: G. P. Putnam's Sons, 1961), p. 21.

4 'Garry Davis, Gadfly and World Citizen No. 1, Dies at 91', *Washington Post*, 6 August 2013; Davis, *The World is My Country*, pp. 18–19.

5 Paul Gallico, 'What Makes Americans Renounce Citizenship?', *St Petersburg Times*, 1 June 1948.

6 *Pravda*, quoted in Davis, *The World is My Country*, p. 49.

7 Herbert V. Evatt, *The Task of Nations* (New York: Duell, Sloan & Pearce, 1949), pp. 223–5.

8 'The Drop-Outs', *Times of India*, 4 February 1975, p. 6; 'World Citizen', *Manchester Guardian*, 10 December 1948, p. 4; 'The First Citizen of the World', *The World's News*, 4 June 1949, p. 6; *New Yorker* quoted in Davis, *The World is My Country*, p. 49.

9 'Man of No Nation Saw One World of No War', obituary, *New York Times*, 28 July 2013; Davis, *The World is My Country*, pp. 18, 48–9; Garry Davis's blog http://blog.worldservice.org/2010/05/world-thought-corollary-to-world-action.html.

10 Davis, *The World is My Country*, p. 18.

11 Garry Davis, speech at City Hall, Ellsworth, Maine, 4 September 1953, reproduced ibid., pp. 220–21.

12 Wendell Willkie, *One World* (London: Cassell & Co., 1943), pp. 140, 165–6.

13 Ibid., p. 165.

14 Thomas G. Weiss, *Global Governance: Why? What? Whither?* (Cambridge: Polity Press, 2013), p. 23.

15 Emery Reves, *The Anatomy of Peace* (London: George Allen & Unwin, 1946), p. v. For a biography of Reves, and sales figures, see Silvan S. Schweber, *Einstein and Oppenheimer: The Meaning of Genius* (Cambridge, MA: Harvard University Press, 2009), pp. 64–5 and 336, fn 85.

16 Reves, *The Anatomy of Peace*, pp. 107, 160.

17 Ibid., pp. 165, 108.

18 'Open Letter to the American People', *New York Times*, 10 October 1945; see also Schweber, *Einstein and Oppenheimer*, p. 66.

19 Committee to Frame a World Constitution, *The Preliminary Draft of a World Constitution* (University of Chicago Press, 1948).

20 R. M. Douglas, *The Labour Party, Nationalism and Internationalism, 1939–1951* (London: Routledge, 2004), p. 159.

21 World Movement for World Federal Government (WMWFG), reply to UN questionnaire on non-governmental organizations, 25 October 1950: UN Archives, S-0441-0057-04 Part A. See also the Movement's 'Montreux Declaration', www.wfm-igp.org/our-movement/history.

22 Opening address at the Moral Re-Armament World Assembly, Caux, Switzerland, 15 July 1947, quoted in Frank N. D. Buchman, *Remaking the World: The Speeches of Frank N. D. Buchman* (London: Blandford, 1947), p. 157.

23 Jan Smuts, speech at the Sixth Plenary Session of the UN San Francisco Conference, 1945, in UN, *The United Nations Conference on International Organization: Selected Documents* (Washington, DC: US Government Printing Office, 1946), p. 338.

24 The Federation of American Scientists' compilation of gloomy essays on the atomic bomb was also a *New York Times* bestseller in 1946. See Dexter Masters and Katharine Way (eds), *One World or None* (New York: McGraw-Hill, 1946). See also the 1946 film of the same name, available online http://publicdomainreview.org/collections/one-world-or-none-1946/.

25 A complete copy of the UN Charter is given in an appendix to Paul Kennedy's *The Parliament of Man* (London: Allen Lane, 2006), pp. 313–41.

26 Brian Urquhart, *A Life in Peace and War* (London: Weidenfeld & Nicolson, 1987), p. 93. See also Jean Richardot, *Journeys for a Better World: A Personal Adventure in War and Peace* (Lanham, MD: University Press of America, 1994), pp. 85–6, 111–13.

27 Joseph Paul-Boncour, quoted in *Gazette de Lausanne*, 27 June 1945, 'La conference de San-Francisco', p. 6.

28 'A World Charter', *Times of India*, 28 June 1945, p. 4; *Straits Times*, 25 October 1945, p. 4.

29 Eyo Ita, quoted in 'The Last Best Hope of Man on Earth', *West African Pilot*, 6 February 1945, p. 2.

30 *New York Times*, 27 June 1945, p. 10.

31 Senator Tom Connally, *Congressional Record* (Senate), 91 (23 July 1945), p. 7953; Congressman Charles A. Eaton, *Congressional Record* (House), 91 (6 July 1945), pp. 7299–300 – both quoted in Thomas M. Franck, *Nation Against Nation: What Happened to the UN Dream and What the US Can Do About It* (New York: Oxford University Press, 1985), p.9.

32 Ibid., p. 8.

33 UN official website: www.un.org/en/sections/history-united-nations-charter/1945-san-francisco-conference/index.html.

34 Barack Obama, 'Proclamation 8740 – United Nations Day 2011', 24 October 2011. Available online at www.presidency.ucsb.edu/ws/?pid=96946.

35 Mark Mazower, *No Enchanted Palace* (Princeton University Press, 2009), p. 6 and related fnn. on p. 206.

36 See UN, *The United Nations Conference on International Organization: Selected Documents*.

37 Alberto Lleras Camargo, speech at Fifth Plenary Session of the San Francisco Conference, ibid., p. 328.

38 Abdel Hamid Badawi, speech at the Third Plenary Session of the San Francisco Conference, ibid., p. 289.

39 For speeches about the veto by representatives of El Salvador, Greece, the Philippines, Colombia, Ecuador, Iraq, Cuba and New Zealand, see ibid., pp. 301, 304, 306, 328, 333, 356, 363, 370. See also New Zealand Department of External Affairs, *United Nations Conference on International Organization* (Wellington: Department of External Affairs, 1945), pp. 77–9; and Marika Sherwood, ' "There is No New Deal for the Blackman in San Francisco": African Attempts to Influence the Founding Conference of the United Nations, April–July 1945', *International Journal of African Historical Studies*, vol. 29, no. 1 (1996), p. 91.

40 Article 2, paragraph 7, United Nations Charter.

41 Mazower, *No Enchanted Palace*, pp. 142–8.

42 Escott Reid, *On Duty: A Canadian at the Making of the United Nations, 1945–1946* (Kent, OH: Kent State University Press, 1983), p. 24.

43 Kennedy, *The Parliament of Man*, pp. 46–7.

44 'Towards a New World Order', *West African Pilot*, 20 August 1945.

45 Reves, *The Anatomy of Peace*, pp. 166, 177, 191.

46 'Oran Declaration', quoted in Davis, *The World is My Country*, p. 216.

47 For a chronological breakdown of all the Security Council vetoes up to 1990, as well as detailed case histories, see Anjali V. Patil, *The UN Veto in World Affairs, 1946–1990* (London: Mansell, 1992).

48 Benjamin Ferencz lecture on international criminal law, available on the UN website: legal.un.org/avl/ls/Ferencz_CLP_video_5.html.

Chapter 12 – World Law

1 Benjamin Ferencz's story and all quotes are taken from personal correspondence with the author in June 2015; Ferencz's own website, www.benferencz. org/stories.html; and a series of lectures Ferencz gave on international law, available on the United Nations website: http://legal.un.org/avl/ls/Ferencz_ CLP.html. There is also a useful biography written by Tom Hofmann, *Benjamin Ferencz: Nuremberg Prosecutor and Peace Advocate* (Jefferson, NC: McFarland, 2014).

2 Keith Lowe, *Savage Continent* (London: Viking, 2012), pp. 135–41.

3 Ibid., p. 150.

4 Henri Rochat, quoted in Marcel Ophüls documentary film *Le Chagrin et la Pitié*, Part II: 'Le Choix' (1969).

5 Jozo Tomasevich, *War and Revolution in Yugoslavia, 1941–1945* (Stanford University Press, 2001), p. 765; Lowe, *Savage Continent*, pp. 249–65.

6 R. M. Douglas, *Orderly and Humane: The Expulsion of the Germans After the Second World War* (New Haven, CT: Yale University Press, 2012), p. 1; Lowe, *Savage Continent*, pp. 234–42.

7 Lowe, *Savage Continent*, p. 131.

8 Philip Snow, *The Fall of Hong Kong* (New Haven, CT: Yale University Press, 2003), pp. 296–7.

9 Konrad Mitchell Lawson, 'Wartime Atrocities and the Politics of Treason in the Ruins of the Japanese Empire, 1937–1953', PhD thesis, Department of History, Harvard University (2012), p. 129; John W. Dower, *Embracing Defeat: Japan in the Wake of World War II* (New York: W. W. Norton, 2000), p. 449.

10 Haji Buyong Adil, quoted in Cheah Boon Kheng, *Red Star Over Malaya*, 3rd edn (Singapore University Press, 2003), p. 184.

11 *La Terre Vivaroise*, 29 October 1944, quoted in Philippe Bourdrel, *L'épuration sauvage* (Paris: Perrin, 2002), pp. 316–17.

12 Sir Hartley Shawcross, quoted in International Military Tribunal, *Trials of the Major War Criminals Before the International Military Tribunal* (Nuremberg: International Military Tribunal, 1947–9), vol. 3, p. 144.

13 For the trial of Yamashita Tomoyuki and its subsequent influence on international criminal law, see Allan A. Ryan, *Yamashita's Ghost* (Lawrence: University Press of Kansas, 2012), pp. xiv–xv, 250–341.

14 Alpheus Thomas Mason, *Harlan Fiske Stone: Pillar of the Law* (Hamden, CT: Archon Books, 1968), p. 716.

15 International Military Tribunal, *Trials of the Major War Criminals*, vol. 1: *Official Documents*, p. 186. Available online at www.loc.gov/rr/frd/ Military_Law/pdf/NT_Vol-I.pdf.

16 William C. Chase, *Front Line General: The Commands of Maj. Gen. Wm. C. Chase* (Houston: Pacesetter Press, 1975), p. 144.

17 B. V. A. Röling and C. F. Rüter (eds), *The Tokyo Judgment* (APA-University Press Amsterdam, 1977), vol. 1, p. 496.

18 Jackson, quoted in Robert E. Conot, *Justice at Nuremberg* (London: Weidenfeld & Nicolson, 1983), p. 68.

19 http://benferencz.org/1946-1949.html.

20 International Military Tribunal, *Trials of the Major War Criminals*, vol. 4, pp. 30, 53. Available online at www.loc.gov/rr/frd/Military_Law/pdf/ NT_war-criminals_Vol-IV.pdf.

21 Ibid., p. 413.

22 Email correspondence with author, 18 June 2015.

23 http://benferencz.org/1943-1946.html.

24 James K. Pollock, James H. Meisel and Henry L. Bretton, *Germany Under Occupation: Illustrative Materials and Documents* (Ann Arbor: George Wahr Publishing Co., 1949), p. 173.

25 Eugene Davidson, *The Death and Life of Germany* (London: Jonathan Cape, 1959), p. 128.

26 Lowe, *Savage Continent*, pp. 150, 153, 161.

27 Dennis Deletant, *Communist Terror in Romania* (London: Hurst & Co., 1999), pp. 72–6; Peter Kenez, *Hungary from the Nazis to the Soviets* (New York: Cambridge University Press, 2006), p. 149; Tony Judt, *Postwar* (London: Pimlico, 2007), p. 60.

28 Dower, *Embracing Defeat*, p. 454.

29 Philip R. Piccigallo, *The Japanese on Trial* (Austin: University of Texas Press, 1979), pp. 263–5.

30 Dower, *Embracing Defeat*, pp. 525–6.

31 Lawson, 'Wartime Atrocities and the Politics of Treason', pp. 43–94, 130–32.

32 According to the UN website: https://treaties.un.org/Pages/ViewDetails. aspx?src=TREATY&mtdsg_no=IV-1&chapter=4&clang=_en.

33 For this, and subsequent quotes, see Ferencz lecture, available on the United Nations website: http://legal.un.org/avl/ls/Ferencz_CLP_video_ 5.html.

Chapter 13 – USA

1 Cord Meyer, *Facing Reality* (New York: Harper & Row, 1980), pp. 5–6. For the following, see also pp. 1–33; 'A Hidden Liberal', *New York Times*, 30 March 1967; Merle Miller, 'One Man's Long Journey – from a One-World Crusade to the "Department of Dirty Tricks"', *New York Times Magazine*, 7 January 1973; obituary, *New York Times*, 16 March 2001.

2 Cord Meyer, *Peace or Anarchy* (Boston, MA: Little, Brown, 1947), p. 5.

3 Meyer, *Facing Reality*, p. 39.

4 Meyer, *Peace or Anarchy*, pp. 209–10.

5 Meyer, *Facing Reality*, p. 50.

6 Ibid., pp. 50, 56–7.

7 Ibid., pp. 61–4.

8 'A Hidden Liberal', p. 30. See also Miller, 'One Man's Long Journey'; Godfrey Hodgson, 'Cord Meyer: Superspook', *Sunday Times Magazine*, 15 June 1975.

9 Meyer, *Facing Reality*, p. xiv.

10 Vandenberg's speech in Cleveland, 11 January 1947, reported in *Washington Post*, 12 January 1947.

11 Truman, radio address to the American people, 1 September 1945; available online at www.presidency.ucsb.edu/ws/?pid=12366; Churchill, speech to House of Commons, 16 August 1945, in David Cannadine (ed.), *Blood, Toil, Tears and Sweat: Winston Churchill's Famous Speeches* (London: Cassell & Co., 1989), p. 282.

12 Charles E. Bohlen, *Witness to History* (New York: W. W. Norton, 1973), p. 215.

13 Wendell Willkie, *One World* (London: Cassell & Co., 1943), p. 72.

14 Stimson memorandum to Truman, 11 September 1945, US Department of State, *Foreign Relations of the United States* (Washington, DC: US Government Printing Office) (hereafter *FRUS*), 1945, vol. 2, p. 42; http://digicoll.library.wisc.edu/cgi-bin/FRUS/FRUS-idx?type=turn&entity=FRUS.FRUS1945v02.p0052&id=FRUS.FRUS1945v02&isize=M.

15 Simon Sebag Montefiori, *Stalin: The Court of the Red Tsar* (London: Weidenfeld & Nicolson, 2003), p. 34; Gromyko obituary, *New York Times*, 4 July 1989.

16 Lucius D. Clay, *Decision in Germany* (London: William Heinemann, 1950), p. 26.

17 According to Republican Senator Tom Connally, quoted in Edward R. Stettinius, *Roosevelt and the Russians* (Garden City, NY: Doubleday, 1949), p. 306.

18 Ed Conway, *The Summit* (London: Little, Brown, 2014), pp. 274, 275.

19 See, for example, Lane to Secretary of State, 13 November 1945, *FRUS 1945*, vol. 2, pp. 412–14; and Arthur Bliss Lane, *I Saw Poland Betrayed* (New York: Bobbs-Merrill, 1948), pp. 193–6.

20 Memorandum of conversation by Charles E. Bohlen, *FRUS 1945*, vol. 5, pp. 231–4; W. Averell Harriman and Elie Abel, *Special Envoy to Churchill and Stalin, 1941–1946* (London: Hutchinson, 1976), p. 448.

21 See Keith Lowe, *Savage Continent* (London: Viking, 2012), pp. 321–30; and Churchill's complaint to Stalin at Potsdam, 24 July 1945, *FRUS: Diplomatic Papers: The Conference at Berlin (the Potsdam Conference) 1945*, vol. 2, p. 362.

22 Crane to Truman, 3 May 1945, *FRUS 1945*, vol. 4, pp. 205–7.

23 Bohlen, *Witness to History*, p. 214.

24 Meyer, *Facing Reality*, p. 82.

25 Quoted in Albert Eugene Kahn, *High Treason: The Plot Against the People* (New York: Lear Publishers, 1950), p. 331.

26 Bill Mauldin, quoted in Studs Terkel, *'The Good War': An Oral History of World War Two* (London: Hamish Hamilton, 1984), p. 363.

27 Ted Morgan, *Reds: McCarthyism in Twentieth-Century America* (New York: Random House, 2003), pp. 224–5.

28 Angus Maddison, *The World Economy: Historical Statistics* (Paris: OECD, 2003), pp. 174, 232.

29 Denis Brogan, 'The Illusion of American Omnipotence', *Harper's Magazine*, December 1952, p. 205.

30 Republican candidates William Jenner (Indiana), George B. Schwabe (Oklahoma), Hugh Butler (Nebraska) and the Republican National Committee, quoted in Morgan, *Reds*, pp. 301–2.

31 Howard Laski, 'America – 1947', *Nation*, 13 December 1947, p. 641.

32 Robert J. Donovan, *Conflict and Crisis: The Presidency of Harry S. Truman, 1945–48* (New York: W. W. Norton, 1977), pp. 163–76, 332–7; Ronald Allen Goldberg, *America in the Forties* (Syracuse University Press, 2012), p. 123.

33 Morgan, *Reds*, pp. 299–300.

34 Daniel Bell, *The End of Ideology* (New York: The Free Press, 1965), p. 123.

35 See Godfrey Hodgson, *America in Our Time* (Garden City, NY: Doubleday, 1976), p. 93; Hamilton Fish, *The Challenge of World Communism* (Milwaukee: Bruce Publishing Co., 1946), pp. 47, 109, 139, 144; Larry Ceplair, *Anti-Communism in Twentieth-Century America* (Santa Barbara, CA: Praeger, 2011), p. 119.

36 Letter to George H. Earl, 28 February 1947, quoted in Morgan, *Reds*, p. 304.

37 Karl H. Von Wiegand, 'Red Tidal Wave Menaces Christian Civilization', article for Hearst Newspapers, 12 May 1945, quoted in Fish, *The Challenge of World Communism*, p. 23.

38 J. Edgar Hoover, 'Red Fascism in the United States Today', *The American Magazine* (1947); 'Communists Penetrate Wall Street', *Commercial and Financial Chronicle*, 6 November 1947; Harry D. Gideonse, 'The Reds Are After Your Child', *The American Magazine* (1948).

39 See, for example, 'Red Fascism's Goal', in New York's *Daily Mirror*, 15 February 1946; Hoover, 'Red Fascism in the United States Today'; Jack B. Tenney, *Red Fascism* (Los Angeles: Federal Printing Co., 1947) and Norman Thomas 'Which Way America – Fascism, Communism, Socialism or Democracy?', *Town Meeting Bulletin*, 16 March 1948, pp. 19–20.

40 George Meany and H. V. Kaltenborn, quoted in Les K. Adler and Thomas G. Paterson, 'Red Fascism: The Merger of Nazi Germany and Soviet Russia in the American Image of Totalitarianism, 1930s–1950s', in Walter L. Hixson (ed.), *The American Experience in World War II*, vol. 12: *The United States Transformed: The Lessons and Legacies of the Second World War* (London: Routledge, 2003), pp. 24, 28.

41 Arthur Bliss Lane, quoted in Adler and Paterson, 'Red Fascism', p. 22.

42 Louis C. Wyman, quoted ibid., p. 20.

43 Truman news conference at Key West, 30 March 1950; available online at www.presidency.ucsb.edu/ws/?pid=13755.

44 Landon R. Y. Storrs, *The Second Red Scare and the Unmaking of the New Deal Left* (Princeton University Press, 2013), p. 2. Different statistics for differing periods of time are also given in Morgan, *Reds*, p. 305; and Tim Weiner, *Enemies: A History of the FBI* (London: Allen Lane, 2012), p. 149.

45 Meyer, *Facing Reality*, p. 79.

46 See, for example, the repeated investigations of Thomas Blaisdell, Esther Brunauer, Leon and Mary Keyserling and many others in Storrs, *The Second Red Scare*, pp. 268–85.

47 Meyer, *Facing Reality*, pp. 70–81.

48 Bernice Bernstein and Esther Peterson, quoted in Storrs, *The Second Red Scare*, p. 180.

49 Pauli Murray, quoted ibid., p. 183.

50 Hodgson, *America in Our Time*, p. 45; Storrs, *The Second Red Scare*, pp. 1–7; Richard Hofstadter, *Anti-Intellectualism in American Life* (New York: Knopf, 1963), pp. 41–2; Michella M. Marino, 'Mothers, Spy Queens, and Subversives: Women in the McCarthy Era', in Caroline S. Emmons (ed.),

Cold War and McCarthy Era: People and Perspectives (Santa Barbara, CA: ABC-Clio, 2010), pp. 130, 141.

51 Hodgson, *America in Our Time*, p. 26.

52 The text of George Kennan's 'long telegram' is reproduced in George Kennan, *Memoirs, 1925–1950* (Boston, MA: Little, Brown, 1967), p. 557.

53 Kennan, *Memoirs*, pp. 294–5.

54 Vandenberg, quoted in James T. Patterson, *Grand Expectations: The United States, 1945–1974* (New York: Oxford University Press, 1996), p. 128.

55 Truman, speech to Congress, 12 March 1947; available online at www.presidency.ucsb.edu/ws/?pid=12846.

56 Kennan, *Memoirs*, pp. 319–20.

57 Michael Burleigh, *Small Wars, Far Away Places* (London: Macmillan, 2013), p. 64.

58 Hodgson, *America in Our Time*, p. 32; Walter LaFeber, *America, Russia and the Cold War, 1945–2002* (New York: McGraw-Hill, 2002), p. 1; Craig Calhoun (ed.), *Dictionary of the Social Sciences* (New York: Oxford University Press, 2002), p. 76.

59 See David Halberstam, *War in a Time of Peace: Bush, Clinton and the Generals* (London: Bloomsbury, 2003), p. 326; Robert Kagan, 'Superpowers Don't Get to Retire', *The New Republic*, 26 May 2014.

60 A. M. Meerloo, *Aftermath of Peace: Psychological Essays* (New York: International Universities Press, 1946), pp. 163–4.

61 For psychoanalytic points of view on the uses of national enemies, particularly in the case of America during the Cold War, see Hanna Segal, 'From Hiroshima to the Gulf War and After: A Psychoanalytic Perspective', in Anthony Elliott and Stephen Frosh (eds), *Psychoanalysis in Contexts: Paths Between Theory and Modern Culture* (London and New York: Routledge, 1995), p. 194; and Michael Rustin, 'Why are We More Afraid Than Ever? The Politics of Anxiety After Nine Eleven', in Susan Levy and Alessandra Lemma (eds), *The Perversion of Loss: Psychoanalytic Perspectives on Trauma* (New York: Brunner-Routledge, 2004), pp. 21–36.

Chapter 14 – USSR

1 Andrei Sakharov, *Memoirs* (London: Hutchinson, 1990), p. 40.

2 Ibid., pp. 97, 111, 164, 204; see also Jay Bergman, *Meeting the Demands of Reason: The Life and Thought of Andrei Sakharov* (Ithaca, NY: Cornell University Press, 2009), pp. 68–9.

3 Sakharov, *Memoirs*, pp. 36, 164, 225.

4 Ibid., p. 288.

5 Quoted in Bergman, *Meeting the Demands of Reason*, pp. 71–7. See also Andrei Sakharov, 'I Tried to be on the Level of My Destiny', *Molodezh Estonii*, 11 October 1988, reprinted in Jonathan Eisen (ed.), *The Glasnost Reader* (New York: New American Library, 1990), pp. 330–31.

6 Boris Galin, quoted in Elena Zubkova, *Russia After the War*, trans. Hugh Ragsdale (Armonk, NY: M. E. Sharpe, 1998), p. 34.

7 Quoted by Sheila Fitzpatrick, 'Postwar Soviet Society', in Susan J. Linz (ed.), *The Impact of World War II on the Soviet Union* (Totowa, NJ: Rowman & Allanheld, 1985), p. 130.

8 Ibid., p. 137; Orlando Figes, *The Whisperers* (London: Allen Lane, 2007), p. 457; Sakharov, *Memoirs*, pp. 76–7.

9 Figes, *The Whisperers*, p. 456; Robert Service, *A History of Modern Russia* (Harmondsworth: Penguin, 2003), p. 295.

10 G. F. Krivosheev (ed.), *Soviet Casualties and Combat Losses in the Twentieth Century* (London: Greenhill Books, 1997), pp. 91, 97; Keith Lowe, *Savage Continent* (London: Viking 2012), p. 16; Figes, *The Whisperers*, p. 465; Zubkova, *Russia After the War*, p. 24.

11 Fitzpatrick, 'Postwar Soviet Society', p. 130; Mark Spoerer, *Zwangsarbeit unter dem Hakenkreuz* (Stuttgart and Munich: Deutsche Verlags-Anstalt, 2001), p. 222.

12 See, for example, testimonies by Lilia Budko, Natalia Melnichenko, Vera Odinets, Tamara Kuraeva and Tamara Umnyagina in Svetlana Alexiyevich, *War's Unwomanly Face*, trans. Keith Hammond and Lyudmila Lezhneva (Moscow: Progress, 1988), pp. 195, 237, 238, 243.

13 Zubkova, *Russia After the War*, p. 69.

14 Alexander Werth, *Russia at War* (London: Barrie & Rockliff, 1964), p. 1037.

15 Zubkova, *Russia After the War*, pp. 44, 84.

16 Molotov interview with Felix Chuev, 28 November 1974, in Albert Resis (ed.), *Molotov Remembers* (Chicago: Ivan R. Dee, 1993), p. 59.

17 Milovan Djilas, *Conversations with Stalin*, trans. Michael B. Petrovich (New York: Harcourt Brace Jovanovich, 1962), p. 114.

18 All three of these agreements are available online at http://avalon.law.yale.edu/subject_menus/wwii.asp.

19 Mark Mazower (ed.), *After the War Was Over* (Princeton University Press, 2000), p. 7; Bethell and Roxborough (eds), *Latin America*, p. 6; Lowe, *Savage Continent*, pp. 154–8, 291–2.

20 See UN, *The United Nations Conference on International Organization: Selected Documents* (Washington, DC: US Government Printing Office, 1946), p. 317; New Zealand Department of External Affairs, *United Nations Conference on International Organization* (Wellington: Department of External Affairs, 1945), p. 4; Anthony Gaglione, *The United Nations Under Trygve Lie, 1945–1953* (Lanham, MD: Scarecrow Press, 2001), p. 112.

21 See Zhdanov's report to Communist Parties conference at Szklarska Poręba, 22 September 1947. This is available in Russian, German and French at www.cvce.eu/obj/le_rapport_jdanov_22_septembre_1947-fr-914edbc9-abdf-48a6-9c4a-02f3d6627a24.html.

22 Nikita Khrushchev, *Khrushchev Remembers*, trans. and ed. Strobe Talbott (Boston, MA: Little, Brown, 1970), p. 362.

23 Molotov interview with Felix Chuev, 1 July 1979, in Resis (ed.), *Molotov Remembers*, p. 58.

24 Sir Archibald Clerk Kerr, telegram to Ernest Bevin, 3 December 1945, *FRUS 1945*, vol. 2, p. 83.

25 W. Averell Harriman and Elie Abel, *Special Envoy to Churchill and Stalin, 1941–1946* (London: Hutchinson, 1976), p. 519; Khrushchev, *Khrushchev Remembers*, p. 225. See also David Holloway, *Stalin and the Bomb* (New Haven, CT: Yale University Press, 1994), p. 169.

26 Replies to questions put by Alexander Werth, 24 September 1946; available online at www.marxists.org/reference/archive/stalin/works/1946/09/24.htm.

27 Holloway, *Stalin and the Bomb*, pp. 148–9; Zubkova, *Russia After the War*, p. 86.

28 Konstantin Simonov, quoted in Zubkova, *Russia After the War*, p. 95; Sakharov, *Memoirs*, p. 41; Jerry F. Hough, 'Debates about the Postwar World', in Susan J. Linz (ed.), *The Impact of World War II on the Soviet Union* (Totowa, NJ: Rowman & Allanheld, 1985), pp. 260–62, 268–70.

29 Zubkova, *Russia After the War*, p. 36.

30 Ibid., p. 36; Figes, *The Whisperers*, pp. 458–9.

31 V. F. Zima, *Golod v SSSR, 1946–1947 godov: Proiskhozhdenie i posledstviia* (Moscow: Institut rossiiskoi istorii RAN, 1996), p. 11; see also Nicholas Ganson, *The Soviet Famine of 1946–47 in Global and Historical Perspective* (Basingstoke: Palgrave Macmillan, 2009), pp. xv–xvi.

32 Zubkova, *Russia After the War*, p. 60.

33 Figes, *The Whisperers*, p. 459.

34 Alexander Statiev, *The Soviet Counterinsurgency in the Western Borderlands* (New York: Cambridge University Press, 2010), p. 106; Lowe, *Savage Continent*, pp. 344; programme of Estonian Armed Resistance League, quoted in Mart Laar, *War in the Woods: Estonia's Struggle for Survival, 1944–1956*, trans. Tiina Ets (Washington, DC: The Compass Press, 1992), p. 108.

35 Stalin, interview with *Pravda*, 13 March 1946; Molotov, quoted in Gerhard Wettig, *Stalin and the Cold War in Europe* (Lanham, MD: Rowman & Littlefield, 2008), p. 139; Andrei Vyshinsky, speech to Foreign Press Association in New York, 11 November 1947 – see Australian Associated Press report in *The Cairns Post*, 13 November 1947; Georgy Malenkov, speech to the Moscow Soviet, 6 November 1949, in *World News and Views*, vol. 29, no. 46 (1949).

36 Anne Applebaum, *Gulag* (London: Allen Lane, 2003), pp. 395–6; Alexander Solzhenitsyn, *The Gulag Archipelago*, vol. 1 (London: Collins & Harvill, 1974), pp. 237–76.

37 Yuri Teplyakov, 'Stalin's War Against His Own Troops: The Tragic Fate of Soviet Prisoners of War in German Captivity', *Journal of Historical Review*, vol. 14, no. 4 (1994), p. 8; Zubkova, *Russia After the War*, p. 105.

38 Statiev, *The Soviet Counterinsurgency in the Western Borderlands*, pp. 176–7; Lowe, *Savage Continent*, pp. 354–8.

39 Stalin, quoted in Simon Sebag Montefiore, *Stalin: The Court of the Red Tsar* (London: Weidenfeld & Nicolson, 2003), p. 482.

40 Figes, *The Whisperers*, pp. 488–92; Hough, 'Debates about the Postwar World', pp. 268–70.

41 Sakharov, *Memoirs*, p. 93.

42 Figes, *The Whisperers*, p. 488; Sakharov, *Memoirs*, p. 123.

43 Vladimir Shlapentokh, *A Normal Totalitarian Society* (Armonk, NY: M. E. Sharp, 2001), p. 159; see also Frederick Charles Barghoorn, *Soviet Russian Nationalism* (New York: Oxford University Press, 1956), passim.

44 Khrushchev, *Khrushchev Remembers*, p. 262; Figes, *The Whisperers*, p. 509.

45 Khrushchev, *Khrushchev Remembers*, p. 258.

46 Sakharov, *Memoirs*, p. 146.

47 Andrei Sakharov, *Progress, Coexistence and Intellectual Freedom*, ed. Harrison E. Salisbury (New York: W. W. Norton, 1968), p. 84. See also Bergman, *Meeting the Demands of Reason*, pp. 135–49.

48 Sakharov, *Memoirs*, pp. 194–5.

Chapter 15 – World Polarization

1 Andrei Zhdanov, Report on the International Situation, 22 September 1947, to Cominform conference at Szklarska Poręba, available at www. cvce.eu/en/obj/le_rapport_jdanov_22_septembre_1947-fr-914edbc9-abdf-48a6-9c4a-02f3d6627a24.html. See also the joint declaration of the European Communist Parties after the conference at www.cvce.eu/obj/declaration_sur_les_problemes_de_la_situation_internationale_septembre_1947-fr-e6e79de9-03b6-4632-ac96-53760cec8643.html.

2 George Kennan (under the pseudonym 'X'), 'The Sources of Soviet Conduct', *Foreign Affairs*, vol. 25, no. 4 (1947), pp. 566–82. For the way this article was misunderstood, see also George Kennan, *Memoirs, 1925–1950* (Boston, MA: Little, Brown, 1967), pp. 354–67.

3 See A. W. Singham and Shirley Hune, *Non-Alignment in an Age of Alignments* (London: Zed Books, 1986), p. 68.

4 Anthony Curwen, interview with the Imperial War Museum's Lyn Smith, May 1987, IWM Sound Archive 9810.

5 For Sweden see Carl-Gustaf Scott, 'The Swedish Midsummer Crisis of 1941: The Crisis that Never Was', *Journal of Contemporary History*, vol. 37, no. 3 (2002), pp. 371–94; for Portugal see Luís Rodrigues and Sergiy Glebov, *Military Bases: Historical Perspectives, Contemporary Challenges* (Amsterdam: IOS Press, 2009), p. 152; for Switzerland see Independent Commission of Experts – Second World War, *Switzerland, National Socialism and the Second World War: Final Report*, trans. Rosamund Bandi et al. (Zürich: Pendo Verlag, 2002), p. 189, available at www.uek.ch/en/schluss-bericht/synthesis/ueke.pdf.

6 For Sweden see Heinrich August Winkler, *The Age of Catastrophe* (New Haven, CT: Yale University Press, 2015), p. 790; for Spain see Stanley G. Payne, *Franco and Hitler* (New Haven, CT: Yale University Press, 2009); for the Vatican see Gerald Steinacher, *Nazis on the Run* (New York: Oxford University Press, 2012), pp. 101–48.

7 For a good history of NATO, see Peter Duignan, *NATO: Its Past, Present, and Future* (Stanford: Hoover Institution Press, 2000).

8 For Latin America in general see Bethell and Roxborough (eds), *Latin America*, pp. 1–32; for Cuba specifically, see Alex von Tunzelmann, *Red Heat* (London: Simon & Schuster, 2011), p. 256.

9 Marco Wyss, *Arms Transfers, Neutrality and Britain's Role in the Cold War* (Boston, MA: Brill, 2012), pp. 25–6; 'Spy Plane Shot Down in Baltic Found', *Telegraph*, 20 June 2003.

10 See Jakob Tanner, 'Switzerland and the Cold War: A Neutral Country Between the "American Way of Life" and "Geistige Landesverteidigung"', in Joy Charnley and Malcolm Pender (eds), *Switzerland and War* (Bern: Peter Lang, 1999), pp. 113–28; Wyss, *Arms Transfers*, passim; Daniel A. Neval, '*Mit Atombomben bis nach Moskau': gegenseitige Wahrnehmung der Schweiz und des Ostblocks im Kalten Krieg, 1945–1968* (Zürich: Chronos, 2003), passim.

11 'Der gefrässige Staat', *Neue Zürcher Zeitung*, 22 November 2014; Dominique Grisard, 'Female Terrorists and Vigilant Citizens: Gender, Citizenship and Cold War Direct-Democracy', in Jadwiga E. Pieper Mooney and Fabio Lanza (eds), *De-Centering Cold War History* (Oxford: Routledge, 2013), pp. 123–44.

12 Paul Kennedy, *The Parliament of Man* (London: Allen Lane, 2006), pp. 54, 74.

13 Nehru, speech of 7 September 1947, quoted in H. M. Wajid Ali, *India and the Non-Aligned Movement* (New Delhi: Adam Publishers & Distributors, 2004), p. 12.

14 Nehru, speech to Indian Parliament, 1951, quoted in Kristin S. Tassin, '"Lift up Your Head, My Brother": Nationalism and the Genesis of the Non-Aligned Movement', *Journal of Third World Studies*, vol. 23, no. 1 (2006), p. 148.

15 See, for example, his speech before the United Nations, 30 September 1960 in Sukarno, *Toward Freedom and the Dignity of Man: A Collection of Five Speeches . . .* (Jakarta: Department of Foreign Affairs, 1961), pp. 127–9; and speech before the Belgrade Conference in September 1961, printed in the conference journal *Belgrade Conference 1961*, no. 3, pp. 7–9.

16 Egypt's Gamal Abdel Nasser, quoted in Tassin, '"Lift up Your Head, My Brother"', p. 158; and Sudan's Ibrahim Abboud, speaking at the Belgrade Conference in September 1961, printed in the conference journal *Belgrade Conference 1961*, no. 4, p. 5.

17 William Potter and Gaukhar Mukhatzhanova, *Nuclear Politics and the Non-Aligned Movement: Principles vs. Pragmatism* (London: Routledge, 2012), pp. 17–36.

18 See the principles of non-alignment agreed at the preparatory Cairo conference, 5–18 June 1960, in P. M. H. Bell, *The World Since 1945* (London: Bloomsbury Academic, 2010), pp. 253–4.

19 Geir Lundestad, *East, West, North, South* (London: Sage, 2014), p. 274; Odd Arne Westad, *The Global Cold War* (Cambridge University Press, 2007), pp. 108–9.

20 Bell, *The World Since 1945*, p. 258.

21 Tanner, 'Switzerland and the Cold War', pp. 113–26.

22 Lecture by Michael Manley to the Third World Foundation, London, 29 October 1979, *International Foundation for Development Alternatives Dossier*, vol. 16 (1980); available online at www.burmalibrary.org/docs19/ifda_dossier-16.pdf.

23 Sukarno's speech in *Belgrade Conference 1961*, no. 3, pp. 8, 9; see also his similar speech to the United Nations, 30 September 1960, Sukarno, *Toward Freedom and the Dignity of Man*, p. 129.

24 Title of Sukarno's speech to the United Nations, 30 September 1960, ibid., p. 121.

25 Bourgwiba's speech in Belgrade Conference 1961, no. 4, p. 8.

Chapter 16 – The Birth of an Asian Nation

1 Adrian Vickers, *A History of Modern Indonesia* (New York: Cambridge University Press, 2013), pp. 1, 9, 14; Joseph H. Daves, *The Indonesian Army from Revolusi to Reformasi*, vol. 1: *The Struggle for Independence and the Sukarno Era* (Self published: printed by CreateSpace, Charleston, 2013).

2 Quoted in S. K. Trimurti, *95 Tahun S. K. Trimurti: Pejuang Indonesia* (Jakarta: Yayasan Bung Karno, 2007), p. 15. Trimurti's story has been compiled from this collection of her writings, along with a biography written by I. N. Soebagijo, *S. K. Trimurti: Wanita Pengabdi Bangsa* (Jakarta: Gunung Agung, 1982).

3 Trimurti, *95 Tahun*, p. 18.

4 Ibid., p. 19.

5 Ibid., p. 24.

6 Vickers, *A History of Modern Indonesia*, pp. 100, 106–7, 114; Daves, *The Indonesian Army*, vol. 1, pp. 42–4; Ian Buruma, *Year Zero: A History of 1945* (London: Atlantic, 2013), pp. 114–20; Anthony Reid, *The Indonesian National Revolution, 1945–1950* (Hawthorn: Longman Australia, 1974), pp. 115–16; Jan Ruff-O'Herne, *Fifty Years of Silence* (Sydney: Heinemann Australia, 2008), p. 135.

7 Benedict R. O'G. Anderson, *Java in a Time of Revolution: Occupation and Resistance, 1944–1946* (Ithaca, NY: Cornell University Press, 1972), pp. 132–3; Buruma, *Year Zero*, p. 115.

8 John W. Dower, *War Without Mercy: Race and Power in the Pacific War* (New York: Pantheon, 1986), p. 296; Vickers, *A History of Modern Indonesia*, pp. 91–5; Saskia Wieringa, *Sexual Politics in Indonesia* (Basingstoke: Palgrave Macmillan, 2002), pp. 82, 95; Yuki Tanaka, '"Comfort Women" in the Dutch East Indies', in Margaret Stetz and Bonnie B. C. Oh (eds), *Legacies of the Comfort Women of World War II* (Armonk, NY: M. E. Sharp, 2001), pp. 63–4.

9 Daves, *The Indonesian Army*, vol. 1, pp. 40, 67; Mbeligai Bangun, quoted in Mary Margaret Steedly, *Rifle Reports: A Story of Indonesian Independence* (Berkeley and Los Angeles: University of California Press, 2013), p. 43.

10 Anderson, *Java in a Time of Revolution*, p. 128.

11 For this, and subsequent description of the battle, see Daves, *The Indonesian Army*, vol. 1, pp. 74–84; William H. Frederick, *Visions and Heat: The Making of the Indonesian Revolution* (Athens: Ohio University Press, 1989), pp. 197–202, 255–67, 278–80; and Anderson, *Java in a Time of Revolution*, pp. 151–66.

12 Sutomo, radio broadcast, quoted in Frederick, *Visions and Heat*, p. 255; see also similar broadcasts by Sumarsono; Anderson, *Java in a Time of Revolution*, p. 161; Buruma, *Year Zero*, p. 119.

13 Frederick, *Visions and Heat*, p. 279; Vickers, *A History of Modern Indonesia*, pp. 102–3.

14 Frederick, *Visions and Heat*, pp. 278–9; Daves, *The Indonesian Army*, vol. 1, p. 83.

15 Vickers, *A History of Modern Indonesia*, p. 103; Daves, *The Indonesian Army*, vol. 1, p. 73; Steedly, *Rifle Reports*, p. 231.

16 Reid, *The Indonesian National Revolution*, pp. 107–8 and 119, n.7; Vickers, *A History of Modern Indonesia*, p. 105.

17 Vickers, *A History of Modern Indonesia*, pp. 115–16; Michael Burleigh, *Small Wars, Far Away Places* (London: Macmillan, 2013), pp. 46–7.

18 D. R. SarDesai, *Southeast Asia: Past and Present* (Boulder, CO: Westview Press, 1997), pp. 200–203.

19 Ho Chi Minh, 'Declaration of Independence of the Democratic Republic of Vietnam', in Gregory Allen Olson (ed.), *Landmark Speeches on the Vietnam War* (College Station: Texas A&M University Press, 2010), pp. 17–18.

20 Burleigh, *Small Wars, Far Away Places*, p. 243.

21 Ibid., p. 243; P. M. H. Bell, *The World Since 1945* (London: Bloomsbury Academic, 2010), p. 298.

22 Bell, *The World Since 1945*, p. 298.

23 Vickers, *A History of Modern Indonesia*, p. 103; Daves, *The Indonesian Army*, vol. 1, p. 84.

24 SarDesai, *Southeast Asia: Past and Present*, p. 234; Cheah Boon Kheng, *Red Star Over Malaya*, 3rd edn (Singapore University Press, 2003), pp. 177–84, 232–9.

25 Ian Talbot and Gurharpal Singh, *The Partition of India* (Cambridge University Press, 2009), pp. 2–3, 154–75.

26 Eben Hezer and E. H. Sinuraya, quoted in Steedly, *Rifle Reports*, p. 259.

27 Sukarno, speech of 19 September 1948, quoted in J. D. Legge, *Sukarno: A Political Biography* (London: Allen Lane, 1972), p. 231; Vickers, *A History of Modern Indonesia*, p. 114.

28 Daves, *The Indonesian Army*, vol. 1, pp. 233–68, 412; Vickers, *A History of Modern Indonesia*, pp. 123, 143; Cees van Dijk, *Rebellion Under the Banner of Islam: The Darul Islam in Indonesia* (The Hague: Martinus Nijhoff, 1981), passim.

29 Daves, *The Indonesian Army*, vol. 1, pp. 338–9; Vickers, *A History of Modern Indonesia*, p. 148.

30 Daves, *The Indonesian Army*, vol. 1, pp. 357, 369, 388–95; Vickers, *A History of Modern Indonesia*, p. 144.

31 Wieringa, *Sexual Politics in Indonesia*, pp. 280–89; Joseph H. Daves, *The Indonesian Army from Revolusi to Reformasi*, vol. 2: *Soeharto and the New Order* (Self published: printed by CreateSpace, Charleston, 2013), pp. 72, 75, 149; Vickers, *A History of Modern Indonesia*, pp. 161–2.

32 Daves, *The Indonesian Army*, vol. 2, p. 156; Vickers, *A History of Modern Indonesia*, pp. 162, 172–3.

Chapter 17 – The Birth of an African Nation

1 The majority of the following story is taken from Waruhiu Itote's memoirs, *'Mau Mau' General* (Nairobi: East African Publishing House, 1967). Supplementary primary material is from Myles Osborne (ed.), *The Life and Times of General China* (Princeton, NJ: Marcus Wiener Publishers, 2015).

2 Itote, *'Mau Mau' General*, p. 14.

3 Ibid., p. 13.

4 Ibid., p. 27.

5 Ibid., p. 39.

6 Ibid., p. 40.

7 Ibid., p. 45.

8 Henry Kahinga Wachanga, *The Swords of Kirinyaga* (Nairobi: East African Literature Bureau, 1975), p. 87; John Lonsdale, 'The Moral Economy of

Mau Mau: Wealth, Poverty and Civic Virtue in Kikuyu Political Thought', in Bruce Berman and John Lonsdale, *Unhappy Valley: Conflict in Kenya & Africa* (London: James Currey, 1992), p. 443.

9 Itote, *'Mau Mau' General*, pp. 216–17.

10 For a list of grievances, see Wachanga, *The Swords of Kirinyaga*, p. xxv, but for greater detail see David Anderson, *Histories of the Hanged* (London: Weidenfeld & Nicolson, 2005), pp. 9–41, and Lonsdale, 'The Moral Economy of Mau Mau', pp. 315–468.

11 Anderson, *Histories of the Hanged*, p. 9.

12 For statistics, see David Killingray, 'African Civilians in the Era of the Second World War, *c.*1939–1950', in John Laband (ed.), *Daily Lives of Civilians in Wartime Africa* (Westport, CT: Greenwood Press, 2007), p. 146; and Elizabeth Schmidt, 'Popular Resistance and Anticolonial Mobilization: The War Effort in French Guinea', in Judith A. Byfield et al. (eds), *Africa and World War II* (New York: Cambridge University Press, 2015), p. 446.

13 John Iliffe, *A Modern History of Tanganyika* (Cambridge University Press, 1979), p. 370.

14 Geoffrey I. Nwaka, 'Rebellion in Umuahia, 1950–1951: Ex-Servicemen and Anti-Colonial Protest in Eastern Nigeria', *Transafrican Journal of History*, vol. 16 (1987), pp. 47–62.

15 Adrienne M. Israel, 'Ex-Servicemen at the Crossroads: Protest and Politics in Postwar Ghana', *Journal of Modern African Studies*, vol. 30, no. 2 (1992), pp. 359–68. For eyewitness accounts of these events, see the BBC World Service production *Witness: Ghana Veterans and the 1948 Accra Riots* (2014).

16 Antoine Lumenganeso and 'Kalubi', quoted in François Ryckmans, *Mémoires noires: Les Congolais racontent le Congo belge, 1940–1960* (Brussels: Éditions Racine, 2010), pp. 24–6.

17 Schmidt, 'Popular Resistance and Anticolonial Mobilization', pp. 454–7.

18 Nancy Ellen Lawler, *Soldiers of Misfortune: Ivoirien Tirailleurs of World War II* (Athens: Ohio University Press, 1992), pp. 15, 208–18.

19 Ashley Jackson, *Botswana, 1939–1945* (Oxford: Clarendon Press, 1999), pp. 237–55.

20 For the compelling argument that Second World War veterans did not play a major *practical* role in the independence struggles see Eugene P. A. Schleh, 'The Post-War Careers of Ex-Servicemen in Ghana and Uganda', *Journal of Modern African Studies* (*JMAS*), vol. 6, no. 2 (1968), pp. 203–20; Gabriel Olusanya, 'The Role of Ex-Servicemen in Nigerian Politics', ibid.,

pp. 221–32; David Killingray, 'Soldiers, Ex-Servicemen and Politics in the Gold Coast, 1939–50', *JMAS*, vol. 21, no. 3 (1983), pp. 523–34.

21 Robert Kakembo, *An African Soldier Speaks* (London: Edinburgh House Press, 1946), pp. 9–10, 22.

22 Lawler, *Soldiers of Misfortune*, p. 220.

23 Namble Silué, quoted ibid., p. 15.

24 Lizzie Collingham, *The Taste of War* (London: Allen Lane, 2011), pp. 133–7; Lonsdale, 'The Moral Economy of Mau Mau', pp. 315–468.

25 Collingham, *The Taste of War*, p. 133; Anderson, *Histories of the Hanged*, p. 26. For Mau Mau as a peasant revolt see Donald L. Barnett and Karari Njama, *Mau Mau from Within* (New York: Modern Reader Paperbacks, 1970); and Wunyabari O. Maloba, *Mau Mau and Kenya: An Analysis of a Peasant Revolt* (Bloomington: Indiana University Press, 1993).

26 John Lonsdale, 'The Depression and the Second World War in the Transformation of Kenya', in David Killingray and Richard Rathbone (eds), *Africa and the Second World War* (Basingstoke: Macmillan, 1986), p. 128.

27 Anderson, *Histories of the Hanged*, pp. 181–90.

28 See David Hyde, 'The Nairobi General Strike (1950): From Protest to Insurgency', in Andrew Burton (ed.), *The Urban Experience in Eastern Africa c.1750–2000* (Nairobi: British Institute in Eastern Africa, 2002), pp. 235–53; and Marshall S. Clough's description of Kenyan Marxist interpretations in his *Mau Mau Memoirs: History Memory and Politics* (Boulder, CO: Lynne Rienner, 1998), p. 243.

29 Nicholas Westcott, 'The Impact of the Second World War on Tanganyika, 1939–49', in Killingray and Rathbone (eds), *Africa and the Second World War*, pp. 146–7.

30 Ashley Jackson, *The British Empire and the Second World War* (London: Hambledon Continuum, 2006), p. 45.

31 Carolyn A. Brown, 'African Labor in the Making of World War II', in Byfield et al. (eds), *Africa and World War II*, p. 62.

32 Allen Isaacman, 'Peasants and Rural Social Protests in Africa', *African Studies Review*, vol. 33, no. 2 (1990), especially pp. 53–8.

33 General Rocafort, quoted in Catherine Bogosian Ash, 'Free to Coerce: Forced Labor During and After the Vichy Years in French West Africa', in Byfield et al. (eds), *Africa and World War II*, p. 123.

34 Hein Marais, *South Africa: Limits to Change* (London: Zed Books, 2001), pp. 12–13.

35 Brown, 'African Labor in the Making of World War II', p. 67.

36 'Kalubi', quoted in Ryckmans, *Mémoires noires*, p. 25.

37 Caroline Elkins, *Britain's Gulag: The Brutal End of Empire in Kenya* (London: Bodley Head, 2014), pp. 38, 42–3; Anderson, *Histories of the Hanged*, pp. 88–95. For press reports of the Ruck killings, see, for example, 'Murder Raid in Kenya', *The Times*, 26 January 1953; 'Family of Three Found Slashed to Death', *Daily Mirror*, 26 January 1953; 'A Vile, Brutal Wickedness', *Illustrated London News*, 7 February 1953, pp. 190–91.

38 Ruck memorial service quoted in 'A Vile, Brutal Wickedness', *Illustrated London News*, 7 February 1953, pp. 190–91; Itote, *'Mau Mau' General*, p. 277.

39 J. F. Lipscomb, *White Africans* (London: Faber & Faber, 1955), p. 142; Elkins, *Britain's Gulag*, pp. 43, 46–51.

40 Anderson, *Histories of the Hanged*, p. 4.

41 Ibid., pp. 125–32; Elkins, *Britain's Gulag*, p. 45. For eyewitness accounts of the massacre see Karigo Muchai, *The Hardcore* (Richmond, BC: LSM Information Center, 1973), pp. 23–4; and Peter Evans, *Law and Disorder: Scenes from Life in Kenya* (London: Secker & Warburg, 1956), pp. 170–88.

42 For discipline of British forces see, for example, the trial of Captain G. S. L. Griffiths of the King's African Rifles, in Anderson, *Histories of the Hanged*, p. 259. For statistics on internment see ibid., p. 5; Elkins, *Britain's Gulag*, p. xi.

43 Figures according to Itote himself: see Osborne (ed.), *The Life and Times of General China*, p. 17. Anderson, *Histories of the Hanged*, p. 233, puts Itote's operational strength at 4,000 men.

44 Anderson, *Histories of the Hanged*, pp. 92, 232.

45 Itote, *'Mau Mau' General*, pp. 43, 129–38.

46 For Itote's interrogation, see Osborne (ed.), *The Life and Times of General China*, pp. 145–99.

47 Itote, *'Mau Mau' General*, p. 40.

48 John Nottingham's eulogy for Waruhiu Itote, in Osborne (ed.), *The Life and Times of General China*, p. 251.

49 For Algeria during the Second World War, see Mohamed Khenouf and Michael Brett, 'Algerian Nationalism and the Allied Military Strategy and Propaganda During the Second World War: The Background to Sétif', in Killingray and Rathbone (eds), *Africa and the Second World War*, pp. 258–74. For Sétif and Algerian War statistics, see Alistair Horne, *A Savage War of Peace* (London: Macmillan, 1977), pp. 26–8, 538.

50 Norrie MacQueen, *The Decolonization of Portuguese Africa* (Harlow: Longman, 1997), pp. 124–204, 223–31; James W. Martin III, *A Political History of*

the Civil War in Angola, 1974–1990 (New Brunswick, NJ: Transaction Books, 2011), pp. ix–x.

51 W. M. Spellman, *A Concise History of the World Since 1945* (Basingstoke: Palgrave Macmillan, 2006), p. 83.

52 P. M. H. Bell, *The World Since 1945* (London: Bloomsbury Academic, 2010), p. 447.

53 Mohamed Mathu, *The Urban Guerrilla* (Richmond, BC: LSM Information Center, 1974), p. 87.

54 Kwame Nkrumah, *Neo-Colonialism: The Last Stage of Imperialism* (London: Nelson, 1965).

55 'Opening the Secret Files on Lumumba's Murder', *Washington Post*, 21 July 2002; 'Revealed: How Israel Helped Amin to Take Power', *Independent*, 16 August 2003.

56 Godfrey Mwakikagile, *Africa is in a Mess: What Went Wrong and What Should be Done* (Dar es Salaam: New Africa Press, 2006), pp. 22–5.

57 Ibid., pp. 26–7.

Chapter 18 – Democracy in Latin America

1 Ocarina Castillo D'Imperio, *Carlos Delgado Chalbaud* (Caracas: El Nacional, 2006), pp. 48, 65–7.

2 Ibid., p. 56.

3 Robert J. Alexander, *Rómulo Betancourt and the Transformation of Venezuela* (New Brunswick, NJ: Transaction Books, 1982), p. 214.

4 Communiqué quoted ibid., pp. 217–18.

5 Ibid., pp. 228–33, 236; Maleady to Secretary of State, 7 January 1947, US Department of State, *Foreign Relations of the United States* (Washington, DC: US Government Printing Office) (hereafter *FRUS*) *1947*, vol. 8, p. 1055.

6 Alexander, *Rómulo Betancourt*, pp. 239–42; Angus Maddison, *The World Economy: Historical Statistics* (Paris: OECD, 2003), p. 122.

7 Alexander, *Rómulo Betancourt*, pp. 258–65.

8 Muriel Emanuel (ed.), *Contemporary Architects* (Basingstoke: Macmillan, 1980), pp. 852–3; Miguel Tinker Salas, *Venezuela: What Everyone Needs to Know* (New York: Oxford University Press, 2015), pp. 73, 87.

9 Alexander, *Rómulo Betancourt*, pp. 276–8.

10 Alexander, *Rómulo Betancourt*, pp. 273–5; Sean M. Griffing et al., 'Malaria Control and Elimination, Venezuela, 1800s–1970s', *Emerging Infectious*

Diseases, vol. 20, no. 10 (2014), available online at http://dx.doi.org/10.3201/eid2010.130917.

11 Delgado, speech of 24 June 1946, quoted in Castillo D'Imperio, *Carlos Delgado Chalbaud*, p. 71; see also pp. 73–4.

12 Bethell and Roxborough (eds), *Latin America*, p. 14.

13 Castillo D'Imperio, *Carlos Delgado Chalbaud*, p. 83.

14 Ibid., p. 84.

15 Alexander, *Rómulo Betancourt*, pp. 296, 314–15.

16 Sheldon T. Mills, Chief of Division of North and West Coast Affairs, memo to Director of Office of American Republics Affairs, 22 November 1948, *FRUS 1948*, vol. 9, pp. 126–7.

17 Alexander, *Rómulo Betancourt*, pp. 283–4.

18 Secretary of State Byrnes to Chargé d'Affaires in Venezuela, 7 January 1946, *FRUS 1946*, vol. 11, p. 1331.

19 Sheldon B. Liss, *Diplomacy and Dependency: Venezuela, the United States, and the Americas* (Salisbury, NC: Documentary, 1978), p. 134.

20 Acting Secretary of State Acheson to Secretary of War Patterson, 17 June 1946, *FRUS 1946*, vol. 11, p. 1346.

21 Castillo D'Imperio, *Carlos Delgado Chalbaud*, p. 90; Alexander, *Rómulo Betancourt*, p. 296.

22 Confidential report of Acting Secretary of State Lovett, 3 December 1948, and Ambassador Donnelly to Secretary of State, 4 December 1948, *FRUS 1948*, vol. 9, pp. 133, 134; Alexander, *Rómulo Betancourt*, pp. 314–15; Castillo D'Imperio, *Carlos Delgado Chalbaud*, pp. 82–90.

23 Delgado communiqué, 24 June 1948, quoted in Castillo D'Imperio, *Carlos Delgado Chalbaud*, p. 92.

24 Castillo D'Imperio, *Carlos Delgado Chalbaud*, pp. 84, 93, 97–8; Alexander, *Rómulo Betancourt*, pp. 312–13.

25 Delgado interview with Gonzalo de la Parra of *El Universal* (Mexico), quoted in Venezuela, Junta Militar de Gobierno, *Saludo de la Junta Militar de Gobierno a los Venezolanos con Ocasion del Año Nuevo* (Caracas: Oficina Nacional de Información y Publicaciones, 1950), p. 28.

26 Delgado quoted in Castillo D'Imperio, *Carlos Delgado Chalbaud*, p. 109; Delgado interview with Rafael Gómez Picón of *Sábado* (Bogotá), quoted in Venezuela, *Saludo*, p. 14.

27 Bethell and Roxborough (eds), *Latin America*, pp. 4–6; William Ebenstein, 'Political and Social Thought in Latin America', in Arthur P. Whitaker

(ed.), *Inter-American Affairs 1945* (New York: Columbia University Press, 1946), p. 137.

28 UN Department of Economic Affairs, *Economic Report: Salient Features of the World Economic Situation, 1945–47* (Lake Success, NY: UN, 1948), p. 18; Maddison, *The World Economy*, pp. 133, 135.

29 See Leslie Bethell's essay on 'Brazil', Andrew Barnard on 'Chile', and Nigel Haworth on 'Peru', in Bethell and Roxborough (eds), *Latin America*, pp. 45, 70, 184; see also the editors' introduction, ibid., pp. 13–14.

30 Alexander, *Rómulo Betancourt*, pp. 284–5; Liss, *Diplomacy and Dependency*, pp. 132, 136.

31 Bethell and Roxborough (eds), *Latin America*, pp. 9–10.

32 US Department of State policy statement, 30 June 1950, *FRUS 1950*, vol. 2, pp. 1029–30.

33 Bethell and Roxborough (eds), *Latin America*, pp. 18–19.

34 Braden, quoted in Stephen G. Rabe, *Eisenhower and Latin America: The Foreign Policy of Anticommunism* (Chapel Hill: University of North Carolina Press, 1988), p. 14.

35 For contemporary suspicions, see US State Department press release, 13 December 1948, *FRUS 1948*, vol. 9, pp. 144–5; for historians who maintain suspicions, see Steve Ellner, 'Venezuela', in Bethell and Roxborough (eds), *Latin America*, p. 166; and Salas, *Venezuela*, p. 85.

36 Tim Weiner, *Legacy of Ashes* (London: Allen Lane, 2007), pp. 93–104; Stephen Schlesinger and Stephen Kinzer, *Bitter Fruit: The Story of the American Coup in Guatemala* (Boston, MA: Harvard University Press, 2005), pp. 96–7; Nick Cullather, *Secret History: The CIA's Classified Account of Its Operations in Guatemala, 1952–1954* (Stanford University Press, 1999).

37 In 1954, for example, Venezuela's dictator Marcos Pérez Jiménez was awarded the Legion of Merit: see Operations Coordinating Board to National Security Council, 19 January 1955, 'Progress Report on NSC 5432/1 United States Objectives and Courses of Action with Respect to Latin America', *FRUS 1952–54*, vol. 4, p. 95.

38 Francesca Miller, *Latin American Women and the Search for Social Justice* (Hanover, NH: University Press of New England, 1991), pp. 154, 185.

39 Weiner, *Legacy of Ashes*, pp. 380–81.

40 See the Charter of the Organization of American States, signed in Bogotá in 1948, Articles 1 to 3: www.oas.org/en/sla/dil/inter_american_treaties_

A-41_charter_OAS.asp; and the UN Charter, particularly Article 2, Clause 7: www.un.org/en/charter-united-nations/.

41 Acting Secretary of State Lovett to Diplomatic Representatives in the American Republics, 28 December 1948, *FRUS 1948*, vol. 9, p. 150.

42 Castillo D'Imperio, *Carlos Delgado Chalbaud*, p. 112.

43 Delgado, interview, *Sábado*, quoted in Venezuela, *Saludo*, p. 15.

44 Delgado, quoted in Castillo D'Imperio, *Carlos Delgado Chalbaud*, p. 109.

45 Ibid., p. 111.

46 Delgado, quoted in Ambassador Donnelly's report to Secretary of State, *FRUS 1948*, vol. 9, p. 130.

Chapter 19 – Israel: Nation of Archetypes

1 Unless otherwise indicated, all quotes come from an interview with the author, 13 September 2016. Additional material was gleaned from Aharon Appelfeld's autobiographical books, *The Story of a Life* (Harmondsworth: Penguin, 2006); *Table for One* (New Milford, CT: The Toby Press, 2007); and an interview for Ari Shavit in his book *My Promised Land* (London: Scribe, 2015).

2 Quoted in Shavit, *My Promised Land*, pp. 140–41.

3 Appelfeld, *The Story of a Life*, pp. 114, 116.

4 For the existentialist thinking of early pioneers, see diary entries by kibbutzniks in Ein Harod, quoted in Shavit, *My Promised Land*, pp. 36–7.

5 See, for example, David Ben-Gurion, *Israel: A Personal History* (New York: Funk & Wagnalls, 1971), p. 135.

6 Tom Segev, *The Seventh Million* (New York: Hill & Wang, 1993), pp. 84–96.

7 Yitzhak Gruenbaum, quoted ibid., p. 71.

8 For English text of the declaration, see the Israeli Ministry of Foreign Affairs website: www.mfa.gov.il/mfa/foreignpolicy/peace/guide/pages/declaration%20of%20establishment%20of%20state%20of%20israel.aspx.

9 David Ben-Gurion, quoted in Martin Gilbert, *Israel: A History* (London: Black Swan, 1999), p. 251.

10 Ibid., p. 187.

11 Anita Shapira, *Israel: A History* (Waltham, MA: Brandeis University Press, 2012), pp. 212–15, 220; Gilbert, *Israel*, p. 267.

12 Shavit, *My Promised Land*, pp. 150–51; Gilbert, *Israel*, p. 267; Shapira, *Israel*, p. 212. See also David Kroyanker, 'Fifty Years of Israeli Architecture as Reflected in Jerusalem's Buildings', 26 May 1999, published on the Israeli Ministry of Foreign Affairs website, www.mfa.gov.il/mfa/abouttheministry/publications/pages/fifty%20years%20of%20israeli%20architecture%20as%20reflected%20i.aspx.

13 Reparations agreement between Israel and West Germany, quoted in Gilbert, *Israel*, p. 283.

14 Shapira, *Israel*, pp. 212–15; Gilbert, *Israel*, p. 267.

15 Uri Yadin of the Attorney General's office, diary entry for 5 April 1948, quoted in Shapira, *Israel*, p. 180.

16 Shapira, *Israel*, p. 210; 'Beersheba', *Canadian Jewish Chronicle*, 7 October 1955, p. 9.

17 Quote from the famous first line of Moshe Shamir's *With His Own Hands* (Jerusalem: Israel Universities Press, 1970): 'Elik was born from the sea.'

18 For example, Yigal Mossinsohn's *Way of a Man* (Tel Aviv: N. Tversky Publishers, 1953); and S. Yizhar's 1948 story 'The Prisoner', reproduced in Robert Alter (ed.), *Modern Hebrew Literature* (West Orange, NJ: Behrman House, 1975).

19 Shlomo Nitzan, *Togetherness* (Tel Aviv: Hakibbutz Hameuchad, 1956); Moshe Shamir, *He Walked Through the Fields* (Merhavia: Sifriat Poalim, 1947).

20 Shamir, *He Walked Through the Fields*; Hanoch Bartov, *Each Had Six Wings* (Merhavia: Sifriat Poalim, 1954).

21 For essays on Israeli literature from this period, see Bryan Cheyette, 'Israel', in John Sturrock (ed.), *The Oxford Guide to Contemporary World Literature* (Oxford University Press, 1996), pp. 238–9; Gila Ramras-Rauch, *The Arab in Israeli Literature* (London: I. B. Tauris, 1989), pp. 55–112; Avner Holtzman, '"They Are Different People": Holocaust Survivors as Reflected in the Fiction of the Generation of 1948', *Yad Vashem Studies*, vol. 30 (2002), pp. 337–68 (English translation available online: www.yadvashem.org/odot_pdf/Microsoft%20Word%20-%205424.pdf).

22 Shapira, *Israel*, p. 208; Shavit, *My Promised Land*, p. 148; Gilbert, *Israel*, pp. 257, 275.

23 Arieh Geldblum, 'Fundamental Problems of Immigrant Absorption', *Haaretz*, 28 September 1945, p. 3; see also Segev, *The Seventh Million*, p. 180.

24 Ehud Loeb, Eliezer Ayalon and Walter Zwi Bacharach, quoted on the Yad Vashem website: www.yadvashem.org/yv/en/education/interviews/

road_ahead.asp; www.yadvashem.org/yv/en/education/interviews/ayalon. asp; www.yadvashem.org/yv/en/education/interviews/bacharach.asp.

25 Aharon Barak, quoted in Shavit, *My Promised Land*, p. 145.

26 Segev, *The Seventh Million*, pp. 168–70; Appelfeld, *The Story of a Life*, pp. 111–12.

27 Segev, *The Seventh Million*, p. 180.

28 Ibid., pp. 170, 172, 174.

29 Ben Shephard, *The Long Road Home: The Aftermath of the Second World War* (London: Bodley Head, 2010), p. 361; Segev, *The Seventh Million*, p. 177.

30 Ben-Gurion, quoted in Hannah Starman, 'Israel's Confrontation with the Holocaust: A Journey of Uncertain Identity', in C. J. A. Stewart et al. (eds), *The Politics of Contesting Identity* (Edinburgh: Politics, University of Edinburgh, 2003), p. 130.

31 Simha Rotem, quoted in Segev, *The Seventh Million*, p. 160.

32 For the text of this homily, and a comprehensive reading of its cultural subtext, see Idith Zertal, *From Catastrophe to Power: The Holocaust Survivors and the Emergence of Israel* (Berkeley and Los Angeles: University of California Press, 1998), pp. 264–9.

33 Segev, *The Seventh Million*, p. 120; Shapira, *Israel*, p. 230; Ronit Lentin, *Israel and the Daughters of the Shoah* (New York: Berghahn Books, 2000).

34 Yehudit Hendel, interviewed for Israeli TV documentary *Cloudburst*, first broadcast in June 1989: see Segev, *The Seventh Million*, p. 179.

35 Shmuel Ussishkin in *Haboker*, 16 November 1951; Eliezer Livneh in *Davar*, 9 November 1951; David Ben-Gurion, quoted in Shapira, *Israel*, pp. 229–30.

36 Yoel Palgi, *Into the Inferno*, trans. Phyllis Palgi (New Brunswick, NJ: Rutgers University Press, 2003), p. 259; Segev, *The Seventh Million*, pp. 121, 183.

37 Palgi, *Into the Inferno*, pp. 258–9.

38 See, for example, Lentin, *Israel and the Daughters of the Shoah*, pp. 176–212; Ruth Amir, *Who is Afraid of Historical Redress?* (Boston, MA: Academic Studies Press, 2012), pp. 245–9; and Rafael Moses, 'An Israeli View', in Rafael Moses (ed.), *Persistent Shadows of the Holocaust* (Madison, CT: International Universities Press, 1993), pp. 130–31.

39 Haike Grossman and Egon Rott, quoted in Segev, *The Seventh Million*, pp. 87–8.

40 Teddy Kollek, *For Jerusalem* (London: Weidenfeld & Nicolson, 1978), p. 46.

41 Dalia Ofer, *Escaping the Holocaust* (New York: Oxford University Press, 1990), pp. 317, 319; Segev, *The Seventh Million*, pp. 84–96.

42 Josef Rosensaft, quoted in Shephard, *The Long Road Home*, p. 363.

43 See, for example, the stormy debates over whether to accept reparations payments from Germany, or the long-running Kastner Affair.

44 Shapira, *Israel*, p. 265.

45 Ben-Gurion, *Israel*, p. 599.

46 Anon., *The Seventh Day: Soldiers Talk About the Six-Day War* (London: André Deutsch, 1970), pp. 217–18.

47 Colonel Ehud Praver, quoted in Segev, *The Seventh Million*, pp. 394–5.

48 For 1930s comparisons see, for example, Yitzhak Tabenkin as well as Arab commentators quoted in Benny Morris, *Righteous Victims* (New York: Vintage, 2001), pp. 133, 136.

49 David Ben-Gurion, 4 July 1947, quoted in Gilbert, *Israel*, p. 146; Ariel Sharon, speech in the Knesset, 26 January 2005, quoted in *Haaretz*, 27 January 2005.

50 Ben-Gurion, quoted in Ilan Pappé, *The Ethnic Cleansing of Palestine* (London: Oneworld, 2007), p. 72; Segev, *The Seventh Million*, pp. 448–51.

51 'Without Intermediaries', *Maariv*, 5 November 1956, p. 4, quoted in Segev, *The Seventh Million*, p. 297.

52 Menachem Begin, quoted in Shapira, *Israel*, p. 380.

53 Ronald J. Berger, *The Holocaust, Religion and the Politics of Collective Memory* (New Brunswick, NJ: Transaction Books, 2013), p. 207.

54 Netanyahu, speech to the United Jewish Communities General Assembly, quoted in Michael Marrus, *Lessons of the Holocaust* (University of Toronto Press, 2016), p. 109.

55 See, for example, Shmaryahu Gutman, military commander of Lydda in 1948, quoted in Shavit, *My Promised Land*, pp. 118–27.

56 Shavit, *My Promised Land*, p. 114.

57 For credible descriptions of Deir Yassin, see Morris, *Righteous Victims*, p. 208 and related notes. For a wide variety of disputed statistics related to the massacre, see also Gilbert, *Israel*, p. 169; and Pappé, *The Ethnic Cleansing of Palestine*, p. 91.

58 Pappé, *The Ethnic Cleansing of Palestine*, pp. 196–7.

59 For Kafr Qasim see Amir, *Who is Afraid of Historical Redress?*, pp. 243–5.

60 See, for example, Anon., *The Seventh Day*, p. 90.

61 Shavit, *My Promised Land*, pp. 230–36.

62 'HRW: Israel committed war crimes in Gaza', *The Times of Israel*, 12 September 2014.

63 See, for example, works on the Israel–Palestine conflict by Edward W. Said, Rashid Khalidi, Norman G. Finkelstein and Noam Chomsky.

64 Pappé, *The Ethnic Cleansing of Palestine*, p. xvii.

65 'German Protesters Dare to Compare Israelis to Nazis', *The Week*, 6 January 2008.

66 For the Chakrabarti report into anti-Semitism in the British Labour Party, see www.labour.org.uk/page/-/party-documents/ChakrabartiInquiry.pdf.

67 Yeshayahu Leibowitz, quoted in Segev, *The Seventh Million*, p. 401; see also pp. 409–10.

68 Shavit, *My Promised Land*, p. 231.

69 Appelfeld, *Table for One*, pp. 97, 105.

70 This is not only a perpetual European, American and Middle Eastern problem: for the demonization of Israel in Southeast Asia, see Anthony Reid, *To Nation by Revolution: Indonesia in the Twentieth Century* (Singapore: NUS Press, 2011), pp. 262–4.

71 Keith Lowe, *Savage Continent* (London: Viking, 2012), pp. 222, 243, 248; Ian Talbot and Gurharpal Singh, *The Partition of India* (Cambridge University Press, 2009), pp. 2–3.

Chapter 20 – European Nationalism

1 For Spinelli's story, see his autobiography: Altiero Spinelli, *Come ho tentato di diventare saggio*, 2 vols (Bologna: Società editrice il Mulino, 1984 and 1987). For the Ventotene Manifesto and other writings, see Altiero Spinelli, *From Ventotene to the European Constitution*, ed. Agustín José Menéndez (Oslo: Centre for European Studies, 2007).

2 Spinelli, 'Ventotene Manifesto', in *From Ventotene to the European Constitution*, p. 18; *Come ho tentato di diventare saggio*, vol. 1, p. 308.

3 Spinelli, 'Ventotene Manifesto', p. 23; *Come ho tentato di diventare saggio*, vol. 1, p. 309.

4 Nobel Peace Prize citation, 12 October 2012, Nobel Peace Centre exhibition, Oslo.

5 See, for example, the collection of essays written by the group 'Historians for Britain', *Peace-Makers or Credit-Takers?: The EU and Peace in Europe*, published on their website, historiansforbritain.org/research.

6 'Euro Federalists Financed by US Spy Chiefs', *Telegraph*, 19 Sept 2000. See also 'The European Union Always Was a CIA Project, as Brexiteers Discover', *Telegraph*, 27 April 2016.

7 De Gaulle, quoted in Richard Mayne, *Postwar: The Dawn of Today's Europe* (London: Thames & Hudson, 1983), p. 314.

8 Nicholas Ridley's interview with Dominic Lawson in the *Spectator*, 14 July 1990.

9 Keith Lowe, *Savage Continent* (London: Viking, 2012), particularly pp. 187–268.

10 Kwaśniewski, speech of 16 April 2003, published on the Polish presidential website: www.president.pl/en/archive/news-archive/news-2003/art,79,-poland-has-signed-the-accession-treaty.html; Evald Mikkel and Geoffrey Pridham, 'Clinching the "Return to Europe": The Referendums on EU Accession in Estonia and Latvia', in Aleks Szczerbiak and Paul Taggart (eds), *EU Enlargement and Referendums* (Abingdon: Routledge, 2005), p. 179.

11 See essays ibid., pp. 123, 150, 178; *Wprost*, 11–17 January 2016.

12 Polish finance minister Jacek Rostowski, quoted in 'Germany and France: Eurozone Will Not Force Out Greece', *Telegraph*, 15 September 2011.

13 Cameron, speech at the British Museum, 9 May 2016, broadcast live on Sky News Channel.

14 Barack Obama, '"As your friend, I tell you that the EU makes Britain even greater"', *Telegraph*, 22 April 2016.

15 Penny Mordaunt, writing in the *Telegraph*, 25 February 2016; Nigel Farage's theme music in 'Brexit Debate Brings Out Britain's World War Two Fixation', *Daily Mail* (online edition), 3 June 2016.

16 *Telegraph*, 15 May 2016; *Daily Express*, 2 June 2016; 'Boris Johnson's Abuse of Churchill', *History Today* website, 1 June 2016: www.historytoday.com/felix-klos/boris-johnsons-abuse-churchill.

17 Alan Sked, quoted in *Daily Express*, 9 June 2016; Michael Gove, quoted in *Daily Express*, 22 June 2016.

18 Boris Johnson interview, *Telegraph*, 15 May 2016.

19 'The Secret History of the EU', *Telegraph*, 27 August 2016.

20 'EU Referendum: The Claims that Won it for Brexit, Fact Checked', *Telegraph*, 29 June 2016.

21 Full letter published on www.historiansforbritainineurope.org and reported in the *Guardian*, 25 May 2016.

22 Remarks by Paweł Machcewicz during his presentation of the permanent exhibition of the museum, 22 January 2017; 'A Museum Becomes a Battlefield Over Poland's History', *New York Times*, 9 November 2016.

Chapter 21 – Trauma

1 Choi Myeong-sun's story is outlined in more detail in Keith Howard (ed.), *True Stories of the Korean Comfort Women*, trans. Young Joo Lee (London: Cassell, 1995), pp. 168–76.

2 For a more detailed description of trauma and its effects, see Caroline Garland (ed.), *Understanding Trauma: A Psychoanalytical Approach* (London: Karnac Books, 2002); and Susan Levy and Alessandra Lemma (eds), *The Perversion of Loss: Psychoanalytic Perspectives on Trauma* (New York: Brunner-Routledge, 2004).

3 Ustinia Dolgopol and Snehal Paranjape, *Comfort Women: An Unfinished Ordeal: Report of a Mission* (Geneva: International Commission of Jurists, 1994), pp. 23–4.

4 'Japanese Charge Russian Abuses', *New York Times*, 4 November 1945; Yoshimi Yoshiaki, *Comfort Women*, trans. Suzanne O'Brien (New York: Columbia University Press, 2002), pp. 188–9; Sheila Miyoshi Jager, *Brothers at War: The Unending Conflict in Korea* (New York: W. W. Norton, 2013), p. 20; Mun Pilgi, quoted in Howard (ed.), *True Stories of the Korean Comfort Women*, p. 86.

5 Pak Duri, quoted in Joshua D. Pilzer, *Hearts of Pine: Songs in the Lives of Three Korean Survivors of the Japanese 'Comfort Women'* (New York: Oxford University Press, 2012), p. 34.

6 Jager, *Brothers at War*, pp. 26–35, 489; H. Merrell Benninghoff to Secretary of State, 15 September 1945, US Department of State, *Foreign Relations of the United States* (Washington, DC: US Government Printing Office) (hereafter *FRUS*) *1945*, vol. 6, pp. 1049–53.

7 Jager, *Brothers at War*, pp. 39–41; Robert Scalapino and Chong-Sik Lee, *Communism in Korea* (Berkeley: University of California Press, 1972), pp. 338–40; Allan R. Millett, *The War for Korea, 1945–1950: A House Burning* (Lawrence: University Press of Kansas, 2005), p. 69; Andrei Lankov, *From Stalin to Kim Il Sung: The Formation of North Korea, 1945–1960* (London: Hurst & Co., 2002), pp. 23–4.

8 For statistics see 'Double Problem Faced in Korea', *New York Times*, 6 December 1945, and 'Korean Population Soars', *New York Times*, 9 July 1947.

9 Paul Kennedy, *The Parliament of Man* (London: Allen Lane, 2006), pp. 56–7; Jager, *Brothers at War*, pp. 64, 124.

10 Bethany Lacina and Nils Petter Gleditsch, 'Monitoring Trends in Global Combat: A New Dataset of Battle Deaths', *European Journal of Population*,

vol. 21, nos 2–3 (2005), p. 154; Jager, *Brothers at War*, pp. 85–97; 'Reds Kill 700 at a Korean "Buchenwald"', and '82 Slain with Bamboo Spears as Reds Attack Loyal Koreans', *Washington Post*, 4 October 1950.

11 C. Sarah Soh, *The Comfort Women* (University of Chicago Press, 2008), pp. 193, 215–17.

12 Park and Kim, quoted in Jager, *Brothers at War*, p. 341.

13 US Army Military Government in Korea, *Summation of the United States Military Government Activities in Korea*, no. 33 (Seoul: National Economic Board, 1948), p. 181; *Chosun Ilbo*, 9 June 1948; *Korean Independence*, 21 July 1948; *Chayu Sinmun*, 25 June 1948. See also summary in Sung-Hwa Cheong, *The Politics of Anti-Japanese Sentiment in Korea* (Westport, CT: Greenwood Press, 1991), pp. 6–8.

14 Dolgopol and Paranjape, *Comfort Women*, p. 138; Pilzer, *Hearts of Pine*, pp. 8, 116; Cheong, *The Politics of Anti-Japanese Sentiment in Korea*, p. 136; Jin-kyung Lee, *Service Economies: Militarism, Sex Work, and Migrant Labor in South Korea* (Minneapolis: University of Minnesota Press, 2010), pp. 25–6.

15 For the history of the 'comfort women' issue to 2016 see Aniko Varga, 'National Bodies: The "Comfort Women" Discourse and Its Controversies in South Korea', *Studies in Ethnicity and Nationalism*, vol. 9, no. 2 (2009), pp. 287–303; Mikyoung Kim, 'Memorializing Comfort Women: Memory and Human Rights in Korea–Japan Relations', *Asian Politics and Policy*, vol. 6, no. 1 (2014), pp. 83–96; and Naoko Kumagai, 'The Background to the Japan–Republic of Korea Agreement: Compromises Concerning the Understanding of the Comfort Women Issue', *Asia-Pacific Review*, vol. 23, no. 1 (2016), pp. 65–99.

16 Young-Hee Shim, *Sexual Violence and Feminism in Korea* (Seoul: Hanyang University Press, 2004), pp. 156–62, 177–82.

17 Lee, *Service Economies*, pp. 5–8, 25–6.

18 Memorials and statues to the comfort women have been erected in several countries: more than half a dozen in the USA, but also in China, Taiwan, the Philippines and Australia.

Chapter 22 – Loss

1 Evgeniia Kiseleva's story is taken from her autobiography, reproduced in N. N. Kozlova and I. I. Sandomirskaia, *Ia tak khochu nazvat'kino: 'Naivnoe pis'mo'. Opyt lingvo-sotsiologicheskogo chteniia* (Moscow: Gnozis, 1996), p. 89. Kiseleva's 'naive' style is almost untranslatable: since I am concerned here only with

her story, I have used correct spellings and added punctuation in this and each subsequent quote. For a brilliant companion to this memoir and discussion of her unique style, see Irina Paperno, *Stories of the Soviet Experience: Memoirs, Diaries, Dreams* (Ithaca, NY: Cornell University Press, 2009), pp. 118–58.

2 Kozlova and Sandomirskaia, *Ia tak khochu nazvat' kino*, pp. 91–4.

3 Ibid., p. 101.

4 Ibid., p. 122.

5 Ibid., p. 145.

6 USSR Central Statistical Office, *Soviet Census 1959: Preliminary Results* (London: Soviet Booklets, 1959), p. 4. Other historians and economists put the excess of women over men lower, at about 13 million: see summary in Keith Lowe, *Savage Continent* (London: Viking, 2012), p. 24.

7 IWM Docs, 06/126/1, Major A. G. Moon, typescript memoir.

8 The official number of wounded was 15,205,592, but the real figure might be much lower due to double counting. On the other hand, many casualties, especially from the beginning of the war, went unreported. See G. F. Krivosheev (ed.), *Soviet Casualties and Combat Losses in the Twentieth Century* (London: Greenhill Books, 1997), pp. 87–8.

9 Charles Glass, *Deserter* (London: HarperPress, 2013), pp. xiii, 228.

10 Studies into PTSD after the Vietnam War found that 15 per cent of veterans continued to suffer symptoms ten years later: see Marc Pilisuk, *Who Benefits from Global Violence and War: Uncovering a Destructive System* (Westport, CT: Praeger Security International, 2008), pp. 12–15.

11 C. A. Merridale, report funded by the British Economic and Social Research Council on 'Death, Mourning and Memory in Modern Russia: A Study in Large-Scale Trauma and Social Change' (2000).

12 Lowe, *Savage Continent*, pp. 16, 402.

13 Robert A. Lewis, Richard H. Rowland and Ralph S. Clem, *Nationality and Population Change in Russia and the USSR: An Evaluation of Census Data, 1897–1970* (New York: Praeger, 1976), p. 275.

14 Thérèse Brosse, *War-Handicapped Children* (Paris: UNESCO, 1950), p. 28.

15 Sergey Afontsev et al., 'The Urban Household in Russia and the Soviet Union, 1900–2000: Patterns of Family Formation in a Turbulent Century', *History of the Family*, vol. 13, no. 2 (2008), pp. 187–8.

16 For US statistics see the government census website, www.census.gov, particularly www.census.gov/prod/2014pubs/p25-1141.pdf on the baby-boom generation. See also Diane J. Macunovich, *Birth Quake: The Baby Boom and its Aftershocks* (University of Chicago Press, 2002).

17 Lowe, *Savage Continent*, p. 16.

18 For a more detailed description, see ibid., pp. 212–19. Crimea was not at this point a part of Ukraine, but would become so in 1954.

19 Alexander Statiev, *The Soviet Counterinsurgency in the Western Borderlands* (New York: Cambridge University Press, 2010), pp. 117, 178.

Chapter 23 – Outcasts

1 Mathias Mendel's story comes from a series of conversations with his son, Dittmann Mendel, in May 2015, and email correspondence in November 2016.

2 Keith Lowe, *Savage Continent* (London: Viking, 2012), p. 27; Adam Tooze, *The Wages of Destruction* (Harmondsworth: Penguin, 2007), p. 672; Mark Wyman, *DPs: Europe's Displaced Persons, 1945–1951* (Ithaca, NY: Cornell University Press, 1998), pp. 41–4.

3 Lowe, *Savage Continent*, p. 27. I have erred on the conservative side: Adam Tooze lists some much higher estimates. See his *The Wages of Destruction*, p. 672.

4 Lowe, *Savage Continent*, pp. 231, 243.

5 Article XII of the Potsdam Agreement, 1945, available online on the Yale Law School website, http://avalon.law.yale.edu/20th_century/decade17. asp. See also Lowe, *Savage Continent*, pp. 125–44, 230–48; R. M. Douglas, *Orderly and Humane: The Expulsion of the Germans After the Second World War* (New Haven, CT: Yale University Press, 2012), p. 1.

6 Lowe, *Savage Continent*, pp. 247–8.

7 Ibid., pp. 222, 224–9.

8 Ibid., pp. 222, 248.

9 Raymond Pearson, *National Minorities in Eastern Europe, 1848–1945* (London: Macmillan, 1983), p. 229.

10 Lori Watt, *When Empire Comes Home: Repatriation and Reintegration in Postwar Japan* (Cambridge, MA: Harvard University Asia Center, 2009), pp. 2, 17–18; John W. Dower, *Embracing Defeat: Japan in the Wake of World War II* (New York: W. W. Norton, 2000), pp. 48–50.

11 Watt, *When Empire Comes Home*, pp. 205–7; Dower, *Embracing Defeat*, pp. 50–58.

12 Dower, *Embracing Defeat*, pp. 45–53.

13 Ibid., pp. 54, 393–4; Sonia Ryang, *Koreans in Japan* (London: Routledge, 2000), p. 4; Watt, *When Empire Comes Home*, p. 196.

14 According to census reports, there were 155,000 British subjects living in India in 1931; but by 1951 there were fewer than 31,000 remaining in India and Pakistan. See J. H. Hutton (ed.), *Census of India: Part I Report* (Delhi: Manager of Publications, 1933), p. 425; R. A. Gopalaswami (ed.), *Census of India, 1951* (Delhi: Government of India Press, 1955), vol. 1, Part II-A, pp. 308–23; and E. H. Slade (ed.), *Census of Pakistan, 1951* (Karachi: Government of Pakistan, 1951), vol. 1, table 10.

15 Ceri Peach, 'Postwar Migration to Europe: Reflux, Influx, Refuge', *Social Science Quarterly*, vol. 78, no. 2 (1997), pp. 271–2.

16 Ibid., p. 271; Trudy T. M. Mooren, *The Impact of War: Studies on the Psychological Consequences of War and Migration* (Delft: Eburon, 2001), pp. 84, 91; Watt, *When Empire Comes Home*, p. 199.

17 Mooren, *The Impact of War*, pp. 84, 91; Peach, 'Postwar Migration to Europe', pp. 271–2; Benjamin Stora, *Algeria, 1830–2000: A Short History*, trans. Jane Marie Todd (Ithaca: Cornell University Press, 2001), p. 8; Norrie MacQueen, *The Decolonization of Portuguese Africa* (Harlow: Longman, 1997), pp. 124–204, 223–31; Ricardo E. Ovalle-Bahamón, 'The Wrinkles of Decolonization and Nationness: White Angolans as *Retornados* in Portugal', in Andrea L. Smith (ed.), *Europe's Invisible Migrants* (Amsterdam University Press, 2003), p. 158.

18 UN General Assembly resolution 319 (IV), 265th plenary meeting, 3 December 1949.

19 For a good introduction to the UNHCR and its work see their study booklet, *An Introduction to International Protection* (Geneva: UNHCR, 2005), available online at www.refworld.org/docid/4214cb4f2.html.

20 'UNHCR Global Trends: Forced Displacement in 2014', available online at www.unhcr.org/556725e69.html.

21 Article 16, later amended to 16a, Basic Law of the Federal Republic of Germany, available in English on http://www.bundestag.de/. See also Kay Hailbronner, 'Asylum Law Reform in the German Constitution', *American University International Law Review*, vol. 9, no. 4 (1994), pp. 159–79.

22 Stephen Castles and Mark J. Miller, *The Age of Migration*, 3rd edn (New York: Palgrave Macmillan, 2003), pp. 201, 203; Friedrich Kern, *Österreich: Offene Grenze der Menschlichkeit* (Vienna: Bundesministeriums für Inneres, 1959), p. 68; Anthony M. Messina, *The Logics and Politics of Post-WWII Migration to Western Europe* (New York: Cambridge University Press, 2007), pp. 43–4.

23 'Germany on Course to Accept One Million Refugees in 2015', *Guardian*, 8 December 2015; 'One Year Ago, Angela Merkel Dared to Stand Up for Refugees in Europe. Who Else Even Tried?', *Telegraph*, 24 August 2016.

24 'Germany's Refugee Response Not Guilt-Driven, Says Wolfgang Schäuble', *Guardian*, 4 March 2016; 'Orban Accuses Germany of "Moral Imperialism" on Migrants', *Wall Street Journal*, 23 September 2015.

25 Correspondence with the author, 22 November 2016.

Chapter 24 – The Globalization of Peoples

1 Interview on Windrush Foundation website, www.windrushfoundation. org/profiles/sam-king/sam-king/.

2 Samuel Beaver King interview, Imperial War Museums, IWM Sound 30021, reel 1; available online at www.iwm.org.uk/collections/item/object/ 80028544.

3 IWM Sound 30021, reel 1; BBC interview, 'Black Soldiers' Role in World War II "should be taught in schools"', 11 November 2015, www.bbc.co.uk/ newsbeat/article/34638038/black-soldiers-role-in-world-war-two-should-be-taught-in-schools.

4 IWM Sound 30021, reel 3.

5 Tracey Connolly, 'Emigration from Ireland to Britain During the Second World War', in Andy Bielenberg (ed.), *The Irish Diaspora* (London: Pearson Education, 2000), p. 56.

6 According to the 1951 census, there were 162,339 Poles in Britain, up from around 44,000 in 1931. See Colin Holmes, *John Bull's Island: Immigration and British Society* (Basingstoke: Macmillan, 1988), pp. 168, 211–12.

7 Edna Delaney, 'Placing Irish Postwar Migration to Britain in a Comparative European Perspective, 1945–1981', in Bielenberg (ed.), *The Irish Diaspora*, p. 332; Ben Shephard, *The Long Road Home: The Aftermath of the Second World War* (London: Bodley Head, 2010), pp. 329–32.

8 Shephard, *The Long Road Home*, p. 332; Delaney, 'Irish Postwar Migration to Britain', p. 333; Ceri Peach, 'Postwar Migration to Europe: Reflux, Influx, Refuge', *Social Science Quarterly*, vol. 78, no. 2 (1997), p. 275.

9 Interview on Windrush Foundation website.

10 IWM Sound 30021, reel 2.

11 According to 1971 census figures: see Ceri Peach, 'Patterns of Afro-Caribbean Migration and Settlement in Great Britain, 1945–1981', in

Colin Brock (ed.), *The Caribbean in Europe* (London: Frank Cass, 1986), p. 64.

12 Figures for 1970 in Stephen Castles and Mark J. Miller, *The Age of Migration*, 3rd edn (New York: Palgrave Macmillan, 2003), pp. 73–5.

13 David Lowenthal, 'West Indian Emigrants Overseas', in Colin G. Clarke (ed.), *Caribbean Social Relations* (Liverpool: Centre for Latin American Studies, University of Liverpool, 1978), p. 84.

14 Castles and Miller, *The Age of Migration*, pp. 144–7; Miguel Tinker Salas, *Venezuela: What Everyone Needs to Know* (New York: Oxford University Press, 2015), p. 80.

15 Anthony M. Messina, *The Logics and Politics of Post-WWII Migration to Western Europe* (New York: Cambridge University Press, 2007), p. 27.

16 Hansard, 8 June 1948, col. 1851.

17 David Kynaston, *Austerity Britain, 1945–51* (London: Bloomsbury, 2007), pp. 274–5.

18 Quoted ibid., p. 275.

19 'Thames Welcome for West Indians: Start of "Invasion"', *Daily Graphic and Daily Sketch*, 22 June 1948.

20 Shephard, *The Long Road Home*, pp. 329–32.

21 Sam King, *Climbing Up the Rough Side of the Mountain* (Peterborough: Upfront, 1998), pp. 64, 101, 114, 118, 127–9, 256; *Guardian* obituary, 30 June 2016.

22 King, *Climbing Up the Rough Side of the Mountain*, p. 156.

23 IWM Sound 30021, reel 2.

24 J. Enoch Powell, *Still to Decide* (London: B. T. Batsford, 1972), pp. 184–5; Gary P. Freeman, *Immigrant Labor and Racial Conflict in Industrial Societies: The French and British Experience, 1945–1975* (Princeton University Press, 2015), pp. 286–90.

25 National Front, *For a New Britain: The Manifesto of the National Front* (Croydon: National Front, 1974), p. 18.

26 Stan Taylor, *The National Front in English Politics* (London: Macmillan, 1982), pp. 130–40.

27 Messina, *The Logics and Politics of Post-WWII Migration to Western Europe*, pp. 60–61.

28 'Hungary Election: Concerns as Neo-Nazi Jobbik Party Wins 20% of Vote', *Independent*, 7 April 2014.

29 'Conservatives' EU Alliance in Turmoil as Michał Kamiński Leaves "Far Right" Party', *Guardian*, 22 November 2010.

30 Calwell quoted in Shephard, *The Long Road Home*, p. 337; Pauline Hanson, speech to House of Representatives, 10 September 1996, available on http://australianpolitics.com/1996/09/10/pauline-hanson-maiden-speech. html; 'Australia Asylum: UN Criticises "Cruel" Conditions on Nauru', www.bbc.co.uk/news/world-australia-38022204.

31 Messina, *The Logics and Politics of Post-WWII Migration to Western Europe*, pp. 76–7.

32 Powell, *Still to Decide*, pp. 185, 201.

33 Roland Wilson (ed.), *Census of the Commonwealth of Australia, 30 June, 1947* (Canberra: Commonwealth Government Printer, 1947), Part XII, pp. 642–3. For 2015 see Australian Bureau of Statistics, Media Release, 30 March 2016, Catalogue no. 3412.0, 'Migration, Australia, 2014–15', available online at www.abs.gov.au/ausstats/abs@.nsf/mf/3412.0/.

34 Figures for 2013, according to the OECD (2016), 'Foreign-Born Population (Indicator)' doi: 10.1787/5a368e1b-en. See https://data.oecd.org/migration/foreign-born-population.htm.

35 Ibid.

36 Ibid. See also Arlie Russell Hochschild, *Strangers in Their Own Land* (New York: New Press, 2016).

37 Census figures, 2001, reported in 'Every Race, Colour, Nation and Religion on Earth', *Guardian*, 21 January 2005; ethnicity figures from 2011 census from Office of National Statistics website, table QS201 EW; for Boris Johnson claim, and how it was misleading (London was possibly the 23rd biggest French city) see www.bbc.co.uk/news/magazine-26823489.

38 *Independent*, 28 January 2016.

39 'Trump Reveals How He Would Force Mexico to Build Border Wall', *Washington Post*, 5 April, 2016; 'Trump Vows to Stop Immigration from Nations "Compromised" by Terrorism', *New York Times*, 22 July 2016.

40 One Trump supporter even made a billboard containing this slogan: see ' "Make America White Again": A Politician's Billboard Ignites Uproar', *Washington Post*, 23 June 2016.

41 Hochschild, *Strangers in Their Own Land*.

42 'Hungary PM Predicts "Parallel Muslim Society" Due to Migration', *Daily Express*, 27 September 2016; 'The Netherlands' Most Popular Party Wants to Ban All Mosques', *Independent*, 28 August 2016.

43 Jean-Paul Sartre, *Anti-Semite and Jew*, trans. George J. Becker (New York: Schocken Books, 1948), particularly chapters 3 and 4. Sartre makes it clear that his thesis applies as much to black people and Arabs as it does to Jews (p. 146).

Epilogue

1 Ed Murrow, broadcast, 15 September 1940, quoted in James Owen and Guy Walters (eds), *The Voice of War* (London: Viking, 2004), p. 80.
2 Interview with the author, 10 August 2015.

Index

Page references in *italic* indicate tables and illustrations or their captions.